KIA
SORENTO
2003-13 REPAIR MANUAL
Deleted

Covers all U.S. and Canadian models of Kia Sorento
2003 through 2013

by Jeff Killingsworth

CHILTON *Automotive Books*

PUBLISHED BY **HAYNES NORTH AMERICA, Inc.**

Haynes

APA
AUTOMOTIVE
PARTS &
ACCESSORIES
ASSOCIATION MEMBER

Manufactured in USA
©2013 Haynes North America, Inc.
ISBN-13: 978-1-62092-058-9
ISBN-10: 1-62092-058-1
Library of Congress Control Number: 2013949319

Haynes Publishing Group
Sparkford Nr Yeovil
Somerset BA22 7JJ England

Haynes North America, Inc
861 Lawrence Drive
Newbury Park
California 91320 USA

ABCDE
FGHIJ
KLMNO
PQRST

D0814347

Contents

Mechanic and photographer with a 2004 KIA Sorento

ACKNOWLEDGEMENTS

We are grateful to Bosch Automotive Service Solutions for providing Wiring Diagrams.

About this manual

ITS PURPOSE

The purpose of this manual is to help you get the best value from your vehicle. It can do so in several ways. It can help you decide what work must be done, even if you choose to have it done by a dealer service department or a repair shop; it provides information and procedures for routine maintenance and servicing; and it offers diagnostic and repair procedures to follow when trouble occurs.

We hope you use the manual to tackle the work yourself. For many simpler jobs, doing it yourself may be quicker than arranging an appointment to get the vehicle into a shop and making the trips to leave it and pick it up. More importantly, a lot of money can be saved by avoiding the expense the shop must pass on to you to cover its labor and overhead costs. An added benefit is the sense of satisfaction and accomplishment that you feel after doing the job yourself.

USING THE MANUAL

The manual is divided into Chapters. Each Chapter is divided into numbered Sections. Each Section consists of consecutively numbered paragraphs.

At the beginning of each numbered Section you will be referred to any illustrations which apply to the procedures in that Section. The reference numbers used in illustration captions pinpoint the pertinent Section and the Step within that Section. That is, illustration 3.2 means the illustration refers to Section 3 and Step (or paragraph) 2 within that Section.

Procedures, once described in the text, are not normally repeated. When it's necessary to refer to another Chapter, the reference will be given as Chapter and Section number. Cross references given without use of the word "Chapter" apply to Sections and/or paragraphs in the same Chapter. For example, "see Section 8" means in the same Chapter.

References to the left or right side of the vehicle assume you are sitting in the driver's seat, facing forward.

Even though we have prepared this manual with extreme care, neither the publisher nor the author can accept responsibility for any errors in, or omissions from, the information given.

➡ NOTE

A *Note* provides information necessary to properly complete a procedure or information which will make the procedure easier to understand.

✳✳ CAUTION

A *Caution* provides a special procedure or special steps which must be taken while completing the procedure where the Caution is found. Not heeding a Caution can result in damage to the assembly being worked on.

✳✳ WARNING

A *Warning* provides a special procedure or special steps which must be taken while completing the procedure where the Warning is found. Not heeding a Warning can result in personal injury.

Introduction

This manual covers 2003 through 2009 and 2011 through 2013 Kia Sorento models. These vehicles are equipped with either a 2.4L four-cylinder engine, or a 3.3L, 3.5L or 3.8L V6 engine.

2009 and earlier models are either rear wheel drive (RWD) or all-wheel drive (AWD); the engine drives the rear wheels through either a four or five-speed automatic or a five-speed manual transmission via a driveshaft and a solid rear axle.

On AWD models, the front wheels are also propelled, via a transfer case, driveshaft, front differential, and front driveaxles. 2011 and later models are either front wheel drive (FWD) or all-wheel drive (AWD); the engine drives the front wheels through either a five or six-speed automatic or manual transaxle via independent driveaxles.

On AWD models, the rear wheels are also propelled, via a transfer case, driveshaft, rear differential, and rear driveaxles.

On 2009 and earlier models, suspension is independent at the front, using upper and lower control arms and coil-over shock absorbers. The rear suspension uses a solid axle, coil springs, upper and lower arms, a lateral rod, and conventional shock absorbers. On 2011 and later models, suspension is independent at all four wheels, with MacPherson struts used at the front and coil springs with conventional shock absorbers at the rear.

The brakes are disc at the front and rear on all models. Power assist is standard on all models. An Anti-lock Brake System (ABS) is standard equipment on some models and is available as an option on others.

Vehicle identification numbers

Modifications are a continuing and unpublicized process in vehicle manufacturing. Since spare parts manuals and lists are compiled on a numerical basis, the individual vehicle numbers are essential to correctly identify the component required.

VEHICLE IDENTIFICATION NUMBER (VIN)

This very important identification number is stamped on a plate attached to the dashboard inside the windshield on the driver's side of the vehicle (see illustration). It can also be found on the certification label located on the driver's side door post and on the right (passenger's) side of the firewall. The VIN also appears on the Vehicle Certificate of Title and Registration. It contains information such as where and when the vehicle was manufactured, the model year and the body style.

VIN ENGINE AND MODEL YEAR CODES

Two particularly important pieces of information found in the VIN are the engine code and the model year code. Counting from the left, the engine code letter designation is the 8th digit and the model year code letter designation is the 10th digit.

On the models covered by this manual the engine codes are:

1 2.4L four-cylinder, 2011 and later (Theta II MPI)
6 2.4L four-cylinder, 2012 and later (Theta II GDI)
2 3.5L DOHC V6, 2011 and later (Lambda II MPI)
5 3.3L DOHC V6, 2008-2009 (Lambda MPI)
6 3.8L DOHC V6, 2007-2009 (Lambda MPI)
3 3.5L DOHC V6, 2006 and earlier (Lambda MPI)

On the models covered by this manual the model year codes are:

3 2003
4 2004
5 2005
6 2006
7 2007
8 2008
9 2009
A 2010
B 2011
C 2012
D 2013

CERTIFICATION LABEL

The certification label is attached to the end of the driver's door post (see illustration). The plate contains the name of the manufacturer, the month and year of production, the Gross Vehicle Weight Rating (GVWR), the Gross Axle Weight Rating (GAWR) and the certification statement.

ENGINE NUMBER

On four-cylinder models, the engine identification number is stamped into a machined pad on the front passenger's side of the engine block, under the exhaust manifold.

On V6 models, the engine identification number is stamped into a machined pad on the front left end (driver's side) of the engine block.

3.2 The Vehicle Identification Number (VIN) is located on a plate on top of the dash (visible through the windshield)

3.6 The vehicle certification label is located at the bottom of the driver's door post

Recall information

Vehicle recalls are carried out by the manufacturer in the rare event of a possible safety-related defect. The vehicle's registered owner is contacted at the address on file at the Department of Motor Vehicles and given the details of the recall. Remedial work is carried out free of charge at a dealer service department.

If you are the new owner of a used vehicle which was subject to a recall and you want to be sure that the work has been carried out, it's best to contact a dealer service department and ask about your individual vehicle - you'll need to furnish them your Vehicle Identification Number (VIN).

The table below is based on information provided by the National Highway Traffic Safety Administration (NHTSA), the body which oversees vehicle recalls in the United States. The recall database is updated constantly.

For the latest information on vehicle recalls, check the NHTSA website at www.nhtsa.gov, www.safercar.gov, or call the NHTSA hotline at 1-888-327-4236.

Recall date	Recall campaign number	Model(s) affected	Concern
AUG 04, 2005	05V353000	2003 Sorento	Some models may experience a fuel leak from fuel tubes near the fuel tank due to an interference fit with the vehicle floor panel. Fuel leakage, in the presence of an ignition source, could result in a fire.
APR 17, 2009	09V130000	2006, 2007 Sorento	On some models, the brake light switch might malfunction. This may cause the brake lights to not illuminate when the brake pedal is depressed or may cause the brake lights to remain illuminated when the brake pedal is released. It may also affect the operation of the brake-transmission shift interlock feature so the transmission shifter would not be able to be shifted out of the park position. It may also cause the Electronic Stability Control (ESC) malfunction light to illuminate, and it may not deactivate the cruise control when the brake pedal is depressed. Any of these malfunctions, alone or in combination, may lead to a crash.

Recall date	Recall campaign number	Model(s) affected	Concern
APR 01, 2013	13V114000	2007, 2008, 2009, 2011 Sorento	On some models, the brake light switch may malfunction. This may cause the brake lights to not illuminate when the brake pedal is depressed or may cause an inability to deactivate the cruise control by depressing the brake pedal. Additionally, it may also result in intermittent operation of the push-button start feature, affect the operation of the brake-transmission shift interlock feature preventing the shifter from being moved out of the PARK position and causing the Electronic Stability Control (ESC) malfunction light to illuminate. Failure to illuminate the stop lamps during braking or inability to disengage the cruise control could increase the risk of a crash. Additionally, when the ignition is in the 'ON' position, the transmission shifter may be able to be moved out of PARK without first applying the brake. This may lead to unintentional movement of the car which may increase the risk of a crash.
SEP 07, 2011	11V473000	2007, 2008 Sorento	On some models, the front passenger airbag may be turned off when an adult is in the passenger seat. The front passenger airbag is designed to be turned off in limited circumstances including when children and small adults are seated in the front passenger seat, there is a child restraint in that seat or the seat is not occupied. The vehicle's Occupant Classification System (OCS), which classifies the occupant in the front passenger seat, may misclassify an adult passenger as a child or child seat and improperly turn off the passenger side airbag. When the airbag is deactivated the "Passenger Air Bag Off" light will illuminate on the center instrument panel. The passenger side airbag is turned off when the OCS misclassifies an adult passenger. With the front passenger airbag off, the front passenger will not have the protection of the passenger airbags in some frontal collisions, thus increasing the risk of occupant injury.
APR 25, 2011	11V258000	2011 Sorento	On some models equipped with automatic transmissions and 2.4L engines, the intermediate shaft may suffer from noise and excessive wear due to a misalignment of the intermediate shaft with the right side output gear. Continuing to drive the vehicle in this condition leads to the development of a whirring/whining noise and can eventually cause damage to the automatic transmission. Damage to the transmission may cause loss of motive power, increasing the risk of a crash.

Recall date	Recall campaign number	Model(s) affected	Concern
NOV 24, 2010	10V599000	2011 Sorento	On some models, the rear brake calipers may not have been properly machined. As a result, brake fluid will leak, followed by illumination of the malfunction indicator light indicating the brake fluid level is low and should be checked, then a soft or spongy brake pedal feel, and if not serviced, reduced braking power which could increase the risk of a crash.
AUG 31, 2010	10V388000	2011 Sorento	On some models, the wiring harness used for the lighting in the interior accent illumination, located in the front and rear door trim panels, may have been improperly soldered. When the lights are illuminated under certain conditions, an electrical short may occur that can result in a fire.

Buying parts

Replacement parts are available from many sources, which generally fall into one of two categories - authorized dealer parts departments and independent retail auto parts stores. Our advice concerning these parts is as follows:

Retail auto parts stores: Good auto parts stores will stock frequently needed components which wear out relatively fast, such as clutch components, exhaust systems, brake parts, tune-up parts, etc. These stores often supply new or reconditioned parts on an exchange basis, which can save a considerable amount of money. Discount auto parts stores are often very good places to buy materials and parts needed for general vehicle maintenance such as oil, grease, filters, spark plugs, belts, touch-up paint, bulbs, etc. They also usually sell tools and general accessories, have convenient hours, charge lower prices and can often be found not far from home.

Authorized dealer parts department: This is the best source for parts which are unique to the vehicle and not generally available elsewhere (such as major engine parts, transmission parts, trim pieces, etc.).

Warranty information: If the vehicle is still covered under warranty, be sure that any replacement parts purchased - regardless of the source - do not invalidate the warranty!

To be sure of obtaining the correct parts, have engine and chassis numbers available and, if possible, take the old parts along for positive identification.

Maintenance techniques, tools and working facilities

MAINTENANCE TECHNIQUES

There are a number of techniques involved in maintenance and repair that will be referred to throughout this manual. Application of these techniques will enable the home mechanic to be more efficient, better organized and capable of performing the various tasks properly, which will ensure that the repair job is thorough and complete.

Fasteners

Fasteners are nuts, bolts, studs and screws used to hold two or more parts together. There are a few things to keep in mind when working with fasteners. Almost all of them use a locking device of some type, either a lockwasher, locknut, locking tab or thread adhesive. All threaded fasteners should be clean and straight, with undamaged threads and undamaged corners on the hex head where the wrench fits. Develop the habit of replacing all damaged nuts and bolts with new ones. Special locknuts with nylon or fiber inserts can only be used once. If they are removed, they lose their locking ability and must be replaced with new ones.

Rusted nuts and bolts should be treated with a penetrating fluid to ease removal and prevent breakage. Some mechanics use turpentine in a spout-type oil can, which works quite well. After applying the rust penetrant, let it work for a few minutes before trying to loosen the nut or bolt. Badly rusted fasteners may have to be chiseled or sawed off or removed with a special nut breaker, available at tool stores.

If a bolt or stud breaks off in an assembly, it can be drilled and removed with a special tool commonly available for this purpose. Most automotive machine shops can perform this task, as well as other repair procedures, such as the repair of threaded holes that have been stripped out.

Flat washers and lockwashers, when removed from an assembly, should always be replaced exactly as removed. Replace any damaged washers with new ones. Never use a lockwasher on any soft metal surface (such as aluminum), thin sheet metal or plastic.

Fastener sizes

For a number of reasons, automobile manufacturers are making wider and wider use of metric fasteners. Therefore, it is important to be able to tell the difference between standard (sometimes called U.S. or SAE) and metric hardware, since they cannot be interchanged.

All bolts, whether standard or metric, are sized according to diameter, thread pitch and length. For example, a standard 1/2 - 13 x 1 bolt is 1/2 inch in diameter, has 13 threads per inch and is 1 inch long. An M12 - 1.75 x 25 metric bolt is 12 mm in diameter, has a thread pitch of 1.75 mm (the distance between threads) and is 25 mm long. The two bolts are nearly identical, and easily confused, but they are not interchangeable.

In addition to the differences in diameter, thread pitch and length, metric and standard bolts can also be distinguished by examining the bolt heads. To begin with, the distance across the flats on a standard bolt head is measured in inches, while the same dimension on a metric bolt is sized in millimeters (the same is true for nuts). As a result, a standard wrench should not be used on a metric bolt and a metric wrench should not be used on a standard bolt. Also, most standard bolts have slashes radiating out from the center of the head to denote the grade or strength

of the bolt, which is an indication of the amount of torque that can be applied to it. The greater the number of slashes, the greater the strength of the bolt. Grades 0 through 5 are commonly used on automobiles. Metric bolts have a property class (grade) number, rather than a slash, molded into their heads to indicate bolt strength. In this case, the higher the number, the stronger the bolt. Property class numbers 8.8, 9.8 and 10.9 are commonly used on automobiles.

Strength markings can also be used to distinguish standard hex nuts from metric hex nuts. Many standard nuts have dots stamped into one side, while metric nuts are marked with a number. The greater the number of dots, or the higher the number, the greater the strength of the nut.

Metric studs are also marked on their ends according to property class (grade). Larger studs are numbered (the same as metric bolts), while smaller studs carry a geometric code to denote grade.

It should be noted that many fasteners, especially Grades 0 through 2, have no distinguishing marks on them. When such is the case, the only way to determine whether it is standard or metric is to measure the thread pitch or compare it to a known fastener of the same size.

Standard fasteners are often referred to as SAE, as opposed to metric. However, it should be noted that SAE technically refers to a non-metric fine thread fastener only. Coarse thread non-metric fasteners are referred to as USS sizes.

Since fasteners of the same size (both standard and metric) may have different strength ratings, be sure to reinstall any bolts, studs or nuts removed from your vehicle in their original locations. Also, when replacing a fastener with a new one, make sure that the new one has a strength rating equal to or greater than the original.

Tightening sequences and procedures

Most threaded fasteners should be tightened to a specific torque value (torque is the twisting force applied to a threaded component such as a nut or bolt). Overtightening the fastener can weaken it and cause it to break, while undertightening can cause it to eventually come loose. Bolts, screws and studs, depending on the material they are made of and their thread diameters, have specific torque values, many of which are noted in the Specifications at the end of each Chapter. Be sure to follow the torque recommendations closely. For fasteners not assigned a specific torque, a general torque value chart is presented here as a guide. These torque values are for dry (unlubricated) fasteners threaded into steel or cast iron (not aluminum). As was previously mentioned, the size and grade of a fastener determine the amount of torque that can safely be applied to it. The figures listed here are approximate for Grade 2 and Grade 3 fasteners. Higher grades can tolerate higher torque values.

Fasteners laid out in a pattern, such as cylinder head bolts, oil pan bolts, differential cover bolts, etc., must be loosened or tightened in sequence to avoid warping the component. This sequence will normally be shown in the appropriate Chapter. If a specific pattern is not given, the following procedures can be used to prevent warping.

Initially, the bolts or nuts should be assembled finger-tight only. Next, they should be tightened one full turn each, in a criss-cross or diagonal pattern. After each one has been tightened one full turn, return to the first one and tighten them all one-half turn, following the same

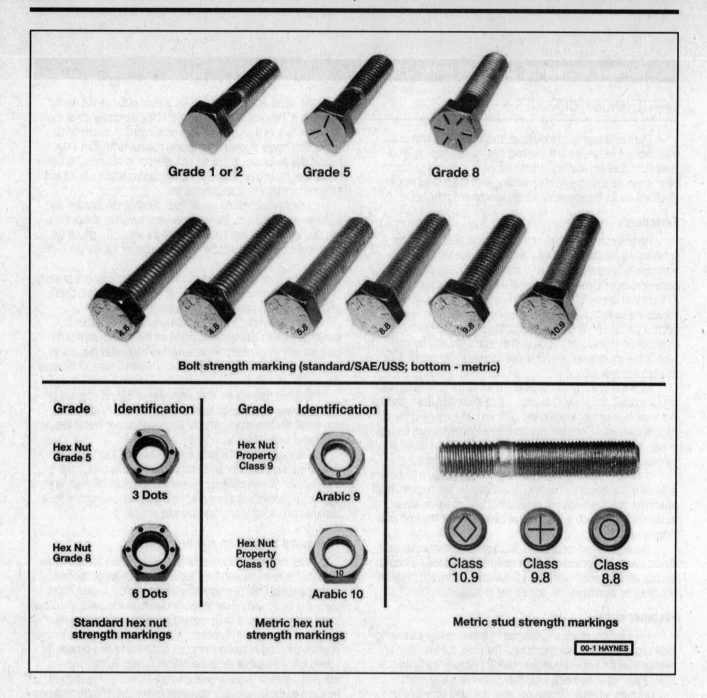

Grade 1 or 2 Grade 5 Grade 8

Bolt strength marking (standard/SAE/USS; bottom - metric)

Grade	Identification
Hex Nut Grade 5	3 Dots
Hex Nut Grade 8	6 Dots

Standard hex nut strength markings

Grade	Identification
Hex Nut Property Class 9	Arabic 9
Hex Nut Property Class 10	Arabic 10

Metric hex nut strength markings

Class 10.9 Class 9.8 Class 8.8

Metric stud strength markings

00-1 HAYNES

pattern. Finally, tighten each of them one-quarter turn at a time until each fastener has been tightened to the proper torque. To loosen and remove the fasteners, the procedure would be reversed.

Component disassembly

Component disassembly should be done with care and purpose to help ensure that the parts go back together properly. Always keep track of the sequence in which parts are removed. Make note of special characteristics or marks on parts that can be installed more than one way, such as a grooved thrust washer on a shaft. It is a good idea to lay the disassembled parts out on a clean surface in the order that they were removed. It may also be helpful to make sketches or take instant photos of components before removal.

When removing fasteners from a component, keep track of their locations. Sometimes threading a bolt back in a part, or putting the washers and nut back on a stud, can prevent mix-ups later. If nuts and bolts cannot be returned to their original locations, they should be kept in a compartmented box or a series of small boxes. A cupcake or muffin tin is ideal for this purpose, since each cavity can hold the bolts and nuts from a particular area (i.e. oil pan bolts, valve cover bolts, engine

Metric thread sizes

	Ft-lbs	Nm
M-6	6 to 9	9 to 12
M-8	14 to 21	19 to 28
M-10	28 to 40	38 to 54
M-12	50 to 71	68 to 96
M-14	80 to 140	109 to 154

Pipe thread sizes

1/8	5 to 8	7 to 10
1/4	12 to 18	17 to 24
3/8	22 to 33	30 to 44
1/2	25 to 35	34 to 47

U.S. thread sizes

1/4 - 20	6 to 9	9 to 12
5/16 - 18	12 to 18	17 to 24
5/16 - 24	14 to 20	19 to 27
3/8 - 16	22 to 32	30 to 43
3/8 - 24	27 to 38	37 to 51
7/16 - 14	40 to 55	55 to 74
7/16 - 20	40 to 60	55 to 81
1/2 - 13	55 to 80	75 to 108

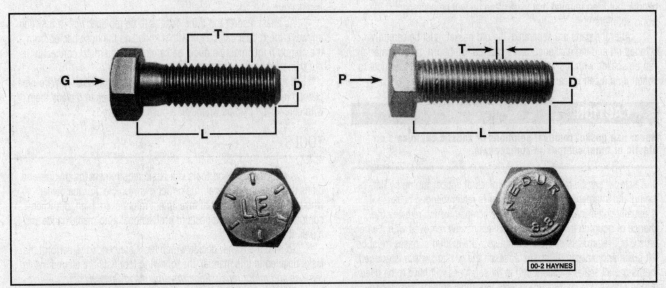

Standard (SAE and USS) bolt dimensions/grade marks

G   Grade marks (bolt strength)
L   Length (in inches)
T   Thread pitch (number of threads per inch)
D   Nominal diameter (in inches)

Metric bolt dimensions/grade marks

P   Property class (bolt strength)
L   Length (in millimeters)
T   Thread pitch (distance between threads in millimeters)
D   Diameter

mount bolts, etc.). A pan of this type is especially helpful when working on assemblies with very small parts, such as the carburetor, alternator, valve train or interior dash and trim pieces. The cavities can be marked with paint or tape to identify the contents.

Whenever wiring looms, harnesses or connectors are separated, it is a good idea to identify the two halves with numbered pieces of masking tape so they can be easily reconnected.

Gasket sealing surfaces

Throughout any vehicle, gaskets are used to seal the mating surfaces between two parts and keep lubricants, fluids, vacuum or pressure contained in an assembly.

Many times these gaskets are coated with a liquid or paste-type gasket sealing compound before assembly. Age, heat and pressure can sometimes cause the two parts to stick together so tightly that they are very difficult to separate. Often, the assembly can be loosened by striking it with a soft-face hammer near the mating surfaces. A regular hammer can be used if a block of wood is placed between the hammer and the part. Do not hammer on cast parts or parts that could be easily damaged. With any particularly stubborn part, always recheck to make sure that every fastener has been removed.

Avoid using a screwdriver or bar to pry apart an assembly, as

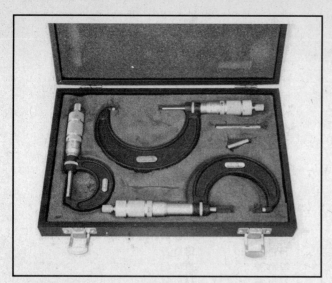

Micrometer set

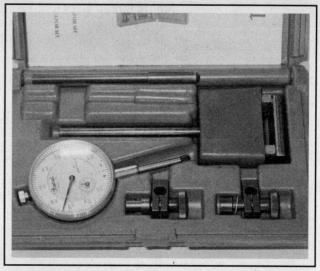

Dial indicator set

they can easily mar the gasket sealing surfaces of the parts, which must remain smooth. If prying is absolutely necessary, use an old broom handle, but keep in mind that extra clean up will be necessary if the wood splinters.

After the parts are separated, the old gasket must be carefully scraped off and the gasket surfaces cleaned. Stubborn gasket material can be soaked with rust penetrant or treated with a special chemical to soften it so it can be easily scraped off.

⁕ CAUTION:

Never use gasket removal solutions or caustic chemicals on plastic or other composite components.

A scraper can be fashioned from a piece of copper tubing by flattening and sharpening one end. Copper is recommended because it is usually softer than the surfaces to be scraped, which reduces the chance of gouging the part. Some gaskets can be removed with a wire brush, but regardless of the method used, the mating surfaces must be left clean and smooth. If for some reason the gasket surface is gouged, then a gasket sealer thick enough to fill scratches will have to be used during reassembly of the components. For most applications, a non-drying (or semi-drying) gasket sealer should be used.

Hose removal tips

⁕ WARNING:

If the vehicle is equipped with air conditioning, do not disconnect any of the A/C hoses without first having the system depressurized by a dealer service department or a service station.

Hose removal precautions closely parallel gasket removal precautions. Avoid scratching or gouging the surface that the hose mates against or the connection may leak. This is especially true for radiator hoses. Because of various chemical reactions, the rubber in hoses can bond itself to the metal spigot that the hose fits over. To remove a hose, first loosen the hose clamps that secure it to the spigot. Then, with slip-joint pliers, grab the hose at the clamp and rotate it around the spigot. Work it back and forth until it is completely free, then pull it off. Silicone or other lubricants will ease removal if they can be applied

between the hose and the outside of the spigot. Apply the same lubricant to the inside of the hose and the outside of the spigot to simplify installation.

As a last resort (and if the hose is to be replaced with a new one anyway), the rubber can be slit with a knife and the hose peeled from the spigot. If this must be done, be careful that the metal connection is not damaged.

If a hose clamp is broken or damaged, do not reuse it. Wire-type clamps usually weaken with age, so it is a good idea to replace them with screw-type clamps whenever a hose is removed.

TOOLS

A selection of good tools is a basic requirement for anyone who plans to maintain and repair his or her own vehicle. For the owner who has few tools, the initial investment might seem high, but when compared to the spiraling costs of professional auto maintenance and repair, it is a wise one.

To help the owner decide which tools are needed to perform the tasks detailed in this manual, the following tool lists are offered: *Maintenance and minor repair, Repair/overhaul and Special.*

The newcomer to practical mechanics should start off with the *maintenance and minor repair* tool kit, which is adequate for the simpler jobs performed on a vehicle. Then, as confidence and experience grow, the owner can tackle more difficult tasks, buying additional tools as they are needed. Eventually the basic kit will be expanded into the *repair and overhaul* tool set. Over a period of time, the experienced do-it-yourselfer will assemble a tool set complete enough for most repair and overhaul procedures and will add tools from the special category when it is felt that the expense is justified by the frequency of use.

Maintenance and minor repair tool kit

The tools in this list should be considered the minimum required for performance of routine maintenance, servicing and minor repair work. We recommend the purchase of combination wrenches (box-end and open-end combined in one wrench). While more expensive than open end wrenches, they offer the advantages of both types of wrench.

Combination wrench set (1/4-inch to 1 inch or 6 mm to 19 mm)
Adjustable wrench, 8 inch
Spark plug wrench with rubber insert

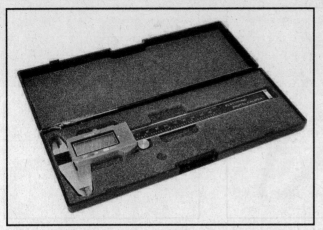

Dial caliper

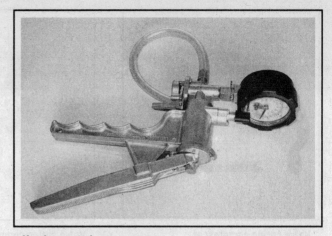

Hand-operated vacuum pump

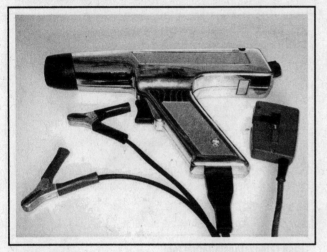

Timing light

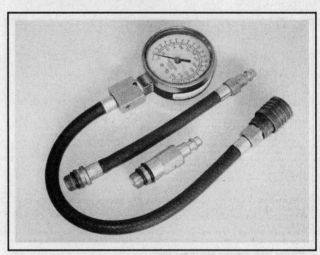

Compression gauge with spark plug hole adapter

Damper/steering wheel puller

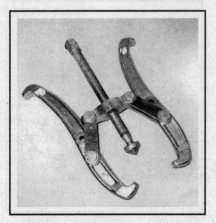

General purpose puller

Hydraulic lifter removal tool

Spark plug gap adjusting tool
Feeler gauge set
Brake bleeder wrench
Standard screwdriver (5/16-inch x 6 inch)
Phillips screwdriver (No. 2 x 6 inch)
Combination pliers - 6 inch
Hacksaw and assortment of blades
Tire pressure gauge
Grease gun

Oil can
Fine emery cloth
Wire brush
Battery post and cable cleaning tool
Oil filter wrench
Funnel (medium size)
Safety goggles
Jackstands (2)
Drain pan

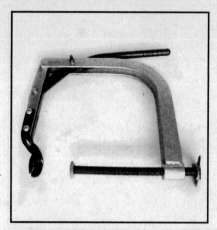

Valve spring compressor

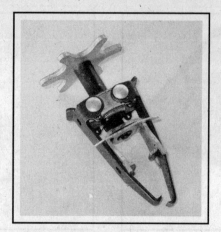

Valve spring compressor

Ridge reamer

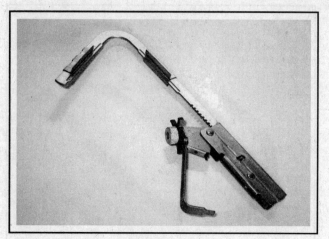

Piston ring groove cleaning tool

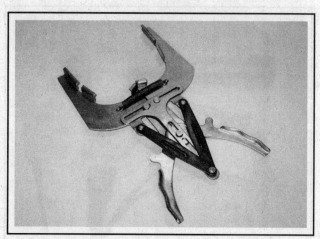

Ring removal/installation tool

Ring compressor

Cylinder hone

Brake hold-down spring tool

➡ **Note:** If basic tune-ups are going to be part of routine maintenance, it will be necessary to purchase a good quality stroboscopic timing light and combination tachometer/dwell meter. Although they are included in the list of special tools, it is mentioned here because they are absolutely necessary for tuning most vehicles properly.

Repair and overhaul tool set

These tools are essential for anyone who plans to perform major repairs and are in addition to those in the maintenance and minor repair tool kit. Included is a comprehensive set of sockets which, though expensive, are invaluable because of their versatility, especially when various extensions and drives are available. We recommend the 1/2-inch drive over the 3/8-inch drive. Although the larger drive is bulky and more expensive, it has the capacity of accepting a very wide range of large sockets. Ideally, however, the mechanic should have a 3/8-inch drive set and a 1/2-inch drive set.

Torque angle gauge

Clutch plate alignment tool

Socket set(s)
Reversible ratchet
Extension - 10 inch
Universal joint
Torque wrench (same size drive as sockets)
Ball peen hammer - 8 ounce
Soft-face hammer (plastic/rubber)
Standard screwdriver (1/4-inch x 6 inch)
Standard screwdriver (stubby - 5/16-inch)
Phillips screwdriver (No. 3 x 8 inch)
Phillips screwdriver (stubby - No. 2)
Pliers - vise grip
Pliers - lineman's
Pliers - needle nose
Pliers - snap-ring (internal and external)
Cold chisel - 1/2-inch
Scribe
Scraper (made from flattened copper tubing)
Centerpunch
Pin punches (1/16, 1/8, 3/16-inch)
Steel rule/straightedge - 12 inch
Allen wrench set (1/8 to 3/8-inch or 4 mm to 10 mm)
A selection of files
Wire brush (large)
Jackstands (second set)
Jack (scissor or hydraulic type)

➡ **Note: Another tool which is often useful is an electric drill with a chuck capacity of 3/8-inch and a set of good quality drill bits.**

Special tools

The tools in this list include those which are not used regularly, are expensive to buy, or which need to be used in accordance with their manufacturer's instructions. Unless these tools will be used frequently, it is not very economical to purchase many of them. A consideration would be to split the cost and use between yourself and a friend or friends. In addition, most of these tools can be obtained from a tool rental shop on a temporary basis.

This list primarily contains only those tools and instruments widely available to the public, and not those special tools produced by the vehicle manufacturer for distribution to dealer service departments. Occasionally, references to the manufacturer's special tools are included in the text of this manual. Generally, an alternative method of doing the job without the special tool is offered. However, sometimes

there is no alternative to their use. Where this is the case, and the tool cannot be purchased or borrowed, the work should be turned over to the dealer service department or an automotive repair shop.

Valve spring compressor
Piston ring groove cleaning tool
Piston ring compressor
Piston ring installation tool
Cylinder compression gauge
Cylinder ridge reamer
Cylinder surfacing hone
Cylinder bore gauge
Micrometers and/or dial calipers
Hydraulic lifter removal tool
Balljoint separator
Universal-type puller
Impact screwdriver
Dial indicator set
Stroboscopic timing light (inductive pick-up)
Hand operated vacuum/pressure pump
Tachometer/dwell meter
Universal electrical multimeter
Cable hoist
Brake spring removal and installation tools
Floor jack

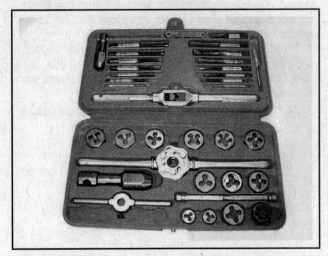

Tap and die set

Buying tools

For the do-it-yourselfer who is just starting to get involved in vehicle maintenance and repair, there are a number of options available when purchasing tools. If maintenance and minor repair is the extent of the work to be done, the purchase of individual tools is satisfactory. If, on the other hand, extensive work is planned, it would be a good idea to purchase a modest tool set from one of the large retail chain stores. A set can usually be bought at a substantial savings over the individual tool prices, and they often come with a tool box. As additional tools are needed, add-on sets, individual tools and a larger tool box can be purchased to expand the tool selection. Building a tool set gradually allows the cost of the tools to be spread over a longer period of time and gives the mechanic the freedom to choose only those tools that will actually be used.

Tool stores will often be the only source of some of the special tools that are needed, but regardless of where tools are bought, try to avoid cheap ones, especially when buying screwdrivers and sockets, because they won't last very long. The expense involved in replacing cheap tools will eventually be greater than the initial cost of quality tools.

Care and maintenance of tools

Good tools are expensive, so it makes sense to treat them with respect. Keep them clean and in usable condition and store them properly when not in use. Always wipe off any dirt, grease or metal chips before putting them away. Never leave tools lying around in the work area. Upon completion of a job, always check closely under the hood for tools that may have been left there so they won't get lost during a test drive.

Some tools, such as screwdrivers, pliers, wrenches and sockets, can be hung on a panel mounted on the garage or workshop wall, while others should be kept in a tool box or tray. Measuring instruments, gauges, meters, etc. must be carefully stored where they cannot be damaged by weather or impact from other tools.

When tools are used with care and stored properly, they will last a very long time. Even with the best of care, though, tools will wear out if used frequently. When a tool is damaged or worn out, replace it. Subsequent jobs will be safer and more enjoyable if you do.

HOW TO REPAIR DAMAGED THREADS

Sometimes, the internal threads of a nut or bolt hole can become stripped, usually from overtightening. Stripping threads is an all-too-common occurrence, especially when working with aluminum parts, because aluminum is so soft that it easily strips out.

Usually, external or internal threads are only partially stripped. After they've been cleaned up with a tap or die, they'll still work. Sometimes, however, threads are badly damaged. When this happens, you've got three choices:

1) *Drill and tap the hole to the next suitable oversize and install a larger diameter bolt, screw or stud.*
2) *Drill and tap the hole to accept a threaded plug, then drill and tap the plug to the original screw size. You can also buy a plug already threaded to the original size. Then you simply drill a hole to the specified size, then run the threaded plug into the hole with a bolt and jam nut. Once the plug is fully seated, remove the jam nut and bolt.*
3) *The third method uses a patented thread repair kit like Heli-Coil or Slimsert. These easy-to-use kits are designed to repair damaged threads in straight-through holes and blind holes. Both are available as kits which can handle a variety of sizes and thread patterns. Drill the hole, then tap it with the special included tap. Install the Heli-Coil and the hole is back to its original diameter and thread pitch.*

Regardless of which method you use, be sure to proceed calmly and carefully. A little impatience or carelessness during one of these relatively simple procedures can ruin your whole day's work and cost you a bundle if you wreck an expensive part.

WORKING FACILITIES

Not to be overlooked when discussing tools is the workshop. If anything more than routine maintenance is to be carried out, some sort of suitable work area is essential.

It is understood, and appreciated, that many home mechanics do not have a good workshop or garage available, and end up removing an engine or doing major repairs outside. It is recommended, however, that the overhaul or repair be completed under the cover of a roof.

A clean, flat workbench or table of comfortable working height is an absolute necessity. The workbench should be equipped with a vise that has a jaw opening of at least four inches.

As mentioned previously, some clean, dry storage space is also required for tools, as well as the lubricants, fluids, cleaning solvents, etc. which soon become necessary.

Sometimes waste oil and fluids, drained from the engine or cooling system during normal maintenance or repairs, present a disposal problem. To avoid pouring them on the ground or into a sewage system, pour the used fluids into large containers, seal them with caps and take them to an authorized disposal site or recycling center. Plastic jugs, such as old antifreeze containers, are ideal for this purpose.

Always keep a supply of old newspapers and clean rags available. Old towels are excellent for mopping up spills. Many mechanics use rolls of paper towels for most work because they are readily available and disposable. To help keep the area under the vehicle clean, a large cardboard box can be cut open and flattened to protect the garage or shop floor.

Whenever working over a painted surface, such as when leaning over a fender to service something under the hood, always cover it with an old blanket or bedspread to protect the finish. Vinyl covered pads, made especially for this purpose, are available at auto parts stores.

Jacking and towing

JACKING

> ✳ **WARNING:**
>
> **The jack supplied with the vehicle should only be used for changing a tire or placing jackstands under the frame. Never work under the vehicle or start the engine while this jack is being used as the only means of support.**

The jack supplied with the vehicle should only be used for raising the vehicle when changing a tire or placing jackstands under the frame.

2009 and earlier models

The vehicle should be on level ground with the hazard flashers on, the wheels blocked, the parking brake applied and the transmission in Park (automatic) or Reverse (manual). If a tire is being changed, loosen the lug nuts one-half turn and leave them in place until the wheel is raised off the ground.

Place the jack under the vehicle **(see illustrations)** :

Front: Under the frame rail, where the crossmember is attached.

Rear: Under the axle tube nearest the wheel being removed.

Operate the jack with a slow, smooth motion until the wheel is raised off the ground. Remove the lug nuts, pull off the wheel, install the spare and thread the lug nuts back on with the beveled sides facing in. Tighten them snugly, but wait until the vehicle is lowered to tighten them completely.

Lower the vehicle, remove the jack and tighten the nuts (if loosened or removed) in a criss-cross pattern.

2011 and later models

When jacking the vehicle, the jack should be engaged with the rocker panel seam, between the two notches **(see illustration)**.

The vehicle should be on level ground with the wheels blocked and the transmission in Park (automatic). Pry off the hub cap (if equipped) using the tapered end of the lug wrench. Loosen the lug nuts one-half turn and leave them in place until the wheel is raised off the ground.

Place the jack under the side of the vehicle in the indicated position. Use the supplied wrench to turn the jackscrew clockwise until the wheel is raised off the ground. Remove the lug nuts, pull off the wheel and replace it with the spare.

With the beveled side in, reinstall the lug nuts and tighten them until snug. Lower the vehicle by turning the jackscrew counterclockwise. Remove the jack and tighten the nuts in a diagonal pattern to the torque listed in the Chapter 1 Specifications. If a torque wrench is not available, have the torque checked by a service station as soon as possible. Install the hubcap by placing it in position and using the heel of your hand or a rubber mallet to seat it.

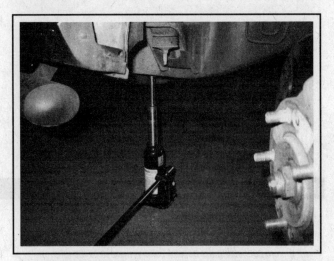

7.3a Front jacking point

7.3b Rear jacking point

7.6 The jack fits between the notches in the rocker panel pinch-weld (there are two jacking points on each side of the vehicle)

TOWING

2009 and earlier models

As a general rule, the vehicle should be towed with professional towing equipment. If towed from the front, the rear wheels should be placed on a towing dolly. If a 4WD model is towed from the rear, the front wheels should be placed on a towing dolly; if a dolly is not available, turn the ignition key to the ACC position, place the transfer case in the 2H position and the transmission in Neutral.

When a vehicle is towed with the rear wheels raised, the steering wheel must be clamped in the straight ahead position with a special device designed for use during towing. The ignition key must not be in the LOCK position, since the steering lock mechanism isn't strong enough to hold the front wheels straight while towing.

Equipment specifically designed for towing should be used. It should be attached to the main structural members of the vehicle, not the bumpers or brackets. Safety is a major consideration when towing and all applicable state and local laws must be obeyed. A safety chain system must be used at all times. Remember that power steering and power brakes will not work with the engine off.

2011 and later models

Two-wheel drive models can be towed from the front with the front wheels off the ground, using a wheel lift type tow truck. If towed from the rear, the front wheels must be placed on a dolly. All-wheel-drive models must be towed with all four wheels off the ground. A sling-type tow truck cannot be used, as body damage will result. The best way to tow the vehicle is with a flat-bed car carrier.

In an emergency the vehicle can be towed a very short distance with a cable or chain attached to one of the towing eyelets located under the front or rear bumpers. The driver must remain in the vehicle to operate the steering and brakes (remember that power steering and power brakes will not work with the engine off). Make certain that the vehicle is in neutral with the parking brake off.

Booster battery (jump) starting

Observe these precautions when using a booster battery to start a vehicle:

a) *Before connecting the booster battery, make sure the ignition switch is in the Off position.*

b) *Turn off the lights, heater and other electrical loads.*

c) *Your eyes should be shielded. Safety goggles are a good idea.*

d) *Make sure the booster battery is the same voltage as the dead one in the vehicle.*

e) *The two vehicles MUST NOT TOUCH each other!*

f) *Make sure the transaxle is in Neutral (manual) or Park (automatic).*

g) *If the booster battery is not a maintenance-free type, remove the vent caps and lay a cloth over the vent holes.*

Connect the red jumper cable to the positive (+) terminals of each battery (see illustration).

Connect one end of the black jumper cable to the negative (-) terminal of the booster battery. The other end of this cable should be connected to a good ground on the vehicle to be started, such as a bolt or bracket on the body.

Start the engine using the booster battery, then, with the engine running at idle speed, disconnect the jumper cables in the reverse order of connection.

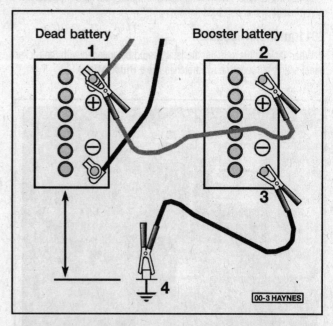

Make the booster battery cable connections in the numerical order shown (note that the negative cable of the booster battery is NOT attached to the negative terminal of the dead battery)

Automotive chemicals and lubricants

A number of automotive chemicals and lubricants are available for use during vehicle maintenance and repair. They include a wide variety of products ranging from cleaning solvents and degreasers to lubricants and protective sprays for rubber, plastic and vinyl.

CLEANERS

Carburetor cleaner and choke cleaner is a strong solvent for gum, varnish and carbon. Most carburetor cleaners leave a dry-type lubricant film which will not harden or gum up. Because of this film it is not recommended for use on electrical components.

Brake system cleaner is used to remove brake dust, grease and brake fluid from the brake system, where clean surfaces are absolutely necessary. It leaves no residue and often eliminates brake squeal caused by contaminants.

Electrical cleaner removes oxidation, corrosion and carbon deposits from electrical contacts, restoring full current flow. It can also be used to clean spark plugs, carburetor jets, voltage regulators and other parts where an oil-free surface is desired.

Demoisturants remove water and moisture from electrical components such as alternators, voltage regulators, electrical connectors and fuse blocks. They are non-conductive and non-corrosive.

Degreasers are heavy-duty solvents used to remove grease from the outside of the engine and from chassis components. They can be sprayed or brushed on and, depending on the type, are rinsed off either with water or solvent.

LUBRICANTS

Motor oil is the lubricant formulated for use in engines. It normally contains a wide variety of additives to prevent corrosion and reduce foaming and wear. Motor oil comes in various weights (viscosity ratings) from 0 to 50. The recommended weight of the oil depends on the season, temperature and the demands on the engine. Light oil is used in cold climates and under light load conditions. Heavy oil is used in hot climates and where high loads are encountered. Multi-viscosity oils are designed to have characteristics of both light and heavy oils and are available in a number of weights from 0W-20 to 20W-50.

Gear oil is designed to be used in differentials, manual transmissions and other areas where high-temperature lubrication is required.

Chassis and wheel bearing grease is a heavy grease used where increased loads and friction are encountered, such as for wheel bearings, ball-joints, tie-rod ends and universal joints.

High-temperature wheel bearing grease is designed to withstand the extreme temperatures encountered by wheel bearings in disc brake equipped vehicles. It usually contains molybdenum disulfide (moly), which is a dry-type lubricant.

White grease is a heavy grease for metal-to-metal applications where water is a problem. White grease stays soft under both low and high temperatures (usually from -100 to +190-degrees F), and will not wash off or dilute in the presence of water.

Assembly lube is a special extreme pressure lubricant, usually containing moly, used to lubricate high-load parts (such as main and rod bearings and cam lobes) for initial start-up of a new engine. The assembly lube lubricates the parts without being squeezed out or washed away until the engine oiling system begins to function.

Silicone lubricants are used to protect rubber, plastic, vinyl and nylon parts.

Graphite lubricants are used where oils cannot be used due to contamination problems, such as in locks. The dry graphite will lubricate metal parts while remaining uncontaminated by dirt, water, oil or acids. It is electrically conductive and will not foul electrical contacts in locks such as the ignition switch.

Moly penetrants loosen and lubricate frozen, rusted and corroded fasteners and prevent future rusting or freezing.

Heat-sink grease is a special electrically non-conductive grease that is used for mounting electronic ignition modules where it is essential that heat is transferred away from the module.

SEALANTS

RTV sealant is one of the most widely used gasket compounds. Made from silicone, RTV is air curing, it seals, bonds, waterproofs, fills surface irregularities, remains flexible, doesn't shrink, is relatively easy to remove, and is used as a supplementary sealer with almost all low and medium temperature gaskets.

Anaerobic sealant is much like RTV in that it can be used either to seal gaskets or to form gaskets by itself. It remains flexible, is solvent resistant and fills surface imperfections. The difference between an anaerobic sealant and an RTV-type sealant is in the curing. RTV cures when exposed to air, while an anaerobic sealant cures only in the absence of air. This means that an anaerobic sealant cures only after the assembly of parts, sealing them together.

Thread and pipe sealant is used for sealing hydraulic and pneumatic fittings and vacuum lines. It is usually made from a Teflon compound, and comes in a spray, a paint-on liquid and as a wrap-around tape.

CHEMICALS

Anti-seize compound prevents seizing, galling, cold welding, rust and corrosion in fasteners. High-temperature anti-seize, usually made with copper and graphite lubricants, is used for exhaust system and exhaust manifold bolts.

Anaerobic locking compounds are used to keep fasteners from vibrating or working loose and cure only after installation, in the absence of air. Medium strength locking compound is used for small nuts, bolts and screws that may be removed later. High-strength locking compound is for large nuts, bolts and studs which aren't removed on a regular basis.

Oil additives range from viscosity index improvers to chemical treatments that claim to reduce internal engine friction. It should be noted that most oil manufacturers caution against using additives with their oils.

Gas additives perform several functions, depending on their chemical makeup. They usually contain solvents that help dissolve gum and varnish that build up on carburetor, fuel injection and intake parts. They also serve to break down carbon deposits that form on the inside surfaces of the combustion chambers. Some additives contain upper cylinder lubricants for valves and piston rings, and others contain chemicals to remove condensation from the gas tank.

MISCELLANEOUS

Brake fluid is specially formulated hydraulic fluid that can withstand the heat and pressure encountered in brake systems. Care must be taken so this fluid does not come in contact with painted surfaces or plastics. An opened container should always be resealed to prevent contamination by water or dirt.

Weatherstrip adhesive is used to bond weatherstripping around doors, windows and trunk lids. It is sometimes used to attach trim pieces.

Undercoating is a petroleum-based, tar-like substance that is designed to protect metal surfaces on the underside of the vehicle from corrosion. It also acts as a sound-deadening agent by insulating the bottom of the vehicle.

Waxes and polishes are used to help protect painted and plated surfaces from the weather. Different types of paint may require the use of different types of wax and polish. Some polishes utilize a chemical or abrasive cleaner to help remove the top layer of oxidized (dull) paint on older vehicles. In recent years many non-wax polishes that contain a wide variety of chemicals such as polymers and silicones have been introduced. These non-wax polishes are usually easier to apply and last longer than conventional waxes and polishes.

CONVERSION FACTORS

LENGTH (distance)
Inches (in)	X	25.4	= Millimeters (mm)	X 0.0394	= Inches (in)
Feet (ft)	X	0.305	= Meters (m)	X 3.281	= Feet (ft)
Miles	X	1.609	= Kilometers (km)	X 0.621	= Miles

VOLUME (capacity)
Cubic inches (cu in; in^3)	X	16.387	= Cubic centimeters (cc; cm^3)	X 0.061	= Cubic inches (cu in; in^3)
Imperial pints (Imp pt)	X	0.568	= Liters (l)	X 1.76	= Imperial pints (Imp pt)
Imperial quarts (Imp qt)	X	1.137	= Liters (l)	X 0.88	= Imperial quarts (Imp qt)
Imperial quarts (Imp qt)	X	1.201	= US quarts (US qt)	X 0.833	= Imperial quarts (Imp qt)
US quarts (US qt)	X	0.946	= Liters (l)	X 1.057	= US quarts (US qt)
Imperial gallons (Imp gal)	X	4.546	= Liters (l)	X 0.22	= Imperial gallons (Imp gal)
Imperial gallons (Imp gal)	X	1.201	= US gallons (US gal)	X 0.833	= Imperial gallons (Imp gal)
US gallons (US gal)	X	3.785	= Liters (l)	X 0.264	= US gallons (US gal)

MASS (weight)
Ounces (oz)	X	28.35	= Grams (g)	X 0.035	= Ounces (oz)
Pounds (lb)	X	0.454	= Kilograms (kg)	X 2.205	= Pounds (lb)

FORCE
Ounces-force (ozf; oz)	X	0.278	= Newtons (N)	X 3.6	= Ounces-force (ozf; oz)
Pounds-force (lbf; lb)	X	4.448	= Newtons (N)	X 0.225	= Pounds-force (lbf; lb)
Newtons (N)	X	0.1	= Kilograms-force (kgf; kg)	X 9.81	= Newtons (N)

PRESSURE
Pounds-force per square inch (psi; lbf/in^2; lb/in^2)	X	0.070	= Kilograms-force per square centimeter (kgf/cm^2; kg/cm^2)	X 14.223	= Pounds-force per square inch (psi; lbf/in^2; lb/in^2)
Pounds-force per square inch (psi; lbf/in^2; lb/in^2)	X	0.068	= Atmospheres (atm)	X 14.696	= Pounds-force per square inch (psi; lbf/in^2; lb/in^2)
Pounds-force per square inch (psi; lbf/in^2; lb/in^2)	X	0.069	= Bars	X 14.5	= Pounds-force per square inch (psi; lbf/in^2; lb/in^2)
Pounds-force per square inch (psi; lbf/in^2; lb/in^2)	X	6.895	= Kilopascals (kPa)	X 0.145	= Pounds-force per square inch (psi; lbf/in^2; lb/in^2)
Kilopascals (kPa)	X	0.01	= Kilograms-force per square centimeter (kgf/cm^2; kg/cm^2)	X 98.1	= Kilopascals (kPa)

TORQUE (moment of force)
Pounds-force inches (lbf in; lb in)	X	1.152	= Kilograms-force centimeter (kgf cm; kg cm)	X 0.868	= Pounds-force inches (lbf in; lb in)
Pounds-force inches (lbf in; lb in)	X	0.113	= Newton meters (Nm)	X 8.85	= Pounds-force inches (lbf in; lb in)
Pounds-force inches (lbf in; lb in)	X	0.083	= Pounds-force feet (lbf ft; lb ft)	X 12	= Pounds-force inches (lbf in; lb in)
Pounds-force feet (lbf ft; lb ft)	X	0.138	= Kilograms-force meters (kgf m; kg m)	X 7.233	= Pounds-force feet (lbf ft; lb ft)
Pounds-force feet (lbf ft; lb ft)	X	1.356	= Newton meters (Nm)	X 0.738	= Pounds-force feet (lbf ft; lb ft)
Newton meters (Nm)	X	0.102	= Kilograms-force meters (kgf m; kg m)	X 9.804	= Newton meters (Nm)

VACUUM
Inches mercury (in. Hg)	X	3.377	= Kilopascals (kPa)	X 0.2961	= Inches mercury
Inches mercury (in. Hg)	X	25.4	= Millimeters mercury (mm Hg)	X 0.0394	= Inches mercury

POWER
Horsepower (hp)	X	745.7	= Watts (W)	X 0.0013	= Horsepower (hp)

VELOCITY (speed)
Miles per hour (miles/hr; mph)	X	1.609	= Kilometers per hour (km/hr; kph)	X 0.621	= Miles per hour (miles/hr; mph)

FUEL CONSUMPTION *
Miles per gallon, Imperial (mpg)	X	0.354	= Kilometers per liter (km/l)	X 2.825	= Miles per gallon, Imperial (mpg)
Miles per gallon, US (mpg)	X	0.425	= Kilometers per liter (km/l)	X 2.352	= Miles per gallon, US (mpg)

TEMPERATURE
Degrees Fahrenheit = (°C x 1.8) + 32   Degrees Celsius (Degrees Centigrade; °C) = (°F - 32) x 0.56

*It is common practice to convert from miles per gallon (mpg) to liters/100 kilometers (l/100km), where mpg (Imperial) x l/100 km = 282 and mpg (US) x l/100 km = 235

FRACTION/DECIMAL/MILLIMETER EQUIVALENTS

DECIMALS TO MILLIMETERS

Decimal	mm	Decimal	mm
0.001	0.0254	0.500	12.7000
0.002	0.0508	0.510	12.9540
0.003	0.0762	0.520	13.2080
0.004	0.1016	0.530	13.4620
0.005	0.1270	0.540	13.7160
0.006	0.1524	0.550	13.9700
0.007	0.1778	0.560	14.2240
0.008	0.2032	0.570	14.4780
0.009	0.2286	0.580	14.7320
		0.590	14.9860
0.010	0.2540		
0.020	0.5080		
0.030	0.7620		
0.040	1.0160	0.600	15.2400
0.050	1.2700	0.610	15.4940
0.060	1.5240	0.620	15.7480
0.070	1.7780	0.630	16.0020
0.080	2.0320	0.640	16.2560
0.090	2.2860	0.650	16.5100
		0.660	16.7640
0.100	2.5400	0.670	17.0180
0.110	2.7940	0.680	17.2720
0.120	3.0480	0.690	17.5260
0.130	3.3020		
0.140	3.5560		
0.150	3.8100		
0.160	4.0640	0.700	17.7800
0.170	4.3180	0.710	18.0340
0.180	4.5720	0.720	18.2880
0.190	4.8260	0.730	18.5420
		0.740	18.7960
0.200	5.0800	0.750	19.0500
0.210	5.3340	0.760	19.3040
0.220	5.5880	0.770	19.5580
0.230	5.8420	0.780	19.8120
0.240	6.0960	0.790	20.0660
0.250	6.3500		
0.260	6.6040		
0.270	6.8580	0.800	20.3200
0.280	7.1120	0.810	20.5740
0.290	7.3660	0.820	21.8280
		0.830	21.0820
0.300	7.6200	0.840	21.3360
0.310	7.8740	0.850	21.5900
0.320	8.1280	0.860	21.8440
0.330	8.3820	0.870	22.0980
0.340	8.6360	0.880	22.3520
0.350	8.8900	0.890	22.6060
0.360	9.1440		
0.370	9.3980		
0.380	9.6520		
0.390	9.9060		
		0.900	22.8600
0.400	10.1600	0.910	23.1140
0.410	10.4140	0.920	23.3680
0.420	10.6680	0.930	23.6220
0.430	10.9220	0.940	23.8760
0.440	11.1760	0.950	24.1300
0.450	11.4300	0.960	24.3840
0.460	11.6840	0.970	24.6380
0.470	11.9380	0.980	24.8920
0.480	12.1920	0.990	25.1460
0.490	12.4460	1.000	25.4000

FRACTIONS TO DECIMALS TO MILLIMETERS

Fraction	Decimal	mm	Fraction	Decimal	mm
1/64	0.0156	0.3969	33/64	0.5156	13.0969
1/32	0.0312	0.7938	17/32	0.5312	13.4938
3/64	0.0469	1.1906	35/64	0.5469	13.8906
1/16	0.0625	1.5875	9/16	0.5625	14.2875
5/64	0.0781	1.9844	37/64	0.5781	14.6844
3/32	0.0938	2.3812	19/32	0.5938	15.0812
7/64	0.1094	2.7781	39/64	0.6094	15.4781
1/8	0.1250	3.1750	5/8	0.6250	15.8750
9/64	0.1406	3.5719	41/64	0.6406	16.2719
5/32	0.1562	3.9688	21/32	0.6562	16.6688
11/64	0.1719	4.3656	43/64	0.6719	17.0656
3/16	0.1875	4.7625	11/16	0.6875	17.4625
13/64	0.2031	5.1594	45/64	0.7031	17.8594
7/32	0.2188	5.5562	23/32	0.7188	18.2562
15/64	0.2344	5.9531	47/64	0.7344	18.6531
1/4	0.2500	6.3500	3/4	0.7500	19.0500
17/64	0.2656	6.7469	49/64	0.7656	19.4469
9/32	0.2812	7.1438	25/32	0.7812	19.8438
19/64	0.2969	7.5406	51/64	0.7969	20.2406
5/16	0.3125	7.9375	13/16	0.8125	20.6375
21/64	0.3281	8.3344	53/64	0.8281	21.0344
11/32	0.3438	8.7312	27/32	0.8438	21.4312
23/64	0.3594	9.1281	55/64	0.8594	21.8281
3/8	0.3750	9.5250	7/8	0.8750	22.2250
25/64	0.3906	9.9219	57/64	0.8906	22.6219
13/32	0.4062	10.3188	29/32	0.9062	23.0188
27/64	0.4219	10.7156	59/64	0.9219	23.4156
7/16	0.4375	11.1125	15/16	0.9375	23.8125
29/64	0.4531	11.5094	61/64	0.9531	24.2094
15/32	0.4688	11.9062	31/32	0.9688	24.6062
31/64	0.4844	12.3031	63/64	0.9844	25.0031
1/2	0.5000	12.7000	1	1.0000	25.4000

Safety first!

Regardless of how enthusiastic you may be about getting on with the job at hand, take the time to ensure that your safety is not jeopardized. A moment's lack of attention can result in an accident, as can failure to observe certain simple safety precautions. The possibility of an accident will always exist, and the following points should not be considered a comprehensive list of all dangers. Rather, they are intended to make you aware of the risks and to encourage a safety conscious approach to all work you carry out on your vehicle.

ESSENTIAL DOS AND DON'TS

DON'T rely on a jack when working under the vehicle. Always use approved jackstands to support the weight of the vehicle and place them under the recommended lift or support points.

DON'T attempt to loosen extremely tight fasteners (i.e. wheel lug nuts) while the vehicle is on a jack - it may fall.

DON'T start the engine without first making sure that the transmission is in Neutral (or Park where applicable) and the parking brake is set.

DON'T remove the radiator cap from a hot cooling system - let it cool or cover it with a cloth and release the pressure gradually.

DON'T attempt to drain the engine oil until you are sure it has cooled to the point that it will not burn you.

DON'T touch any part of the engine or exhaust system until it has cooled sufficiently to avoid burns.

DON'T siphon toxic liquids such as gasoline, antifreeze and brake fluid by mouth, or allow them to remain on your skin.

DON'T inhale brake lining dust - it is potentially hazardous (see Asbestos below).

DON'T allow spilled oil or grease to remain on the floor - wipe it up before someone slips on it.

DON'T use loose fitting wrenches or other tools which may slip and cause injury.

DON'T push on wrenches when loosening or tightening nuts or bolts. Always try to pull the wrench toward you. If the situation calls for pushing the wrench away, push with an open hand to avoid scraped knuckles if the wrench should slip.

DON'T attempt to lift a heavy component alone - get someone to help you.

DON'T rush or take unsafe shortcuts to finish a job.

DON'T allow children or animals in or around the vehicle while you are working on it.

DO wear eye protection when using power tools such as a drill, sander, bench grinder, etc. and when working under a vehicle.

DO keep loose clothing and long hair well out of the way of moving parts.

DO make sure that any hoist used has a safe working load rating adequate for the job.

DO get someone to check on you periodically when working alone on a vehicle.

DO carry out work in a logical sequence and make sure that everything is correctly assembled and tightened.

DO keep chemicals and fluids tightly capped and out of the reach of children and pets.

DO remember that your vehicle's safety affects that of yourself and others. If in doubt on any point, get professional advice.

STEERING, SUSPENSION AND BRAKES

These systems are essential to driving safety, so make sure you have a qualified shop or individual check your work. Also, compressed suspension springs can cause injury if released suddenly - be sure to use a spring compressor.

AIRBAGS

Airbags are explosive devices that can CAUSE injury if they deploy while you're working on the vehicle. Follow the manufacturer's instructions to disable the airbag whenever you're working in the vicinity of airbag components.

ASBESTOS

Certain friction, insulating, sealing, and other products - such as brake linings, brake bands, clutch linings, torque converters, gaskets, etc. - may contain asbestos or other hazardous friction material. Extreme care must be taken to avoid inhalation of dust from such products, since it is hazardous to health. If in doubt, assume that they do contain asbestos.

FIRE

Remember at all times that gasoline is highly flammable. Never smoke or have any kind of open flame around when working on a vehicle. But the risk does not end there. A spark caused by an electrical short circuit, by two metal surfaces contacting each other, or even by static electricity built up in your body under certain conditions, can ignite gasoline vapors, which in a confined space are highly explosive. Do not, under any circumstances, use gasoline for cleaning parts. Use an approved safety solvent.

Always disconnect the battery ground (-) cable at the battery before working on any part of the fuel system or electrical system. Never risk spilling fuel on a hot engine or exhaust component. It is strongly recommended that a fire extinguisher suitable for use on fuel and electrical fires be kept handy in the garage or workshop at all times. Never try to extinguish a fuel or electrical fire with water.

FUMES

Certain fumes are highly toxic and can quickly cause unconsciousness and even death if inhaled to any extent. Gasoline vapor falls into this category, as do the vapors from some cleaning solvents. Any draining or pouring of such volatile fluids should be done in a well ventilated area.

When using cleaning fluids and solvents, read the instructions on the container carefully. Never use materials from unmarked containers.

Never run the engine in an enclosed space, such as a garage. Exhaust fumes contain carbon monoxide, which is extremely poisonous. If you need to run the engine, always do so in the open air, or at least have the rear of the vehicle outside the work area.

THE BATTERY

Never create a spark or allow a bare light bulb near a battery. They normally give off a certain amount of hydrogen gas, which is highly explosive.

Always disconnect the battery ground (-) cable at the battery before working on the fuel or electrical systems.

If possible, loosen the filler caps or cover when charging the battery from an external source (this does not apply to sealed or maintenance-free batteries). Do not charge at an excessive rate or the battery may burst.

Take care when adding water to a non maintenance-free battery and when carrying a battery. The electrolyte, even when diluted, is very corrosive and should not be allowed to contact clothing or skin.

Always wear eye protection when cleaning the battery to prevent the caustic deposits from entering your eyes.

HOUSEHOLD CURRENT

When using an electric power tool, inspection light, etc., which operates on household current, always make sure that the tool is correctly connected to its plug and that, where necessary, it is properly grounded. Do not use such items in damp conditions and, again, do not create a spark or apply excessive heat in the vicinity of fuel or fuel vapor.

SECONDARY IGNITION SYSTEM VOLTAGE

A severe electric shock can result from touching certain parts of the ignition system (such as the spark plug wires) when the engine is running or being cranked, particularly if components are damp or the insulation is defective. In the case of an electronic ignition system, the secondary system voltage is much higher and could prove fatal.

HYDROFLUORIC ACID

This extremely corrosive acid is formed when certain types of synthetic rubber, found in some O-rings, oil seals, fuel hoses, etc. are exposed to temperatures above 750-degrees F (400-degrees C). The rubber changes into a charred or sticky substance containing the acid. *Once formed, the acid remains dangerous for years. If it gets onto the skin, it may be necessary to amputate the limb concerned.*

When dealing with a vehicle which has suffered a fire, or with components salvaged from such a vehicle, wear protective gloves and discard them after use.

Troubleshooting

CONTENTS

1   This Section provides an easy reference guide to the more common problems which may occur during the operation of your vehicle. These problems and their possible causes are grouped under headings denoting various components or systems, such as Engine, Cooling system, etc. They also refer you to the Chapter and/or Section which deals with the problem.

2   Remember that successful troubleshooting is not a mysterious art practiced only by professional mechanics. It is simply the result of the right knowledge combined with an intelligent, systematic approach to the problem. Always work by a process of elimination, starting with the simplest solution and working through to the most complex - and never overlook the obvious. Anyone can run the gas tank dry or leave the lights on overnight, so don't assume that you are exempt from such oversights.

3   Finally, always establish a clear idea of why a problem has occurred and take steps to ensure that it doesn't happen again. If the electrical system fails because of a poor connection, check the other connections in the system to make sure that they don't fail as well. If a particular fuse continues to blow, find out why - don't just replace one fuse after another. Remember, failure of a small component can often be indicative of potential failure or incorrect functioning of a more important component or system.

ENGINE

1   Engine will not rotate when attempting to start

4   Battery terminal connections loose or corroded (Chapter 1).
5   Battery discharged or faulty (Chapter 1).
6   Automatic transaxle not completely engaged in Park (Chapter 7B).
7   Broken, loose or disconnected wiring in the starting circuit (Chapters 5 and 12).
8   Starter motor pinion jammed in flywheel ring gear (Chapter 5).
9   Starter solenoid faulty (Chapter 5).
10 Starter motor faulty (Chapter 5).
11 Ignition switch faulty (Chapter 12).
12 Starter pinion or flywheel teeth worn or broken (Chapter 5).

2   Engine rotates but will not start

13 Fuel tank empty.
14 Fuel cut switch activated due to vehicle impact (Chapter 4).
15 Battery discharged (engine rotates slowly) (Chapter 5).
16 Battery terminal connections loose or corroded (Chapter 1).
17 Leaking fuel injector(s), faulty fuel pump, pressure regulator, etc. (Chapter 4).
18 Fuel not reaching fuel rail (Chapter 4).
19 Ignition components damp or damaged (Chapter 5).
20 Worn, faulty or incorrectly gapped spark plugs (Chapter 1).
21 Broken, loose or disconnected wiring in the starting circuit (Chapter 5).
22 Broken, loose or disconnected wires at the ignition coil(s) or faulty coil(s) (Chapter 5).
23 Faulty camshaft or crankshaft position sensor (Chapter 6).

3   Engine hard to start when cold

24 Battery discharged or low (Chapter 1).
25 Malfunctioning fuel system (Chapter 4).
26 Faulty cold start injector (Chapter 4).
27 Injector(s) leaking (Chapter 4).
28 Faulty coolant temperature sensor (Chapter 6).

4   Engine hard to start when hot

29 Air filter clogged (Chapter 1).
30 Faulty fuel pump/low fuel pressure (Chapter 4).
31 Corroded battery connections, especially ground (Chapter 1).

5   Starter motor noisy or excessively rough in engagement

32 Pinion or flywheel gear teeth worn or broken (Chapter 5).
33 Starter motor mounting bolts loose or missing (Chapter 5).

6   Engine starts but stops immediately

34 Loose or faulty electrical connections at coil(s) or alternator (Chapter 5).
35 Faulty fuel pump/low fuel pressure (Chapters 1 and 4).
36 Vacuum leak at the gasket between the intake manifold/plenum and throttle body (Chapters 1 and 4).

7   Oil puddle under engine

37 Oil pan gasket and/or oil pan drain bolt washer leaking (Chapter 2).
38 Oil pressure sending unit leaking (Chapter 2).
39 Valve covers leaking (Chapter 2).
40 Engine oil seals leaking (Chapter 2).
41 Oil pump housing leaking (Chapter 2).

8   Engine lopes while idling or idles erratically

42 Vacuum leakage (Chapters 2 and 4).
43 Leaking EGR valve (Chapter 6).
44 Air filter clogged (Chapter 1).
45 Faulty fuel pump/low fuel pressure (Chapter 4).
46 Leaking head gasket (Chapter 2).
47 Timing belt and/or sprockets worn (Chapter 2).
48 Camshaft lobes worn (Chapter 2).

9   Engine misses at idle speed

49 Spark plugs worn or faulty (Chapter 1).
50 Faulty spark plug wires (Chapter 1).
51 Vacuum leaks (Chapter 1).
52 Fault in engine management system (Chapter 6).
53 Uneven or low compression (Chapter 2).

10 Engine misses throughout driving speed range

54 Fuel filter clogged and/or impurities in the fuel system (Chapter 1).
55 Low fuel output at the injector(s) (Chapter 4).
56 Faulty or worn spark plugs (Chapter 1).

57 Fault in engine management system (Chapter 6).
58 Faulty emission system components (Chapter 6).
59 Low or uneven cylinder compression pressures (Chapter 2).
60 Weak or faulty ignition coil(s) (Chapter 5).
61 Vacuum leak in fuel injection system, intake manifold/plenum, air control valve or vacuum hoses (Chapter 4).

11   Engine stumbles on acceleration

62 Spark plugs fouled (Chapter 1).
63 Fuel injection system faulty (Chapter 4).
64 Fuel filter clogged (Chapters 1 and 4).
65 Fault in engine management system (Chapter 6).
66 Intake manifold or plenum air leak (Chapters 2 and 4).

12   Engine surges while holding accelerator steady

67 Intake air leak (Chapter 4).
68 Fuel pump faulty (Chapter 4).
69 Loose fuel injector wire harness connectors (Chapter 4).
70 Defective ECM or information sensor (Chapter 6).

13   Engine stalls

71 Fuel filter clogged and/or water and impurities in the fuel system (Chapters 1 and 4).
72 Ignition components damp or damaged (Chapter 5).
73 Faulty emissions system components (Chapter 6).
74 Faulty or incorrectly gapped spark plugs (Chapter 1).
75 Vacuum leak in the fuel injection system, intake manifold or vacuum hoses (Chapters 2 and 4).
76 Valve clearances incorrectly set (Chapter 1).

14   Engine lacks power

77 Fault in engine management system (Chapter 6).
78 Faulty or worn spark plugs (Chapter 1).
79 Fuel injection system malfunction (Chapter 4).
80 Faulty coil(s) (Chapter 5).
81 Brakes binding (Chapter 9).
82 Automatic transaxle fluid level incorrect (Chapter 1).
83 Fuel filter clogged and/or impurities in the fuel system (Chapters 1 and 4).
84 Emissions control systems not functioning properly (Chapter 6).
85 Low or uneven cylinder compression pressures (Chapter 2).
86 Obstructed exhaust system (Chapter 4).

15   Engine backfires

87 Emission control system not functioning properly (Chapter 6).
88 Fault in engine management system (Chapter 6).
89 Faulty spark plug insulator (Chapter 1).
90 Fuel injection system malfunction (Chapter 4).

91 Vacuum leak at fuel injector(s), intake manifold, air control valve or vacuum hoses (Chapters 2 and 4).
92 Valve clearances incorrectly set and/or valves sticking (Chapter 1).

16   Pinging or knocking engine sounds during acceleration or uphill

93 Incorrect grade of fuel.
94 Fault in engine management system (Chapter 6).
95 Fuel injection system faulty (Chapter 4).
96 Improper or damaged spark plug(s) (Chapter 1).
97 Vacuum leak (Chapters 2 and 4).
98 Defective knock sensor (Chapter 6).

17   Engine runs with oil pressure light on

99 Low oil level (Chapter 1).
100 Short in wiring circuit (Chapter 12).
101 Faulty oil pressure sender (Chapter 2).
102 Worn engine bearings and/or oil pump (Chapter 2).

18   Engine diesels (continues to run) after switching off

103 Excessive engine operating temperature (Chapter 3).
104 Fault in engine management system (Chapter 6).

ENGINE ELECTRICAL SYSTEM

19   Battery will not hold a charge

105 Alternator drivebelt defective or not adjusted properly (Chapter 1).
106 Battery electrolyte level low (Chapter 1).
107 Battery terminals loose or corroded (Chapter 1).
108 Alternator not charging properly (Chapter 5).
109 Loose, broken or faulty wiring in the charging circuit (Chapter 5).
110 Internally defective battery (Chapters 1 and 5).

20   Alternator light fails to go out

111 Faulty alternator or charging circuit (Chapter 5).
112 Alternator drivebelt defective or out of adjustment (Chapter 1).
113 Alternator voltage regulator inoperative (Chapter 5).

21   Alternator light fails to come on when key is turned on

114 Warning light bulb defective (Chapter 12).
115 Fault in the printed circuit, dash wiring or bulb holder (Chapter 12).

FUEL SYSTEM

22 Excessive fuel consumption

116 Dirty or clogged air filter element (Chapter 1).
117 Fault in engine management system (Chapter 6).
118 Emissions systems not functioning properly (Chapter 6).
119 Fuel injection system not functioning properly (Chapter 4).
120 Low tire pressure or incorrect tire size (Chapter 1).

23 Fuel leakage and/or fuel odor

121 Leaking fuel feed or return line (Chapters 1 and 4).
122 Tank overfilled.
123 Evaporative canister filter clogged (Chapters 1 and 6).
124 Fuel injection system not functioning properly (Chapter 4).

COOLING SYSTEM

24 Overheating

125 Insufficient coolant in system (Chapter 1).
126 Water pump defective (Chapter 3).
127 Radiator core blocked or grille restricted (Chapter 3).
128 Thermostat faulty (Chapter 3).
129 Electric coolant fan blades broken or cracked (Chapter 3).
130 Radiator cap not maintaining proper pressure (Chapter 3).
131 Fault in engine management system (Chapter 6).

25 Overcooling

132 Faulty thermostat (Chapter 3).
133 Inaccurate temperature gauge sending unit (Chapter 3)

26 External coolant leakage

134 Deteriorated/damaged hoses; loose clamps (Chapters 1 and 3).
135 Water pump defective (Chapter 3).
136 Leakage from radiator core or coolant reservoir bottle (Chapter 3).
137 Engine drain or water jacket core plugs leaking (Chapter 2).

27 Internal coolant leakage

138 Leaking cylinder head gasket (Chapter 2).
139 Cracked cylinder bore or cylinder head (Chapter 2).

28 Coolant loss

140 Too much coolant in system (Chapter 1).
141 Coolant boiling away because of overheating (Chapter 3).
142 Internal or external leakage (Chapter 3).
143 Faulty radiator cap (Chapter 3).

29 Poor coolant circulation

144 Inoperative water pump (Chapter 3).
145 Restriction in cooling system (Chapters 1 and 3).
146 Water pump drivebelt defective/out of adjustment (Chapter 1).
147 Thermostat sticking (Chapter 3).

CLUTCH

➡ **Note: All clutch service information is located in Chapter 8, unless otherwise noted.**

30 Fails to release (pedal pressed to the floor - shift lever does not move freely in and out of Reverse)

148 Freeplay incorrectly adjusted.
149 Clutch contaminated with oil. Remove clutch plate and inspect.
150 Clutch plate warped, distorted or otherwise damaged.
151 Diaphragm spring fatigued. Remove clutch cover/pressure plate assembly and inspect.
152 Leakage of fluid from clutch hydraulic system. Inspect master cylinder, operating cylinder and connecting lines.
153 Air in clutch hydraulic system. Bleed the system.
154 Insufficient pedal stroke. Check and adjust as necessary.
155 Piston seal in master or release cylinder deformed or damaged.
156 Lack of grease on pilot bearing.

31 Clutch slips (engine speed increases with no increase in vehicle speed)

157 Worn or oil-soaked clutch plate.
158 Diaphragm spring weak or damaged. Remove clutch cover/pressure plate assembly and inspect.
159 Clutch hydraulic line damaged internally (not allowing fluid to return to the clutch master cylinder).
160 Binding in the release mechanism.

32 Grabbing (chattering) as clutch is engaged

161 Oil on clutch plate. Remove and inspect. Repair any leaks.
162 Worn or loose engine or transmission mounts. They may move slightly when clutch is released. Inspect mounts and bolts.
163 Worn splines on transmission input shaft. Remove clutch components and inspect.
164 Warped pressure plate or flywheel. Remove clutch components and inspect.
165 Diaphragm spring fatigued. Remove clutch cover/pressure plate assembly and inspect.
166 Clutch linings hardened or warped.
167 Clutch lining rivets loose.

33 Squeal or rumble with clutch engaged (pedal released)

168 Improper pedal adjustment. Adjust pedal freeplay.
169 Release bearing binding on transmission shaft. Remove clutch components and check bearing. Remove any burrs or nicks, clean and relubricate before reinstallation.
170 Clutch rivets loose.
171 Clutch plate cracked.
172 Fatigued clutch plate torsion springs. Replace clutch plate.

34 Squeal or rumble with clutch disengaged (pedal depressed)

173 Worn or damaged release bearing.
174 Worn or broken pressure plate diaphragm fingers.
175 Pilot bearing worn or damaged.

35 Clutch pedal stays on floor when disengaged

176 Binding release bearing.

MANUAL TRANSMISSION/TRANSAXLE

36 Noisy in Neutral with engine running

177 Input shaft bearing worn.
178 Damaged main drive gear bearing.
179 Insufficient transmission oil (Chapter 1).
180 Transmission oil in poor condition. Drain and fill with proper grade oil. Check old oil for water and debris (Chapter 1).
181 Noise can be caused by variations in engine torque. Change the idle speed and see if noise disappears.

37 Noisy in all gears

182 Any of the above causes, and/or:
183 Worn or damaged output gear bearings or shaft.

38 Noisy in one particular gear

184 Worn, damaged or chipped gear teeth.
185 Worn or damaged synchronizer.

39 Slips out of gear

186 Stiff shift lever seal.
187 Shift linkage binding.
188 Broken or loose input gear bearing retainer.
189 Dirt between clutch lever and engine housing.
190 Worn linkage.

191 Damaged or worn check balls, fork rod ball grooves or check springs.
192 Worn mainshaft or countershaft bearings.
193 Loose engine mounts (Chapter 2A).
194 Excessive gear endplay.
195 Worn synchronizers.

40 Oil leaks

196 Excessive amount of lubricant in transmission (Chapter 1). Drain lubricant as required.
197 Rear oil seal or speedometer oil seal damaged.
198 To pinpoint a leak, first remove all built-up dirt and grime from the transmission. Degreasing agents and/or steam cleaning will achieve this. With the underside clean, drive the vehicle at low speeds so the air flow will not blow the leak far from its source. Raise the vehicle and determine where the leak is located.

41 Difficulty engaging gears

199 Clutch not releasing completely.
200 Loose or damaged shift linkage. Make a thorough inspection, replacing parts as necessary.
201 Insufficient transmission oil (Chapter 1).
202 Transmission oil in poor condition. Drain and fill with proper grade oil. Check oil for water and debris (Chapter 1).
203 Worn or damaged striking rod.
204 Sticking or jamming gears.

42 Noise occurs while shifting gears

205 Check for proper operation of the clutch (Chapter 8).
206 Faulty synchronizer assemblies.

AUTOMATIC TRANSMISSION/TRANSAXLE

43 Fluid leakage

207 Automatic transmission/transaxle fluid is a deep red color. Fluid leaks should not be confused with engine oil, which can easily be blown onto the transmission/transaxle by air flow.
208 To pinpoint a leak, first remove all built-up dirt and grime from the transmission/transaxle housing with degreasing agents and/or steam cleaning. Then drive the vehicle at low speeds so air flow will not blow the leak far from its source. Raise the vehicle and determine where the leak is coming from. Common areas of leakage are:

Pan (Chapters 1 and 7B)
Dipstick tube (Chapters 1 and 7B)
Transmission/transaxle oil lines (Chapter 7B)
Speed sensor (Chapter 7B)
Differential drain plug (Chapter 1)

44 Transmission/transaxle fluid brown or has a burned smell

209 Transmission/transaxle fluid overheated (Chapter 1).
210 Clutch friction discs and/or bands burned.

45 General shift mechanism problems

211 Chapter # deals with checking and adjusting the shift linkage on automatic transmission/transaxles. Common problems which may be attributed to poorly adjusted linkage are:

Engine starting in gears other than Park or Neutral.
Indicator on shifter pointing to a gear other than the one actually being used.
Vehicle moves when in Park.

212 Refer to Chapter 7A for the shift linkage procedure.

46 Transmission/transaxle will not downshift with accelerator pedal pressed to the floor

213 These transmission/transaxles are electronically controlled. Check for trouble codes stored in the PCM (Chapter 6).

47 Engine will start in gears other than Park or Neutral

214 Transmission Range (TR) sensor malfunctioning (Chapter 6).

48 Transmission/transaxle slips, shifts roughly, is noisy or has no drive in forward or reverse gears

215 There are many probable causes for the above problems, but the home mechanic should be concerned with only one possibility - fluid level. Before taking the vehicle to a repair shop, check the level and condition of the fluid (Chapter 1). Correct the fluid level as necessary or change the fluid and filter if needed. If the problem persists, have a professional diagnose the cause.

DRIVEAXLES

49 Clicking noise in turns

216 Worn or damaged outboard CV joint (Chapter 8).

50 Shudder or vibration during acceleration

217 Excessive toe-in (Chapter 10).
218 Worn or damaged inboard or outboard CV joints (Chapter 8).
219 Sticking inboard CV joint assembly (Chapter 8).

51 Vibration at highway speeds

220 Out-of-balance front wheels and/or tires (Chapters 1 and 10).
221 Out-of-round front tires (Chapters 1 and 10).
222 Worn CV joint(s) (Chapter 8).

BRAKES

52 Vehicle pulls to one side during braking

223 Incorrect tire pressures (Chapter 1).
224 Front end out of alignment (have the front end aligned).
225 Front or rear tires not matched to one another.
226 Restricted brake lines or hoses (Chapter 9).
227 Malfunctioning caliper assembly (Chapter 9).
228 Loose suspension parts (Chapter 10).
229 Excessive wear of brake pad material or disc on one side.

53 Noise (high-pitched squeal when the brakes are applied)

230 Front and/or rear disc brake pads worn out. Replace pads with new ones immediately (Chapter 9).

54 Brake roughness or chatter (pedal pulsates)

231 Excessive lateral runout (Chapter 9).
232 Uneven pad wear (Chapter 9).
233 Defective disc (Chapter 9).

55 Excessive brake pedal effort required to stop vehicle

234 Malfunctioning power brake booster (Chapter 9).
235 Partial system failure (Chapter 9).
236 Excessively worn pads (Chapter 9).
237 Piston in caliper stuck or sluggish (Chapter 9).
238 Brake pads contaminated with oil, grease or brake fluid (Chapter 9).
239 New pads installed and not yet seated. It will take a while for the new material to seat against the disc.

56 Excessive brake pedal travel

240 Partial brake system failure (Chapter 9).
241 Insufficient fluid in master cylinder (Chapters 1 and 9).
242 Air trapped in system (Chapters 1 and 9).

57 Dragging brakes

243 Incorrect adjustment of brake light switch (Chapter 9).
244 Master cylinder pistons not returning correctly (Chapter 9).
245 Restricted brakes lines or hoses (Chapters 1 and 9).
246 Incorrect parking brake adjustment (Chapter 9).

58 Grabbing or uneven braking action

247 Contaminated brake pad lining (Chapter 9).
248 Binding brake pedal mechanism (Chapter 9).

59   Brake pedal feels spongy when depressed

249   Air in hydraulic lines (Chapter 9).
250   Master cylinder mounting bolts loose (Chapter 9).
251   Master cylinder defective (Chapter 9).

60   Brake pedal travels to the floor with little resistance

252   Little or no fluid in the master cylinder reservoir caused by leaking caliper piston(s) (Chapter 9).
253   Loose, damaged or disconnected brake lines (Chapter 9).
254   Defective master cylinder (Chapter 9).

61   Parking brake does not hold

255   Parking brake improperly adjusted (Chapters 1 and 9).

SUSPENSION AND STEERING SYSTEMS

62   Vehicle pulls to one side

256   Mismatched or uneven tires (Chapter 10).
257   Broken or sagging springs (Chapter 10).
258   Wheel alignment (Chapter 10).
259   Front brake dragging (Chapter 9).

63   Abnormal or excessive tire wear

260   Wheel alignment (Chapter 10).
261   Sagging or broken springs (Chapter 10).
262   Tire out of balance (Chapter 10).
263   Worn strut damper (Chapter 10).
264   Overloaded vehicle.
265   Tires not rotated regularly.

64   Wheel makes a thumping noise

266   Blister or bump on tire (Chapter 10).
267   Improper strut damper action (Chapter 10).

65   Shimmy, shake or vibration

268   Tire or wheel out-of-balance or out-of-round (Chapter 10).
269   Loose or worn wheel bearings (Chapter 10).
270   Worn tie-rod ends (Chapter 10).
271   Worn balljoints (Chapters 1 and 10).
272   Excessive wheel runout (Chapter 10).
273   Blister or bump on tire (Chapter 10).

66   Hard steering

274   Lack of lubrication at balljoints, tie-rod ends and steering gear assembly (Chapter 10).
275   Front wheel alignment (Chapter 10).
276   Low tire pressure(s) (Chapters 1 and 10).

67   Poor returnability of steering to center

277   Lack of lubrication at balljoints and tie-rod ends (Chapter 10).
278   Binding in balljoints (Chapter 10).
279   Binding in steering column (Chapter 10).
280   Lack of lubricant in steering gear assembly (Chapter 10).
281   Front wheel alignment (Chapter 10).

68   Abnormal noise at the front end

282   Lack of lubrication at balljoints and tie-rod ends (Chapters 1 and 10).
283   Damaged strut mounting (Chapter 10).
284   Worn control arm bushings or tie-rod ends (Chapter 10).
285   Loose stabilizer bar (Chapter 10).
286   Loose wheel nuts (Chapters 1 and 10).
287   Loose suspension bolts (Chapter 10)

69   Wander or poor steering stability

288   Mismatched or uneven tires (Chapter 10).
289   Lack of lubrication at balljoints and tie-rod ends (Chapters 1 and 10).
290   Worn strut assemblies (Chapter 10).
291   Loose stabilizer bar (Chapter 10).
292   Broken or sagging springs (Chapter 10).
293   Wheels out of alignment (Chapter 10).

70   Erratic steering when braking

294   Wheel bearings worn (Chapter 10).
295   Broken or sagging springs (Chapter 10).
296   Leaking wheel cylinder or caliper (Chapter 9).
297   Warped brake discs (Chapter 9).

71   Excessive pitching and/or rolling around corners or during braking

298   Loose stabilizer bar (Chapter 10).
299   Worn strut dampers or mountings (Chapter 10).
300   Broken or sagging springs (Chapter 10).
301   Overloaded vehicle.

72   Suspension bottoms

302   Overloaded vehicle.
303   Worn strut dampers (Chapter 10).
304   Incorrect, broken or sagging springs (Chapter 10).

73   Cupped tires

305   Front wheel or rear wheel alignment (Chapter 10).
306   Worn strut dampers (Chapter 10).
307   Wheel bearings worn (Chapter 10).
308   Excessive tire or wheel runout (Chapter 10).
309   Worn balljoints (Chapter 10).

74　Excessive tire wear on outside edge

310　Inflation pressures incorrect (Chapter 1).
311　Excessive speed in turns.
312　Front end alignment incorrect (excessive toe-in). Have professionally aligned.
313　Suspension arm bent or twisted (Chapter 10).

75　Excessive tire wear on inside edge

314　Inflation pressures incorrect (Chapter 1).
315　Front end alignment incorrect (toe-out). Have professionally aligned.
316　Loose or damaged steering components (Chapter 10).

76　Tire tread worn in one place

317　Tires out of balance.
318　Damaged wheel. Inspect and replace if necessary.
319　Defective tire (Chapter 1).

77　Excessive play or looseness in steering system

320　Wheel bearing(s) worn (Chapter 10).
321　Tie-rod end loose (Chapter 10).
322　Steering gear loose (Chapter 10).
323　Worn or loose steering intermediate shaft (Chapter 10).

78　Rattling or clicking noise in steering gear

324　Steering gear loose (Chapter 10).
325　Steering gear defective.

1

TUNE-UP AND ROUTINE MAINTENANCE

1 KIA Sorento Maintenance Schedule

1 The maintenance intervals in this manual are provided with the assumption that you, not the dealer, will be doing the work. These are the minimum maintenance intervals recommended by the factory for vehicles that are driven daily. If you wish to keep your vehicle in peak condition at all times, you may wish to perform some of these procedures even more often. Because frequent maintenance enhances the efficiency, performance and resale value of your car, we encourage you to do so. If you drive in dusty areas, tow a trailer, idle or drive at low speeds for extended periods or drive for short distances (less than four miles) in below freezing temperatures, shorter intervals are also recommended.

2 When your vehicle is new, it should be serviced by a factory authorized dealer service department to protect the factory warranty. In many cases, the initial maintenance check is done at no cost to the owner.

EVERY 250 MILES (400 KM) OR WEEKLY, WHICHEVER COMES FIRST

3 Check the engine oil level (Section 4)
4 Check the engine coolant level (Section 4)
5 Check the windshield washer fluid level (Section 4)
6 Check the brake fluid level (Section 4)
7 Check the power steering fluid level (Section 4)
8 Check the automatic transmission/transaxle fluid level (2009 and earlier models only) (Section 4)
9 Check the tires and tire pressures (Section 5)

EVERY 3000 MILES (4,800 KM) OR 3 MONTHS, WHICHEVER COMES FIRST

10 *All items listed above plus*:
11 Change the engine oil and oil filter (Section 6)

EVERY 5000 MILES (8000 KM) OR 6 MONTHS, WHICHEVER COMES FIRST

12 *All items listed above plus*:
13 Check and service the battery (Section 7)
14 Rotate the tires (Section 8)
15 Inspect and replace (if necessary) the windshield wiper blades (Section 9)
16 Inspect and replace (if necessary) all underhood hoses (Section 10)
17 Check the cooling system (Section 11)
18 Inspect the brake system (Section 12)

EVERY 15,000 MILES (24,000 KM) OR 18 MONTHS, WHICHEVER COMES FIRST

19 *All items listed above plus*:
20 Inspect the suspension, steering components and driveaxle boots (Section 13)*
21 Inspect the exhaust system (Section 14)
22 Check the tranfer case/rear differential/front differential/manual transaxle lubricant levels, as applicable (Section 4).

EVERY 30,000 MILES (48,000 KM) OR 36 MONTHS, WHICHEVER COMES FIRST

23 *All items listed above plus:*
24 Replace the air filter (Section 15)*
25 Inspect the fuel system (Section 16)
26 Replace the interior ventilation filter (Section 17)*
27 Check and replace (if necessary) the PCV valve (Section 18)
28 Change the brake fluid (Section 19)

EVERY 50,000 MILES (80,500 KM) OR 60 MONTHS, WHICHEVER COMES FIRST

29 Service the cooling system (drain, flush and refill) (Section 25) (after the initial 100,000-mile [160,000 km] or 120-month service)

EVERY 60,000 MILES (96,000 KM) OR 72 MONTHS, WHICHEVER COMES FIRST

30 *All items listed above plus:*
31 Check and adjust if necessary the engine drivebelts (Section 20) (after the initial 60,000-mile [96,000 km] or 72-month check)
32 Change the automatic transmission/transaxle fluid (2009 and earlier models only) (Section 21)**
33 Change the transfer case (AWD models) and manual transmission/transaxle lubricant (Section 22)**
34 Change the rear differential lubricant (AWD models) (Section 23)**

100,000 MILES (160,000 KM) OR 120 MONTHS, WHICHEVER COMES FIRST - THEREAFTER EVERY 50,000 MILES (80,500 KM) OR 60 MONTHS, WHICHEVER COMES FIRST

35 Service the cooling system (drain, flush and refill) (Section 25)

EVERY 120,000 MILES (193,000 KM) OR 144 MONTHS, WHICHEVER COMES FIRST

36 Replace the spark plugs (Section 26)
37 Check the ignition system components (Section 27)

* This item is affected by "severe" operating conditions as described below. If your vehicle is operated under severe conditions, inspect all maintenance indicated with an asterisk (*) at 3000 mile/3 month intervals and perform maintenance or replace parts as necessary. Severe conditions are indicated if you mainly operate your vehicle under one or more of the following conditions:
Operating in dusty areas
Idling for extended periods and/or low speed operation
Operating when outside temperatures remain below freezing and when most trips are less than 4 miles

** If used for trailer towing, change the transaxle, transfer case or rear differential fluid lubricant every 30,000 miles (Section 21, Section 22 or Section 23)

2006 and earlier 3.5L V6 engine compartment (2007 through 2009 models similar)

1 Brake fluid reservoir	5 Engine oil filler cap	8 Air filter housing
2 Fuse/relay box	6 Windshield washer fluid reservoir	9 Engine coolant reservoir
3 Battery	7 Power steering fluid reservoir	10 Automatic transmission fluid dipstick
4 Engine oil dipstick		

2011 and later 2.4L four-cylinder MPI engine compartment

1	Brake fluid reservoir	4	Battery	7	Power steering fluid reservoir
2	Air filter housing	5	Engine oil dipstick	8	Windshield washer fluid reservoir
3	Fuse/relay box	6	Engine oil filler cap	9	Engine coolant reservoir

Typical 2009 and earlier V6 4WD front underside components

1	Engine oil pan drain plug	5	Inner driveaxle boot	8	Outer driveaxle boot
2	Radiator drain plug	6	Steeering gear boot	9	Brake caliper
3	Front differential drain plug	7	Lower balljoint	10	Coil-over shock absorber assembly
4	Steering gear				

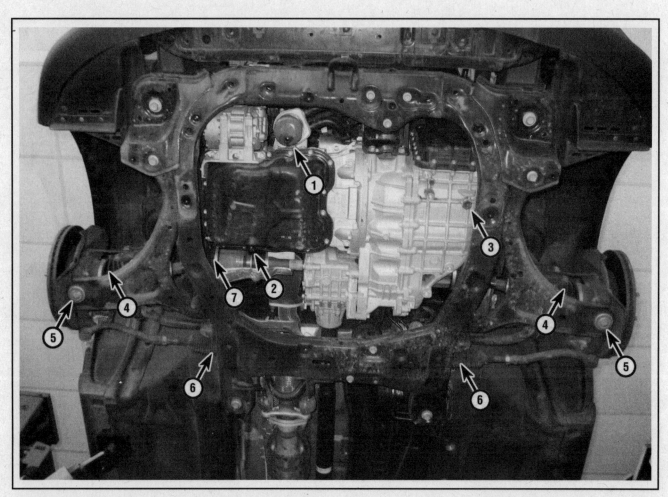

Typical 2011 and later four-cylinder front underside components

1	Oil filter	3	Transaxle drain plug	5	Balljoint
2	Engine oil drain plug	4	Outer driveaxle boot	6	Steering gear boot

Typical 2011 and later four-cylinder 4WD rear underside components

1	Rear differential drain plug	3	Inner driveaxle boot	5	Shock absorber
2	Muffler	4	Coil spring	6	Outer driveaxle boot

Typical 2009 and earlier V6 rear underside components

1	Rear differential drain plug	3	Rear disc brake caliper	5	Shock absorber
2	Stabilizer bar	4	Coil spring	6	Muffler

2 Introduction

1 This Chapter is designed to help the home mechanic maintain his vehicle for peak performance, economy, safety and long life.

2 Included is a master maintenance schedule, followed by sections dealing specifically with each item on the schedule. Visual checks, adjustments, component replacement and other helpful items are included. Refer to the accompanying illustrations of the engine compartment and the underside of the vehicle for the location of various components.

3 Servicing your vehicle in accordance with the mileage/time maintenance schedule and the following Sections will provide it with a planned maintenance program that should result in a long and reliable service life. This is a comprehensive plan, so maintaining some items but not others at the specified service intervals won't produce the same results.

4 As you service your vehicle, you will discover that many of the procedures can - and should - be grouped together because of the nature of the particular procedure you're performing or because of the close proximity of two otherwise unrelated components to one another.

5 For example, if the vehicle is raised for any reason, you should inspect the exhaust, suspension, steering and fuel systems while you're under the vehicle. When you're rotating the tires, it makes good sense to check the brakes and wheel bearings since the wheels are already removed.

6 Finally, let's suppose you have to borrow or rent a torque wrench. Even if you only need to tighten the spark plugs, you might as well check the torque of as many critical fasteners as time allows.

7 The first step of this maintenance program is to prepare yourself before the actual work begins. Read through all Sections pertinent to the procedures you're planning to do, then make a list of and gather together all the parts and tools you will need to do the job. If it looks as if you might run into problems during a particular segment of some procedure, seek advice from your local parts man or dealer service department.

3 Tune-up general information

1 The term tune-up is used in this manual to represent a combination of individual operations rather than one specific procedure.

2 If, from the time the vehicle is new, the routine maintenance schedule is followed closely and frequent checks are made of fluid levels and high wear items, as suggested throughout this manual, the engine will be kept in relatively good running condition and the need for additional work will be minimized.

3 More likely than not, however, there will be times when the engine is running poorly due to lack of regular maintenance. This is even more likely if a used vehicle, which has not received regular and frequent maintenance checks, is purchased. In such cases, an engine tune-up will be needed outside of the regular routine maintenance intervals.

4 The first step in any tune-up or engine diagnosis to help correct a poor running engine would be a cylinder compression check. A check of the engine compression (see Chapter 2C) will give you valuable information regarding the overall performance of many internal components and should be used as a basis for tune-up and repair procedures. If, for instance, a compression check indicates serious internal engine wear, a conventional tune-up will not help the running condition of the engine and would be a waste of time and money. Also included in Chapter 2C is information on checking engine vacuum, which also gives information on the engine's state-of-tune and condition.

5 The following series of operations are those most often needed to bring a generally poor-running engine back into a proper state of tune.

MINOR TUNE-UP

Check all engine related fluids (Section 4)
Clean, inspect and test the battery (Section 7)
Check all underhood hoses (Section 10)
Check the cooling system (Section 11)
Check the air filter (Section 15)
Check and adjust the drivebelts (Section 20)

MAJOR TUNE-UP

All items listed under *Minor tune-up*, plus . . .
Replace the air filter (Section 15)
Check the fuel system (Section 16)
Replace the spark plugs (Section 26)
Check the charging system (Chapter 5)

4 Fluid level checks (every 250 miles [400 km] or weekly)

1 Fluids are an essential part of the lubrication, cooling, brake, clutch and other systems. Because these fluids gradually become depleted and/or contaminated during normal operation of the vehicle, they must be periodically replenished. See *Recommended lubricants and fluids* and *Capacities* in this Chapter's Specifications before adding fluid to any of the following components.

➡ **Note: The vehicle must be on level ground before fluid levels can be checked.**

ENGINE OIL

2 The engine oil level is checked with a dipstick located on the driver's side (2009 and earlier models), or the front side (2011 and later models) of the engine **(see illustration)**. The dipstick extends through a metal tube from which it protrudes down into the engine oil pan.

3 The oil level should be checked before the vehicle has been driven, or about 5 minutes after the engine has been shut off. If the oil is checked immediately after driving the vehicle, some of the oil will remain in the upper engine components, producing a low reading on the dipstick.

4 Pull the dipstick from the tube and wipe all the oil from the end with a clean rag or paper towel. Insert the clean dipstick all the way back into its metal tube and pull it out again. Observe the oil at the end of the dipstick. At its highest point, the level should be between the lower and upper marks **(see illustration)**.

5 It takes one quart of oil to raise the level from the lower mark to the upper mark on the dipstick. Do not allow the level to drop below the lower mark or oil starvation may cause engine damage. Conversely, overfilling the engine (adding oil above the upper mark) may cause oil-fouled spark plugs, oil leaks or oil seal failures.

6 Remove the threaded cap from the valve cover to add oil **(see illustration 4.2a or 4.2b).** Use a funnel to prevent spills. After adding the oil, install the filler cap hand tight. Start the engine and look carefully for any small leaks around the oil filter or drain plug. Stop the engine and check the oil level again after it has had sufficient time to drain from the upper block and cylinder head galleys.

7 Checking the oil level is an important preventive maintenance step. A continually dropping oil level indicates oil leakage through damaged seals, from loose connections, or past worn rings or valve guides. If the oil looks milky in color or has water droplets in it, a cylinder head gasket may be blown. The engine should be checked immediately. The condition of the oil should also be checked. Each time you check the oil level, slide your thumb and index finger up the dipstick before wiping off the oil. If you see small dirt or metal particles clinging to the dipstick, the oil should be changed (see Section 6).

ENGINE COOLANT

✳ WARNING:

Do not allow antifreeze to come in contact with your skin or painted surfaces of the vehicle. Flush contaminated areas immediately with plenty of water. Don't store new coolant or leave old coolant lying around where it's accessible to children or pets - they're attracted by its sweet smell. Ingestion of even a small amount of coolant can be fatal! Wipe up garage floor and drip pan spills immediately. Keep antifreeze containers covered and repair cooling system leaks as soon as they're noticed.

✳ WARNING:

Never remove the cap from the coolant surge tank unless the engine is completely cool. Serious burns can result.

4.2a On 2009 and earlier models, the oil dipstick is on the left side of the engine; on all models, the oil filler cap is located on the valve cover - make sure the area around this opening is clean before removing the cap

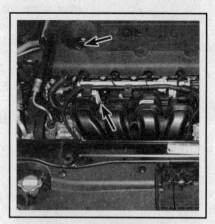

4.2b Engine oil dipstick and oil filler cap - 2011 and later four-cylinder engines

4.4 The oil level should be at or near the upper mark on the dipstick - if it isn't, add enough oil to bring the level to or near the upper mark (it takes one quart to raise the level from the lower mark to the upper mark)

8 All models use a coolant surge tank connected to the top of the radiator **(see illustration)**.

9 The coolant level should be checked regularly. It must be between the Full and Low lines on the tank. The level will vary with the temperature of the engine. When the engine is cold, the coolant level should be at or slightly above the Low mark on the tank. Once the engine has warmed up, the level should be at or near the Full mark. If it isn't, allow the fluid in the tank to cool, then remove the cap from the reservoir and add coolant to bring the level up to the Full line. Use only the type of coolant listed in this Chapter's Specifications or in your owner's manual. Do not use supplemental inhibitors or additives. If only a small amount of coolant is required to bring the system up to the proper level, water can be used. However, repeated additions of water will dilute the recommended antifreeze and water solution. In order to maintain the proper ratio of antifreeze and water, it is advisable to top up the coolant level with the correct mixture. If the coolant level drops within a short time after replenishment, there may be a leak in the system. Inspect the radiator, hoses, coolant surge tank cap, drain plugs, air bleeder plugs and water pump. If no leak is evident, have the surge tank cap pressure tested.

❊❊ WARNING:

Never remove the surge tank cap when the engine is running or has just been shut down, because the cooling system is hot. Escaping steam and scalding liquid could cause serious injury.

10 If it is necessary to open the surge tank cap, wait until the system has cooled completely, then wrap a thick cloth around the cap and turn it to the first stop (or slowly unscrew it, as applicable). If any steam escapes, wait until the system has cooled further, then remove the cap.

11 When checking the coolant level, always note its condition. It should be relatively clear. If it is brown or rust colored, the system should be drained, flushed and refilled. Even if the coolant appears to be normal, the corrosion inhibitors wear out with use, so it must be replaced at the specified intervals.

12 Do not allow antifreeze to come in contact with your skin or painted surfaces of the vehicle. Flush contacted areas immediately with plenty of water.

WINDSHIELD WASHER FLUID

13 Fluid for the windshield washer system is stored in a plastic reservoir that is located at the right front corner of the engine compartment **(see illustration)**. In milder climates, plain water can be used to top up the reservoir, but the reservoir should be kept no more than two-thirds full to allow for expansion should the water freeze. In colder climates, the use of a specially designed windshield washer fluid, available at your dealer and any auto parts store, will help lower the freezing point of the fluid. Mix the solution with water in accordance with the manufacturer's directions on the container. Do not use regular antifreeze. It will damage the vehicle's paint.

BRAKE FLUID

14 The brake master cylinder is mounted on the front of the power booster unit in the engine compartment.

15 To check the fluid level of the brake master cylinder reservoir, simply look at the MAX and MIN marks on the reservoir **(see illustration).** The level should be near the MAX mark.

16 If the level is low, wipe the top of the reservoir cover with a clean rag to prevent contamination of the brake system before lifting the cover.

❊❊ WARNING:

Use caution when filling the reservoir - brake fluid can harm your eyes and damage painted surfaces. Do not use brake fluid that has been opened for more than one year or has been left open. Brake fluid absorbs moisture from the air. Excess moisture can cause a dangerous loss of braking.

17 Add only the specified brake fluid to the brake reservoir (refer to *Recommended lubricants and fluids* in this Chapter's Specifications or your owner's manual). Mixing different types of brake fluid can damage the system. Fill the brake master cylinder reservoir only to the dotted line - this brings the fluid to the correct level when you put the cover back on.

18 While the reservoir cap is removed, inspect the master cylinder reservoir for contamination. If deposits, dirt particles or water droplets are present, the system should be drained and refilled (see Chapter 9).

4.8 The coolant reservoir (surge tank) is located at the passenger's side of the engine compartment

4.13 The windshield washer fluid reservoir is located at the right front corner of the engine compartment

4.15 The brake fluid should be kept between the Min and Max marks on the reservoir

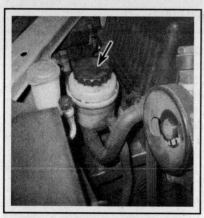

4.25 The power steering fluid reservoir is located on the right side of the engine compartment - the reservoir is translucent, so the fluid level can be checked either hot or cold without removing the cap

4.32a The automatic transmission fluid dipstick is located next to the power brake booster

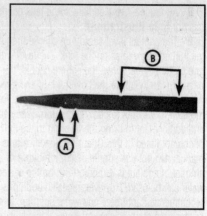

4.32b Automatic transmission fluid COLD range (A) and HOT range (B)

19 After filling the reservoir to the proper level, make sure the lid is properly seated to prevent fluid leakage and/or system pressure loss.

20 The brake fluid in the master cylinder will drop slightly as the brake pads at each wheel wear down during normal operation. If the master cylinder requires repeated replenishing to keep it at the proper level, this is an indication of leakage in the brake system, which should be corrected immediately. Check all brake lines and connections, along with the wheel cylinders and booster (see Section 12 for more information).

21 If, upon checking the master cylinder fluid level, you discover the reservoir empty or nearly empty, the brake system should be thoroughly inspected for leaks (see Chapter 9 for more information on the brake system).

POWER STEERING FLUID

22 The power steering system relies on fluid that may, over a period of time, require replenishing.

23 The fluid reservoir for the power steering pump is located near the front of the engine.

24 For the check, the front wheels should be pointed straight ahead and the engine should be off.

25 The reservoir is translucent plastic and the fluid level can be checked visually **(see illustration).**

26 If additional fluid is required, pour the specified type into the reservoir, using a funnel to prevent spills.

27 If the reservoir requires frequent fluid additions, all power steering hoses, hose connections, the power steering pump and the steering gear assembly should be carefully checked for leaks.

AUTOMATIC TRANSMISSION FLUID (2009 AND EARLIER MODELS ONLY)

➡ **Note: On 2011 and later models, transaxle fluid level check is not a routine maintenance item. Refer to Chapter 7B for the transaxle fluid level check (which would normally only be done if a leak is suspected).**

28 The level of the automatic transmission fluid should be carefully maintained. Low fluid level can lead to slipping or loss of drive, while overfilling can cause foaming, loss of fluid and transmission damage.

✳ CAUTION:

If the vehicle has just been driven for a long time at high speed or in city traffic in hot weather, or if it has been pulling a trailer, an accurate fluid level reading cannot be obtained. Allow the fluid to cool down for about 30 minutes.

29 The transmission fluid level should only be checked when the transmission is hot (at its normal operating temperature). If the vehicle has just been driven over 10 miles (15 miles in a frigid climate), and the fluid temperature is 160 to 175-degrees F, the transmission is hot.

30 If the vehicle has not just been driven, park the vehicle on level ground, set the parking brake and start the engine.

31 While the engine is idling, depress the brake pedal and move the selector lever through all the gear ranges, beginning and ending in Park.

32 With the engine still idling, remove the dipstick from its tube **(see illustration).** Check the level of the fluid on the dipstick **(see illustrations)** and note its condition.

33 Wipe the fluid from the dipstick with a clean rag and reinsert it back into the filler tube until the cap seats.

34 Pull the dipstick out again and note the fluid level. If the transmission is cold, the level should be in the COLD or COOL range on the dipstick. If it is hot, the fluid level should be in the HOT range. If the level is at the low side of either range, add the specified automatic transmission fluid through the dipstick tube with a funnel.

35 Add just enough of the recommended fluid to fill the transaxle to the proper level. It takes about one pint to raise the level from the low mark to the high mark when the fluid is hot, so add the fluid a little at a time and keep checking the level until it is correct.

36 The condition of the fluid should also be checked along with the level. If the fluid at the end of the dipstick is black or a dark reddish brown color, or if it emits a burned smell, the fluid should be changed (see Section 21). If you are in doubt about the condition of the fluid, purchase some new fluid and compare the two for color and smell.

TRANSFER CASE LUBRICANT (2009 AND EARLIER MODELS)

➡ **Note: It is not necessary to check the transfer case lubricant level weekly; every 15,000 miles (24,000 km)/18 months is adequate (unless a leak is suspected).**

4.37 Transfer case check/fill plug (A) and drain plug (B)

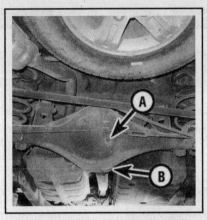

4.41a Rear differential check/fill plug (A) and drain plug (B) - 2009 and earlier models

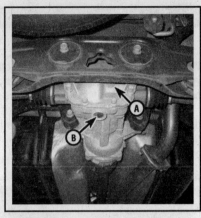

4.41b Rear differential check/fill plug (A) and drain plug (B) - 2011 and later models

37 The transfer case does not have a dipstick. To check the fluid level, raise the vehicle and support it securely on jackstands. Remove the damper weight from the back of the transfer case, if equipped. On the rear of the transfer case housing, you will see two plugs - remove remove the upper plug. If the lubricant level is correct, it should be up to the lower edge of the hole.

38 If the transaxle needs more lubricant (if the level is not up to the hole), use a syringe or a gear oil pump to add more. Stop filling the transaxle when the lubricant begins to run out the hole.

39 Install the plug and tighten it securely. Drive the vehicle a short distance, then check for leaks.

REAR DIFFERENTIAL LUBRICANT LEVEL (RWD/AWD MODELS)

➡ **Note: It is not necessary to check the rear differential lubricant level weekly; every 15,000 miles (24,000 km)/18 months is adequate (unless a leak is suspected).**

40 Raise the vehicle and support it securely on jackstands.

41 Using the appropriate wrench, unscrew the check/fill plug from the rear differential **(see illustrations).**

42 Use your little finger to reach inside the housing to feel the lubricant level. The level should be at or near the bottom of the plug hole. If it isn't, add the recommended lubricant through the plug hole with a syringe or squeeze bottle.

43 Install the plug and tighten it securely. Check for leaks after the first few miles of driving.

FRONT DIFFERENTIAL LUBRICANT LEVEL (2009 AND EARLIER 4WD MODELS)

➡ **Note: It is not necessary to check the front differential lubricant level weekly; every 15,000 miles (24,000 km)/18 months is adequate (unless a leak is suspected).**

44 Raise the vehicle and support it securely on jackstands.

45 Remove the check/fill plug from the front differential.

46 Use your little finger to reach inside the housing to feel the lubricant level. The level should be at or near the bottom of the plug hole.

4.45 Front differential check/fill plug (A) and drain plug (B)

If it isn't, add the recommended lubricant through the plug hole with a syringe or squeeze bottle.

47 Install the check/fill plug and tighten it securely. Check for leaks after the first few miles of driving.

MANUAL TRANSMISSION/TRANSAXLE LUBRICANT LEVEL CHECK

➡ **Note: It is not necessary to check the manual transmission/ transaxle lubricant level weekly; every 15,000 miles (24,000 km)/18 months is adequate (unless a leak is suspected).**

48 Raise the vehicle and support it securely on jackstands.

49 Remove the check/fill plug from the transmission/transaxle. On 2004 through 2006 models, the check fill plug is located on the right side of the transmission case. On 2011 and later models, the check/fill plug is located on the front side of the transaxle.

50 Use your little finger to reach inside the housing to feel the lubricant level; it should be at or near the bottom of the hole. If it isn't, add the recommended lubricant with a syringe or squeeze bottle.

51 Install the check/fill plug and tighten it to the torque listed in this Chapter's Specifications.

5 Tire and tire pressure checks (every 250 miles [400 km] or weekly)

1 Periodic inspection of the tires may spare you from the inconvenience of being stranded with a flat tire. It can also provide you with vital information regarding possible problems in the steering and suspension systems before major damage occurs.

2 Normal tread wear can be monitored with a simple, inexpensive device known as a tread depth indicator **(see illustration).** When the tread depth reaches approximately 1/16-inch, replace the tire(s) (preferably long before that).

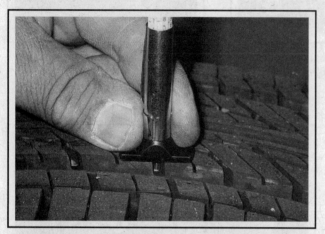

5.2 Use a tire tread depth gauge to monitor tire wear - they are available at auto parts stores and service stations and cost very little

3 Note any abnormal tread wear **(see illustration).** Tread pattern irregularities such as cupping, flat spots and more wear on one side than the other are indications of front end alignment and/or balance problems. If any of these conditions are noted, take the vehicle to a tire shop or service station to correct the problem.

4 Look closely for cuts, punctures and embedded nails or tacks. Sometimes a tire will hold its air pressure for a short time or leak down very slowly even after a nail has embedded itself into the tread. If a slow leak persists, check the valve stem core to make sure it is tight **(see illustration).** Examine the tread for an object that may have embedded itself into the tire or for a plug that may have begun to leak (radial tire punctures are repaired with a plug that is inserted into the hole). If a puncture is suspected, it can be easily verified by spraying a solution of soapy water onto the puncture area **(see illustration).** The soapy solution will bubble if there is a leak. Unless the puncture is inordinately large, a tire shop or gas station can usually repair the punctured tire.

5 Carefully inspect the inner sidewall of each tire for evidence of brake fluid leakage. If you see any, inspect the brakes immediately.

6 Correct tire air pressure adds miles to the lifespan of the tires, improves mileage and enhances overall ride quality. Tire pressure cannot be accurately estimated by looking at a tire, particularly if it is a radial. A tire pressure gauge is therefore essential. Keep an accurate gauge in the glove box. The pressure gauges fitted to the nozzles of air hoses at gas stations are often inaccurate.

7 Always check tire pressure when the tires are cold. "Cold," in this case, means the vehicle has not been driven over a mile in the three

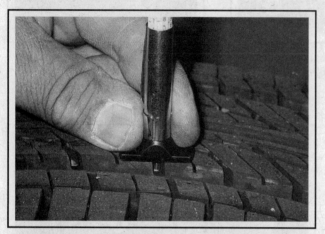

UNDERINFLATION

CUPPING

OVERINFLATION

Cupping may be caused by:
- Underinflation and/or mechanical irregularities such as out-of-balance condition of wheel and/or tire, and bent or damaged wheel.
- Loose or worn steering tie-rod or steering idler arm.
- Loose, damaged or worn front suspension parts.

INCORRECT TOE-IN OR EXTREME CAMBER

FEATHERING DUE TO MISALIGNMENT

5.3 This chart will help you determine the condition of your tires, the probable cause(s) of abnormal wear and the corrective action necessary

5.4a If a tire loses air on a steady basis, check the valve core first to make sure it's snug (special inexpensive wrenches are commonly available at auto parts stores)

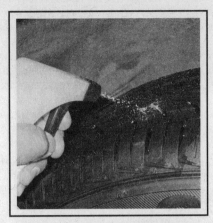

5.4b If the valve core is tight, raise the corner of the vehicle with the low tire and spray a soapy water solution onto the tread as the tire is turned slowly - slow leaks will cause small bubbles to appear

5.8 To extend the life of your tires, check the air pressure at least once a week with an accurate gauge (don't forget the spare!)

hours preceding a tire pressure check. A pressure rise of four to eight pounds is not uncommon once the tires are warm.

8   Unscrew the valve cap protruding from the wheel or hubcap and push the gauge firmly onto the valve **(see illustration)**. Note the reading on the gauge and compare this figure to the recommended tire pressure shown on the tire placard in the glove box. Be sure to reinstall the valve cap to keep dirt and moisture out of the valve stem mechanism. Check all four tires and, if necessary, add enough air to bring them up to the recommended pressure levels.

9   Don't forget to keep the spare tire inflated to the specified pressure (consult your owner's manual).

6   Engine oil and oil filter change (every 3000 miles [4,800 km] or 3 months)

⁑ WARNING:

If the vehicle is equipped with electronically modulated air suspension, make sure that the height control switch is turned off.

1   Frequent oil changes are the best preventive maintenance the home mechanic can give the engine, because aging oil becomes diluted and contaminated, which leads to premature engine wear.

2   Make sure that you have all the necessary tools before you begin this procedure **(see illustration)**. You should also have plenty of rags or newspapers handy for mopping up any spills.

⁑ WARNING:

Do not work under a vehicle which is supported only by a bumper, hydraulic or scissors-type jack.

6.2 These tools are required when changing the engine oil and filter

*1 **Drain pan** - It should be fairly shallow in depth, but wide in order to prevent spills*
*2 **Rubber gloves** - When removing the drain plug and filter, it is inevitable that you will get oil on your hands (the gloves will prevent burns)*
*3 **Breaker bar** - Sometimes the oil drain plug is pretty tight and a long breaker bar is needed to loosen it*
*4 **Socket** - To be used with the breaker bar or a ratchet (must be the correct size to fit the drain plug)*
*5 **Filter wrench** - This is a metal band-type wrench, which requires clearance around the filter to be effective*
*6 **Filter wrench** - This type fits on the bottom of the filter and can be turned with a ratchet or beaker bar (different size wrenches are available for different types of filters)*

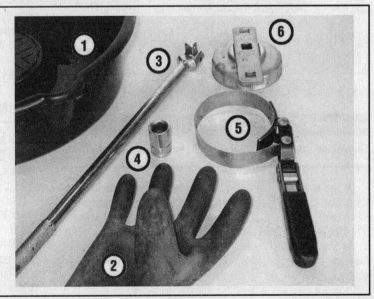

6.6 Use the proper size box-end wrench or socket to remove the oil drain plug without rounding off the corners

6.10 Typical oil filter location (lower engine splash shield removed for clarity; the filter is accessible without removing the shield)

6.12 Lubricate the oil filter gasket with clean engine oil before installing the filter on the engine

3   Access to the underside of the vehicle is greatly improved if the vehicle can be lifted on a hoist, driven onto ramps or supported by jackstands.

4   If this is your first oil change, get under the vehicle and familiarize yourself with the location of the oil drain plug. The engine and exhaust components will be warm during the actual work, so try to anticipate any potential problems before the engine and accessories are hot.

5   Park the vehicle on a level spot. Start the engine and allow it to reach its normal operating temperature (the needle on the temperature gauge should be at least above the bottom mark). Warm oil and sludge will flow out more easily. Turn off the engine once it's warmed up. Remove the filler cap.

6   Being careful not to touch the hot exhaust components, place a drain pan under the drain plug in the bottom of the pan and remove the plug **(see illustration)**. You may want to wear gloves while unscrewing the plug the final few turns if the engine is really hot.

7   Allow the old oil to drain into the pan. It may be necessary to move the pan farther under the engine as the oil flow slows to a trickle. Inspect the old oil for presence of metal shavings and chips.

8   After all the oil is drained, wipe off the drain plug opening, reinstall the plug and tighten it securely, but do not strip the threads.

ALL FOUR-CYLINDER ENGINES, AND 2006 AND EARLIER 3.5L V6 ENGINES

9   Move the drain pan into position under the oil filter.

❋❋ WARNING:

The engine exhaust manifold may still be hot, so be careful.

10   The oil filter is visible from underneath the engine **(see illustration)**. Loosen the oil filter by turning it counterclockwise with an oil filter wrench. On most engines you will have to use the type of wrench that slips over the bottom of the filter and is turned with a ratchet. Just as the filter is detached from the block, immediately tilt the open end up to prevent the oil inside the filter from spilling out. Make sure that the old filter gasket does not remain stuck to the block.

11   With a clean rag, wipe off the mounting surface on the block. If a residue of old oil is allowed to remain, it will smoke when the block is heated up. It will also prevent the new filter from seating properly. Also make sure that none of the old gasket remains stuck to the mounting surface. It can be removed with a scraper if necessary.

12   Compare the old filter with the new one to make sure they are the same type. Smear some engine oil on the rubber gasket of the new filter and screw it into place **(see illustration)**. Overtightening the filter will damage the gasket, so don't use a filter wrench. Most filter manufacturers recommend tightening the filter by hand only. Normally they should be tightened 3/4-turn after the gasket contacts the block, but be sure to follow the directions on the filter or container. Once the filter is installed, lower the vehicle and proceed to Step 17.

3.3L, 3.8L, AND 2011 AND LATER 3.5L V6 ENGINES

13   Remove all the tools, rags, etc. from under the vehicle, being careful not to spill the oil in the drain pan, then lower the vehicle.

14   Working in the engine compartment, remove the engine cover, then locate the oil filter/housing on the end of the engine **(see illustration)**. Place a rag around the housing to absorb any spilled oil, then unscrew the oil filter cap **(see illustration)**. The element is withdrawn with the oil filter cap, and can then be separated and discarded **(see illustration)**.

15   Wipe out the oil filter housing and cap using a clean rag, then install a new O-ring on the cap and stem **(see illustrations)**.

16   Install the filter element onto the cap **(see illustration)**.

ALL MODELS

17   Add new oil to the engine through the oil filler cap in the valve cover. Use a funnel to prevent oil from spilling onto the top of the engine. Pour three quarts of fresh oil into the engine. Wait a few minutes to allow the oil to drain into the pan, then check the level on the oil dipstick (see Section 4 if necessary). If the oil level is at or near the F mark, install the filler cap hand tight, start the engine and allow the new oil to circulate.

18   Allow the engine to run for about a minute. While the engine is running, look under the vehicle and check for leaks at the oil pan drain plug and around the oil filter. If either is leaking, stop the engine and tighten the plug or filter slightly.

6.14a Location of the oil filter housing

6.14b Use an oil filter wrench like this to remove the filter cap

19 Wait a few minutes to allow the oil to trickle down into the pan, then recheck the level on the dipstick and, if necessary, add enough oil to bring the level to the F mark.

20 During the first few trips after an oil change, make it a point to check frequently for leaks and proper oil level.

21 The old oil drained from the engine cannot be reused in its present state and should be disposed of. Check with your local auto parts store, disposal facility or environmental agency to see if they will accept the oil for recycling. After the oil has cooled it can be drained into a container (capped plastic jugs, topped bottles, milk cartons, etc.) for transport to one of these disposal sites. Don't dispose of the oil by pouring it on the ground or down a drain!

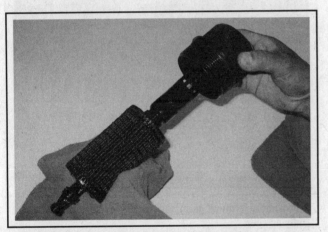

6.14c Pull the used element off of the filter cap stem

6.15a Install a new O-rig on the cap . . .

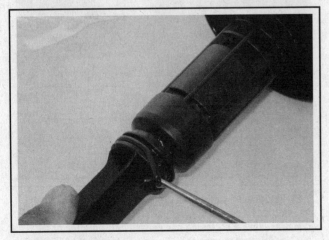

6.15b . . . and stem

6.16 Install the new filter element

7   Battery check, maintenance and charging (every 5000 miles [8000 km] or 6 months)

⁂ WARNING:

Certain precautions must be followed when checking and servicing the battery. Hydrogen gas, which is highly flammable, is always present in the battery cells, so keep lighted tobacco and all other open flames and sparks away from the battery. The electrolyte inside the battery is actually dilute sulfuric acid, which will cause injury if splashed on your skin or in your eyes. It will also ruin clothes and painted surfaces. When removing the battery cables, always detach the negative cable first and hook it up last!

MAINTENANCE

1   A routine preventive maintenance program for the battery in your vehicle is the only way to ensure quick and reliable starts. But before performing any battery maintenance, make sure that you have the proper equipment necessary to work safely around the battery **(see illustration)**.

2   There are also several precautions that should be taken whenever battery maintenance is performed. Before servicing the battery, always turn the engine and all accessories off and disconnect the cable from the negative terminal of the battery.

3   The battery produces hydrogen gas, which is both flammable and explosive. Never create a spark, smoke or light a match around the battery. Always charge the battery in a ventilated area.

4   Electrolyte contains poisonous and corrosive sulfuric acid. Do not allow it to get in your eyes, on your skin on your clothes. Never ingest it. Wear protective safety glasses when working near the battery. Keep children away from the battery.

5   Note the external condition of the battery. If the positive terminal and cable clamp on your vehicle's battery is equipped with a rubber protector, make sure that it's not torn or damaged. It should completely cover the terminal. Look for any corroded or loose connections, cracks in the case or cover or loose hold-down clamps. Also check the entire length of each cable for cracks and frayed conductors.

6   If corrosion, which looks like white, fluffy deposits **(see illustration)** is evident, particularly around the terminals, the battery should be removed for cleaning. Loosen the cable clamp bolts with a wrench, being careful to remove the ground cable first, and slide them off the terminals **(see illustration)**. Then disconnect the hold-down clamp bolt and nut, remove the clamp and lift the battery from the engine compartment.

7.6a Battery terminal corrosion usually appears as light, fluffy powder

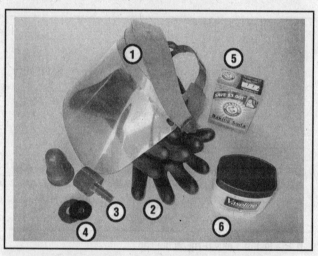

7.1 Tools and materials required for battery maintenance

1 *Face shield/safety goggles* - *When removing corrosion with a brush, the acidic particles can easily fly up into your eyes*
2 *Baking soda* - *A solution of baking soda and water can be used to neutralize corrosion*
3 *Petroleum jelly* - *A layer of this on the battery posts will help prevent corrosion*
4 *Battery post/cable cleaner* - *This wire brush cleaning tool will remove all traces of corrosion from the battery posts and cable clamps*
5 *Treated felt washers* - *Placing one of these on each post, directly under the cable clamps, will help prevent corrosion*
6 *Puller* - *Sometimes the cable clamps are very difficult to pull off the posts, even after the nut/bolt has been completely loosened. This tool pulls the clamp straight up and off the post without damage*
7 *Battery post/cable cleaner*- *Here is another cleaning tool that is a slightly different version of number 4 above, but it does the same thing*
8 *Rubber gloves* - *Another safety item to consider when servicing the battery; remember that's acid inside the battery*

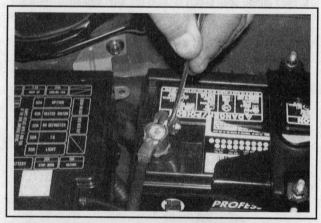

7.6b Removing a cable from the battery post with a wrench - sometimes a pair of special battery pliers are required for this procedure if corrosion has caused deterioration of the nut hex (always remove the ground (-) cable first and hook it up last!)

7.7a When cleaning the cable clamps, all corrosion must be removed (the inside of the clamp is tapered to match the taper on the post, so don't remove too much material)

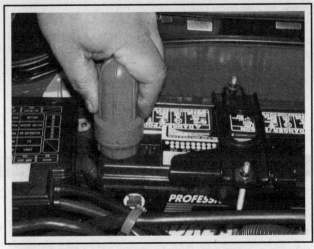

7.7b Regardless of the type of tool used to clean the battery posts, a clean, shiny surface should be the result

7 Clean the cable clamps thoroughly with a battery brush or a terminal cleaner and a solution of warm water and baking soda **(see illustration).** Wash the terminals and the top of the battery case with the same solution but make sure that the solution doesn't get into the battery. When cleaning the cables, terminals and battery top, wear safety goggles and rubber gloves to prevent any solution from coming in contact with your eyes or hands. Wear old clothes too - even diluted, sulfuric acid splashed onto clothes will burn holes in them. If the terminals have been extensively corroded, clean them up with a terminal cleaner **(see illustration).** Thoroughly wash all cleaned areas with plain water.

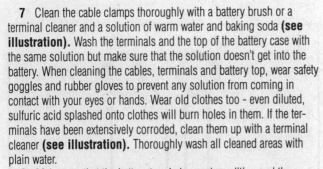

8 Make sure that the battery tray is in good condition and the hold-down clamp bolts are tight. If the battery is removed from the tray, make sure no parts remain in the bottom of the tray when the battery is reinstalled. When reinstalling the hold-down clamp bolts, do not over-tighten them.

9 Any metal parts of the vehicle damaged by corrosion should be covered with a zinc-based primer, then painted.

10 Information on removing and installing the battery can be found in Chapter 5. Information on jump starting can be found at the front of this manual.

CHARGING

❋❋ WARNING:

When batteries are being charged, hydrogen gas, which is very explosive and flammable, is produced. Do not smoke or allow open flames near a battery. Wear eye protection when near the battery during charging. Also, make sure the charger is unplugged before connecting or disconnecting the battery from the charger.

➡ **Note: The manufacturer recommends the battery be removed from the vehicle for charging because the gas that escapes during this procedure can damage the paint. Fast charging with the** battery cables connected can result in damage to the electrical system.

11 Slow-rate charging is the best way to restore a battery that's discharged to the point where it will not start the engine. It's also a good way to maintain the battery charge in a vehicle that's only driven a few miles between starts. Maintaining the battery charge is particularly important in the winter when the battery must work harder to start the engine and electrical accessories that drain the battery are in greater use.

12 It's best to use a one or two-amp battery charger (sometimes called a trickle charger). They are the safest and put the least strain on the battery. They are also the least expensive. For a faster charge, you can use a higher amperage charger, but don't use one rated more than 1/10th the amp/hour rating of the battery. Rapid boost charges that claim to restore the power of the battery in one to two hours are hardest on the battery and can damage batteries not in good condition. This type of charging should only be used in emergency situations.

13 The average time necessary to charge a battery should be listed in the instructions that come with the charger. As a general rule, a trickle charger will charge a battery in 12 to 16 hours.

14 Remove all the cell caps (if equipped) and cover the holes with a clean cloth to prevent spattering electrolyte. Disconnect the negative battery cable and hook the battery charger cable clamps up to the battery posts (positive to positive, negative to negative), then plug in the charger. Make sure it is set at 12-volts if it has a selector switch.

15 If you're using a charger with a rate higher than two amps, check the battery regularly during charging to make sure it doesn't overheat. If you're using a trickle charger, you can safely let the battery charge overnight after you've checked it regularly for the first couple of hours.

16 If the battery has removable cell caps, measure the specific gravity with a hydrometer every hour during the last few hours of the charging cycle. Hydrometers are available inexpensively from auto parts stores - follow the instructions that come with the hydrometer. Consider the battery charged when there's no change in the specific gravity reading for two hours and the electrolyte in the cells is gassing (bubbling) freely. The specific gravity reading from each cell should be very close to the others. If not, the battery probably has a bad cell(s).

17 Some batteries with sealed tops have built-in hydrometers on the top that indicate the state of charge by the color displayed in the hydrometer window. Normally, a bright-colored hydrometer indicates a full charge and a dark hydrometer indicates the battery still needs charging.

18 If the battery has a sealed top and no built-in hydrometer, you can hook up a voltmeter across the battery terminals to check the charge. A fully charged battery should read 12.6 volts or higher after the surface charge has been removed.

19 Further information on the battery and jump starting can be found in Chapter 5 and *Booster battery jump starting*.

8   Tire rotation (every 5000 miles [8000 km] or 6 months)

1 The tires should be rotated at the specified intervals and whenever uneven wear is noticed. Since the vehicle will be raised and the tires removed anyway, check the brakes (see Section 12) at this time.

2 Radial tires must be rotated in a specific pattern **(see illustrations)**.

3 Refer to the information in *Jacking and towing* for the proper procedures to follow when raising the vehicle and changing a tire. If the brakes are to be checked, do not apply the parking brake as stated. Make sure the tires are blocked to prevent the vehicle from rolling.

4 Preferably, the entire vehicle should be raised at the same time. This can be done on a hoist or by jacking up each corner and then lowering the vehicle onto jackstands placed under the frame rails. Always use four jackstands and make sure the vehicle is firmly supported.

5 After rotation, check and adjust the tire pressures as necessary and be sure to check the lug nut tightness.

6 For further information on the wheels and tires, refer to Chapter 10.

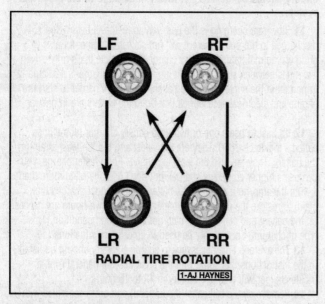

8.2a Four-tire rotation pattern

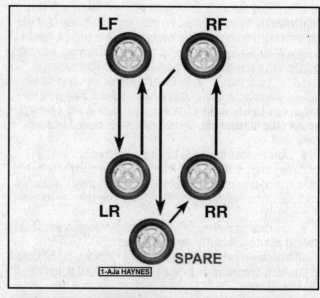

8.2b Five-tire rotation pattern (to be used only if the spare tire is the same as the other four)

9   Windshield/rear wiper blade inspection and replacement (every 5000 miles [8000 km] or 6 months)

1 The wiper and blade assemblies should be inspected periodically for damage, loose components and cracked or worn blade elements.

2 Road film can build up on the wiper blades and affect their efficiency, so they should be washed regularly with a mild detergent solution.

3 The action of the wiping mechanism can loosen bolts, nuts and fasteners, so they should be checked and tightened, as necessary, at the same time the wiper blades are checked.

4 If the wiper blade elements are cracked, worn or warped, or no longer clean adequately, they should be replaced with new ones.

5 Lift the arm assembly away from the glass for clearance, press the release lever, then slide the wiper blade assembly out of the hook at the end of the arm **(see illustrations)**.

6 Attach the new wiper to the arm. Connection can be confirmed by an audible click.

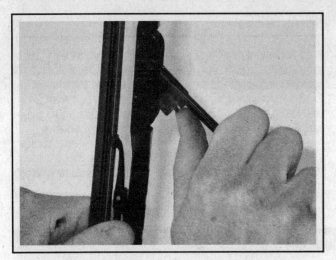

9.5a To release the blade holder, push the release pin . . .

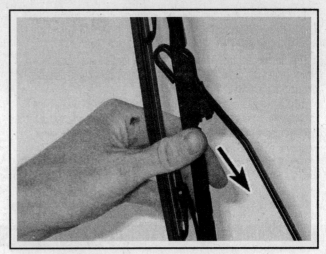

9.5b . . . and pull the wiper blade in the direction of the arrow to separate it from the arm

10 Underhood hose check and replacement (every 5000 miles [8000 km] or 6 months)

※※ WARNING:

Replacement of air conditioning hoses must be left to a dealer service department or air conditioning shop that has the equipment to depressurize the system safely. Never remove air conditioning components or hoses until the system has been evacuated and the refrigerant recovered by a dealer service department or air conditioning shop.

GENERAL

1 High temperatures in the engine compartment can cause the deterioration of the rubber and plastic hoses used for engine, accessory and emission systems operation. Periodic inspection should be made for cracks, loose clamps, material hardening and leaks.

2 Information specific to the cooling system hoses can be found in Section 11.

3 Some, but not all, hoses are secured to the fittings with clamps. Where clamps are used, check to be sure they haven't lost their tension, allowing the hose to leak. If clamps aren't used, make sure the hose has not expanded and/or hardened where it slips over the fitting, allowing it to leak.

VACUUM HOSES

4 It's quite common for vacuum hoses, especially those in the emissions system, to be color coded or identified by colored stripes molded into them. Various systems require hoses with different wall thickness, collapse resistance and temperature resistance. When replacing hoses, be sure the new ones are made of the same material.

5 Often the only effective way to check a hose is to remove it completely from the vehicle. If more than one hose is removed, be sure to label the hoses and fittings to ensure correct installation.

6 When checking vacuum hoses, be sure to include any plastic T-fittings in the check. Inspect the fittings for cracks and the hose where it fits over the fitting for distortion, which could cause leakage.

※※ WARNING:

When probing with the vacuum hose stethoscope, be very careful not to come into contact with moving engine components such as the drivebelts, cooling fan, etc.

7 A small piece of vacuum hose (1/4-inch inside diameter) can be used as a stethoscope to detect vacuum leaks. Hold one end of the hose to your ear and probe around vacuum hoses and fittings, listening for the hissing sound characteristic of a vacuum leak.

FUEL HOSE

※※ WARNING:

Gasoline is extremely flammable, so take extra precautions when you work on any part of the fuel system. Don't smoke or allow open flames or bare light bulbs near the work area, and don't work in a garage where a gas-type appliance (such as a water heater or a clothes dryer) is present. Since gasoline is carcinogenic, wear fuel resistant gloves when there's a possibility of being exposed to fuel, and, if you spill any fuel on your skin, rinse it off immediately with soap and water. Mop up any spills immediately and do not store fuel-soaked rags where they could ignite. The fuel system is under constant pressure, so, if any fuel lines are to be disconnected, the fuel pressure in the system must be relieved first. When you perform any kind of work on the fuel system, wear safety glasses and have a Class B type fire extinguisher on hand.

8 Check all rubber fuel lines for deterioration and chafing. Check especially for cracks in areas where the hose bends and just before fittings, such as where a hose attaches to the fuel filter.

9 High quality fuel line should be used for fuel line replacement. Never, under any circumstances, use unreinforced vacuum line, clear plastic tubing or water hose for fuel lines.

10 Spring-type clamps are commonly used on fuel lines. These clamps often lose their tension over a period of time, and can be sprung during removal. Replace all spring-type clamps with screw clamps whenever a hose is replaced.

METAL LINES

11 Sections of metal line are often used for fuel line between the fuel pump and fuel injection unit. Check carefully to be sure the line has not been bent or crimped and that cracks have not started in the line.

12 If a section of metal fuel line must be replaced, only seamless steel tubing should be used, since copper and aluminum tubing don't have the strength necessary to withstand normal engine vibration.

13 Check the metal brake lines where they enter the master cylinder and brake proportioning unit (if used) for cracks in the lines or loose fittings. Any sign of brake fluid leakage calls for an immediate thorough inspection of the brake system.

11 Cooling system check (every 5000 miles [8000 km] or 6 months)

1 Many major engine failures can be attributed to a faulty cooling system. If the vehicle is equipped with an automatic transaxle, the cooling system also cools the transaxle fluid and thus plays an important role in prolonging transaxle life.

✳ WARNING:

Never remove the cooling system pressure cap when the engine is running or has just been shut down, because the cooling system is hot. Escaping steam and scalding liquid could cause serious injury.

2 The cooling system should be checked with the engine cold. Do this before the vehicle is driven for the day or after the engine has been shut off for at least three hours.

3 Remove the surge tank pressure cap by turning it to the left until it reaches a stop. If you hear a hissing sound (indicating there is still pressure in the system), wait until it stops. Now press down on the cap with the palm of your hand and continue turning to the left until the cap can be removed. Thoroughly clean the cap, inside and out, with clean water. Also clean the filler neck on the tank. All traces of corrosion should be removed. The coolant inside should be relatively transparent. If it's rust colored, the system should be drained and refilled (see Section 25). If the coolant level isn't up to the top, add additional antifreeze/coolant mixture (see Section 4).

4 Carefully check the large upper and lower radiator hoses along with the smaller diameter heater hoses which run from the engine to the firewall. Inspect each hose along its entire length, replacing any hose that is cracked, swollen or shows signs of deterioration. Cracks may become more apparent if the hose is squeezed **(see illustration)**. Regardless of condition, it's a good idea to replace hoses with new ones every two years.

5 Make sure that all hose connections are tight. A leak in the cooling system will usually show up as white or rust colored deposits on the areas adjoining the leak. If wire-type clamps are used at the ends of the hoses, it may be a good idea to replace them with more secure screw-type clamps.

6 Use compressed air or a soft brush to remove bugs, leaves, etc. from the front of the radiator or air conditioning condenser. Be careful not to damage the delicate cooling fins or cut yourself on them.

7 Every other inspection, or at the first indication of cooling system problems, have the cap and system pressure tested. If you don't have a pressure tester, most gas stations and garages will do this for a minimal charge.

Check for a chafed area that could fail prematurely.

Check for a soft area indicating the hose has deteriorated inside.

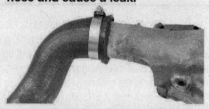
Overtightening the clamp on a hardened hose will damage the hose and cause a leak.

Check each hose for swelling and oil-soaked ends. Cracks and breaks can be located by squeezing the hose.

11.4 Hoses, like drivebelts, have a habit of failing at the worst possible time - to prevent the inconvenience of a blown radiator or heater hose, inspect them carefully as shown here

12 Brake check (every 5000 miles [8000 km] or 6 months)

※ WARNING:

The dust created by the brake system is harmful to your health. Never blow it out with compressed air and don't inhale any of it. An approved filtering mask should be worn when working on the brakes. Do not, under any circumstances, use petroleum-based solvents to clean brake parts. Use brake system cleaner only!

➡ **Note: For detailed photographs of the brake system, refer to Chapter 9.**

1 In addition to the specified intervals, the brakes should be inspected every time the wheels are removed or whenever a defect is suspected.

2 Any of the following symptoms could indicate a potential brake system defect: The vehicle pulls to one side when the brake pedal is depressed; the brakes make squealing or dragging noises when applied; brake pedal travel is excessive; the pedal pulsates; or brake fluid leaks, usually onto the inside of the tire or wheel.

3 Loosen the wheel lug nuts.

4 Raise the vehicle and place it securely on jackstands.

5 Remove the wheels (see *Jacking and towing*, or your owner's manual, if necessary).

DISC BRAKES

6 There are two pads (an outer and an inner) in each caliper. The pads are visible with the wheels removed. The vehicles covered by this manual have disc brakes front and rear, with a mechanical, drum-type parking brake mechanism inside the rear discs.

7 Check the pad thickness by looking at each end of the caliper and through the inspection window in the caliper body **(see illustrations)**. If the lining material is less than the thickness listed in this Chapter's Specifications, replace the pads.

➡ **Note: Keep in mind that the lining material is riveted or bonded to a metal backing plate and the metal portion is not included in this measurement.**

8 If it is difficult to determine the exact thickness of the remaining pad material by the above method, or if you are at all concerned about the condition of the pads, remove the caliper(s), then remove the pads

from the calipers for further inspection (see Chapter 9).

9 Once the pads are removed from the calipers, clean them with brake cleaner and re-measure them with a ruler or a vernier caliper.

10 Measure the disc thickness with a micrometer to make sure that it still has service life remaining. If any disc is thinner than the specified minimum thickness, replace it (see Chapter 9). Even if the disc has service life remaining, check its condition. Look for scoring, gouging and burned spots. If these conditions exist, remove the disc and have it resurfaced (see Chapter 9).

11 Before installing the wheels, check all brake lines and hoses for damage, wear, deformation, cracks, corrosion, leakage, bends and twists, particularly in the vicinity of the rubber hoses at the calipers. Check the clamps for tightness and the connections for leakage. Make sure that all hoses and lines are clear of sharp edges, moving parts and the exhaust system. If any of the above conditions are noted, repair, reroute or replace the lines and/or fittings as necessary (see Chapter 9).

BRAKE BOOSTER CHECK

12 Sit in the driver's seat and perform the following sequence of tests.

13 With the brake fully depressed, start the engine - the pedal should move down a little when the engine starts.

14 With the engine running, depress the brake pedal several times - the travel distance should not change.

15 Depress the brake, stop the engine and hold the pedal in for about 30 seconds - the pedal should neither sink nor rise.

16 Restart the engine, run it for about a minute and turn it off. Then firmly depress the brake several times - the pedal travel should decrease with each application.

17 If your brakes do not operate as described, the brake booster has failed. Refer to Chapter 9 for the replacement procedure.

PARKING BRAKE

18 One method of checking the parking brake is to park the vehicle on a steep hill with the parking brake set and the transmission in Neutral (be sure to stay in the vehicle for this check). If the parking brake cannot prevent the vehicle from rolling, it's in need of attention (see Chapter 9).

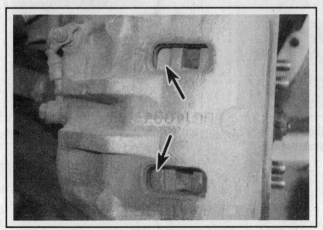

12.7a You'll find an inspection hole like this in each caliper through which you can view the inner brake pad lining

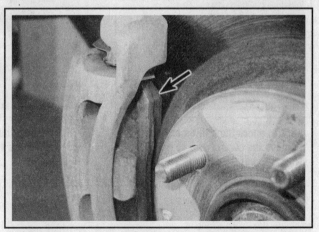

12.7b The outer pad is more easily checked at the edge of the caliper

13 Steering, suspension and driveaxle boot check (every 15,000 miles [24,000 km] or 18 months)

STEERING CHECK

➡ **Note: For detailed illustrations of the steering and suspension components, refer to Chapter 10.**

1 With the vehicle on the ground and the front wheels pointed straight ahead, rock the steering wheel gently back and forth. If freeplay is excessive, a front wheel bearing, main shaft yoke, intermediate shaft yoke, lower arm balljoint or steering system joint is worn or the steering gear is out of adjustment or broken. Steering wheel freeplay is the amount of travel (measured at the rim of the steering wheel) between the initial steering input and the point at which the front wheels begin to turn (indicated by slight resistance). Refer to Chapter 10 for the appropriate repair procedure.

2 Other symptoms, such as excessive vehicle body movement over rough roads, swaying (leaning) around corners and binding as the steering wheel is turned, may indicate faulty steering and/or suspension components.

SUSPENSION CHECK

3 Check the shock absorbers/struts by pushing down and releasing the vehicle several times at each corner. If the vehicle does not come back to a level position within one or two bounces, the shocks/struts are worn and must be replaced. When bouncing the vehicle up and down, listen for squeaks and noises from the suspension components. Additional information on suspension components can be found in Chapter 10.

4 Raise the vehicle with a floor jack and support it securely on jackstands. See *Jacking and towing* for the proper jacking points.

5 Check the tires for irregular wear patterns and proper inflation.

See Section 5 in this Chapter for information regarding tire wear and Chapter 10 for the wheel bearing replacement procedures.

6 Inspect the universal joint between the steering shaft and the steering gear housing. Check the steering gear housing for lubricant leakage or oozing. Make sure that the dust seals and boots are not damaged and that the boot clamps are not loose. Check the steering linkage for looseness or damage. Check the track rod ends for excessive play. Look for loose bolts, broken or disconnected parts and deteriorated rubber bushings on all suspension and steering components. While an assistant turns the steering wheel from side to side, check the steering components for free movement, chafing and binding. If the steering components do not seem to be reacting with the movement of the steering wheel, try to determine where the slack is located.

7 Check the balljoints for wear by trying to move each control arm up and down with a prybar **(see illustration)** to ensure that its balljoint has no play. If any balljoint does have play, replace it. See Chapter 10 for the front balljoint replacement procedure.

8 Inspect the balljoint boots for damage and leaking grease **(see illustration).** Replace the balljoints with new ones if they are damaged (see Chapter 10).

DRIVEAXLE BOOT CHECK

9 The driveaxle boots are very important because they prevent dirt, water and foreign material from entering and damaging the constant velocity (CV) joints. Oil and grease can cause the boot material to deteriorate prematurely, so it's a good idea to wash the boots with soap and water.

10 Inspect the boots for tears and cracks as well as loose clamps **(see illustration).** If there is any evidence of cracks or leaking lubricant, they must be replaced as described in Chapter 8.

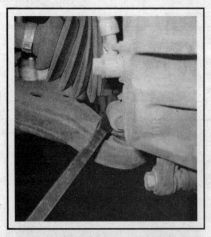

13.7 To check the balljoints, attempt to move the control arm up and down with a prybar to make sure there is no play in the balljoint (if there is, replace it)

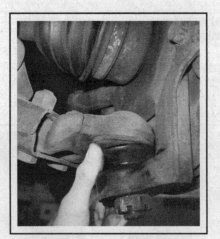

13.8 Push on the balljoint boot to check for tears and grease leaks

13.10 Flex the driveaxle boots by hand to check for tears, cracks and leaking grease

14 Exhaust system check (every 15,000 miles [24,000 km] or 18 months)

1 With the engine cold (at least three hours after the vehicle has been driven), check the complete exhaust system from its starting point at the engine to the end of the tailpipe. Preferably this should be done on a hoist where unrestricted access is available.

2 Check the pipes and connections for evidence of leaks, severe corrosion or damage. Make sure that all brackets and hangers are in good condition and tight **(see illustration).**

3 At the same time, inspect the underside of the body for holes, corrosion, open seams, etc. that may allow exhaust gases to enter the passenger compartment. Seal all body openings with silicone or body putty.

4 Rattles and other noises can often be traced to the exhaust system, especially the mounts and hangers. Try to move the pipes, silencer and catalytic converter. If the components can come in contact with the body or suspension parts, secure the exhaust system with new mounts.

5 Check the running condition of the engine by inspecting inside the end of the tailpipe. The exhaust deposits here are an indication of engine state-of-tune. If the pipe is black and sooty or coated with white deposits, the engine is in need of a tune-up, including a thorough fuel system inspection.

14.2 Check the exhaust system rubber hangers for damage

15 Air filter replacement (every 30,000 miles [48,000 km] or 36 months)

1 The air filter is located inside a housing at the side of the engine compartment. To remove the air filter, release the clamps retaining the two halves of the air filter housing **(see illustration).** Disconnect the wiring from the Mass Airflow (MAF) sensor in order to get enough clearance to raise the lid.

2 Lift the cover up and remove the air filter element **(see illustration).**

❋ CAUTION:

Never drive the vehicle with the air filter removed. Excessive engine wear could result and backfiring could even cause a fire under the hood.

3 Inspect the outer surface of the filter element. If it is dirty, replace it. If it is only moderately dusty, it can be reused by blowing it clean from the back to the front surface with compressed air.

❋ WARNING:

Always wear eye protection when using compressed air!

4 Because it is a pleated paper type filter, it cannot be washed or oiled. If it cannot be cleaned satisfactorily with compressed air, discard and replace it.

5 Installation is the reverse of removal. Make sure the hinge tabs on the housing cover engage properly with the lower part of the housing.

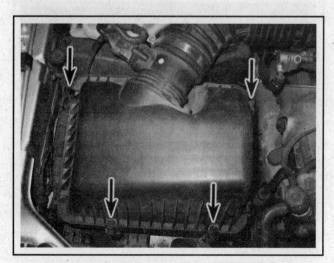

15.1 Release the latches securing the air filter housing lid

15.2 Lift the cover up, remove the filter element and install the new one

16 Fuel system check (every 30,000 miles [48,000 km] or 36 months)

✳✳ WARNING:

Gasoline is extremely flammable, so take extra precautions when you work on any part of the fuel system. Don't smoke or allow open flames or bare light bulbs near the work area, and don't work in a garage where a gas-type appliance (such as a water heater or a clothes dryer) is present. Since gasoline is carcinogenic, wear fuel resistant gloves when there's a possibility of being exposed to fuel, and, if you spill any fuel on your skin, rinse it off immediately with soap and water. Mop up any spills immediately and do not store fuel-soaked rags where they could ignite. The fuel system is under constant pressure, so, if any fuel lines are to be disconnected, the fuel pressure in the system must be relieved first. When you perform any kind of work on the fuel system, wear safety glasses and have a Class B type fire extinguisher on hand.

1 If you smell fuel while driving or after the vehicle has been sitting in the sun, inspect the fuel system immediately.

2 Remove the fuel filler cap and inspect it for damage and corrosion. The gasket should have an unbroken sealing imprint. If the gasket is damaged or corroded, remove it and install a new one.

3 Inspect the fuel feed and return lines for cracks. Make sure that the threaded flare nut type connectors (which secure the metal fuel lines to the fuel injection system) and the fittings on the in-line fuel filter are tight.

4 Since some components of the fuel system - the fuel tank and part of the fuel feed and return lines, for example - are underneath the vehicle, they can be inspected more easily with the vehicle raised on a hoist. If that's not possible, raise the vehicle and support it securely on jackstands.

✳✳ WARNING:

Do not, under any circumstances, try to repair a fuel tank (except rubber components). A welding torch or any open flame can easily cause fuel vapors inside the tank to explode.

5 With the vehicle raised and safely supported, inspect the fuel tank and filler neck for punctures, cracks and other damage. The connection between the filler neck and the tank is particularly critical. Sometimes a rubber filler neck will leak because of loose clamps or deteriorated rubber. These are problems a home mechanic can usually rectify.

6 Carefully check all rubber hoses and metal lines leading away from the fuel tank. Check for loose connections, deteriorated hoses, crimped lines and other damage. Carefully inspect the lines from the tank to the fuel injection system. Repair or replace damaged sections as necessary (see Chapter 4).

17 Interior ventilation filter replacement (every 30,000 miles [48,000 km] or 36 months)

1 On some models, there is a filter in the blower housing that cleans the air before it enters the passenger's compartment.

2 To remove the air filter, open the glove box and disconnect the support cable from the right side, if equipped.

3 Remove the stoppers from both sides of the box and lower the door.

4 Press the filter cover retaining clips and remove the cover (see illustration).

5 Lift off the cover and remove the air filter element (see illustration).

6 Installation is the reverse of removal.

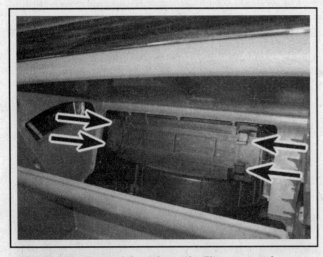

17.4 Depress the retaining tabs on the filter cover and remove the cover

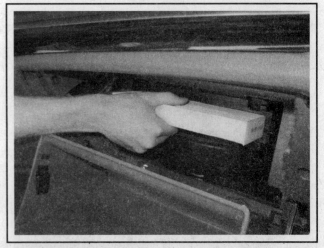

17.5 Remove the filter

18 Positive Crankcase Ventilation (PCV) valve check and replacement (every 30,000 miles [48,000 km] or 36 months)

1   The PCV valve and hose are located at the rear of the left valve cover on 2006 and earlier 3.5L V6 engines; it will be necessary to remove the upper intake manifold for access (see Chapter 2B). On 2007 through 2009 3.3L and 3.8L engines, it's located under the upper intake manifold at the front of the engine. On four-cylinder engines, it's located at the right front corner of the valve cover. On 2011 and later 3.5L V6 engines, it's located at the left end of the rear valve cover.

2   Disconnect the hose and unscrew the PCV valve **(see illustrations).**

3   Use a toothpick inserted into the valve and depress the plunger inside. If you can feel the plunger moving, and some spring resistance, the valve is ok. If not, replace it. The valve can be cleaned with carburetor cleaner, which might free-up a sticky plunger.

4   When purchasing a replacement PCV valve, make sure it's for your particular vehicle and engine size. Compare the old valve with the new one to make sure they're the same.

5   Installation is the reverse of removal.

18.2a PCV valve location - 2006 and earlier V6 models

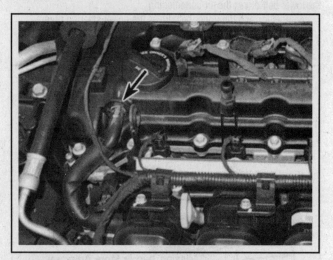

18.2b PCV valve location - four-cylinder engines

19 Brake fluid change (every 30,000 miles [48,000 km] or 36 months)

✳✳ WARNING:

Brake fluid can harm your eyes and damage painted surfaces, so use extreme caution when handling or pouring it. Do not use brake fluid that has been standing open or is more than one year old. Brake fluid absorbs moisture from the air. Excess moisture can cause a dangerous loss of braking effectiveness.

1   At the specified intervals, the brake fluid should be drained and replaced. Since the brake fluid may drip or splash when pouring it, place plenty of rags around the master cylinder to protect any surrounding painted surfaces.

2   Before beginning work, purchase the specified brake fluid (see *Recommended lubricants and fluids* in this Chapter's Specifications).

3   Remove the cap from the master cylinder reservoir.

4   Using a hand suction pump or similar device, withdraw the fluid from the master cylinder reservoir.

5   Add new fluid to the master cylinder until it rises to the base of the filler neck.

6   Bleed the brake system (see Chapter 9) at all four brakes until new and uncontaminated fluid is expelled from the bleeder screw. Be sure to maintain the fluid level in the master cylinder as you perform the bleeding process. If you allow the master cylinder to run dry, air will enter the system.

7   Refill the master cylinder with fluid and check the operation of the brakes. The pedal should feel solid when depressed, with no sponginess.

✳✳ WARNING:

Do not operate the vehicle if you are in doubt about the effectiveness of the brake system.

20   Drivebelt check, adjustment and replacement (60,000 miles [96,000 km] or 72 months

CHECK

1   The drivebelt(s) is/are located at the front of the engine. The good condition and proper adjustment of the belts is critical to the operation of the engine. Because of their composition and the high stresses to which they are subjected, drivebelts stretch and deteriorate as they get older. They must therefore be periodically inspected.

2   On four-cylinder models and all V6 engines except 2006 and earlier 3.5L models, one belt transmits power to all accessories. On 2006 and earlier 3.5L V6 engines, the inner belt drives the alternator, the lower belt drives the air conditioning compressor, and the upper belt drives the power steering pump.

3   With the engine off, open the hood and locate the drivebelts.

With a flashlight, check each belt for separation of the adhesive rubber on both sides of the core, core separation from the belt side, a severed core, separation of the ribs from the adhesive rubber, cracking or separation of the ribs, and torn or worn ribs or cracks in the inner ridges of the ribs **(see illustration)**. Also check for fraying and glazing, which gives the belt a shiny appearance. Both sides of the belt should be inspected, which means you will have to twist the belt to check the underside. Use your fingers to feel the belt where you can't see it. If any of the above conditions are evident, replace the belt.

4   The tension of each belt is checked by pushing on the belt at a distance halfway between the pulleys. Push firmly with your thumb and see how much the belt moves (deflects) **(see illustration)**. The belt should deflect approximately 1/4-inch.

ADJUSTMENT (2006 AND EARLIER 3.5L V6 ENGINES)

5   All the belts are adjusted in the same manner, although each has its own tensioner **(see illustrations)**. The adjustment bolts are located at the top or bottom of each tensioner.

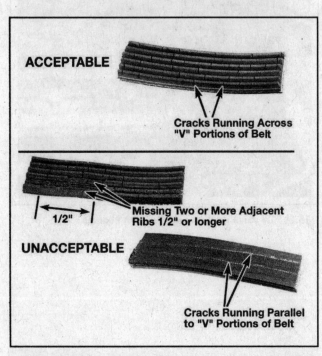

20.3 Check a multi-ribbed belt for signs like these - if the belt looks worn, replace it

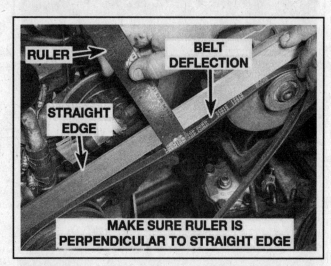

20.4 Measuring drivebelt deflection with a straightedge and ruler

20.5a Tensioner adjustment bolt for the power steering belt . . .

20.5b . . . the alternator belt . . .

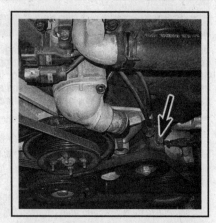

20.5c . . . and the air conditioning compressor belt

6 Loosen the tensioner pulley nut, then turn the tensioner adjustment bolts in or out to achieve the proper belt tension. When proper tension is achieved, tighten the pulley nut securely.

REPLACEMENT

7 Remove any interfering components such as engine covers and engine brackets.

8 On 2006 and earlier 3.5L V6 engines, release tension on the belt(s). Refer to the adjustment procedures above. Loosen the tension so that the belt will slip off the pulleys.

9 All other engines use a self-adjusting spring-loaded tensioner. Use a breaker bar or a long-handle ratchet to rotate the tensioner and release tension on the belt. Slip the belt from the pulleys while the tension is released.

10 Take the old belts to the parts store in order to make a direct comparison for length, width and design.

11 After replacing the drivebelt, make sure that it fits properly in the ribbed grooves in the pulleys. It is essential that the belt be properly centered.

12 To replace a belt, follow the procedures for drivebelt adjustment, but slip the belt off the crankshaft pulley and remove it. Because belts tend to wear out more or less together, it is a good idea to replace both belts at the same time. Mark each belt and its appropriate pulley groove so the replacement belts can be installed in their proper positions.

13 Adjust the belt(s) in accordance with the procedures outlined earlier in this Section.

➡ **Note: The self-adjusting tensioner used on all models except 2006 and earlier V6 engines has a scale that indicates minimum and maximum allowable positions. If the belt has stretched enough to be more than the maximum length, replace it with a new one.**

21 Automatic transmission/transaxle fluid and filter change (60,000 miles [96,000 km] or 72 months)

1 At the specified time intervals, the automatic transmission or automatic transaxle and differential fluid should be drained and replaced.

➡ **Note: Although the manufacturer doesn't specify it, it is a good idea to replace the transaxle fluid filter periodically to remove accumulated dirt and metal particles.**

2 Before beginning work, purchase the specified fluid (see *Recommended lubricants and fluids* in this Chapter's Specifications).

3 Other tools necessary for this job include jackstands to support the vehicle in a raised position, an appropriate wrench, a drain pan, newspapers and clean rags.

✳ WARNING:

Fluid temperature can exceed 350-degrees F in a hot transaxle. Wear protective gloves.

4 The fluid should be drained immediately after the vehicle has been driven. Hot fluid is more effective than cold fluid at removing built up sediment.

5 After the vehicle has been driven to warm up the fluid, raise it and place it on jackstands.

6 Move the necessary equipment under the vehicle, being careful not to touch any of the hot exhaust components.

7 Place the drain pan under the drain plug and remove the drain plug **(see illustration)**. Once the fluid is drained, reinstall the drain plug and tighten it to the torque listed in this Chapter's Specifications.

2009 AND EARLIER MODELS

8 Remove the transmission oil pan bolts, pan and gasket. Carefully

21.7 Automatic transmission fluid drain plug

clean the gasket surface of the transmission to remove all traces of old gasket and sealant.

9 Drain any fluid still left in the transmission pan, clean it with solvent and dry it.

10 Unclip the filter from the valve body and lower the filter; some models may have filter mounting bolts that must be removed before the filter can be lowered.

11 Install a new filter and seal if equipped.

12 Make sure the gasket surface on the transmission pan is clean, then fit a new gasket on the pan. Put the pan in place against the transmission and working around the pan, tighten each bolt a little at a time until the final torque is reached (see this Chapter's Specifications). Keep in mind that the correct torque to avoid leaks is very low.

2011 AND LATER MODELS

13 Early-production 2011 models have a cartridge-type transmission fluid filter located on top of the transaxle case; remove the air filter housing for access (see Chapter 4). Using an oil filter wrench, unscrew the filter. Lubricate the O-ring of the new filter with clean transmission fluid, then install the new filter, tightening it hand-tight.

ALL MODELS

14 Add new fluid to the transmission/transaxle through the dipstick tube (see *Recommended lubricants and fluids in* this Chapter's Specifications for the recommended fluid type and capacity). Use a funnel to prevent spills. It is best to add a little fluid at a time, continually checking the level with the dipstick (see Section 4).

❋ WARNING:

It's important not to overfill the transmission/transaxle.

15 Start the engine and shift into all positions from P through L, then shift into N and apply the parking brake.
16 With the engine idling, check the fluid level. Add fluid up to the Cool (or lower) level mark on the dipstick.
17 Drive the vehicle to warm up the transaxle to normal operating temperature, then recheck the fluid level.

22 Transfer case (2009 and earlier models) and manual transmission / transaxle lubricant change (60,000 miles [96,000 km] or 72 months)

1 Raise the vehicle and support it securely on jackstands.
2 Remove the check/fill plug, then remove the drain plug and drain the lubricant **(see illustration 4.37)**.
3 Reinstall the drain plug and tighten it securely.

4 Add new lubricant until it is even with the lower edge of the filler hole. See *Recommended lubricantsand fluids* in this Chapter's Specifications for the specified lubricant type.
5 Reinstall the check/fill plug and tighten it securely.

23 Rear differential lubricant change (RWD/AWD models) (60,000 miles [96,000 km] or 72 months)

1 Raise the rear of the vehicle and support it securely on jackstands.
2 Remove the check/fill plug, then remove the drain plug and drain the lubricant **(see illustration 4.41a or 4.41b)**.
3 Reinstall the drain plug and tighten it securely.

4 Add new lubricant until it is even with the lower edge of the filler hole (see Section 4). See *Recommended lubricants and fluids* in this Chapter's Specifications for the specified lubricant type.
5 Reinstall the check/fill plug and tighten it securely.

24 Front differential lubricant change (2009 and earlier 4WD models) (60,000 miles [96,000 km] or 72 months)

1 Raise the front of the vehicle and support it securely on jackstands.
2 Remove the check/fill plug, then remove the drain plug and drain the lubricant **(see illustration 4.45)**.
3 Reinstall the drain plug and tighten it securely.

4 Add new lubricant until it is even with the lower edge of the filler hole (see Section 4). See *Recommended lubricants and fluids* in this Chapter's Specifications for the specified lubricant type.
5 Reinstall the check/fill plug and tighten it securely.

25 Cooling system servicing (draining, flushing and refilling) (at 100,000 miles [160,000 km] or 120 months and every 50,000 miles [80,500 km] or 60 months thereafter)

❋ WARNING:

Wait until the engine is completely cool before beginning this procedure.

❋ WARNING:

Do not allow engine coolant (antifreeze) to come in contact with your skin or painted surfaces of the vehicle. Rinse off spills immediately with plenty of water. Antifreeze is highly toxic if ingested. Never leave antifreeze lying around in an open con-tainer or in puddles on the floor; children and pets are attracted by its sweet smell and may drink it. Check with local authorities about disposing of used antifreeze. Many communities have collection centers that will see that antifreeze is disposed of safely.

1 Periodically, the cooling system should be drained, flushed and refilled to replenish the antifreeze mixture and prevent formation of rust and corrosion, which can impair the performance of the cooling system and cause engine damage. When the cooling system is serviced, all hoses and the radiator cap should be checked and replaced if necessary.

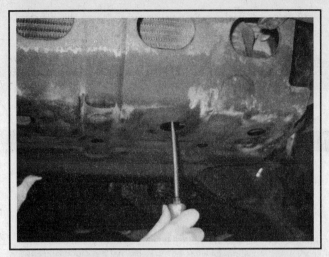

25.4 The radiator drain is accessible through this hole in the front radiator support (2009 and earlier models)

25.5 The V6 engine has a coolant drain plug located on each side of the block

DRAINING

2 Apply the parking brake and block the wheels. If the vehicle has just been driven, wait several hours to allow the engine to cool down before beginning this procedure.

3 Once the engine is completely cool, remove the surge tank cap.

4 Move a large container under the radiator drain to catch the coolant. Attach a 3/8-inch inner diameter hose to the drain fitting to direct the coolant into the container (some models are already equipped with a hose), then open the drain fitting **(see illustration)**.

5 After the coolant stops flowing out of the radiator, move the container under the engine block drain plug(s). Loosen the plug(s) and allow the coolant in the block to drain. On four-cylinder models, the block drain plug is on the front side of the engine block. On V6 models, there's one on each side of the block **(see illustration)**.

6 While the coolant is draining, check the condition of the radiator hoses, heater hoses and clamps (see Section 11 if necessary).

7 Replace any damaged clamps or hoses (see Chapter 3).

FLUSHING

8 Once the system is completely drained, remove the thermostat from the engine (see Chapter 3). Temporarily reinstall the thermostat housing without the thermostat. This will allow the system to be flushed.

9 Reinstall the engine block drain plug(s) and tighten the radiator drain plug. Turn your heating system controls to Hot, so that the heater core will be flushed at the same time as the rest of the cooling system.

10 Disconnect the upper radiator hose from the radiator. Place a garden hose in the upper radiator inlet, turn the water on and flush the system until the water runs clear out of the upper radiator hose **(see illustration)**.

11 In severe cases of contamination or clogging of the radiator, remove the radiator (see Chapter 3) and have a radiator repair facility clean and repair it if necessary. Many deposits can be removed by the chemical action of a cleaner available at auto parts stores. Follow the

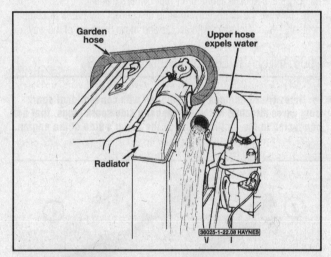

25.10 With the thermostat removed, disconnect the upper radiator hose and flush the radiator and engine block with a garden hose

procedure outlined in the manufacturer's instructions.

➡ **Note: When the coolant is regularly drained and the system refilled with the correct antifreeze/water mixture, there should be no need to use chemical cleaners or descalers.**

12 After flushing, drain the radiator and remove the block drain plugs once again to drain the water from the system.

REFILLING

13 Close and tighten the radiator drain. Install and tighten the block drain plug(s). Replace the thermostat (see Chapter 3).

14 Place the heater temperature control in the maximum heat position.

15 Slowly add new coolant to the surge tank until it's between the MAX and MIN marks.

16 Leave the surge tank cap off and run the engine in a well-ventilated area until the thermostat opens (coolant will begin flowing through the radiator and the upper radiator hose will become hot).
17 Turn the engine off and let it cool. Add more coolant mixture to bring the level back up between the MAX and MIN marks on the surge tank.

18 Squeeze the upper radiator hose to expel air, then add more coolant mixture if necessary. Replace the surge tank cap.
19 Start the engine, allow it to reach normal operating temperature and check for leaks.

26 Spark plug check and replacement (every 120,000 miles [193,000 km] or 144 months)

1 Spark plug replacement requires a spark plug socket that fits onto a ratchet. This socket is lined with a rubber grommet to protect the porcelain insulator of the spark plug and to hold the plug while you insert it into the spark plug hole **(see illustration)**.
2 If you are replacing the plugs, purchase the new plugs and replace each plug one at a time.
3 Inspect each of the new plugs for defects. If there are any signs of cracks in the porcelain insulator of a plug, don't use it.
4 Check the gaps of the new spark plugs by inserting the proper thickness gauge between the electrodes at the tip of the plug **(see illustration)**. The gap between the electrodes should be as listed in this Chapter's Specifications or in your owner's manual.
5 Remove the engine cover(s) and disconnect any hoses or components that would interfere with access and move them out of the way.

2006 AND EARLIER 3.5L ENGINE MODELS

➡ **Note: These engines are equipped with conventional spark plug wires attached to the passenger's side spark plugs, that are connected to the ignition coils on the driver's side of the engine.**

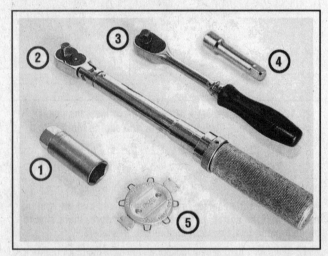

26.1 Tools required for changing spark plugs

*1   **Spark plug socket** - This will have special padding inside to
      protect the spark plug's porcelain insulator*
*2   **Torque wrench** - Although not mandatory, using this tool is the
      best way to ensure the plugs are tightened properly*
*3   **Ratchet** - Standard hand tool to fit the spark plug socket*
*4   **Extension** - Depending on model and accessories, you may need
      special extensions and universal joints to reach one or more of the plugs*
*5   **Spark plug gap gauge** - This gauge for checking the gap comes
      in a variety of styles. Make sure the gap for your engine is included*

6 Remove the intake manifold support bracket fasteners and brackets, if equipped.
7 Remove the ignition coil/spark plug wire cover fasteners and cover from the valve covers **(see illustration)**.
8 To access the spark plugs on the passenger's side, remove the throttle body (see Chapter 4), then pull the spark plug wires from the spark plugs, grasping the wires by the boots, not the wire itself **(see illustration)**.

26.4 Spark plug manufacturers recommend using a wire-type gauge when checking the gap - the wire should slide between the electrodes with a slight drag

26.7 Remove the fasteners securing the ignition coil/spark plug covers

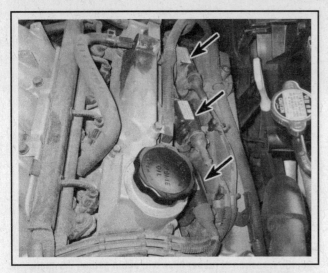

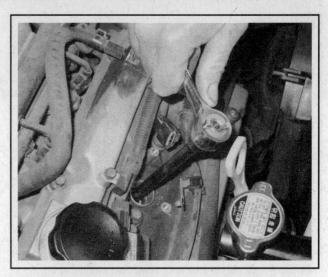

26.8 2006 and earlier 3.5L V6 engines use a combination of ignition coil-on-plug on the front three spark plugs and conventional spark plug wires on the rear three

26.11 Because they are deeply recessed, the proper spark plug socket and an extension will be required when removing or installing the spark plugs

ALL MODELS

9 On models with a coil directly over the spark plugs, disconnect the coil wiring, then unbolt and remove each coil (see Chapter 5, Section 6).

❊ WARNING:

Always wear eye protection when using compressed air!

10 If compressed air is available, blow any dirt or foreign material away from the spark plug area before proceeding.

11 Remove the spark plug **(see illustration)**.

12 Whether you are replacing the plugs at this time or intend to re-use the old plugs, the spark plug to those shown in this chart **(see illustration)** to get an indication of the general running condition of the engine.

13 Apply a small amount of anti-seize compound to the spark plug threads **(see illustration)**. It's often difficult to insert spark plugs into

A **normally worn** spark plug should have light tan or gray deposits on the firing tip.

A **carbon fouled** plug, identified by soft, sooty, black deposits, may indicate an improperly tuned vehicle. Check the air cleaner, ignition components and engine control system.

An **oil fouled** spark plug indicates an engine with worn piston rings and/or bad valve seals allowing excessive oil to enter the chamber.

This spark plug has been **left in the engine too long,** as evidenced by the extreme gap- Plugs with such an extreme gap can cause misfiring and stumbling accompanied by a noticeable lack of power.

A **physically damaged** spark plug may be evidence of severe detonation in that cylinder. Watch that cylinder carefully between services, as a continued detonation will not only damage the plug, but could also damage the engine.

A **bridged or almost bridged** spark plug, identified by a build-up between the electrodes caused by excessive carbon or oil build-up on the plug.

26.12 Inspect the spark plug to determine engine running conditions

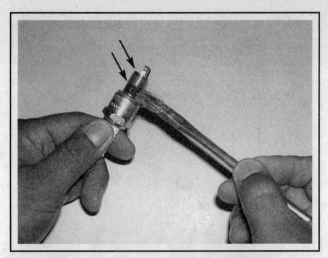

26.13a A light coat of anti-seize compound applied to the threads of the spark plugs will keep the threads in the cylinder head from being damaged the next time the plugs are removed

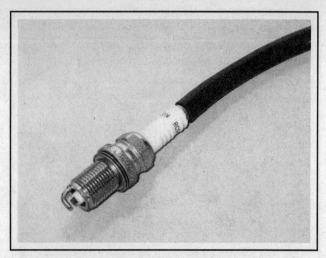

26.13b A section of rubber hose will aid in getting the spark plug threads started

their holes without cross-threading them. To avoid this possibility, fit a short piece of rubber hose over the end of the spark plug **(see illustration).** The flexible hose acts as a universal joint to help align the plug with the spark plug hole. Should the plug begin to cross-thread, the hose will slip on the spark plug, preventing thread damage. Tighten

the plug to the torque listed in this Chapter's Specifications.

14 Attach the plug wires to the spark plugs, making sure that they're securely snapped in place.

15 Reinstall the removed interfering components.

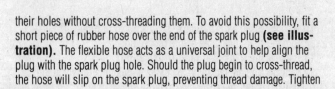

27 Ignition system component check and replacement (every 120,000 miles [193,000 km] or 144 months)

➡ **Note: Some models don't use spark plug wires; instead they use an ignition coil mounted on each spark plug. 2006 and earlier 3.5L V6 models use spark plug wires on the rear three cylinders and direct-mounted ignition coils on the front three.**

1 The spark plug wires should be checked whenever new spark plugs are installed.

2 Begin this procedure by making a visual check of the spark plug wires while the engine is running. In a darkened garage (make sure there is adequate ventilation), start the engine and observe each plug wire. Be careful not to come into contact with any moving engine parts. If there is a break in the wire, you will see arcing or a small spark at the damaged area. If arcing is noticed, make a note to obtain new wires, then allow the engine to cool and check the ignition coil packs.

3 The spark plug wires should be inspected one at a time to prevent mixing up the order, which is essential for proper engine operation. Each original plug wire should be numbered to help identify its location. If the number is illegible, a piece of tape can be marked with the correct number and wrapped around the plug wire.

4 Disconnect the plug wire from the spark plug. Grasp the rubber boot, twist the boot half a turn and pull the boot free. Do not pull on the wire itself.

5 Check inside the boot for corrosion, which will look like a white crusty powder. Light corrosion can be removed with a small wire brush,

but replace the wires if corrosion is heavy.

6 Push the wire and boot back onto the end of the spark plug. It should fit tightly onto the end of the plug. If it doesn't, remove the wire and use pliers to carefully crimp the metal connector inside the wire boot until the fit is snug.

7 Using a clean rag, wipe the entire length of the wire to remove built-up dirt and grease. Once the wire is clean, check for burns, cracks and other damage. Do not bend the wire sharply, because the conductor might break.

8 Disconnect the wire from the ignition coil pack. Pull only on the rubber boot. Check for corrosion and a tight fit. Replace the wire in the coil pack.

9 Inspect the remaining spark plug wires, making sure that each one is securely fastened at the coil pack and spark plug when the check is complete.

10 If new spark plug wires are required, purchase a set for your specific engine model. Remove and replace the wires one at a time to avoid mix-ups in the firing order.

11 Clean the coil pack with a dampened cloth and dry it thoroughly.

12 Inspect the coil pack for cracks, damage and carbon tracking. Carbon tracks can usually be removed. If damage exists, refer to Chapter 5 for the replacement procedure.

Specifications

Recommended lubricants and fluids

→ Note: Listed here are manufacturer recommendations at the time this manual was written. Manufacturers occasionally upgrade their fluid and lubricant specifications, so check with your auto parts store for current recommendations.

Engine oil	
Type	API "certified for gasoline engines"
Viscosity	SAE 5W-30
Fuel	Unleaded gasoline, 87 octane
Automatic transaxle fluid (2011 and later models)	MICHANG SP-IV, SK SP-IV, NOCA SP-IV or KIA genuine SP-IV Automatic Transaxle Fluid
Automatic transmission fluid (2009 and earlier models)	
30-40LEi transmissions	Mobil D-II Automatic transmission fluid
A5SR1 transmissions	Mobil Oil ATF RED-1 Automatic transmission fluid
Manual transaxle fluid (2011 and later models)	GL-4 SAE, 75W-85
Manual transmission fluid* (2009 and earlier models)	GL-4 SAE, 75W-85
Brake fluid type	DOT 3 or DOT 4 brake fluid
Power steering system fluid	PSF III power steering fluid
Transfer case (AWD models)	
2009 and earlier models*	DEXRON III Automatic Transmission Fluid
2011 and later models	API GL-5, SAE 75W-90 Hypoid gear oil
Front differential lubricant	
(2009 and earlier 4WD models)	GL-5, SAE 90 Hypoid gear oil
Rear differential lubricant	
2009 and earlier models	
Without limited slip differential	GL-5 SAE 90 gear lubricant
With limited slip differential	GL-5 SAE 85W-90 (INFILREX 33) gear lubricant
2011 and later models	API GL-5, SAE 75W-90 Hypoid gear oil
Engine coolant	50/50 mix of ethylene-glycol based coolant for use with aluminum and distilled water

* Filled for life unless there is a leak or a repair has been done.

Capacities*

Engine oil (including filter)		
Four-cylinder engines	4.86 quarts	4.6 liters
V6 engines		
2006 and earlier 3.5L engines	4.7 quarts	4.4 liters
All other V6 engines	5.5 quarts	5.2 liters
Coolant		
Four-cylinder engines		
With manual transmission	6.87 quarts	6.5 liters
With automatic transmission	6.97 quarts	6.6 liters
V6 engines		
2006 and earlier models	4.7 quarts	4.4 liters
2007 through 2009 models	9.4 quarts	9.0 liters
2011 and later models	9.1 quarts	8.6 liters
Automatic transaxle ** (2011 and later models)		
Four-cylinder engines	7.5 quarts	7.1 liters
3.5L V6 engines	8.24 quarts	7.8 liters

Capacities* (continued)

Automatic transmission ** (2009 and earlier models)

2006 and earlier models

30-40LEi transmissions	11.5 quarts	10.88 liters
A5SR1 transmissions	10.0 quarts	9.46 liters
2007 through 2009 models	10.57 quarts	10.0 liters
Manual transaxle (2011 and later four-cylinder models)	1.9 quarts	1.8 liters

Manual transmission (2006 and earlier models)

2WD models	3.2 quarts	3.0 liters
4WD models	2.7 quarts	2.55 liters
Front differential lubricant (AWD models)	Up to 1.37 quarts	Up to 1.3 liters

Rear differential lubricant

Without limited slip differential	Up to 1.37 quarts	Up to 1.3 liters
With limited slip differential	Up to 1.69 quarts	Up to 1.6 liters
2011 and later AWD models	Up to 0.74 quarts	Up to 0.7 liters

Transfer case

2009 and earlier RWD models	Up to 1.5 quarts	Up to 1.42 liters

2011 and later AWD models

Four-cylinder engine	Up to 0.63 quarts	Up to 0.6 liters
3.5L V6 engine	Up to 0.74 quarts	Up to 0.7 liters

* All capacities approximate. Add as necessary to bring to the appropriate level.

** This is a dry-fill specification; the amount required during a routine fluid change will be substantially less. The best way to determine the amount of fluid to add during a routine fluid change is to measure the amount drained. Begin the refill procedure by initially adding 1/3 of the amount drained. Then, with the engine running, add 1/2-pint at a time (cycling the shifter through each gear position between additions) until the level is correct on the dipstick. It is important not to overfill the transaxle or transmission. You will, however, need to purchase a few extra quarts, since the fluid replacement procedure involves flushing the torque converter (see Section 21).

Ignition system

Spark plug type and gap

Type

Four-cylinder engines

2.4L MPI	FK16HQR11 or equivalent
2.4L GDI	FXU16HR11 or equivalent

V6 engines

2006 and earlier 3.5L	PFR5N-11 or equivalent
2011 and later 3.5L	SILIKR7B11/REP8WMPB4 or equivalent
3.3L and 3.8L	IFR5G-11 or equivalent
Gap	0.0394 to 0.0433 inch (1.0 to 1.1 mm)

Engine firing order

Four-cylinder engines	1-3-4-2
V6 engines	1-2-3-4-5-6

Cylinder numbering - four-cylinder engine

Cylinder numbering - 2009 and earlier V6 engines

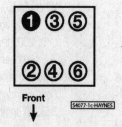

Cylinder numbering - 2011 and later V6 engines

Brakes

Disc brake pad lining thickness (minimum)	1/8 inch (3 mm)
Parking brake adjustment	
Lever travel	
2006 and earlier models	6 to 8 clicks
2011 and later models	5 to 6 clicks
Pedal travel	4 to 5 clicks

Torque specifications	Ft-lbs (unless otherwise indicated)	Nm

➡ **Note: One foot-pound (ft-lb) of torque is equivalent to 12 inch-pounds (in-lbs) of torque. Torque values below approximately 15 foot-pounds are expressed in inch-pounds, because most foot-pound torque wrenches are not accurate at these smaller values.**

Engine oil drain plug	26 to 32	35 to 44
Automatic transaxle drain plug	65 in-lbs	7
Front differential cover bolts (2009 and		
earlier AWD models)	27 to 38	38 to 52
Rear differential cover bolts (AWD models)	29 to 39	40 to 49
Differential check/fill plug (front and rear)	27 to 38	38 to 52
Manual transmission check/fill plug	43 to 48	60 to 65
Manual transaxle check/fill plug	22 to 25	30 to 33
Manual transaxle drain plug	44 to 57	59 to 77
Transfer case check/fill plug and drain plug	14 to 22	19 to 30
Spark plugs		
Four-cylinder engines	Not available	
2006 and earlier 3.5L V6 engines	15	20
3.3L and 3.8L V6 engines	18	25
Drivebelt tensioner nut/bolts		
Four-cylinder engines	40 to 47	54 to 63
3.3L and 3.8L V6 engines		
10 mm (upper) bolt	22 to 24	30 to 33
12 mm (lower) bolt	60 to 62	82 to 85
3.5L V6 engines		
2006 and earlier models (nut)	33 to 37	45 to 50
2011 and later models		
10 mm (upper) bolt	13 to 15.5	18 to 21
12 mm (lower) bolt	60 to 62	81 to 84
Wheel lug nuts		
2009 and earlier models	65 to 86	88 to 117
2011 and later models	66 to 79	89 to 107

Notes

Section

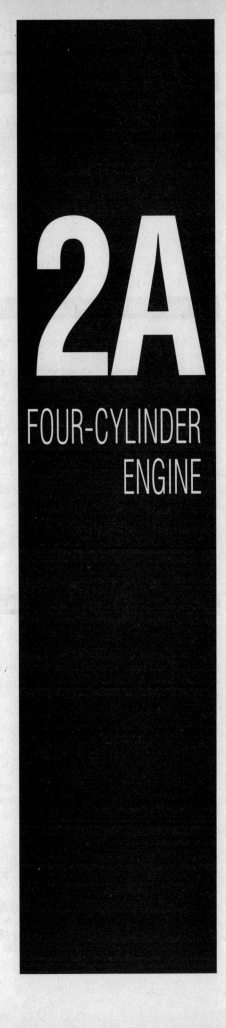

2A

FOUR-CYLINDER ENGINE

1   General Information

1   This Part of Chapter 2 is devoted to in-vehicle repair procedures for the 2.4L MPI (Multi-Port Injection) and 2.4L GDI (Gasoline Direct Injection) four-cylinder engines. Information concerning engine removal, installation and overhaul can be found in Chapter 2C.

2   The following repair procedures are based on the assumption that the engine is installed in the vehicle. If the engine has been removed from the vehicle and mounted on a stand, many of the steps outlined in this Part of Chapter 2 will not apply. This Chapter's Specifications apply only to the in-vehicle procedures contained in this Part.

3   This engine incorporates an aluminum cylinder block with an aluminum ladder frame for crankshaft support. The aluminum cylinder head utilizes Dual OverHead Camshafts (DOHC). The camshafts are driven from a single timing chain off the crankshaft.

2   Repair operations possible with the engine in the vehicle

1   Many major repair operations can be accomplished without removing the engine from the vehicle.

2   Clean the engine compartment and the exterior of the engine with some type of degreaser before any work is done. It will make the job easier and help keep dirt out of the internal areas of the engine.

3   Depending on the components involved, it may be helpful to remove the hood to improve access to the engine as repairs are performed (refer to Chapter 11 if necessary). Cover the fenders to prevent damage to the paint. Special pads are available, but an old bedspread or blanket will also work.

4   If vacuum, exhaust, oil or coolant leaks develop, indicating a need for gasket or seal replacement, the repairs can generally be made with the engine in the vehicle. The intake and exhaust manifold gaskets, oil pan gasket, crankshaft oil seals and cylinder head gasket are all accessible with the engine in place.

5   Exterior engine components, such as the intake and exhaust manifolds, the oil pan, the oil pump, the water pump, the starter motor, the alternator and the fuel system components can be removed for repair with the engine in place.

6   Since the cylinder head can be removed without pulling the engine, camshaft and valve component servicing can also be accomplished with the engine in the vehicle. Replacement of the timing belt and sprockets is also possible with the engine in the vehicle.

3   Top Dead Center (TDC) for number one piston - locating

1   Top Dead Center (TDC) is the highest point in the cylinder that each piston reaches as it travels up the cylinder bore. Each piston reaches TDC on the compression stroke and again on the exhaust stroke, but TDC generally refers to piston position on the compression stroke.

2   Positioning the piston(s) at TDC is an essential part of certain procedures such as camshaft and timing chain/sprocket removal.

3   Place the transmission in Neutral and apply the parking brake or block the rear wheels. Disconnect the cable from the negative terminal of the battery (see Chapter 5).

4   In order to bring any piston to TDC, the crankshaft must be turned using a large breaker bar or ratchet and socket placed on the crankshaft pulley bolt. When looking at the front of the engine, normal crankshaft rotation is clockwise.

5   Remove the spark plugs (see Chapter 1) and install a compression gauge in the number one spark plug hole. It should be a gauge with a screw-in fitting and a hose at least six inches long **(see illustration)**.

➡ **Note: If a compression gauge is not available, you can simply place a blunt object over the spark plug hole and listen for compression as the engine is rotated. Once compression at the No. 1 spark plug hole is noted, the remainder of the Step is the same.**

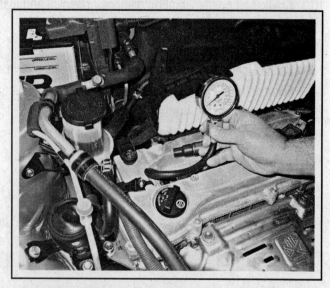

3.5 A compression gauge can be used in the number one spark plug hole to assist in finding TDC

6 Rotate the crankshaft while observing for pressure on the compression gauge. The moment the gauge shows pressure indicates that the number one cylinder has begun the compression stroke.

7 Once the compression stroke has begun, TDC for the compression stroke is reached by bringing the piston to the top of the cylinder.

8 Continue to turn the crankshaft until the groove in the crankshaft pulley is aligned with the timing mark on the timing chain cover **(see illustration)**.

9 After the number one piston has been positioned at TDC on the compression stroke, TDC for any of the remaining cylinders can be located by turning the crankshaft 180-degrees and following the firing order (see this Chapter's Specifications). For example, rotating the engine 180-degrees past TDC 1 will put the engine at TDC compression for cylinder 3.

3.8 The mark on the crankshaft pulley will align with the 0 mark on the timing chain cover when the engine is at TDC on the compression stroke for cylinder number 1

---

4 Valve cover - removal and installation

REMOVAL

1 Disconnect the cable from the negative terminal of the battery (see Chapter 5).

2 Remove the engine cover from the top of the valve cover.

3 Remove the ignition coils (see Chapter 5).

4 Detach the PCV hoses from the valve cover.

5 Disconnect any other interfering components. Label hoses and wires so you can connect them later with no confusion.

6 Remove the valve cover mounting bolts and nuts, then detach the valve cover and gasket from the cylinder head. If the valve cover is stuck to the cylinder head, bump the end with a wood block and a hammer to jar it loose. If that doesn't work, try to slip a flexible putty knife between the cylinder head and valve cover to break the seal.

❊❊❊ CAUTION:

Don't pry at the valve cover-to-cylinder head joint or damage to the sealing surfaces may occur, leading to oil leaks after the valve cover is reinstalled.

INSTALLATION

7 Remove the valve cover gasket from the valve cover and clean the mating surfaces with brake system cleaner. Install a new rubber gasket, pressing it evenly into the grooves around the underside of the valve cover.

➡ **Note: Make sure the spark plug tube seals are in place on the bottom of the valve cover before reinstalling it.**

8 The mating surfaces of the timing belt cover, the cylinder head and valve cover must be perfectly clean when the valve cover is installed. If there's residue or oil on the mating surfaces when the valve cover is installed, oil leaks may develop.

9 Apply RTV sealant at the timing chain cover-to-cylinder head joints and also around the semi-circular rubber rear seal, then install the valve cover and fasteners.

10 Tighten the nuts/bolts in sequence **(see illustrations)** to the torque listed in this Chapter's Specifications.

11 Reinstall the remaining parts, run the engine and check for oil leaks.

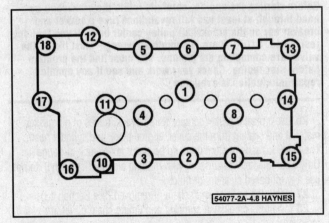

4.10a Valve cover bolt tightening sequence - 2.4L MPI engine

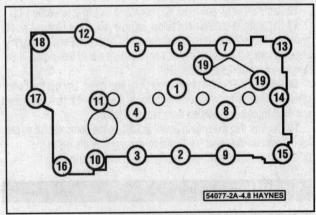

4.10b Valve cover bolt tightening sequence - 2.4L GDI engine

5 Timing chain and sprockets - removal, inspection and installation

❊❊ WARNING:

Wait until the engine is completely cool before beginning this procedure.

❊❊ CAUTION:

The timing system is complex, and severe engine damage will occur if you make any mistakes. Do not attempt this procedure unless you are highly experienced with this type of repair. If you are at all unsure of your abilities, be sure to consult an expert. Double check all your work and be sure everything is correct before you attempt to start the engine.

REMOVAL

1 Relieve the fuel system pressure (see Chapter 4), then detach the cable from the negative terminal of the battery (see Chapter 5). Position the number one piston at TDC on the compression stroke (see Section 3). The marks on the camshafts and the valve cover should be aligned. The dowels on the camshaft sprockets should be facing upward.

2 Remove the drivebelt, drivebelt tensioner, idler pulley (see Chapter 1) and the alternator (see Chapter 5).

3 Remove the air filter housing inlet duct and the air filter assembly (see Chapter 4).

4 Raise the vehicle and support it securely on jack stands, then remove the lower engine cover.

5 Disconnect the electrical connectors to the ignition coils, fuel injectors and the camshaft position (CMP) sensor from the top of the engine. If you're working on a GDI engine, remove the high-pressure fuel pump (see Chapter 4).

6 Disconnect the PCV hose (see Chapter 1).

7 Remove the ignition coils (see Chapter 5).

8 Remove the valve cover (see Section 4).

9 Remove the crankshaft damper/vibration damper (see Section 10). Also remove the water pump pulley.

10 Remove the two lower compressor bolts (see Chapter 3) then remove the compressor bracket bolts and the bracket.

11 Drain the engine oil (see Chapter 1).

12 Remove the oil pan mounting bolts and oil pan (see Section 12).

13 Support the engine from below, using a jack and a block of wood under the ladder frame (crankshaft support). Jack up the engine slightly and disconnect the engine mount from the right end of the engine, then remove the mount (see Section 16).

14 Remove the timing chain cover bolts and cover. Lay out the bolts carefully (in order) as you remove them, as there are different sizes used and each must be reinstalled in its proper position.

15 Confirm that the engine is still at TDC on the compression stroke for cylinder number one. Verify this by making sure the key of the crankshaft is aligned with the mating face of main bearing cap.

❊❊ CAUTION:

If the crankshaft is rotated while the timing chain is removed, the pistons may contact the valves and bend them.

16 Locate the access hole on the side of the tensioner. Working through the hole, lift and hold the pawl off of the rack of the plunger in the tensioner. Press the plunger in until a 3 mm Allen wrench can be inserted through both small holes in the top and bottom of the tensioner body, holding the plunger in the compressed position.

17 With the tensioner in the compressed position, remove the mounting fasteners, then remove the tensioner and chain guide.

18 Before removing the timing chain, mark the chain-to-sprockets relationship at TDC (this isn't necessary if a new chain is to be installed).

19 Remove the timing chain from the sprockets.

20 Remove the timing chain oil jet mounting bolt and oil jet.

21 Slide the crankshaft chain sprocket off of the crankshaft. If the balance shaft sprocket is being removed, see Section 13.

22 The camshaft sprockets can be removed at this time if necessary. To remove the camshaft sprockets, loosen the CVVT center bolt while holding the lug on the camshaft with a wrench, on the hex portion of the camshaft only. Note the identification marks on the camshaft CVVT sprockets before removal, then remove the bolts. Pull the sprockets by hand until they slip off the dowels.

INSPECTION

23 Inspect the components for wear and damage. Look for teeth that are deformed, chipped, pitted, and cracked; if there is any doubt, replace it now. The timing chain and sprockets should be replaced with a new ones if the engine has high mileage or the chain or sprocket(s) has visible damage. Failure to replace a worn timing chain and sprockets may result in erratic engine performance, loss of power, and decreased fuel mileage. Loose chains can jump timing. In the worst case, chain jumping or breakage will result in severe engine damage.

24 If the timing chain is to be replaced, replace the balance shaft chain at the same time.

25 Check the tensioner for leakage and wear.

INSTALLATION

❊❊ CAUTION:

Before starting the engine, carefully rotate the crankshaft by hand through at least two full revolutions (use a socket and breaker bar on the crankshaft pulley center bolt). If you feel any resistance, STOP! There is something wrong - most likely, the valves are contacting the pistons. You must find the problem before proceeding. Check your work and see if any updated repair information is available.

26 Use a plastic gasket scraper to remove all traces of old gasket material and sealant from the cover, engine block and cylinder head. The cover is made of aluminum, so be carful not to nick or gouge it. Only clean the sealing surfaces with rubbing alcohol (isopropyl) do not use any oil based cleaners or fluids.

27 Install the balance shaft chain, if removed (see Section 13).

28 Install the crankshaft sprocket and timing chain oil jet, if removed.

➡ Note: On 2.4L GDI models, the crankshaft sprocket timing mark should be pointing towards the 6 o'clock position.

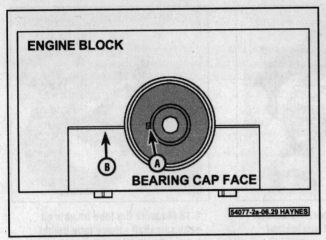

5.29 Align the crankshaft keyway (A) with the mating surface line of the main bearing cap (B)

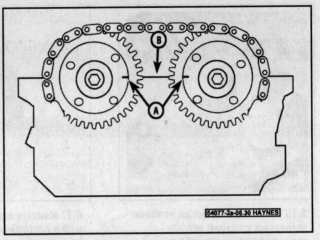

5.30 Align the camshaft timing TDC marks (A) with each other and inline with the surface of the cylinder head (B)

29 Set the crankshaft so that the keyway of crankshaft will be aligned with the line made where the engine block and bearing cap meet **(see illustration)**.

30 Make sure the intake and exhaust camshaft marks on the CVVT sprockets are aligned with the top surface of the cylinder head **(see illustration)**.

31 Install the right side timing chain guide. Tighten the sprocket bolt to the torque listed in this Chapter's Specifications.

32 Install the timing chain, looping the chain under the crankshaft sprocket, around the intake CVVT sprocket, then over the exhaust CVVT sprocket, aligning the colored links on the chain with the timing marks on the camshaft sprockets **(see illustration)**.

➡ **Note: On 2.4L GDI models, align the first colored link with the timing mark on the crankshaft sprocket then align the colored links with the camshaft marks**

33 Install the inner tensioner. The pulley should be on the left of the mounting bolt.

34 Install the primary chain guide and tensioner, and tighten the fasteners to the torque listed in this Chapter's Specifications. Remove the 3 mm Allen wrench from the tensioner plunger.

35 Confirm that all of the timing marks are still lined up. Rotate the engine two complete turns using the machined mark on the crankshaft with the line made where the engine block and bearing caps meet as the reference. Verify all the marks are aligned if the marks are off rotate the engine two more complete turns and check again.

36 Apply a 1/8-inch wide by 1/16-inch, bead of RTV sealant to the sealing surface of the cover then install the cover.

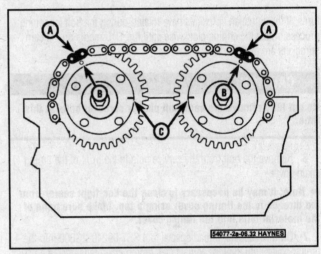

5.32 Align the colored or plated links (A) with the marks on the camshaft sprocket (B) making sure the TDC marks (C) are still aligned

37 Install the timing chain cover bolts and tighten them in a criss-cross pattern, in three steps, to the torque listed in this Chapter's Specifications.

38 The remainder of the installation is the reverse of removal.

39 Add oil and coolant (see Chapter 1), start the engine and check for leaks.

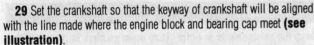

6   Camshafts - removal, inspection, installation and adjustment

➡ **Note: The camshafts should always be thoroughly inspected before installation and camshaft endplay should always be checked prior to camshaft removal (see Step 15).**

REMOVAL

1 Disconnect the cable from the negative terminal of the battery

(see Chapter 5).

2 Place the engine on TDC for number 1 cylinder (see Section 3).

3 On GDI models, remove the high pressure fuel pump (see Chapter 4).

4 Remove the valve cover (see Section 4).

5 With the TDC marks aligned **(see illustration 5.30)**, use a large wrench (on the hex portion of the camshaft only) to hold the camshaft from turning, then loosen the camshaft phaser sprocket bolts several

6.15 Mount a dial indicator as shown to measure camshaft endplay - pry the camshaft forward and back and read the endplay on the dial

6.17 Measure each journal diameter with a micrometer - if any journal measures less than the specified limit, replace the camshaft

6.18 Measure the lobe heights on each camshaft - if any lobe height is less than the specified allowable minimum, replace that camshaft

turns. If the camshaft sprockets have rotated during the bolt loosening process, rotate the engine clockwise until the TDC marks on the cam sprockets are realigned.

※※ CAUTION:

Do not fully remove the camshaft phaser sprocket bolts at this time.

6   Remove the bolt from the service hole in the front of the timing chain cover.

➡ **Note: It may be necessary to clean the Loc-tight sealer from the threads in the timing cover using a tap. Make sure none of the material falls into the timing cover.**

7   On MPI models, thread special tool SST 09240-2G000 into the timing cover until the tool contacts the timing chain tensioner, then back the tool out approximately one turn. Unlock the tool following the tool manufacturers instructions, then slowly turn the tool counterclockwise until you can feel the spring loaded pawl on the tensioner begin to lift. Once the pawl is lifted, lock the tool in place.

8   On GDI models, insert a small screwdriver through the service hole, and pull the link down on the tensioner to release the tensioner ratchet.

9   Lift the chain off the sprocket and onto the camshafts.

10   Loosen the front bearing cap bolts in several stages starting from the inside out and remove the bearing cap and upper bearing.

11   Loosen the remaining camshaft cap bolts in two or three steps starting with the outer camshaft caps and work toward the center (opposite of the tightening sequence). Remove the cap bolts and the camshafts from the cylinder head.

※※ CAUTION:

Keep the caps in order. They must go back in the same location from which they were removed. It is very important that the camshafts are returned to their original locations during installation. The exhaust camshaft has a slot in its end to drive the Camshaft Position (CMP) sensor.

12   Remove the lifters.

※※ CAUTION:

Keep the components in order. They must go back in the positions from which they were removed, facing the same direction.

13   If necessary, remove the camshaft phaser sprocket from the camshafts.

14   Inspect the camshafts, camshaft bearing caps and lifters as described below. Also inspect the camshaft sprockets for wear on the teeth. Inspect the chain for cracks or excessive wear. If any of the components show signs of excessive wear, they must be replaced.

INSPECTION

15   Before the camshafts are removed from the engine, check the camshaft endplay by placing a dial indicator with the stem in line with the camshaft and touching the snout **(see illustration)**. Push the camshaft all the way to the rear and zero the dial indicator. Next, pry the camshaft to the front as far as possible and check the reading on the dial indicator. The distance it moves is the endplay. If the endplay for either camshaft is greater than this Chapter's Specifications, the camshaft or the cylinder head (or both) may need to be replaced.

16   With the camshafts removed, visually check the camshaft bearing surfaces in the cylinder head for pitting, score marks, galling and abnormal wear. If the bearing surfaces are damaged, the cylinder head or the journal bearings of the camshafts may have to be replaced.

17   Measure the outside diameter of each camshaft bearing journal and record your measurements **(see illustration)**. Compare them to the journal outside diameter listed in this Chapter's Specifications, then measure the inside diameter of each corresponding camshaft bearing and record the measurements. Subtract each cam journal outside diameter from its respective cam bearing bore inside diameter to determine the oil clearance for each bearing. Compare the results to the specified journal-to-bearing clearance. If any of the measurements fall outside the standard specified wear limits, either the camshaft or the cylinder head, or both, must be replaced.

➡ **Note: If precision measuring tools are not available, Plastigage may be used to determine the bearing journal oil clearance.**

18   Using a micrometer, measure the height of each camshaft lobe **(see illustration)**. Compare your measurements with this Chapter's

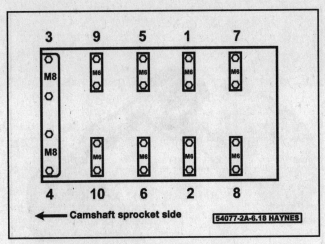

6.27 Camshaft bearing cap bolt size location and TIGHTENING sequence

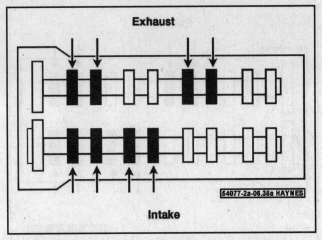

6.35a When the no. 1 piston is at TDC on the compression stroke, the valve clearance for the no.1 intake and exhaust valves, the number 2 intake valves and the number 3 exhaust valves can be measured

6.35b Measure the clearance for each valve with a feeler gauge of the specified thickness - if the clearance is correct, you should feel a slight drag on the gauge as you pull it out

Specifications. If the height for any one lobe is less than the specified minimum, replace the camshaft.

19 Check the camshaft runout by placing the camshaft back into the cylinder head and set up a dial indicator on the center journal. Zero the dial indicator. Turn the camshaft slowly and note the dial indicator readings. Runout should not exceed 0.0012 inch (0.03 mm). If the measured runout exceeds the specified runout, replace the camshaft.

20 Inspect each lifter for scuffing and score marks.

INSTALLATION

21 Coat the lifters with clean engine oil and install the lifters in their original locations.

22 Install the exhaust camshaft lower bearing into the cylinder head then coat the bearing with moly-based engine lubricant.

23 Install the camshaft phaser sprockets onto the camshaft phaser sprocket and tighten the mounting bolts by hand.

24 Apply moly-based engine assembly lubricant to the camshaft lobes and journals and install the camshaft into the cylinder head with the TDC marks facing towards each other (see Section 5). If the old camshafts are being used, make sure they're installed in their original locations.

25 Install the exhaust camshaft upper bearing into the camshaft bearing cap and coat the bearing with moly-based engine lubricant.

26 Install the bearing caps and bolts and tighten them hand tight. Each cap is marked with either an "I" or an "E," indicating if it is for the intake or exhaust side. They are also numbered.

27 Tighten the bearing cap bolts in several equal steps, using the proper tightening sequence **(see illustration)**, to the torque listed in this Chapter's Specifications. If a camshaft oil seal needs to be replaced, do it at this time. Oil the outside of the seal and use a large socket to drive the new seal flush.

28 Place the timing chain over the camshaft sprockets with the TDC marks pointing towards each other and the plated links aligned to the chain, or matching marks aligned. Use a large wrench (on the hex portion of the camshaft only) to hold the camshaft from turning and tighten the camshaft phaser sprocket bolts to the torque listed in this Chapter's Specifications.

29 On MPI models, remove the special tool from the front of the timing cover and slowly rotate the engine several times and recheck the timing marks are aligned.

30 On GDI models, use a small screwdriver and lift the link on the tensioner to allow the ratchet to move.

31 Install a new service hole bolt into the cover and tighten it the torque listed in this Chapter's Specifications.

32 The remainder of installation is the reverse of removal; refer to Sections 4 and 5.

ADJUSTMENT

33 Remove the valve cover (see Section 4).

34 Set number one cylinder to TDC on the compression stroke (see Section 3).

35 Use a feeler gauge to measure the clearance between the camshaft lobes and the lifters on the indicated cylinders **(see illustrations)**. There should be a light drag on the blade as it's pulled out. Carefully write down the figures.

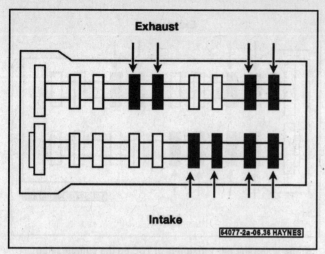

6.36 When the no.4 piston is at TDC on the compression stroke, the valve clerance for the number 2 exhaust valves, number 3 intake valves and the intake and exhaust valves for number 4 cylinder can be measured

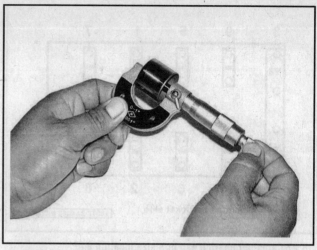

6.39 Measure the thickness of the lifter head with a micrometer

36 Rotate the engine exactly one turn clockwise and repeat the procedure on the remaining valves (see illustration).

37 If the clearances are outside of the limits the camshaft(s) will have to be removed, new lifters of the proper thickness will have to be installed in the location(s) with incorrect clearance(s). To do so, proceed to the next step.

38 Remove the camshaft(s) as described earlier in this Section.

39 Remove the lifter from the location with the incorrect clearance and measure it with a micrometer **(see illustration)**.

40 To calculater the correct thickness of a lifter, use this formula:

$N = T + (A - V)$

N = Thickness of the-new lifter
T = Thickness of the old lifter
A = Valve clearance measured
V = Valve clearance specified in this Chapter's Specifications

41 Purchase replacement lifters of the correct thickness.

42 After installing the lifters and camshafts, check the clearances again and make sure they are within specification before proceeding.

43 Apply camshaft installation lubricant to the camshaft lobes and bearing journals.

44 Install the lash adjusters in their original positions.

45 Place each camshaft in its original position and verify that the timing marks on the sprockets are lined up with the marks on the engine.

46 Install the bearing caps in its original position, by numerical order with the arrows pointing toward the timing chain end of the engine.

47 Tighten the bearing cap bolts, in sequence **(see illustration 6.27)**, to the torque listed in this Chapter's Specifications.

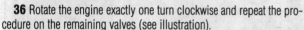

7 Intake manifold - removal and installation

⁂ WARNING:

Wait until the engine is completely cool before beginning this procedure.

REMOVAL

1 Relieve the fuel system pressure (see Chapter 4), then disconnect the negative cable from the battery (see Chapter 5).

2 Remove the engine cover.

3 Remove the air intake duct and resonator (see Chapter 4).

4 Drain the cooling system (see Chapter 1), then remove the upper radiator hose.

5 Disconnect the electrical connectors to the OCV valve, the VIS, oil pressure sending unit, knock sensor, A/C compressor, fuel injectors,

throttle body, MAP sensor, IAT sensor and the VCM.

6 Disconnect the brake booster hose and the PCV hose.

7 Disconnect the canister purge solenoid (see Chapter 6).

8 Relieve the fuel system pressure (see Chapter 4), then disconnect the fuel supply hose from the fuel rail.

9 Remove the intake manifold brace bolts and remove the brace.

10 Remove the intake manifold bolts and nuts, then remove the manifold with the throttle body.

INSTALLATION

11 Clean the mating surfaces of the intake manifold and the cylinder head mounting surface with brake system cleaner. If the gasket shows signs of leaking, check the manifold for warpage with a straightedge and feeler gauges. Compare your readings with those listed in this Chapter's Specifications. If the manifold is warped, it must be surfaced or replaced.

12 Install the manifold and gasket over the studs on the cylinder head.

13 Tighten the manifold-to-cylinder head nuts/bolts in three or four equal steps to the torque listed in this Chapter's Specifications. Work from the middle bolts out to avoid flexing the manifold.

14 Install the remaining parts in the reverse order of removal. Check the coolant level, adding as necessary (see Chapter 1).

15 Run the engine and check for coolant and vacuum leaks.

16 Road test the vehicle and check for proper operation of all accessories, including the cruise control system, if equipped.

8 Exhaust manifold - removal and installation

✳ WARNING:

The engine must be completely cool before beginning this procedure.

➡ **Note: The catalytic converter is an integral part of the exhaust manifold and can't be removed from the manifold.**

REMOVAL

1 Disconnect the negative cable from the battery (see Chapter 5).

2 Remove the air filter housing (see Chapter 4).

3 Disconnect the oxygen sensor electrical connectors and in replacing the exhaust manifold remove the sensors (see Chapter 6).

4 Working in the engine compartment, remove the upper heat shield from the manifold.

5 Raise the front of the vehicle and support it securely on jackstands.

6 Remove the exhaust manifold support bracket bolts and bracket, if equipped.

7 Apply penetrating oil to the nut/bolts retaining the manifold. After the nuts have soaked, remove the nuts/bolts retaining the manifold to the cylinder head. Detach manifold from the cylinder head, being careful not to damage the oxygen sensors, and discard the gasket.

INSTALLATION

8 Use a scraper to remove all traces of old gasket material and carbon deposits from the manifold and cylinder head mating surfaces. If the gasket shows signs of leaking, check the manifold for warpage with a straightedge and compare your readings with those listed in this Chapter's Specifications. If the manifold is warped, it must be resurfaced or replaced.

9 Position a new gasket over the cylinder head studs, noting any directional marks or arrows on the gasket that may be present.

10 Install the manifold and thread the mounting nut/bolts into place.

11 Working from the center out, tighten the nuts/bolts to the torque listed in this Chapter's Specifications in three or four equal steps.

12 Reinstall the remaining parts in the reverse order of removal.

13 Run the engine and check for exhaust leaks.

9 Cylinder head - removal, inspection and installation

✳ WARNING:

The engine must be completely cool before beginning this procedure.

REMOVAL

1 Relieve the fuel system pressure (see Chapter 4), then disconnect the cable from the negative terminal of the battery (see Chapter 5).

2 Drain the engine coolant (see Chapter 1).

3 Perform all the Steps for removing the intake manifold (see Section 7). However, the manifold itself can be left in place if desired.

4 Disconnect the coolant hoses from the cylinder head (see Chapter 3).

5 Remove the timing chain and camshaft sprockets (see Section 5).

6 Raise the vehicle and support it securely on jackstands, then disconnect the exhaust manifold (see Section 8).

7 Label and detach the electrical connections from the cylinder head.

8 Remove the Oil Control Valve (OCV) and both Camshaft Position (CMP) sensors (see Chapter 6).

9 On GDI models, remove the fuel injector and rail assembly (see Chapter 4).

10 Loosen the cylinder head bolts in 1/4-turn increments until they can be removed by hand. Loosen the cylinder head bolts in the reverse order of the recommended tightening sequence **(see illustration 9.24)** to avoid warping or cracking the cylinder head.

➡ **Note: Not all of the head bolts will have washers attached to them. Make sure to note which have them and which do not.**

11 With the help of an assistant, lift the cylinder head off the engine block. If it's stuck, very carefully pry up at the transaxle end, beyond the gasket surface.

12 Remove any remaining external components from the cylinder head to allow for thorough cleaning and inspection.

INSPECTION

13 Use a precision straightedge to check the gasket surfaces of each head. Try to insert a feeler gauge of the correct size between the

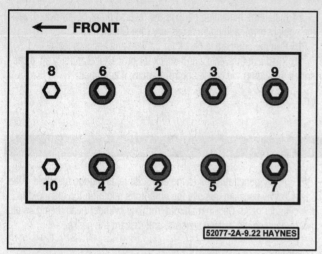

9.24 Cylinder head bolt washer locations and TIGHTENING sequence

straightedge and the head surface. If the clearance is more than that listed in this Chapter's Specifications, the head must be resurfaced or replaced. Check the intake and exhaust manifold surfaces as well as the block surface.

14 Examine all areas of each head for signs of cracks and coolant leakage, especially around the valve seats.

INSTALLATION

15 The mating surfaces of the cylinder head and block must be perfectly clean when the cylinder head is installed.

16 Use a gasket scraper to remove all traces of carbon and old gasket material, then clean the mating surfaces with brake system cleaner. If there's oil on the mating surfaces when the cylinder head is installed, the gasket may not seal correctly and leaks could develop. When working on the block, stuff the cylinders with clean shop rags to keep out debris. Use a vacuum cleaner to remove material that falls into the cylinders.

✳ CAUTION:

The cylinder head is made of aluminum. It is very easy to scratch it, so use care.

17 Check the block and cylinder head mating surfaces for nicks, deep scratches and other damage. If damage is slight, it can be removed with a file; if it's excessive, machining may be the only alternative.

18 Use a tap of the correct size to chase the threads in the cylinder head bolt holes, then clean the holes with compressed air - make sure that nothing remains in the holes.

✳ WARNING:

Wear eye protection when using compressed air!

19 Using a wire brush, clean the threads on each bolt to remove corrosion and restore the threads. Dirt, corrosion, sealant and damaged threads will affect torque readings. If the bolts are damaged in any way, replace them with new cylinder head bolts.

20 Install the components that were removed from the cylinder head.

21 Apply liquid gasket (Loctite 5900H) or equivalent to the front corner edges of the gasket then position the new gasket over the dowel pins in the block. Examine it carefully to verify that is installed in the correct orientation.

22 Carefully set the cylinder head on the block without disturbing the gasket.

➡ **Note: Once the liquid gasket is applied, the cylinder head must be installed within five minutes.**

23 Before installing the cylinder head bolts, apply a small amount of clean engine oil to the threads and under the bolt heads.

24 Install new head bolts and washers (if equipped) then tighten them finger tight. Following the recommended sequence **(see illustration)**, tighten the bolts to the torque listed in this Chapter's Specifications. Later Steps in the tightening sequence require each bolt to be tightened an additional 90-degrees. If you don't have an angle-torque attachment for your torque wrench, simply apply a paint mark on the socket you'll be using and tighten the bolt until that mark is 90-degrees (1/4-turn) from where you started.

25 If you have replaced either the head bolts, the head itself or the block with new, unused parts, be sure to follow the torque sequence for this application.

26 The remainder of installation is the reverse of removal. To ensure correct installation of the timing chain, see Section 5.

27 Change the engine oil and filter (see Chapter 1).

28 Refill the cooling system (see Chapter 1), run the engine and check for leaks.

10 Crankshaft pulley/vibration damper - removal and installation

1 Disconnect the cable from the negative terminal of the battery (see Chapter 5).

2 Remove the drivebelt (see Chapter 1).

3 With the parking brake applied and the shifter in Park (automatic) or in gear (manual), loosen the lug nuts from the right front wheel, then raise the front of the vehicle and support it securely on jackstands. Remove the engine splash shield (if installed), the front wheel and the splash shield from the right wheelwell.

4 Remove all other interfering components that are installed on your particular vehicle.

5 Remove the bolt from the front of the crankshaft. A breaker bar will be necessary, since the bolt is very tight. Use a strap wrench to hold the crankshaft from turning. If one is not available, have an assistant lock the flywheel in place with a prybar or special tool 09231-3D100.

6 A puller should not be necessary but if it in needed use a puller

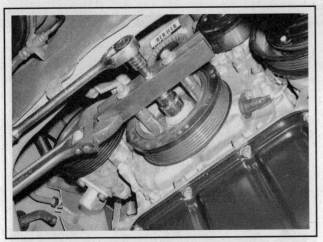

10.6 Use a large wrench to keep the crankshaft from turning as you remove the crankshaft pulley bolt, then the pulley itself

10.8 Align the keyway in the crankshaft pulley hub with the Woodruff key in the crankshaft

that bolts to the crankshaft hub, remove the crankshaft pulley from the crankshaft **(see illustration)**.

7   Do not use a jaw-type puller - it will damage the pulley/damper assembly. Use the proper adapter to prevent damage to the end of the crankshaft.

8   To install the crankshaft pulley, slide the pulley onto the crankshaft as far as it will slide on, then use a vibration damper installation tool to press the pulley onto the crankshaft. Note that the slot (keyway) in the hub must be aligned with the Woodruff key in the end of the crankshaft and that the crankshaft bolt can also be used to press the crankshaft pulley into position **(see illustration)**.

9   Tighten the crankshaft bolt to the torque listed in this Chapter's Specifications.

10 The remainder of installation is the reverse of removal.

11 Crankshaft front oil seal - replacement

1   Remove the crankshaft pulley (see Section 10).

2   Note how the seal is installed - the new one must be installed to the same depth and facing the same way. Carefully pry the oil seal out of the cover with a seal puller or a large screwdriver **(see illustration)**. Be very careful not to distort the cover or scratch the crankshaft! Wrap electrician's tape around the tip of the screwdriver to avoid damage to the crankshaft.

3   Apply clean engine oil or multi-purpose grease to the outer edge of the new seal, then install it in the cover with the lip (spring side)

facing IN. Drive the seal into place with a seal driver or a large socket and a hammer **(see illustration)**. Make sure the seal enters the bore squarely and stop when the front face is at the proper depth.

4   Lubricate the pulley hub with clean engine oil and reinstall the crankshaft pulley (see Section 10).

5   Install the crankshaft pulley retaining bolt and tighten it to the torque listed in this Chapter's Specifications.

6   The remainder of installation is the reverse of the removal.

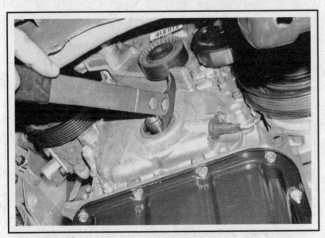

11.2 Carefully pry the old seal out of the timing belt cover - don't damage the crankshaft in the process

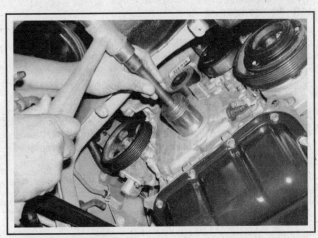

11.3 Drive the new seal into place with a seal driver or a large socket and hammer

12 Oil pan - removal and installation

REMOVAL

1 Disconnect the cable from the negative terminal of the battery (see Chapter 5).

2 Set the parking brake and block the rear wheels. Raise the front of the vehicle and support it securely on jackstands.

3 Remove the engine splash shield, if so equipped

4 Drain the engine oil and remove the oil filter (see Chapter 1). Remove the oil dipstick.

5 Remove the A/C compressor lower mounting bolts then remove the compressor mounting bracket bolts and bracket.

6 Disconnect the exhaust pipe from the exhaust manifold/converter assembly.

7 Remove the pan bolts and detach the oil pan. Different bolt lengths may be used, so note their locations. If the pan is stuck, pry it loose very carefully with a small screwdriver or putty knife **(see illustration)**. Don't damage the mating surfaces of the pan and block or oil leaks could develop.

→ **Note: The lower oil pan can be removed independently of the upper oil pan.**

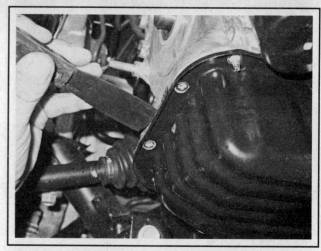

12.7 Pry the oil pan loose with special tool 09215-3C000 or a putty knife - be careful not to damage the mating surfaces of the pan and block or oil leaks may develop

INSTALLATION

8 Use a scraper to remove all traces of old sealant from the block and oil pan. Clean the mating surfaces with lacquer thinner or acetone.

9 Make sure the threaded bolt holes in the block are clean.

10 Check the oil pan flange for distortion, particularly around the bolt holes. Remove any nicks or burrs as necessary.

11 Apply a 3/16-inch wide bead of RTV sealant to the mating surface of the oil pan, following the groove but going to the inside where the

bolt holes are located. Install the pan within 15 minutes.

12 Carefully position the oil pan on the ladder assembly and install the oil pan-to-ladder assembly bolts loosely.

13 Working from the center out, tighten the oil pan-to-ladder bolts, in three or four steps, to the torque listed in this Chapter's Specifications.

14 Install the lower oil pan, tightening the bolts evenly in several steps to the torque listed in this Chapter's Specifications. The remainder of installation is the reverse of removal

15 Run the engine and check for oil pressure and leaks.

13 Balance shaft and oil pump module - removal and installation

REMOVAL

1 Position the number one piston at TDC on the compression stroke (see Section 3).

2 Remove the timing chain (see Section 5).

3 Remove the oil pan and its gasket (see Section 12).

4 Compress the balance shaft chain tensioner and insert a paper clip or 3 mm Allen wrench into the hole of the tensioner.

5 Remove the balance shaft chain tensioner, tensioner arm and guide mounting bolts then remove the components in the same order.

6 Remove the balance shaft and oil pump module mounting bolts and lower the assembly from the ladder assembly.

→ **Note: The balance shaft and oil pump module can not be repaired; if there is a problem, the assembly must be replaced as a unit.**

INSTALLATION

7 Set the crankshaft so that the keyway of crankshaft will be aligned with the line made where the engine block and bearing cap meet **(see illustration 5.29)**.

8 Align the balance shaft sprocket and chain with the cast timing mark on the balance shaft and oil pump module **(see illustration)**.

9 Install the balance shaft and oil pump module with the chain and

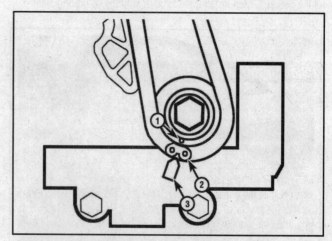

13.8 Align the balance shaft chain sprocket (1) with the colored or plated link (2) and the balance shaft oil pump module timing mark (3)

sprocket at the same time. Verify the timing mark are all aligned, then install the bolts. Tighten the bolts in sequence **(see illustration)** to the torque listed in this Chapter's Specifications.

10 Install the balance shaft and oil pump module timing chain guide, tensioner arm and hydraulic tensioner. Tighten the bolts to the torque listed in this Chapter's Specifications.

11 Remove the pin or Allen wrench from the tensioner, then recheck the timing marks.

12 Reinstall the timing chain (see Section 5).

13 Reinstall the oil pan (see Section 12).

14 Add oil to the proper level, start the engine and check for oil pressure and leaks.

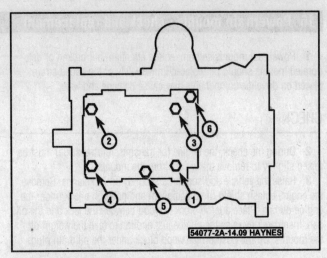

13.9 Balance shaft and oil pump module bolt tightening sequence

14 Flywheel/driveplate - removal and installation

REMOVAL

1 Disconnect the cable from the negative terminal of the battery (see Chapter 5).

2 Remove the transmission/transaxle (see Chapter 7A or 7B).

3 Using a center-punch or paint, apply alignment marks on the crankshaft flange and driveplate to ensure correct alignment on installation.

4 Remove the bolts retaining the driveplate to the crankshaft. Use a driveplate holding tool (available at auto parts stores) or wedge a screwdriver or prybar through one of the holes in the driveplate to keep it from turning while you loosen the bolts.

5 Remove the driveplate, taking note of spacers used and on which side of the driveplate they were installed.

INSTALLATION

6 Inspect the driveplate. Look for any fractures in the driveplate. Inspect the driveplate carefully for any other type of damage.

7 Position the driveplate on the crankshaft flange, aligning the marks made during removal. Align the bolt holes; note that some models may have a staggered bolt pattern to ensure correct installation.

8 Apply non-hardening thread locking compound to the threads of the bolts. Install the bolts and tighten them in a criss cross pattern to the torque listed in this Chapter's Specifications. Work up to the final torque in several steps.

9 Install the transmission/transaxle (see Chapter 7A or 7B).

15 Rear main oil seal - replacement

1 Remove the transmission/transaxle (see Chapter 7A or 7B).

2 Remove the flywheel/driveplate (see Section 14).

3 Pry the oil seal from the rear of the engine with a seal removal tool or a screwdriver. Be careful not to nick or scratch the crankshaft or the seal bore. Thoroughly clean the seal bore in the block with a shop towel. Remove all traces of oil and dirt.

4 Lubricate the outside diameter of the seal and install the seal over the end of the crankshaft. Make sure the lip of the seal points toward the engine. Preferably, a seal installation tool (available at most auto parts

stores) should be used to press the new seal back into place.

➡ **Note: There is a small oil drain in the separator that must be in the lowest position.**

5 If the proper seal installation tool is unavailable, use a large socket and carefully drive the new seal squarely into the seal bore and flush with the edge of the engine block.

6 Install the flywheel/driveplate (see Section 14).

7 Install the transmission/transaxle (see Chapter 7A or 7B).

2A-14 FOUR-CYLINDER ENGINE

16 Powertrain mounts - check and replacement

1 Powertrain mounts seldom require attention, but broken or deteriorated mounts should be replaced immediately or the added strain placed on driveline components may cause damage and wear.

CHECK

2 During the check, the engine (or transmission/transaxle) must be raised slightly to remove the weight from the mounts.

3 Raise the vehicle and support it securely on jackstands. Remove the engine splash shield (if so equipped) and position a jack under the engine oil pan. Place a large block of wood between the jack and the oil pan, then carefully raise the engine just enough to take the weight off the mounts. Do not position the wood block under the oil drain plug.

✳✳ WARNING:

DO NOT place any part of your body under the engine when only a jack supports it!

4 Check the mounts to see if the rubber is cracked, hardened or separated from the bushing in the center of the mount.

5 Check for relative movement between the mount plates and the engine or frame (use a large screwdriver or pry bar to attempt to move the mounts).

6 If movement is noted, lower the engine and tighten the mount fasteners.

REPLACEMENT

7 All engine mounts are replaced in the same manner. Use the jack to securely support the weight of the engine, then use it to remove all force from the mount in question.

8 Remove the bolts from both sides of the mount, then remove the mount.

9 Install the replacement mount and tighten all fasteners securely.

Specifications

General

Engine type	Four-cylinder, in-line, DOHC
Displacement	143.90 cubic inches (2359 cc)
Engine VIN code	
2.4L MPI	1
2.4L GDI	6
Firing order	1-3-4-2
Bore	3.464 inches (88.0 mm)
Stroke	3.819 inches (97.0 mm)
Compression ratio	
2.4L MPI	10.5:1
2.4L GDI	11.3 +/- 0.3:1
Compression pressure	See Chapter 2C
Oil pressure	See Chapter 2C

FRONT OF VEHICLE ① ② ③ ④

1-3-4-2

Cylinder numbering

Camshafts

	Inches	Millimeters
Lobe height		
Intake	1.7401 inches	44.2 mm
Exhaust	1.7716 inches	45.0 mm
Bearing journal diameter		
Number 1 intake camshaft journal	1.1811 inches	30 mm
Number 1 exhaust camshaft journal	1.4173 inches	36 mm
All other journals	0.9449 inch	24 mm
Runout	0.0012 inch	0.03 mm

Valve clearances (engine cold)

Intake	0.0067 to 0.0090 inch	0.17 to 0.23 mm
Exhaust	0.0106 to 0.0129 inch	0.27 to 0.33 mm

Warpage limits

	Inches	Millimeters
Cylinder head gasket surfaces (head and block)	0.0019 inch	0.05 mm
Intake and exhaust manifolds	0.0039 inch	0.10 mm

Torque specifications

	Ft-lbs (unless otherwise indicated)	Nm

➡ **Note: One foot-pound (ft-lb) of torque is equivalent to 12 inch-pounds (in-lbs) of torque. Torque values below approximately 15 foot-pounds are expressed in inch-pounds, because most foot-pound torque wrenches are not accurate at these smaller values.**

	Ft-lbs (unless otherwise indicated)	Nm
Camshaft bearing cap bolts (in sequence - see illustration 6.27)		
Step 1 (M6) bolts	52 in-lbs	6
Step 2 (M8) bolts	130 in-lbs	14.5
Step 3 (M6) bolts	95 to 113 in-lbs	10.5 to 12.5
Step 4 (M8) bolts	20 to 23	27 to 31
Camshaft phaser and sprocket bolts	40 to 47	54 to 64
Crankshaft pulley bolt	123 to 130	167 to 176
Cylinder head bolts (in sequence - see illustration 9.24)		
Step 1	24 to 27	32 to 37
Step 2	Tighten an additional 90 to 95-degrees	
Step 3	Tighten an additional 90 to 95-degrees	

Torque specifications (continued)   Ft-lbs (unless otherwise indicated)   Nm

➡ **Note: One foot-pound (ft-lb) of torque is equivalent to 12 inch-pounds (in-lbs) of torque. Torque values below approximately 15 foot-pounds are expressed in inch-pounds, because most foot-pound torque wrenches are not accurate at these smaller values.**

Continuously Variable Valve Timing (CVVT)		
solenoid bolt	87 to 142 in-lbs	10 to 16
Valve cover bolts		
Step 1	36 to 51 in-lbs	4 to 6
Step 2	70 to 86 in-lbs	8 to 9.5
Engine mount nuts/bolts		
M8 x 30 bolts	15 to 18	20 to 25
M10 x 40 and M10 x 45 bolts	29 to 33	39 to 45
Flywheel/driveplate bolts	87 to 94	118 to 127
Intake manifold bolt/nut	14 to 17	19 to 23
Oil pan bolt		
M6 bolts	87 to 142 in-lbs	10 to 16
M9 bolts	22 to 25	30 to 34
Timing chain cover bolts		
M6 bolts	70 to 86 in-lbs	8 to 9.5
M8 bolts	14 to 17	19 to 23
Timing chain guide bolts	87 to 142 in-lbs	10 to 16
Timing chain tensioner bolts	87 to 142 in-lbs	10 to 16
Transaxle-to-engine bolts		
M10 (lower two) bolts	25 to 30	34 to 40
M12 (upper) bolt	58 to 72	79 to 98

Section

2B

V6 ENGINES

1 General Information

1 2006 and earlier 3.5L engines use a timing belt, while all other V6 engines use timing chains. All the V6 engines in this manual are DOHC (dual overhead cam) with aluminum heads, four valves per cylinder and a two-piece oil pan.

2 This Part of Chapter 2 is devoted to in-vehicle repair procedures for the V6 engine. Information concerning engine removal and installation and engine overhaul can be found in Chapter 2C.

3 The following repair procedures are based on the assumption that the engine is installed in the vehicle. If the engine has been removed from the vehicle and mounted on a stand, many of the steps outlined in this Part of Chapter 2 will not apply.

2 Repair operations possible with the engine in the vehicle

1 Many major repair operations can be accomplished without removing the engine from the vehicle.

2 Clean the engine compartment and the exterior of the engine with some type of degreaser before any work is done. It will make the job easier and help keep dirt out of the internal areas of the engine.

3 Depending on the components involved, it may be helpful to remove the hood to improve access to the engine as repairs are performed (see Chapter 11 if necessary). Cover the fenders to prevent damage to the paint. Special pads are available, but an old bedspread or blanket will also work.

4 If vacuum, exhaust, oil or coolant leaks develop, indicating a need for gasket or seal replacement, the repairs can generally be made with the engine in the vehicle. The intake and exhaust manifold gaskets, oil pan gasket, crankshaft oil seals and cylinder head gaskets are all accessible with the engine in place.

5 Exterior engine components, such as the intake and exhaust manifolds, the oil pan, the oil pump, the water pump, the starter motor, the alternator, and the fuel system components can be removed for repair with the engine in place.

6 Since the cylinder heads can be removed without pulling the engine, valve component servicing can also be accomplished with the engine in the vehicle. Replacement of the camshafts, timing belt/chain and sprockets is also possible with the engine in the vehicle.

3 Top Dead Center (TDC) for number one piston - locating

1 Top Dead Center (TDC) is the highest point in the cylinder that each piston reaches as it travels up the cylinder bore. Each piston reaches TDC on the compression stroke and again on the exhaust stroke, but TDC generally refers to piston position on the compression stroke.

2 Positioning the piston(s) at TDC is an essential part of certain procedures such as valve timing, camshaft, timing chain and timing belt and sprocket removal.

3 Before beginning this procedure, place the transmission/transaxle in Neutral and apply the parking brake or block the rear wheels. Disconnect the cable from the negative terminal of the battery (see Chapter 5).

4 Remove the spark plug and install a compression pressure gauge in the number one spark plug hole. It should be a gauge with a screw-in fitting and a hose at least six inches long **(see illustration)**.

☀ CAUTION:

It is possible to check the compression on cylinder number 1 on the V6 engine with the upper intake manifold and throttle body installed on the engine. The spark plugs can remain in the cylinder heads (except for number 1) if the ignition system and the fuel pump have been disabled.

5 Rotate the crankshaft with a socket and large ratchet or breaker bar while observing the compression gauge. When the compression stroke of the number one cylinder is reached, pressure will begin to show on the gauge; continue to rotate the crankshaft and align the notch on the crankshaft pulley with the 0 mark on the timing plate (3.5L engines) or T mark on the timing chain cover (3.3 and 3.8L engines). If you go past the marks, release the gauge pressure and rotate the crankshaft around two more revolutions.

6 After the number one piston has been positioned at TDC on the compression stroke, TDC for the remaining cylinders can be located by turning the crankshaft 120-degrees (1/3-turn) at a time and following the firing order (see this Chapter's Specifications).

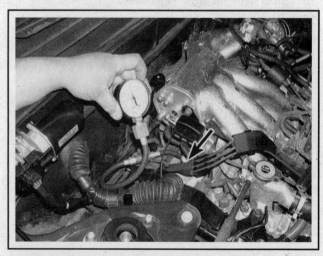

3.4 A compression gauge can be used in the number one plug hole to assist in finding TDC

4 Valve covers - removal and installation

REMOVAL

1 Disconnect the cable from the negative terminal of the battery (see Chapter 5).
2 On 2009 and earlier models, drain the cooling system (see Chapter 1).
3 Remove the engine cover.
4 On 2011 and later models, remove the upper intake manifold if you're working on the rear valve cover (see Section 5). On all other models the upper intake manifold must be removed for access to either valve cover.
5 Detach the engine wiring harnesses and pull them out of the way.
6 Disconnect all interfering wiring and hoses. Label them as you go to prevent confusion later.
7 Remove the retaining bolts, then detach the cover(s). If the cover is stuck to the head, bump the end with a wood block and a hammer to jar it loose. If that doesn't work, try to slip a flexible putty knife between the head and cover to break the seal.

✳✳ CAUTION:

Don't pry at the cover-to-head joint or damage to the sealing surfaces may occur, leading to oil leaks after the cover is reinstalled.

INSTALLATION

8 The mating surfaces of the cylinder head and cover must be clean when the cover is installed. Use a gasket scraper to remove all traces of sealant and old gasket material, then clean the mating surfaces with brake system cleaner. If there's residue or oil on the mating surfaces when the cover is installed, oil leaks may develop.
9 Install new spark plug tube seals.
10 Apply RTV sealant to the gasket/seal joints at the front and rear camshaft-to-head mounts, and timing chain cover joints on 2011 and later models, then install the valve cover with a new gasket.
11 Tighten the bolts a little at a time, working from the center outwards, to the torque listed in this Chapter's Specifications.
12 Reinstall the remaining parts, run the engine and check for oil leaks.

5 Intake manifold - removal and installation

✳✳ WARNING:

Wait until the engine is completely cool before beginning this procedure.

REMOVAL

1 Relieve the fuel system pressure (see Chapter 4), then disconnect the cable from the negative terminal of the battery (see Chapter 5).
2 Remove the engine cover.
3 On 2006 and earlier models, disconnect the accelerator and cruise control cables (see Chapter 4).

Upper intake manifold

4 Remove the air inlet tube and air filter housing (see Chapter 4).
5 Disconnect the PCV hose (see Chapter 1) and the brake booster hose (see Chapter 9).
6 Disconnect the ground strap, the electrical connectors and the vacuum lines from the upper intake manifold. Label each connector using tape and a marker to ensure correct reassembly. Pull the wiring harnesses aside.
7 On 2006 and earlier models, clamp off the coolant lines to the throttle body, then disconnect them.
8 On 2007 and later models, drain the engine coolant (see Chapter 1). Disconnect the heater hoses from the heater core tubes at the firewall.
9 Disconnect and remove the upper intake manifold support brackets.
10 Disconnect the electrical connectors and hoses to the throttle body (see Chapter 4).

✳✳ CAUTION:

Clamp-off the coolant hoses before detaching them, or plug them as soon as they are detached. Be prepared for coolant spillage.

11 Disconnect the electrical connectors to the various sensors and move the harness out of the way.
12 Remove the bolts mounting the upper intake manifold to the lower intake manifold.

Lower intake manifold

13 Drain the cooling system (see Chapter 1).
14 Disconnect the electrical connectors from the fuel injectors (see Chapter 4). Also detach the fuel line from the fuel rail (see Chapter 4). Pull the wiring harness aside.

➡ **Note: The intake manifold can be removed with the injectors and fuel rails in place or removed, depending on the work to be done.**

15 Disconnect any remaining components from the lower manifold.
16 Remove the mounting bolts following the reverse of the tightening sequence **(see illustration 5.19)**, then detach the lower intake manifold from the engine. If the manifold is stuck, don't pry between the gasket mating surfaces or damage may result.

➡ **Note: Make note of each bolt as you remove them; they vary in lengths and must be installed in the same locations.**

17 Check the manifold's surface with a precision straightedge and compare your readings with those listed in this Chapter's Specifications. If it's excessively deformed, it must be replaced.

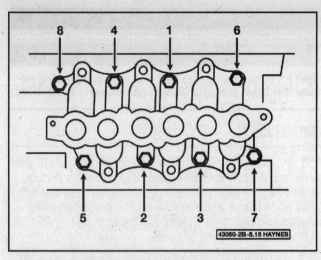

5.19 Lower intake manifold bolt tightening sequence

INSTALLATION

18 Use a scraper to remove all traces of old gasket material and sealant from the lower intake manifold and cylinder heads, then clean the mating surfaces with brake system cleaner.

19 Install new gaskets, then position the lower intake manifold on the engine. Make sure the gaskets haven't shifted, then install the bolts. Tighten the bolts in three or four equal steps, in the correct sequence **(see illustration)**, to the torque listed in this Chapter's Specifications.

20 Install a new gasket between the lower and upper intake manifolds. Place the upper intake manifold on the lower intake manifold. Install the bolts and tighten them, a little at a time, to the torque listed in this Chapter's Specifications.

21 Refill the cooling system (see Chapter 1). Run the engine and check for fuel, vacuum and coolant leaks.

---

6   Exhaust manifold/catalytic converter assemblies - removal and installation

❊❊❊ WARNING:

The engine must be completely cool before beginning this procedure.

➡ **Note: All engines are equipped with exhaust manifold/catalytic converter assemblies; on 2006 and earlier 3.5L engines, the catalytic converters can be unbolted from the exhaust manifolds.**

1 Disconnect the cable from the negative terminal of the battery (see Chapter 5).

2 Spray penetrating oil on the exhaust manifold fasteners and allow it to soak in.

3 If you're removing the rear (firewall side) exhaust manifold, raise the front of the vehicle and support it securely on jackstands, then remove the engine splash shield.

4 Disconnect or remove the heated oxygen sensors from the manifold(s) (see Chapter 6) **(see illustration)**.

5 Remove the bolts and the heat shield over the exhaust manifold.

6 Remove the exhaust manifold brace, if equipped.

7 Remove the nuts retaining the exhaust pipe(s) to the exhaust manifold(s) or catalytic converter(s).

8 Unbolt the exhaust manifold(s) from the cylinder head(s), working from the ends toward the middle. Slip the manifold(s) off the mounting studs.

9 Carefully inspect the manifold(s) and fasteners for cracks and damage.

10 Use a scraper to remove all traces of old gasket material and carbon deposits from the manifold and cylinder head mating surfaces. If the gasket was leaking, check the manifold for warpage on the cylinder head mounting surface by placing a straightedge over the surface and trying to insert a feeler gauge. If the clearance exceeds the limit listed in this Chapter's Specifications, have the manifold resurfaced at an automotive machine shop.

11 Position a new gasket over the cylinder head studs.

12 Install the manifold(s) and thread the mounting nuts into place.

13 Working from the center out, tighten the nuts to the torque listed in this Chapter's Specifications in three or four equal steps.

14 The remainder of installation is the reverse of removal. Use new gaskets when connecting the exhaust pipes.

15 Run the engine and check for exhaust leaks.

6.4 There is an oxygen sensor immediately before and after each catalytic converter (downstream sensor shown)

7   Timing chain and sprockets (all except 2006 and earlier 3.5L engines) - removal, inspection and installation

⁂ CAUTION:

The timing system is complex, and severe engine damage will occur if you make any mistakes. Do not attempt this procedure unless you are highly experienced with this type of repair. If you are at all unsure of your abilities, be sure to consult an expert. Double check all your work and be sure everything is correct before you attempt to start the engine.

REMOVAL

1 Disconnect the cable from the negative terminal of the battery (see Chapter 5).

2 Remove the engine cover.

3 Remove the drivebelt (see Chapter 1).

4 Remove the alternator (see Chapter 5). Also unbolt the power steering pulley and secure it out of the way (don't disconnect the hoses).

5 Remove the tensioner and idler pulley (see Chapter 1).

6 Remove the A/C compressor (see Chapter 3), without opening the refrigerant lines, and secure the compressor out of the way.

7 Remove the intake manifold (see Section 5).

8 Raise the front of the vehicle and support it securely on jackstands. Apply the parking brake and block the rear wheels. Remove the right front wheel.

9 Remove the lower and upper oil pans (see Section 12).

10 Remove the radiator and coolant reservoir (see Chapter 3).

11 On 2011 and later models, support the engine from above using an engine support fixture. Remove the upper engine mounts and loosen the transaxle mount (see Chapter 2A).

12 Remove the valve covers (see Section 4).

13 Support the engine from below, using a jack and a block of wood under the oil pan. Disconnect the power steering hose from the engine mount, then remove the mount.

14 Set the number one cylinder to TDC on the compression stroke (see Section 3).

15 Remove the crankshaft pulley (see Chapter 2A).

16 Lift the engine mount bracket upwards and off of the engine. You may have to rock the engine by hand to do so.

17 Remove the timing chain cover. Lay out the bolts carefully (in order) as you remove them, as there are many different sizes used and each must be reinstalled in its proper position.

18 Verify the number one cylinder is still at TDC on the compression stroke. Paint match marks on the sprockets so the entire assembly can be reinstalled in its original position. There are existing colored links on the chains for this purpose, but very often they become faint or totally erased during use **(see illustration)**.

19 Compress the right chain tensioner and put a small drill bit or other steel pin through the hole to hold it in the retracted position.

20 Remove the right upper chain guide that is between the sprockets.

21 Remove the right tensioner and the tensioner arm, then lift off the right chain.

22 Remove the right chain guide.

23 Remove the oil pump chain cover, chain tensioner, oil pump sprocket and chain (see Section 13).

24 Remove the crankshaft gear for the oil pump and right timing chain.

25 Remove the components for the left timing chain in the same order as for the right chain.

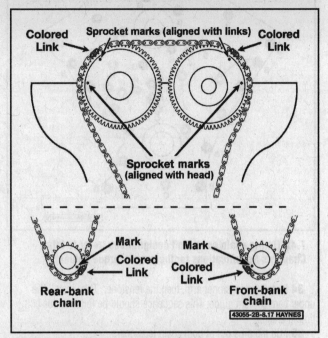

7.18 Camshaft timing chain alignment; the alignment is the same for both chains on both heads - however, the marks on the crankshaft sprocket are in different places

INSPECTION

26 Inspect all parts for wear and damage. Check the timing chain for loose pins, cracks, worn rollers and worn side plates. Check the sprockets for hooked-shaped, chipped and missing teeth. Always replace the timing chain and sprockets as a set if the engine has high mileage or fails inspection of any component.

27 Check the chain guides for excessive wear. Note that some scoring and wear is mormal.

28 Check the automatic tensioners for looseness. The piston should move smoothly when the pawl of the ratchet mechanism has been pushed back using a small Allen wrench or similar rod. All idler and tensioner sprockets must turn smoothly and freely. Again, if any component fails inspection, all other components are suspect.

INSTALLATION

29 Remove all dirt, oil and grease from the timing belt area at the front of the engine.

30 Note that the crankshaft key will be at the 11 o'clock position, aligned with the mark on the block, when the number one piston is at TDC.

31 Align the camshafts with their TDC marks at the top surface of the cylinder heads. Verify that all other marks are set correctly during this procedure. If you are installing new timing chains, align the colored links on the chains with the marks on the camshaft and crankshaft sprockets. If you're reusing the old timing chains, align the paint marks you made.

32 Install the timing chain guide.

33 Install the chains over the crankshaft sprocket first, followed by the guide and the camshaft sprockets. There should be no slack between these components.

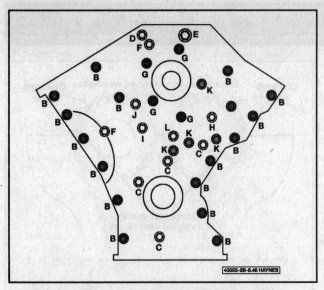

7.42 Timing chain cover bolt designations (refer to this Chapter's Specifications for the proper torque values)

34 Install the tensioner arm, then the tensioner. Then install the upper cam-to-cam guide. This sequence should be followed for both timing chains.
35 Pull the pins out of both chain tensioners.

36 Install the oil pump chain guide and tensioner (see Section 13).
37 Rotate the engine two complete turns clockwise so that the marks are again aligned (use a socket and breaker bar on the crankshaft pulley center-bolt).

⁙ CAUTION:

If you feel any resistance, STOP! There is something wrong - most likely, the valves are contacting the pistons. You must find the problem before proceeding. Check your work and see if any updated repair information is available.

38 Verify that the marks on all six sprockets are properly set. The colored links on the chains will not align with the marks on the sprockets after the engine is rotated because of the design of the chain but the sprocket marks should be exact for the TDC setting **(see illustration 7.18)**.
39 Clean the timing chain cover sealing surfaces and the mating surfaces of the block with brake system cleaner.
40 Apply a small dab of RTV silicone sealant to the four spots where the cylinder heads mate with the block under the timing cover.
41 Apply a continuous 3/16-inch bead of RTV silicone sealant along the sealing surface of the timing chain cover. Also replace the two small upper timing chain cover gaskets, if equipped.
42 There are many timing chain cover bolts **(see illustration)**; tighten them to the torque listed in this Chapter's Specifications.
43 The remainder of installation is the reverse of removal.

---

8   Timing belt and sprockets (2006 and earlier 3.5L engines) - removal, inspection and installation

⁙ CAUTION:

The timing system is complex, and severe engine damage will occur if you make any mistakes. Do not attempt this procedure unless you are highly experienced with this type of repair. If you are at all unsure of your abilities, be sure to consult an expert. Double check all your work and be sure everything is correct before you attempt to start the engine.

REMOVAL

1 Disconnect the cable from the negative terminal of the battery (see Chapter 5).
2 Remove the engine cover.
3 Raise the front of the vehicle and support it securely on jackstands. Apply the parking brake and block the rear wheels.
4 Remove the drivebelt (see Chapter 1), then remove the crankshaft pulley (see Chapter 2A).
5 Loosen the alternator nuts and disconnect the wiring from the alternator. Loosen all the engine mount bracket bolts.
6 Remove the timing belt covers.
7 Set the engine at TDC for number one cylinder (see Section 3). Verify that all timing marks are aligned before proceeding.
8 If you intend to reuse the belt, mark it with an arrow indicating direction of travel and put match marks from the belt to the sprockets so it can be realigned easily.
9 Remove the tensioner and the timing belt.
10 The camshaft sprockets can be removed now, if necessary. Remove the valve covers and hold the hex area of the camshaft securely with a wrench while removing the bolts.

INSPECTION

11 Check the belt for the presence of oil or dirt, and inspect for visible defects **(see illustration)**.
12 Check the belt tensioner for visible oil leakage. If there's only a faint trace of oil on the pushrod side, the tensioner seal is in satisfactory condition.
13 Push the tensioner forcefully against an immovable object **(see illustration)**. If the pushrod moves, replace the tensioner.
14 Check that the idler pulleys turn smoothly.

INSTALLATION

15 Remove all dirt, oil and grease from the timing belt area at the front of the engine.
16 Install the camshaft sprocket(s) (if they were removed) on the camshaft(s). Align the pin hole in the sprocket with the pin in the end of the camshaft.
17 Install the camshaft sprocket bolt(s) and tighten it to the torque listed in this Chapter's Specifications.
18 Carefully align all of the camshaft sprocket marks with the marks on the engine.
19 Install all the sprockets and pulleys if they were removed. Verify that the engine is still at TDC.
20 Make sure that the crankshaft sprocket is installed with the spacer first, then the sensor blade between the spacer and the sprocket.
21 Align the marks on the front (left) camshafts with the marks on the engine. The right camshafts may have to be rotated counterclockwise about 50 degrees before final positioning.

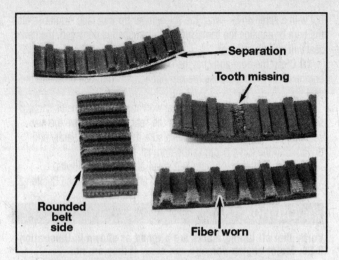

8.11 Check the timing belt for cracked or missing teeth; if the belt is cracked or worn, also check the pulleys for nicks or burrs - wear on one side of the belt indicates pulley misalignment problems

Separation
Tooth missing
Rounded belt side
Fiber worn

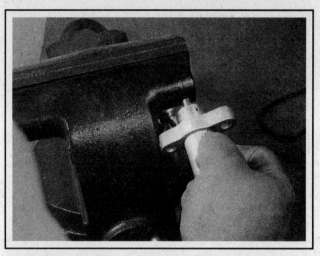

8.13 Check the tensioner for signs of leakage and test for leakdown by forcing it against an immovable object

22 Using a press or vise, compress the timing belt tensioner pushrod extremely slowly. Insert a metal pin, drill bit or Allen wrench through the holes in the pushrod and housing. Remove the tensioner from the press or vise and install it on the engine with the pin in place.

23 Align all of the timing marks and place the timing belt around the sprockets and pulleys in this order **(see illustration)** :

Crankshaft
Idler
Camshafts
Tensioner

24 With the tensioner pulley center bolt loose, use special tool no. 09244-28100 or equivalent to rotate the hub of the tensioner pulley counterclockwise, applying a torque of 44 in-lbs (50 kg-cm). While maintaining this torque on the pulley, tighten the pulley bolt to the torque listed in this Chapter's Specifications.

25 Again verify that all timing marks are aligned, then pull the pin from the tensioner, allowing it to snap into position.

26 Using a socket and breaker bar on the crankshaft pulley bolt, turn the crankshaft slowly (clockwise) through two complete revolutions (720-degrees). Recheck the timing marks.

❋❋ CAUTION:

Stop turning the crankshaft immediately if you feel resistance; the valves could be contacting the pistons.

27 If the timing marks are not aligned exactly as shown in **illustra-**

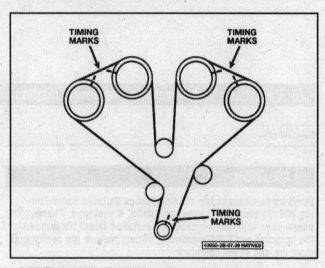

TIMING MARKS
TIMING MARKS
TIMING MARKS
43050-2B-07.36 HAYNES

8.23 Timing belt alignment marks

tion 8.23, repeat the timing belt installation procedure. DO NOT start the engine until you're absolutely certain that the timing belt is installed correctly. Serious and costly engine damage could occur if the belt is installed incorrectly.

28 Let the engine sit for five minutes at TDC, then check the protrusion of the tensioner rod. Compare your measurement to this Chapter's Specifications. If it isn't correct, replace the tensioner or determine if there's another problem.

29 The remainder of installation is the reverse of removal.

9   Oil seals - replacement

CRANKSHAFT FRONT OIL SEAL

1   On 2006 and earlier models, remove the timing belt and crankshaft sprocket (see Section 8). Slip off the sensor ring and the spacer

behind it. On 2007 and later models, remove the crankshaft pulley (see Chapter 2A).

2   Carefully pry the seal out with a screwdriver or seal removal tool. If you use a screwdriver, wrap tape around the tip - don't scratch the

housing bore or damage the crankshaft (if the crankshaft is damaged, the new seal will end up leaking).

3   Clean the bore in the engine and coat the outer edge of the new seal with engine oil or multi-purpose grease. Apply the same lubricant to the seal lip.

4   Using a seal driver or a socket with an outside diameter slightly smaller than the outside diameter of the seal, carefully drive the new seal into place with a hammer. Make sure it's installed squarely and driven in to the same depth as the original. Check the seal after installation to make sure the spring didn't pop out of place.

5   Reinstall the crankshaft timing sprocket and timing belt (see Section 8).

6   Run the engine and check for oil leaks at the front seal.

CAMSHAFT OIL SEALS - 2006 AND EARLIER MODELS

7   Remove the timing belt and camshaft sprocket(s) (see Section 8).
8   Remove the bolts and detach the rear timing belt cover.
9   Note how far the seal is seated in the bore, then carefully pry it

out with a screwdriver. Wrap the screwdriver tip with tape - don't scratch the bore or damage the camshaft (if the camshaft is damaged, the new seal will end up leaking).

10   Clean the bore and coat the outer edge of the new seal with engine oil or multi-purpose grease. Apply multi-purpose grease to the seal lip.

11   Using a seal driver or a socket with an outside diameter slightly smaller than the outside diameter of the seal, carefully drive the new seal into place with a hammer. Make sure it's installed squarely and driven in to the same depth as the original.

12   Reinstall the rear timing belt cover and tighten the bolts.

13   Reinstall the camshaft sprocket(s) and timing belt (see Section 8).

⚹ CAUTION:

Verify that all timing marks are aligned as shown in illustration 8.23. Major engine damage can occur if they are not.

14   Run the engine and check for oil leaks at the camshaft seal.

10 Camshafts and valvetrain - removal, inspection, installation and adjustment

REMOVAL

⚹ CAUTION:

Don't try to disassemble the Continuous Variable Valve Timing (CVVT) assembly on the camshafts, if equipped. These assemblies must be removed and installed intact. To remove the sprocket and CVVT assembly, simply remove the center bolt from the end of the camshaft.

1   Position the engine at TDC (see Section 3), then remove the valve covers (see Section 4), the timing chain or belt and the camshaft sprockets (see Section 7 or 8).

2   Make sure the cam timing marks on the sprockets and engine are in alignment (see Section 7 or 8).

3   Remove the Oil Control Valve (OCV) mounting bolts and remove the valves from the front camshaft bearing caps.

4   The camshafts are not interchangeable. Mark them clearly to avoid confusion later.

5   Loosen the camshaft bearing cap bolts in 1/4-turn increments in the reverse order of the tightening sequence **(see illustration 10.16)** until they can be removed by hand. Start with the outer caps and work inward.

6   The bearing caps are marked I and E for intake and exhaust and numbered. Mark the caps with your own numbers if necessary. Remove the bearing caps and gently lift out the camshaft.

7   Store the bearing caps in the correct order.

8   If necessary, the valve hydraulic adjusters and rocker arms can now be removed on 2006 and earlier 3.5L engines. On all other models, remove the bucket-style lifters. Store them separately so they can be reinstalled in their original locations.

INSPECTION

9   Refer to Chapter 2A, for camshaft, lifter and related component inspection procedures, but use the Specifications in this Chapter.

INSTALLATION

10   Apply camshaft installation lubricant to the camshaft lobes and bearing journals.

11   Install the lifters (2007 and later models) or lash adjusters and rocker arms (2006 and earlier 3.5L engines) in their original positions.

12   On all 2007 and later V6 engines, install the timing chains around the sprockets of each pair of camshafts and set them in their journals. Make sure that the timing marks on the sprockets are aligned with the marks on the timing chains.

13   On 2006 and earlier 3.5L engines, place each camshaft in its original position and verify that the timing marks on the sprockets are lined up with the marks on the engine. The left intake camshaft is marked "I," the left exhaust camshaft is marked "E," the right intake camshaft is marked "J," the right exhaust camshaft is marked "H."

14   Install the bearing caps in numerical order with the arrows pointing toward the timing belt end of the engine.

15   Refer to Section 9 and install a new camshaft oil seal if necessary.

16   Reinstall the remaining components in the reverse order of removal. Tighten the bearing cap bolts, in sequence **(see illustration)**, to the torque listed in this Chapter's Specifications.

17   The remainder of the installation is the reverse of removal.

⚹ CAUTION:

Verify that all timing marks are aligned as shown in Section 7 or Section 8. Major engine damage can occur if they are not.

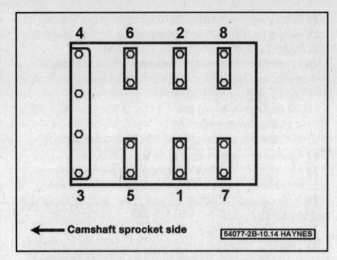

10.16 Camshaft bearing cap bolt tightening sequence

18 Run the engine, then check for leaks and proper operation. If the hydraulic valve adjusters have been somewhat drained, it may take several minutes for valvetrain noise to disappear.

ADJUSTMENT - 2007 AND LATER V6 ENGINES

➡ **Note: Valve clearance on 2006 and earlier 3.5L engines is done automatically by hydraulic lash adjusters. On all other V6 engines, bucket-style lifters are used and must be replaced with ones of the proper head thickness in order to adjust clearance.**

19 Remove the valve cover (see Section 4).
20 Set number one cylinder to TDC on the compression stroke (see Section 3).
21 Use a feeler gauge to measure the clearance between the camshaft lobes and the lifters on the indicated cylinders **(see illustrations)**. There should be a light drag on the blade as it's pulled out. Carefully write down the figures.
22 Rotate the engine exactly one turn clockwise and repeat the procedure on the remaining valves **(see illustration)**.

10.21b Measure the clearance for each valve with a feeler gauge of the specified thickness - if the clearance is correct, you should feel a slight drag on the gauge as you pull it out

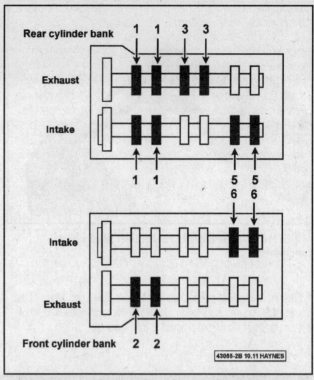

10.21a When the no. 1 piston is at TDC on the compression stroke, the valve clearance for the no.1 intake and exhaust valves, the number 3 exhaust valves, number 5 intake valve, number 2 exhaust valve and number 6 intake valve can be measured

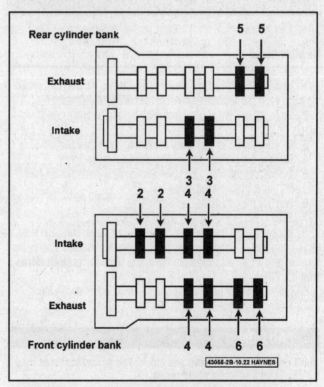

10.22 When the no. 4 piston is at TDC on the compression stroke, the valve clerance for the nos. 2, 3 and 4 intkae valves and the nos. 4, 5 and 6 exhaust valves can be measured

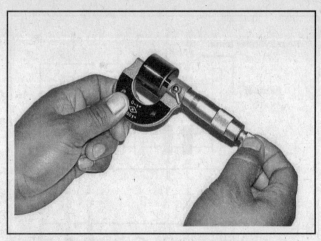

10.25 Measure the thickness of the lifter head with a micrometer

23 If the clearances are outside of the limits (see), new lifters of the proper thickness will have to be installed in the location(s) with incorrect clearance(s). To do so, proceed to the next step.

24 Remove the camshaft(s) as described earlier in this Section.

25 Remove the lifter from the location with the incorrect clearance and measure it with a micrometer **(see illustration)**.

26 To calculater the correct thickness of a lifter, use this formula:

$N = T + (A - V)$
N = Thickness of the new lifter
T = Thickness of the old lifter
A = Valve clearance measured
V = Valve clearance specified in this Chapter's Specifications

27 Purchase replacement lifters of the correct thickness.

28 After installing the lifters and camshafts, check the clearances again and make sure they are within specification before proceeding.

29 Apply camshaft installation lubricant to the camshaft lobes and bearing journals.

30 Install the lash adjusters in their original positions.

31 Place each camshaft in its original position and verify that the timing marks on the sprockets are lined up with the marks on the engine.

32 Install the bearing caps in its original position, by numerical order with the arrows pointing toward the timing chain end of the engine.

33 Tighten the bearing cap bolts in sequence **(see illustration 10.16)**, in 1/4-turn increments, to the torque listed in this Chapter's Specifications.

11 Cylinder heads - removal, inspection and installation

❈❈ WARNING:

Wait until the engine is completely cool before beginning this procedure.

REMOVAL

1 Relieve the fuel system pressure (see Chapter 4), then disconnect the cable from the negative terminal of the battery (see Chapter 5).

2 Drain the cooling system, including the engine block (see Chapter 1).

3 Remove the upper and lower intake manifolds (see Section 5).

4 Remove the exhaust manifold(s) (see Section 6).

5 Disconnect the timing belt (see Section 8) or timing chain (see Section 7) from the camshaft sprockets.

6 Remove the camshafts (see Section 10).

7 Disconnect any remaining sensors or hoses.

8 Loosen the cylinder head bolts in 1/4-turn increments until they can be removed by hand, along with their hardened washers. Follow the reverse order of the recommended tightening sequence **(see illustration 11.22)**.

9 Lift the cylinder head off the engine block. If the head is stuck, place a wood block against it and strike the wood with a hammer.

❈❈ CAUTION:

Don't pry between the head and block. The gasket surfaces may be damaged and leaks could result.

10 Repeat the procedure for the other head if necessary.

INSPECTION

11 Use a precision straightedge to check the gasket surfaces of each head. Try to insert a feeler gauge of the maximum specified size between the straightedge and the head surface. If the clearance is more than that listed in this Chapter's Specifications, the head must be resurfaced or replaced.

12 Check the intake and exhaust manifold surfaces as well as the block surface.

13 Examine all areas of each head for signs of cracks and coolant leakage, especially around the valve seats.

INSTALLATION

14 The mating surfaces of the cylinder heads and block must be perfectly clean when the heads are installed.

15 Use a gasket scraper to remove all traces of carbon and old gasket material, then clean the mating surfaces with brake cleaner. If there's oil on the mating surfaces when the head is installed, the gasket may not seal correctly and leaks could develop. When working on the block, stuff the cylinders with clean shop rags to keep out debris. Use a vacuum cleaner to remove material that falls into the cylinders.

16 Check the block and head mating surfaces for nicks, deep scratches and other damage. If damage is slight, it can be removed with a file; if it's excessive, machining may be the only alternative.

17 Use a tap of the correct size to chase the threads in the cylinder head bolt holes, then clean the holes with compressed air - make sure that nothing remains in the holes.

❈❈ WARNING:

Wear eye protection when using compressed air!

11.19a The new head gaskets must be positioned right side up (check all holes and coolant passages for correct alignment) and over the block dowels

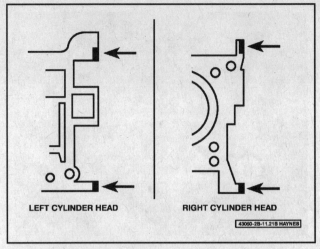

LEFT CYLINDER HEAD   RIGHT CYLINDER HEAD

43050-2B-11.21B HAYNES

11.19b On 2006 and earlier models, apply sealant to the specified areas above and below the cylinder head gasket

18 Mount each bolt in a vise and run a die down the threads to remove corrosion and restore the threads. Dirt, corrosion, sealant and damaged threads will affect torque readings. Replace any bolts that have been worn or damaged.

19 Position the new gaskets over the dowel pins in the block **(see illustration)**. The side of the gasket with the identification mark must face upward. Apply a small dab of RTV sealant to the end of each leg on the gaskets **(see illustration)**.

20 Carefully set the head on the block without disturbing the gasket.

21 Before installing the head bolts, apply a small amount of clean engine oil to the threads.

22 Install the bolts and tighten them finger tight. Following the recommended sequence **(see illustration)**, tighten the bolts to the torque listed in this Chapter's Specifications. If you don't have a torque angle gauge attachment, simply apply a paint mark to the socket you will be using to act as a reference point.

23 Install and tighten the small bolt at the front of the cylinder heads to the torque listed in this Chapter's Specifications.

24 The remainder of installation is the reverse of removal.

25 Refill the cooling system, change the oil and filter (see Chapter 1), run the engine and check for leaks.

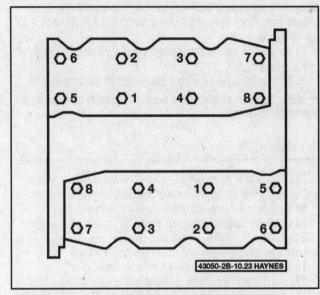

43050-2B-10.23 HAYNES

11.22 V6 cylinder head bolt TIGHTENING sequence

12 Oil pan - removal and installation

REMOVAL

1 Disconnect the cable from the negative terminal of the battery (see Chapter 5).

2 Raise the vehicle and support it securely on jackstands

3 Remove the engine splash shields, if equipped.

4 Drain the engine oil and remove the oil filter (see Chapter 1). The oil pan is a two-piece assembly, with an aluminum casting attached to the block and transmission/transaxle, and a lower stamped-steel pan section at the bottom.

5 Disconnect the exhaust pipe from both exhaust manifolds.

6 On 2009 and earlier 4WD models, lower the front differential

assembly (see Chapter 8).

7 Disconnect the oxygen sensors (if necessary) and support the pipe temporarily. Unbolt the pipe at the rear, disconnect it from the hangers and remove it from the vehicle.

8 On 2011 and later models, remove the two lower bolts holding the upper aluminum oil pan section to the transaxle.

9 Remove any interfering components. These components vary by year and model; be sure you have enough clearance for oil pan removal.

➡ **Note: On 2009 and earlier models, it may be easier to attach an engine hoist and raise the engine (see Chapter 2C) to make enough room to remove the upper oil pan.**

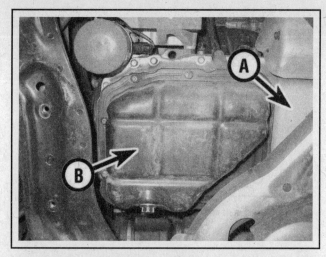

12.10 There are two oil pans: an upper cast aluminum pan (A) and a lower stamped steel pan (B)

10 Remove the bolts and detach the lower steel pan **(see illustration)**. If it's stuck, pry it loose very carefully with a small screwdriver or putty knife. Don't damage the mating surfaces of the pan or oil leaks could develop.

11 Remove the lower baffle (if equipped) and the oil pump strainer/pickup if necessary.

12 Remove the bolts securing the aluminum oil pan to the block.

➡ **Note: Some bolts are within the area formerly covered by the steel pan.**

INSTALLATION

13 Use a scraper to remove all traces of old sealant from the block and oil pan. Clean the mating surfaces with lacquer thinner or acetone.

14 Make sure the threaded bolt holes in the block are clean.

15 Check the flange of the steel pan section for distortion, particularly around the bolt holes. If necessary, place the pan on a wood block and use a hammer to flatten and restore the gasket surface.

16 If the baffle had been removed, reinstall it now.

17 Clean the mating surfaces of the engine block and aluminum pan section, being careful not to gouge the soft metal, which could lead to leaks.

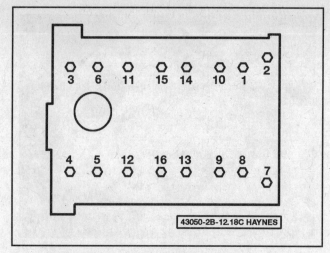

12.19 Upper oil pan bolt TIGHTENING sequence

18 Apply a 3/16-inch wide bead of RTV sealant to the aluminum pan section.

19 Install the aluminum pan section within five minutes, and uniformly tighten the bolts, in several steps, to the torque listed in this Chapter's Specifications. Follow the tightening sequence **(see illustration)**.

20 Inspect the oil pump pick-up/strainer assembly for cracks and a blocked strainer. If the pick-up was removed, clean it with solvent or thinner and install it now, using a new gasket (see Section 13). Tighten the fasteners to the torque listed in this Chapter's Specifications.

21 Apply a 3/16-inch wide bead of RTV sealant to the flange of the steel oil pan section.

➡ **Note: The steel pan section must be installed within five minutes once the sealant has been applied**

22 Carefully position the steel pan on the aluminum section and install the bolts, tightening them, in three or four steps, to the torque listed in this Chapter's Specifications. Follow the tightening sequence **(see illustrations)**.

23 The remainder of installation is the reverse of removal. Allow the sealant to set for at least two hours before adding new oil and a new oil filter.

24 Run the engine and check for oil pressure and leaks.

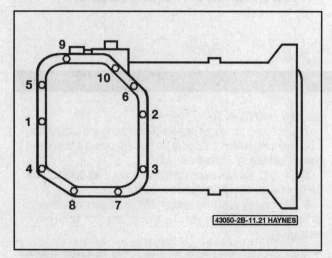

12.22a Lower oil pan bolt TIGHTENING sequence - 2007 and earlier models

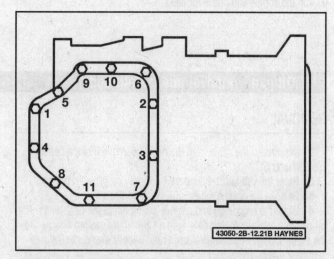

12.22b Lower oil pan bolt tightening sequence - 2008 and later models

13 Oil pump - removal, inspection and installation

REMOVAL

1 Disconnect the cable from the negative battery terminal (see Chapter 5).

2 Drain the engine oil and remove the oil filter (see Chapter 1).

2006 and earlier 3.5L engines

3 Remove the timing belt and sprocket (see Section 8).

4 Remove the oil filter bracket and gasket.

5 Remove the upper oil pan-to-oil pump bolts.

6 Remove the oil pump-to-engine block mounting bolts and remove the pump from the front of the engine.

7 Remove the pump cover fasteners, then remove the cover and pump rotors.

8 Use a gasket scraper to remove all traces of sealant and old gasket material from the pump body and engine block, then clean the mating surfaces with brake cleaner.

➡ **Note: Keep the front of the oil pan covered to prevent debris from falling into the oil pans.**

All other engines

9 Remove the lower oil pan (see Section 12).

10 Remove the oil pump chain cover fasteners and remove the cover.

11 Remove the oil pump sprocket bolt, sprocket and chain and set them to the side.

12 Remove the oil pump mounting bolts and pump. On these models, the oil pump is normally serviced as a unit; don't try to replace individual parts.

INSPECTION

13 Clean all components with solvent, then inspect them for wear and damage.

2006 and earlier 3.5L engines

14 Check the oil pressure relief valve sliding surface and valve spring. If either the spring or the valve is damaged, they must be replaced as a set.

15 Check the clearance of the following components with a feeler gauge and compare the measurements to this Chapter's Specifications **(see illustrations)**:

Driven rotor-to-oil pump body clearance
Rotor side clearance
Rotor tip clearance

All other engines

16 If there is any problem suspected with the pump, replace it with a new one.

13.15a Measure the driven rotor-to-body clearance with a feeler gauge

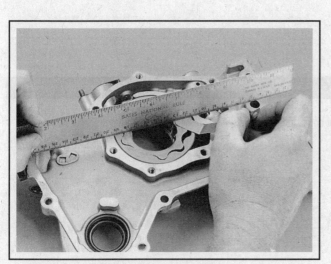

13.15b Measure the rotor side clearance with a precision straightedge and feeler gauge

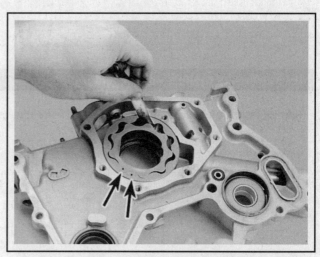

13.15c Measure the rotor tip clearance with a feeler gauge - note the rotor marks are facing out (when the pump body cover is installed, the marks will be against the cover)

INSTALLATION

2006 and earlier 3.5L engines

17 Pry the old crankshaft seal out with a screwdriver.

18 Apply multi-purpose grease or engine oil to the outer edge of the new seal and carefully drive it into place with a seal driver and a hammer. Also apply multi-purpose grease to the seal lip.

19 Place the drive and driven rotors into the pump body.

20 Pack the pump cavity with white grease and install the cover using either a new gasket or RTV sealant. Tighten the screws in a criss-cross pattern to the torque listed in this Chapter's Specifications.

21 Lubricate the oil pressure relief valve with engine oil and install the valve components in the pump body.

22 Use brake cleaner and a clean rag to remove all traces of oil from the case gasket surfaces.

23 Install the oil pump case with a new gasket. Install the mounting bolts and tighten them in a criss-cross pattern to the torque listed in this Chapter's Specifications.

24 Using a new gasket, install the oil pick-up tube and tighten the fasteners to the torque listed in this Chapter's Specifications.

All other engines

25 Replace the oil pump O-ring with a new one.

26 Tighten the oil pump bolts to the torque listed in this Chapter's Specifications.

27 Replace the drive chain and sprocket and tighten the sprocket bolt to the torque listed in this Chapter's Specifications.

All models

28 Reinstall the remaining parts in the reverse order of removal.

29 Add oil, start the engine and check oil pressure and leaks.

30 Recheck the engine oil level.

14 Flywheel/driveplate - removal and installation

Refer to Chapter 2A for this procedure, but use the torque(s) listed in this Chapter's Specifications. On automatic transmission/transaxle vehicles, there is an adapter plate used on the rear of the driveplate.

15 Rear main oil seal - replacement

Refer to Chapter 2A for this procedure. Note that the V6 engine doesn't have a gasket between the seal retainer and the engine block. Instead, apply a 2 to 3 mm wide bead of RTV sealant to the retainer flange before attaching the retainer to the block. Also, use the torque(s) listed in this Chapter's Specifications.

16 Powertrain mounts - check and replacement

Refer to Chapter 2A; the V6 engine mounts are slightly different in ways that don't significantly affect the check and replacement procedures.

Specifications

General

Engine type   DOHC V6

Displacement

    3.3L engine   203.86 cubic inches   3341 cc

    3.5L engine   211.75 cubic inches   3470 cc

    3.8L engine   230.55 cubic inches   3778 cc

Engine VIN code

    3.3L engine   5

    3.5L engine (2006 and earlier)   3

    3.5L engine (2011 and later)   2

    3.8L engine (2006 and earlier)   6

Firing order   1-2-3-4-5-6

Bore

    3.3L and 3.5L engines   3.622 inches   92 mm

    3.8L engine   3.7795 inches   96 mm

Stroke

    3.3L engine   3.2992 inches   83.8 mm

    3.5L and 3.8L engines   3.4252 inches   87 mm

Compression ratio

    3.3L and 3.8L engines   10.4:1

    3.5L engine   10.6:1

Compression pressure   See Chapter 2C

Oil pressure   See Chapter 2C

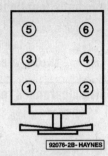

Cylinder numbering - 2009 and earlier models

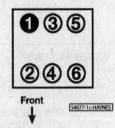

Cylinder numbering - 2011 and later models

Camshafts

Lobe height

    3.3L engine

        Intake   1.8228 inches   46.3 mm

        Exhaust   1.8031 inches   45.8 mm

    3.5L engine

        2006 and earlier

            Intake   1.3818 to 1.3897 inches   35.098 to 35.298 mm

            Exhaust   1.3705 to 1.3783 inches   34.81 to 35.01 mm

        2011 and later

            Intake   1.8582 inches   47.2 mm

            Exhaust   1.8031 inches   45.8 mm

    3.8L engine

        Intake   1.8425 inches   46.8 mm

        Exhaust   1.8031 inches   45.8 mm

Journal diameter

    2006 and earlier 3.5L engines   1.0220 to 1.0224 inches   25.951 to 25.970 mm

    All other V6 engines

        First journal   1.1009 to 1.1015 inches   27.964 to 27.978 mm

        All other journals 0.9430 to 0.9437 inch 23.954 to 23.970 mm

Journal-to-bearing oil clearance (maximum)

    2006 and earlier 3.5L engines   0.0007 to 0.0024 inch   0.018 to 0.06 mm

    All other V6 engines

        First journal   0.0011 to 0.0022 inch   0.027 to 0.057 mm

        All other journals 0.0012 to 0.0026 inch 0.030 to 0.067 mm

Specifications

Camshafts (continued)

Endplay

2006 and earlier 3.5L engines	0.0039 to 0.0059 inch	0.10 to 0.15 mm
All other V6 engines	0.0008 to 0.0071 inch	0.02 to 0.18 mm

Valve clearances (engine cold)

All 2007 and later V6 engines

Intake valve	0.0067 to 0.0090 inch	0.17 to 0.23 mm
Exhaust valve	0.0106 to 0.0129 inch	0.27 to 0.33 mm

Timing belt tensioner

Timing belt tensioner pushrod protrusion (2006 and earlier 3.5L V6 engine)	0.15 to 0.18 inch	3.8 to 4.5 mm

Warpage limits

Cylinder head gasket surface	0.0019 inch	0.05 mm
Cylinder head intake gasket surface	0.0039 inch	0.10 mm
Cylinder head exhaust manifold gasket surface	0.0039 inch	0.10 mm

Torque specifications   Ft-lbs (unless otherwise indicated)   Nm

➡ **Note: One foot-pound (ft-lb) of torque is equivalent to 12 inch-pounds (in-lbs) of torque. Torque values below approximately 15 foot-pounds are expressed in inch-pounds, because most foot-pound torque wrenches are not accurate at these smaller values.**

	Ft-lbs (unless otherwise indicated)	Nm
Camshaft bearing cap bolts		
2006 and earlier 3.5L engines		
Inner bolts	84 to 108 in-lbs	9.5 to 12
Outer bolts	14 to 15	19 to 20
All other V6 engines	87 to 104 in-lbs	10 to 11.5
Camshaft sprocket bolt (2006 and earlier 3.5L engines)	58 to 72	79 to 98
Camshaft sprocket and Variable Camshaft Timing (CVVT) bolt	48 to 56.	65 to 76
Crankshaft pulley bolt*		
2006 and earlier 3.5L engine	130 to 138	176 to 187
All other V6 engines	210 to 224	285 to 304
Cylinder head bolts (in sequence - see illustration 11.22)*		
2006 and earlier 3.5L engines	77 to 85	104 to 115
All other V6 engines		
Main bolts		
Step 1	28 to 30	38 to 40
Step 2	Tighten an additional 118 to 122-degrees	
Step 3	Tighten an additional 88 to 92-degrees	
M6 bolt (at the front of cylinder head)	14 to 17	19 to 23
Drivebelt tensioner (all models except 3.5L engine)		
M8 bolts	22 to 25	30 to 34
M12 bolts	60 to 63	81 to 85
Driveplate bolts (2006 and earlier 3.5L engine)	53 to 55	72 to 75

*Use new bolt(s)

Torque specifications	Ft-lbs (unless otherwise indicated)	Nm
Driveplate fasteners (all except 2006 and earlier 3.5L engine)	53 to 56	72 to 76
Exhaust manifold nuts		
2006 and earlier 3.5L engine	18 to 22	25 to 30
All other V6 engines	29 to 33	35 to 45
Intake manifold assembly (in sequence - see illustration 5.19)		
2006 and earlier 3.5L engine	9 to 15	12 to 20
All other V6 engines		
Bolts	20 to 23	27 to 31
Nuts	14 to 17	19 to 23
Oil control valve bolt	87 to 104 in-lbs	10 to 12
Lower oil pan bolts	87 to 104 in-lbs	10 to 12
Upper oil pan bolts		
3.5L engine		
2006 and earlier		
10 mm x 38 mm bolts	22 to 30	30 to 40
8 mm x 22 mm bolts	14 to 20	19 to 28
Oil pump case bolts	9 to 15	12 to 20
2011 and later	15 to 17	20 to 23
3.3L and 3.8L engines	14 to 17	19 to 23
Timing belt (2006 and earlier 3.5L engine)		
Tensioner pulley bolt	31 to 40	42 to 54
Idler pulley bolt	36 to 43	49 to 58
Tensioner arm (fixed bolt)	26 to 40	35 to 54
Automatic tensioner fixed bolt	14 to 20	19 to 27
Timing chain (all other V6 engines)		
Timing chain cover bolts (in sequence - see illustration 7.42)		
Bolts B	14 to 16	19 to 22
Bolt C	87 to 104 in-lbs	10 to 12
Bolts D and E	43 to 51	58 to 69
Bolt F	18 to 20	25 to 27
Bolt G	16 to 17	22 to 23
Bolts H, I and J	87 to 104 in-lbs	10 to 12
Bolts K	96 in-lbs	11
Bolts L	16 to 19	22 to 26
Timing chain guides	87 to 104 in-lbs	10 to 12
Timing chain tensioner bolts	87 to 104 in-lbs	10 to 12
Valve cover bolts	87 to 104 in-lbs	10 to 12

Notes

Section

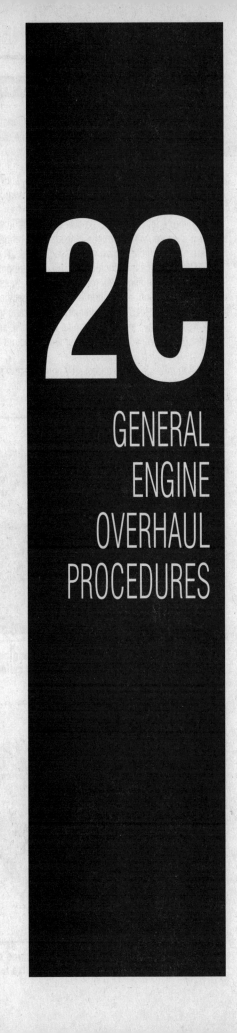

2C

GENERAL
ENGINE
OVERHAUL
PROCEDURES

1 General information - engine overhaul

1 Included in this portion of Chapter 2 are general information and diagnostic testing procedures for determining the overall mechanical condition of your engine.

2 The information ranges from advice concerning preparation for an overhaul and the purchase of replacement parts and/or components to detailed, step-by-step procedures covering removal and installation.

3 The following Sections have been written to help you determine whether your engine needs to be overhauled and how to remove and install it once you've determined it needs to be rebuilt. For information concerning in-vehicle engine repair, see Chapter 2A or 2B.

4 The Specifications included in this Part are general in nature and include only those necessary for testing the oil pressure, checking the engine compression, and bottom-end torque specifications. Refer to Chapter 2A or 2B for additional engine Specifications.

5 It's not always easy to determine when, or if, an engine should be completely overhauled, because a number of factors must be considered.

6 High mileage is not necessarily an indication that an overhaul is needed, while low mileage doesn't preclude the need for an overhaul.

Frequency of servicing is probably the most important consideration. An engine that's had regular and frequent oil and filter changes, as well as other required maintenance, will most likely give many thousands of miles of reliable service. Conversely, a neglected engine may require an overhaul very early in its service life.

7 Excessive oil consumption is an indication that piston rings, valve seals and/or valve guides are in need of attention. Make sure that oil leaks aren't responsible before deciding that the rings and/or guides are bad. Perform a cylinder compression check to determine the extent of the work required (see Section 3). Also check the vacuum readings under various conditions (see Section 4).

8 Check the oil pressure with a gauge installed in place of the oil pressure sending unit and compare it to this Chapter's Specifications (see Section 2). If it's extremely low, the bearings and/or oil pump are probably worn out.

9 Loss of power, rough running, knocking or metallic engine noises, excessive valve train noise and high fuel consumption rates may also point to the need for an overhaul, especially if they're all present at the same time. If a complete tune-up doesn't remedy the situation, major mechanical work is the only solution.

10 An engine overhaul involves restoring the internal parts to the specifications of a new engine. During an overhaul, the piston rings are replaced and the cylinder walls are reconditioned (rebored and/or honed) **(see illustrations 1.10a and 1.10b)**. If a rebore is done by an automotive machine shop, new oversize pistons will also be installed. The main bearings, connecting rod bearings and camshaft bearings are generally replaced with new ones and, if necessary, the crankshaft may be reground to restore the journals **(see illustration 1.10c)**. Generally, the valves are serviced as well, since they're usually in less-than-perfect condition at this point. While the engine is being overhauled, other components, such as the distributor, starter and alternator, can be rebuilt as well. The end result should be a like-new engine that will give many trouble-free miles.

➡ **Note: Critical cooling system components such as the hoses, drivebelts, thermostat and water pump should be replaced with new parts when an engine is overhauled. The radiator should be checked carefully to ensure that it isn't clogged or leaking (see Chapter 3). If you purchase a rebuilt engine or short block, some**

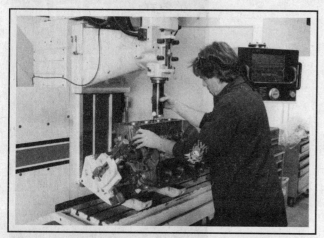
1.10a An engine block being bored - an engine rebuilder will use special machinery to recondition the cylinder bores

1.10b If the cylinders are bored, the machine shop will normally hone the engine on a machine like this

1.10c A crankshaft having a main bearing journal ground

1.11a A machinist checks for a bent connecting rod, using specialized equipment

1.11b A bore gauge being used to check the main bearing bore

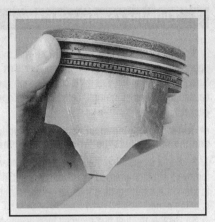

1.11c Uneven piston wear like this indicates a bent connecting rod

rebuilders will not warranty their engines unless the radiator has been professionally flushed. Also, we don't recommend overhauling the oil pump - always install a new one when an engine is rebuilt.

11 Overhauling the internal components on today's engines is a difficult and time-consuming task which requires a significant amount of specialty tools and is best left to a professional engine rebuilder **(see illustrations 1.11a, 1.11b and 1.11c)**. A competent engine rebuilder will handle the inspection of your old parts and offer advice concerning the reconditioning or replacement of the original engine. Never purchase parts or have machine work done on other compo-

nents until the block has been thoroughly inspected by a professional machine shop. As a general rule, time is the primary cost of an overhaul, especially since the vehicle may be tied up for a minimum of two weeks or more. Be aware that some engine builders only have the capability to rebuild the engine you bring them while other rebuilders have a large inventory of rebuilt exchange engines in stock. Also be aware that many machine shops could take as much as two weeks time to completely rebuild your engine depending on shop workload. Sometimes it makes more sense to simply exchange your engine for another engine that's already rebuilt to save time.

2   Oil pressure check

1   Low engine oil pressure can be a sign of an engine in need of rebuilding. A low oil pressure indicator (often called an idiot light) is not a test of the oiling system. Such indicators only come on when the oil pressure is dangerously low. Even a factory oil pressure gauge in the instrument panel is only a relative indication, although much better for driver information than a warning light. A better test is with a mechanical (not electrical) oil pressure gauge.

2   Locate the oil pressure indicator sending unit. On four-cylinder models, it's on the front of the engine, to the right of the intake manifold. On 2006 and earlier V6 models it's located above the oil filter **(see**

illustration). On 3.3L and 3.8L engines, it's located at the rear of the left cylinder head. On 2011 and later 3.5L V6 engines, it's located at the right end of the front-bank cylinder head.

3   Unscrew and remove the oil pressure sending unit, then screw in the hose for your oil pressure gauge **(see illustration)**. If necessary, install an adapter fitting. Use Teflon tape or thread sealant on the threads of the adapter and/or the fitting on the end of your gauge's hose.

4   Check the oil pressure with the engine running (normal operating temperature) at idle, and compare it to this Chapter's Specifications. If it's extremely low, the bearings and/or oil pump are probably worn out.

2.2 On 2006 and earlier 3.5L V6 models, the oil pressure sending unit is located above the oil filter

2.3 The oil pressure can be checked by removing the sending unit and installing a pressure gauge in its place

3 Cylinder compression check

1 A compression check will tell you what mechanical condition the upper end of your engine (pistons, rings, valves, head gaskets) is in. Specifically, it can tell you if the compression is down due to leakage caused by worn piston rings, defective valves and seats or a blown head gasket.

➤ **Note: The engine must be at normal operating temperature and the battery must be fully charged for this check.**

2 Begin by cleaning the area around the spark plugs before you remove them (compressed air should be used, if available). The idea is to prevent dirt from getting into the cylinders as the compression check is being done.

3 Disable the fuel pump circuit by relieving the fuel pressure (see Chapter 4).

4 Remove all of the spark plugs from the engine (see Chapter 1). Disconnect the primary (low voltage) electrical connector(s) from the coil pack(s) (V6 engines).

5 Block the throttle wide open.

6 Install a compression gauge in the spark plug hole **(see illustration)**.

7 Crank the engine over at least seven compression strokes and watch the gauge. The compression should build up quickly in a healthy engine. Low compression on the first stroke, followed by gradually increasing pressure on successive strokes, indicates worn piston rings. A low compression reading on the first stroke, which doesn't build up during successive strokes, indicates leaking valves or a blown head gasket (a cracked head could also be the cause). Deposits on the undersides of the valve heads can also cause low compression. Record the highest gauge reading obtained.

8 Repeat the procedure for the remaining cylinders and compare the results to this Chapter's Specifications.

9 Add some engine oil (about three squirts from a plunger-type oil can) to each cylinder, through the spark plug hole, and repeat the test.

10 If the compression increases after the oil is added, the piston rings are definitely worn. If the compression doesn't increase significantly, the leakage is occurring at the valves or head gasket. Leakage past the valves may be caused by burned valve seats and/or faces or

3.6 Use a compression gauge with a threaded fitting for the spark plug hole, not the type that requires hand pressure to maintain the seal - open the throttle valve as far as possible during the test

warped, cracked or bent valves.

11 If two adjacent cylinders have equally very low compression, there's a strong possibility that the head gasket between them is blown. The appearance of coolant in the combustion chambers or the crankcase would verify this condition.

12 If one cylinder is slightly lower than the others, and the engine has a slightly rough idle, a worn lobe on the camshaft could be the cause.

13 If the compression is unusually high, the combustion chambers are probably coated with carbon deposits. If that's the case, the cylinder head(s) should be removed and decarbonized.

14 If compression is way down or varies greatly between cylinders, it would be a good idea to have a leak-down test performed by an automotive repair shop. This test will pinpoint exactly where the leakage is occurring and how severe it is.

4 Vacuum gauge diagnostic checks

1 A vacuum gauge provides inexpensive but valuable information about what is going on in the engine. You can check for worn rings or cylinder walls, leaking head or intake manifold gaskets, incorrect carburetor adjustments, restricted exhaust, stuck or burned valves, weak valve springs, improper ignition or valve timing and ignition problems.

2 Unfortunately, vacuum gauge readings are easy to misinterpret, so they should be used in conjunction with other tests to confirm the diagnosis.

3 Both the absolute readings and the rate of needle movement are important for accurate interpretation. Most gauges measure vacuum in inches of mercury (in-Hg). The following references to vacuum assume the diagnosis is being performed at sea level. As elevation increases (or atmospheric pressure decreases), the reading will decrease. For every 1,000-foot increase in elevation above approximately 2000 feet, the gauge readings will decrease about one inch of mercury.

4 Connect the vacuum gauge directly to the intake manifold vacuum, not to ported (throttle body) vacuum **(see illustration)**. Be sure no hoses are left disconnected during the test or false readings will result.

4.4 A simple vacuum gauge can be handy in diagnosing engine condition and performance

5 Before you begin the test, allow the engine to warm up completely. Block the wheels and set the parking brake. With the transmission in Park, start the engine and allow it to run at normal idle speed.

※※ WARNING:

Keep your hands and the vacuum gauge clear of the fans and drivebelts.

6 Read the vacuum gauge; an average, healthy engine should normally produce about 17 to 22 in-Hg with a fairly steady needle **(see illustration)**. Refer to the following vacuum gauge readings and what they indicate about the engine's condition:

7 A low steady reading usually indicates a leaking gasket between the intake manifold and cylinder head(s) or throttle body, a leaky vacuum hose, late ignition timing or incorrect camshaft timing. Check ignition timing with a timing light and eliminate all other possible causes, utilizing the tests provided in this Chapter before you remove the timing belt cover to check the timing marks.

8 If the reading is three to eight inches below normal and it fluctuates at that low reading, suspect an intake manifold gasket leak at an intake port or a faulty fuel injector.

9 If the needle has regular drops of about two-to-four inches at a steady rate, the valves are probably leaking. Perform a compression check or leak-down test to confirm this.

10 An irregular drop or down-flick of the needle can be caused by a sticking valve or an ignition misfire. Perform a compression check or leak-down test and read the spark plugs.

11 A rapid vibration of about four in-Hg vibration at idle combined with exhaust smoke indicates worn valve guides. Perform a leak-down test to confirm this. If the rapid vibration occurs with an increase in engine speed, check for a leaking intake manifold gasket or head gasket, weak valve springs, burned valves or ignition misfire.

12 A slight fluctuation, say one inch up and down, may mean ignition problems. Check all the usual tune-up items and, if necessary, run the engine on an ignition analyzer.

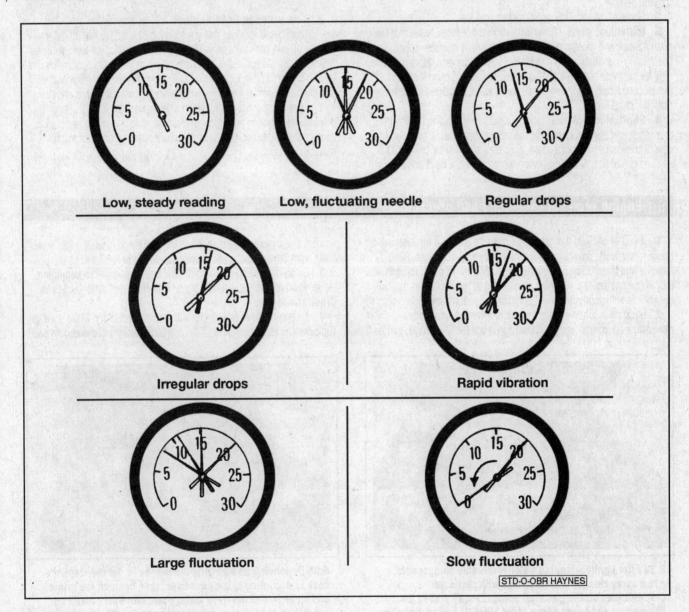

Low, steady reading   Low, fluctuating needle   Regular drops

Irregular drops   Rapid vibration

Large fluctuation   Slow fluctuation

STD-O-OBR HAYNES

4.6 Typical vacuum gauge readings

13 If there is a large fluctuation, perform a compression or leak-down test to look for a weak or dead cylinder or a blown head gasket.

14 If the needle moves slowly through a wide range, check for a clogged PCV system, incorrect idle fuel mixture, throttle body or intake manifold gasket leaks.

15 Check for a slow return after revving the engine by quickly snapping the throttle open until the engine reaches about 2,500 rpm and let it shut. Normally the reading should drop to near zero, rise above normal idle reading (about 5 in-Hg over) and then return to the previous idle reading. If the vacuum returns slowly and doesn't peak when the throttle is snapped shut, the rings may be worn. If there is a long delay, look for a restricted exhaust system (often the muffler or catalytic converter). An easy way to check this is to temporarily disconnect the exhaust ahead of the suspected part and redo the test.

5 Engine rebuilding alternatives

1 The do-it-yourselfer is faced with a number of options when purchasing a rebuilt engine. The major considerations are cost, warranty, parts availability and the time required for the rebuilder to complete the project. The decision to replace the engine block, piston/connecting rod assemblies and crankshaft depends on the final inspection results of your engine. Only then can you make a cost effective decision whether to have your engine overhauled or simply purchase an exchange engine for your vehicle.

2 Some of the rebuilding alternatives include:

3 **Individual parts** - If the inspection procedures reveal that the engine block and most engine components are in reusable condition, purchasing individual parts and having a rebuilder rebuild your engine may be the most economical alternative. The block, crankshaft and piston/connecting rod assemblies should all be inspected carefully by a machine shop first.

4 **Short block** - A short block consists of an engine block with a crankshaft and piston/connecting rod assemblies already installed. All new bearings are incorporated and all clearances will be correct. The existing camshafts, valve train components, cylinder head and external parts can be bolted to the short block with little or no machine shop work necessary.

5 **Long block** - A long block consists of a short block plus an oil pump, oil pan, cylinder head, valve cover, camshaft and valve train components, timing sprockets and belt or gears and timing cover. All components are installed with new bearings, seals and gaskets incorporated throughout. The installation of manifolds and external parts is all that's necessary.

6 **Low mileage used engines** - Some companies now offer low mileage used engines that are a very cost effective way to get your vehicle up and running again. These engines often come from vehicles that have been in totaled in accidents or come from other countries that have a higher vehicle turn over rate. A low mileage used engine also usually has a similar warranty like the newly remanufactured engines.

7 Give careful thought to which alternative is best for you and discuss the situation with local automotive machine shops, auto parts dealers and experienced rebuilders before ordering or purchasing replacement parts.

6 Engine removal - methods and precautions

1 If you've decided that an engine must be removed for overhaul or major repair work, several preliminary steps should be taken. Read all removal and installation procedures carefully prior to committing this job. These engines are removed by lowering to the floor, then raising the vehicle sufficiently to slide it out; this will require a vehicle hoist.

2 Locating a suitable place to work is extremely important. Adequate work space, along with storage space for the vehicle, will be needed. If a shop or garage isn't available, at the very least a flat, level, clean work surface made of concrete or asphalt is required.

3 Cleaning the engine compartment and engine before beginning the removal procedure will help keep tools clean and organized **(see illustrations)**.

4 An engine hoist or A-frame will also be necessary. Make sure the equipment is rated in excess of the combined weight of the engine and

6.3a After tightly wrapping water-vulnerable components, use a spray cleaner on everything, with particular concentration on the greasiest areas, usually around the valve cover and lower edges of the block. If one section dries out, apply more cleaner

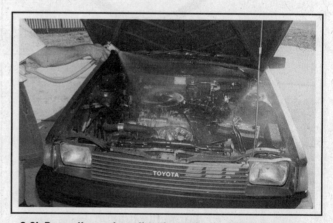

6.3b Depending on how dirty the engine is, let the cleaner soak in according to the directions, then hose off the grime and cleaner. Get the rinse water down into every area you can get at, then dry important components with a hair dryer or paper towels

6.6a Get an engine hoist that's strong enough to easily lift your engine in and out of the engine compartment; an adapter, like the one shown here, can be used to change the angle of the engine as it's being removed or installed

6.6b Get an engine stand sturdy enough to firmly support the engine while you're working on it. Stay away from three-wheeled models - they have a tendency to tip over more easily, so get a four-wheeled unit

transmission. Safety is of primary importance, considering the potential hazards involved in lifting the engine out of the vehicle. On 2011 and later models, a vehicle hoist will be necessary, as the engine and transaxle are removed out from the bottom of the engine compartment.

5 If you're a novice at engine removal, get at least one helper. One person cannot easily do all the things you need to do to lower a big heavy engine out of the engine compartment. Also helpful is to seek advice and assistance from someone who's experienced in engine removal.

6 Plan the operation ahead of time. Arrange for or obtain all of the tools and equipment you'll need prior to beginning the job **(see illustrations)**. Some of the equipment necessary to perform engine removal and installation safely and with relative ease are a heavy duty floor jack, complete sets of wrenches and sockets as described in the front of this manual, wooden blocks, plenty of rags and cleaning solvent for mopping up spilled oil, coolant and gasoline. If the hoist must be rented, make sure that you arrange for it in advance and have everything disconnected and/or removed before bringing the hoist home. This will save you money and time.

7 Plan for the vehicle to be out of use for quite a while. A machine shop can do the work that is beyond the scope of the home mechanic. Machine shops often have a busy schedule, so before removing the engine, consult the shop for an estimate of how long it will take to rebuild or repair the components that may need work.

7 Engine - removal and installation

❋❋ WARNING:

The engine must be completely cool before beginning this procedure.

➡ **Note: 2011 and later models: Engine removal on these vehicles is a difficult job, especially for the do-it-yourself mechanic working at home. Because of the vehicle's design, the manufacturer states that the engine and transaxle have to be removed as a unit from the bottom of the vehicle, not the top. With a floor jack and jackstands, the vehicle can't be raised high enough or supported safely enough for the engine/transaxle assembly to slide out from underneath. The manufacturer recommends that removal of the engine/transaxle assembly only be performed with the use of a frame-contact type vehicle hoist.**

➡ **Note: Keep in mind that during this procedure you'll have to adjust the height of the vehicle with the vehicle hoist to perform certain operations.**

REMOVAL

1 **2011 and later models:** Park the vehicle on a frame-contact type vehicle hoist, then engage the arms of the hoist with the jacking points of the vehicle. Raise the hoist arms until they contact the vehicle, but not so much that the wheels come off the ground. Loosen the front wheel lug nuts and the driveaxle/hub nuts.

2 Relieve the fuel system pressure (see Chapter 4).

3 Remove the battery (see Chapter 5). Remove the air inlet assembly and air filter housing (see Chapter 4).

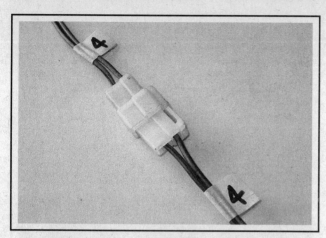

7.4 Label both ends of each wire or hose before disconnecting it

4 Clearly label and disconnect all vacuum lines, emissions hoses, electrical connectors and ground straps connecting the engine and transaxle to the vehicle. Masking tape and/or a touch up paint applicator work well for marking items **(see illustration)**. Take instant photos or sketch the locations of components and brackets, if necessary.

5 Drain the coolant, transmission/transaxle fluid and the engine oil (see Chapter 1).

6 Remove the radiator (see Chapter 3).

7 Disconnect both heater hoses.

8 Disconnect the accelerator and cruise control cables (on models so equipped).

9 Disconnect the fuel lines at the fuel rail (see Chapter 4).

10 Remove the power steering pump and secure it out of the way.

2009 and earlier models

11 Remove the hood (see Chapter 11).

12 Support the transmission with a floor jack, then remove the transmission-to-engine bolts. On automatic transmission vehicles, remove the torque converter-to-driveplate bolts too.

13 Attach an engine hoist to the engine, then disconnect the engine mounts and lift the engine out of the vehicle through the engine compartment. Make sure there is nothing connected or interfering with the engine as it is removed.

14 Raise the engine and attach it to an engine stand.

2011 and later models

15 Detach the shift cable(s) from the transaxle.

16 Raise the vehicle on the hoist and remove the front wheels.

17 Disconnect the steering shaft U-joint after pulling back the plastic cover and making match marks with dabs of paint (see Chapter 10).

18 On manual transmission/transaxle equipped models, remove the clutch release cylinder and support it out of the way with a piece of wire. Don't disconnect the hose from the release cylinder.

➡ **Note: Do not depress the clutch pedal while the release cylinder is removed.**

19 Disconnect the cooler hoses from the automatic transaxle. Plug the hose ends to prevent leakage and contamination.

20 Remove the driveaxles (see Chapter 8).

21 Remove the subframe (see Chapter 10).

22 Disconnect the remaining engine mount. Lower the engine and transaxle assembly with the hoist.

23 Lower the engine/transaxle assembly completely. Once the engine/transaxle assembly is on the floor, disconnect the engine hoist and raise the vehicle until it clears the engine/transaxle assembly.

INSTALLATION

24 Installation is the reverse of removal, noting the following points, as applicable for your model:

a) *Check the engine/transaxle mounts. If they're worn or damaged, replace them.*

b) *2011 and later models: Attach the transaxle to the engine (see Chapter 7A or 7B).*

c) *When installing the subframe, tighten the mounting bolts to the torque listed in the Chapter 10 Specifications.*

d) *Tighten the driveaxle/hub nuts to the torque listed in the Chapter 8 Specifications. Tighten all steering and suspension fasteners to the torque listed in the Chapter 10 Specifications. Tighten the wheel lug nuts to the torque listed in the Chapter 1 Specifications.*

e) *Refill the engine coolant, oil, power steering and transaxle fluids (see Chapter 1).*

f) *Reconnect the battery (see Chapter 5).*

g) *Run the engine and check for proper operation and leaks. Shut off the engine and recheck fluid levels.*

8 Engine overhaul - disassembly sequence

1 It's much easier to disassemble the engine if it's mounted on a portable engine stand. A stand can often be rented quite cheaply from an equipment rental yard. Before the engine is mounted on a stand, the driveplate should be removed from the engine.

2 If a stand isn't available, it's possible to remove the external engine components with it blocked up on the floor. Be extra careful not to tip or drop the engine when working without a stand.

3 If you're going to obtain a rebuilt engine, all external components must come off first, to be transferred to the replacement engine. These components include:

Flywheel/driveplate
Ignition system components
Emissions-related components
Engine mounts and mount brackets
Fuel injection components
Intake/exhaust manifolds
Upper and lower oil pans
Oil filter
Thermostat and housing assembly
Water pump

➡ **Note:** *When removing the external components from the engine, pay close attention to details that may be helpful or important during installation. Note the installed position of gaskets, seals, spacers, pins, brackets, washers, bolts and other small items.*

4   If you're going to obtain a short block (assembled engine block, crankshaft, pistons and connecting rods), you should remove the timing belt/chain, cylinder head, oil pan, oil pump pick-up tube, oil pump and water pump from your engine so that you can turn in your old short block to the rebuilder as a core. See Section 5 for additional information regarding the different possibilities to be considered.

9   Pistons and connecting rods - removal and installation

REMOVAL

➡ **Note:** *Prior to removing the piston/connecting rod assemblies, remove the cylinder head, oil pan, and the upper (aluminum) oil pan (see Chapter 2A or 2B). On four-cylinder engines, also remove the balance shafts (see Chapter 2A).*

1   Use your fingernail to feel if a ridge has formed at the upper limit of ring travel (about 1/4-inch down from the top of each cylinder). If carbon deposits or cylinder wear have produced ridges, they must be completely removed with a special tool **(see illustration)**. Follow the manufacturer's instructions provided with the tool. Failure to remove the ridges before attempting to remove the piston/connecting rod assemblies may result in piston breakage.

2   After the cylinder ridges have been removed, turn the engine so the crankshaft is facing up.

3   Before the pistons and connecting rods are removed, check the connecting rod endplay with feeler gauges. Slide them between the first connecting rod and the crankshaft throw until the play is removed **(see illustration)**. Repeat this procedure for each connecting rod. The endplay is equal to the thickness of the feeler gauge(s). Check with an automotive machine shop for the endplay service limit. If the play exceeds the service limit, new connecting rods will be required. If new rods (or a new crankshaft) are installed, the endplay may fall under the minimum allowable clearance. If it does, the rods will have to be machined to restore it. If necessary, consult an automotive machine shop for advice.

4   Check the connecting rods and caps for identification marks **(see illustration)**. If they aren't plainly marked, use a small center-punch to make the appropriate number of indentations on each rod and cap (1, 2, 3, etc., depending on the cylinder they're associated with).

5   Loosen each of the connecting rod cap bolts 1/2-turn at a time until they can be removed by hand. Remove the number one connecting rod cap and bearing insert. Don't drop the bearing insert out of the cap.

9.1 Before you try to remove the pistons, use a ridge reamer to remove the raised material (ridge) from the top of the cylinders

9.3 Checking the connecting rod endplay (side clearance)

9.4 If the connecting rods and caps are not marked, use a center punch or numbered impression stamps to mark the caps to the rods by cylinder number

9.13 Install the piston ring into the cylinder, then push it down into position using a piston so the ring will be square in the cylinder

9.14 With the ring square in the cylinder, measure the ring end gap with a feeler gauge

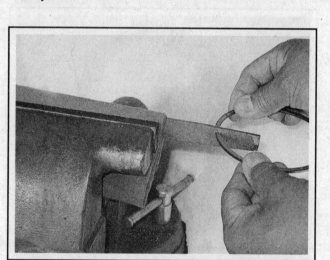

9.15 If the ring end gap is too small, clamp a file in a vise as shown and file the piston ring ends - file the ends squarely and finish by removing all raised material or burrs with a fine stone

6   Remove the bearing insert and push the connecting rod/piston assembly out through the top of the engine. Use a wooden or plastic hammer handle to push on the upper bearing surface in the connecting rod. Be careful to avoid scratching the crankshaft bearing journals with the rod bolts.

➡ Note: Slip a sort section of rubber hose over the rod bolts before pushing the piston/rod assemblies out to make sure the crankshaft isn't damaged.

7   If resistance is felt, double-check to make sure that the entire ridge was removed from the cylinder.

8   Repeat the procedure for the remaining cylinders.

9   After removal, reassemble the connecting rod caps and bearing inserts in their respective connecting rods and install the cap bolts finger tight. Leaving the old bearing inserts in place until reassembly will help prevent the connecting rod bearing surfaces from being accidentally nicked or gouged.

10   The pistons and connecting rods are now ready for inspection and overhaul at an automotive machine shop.

PISTON RING INSTALLATION

11 Before installing the new piston rings, the ring end gaps must be checked. It's assumed that the piston ring side clearance has been checked and verified correct.

➡ Note: Pistons and rods can only be installed after the crankshaft has been installed (see Section 10).

12 Lay out the piston/connecting rod assemblies and the new ring sets so the ring sets will be matched with the same piston and cylinder during the end gap measurement and engine assembly.

13 Insert the top (number one) ring into the first cylinder and square it up with the cylinder walls by pushing it in with the top of the piston (see illustration). The ring should be near the bottom of the cylinder, at the lower limit of ring travel.

14 To measure the end gap, slip feeler gauges between the ends of the ring until a gauge equal to the gap width is found (see illustration). The feeler gauge should slide between the ring ends with a slight amount of drag. Check with an automotive machine shop for the correct end gap for your engine. If the gap is larger or smaller than specified, double-check to make sure you have the correct rings before proceeding.

15 If the gap is too small, it must be enlarged or the ring ends may come in contact with each other during engine operation, which can cause serious damage to the engine. The end gap can be increased by filing the ring ends very carefully with a fine file. Mount the file in a vise equipped with soft jaws, slip the ring over the file with the ends contacting the file face and slowly move the ring to remove material from the ends. When performing this operation, file only by pushing the ring from the outside end of the file towards the vise (see illustration).

16 Excess end gap isn't critical unless it's greater than approximately 0.030-inch. Again, double-check to make sure you have the correct ring type.

17 Repeat the procedure for each ring that will be installed in the first cylinder and for each ring in the remaining cylinders. Remember to keep rings, pistons and cylinders matched up.

18 Once the ring end gaps have been checked/corrected, the rings can be installed on the pistons.

19 The oil control ring (lowest one on the piston) is usually installed

9.19a Installing the spacer/expander in the oil ring groove

9.19b DO NOT use a piston ring installation tool when installing the oil control side rails

first. It's composed of three separate components. Slip the spacer/expander into the groove **(see illustration)**. If an anti-rotation tang is used, make sure it's inserted into the drilled hole in the ring groove. Next, install the upper side rail in the same manner **(see illustration)**. Don't use a piston ring installation tool on the oil ring side rails, as they may be damaged. Instead, place one end of the side rail into the groove between the spacer/expander and the ring land, hold it firmly in place and slide a finger around the piston while pushing the rail into the groove. Finally, install the lower side rail.

20 After the three oil ring components have been installed, check to make sure that both the upper and lower side rails can be rotated smoothly inside the ring grooves.

21 The number two (middle) ring is installed next. It's usually stamped with a mark that must face up, toward the top of the piston. Do not mix up the top and middle rings, as they have different cross-sections.

→ **Note: Always follow the instructions printed on the ring package or box - different manufacturers may require different approaches.**

22 Use a piston ring installation tool and make sure the identification mark is facing the top of the piston, then slip the ring into the middle groove on the piston **(see illustration)**. Don't expand the ring any more than necessary to slide it over the piston.

23 Install the number one (top) ring in the same manner. Make sure the mark is facing up. Be careful not to confuse the number one and number two rings.

24 Repeat the procedure for the remaining pistons and rings.

INSTALLATION

25 Before installing the piston/connecting rod assemblies, the cylinder walls must be perfectly clean, the top edge of each cylinder bore must be chamfered, and the crankshaft must be in place.

26 Remove the cap from the end of the number one connecting rod (refer to the marks made during removal - the bearing locating tangs must be together).

9.22 Use a piston ring installation tool to install the number 2 and the number 1 (top) rings - the directional mark on the piston ring(s) must face toward the top of the piston

27 Remove the original bearing inserts and wipe the bearing surfaces of the connecting rod and cap with a clean, lint-free cloth. They must be kept spotlessly clean.

Connecting rod bearing oil clearance check

28 Clean the rear of the new upper bearing insert, then lay it in place in the connecting rod. Make sure the tab on the bearing fits into the recess in the rod. Don't hammer the bearing insert into place and be very careful not to nick or gouge the bearing face. Don't lubricate the bearing at this time.

29 Clean the back of the other bearing insert and install it in the rod cap. Again, make sure the tab on the bearing fits into the recess in the cap, and don't apply any lubricant. It's critically important that the mating surfaces of the bearing and connecting rod are perfectly clean and oil free when they're assembled.

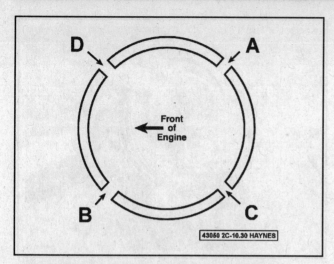

9.30 Position the piston ring end gaps as shown here before installing the piston/connecting rod assemblies into the engine

A Top compression ring gap and oil ring spacer gap
B Second compression ring
C Upper oil ring gap
D Lower oil ring gap

9.37 Place Plastigage on each connecting rod bearing journal parallel to the crankshaft centerline

30 Position the piston ring gaps around the piston as shown **(see illustration)**.

31 Lubricate the piston and rings with clean engine oil and attach a piston ring compressor to the piston. Leave the skirt protruding about 1/4-inch to guide the piston into the cylinder. The rings must be compressed until they're flush with the piston.

➡ **Note: Slip pieces of rubber hose about 6 inches long over each rod bolt. These will guide the connecting rod into position and keep the rod bolts from damaging the crankshaft.**

32 Rotate the crankshaft until the number one connecting rod journal is at Bottom Dead Center (BDC) and apply a liberal coat of engine oil to the cylinder walls.

33 With the mark on top of the piston facing the front (timing belt end) of the engine, gently insert the piston/connecting rod assembly

9.35 Use a plastic or wooden hammer handle to push the piston into the cylinder

into the number one cylinder bore and rest the bottom edge of the ring compressor on the engine block.

➡ **Note: The connecting rod also has a mark on it that must face the correct direction.**

34 Tap the top edge of the ring compressor to make sure it's contacting the block around its entire circumference.

35 Gently tap on the top of the piston with the end of a wooden or plastic hammer handle **(see illustration)** while guiding the end of the connecting rod into place on the crankshaft journal. The piston rings may try to pop out of the ring compressor just before entering the cylinder bore, so keep some downward pressure on the ring compressor. Work slowly, and if any resistance is felt as the piston enters the cylinder, stop immediately. Find out what's hanging up and fix it before proceeding. Do not, for any reason, force the piston into the cylinder - you might break a ring and/or the piston.

36 Once the piston/connecting rod assembly is installed, the connecting rod bearing oil clearance must be checked before the rod cap is permanently installed.

37 Cut a piece of the appropriate size Plastigage slightly shorter than the width of the connecting rod bearing and lay it in place on the number one connecting rod journal, parallel with the journal axis **(see illustration)**.

38 Clean the connecting rod cap bearing face and install the rod cap. Make sure the mating mark on the cap is on the same side as the mark on the connecting rod.

39 Install the rod bolts and tighten them in two steps to the torque listed in this Chapter's Specifications.

➡ **Note: Use a thin-wall socket to avoid erroneous torque readings that can result if the socket is wedged between the rod cap and the bolt. If the socket tends to wedge itself between the fastener and the cap, lift up on it slightly until it no longer contacts the cap. DO NOT rotate the crankshaft at any time during this operation.**

40 Remove the fasteners and detach the rod cap, being very careful not to disturb the Plastigage.

41 Compare the width of the crushed Plastigage to the scale printed on the Plastigage envelope to obtain the oil clearance **(see illustration)**. The connecting rod oil clearance is usually about 0.001 to 0.002 inch. Consult an automotive machine shop for the clearance specified for the rod bearings on your engine.

9.41 Use the scale on the Plastigage package to determine the bearing oil clearance - be sure to measure the widest part of the Plastigage and use the correct scale; it comes with both standard and metric scales

42 If the clearance is not as specified, the bearing inserts may be the wrong size (which means different ones will be required). Before deciding that different inserts are needed, make sure that no dirt or oil was between the bearing inserts and the connecting rod or cap when the clearance was measured. Also, recheck the journal diameter. If the Plastigage was wider at one end than the other, the journal may be tapered. If the clearance still exceeds the limit specified, the bearing will have to be replaced with an undersize bearing.

✳✳ CAUTION:

When installing a new crankshaft always use a standard size bearing.

FINAL INSTALLATION

43 Carefully scrape all traces of the Plastigage material off the rod journal and/or bearing face. Be very careful not to scratch the bearing - use your fingernail or the edge of a plastic card.

44 Make sure the bearing faces are perfectly clean, then apply a uniform layer of clean moly-base grease or engine assembly lube to both of them. You'll have to push the piston into the cylinder to expose the face of the bearing insert in the connecting rod.

45 Slide the connecting rod back into place on the journal, install the rod cap and bolts, tightening them in two steps to the torque listed in this Chapter's Specifications.

46 Repeat the entire procedure for the remaining pistons/connecting rods.

47 The important points to remember are:

a) *Keep the back sides of the bearing inserts and the insides of the connecting rods and caps perfectly clean when assembling them.*

b) *Make sure you have the correct piston/rod assembly for each cylinder.*

c) *The mark on the piston must face the front (timing belt end) of the engine.*

d) *Lubricate the cylinder walls liberally with clean oil.*

e) *Lubricate the bearing faces when installing the rod caps after the oil clearance has been checked.*

48 After all the piston/connecting rod assemblies have been correctly installed, rotate the crankshaft a number of times by hand to check for any obvious binding.

49 As a final step, check the connecting rod endplay again. If it was correct before disassembly and the original crankshaft and rods were

reinstalled, it should still be correct. If new rods or a new crankshaft were installed, the endplay may be inadequate. If so, the rods will have to be removed and taken to an automotive machine shop for resizing.

10 Crankshaft - removal and installation

REMOVAL

➡ **Note: The crankshaft can be removed only after the engine has been removed from the vehicle. It's assumed that the flywheel/driveplate, crankshaft pulley, timing belt/chains, oil pan, oil pump body, oil filter and piston/connecting rod assemblies have already been removed. The rear main oil seal retainer must be unbolted and separated from the block before proceeding with crankshaft removal.**

1 Before the crankshaft is removed, measure the endplay. Mount a dial indicator with the indicator in line with the crankshaft and touching the end of the crankshaft **(see illustration)**.

2 Pry the crankshaft all the way to the rear and zero the dial indica-

10.1 Checking crankshaft endplay with a dial indicator

10.3 Checking crankshaft endplay with feeler gauges at the thrust bearing journal

10.17 Place the Plastigage onto the crankshaft bearing journal as shown

tor. Next, pry the crankshaft to the front as far as possible and check the reading on the dial indicator. The distance traveled is the endplay. A typical crankshaft endplay will fall between 0.003 to 0.010-inch. If it's greater than that, check the crankshaft thrust surfaces for wear after it's removed. If no wear is evident, new main bearings should correct the endplay.

3   If a dial indicator isn't available, feeler gauges can be used. Gently pry the crankshaft all the way to the front of the engine. Slip feeler gauges between the crankshaft and the front face of the thrust bearing or washer to determine the clearance **(see illustration)**.

4   Loosen the main bearing cap bolts (bearing cap assembly on 2006 and earlier 3.5L engines) (and side bolts if equipped), 1/4-turn at a time each, until they can be removed by hand in the reverse order of the tightening sequence **(see illustration 10.19a, 10.19b, 10.19c or 10.19d)**.

5   Gently tap the main bearing caps with a soft-face hammer. Pull the main bearing cap straight up and off the cylinder block. Try not to drop the bearing inserts if they come out with the cap.

➡ **Note: 2006 and earlier 3.5L engines use a mono-bearing cap that be removed as a unit.**

6   Carefully lift the crankshaft out of the engine. It may be a good idea to have an assistant available, since the crankshaft is quite heavy and awkward to handle. With the bearing inserts in place inside the engine block and main bearing caps, reinstall the main bearing caps onto the engine block and tighten the bolts finger tight. Make sure you install the main bearing cap(s) with the arrow facing the front end of the engine.

INSTALLATION - MAIN BEARING OIL CLEARANCE CHECK

7   Crankshaft installation is the first step in engine reassembly. It's assumed at this point that the engine block and crankshaft have been cleaned, inspected and repaired or reconditioned.

8   Position the engine block with the bottom facing up.

9   Remove the mounting bolts and lift off the main bearing cap(s).

10 If they're still in place, remove the original bearing inserts from the block and from the main bearing caps. Wipe the bearing surfaces of the block and main bearing caps with a clean, lint-free cloth. They must be kept spotlessly clean. This is critical for determining the correct bearing oil clearance.

11 Without mixing them up, clean the backs of the new upper main bearing inserts (with grooves and oil holes) and lay one in each main bearing saddle in the block. Each upper bearing has an oil groove and oil hole in it. Install the thrust washers with the grooved side facing out. Clean the back sides of the lower main bearing inserts (without grooves) and lay them in the corresponding caps. Make sure the tab on the bearing insert fits into the recess in the block or main bearing cap.

❈❈ CAUTION:

The oil holes in the block must line up with the oil holes in the upper bearing inserts.

❈❈ CAUTION:

Do not hammer the bearing insert into place and don't nick or gouge the bearing faces. DO NOT apply any lubrication at this time.

12 Clean the faces of the bearing inserts in the block and the crankshaft main bearing journals with a clean, lint-free cloth.

13 Check or clean the oil holes in the crankshaft, as any dirt here

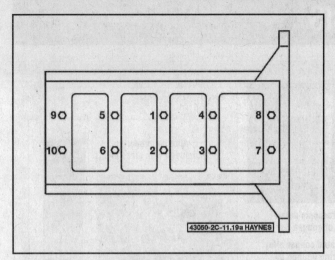

10.19a Main bearing cap bolt tightening sequence - 2.4L four-cylinder models

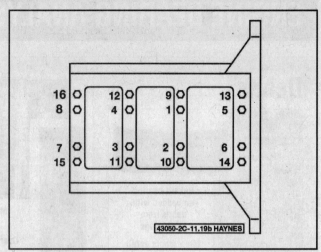

10.19b Main bearing cap bolt tightening sequence - 2006 and earlier 3.5L V6 models

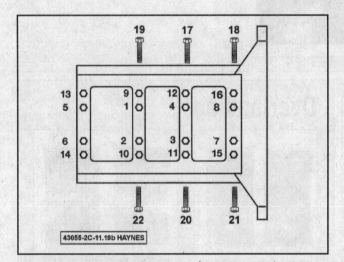

10.19c Main bearing cap bolt tightening sequence - 3.3L and 3.8L V6 models

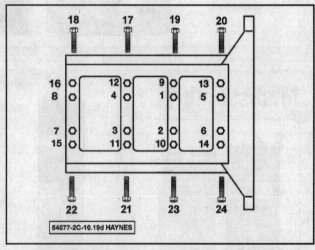

10.19d Main bearing cap bolt tightening sequence - 2011 and later 3.5L V6 models

can go only one way - straight through the new bearings.

14 Once you're certain the crankshaft is clean, carefully lay it in position in the cylinder block.

15 Before the crankshaft can be permanently installed, the main bearing oil clearance must be checked.

16 Cut several strips of the appropriate size of Plastigage (they must be slightly shorter than the width of the main bearing journal).

17 Place one piece on each crankshaft main bearing journal, parallel with the journal axis **(see illustration)**.

18 Clean the faces of the bearing inserts in the main bearing caps. Hold the bearing inserts in place and install the caps onto the crank-

shaft and cylinder block. DO NOT disturb the Plastigage. Make sure you install the main bearing cap with the arrow facing the front of the engine.

19 Apply clean engine oil to all bolt threads prior to installation, then install all bolts finger-tight. Tighten the main bearing cap bolts in two steps in the sequence shown **(see illustrations)**, to the torque listed in this Chapter's Specifications. DO NOT rotate the crankshaft at any time during this operation.

20 Remove the bolts in the *reverse* order of the tightening sequence and carefully lift the main bearing cap straight up and off the block. Do not disturb the Plastigage or rotate the crankshaft. If the main bearing

ENGINE BEARING ANALYSIS

Debris

Babbitt bearing embedded with debris from machinings

Microscopic detail of debris

Microscopic detail of gouges

Overplated copper alloy bearing gouged by cast iron debris

Aluminum bearing embedded with glass beads

Microscopic detail of glass beads

Damaged lining caused by dirt left on the bearing back

Misassembly

Result of a lower half assembled as an upper - blocking the oil flow

Excessive oil clearance is indicated by a short contact arc

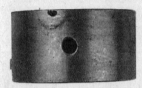

Polished and oil-stained backs are a result of a poor fit in the housing bore

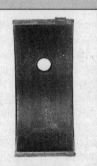

Result of a wrong, reversed, or shifted cap

Overloading

Damage from excessive idling which resulted in an oil film unable to support the load imposed

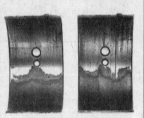

Damaged upper connecting rod bearings caused by engine lugging; the lower main bearings (not shown) were similarly affected

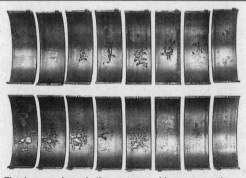

The damage shown in these upper and lower connecting rod bearings was caused by engine operation at a higher-than-rated speed under load

Misalignment

A warped crankshaft caused this pattern of severe wear in the center, diminishing toward the ends

A poorly finished crankshaft caused the equally spaced scoring shown

A tapered housing bore caused the damage along one edge of this pair

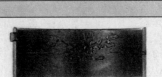

A bent connecting rod led to the damage in the "V" pattern

Lubrication

Result of dry start: The bearings on the left, farthest from the oil pump, show more damage

Result of a low oil supply or oil starvation

Severe wear as a result of inadequate oil clearance

Corrosion

Microscopic detail of corrosion

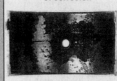

Corrosion is an acid attack on the bearing lining generally caused by inadequate maintenance, extremely hot or cold operation, or inferior oils or fuels

Microscopic detail of cavitation

Example of cavitation - a surface erosion caused by pressure changes in the oil film

Damage from excessive thrust or insufficient axial clearance

Bearing affected by oil dilution caused by excessive blow-by or a rich mixture

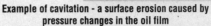

10.21 Use the scale on the Plastigage package to determine the bearing oil clearance - measure the widest part of the Plastigage and use the correct scale; it comes with both standard and metric scales

cap is difficult to remove, tap it gently from side-to-side with a soft-face hammer to loosen it.

21 Compare the width of the crushed Plastigage on each journal to the scale printed on the Plastigage envelope to determine the main bearing oil clearance **(see illustration)**. A typical main bearing oil clearance should fall between 0.0015 to 0.0023-inch. Check with an automotive machine shop for the clearance specified for your engine.

22 If the clearance is not as specified, the bearing inserts may be the wrong size (which means different ones will be required). Before deciding if different inserts are needed, make sure that no dirt or oil was between the bearing inserts and the cap or block when the clearance was measured. If the Plastigage was wider at one end than the other, the crankshaft journal may be tapered. If the clearance still exceeds the limit specified, the bearing insert(s) will have to be replaced with an under-size bearing insert(s).

✼ CAUTION:

When installing a new crankshaft, always install a standard bearing insert set.

23 Carefully scrape all traces of the Plastigage material off the main bearing journals and/or the bearing insert faces. Remove all residue from the oil holes. Use your fingernail or the edge of a plastic card - don't nick or scratch the bearing faces.

FINAL INSTALLATION

24 Carefully lift the crankshaft out of the cylinder block.

25 Clean the bearing insert faces in the cylinder block, then apply a thin, uniform layer of moly-base grease or engine assembly lube to each of the bearing surfaces. Coat the thrust faces as well as the journal face of the thrust bearing.

➡ **Note: The thrust bearings are installed in the no. 3 main cap/saddle position (counting from the front) on all engines covered by this manual.**

26 Make sure the crankshaft journals are clean, then lay the crankshaft back in place in the cylinder block.

27 Clean the bearing insert faces and apply the same lubricant to them.

28 Hold the bearing inserts in place and install the main bearing caps (cap assembly on 2006 and earlier 3.5L engines) on the crankshaft and cylinder block. Tap the bearing caps into place with a brass punch or a soft-face hammer.

29 Apply clean engine oil to the bolt threads, wipe off any excess oil and install the bolts finger-tight.

30 Tighten the main bearing cap bolts, to 10 or 12 foot-pounds, in the correct sequence **(see illustration 10.19a, 10.19b, 10.19c or 10.19d).**

31 Push the crankshaft forward using a screwdriver or prybar to seat the thrust bearing. Once the crankshaft is pushed fully forward to seat the thrust bearing, leave the screwdriver in position so that force stays on the crankshaft until after all main bearing cap bolts have been tightened.

32 Tighten the main bearing cap bolts in two steps, in sequence **(see illustration 10.19a, 10.19b, 10.19c or 10.19d)** and to the torque and angle listed in this Chapter's Specifications.

33 Recheck crankshaft endplay with a feeler gauge or a dial indicator. The endplay should be correct if the crankshaft thrust faces aren't worn or damaged and if new bearings have been installed.

34 Rotate the crankshaft a number of times by hand to check for any obvious binding. It should rotate with a running torque of 50 in-lbs or less. If the running torque is too high, correct the problem at this time.

35 Install a new rear main oil seal (see Chapter 2A or 2B).

11 Engine overhaul - reassembly sequence

1 Before beginning engine reassembly, make sure you have all the necessary new parts, gaskets and seals as well as the following items on hand:

  Common hand tools
  A 1/2-inch drive torque wrench
  New engine oil
  Gasket sealant
  Thread locking compound

2 If you obtained a short block, it will be necessary to install the cylinder head, the oil pump and pick-up tube, the oil pan, the water

  Flywheel and clutch (manual transmission or transaxle)
  Driveplate (automatic transmission or transaxle)

12 Initial start-up and break-in after overhaul

✳✳ WARNING:

Have a fire extinguisher handy when starting the engine for the first time.

1 Once the engine has been installed in the vehicle, double-check the engine oil and coolant levels.
2 With the spark plugs out of the engine and the ignition system and fuel pump disabled (see Section 3 to disable the ignition system and Chapter 4 to disable the fuel pump), crank the engine until oil pressure registers on the gauge or the light goes out.
3 Install the spark plugs and ignition coils and restore the fuel pump and ignition functions.
4 Start the engine. It may take a few moments for the fuel system

pump, the timing belt/chain and timing cover, and the valve cover (see Chapter 2A or 2B). In order to save time and avoid problems, the external components must be installed in the following general order:

  Thermostat and housing cover
  Water pump
  Intake and exhaust manifolds
  Fuel injection components
  Emission control components
  Spark plugs
  Ignition coils
  Oil filter
  Engine mounts and mount brackets

to build up pressure, but the engine should start without a great deal of effort.
5 After the engine starts, it should be allowed to warm up to normal operating temperature. While the engine is warming up, make a thorough check for fuel, oil and coolant leaks.
6 Shut the engine off and recheck the engine oil and coolant levels.
7 Drive the vehicle to an area with minimum traffic, accelerate from 30 to 50 mph, then allow the vehicle to slow to 30 mph with the throttle closed. Repeat the procedure 10 or 12 times. This will load the piston rings and cause them to seat properly against the cylinder walls. Check again for oil and coolant leaks.
8 Drive the vehicle gently for the first 500 miles (no sustained high speeds) and keep a constant check on the oil level. It is not unusual for an engine to use oil during the break-in period.
9 At approximately 500 to 600 miles, change the oil and filter.
10 For the next few hundred miles, drive the vehicle normally. Do not pamper it or abuse it.

GLOSSARY

B

Backlash - The amount of play between two parts. Usually refers to how much one gear can be moved back and forth without moving the gear with which it's meshed.

Bearing Caps - The caps held in place by nuts or bolts which, in turn, hold the bearing surface. This space is for lubricating oil to enter.

Bearing clearance - The amount of space left between shaft and bearing surface. This space is for lubricating oil to enter.

Bearing crush - The additional height which is purposely manufactured into each bearing half to ensure complete contact of the bearing back with the housing bore when the engine is assembled.

Bearing knock - The noise created by movement of a part in a loose or worn bearing.

Blueprinting - Dismantling an engine and reassembling it to EXACT specifications.

Bore - An engine cylinder, or any cylindrical hole; also used to describe the process of enlarging or accurately refinishing a hole with a cutting tool, as to bore an engine cylinder. The bore size is the diameter of the hole.

Boring - Renewing the cylinders by cutting them out to a specified size. A boring bar is used to make the cut.

Bottom end - A term which refers collectively to the engine block, crankshaft, main bearings and the big ends of the connecting rods.

Break-in - The period of operation between installation of new or rebuilt parts and time in which parts are worn to the correct fit. Driving at reduced and varying speed for a specified mileage to permit parts to wear to the correct fit.

Bushing - A one-piece sleeve placed in a bore to serve as a bearing surface for shaft, piston pin, etc. Usually replaceable.

C

Camshaft - The shaft in the engine, on which a series of lobes are located for operating the valve mechanisms. The camshaft is driven by gears or sprockets and a timing chain. Usually referred to simply as the cam.

Carbon - Hard, or soft, black deposits found in combustion chamber, on plugs, under rings, on and under valve heads.

Cast iron - An alloy of iron and more than two percent carbon, used for engine blocks and heads because it's relatively inexpensive and easy to mold into complex shapes.

Chamfer - To bevel across (or a bevel on) the sharp edge of an object.

Chase - To repair damaged threads with a tap or die.

Combustion chamber - The space between the piston and the cylinder head, with the piston at top dead center, in which air-fuel mixture is burned.

Compression ratio - The relationship between cylinder volume (clearance volume) when the piston is at top dead center and cylinder volume when the piston is at bottom dead center.

Connecting rod - The rod that connects the crank on the crankshaft with the piston. Sometimes called a con rod.

Connecting rod cap - The part of the connecting rod assembly that attaches the rod to the crankpin.

Core plug - Soft metal plug used to plug the casting holes for the coolant passages in the block.

Crankcase - The lower part of the engine in which the crankshaft rotates; includes the lower section of the cylinder block and the oil pan.

Crank kit - A reground or reconditioned crankshaft and new main and connecting rod bearings.

Crankpin - The part of a crankshaft to which a connecting rod is attached.

Crankshaft - The main rotating member, or shaft, running the length of the crankcase, with offset throws to which the connecting rods are attached; changes the reciprocating motion of the pistons into rotating motion.

Cylinder sleeve - A replaceable sleeve, or liner, pressed into the cylinder block to form the cylinder bore.

D

Deburring - Removing the burrs (rough edges or areas) from a bearing.

Deglazer - A tool, rotated by an electric motor, used to remove glaze from cylinder walls so a new set of rings will seat.

E

Endplay - The amount of lengthwise movement between two parts. As applied to a crankshaft, the distance that the crankshaft can move forward and back in the cylinder block.

F

Face - A machinist's term that refers to removing metal from the end of a shaft or the face of a larger part, such as a flywheel.

Fatigue - A breakdown of material through a large number of loading and unloading cycles. The first signs are cracks followed shortly by breaks.

Feeler gauge - A thin strip of hardened steel, ground to an exact thickness, used to check clearances between parts.

Free height - The unloaded length or height of a spring.

Freeplay - The looseness in a linkage, or an assembly of parts, between the initial application of force and actual movement. Usually perceived as slop or slight delay.

Freeze plug - See Core plug.

G

Gallery - A large passage in the block that forms a reservoir for engine oil pressure.

Glaze - The very smooth, glassy finish that develops on cylinder walls while an engine is in service.

H

Heli-Coil - A rethreading device used when threads are worn or damaged. The device is installed in a retapped hole to reduce the thread size to the original size.

I

Installed height - The spring's measured length or height, as installed on the cylinder head. Installed height is measured from the spring seat to the underside of the spring retainer.

J

Journal - The surface of a rotating shaft which turns in a bearing.

K

Keeper - The split lock that holds the valve spring retainer in position on the valve stem.

Key - A small piece of metal inserted into matching grooves machined into two parts fitted together - such as a gear pressed onto a shaft - which prevents slippage between the two parts.

Knock - The heavy metallic engine sound, produced in the combustion chamber as a result of abnormal combustion - usually detonation. Knock is usually caused by a loose or worn bearing. Also referred to as detonation, pinging and spark knock. Connecting rod or main bearing knocks are created by too much oil clearance or insufficient lubrication.

L

Lands - The portions of metal between the piston ring grooves.

Lapping the valves - Grinding a valve face and its seat together with lapping compound.

Lash - The amount of free motion in a gear train, between gears, or in a mechanical assembly, that occurs before movement can begin. Usually refers to the lash in a valve train.

Lifter - The part that rides against the cam to transfer motion to the rest of the valve train.

M

Machining - The process of using a machine to remove metal from a metal part.

Main bearings - The plain, or babbitt, bearings that support the crankshaft.

Main bearing caps - The cast iron caps, bolted to the bottom of the block, that support the main bearings.

O

O.D. - Outside diameter.

Oil gallery - A pipe or drilled passageway in the engine used to carry engine oil from one area to another.

Oil ring - The lower ring, or rings, of a piston; designed to prevent excessive amounts of oil from working up the cylinder walls and into the combustion chamber. Also called an oil-control ring.

Oil seal - A seal which keeps oil from leaking out of a compartment. Usually refers to a dynamic seal around a rotating shaft or other moving part.

O-ring - A type of sealing ring made of a special rubberlike material; in use, the O-ring is compressed into a groove to provide the sealing action.

Overhaul - To completely disassemble a unit, clean and inspect all parts, reassemble it with the original or new parts and make all adjustments necessary for proper operation.

P

Pilot bearing - A small bearing installed in the center of the flywheel (or the rear end of the crankshaft) to support the front end of the input shaft of the transmission.

Pip mark - A little dot or indentation which indicates the top side of a compression ring.

Piston - The cylindrical part, attached to the connecting rod, that moves up and down in the cylinder as the crankshaft rotates. When the fuel charge is fired, the piston transfers the force of the explosion to the connecting rod, then to the crankshaft.

Piston pin (or wrist pin) - The cylindrical and usually hollow steel pin that passes through the piston. The piston pin fastens the piston to the upper end of the connecting rod.

Piston ring - The split ring fitted to the groove in a piston. The ring contacts the sides of the ring groove and also rubs against the cylinder wall, thus sealing space between piston and wall. There are two types of rings: Compression rings seal the compression pressure in the combustion chamber; oil rings scrape excessive oil off the cylinder wall.

Piston ring groove - The slots or grooves cut in piston heads to hold piston rings in position.

Piston skirt - The portion of the piston below the rings and the piston pin hole.

Plastigage - A thin strip of plastic thread, available in different sizes, used for measuring clearances. For example, a strip of plastigage is laid across a bearing journal and mashed as parts are assembled. Then parts are disassembled and the width of the strip is measured to determine clearance between journal and bearing. Commonly used to measure crankshaft main-bearing and connecting rod bearing clearances.

Press-fit - A tight fit between two parts that requires pressure to force the parts together. Also referred to as drive, or force, fit.

Prussian blue - A blue pigment; in solution, useful in determining the area of contact between two surfaces. Prussian blue is commonly used to determine the width and location of the contact area between the valve face and the valve seat.

R

Race (bearing) - The inner or outer ring that provides a contact surface for balls or rollers in bearing.

Ream - To size, enlarge or smooth a hole by using a round cutting tool with fluted edges.

Ring job - The process of reconditioning the cylinders and installing new rings.

Runout - Wobble. The amount a shaft rotates out-of-true.

S

Saddle - The upper main bearing seat.

Scored - Scratched or grooved, as a cylinder wall may be scored by abrasive particles moved up and down by the piston rings.

Scuffing - A type of wear in which there's a transfer of material between parts moving against each other; shows up as pits or grooves in the mating surfaces.

Seat - The surface upon which another part rests or seats. For example, the valve seat is the matched surface upon which the valve face rests. Also used to refer to wearing into a good fit; for example, piston rings seat after a few miles of driving.

Short block - An engine block complete with crankshaft and piston and, usually, camshaft assemblies.

Static balance - The balance of an object while it's stationary.

Step - The wear on the lower portion of a ring land caused by excessive side and back-clearance. The height of the step indicates the ring's extra side clearance and the length of the step projecting from the back wall of the groove represents the ring's back clearance.

Stroke - The distance the piston moves when traveling from top dead center to bottom dead center, or from bottom dead center to top dead center.

Stud - A metal rod with threads on both ends.

T

Tang - A lip on the end of a plain bearing used to align the bearing during assembly.

Tap - To cut threads in a hole. Also refers to the fluted tool used to cut threads.

Taper - A gradual reduction in the width of a shaft or hole; in an engine cylinder, taper usually takes the form of uneven wear, more pronounced at the top than at the bottom.

Throws - The offset portions of the crankshaft to which the connecting rods are affixed.

Thrust bearing - The main bearing that has thrust faces to prevent excessive endplay, or forward and backward movement of the crankshaft.

Thrust washer - A bronze or hardened steel washer placed between two moving parts. The washer prevents longitudinal movement and provides a bearing surface for thrust surfaces of parts.

Tolerance - The amount of variation permitted from an exact size of measurement. Actual amount from smallest acceptable dimension to largest acceptable dimension.

U

Umbrella - An oil deflector placed near the valve tip to throw oil from the valve stem area.

Undercut - A machined groove below the normal surface.

Undersize bearings - Smaller diameter bearings used with re-ground crankshaft journals.

V

Valve grinding - Refacing a valve in a valve-refacing machine.

Valve train - The valve-operating mechanism of an engine; includes all components from the camshaft to the valve.

Vibration damper - A cylindrical weight attached to the front of the crankshaft to minimize torsional vibration (the twist-untwist actions of the crankshaft caused by the cylinder firing impulses). Also called a harmonic balancer.

W

Water jacket - The spaces around the cylinders, between the inner and outer shells of the cylinder block or head, through which coolant circulates.

Web - A supporting structure across a cavity.

Woodruff key - A key with a radiused backside (viewed from the side).

11 After 2,000 miles, change the oil and filter again and consider the engine broken in.

Specifications

General

Cylinder compression	Lowest cylinder must be within 75% of the highest cylinder	
Oil pressure		
Four-cylinder engines (hot, @ 1000 rpm)	21 psi or higher	147 kPa or higher
V6 engines		
2006 and earlier 3.5L (@ idle)	11 psi	80 kPa
All other V6 engines (@ 1000 rpm)	18 psi	130 kPa

Torque specifications — Ft-lbs (unless otherwise indicated) — Nm

➡ **Note: One foot-pound (ft-lb) of torque is equivalent to 12 inch-pounds (in-lbs) of torque. Torque values below approximately 15 foot-pounds are expressed in inch-pounds, because most foot-pound torque wrenches are not accurate at these smaller values.**

	Ft-lbs (unless otherwise indicated)	Nm
Balance shaft assembly mounting bolts (four-cylinder engines)		
Step 1	17 to 20	23 to 27
Step 2	Tighten an additional 103 to 107-degrees	
Connecting rod bolts/nuts		
Four-cylinder engines		
Step 1	13 to 16	18 to 22
Step 2	Tighten an additional 88 to 92-degrees	
V6 engines		
2006 and earlier 3.5L engine (nuts)		
Step 1	26	34
Step 2	Tighten an additional 90-degrees	
All other V6 engines		
Step 1	13 to 16	18 to 22
Step 2	Tighten an additional 88 to 92-degrees	
Main bearing bolts		
Four-cylinder engines		
Step 1	130 in-lbs	14.5
Step 2	20 to 23	27 to 31
Step 3	Tighten an additional 120 to 125-degrees	
V6 engines		
2006 and earlier 3.5L engine	51 to 58	69 to 79
All other V6 engines		
Step 1, M11 (inner) bolts	37	50
Step 2, M11 (inner) bolts	Tighten an additional 90-degrees	
Step 3, M8 (outer) bolts	173 in-lbs	19.5
Step 4, M8 (outer) bolts	Tighten an additional 120-degrees	
Step 5, M8 (side) bolts	22 to 23	30 to 31
Baffle plate (3.3L, 3.8L and 2011 and later 3.5L engines)	87 to 104 in-lbs	10 to 11.5
Main bearing cap support brace or ladder (four-cylinder engines)		
Step 1	78 to 86 in-lbs	9 to 9.5
Step 2	13 to 15	18 to 20
Step 3	20 to 23	27 to 31

Section

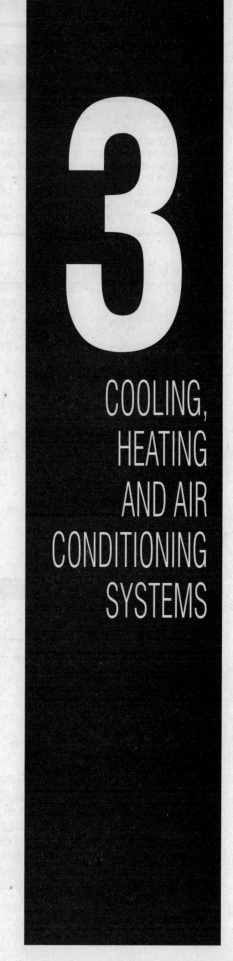

3

COOLING, HEATING AND AIR CONDITIONING SYSTEMS

1 General Information

ENGINE COOLING SYSTEM

1 All modern vehicles employ a pressurized engine cooling system with thermostatically controlled coolant circulation. The cooling system consists of a radiator, an expansion tank or coolant reservoir, a pressure cap (located on the expansion tank or radiator), a thermostat, a cooling fan, and a water pump.

2 The water pump circulates coolant through the engine. The coolant flows around each cylinder and around the intake and exhaust ports, near the spark plug areas and in close proximity to the exhaust valve guides.

3 A thermostat controls engine coolant temperature. During warm up, the closed thermostat prevents coolant from circulating through the radiator. As the engine nears normal operating temperature, the thermostat opens and allows hot coolant to travel through the radiator, where it's cooled before returning to the engine.

HEATING SYSTEM

4 The heating system consists of a blower fan and heater core located in a housing under the dash, the hoses connecting the heater core to the engine cooling system and the heater/air conditioning control head on the dashboard. Hot engine coolant is circulated through the heater core. When the heater mode is activated, a flap door in the housing opens to expose the heater core to the passenger compartment through air ducts. A fan switch on the control head activates the blower motor, which forces air through the core, heating the air.

AIR CONDITIONING SYSTEM

5 The air conditioning system consists of a condenser mounted in front of the radiator, an evaporator mounted adjacent to the heater core, a compressor mounted on the engine, a receiver-drier or accumulator and the plumbing connecting all of the above components.

6 A blower fan forces the warmer air of the passenger compartment through the evaporator core (sort of a radiator-in-reverse), transferring the heat from the air to the refrigerant. The liquid refrigerant boils off into low pressure vapor, taking the heat with it when it leaves the evaporator.

2 Troubleshooting

COOLANT LEAKS

1 A coolant leak can develop anywhere in the cooling system, but the most common causes are:

  a) *A loose or weak hose clamp*
  b) *A defective hose*
  c) *A faulty pressure cap*
  d) *A damaged radiator*
  e) *A bad heater core*
  f) *A faulty water pump*
  g) *A leaking gasket at any joint that carries coolant*

2 Coolant leaks aren't always easy to find. Sometimes they can only be detected when the cooling system is under pressure. Here's where a cooling system pressure tester comes in handy. After the engine has cooled completely, the tester is attached in place of the pressure cap, then pumped up to the pressure value equal to that of the pressure cap rating **(see illustration)**. Now, leaks that only exist when the engine is fully warmed up will become apparent. The tester can be left connected to locate a nagging slow leak.

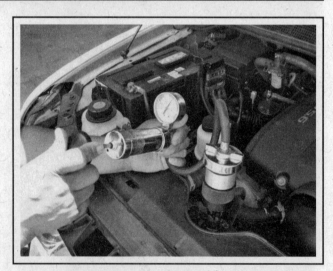

2.2 The cooling system pressure tester is connected in place of the pressure cap, then pumped up to pressurize the system

2.5a The combustion leak detector consists of a bulb, syringe and test fluid

2.5b Place the tester over the cooling system filler neck and use the bulb to draw a sample into the tester

COOLANT LEVEL DROPS, BUT NO EXTERNAL LEAKS

3 If you find it necessary to keep adding coolant, but there are no external leaks, the probable causes include:

   a) *A blown head gasket*
   b) *A leaking intake manifold gasket (only on engines that have coolant passages in the manifold)*
   c) *A cracked cylinder head or cylinder block*

4 Any of the above problems will also usually result in contamination of the engine oil, which will cause it to take on a milkshake-like appearance. A bad head gasket or cracked head or block can also result in engine oil contaminating the cooling system.

5 Combustion leak detectors (also known as block testers) are available at most auto parts stores. These work by detecting exhaust gases in the cooling system, which indicates a compression leak from a cylinder into the coolant. The tester consists of a large bulb-type syringe and bottle of test fluid **(see illustration)**. A measured amount of the fluid is added to the syringe. The syringe is placed over the cooling system filler neck and, with the engine running, the bulb is squeezed and a sample of the gases present in the cooling system are drawn up through the test fluid **(see illustration)**. If any combustion gases are present in the sample taken, the test fluid will change color.

6 If the test indicates combustion gas is present in the cooling system, you can be sure that the engine has a blown head gasket or a crack in the cylinder head or block, and will require disassembly to repair.

PRESSURE CAP

❉ WARNING:

Wait until the engine is completely cool before beginning this check.

7 The cooling system is sealed by a spring-loaded cap, which raises the boiling point of the coolant. If the cap's seal or spring are worn out, the coolant can boil and escape past the cap. With the engine completely cool, remove the cap and check the seal; if it's cracked, hardened or deteriorated in any way, replace it with a new one.

8 Even if the seal is good, the spring might not be; this can be checked with a cooling system pressure tester **(see illustration)**. If the cap can't hold a pressure within approximately 1-1/2 lbs of its rated pressure (which is marked on the cap), replace it with a new one.

9 The cap is also equipped with a vacuum relief spring. When the engine cools off, a vacuum is created in the cooling system. The vacuum relief spring allows air back into the system, which will equalize the pressure and prevent damage to the radiator (the radiator tanks could collapse if the vacuum is great enough). If, after turning the engine off and allowing it to cool down, you notice any of the cooling system hoses collapsing, replace the pressure cap with a new one.

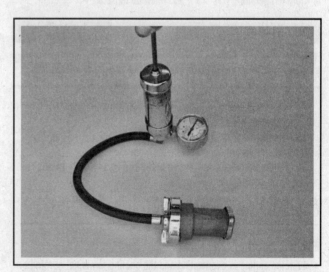

2.8 Checking the cooling system pressure cap with a cooling system pressure tester

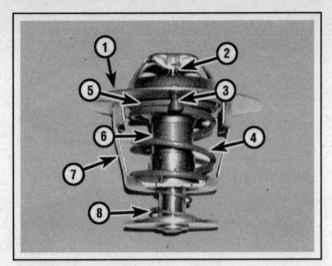

2.10 Typical thermostat:

1	Flange	5	Valve seat
2	Piston	6	Valve
3	Jiggle valve	7	Frame
4	Main coil spring	8	Secondary coil spring

THERMOSTAT

10 Before assuming the thermostat **(see illustration)** is responsible for a cooling system problem, check the coolant level (see Chapter 1), drivebelt tension (see Chapter 1) and temperature gauge (or light) operation.

11 If the engine takes a long time to warm up (as indicated by the temperature gauge or heater operation), the thermostat is probably stuck open. Replace the thermostat with a new one.

12 If the engine runs hot or overheats, a thorough test of the thermostat should be performed.

13 Definitive testing of the thermostat can only be made when it is removed from the vehicle. If the thermostat is stuck in the open position at room temperature, it is faulty and must be replaced.

✳ CAUTION:

Do not drive the vehicle without a thermostat. The computer may stay in open loop and emissions and fuel economy will suffer.

14 To test a thermostat, suspend the (closed) thermostat on a length of string or wire in a pot of cold water.

15 Heat the water on a stove while observing the thermostat. The thermostat should fully open before the water boils.

16 If the thermostat doesn't open and close as specified, or sticks in any position, replace it.

COOLING FAN

Electric cooling fan

17 If the engine is overheating and the cooling fan is not coming on when the engine temperature rises to an excessive level, unplug the fan motor electrical connector(s) and connect the motor directly to the battery with fused jumper wires. If the fan motor doesn't come on, replace the motor.

2.28 The water pump weep hole is generally located on the underside of the pump

18 If the radiator fan motor is okay, but it isn't coming on when the engine gets hot, the fan relay might be defective. A relay is used to control a circuit by turning it on and off in response to a control decision by the Powertrain Control Module (PCM). These control circuits are fairly complex, and checking them should be left to a qualified automotive technician. Sometimes, the control system can be fixed by simply identifying and replacing a bad relay.

19 Locate the fan relays in the engine compartment fuse/relay box.

20 Test the relay (see Chapter 12).

21 If the relay is okay, check all wiring and connections to the fan motor. Refer to the wiring diagrams in Chapter 13. If no obvious problems are found, the problem could be the Engine Coolant Temperature (ECT) sensor or the Powertrain Control Module (PCM). Have the cooling fan system and circuit diagnosed by a dealer service department or repair shop with the proper diagnostic equipment.

Belt-driven cooling fan

22 Disconnect the cable from the negative terminal of the battery and rock the fan back and forth by hand to check for excessive bearing play.

23 With the engine cold (and not running), turn the fan blades by hand. The fan should turn freely.

24 Visually inspect for substantial fluid leakage from the clutch assembly. If problems are noted, replace the clutch assembly.

25 With the engine completely warmed up, turn off the ignition switch and disconnect the negative battery cable from the battery. Turn the fan by hand. Some drag should be evident. If the fan turns easily, replace the fan clutch.

WATER PUMP

26 A failure in the water pump can cause serious engine damage due to overheating.

Drivebelt-driven water pump

27 There are two ways to check the operation of the water pump while it's installed on the engine. If the pump is found to be defective, it should be replaced with a new or rebuilt unit.

28 Water pumps are equipped with weep (or vent) holes **(see illustration)**. If a failure occurs in the pump seal, coolant will leak from the hole.

29 If the water pump shaft bearings fail, there may be a howling sound at the pump while it's running. Shaft wear can be felt with the drivebelt removed if the water pump pulley is rocked up and down (with the engine off). Don't mistake drivebelt slippage, which causes a squealing sound, for water pump bearing failure.

Timing chain or timing belt-driven water pump

30 Water pumps driven by the timing chain or timing belt are located underneath the timing chain or timing belt cover.

31 Checking the water pump is limited because of where it is located. However, some basic checks can be made before deciding to remove the water pump. If the pump is found to be defective, it should be replaced with a new or rebuilt unit.

32 One sign that the water pump may be failing is that the heater (climate control) may not work well. Warm the engine to normal operating temperature, confirm that the coolant level is correct, then run the heater and check for hot air coming from the ducts.

33 Check for noises coming from the water pump area. If the water pump impeller shaft or bearings are failing, there may be a howling sound at the pump while the engine is running.

➡ **Note: Be careful not to mistake drivebelt noise (squealing) for water pump bearing or shaft failure.**

34 It you suspect water pump failure due to noise, wear can be confirmed by feeling for play at the pump shaft. This can be done by rocking the drive sprocket on the pump shaft up and down. To do this you will need to remove the tension on the timing chain or belt as well as access the water pump.

All water pumps

35 In rare cases or on high-mileage vehicles, another sign of water pump failure may be the presence of coolant in the engine oil. This condition will adversely affect the engine in varying degrees.

➡ **Note: Finding coolant in the engine oil could indicate other serious issues besides a failed water pump, such as a blown head gasket or a cracked cylinder head or block.**

36 Even a pump that exhibits no outward signs of a problem, such as noise or leakage, can still be due for replacement. Removal for close examination is the only sure way to tell. Sometimes the fins on the back of the impeller can corrode to the point that cooling efficiency is diminished significantly.

HEATER SYSTEM

37 Little can go wrong with a heater. If the fan motor will run at all speeds, the electrical part of the system is okay. The three basic heater problems fall into the following general categories:

a) Not enough heat
b) Heat all the time
c) No heat

38 If there's not enough heat, the control valve or door is stuck in a partially open position, the coolant coming from the engine isn't hot enough, or the heater core is restricted. If the coolant isn't hot enough, the thermostat in the engine cooling system is stuck open, allowing coolant to pass through the engine so rapidly that it doesn't heat up quickly enough. If the vehicle is equipped with a temperature gauge instead of a warning light, watch to see if the engine temperature rises to the normal operating range after driving for a reasonable distance.

39 If there's heat all the time, the control valve or the door is stuck wide open.

40 If there's no heat, coolant is probably not reaching the heater core, or the heater core is plugged. The likely cause is a collapsed or plugged hose, core, or a frozen heater control valve. If the heater is the type that flows coolant all the time, the cause is a stuck door or a broken or kinked control cable.

AIR CONDITIONING SYSTEM

41 If the cool air output is inadequate:
Inspect the condenser coils and fins to make sure they're clear
a) *Check the compressor clutch for slippage.*
b) *Check the blower motor for proper operation.*
c) *Inspect the blower discharge passage for obstructions.*
d) *Check the system air intake filter for clogging.*

42 If the system provides intermittent cooling air:
a) *Check the circuit breaker, blower switch and blower motor for a malfunction.*
b) *Make sure the compressor clutch isn't slipping.*
c) *Inspect the plenum door to make sure it's operating properly.*
d) *Inspect the evaporator to make sure it isn't clogged.*
e) *If the unit is icing up, it may be caused by excessive moisture in the system.*

43 If the system provides no cooling air:
a) *Inspect the compressor drivebelt. Make sure it's not loose or broken.*
b) *Make sure the compressor clutch engages. If it doesn't, check for a blown fuse.*
c) *Inspect the wire harness for broken or disconnected wires.*
d) *If the compressor clutch doesn't engage, bridge the terminals of the A/C pressure switch(es) with a jumper wire; if the clutch now engages, and the system is properly charged, the pressure switch is bad.*
e) *Make sure the blower motor is not disconnected or burned out.*
f) *Make sure the compressor isn't partially or completely seized.*
g) *Inspect the refrigerant lines for leaks.*
h) *Check the components for leaks.*
i) *Inspect the receiver-drier/accumulator or expansion valve/tube for clogged screens.*

44 If the system is noisy:
a) *Look for loose panels in the passenger compartment.*
b) *Inspect the compressor drivebelt. It may be loose or worn.*
c) *Check the compressor mounting bolts. They should be tight.*
d) *Listen carefully to the compressor. It may be worn out.*
e) *Listen to the idler pulley and bearing and the clutch. Either may be defective.*
f) *The winding in the compressor clutch coil or solenoid may be defective.*
g) *The compressor oil level may be low.*
h) *The blower motor fan bushing or the motor itself may be worn out.*
i) *If there is an excessive charge in the system, you'll hear a rumbling noise in the high pressure line, a thumping noise in the compressor, or see bubbles or cloudiness in the sight glass.*
j) *If there's a low charge in the system, you might hear hissing in the evaporator case at the expansion valve, or see bubbles or cloudiness in the sight glass.*

3   Air conditioning and heating system - check and maintenance

AIR CONDITIONING SYSTEM

> ❄❄ **WARNING:**
>
> The air conditioning system is under high pressure. Do not loosen any hose fittings or remove any components until after the system has been discharged. Air conditioning refrigerant should be properly discharged into an EPA-approved recovery/recycling unit at a dealer service department or an automotive air conditioning repair facility. Always wear eye protection when disconnecting air conditioning system fittings.

> ❄❄ **CAUTION:**
>
> All models covered by this manual use environmentally friendly R-134a. This refrigerant (and its appropriate refrigerant oils) are not compatible with R-12 refrigerant system components and must never be mixed or the components will be damaged.

> ❄❄ **CAUTION:**
>
> When replacing entire components, additional refrigerant oil should be added equal to the amount that is removed with the component being replaced. Always read the can before adding any oil to the system, to make sure it is compatible with the R-134a system.

1   The following maintenance checks should be performed on a regular basis to ensure that the air conditioning continues to operate at peak efficiency.

a) *Inspect the condition of the compressor drivebelt. If it is worn or deteriorated, replace it (see Chapter 1).*

b) *Check the drivebelt tension (see Chapter 1).*

3.9 Insert a thermometer in the center vent, turn on the air conditioning system and wait for it to cool down; depending on the humidity, the output air should be 35 to 40 degrees cooler than the ambient air temperature

c) *Inspect the system hoses. Look for cracks, bubbles, hardening and deterioration. Inspect the hoses and all fittings for oil bubbles or seepage. If there is any evidence of wear, damage or leakage, replace the hose(s).*

d) *Inspect the condenser fins for leaves, bugs and any other foreign material that may have embedded itself in the fins. Use a fin comb or compressed air to remove debris from the condenser.*

e) *Make sure the system has the correct refrigerant charge.*

2   It's a good idea to operate the system for about ten minutes at least once a month. This is particularly important during the winter months because long term non-use can cause hardening, and subsequent failure, of the seals. Note that using the Defrost function operates the compressor.

3   If the air conditioning system is not working properly, proceed to Step 6 and perform the general checks outlined there.

4   Because of the complexity of the air conditioning system and the special equipment necessary to service it, in-depth troubleshooting and repairs beyond checking the refrigerant charge and the compressor clutch operation are not included in this manual. However, simple checks and component replacement procedures are provided in this Chapter.

5   The most common cause of poor cooling is simply a low system refrigerant charge. If a noticeable drop in system cooling ability occurs, one of the following quick checks will help you determine if the refrigerant level is low.

CHECKING THE REFRIGERANT CHARGE

6   Warm the engine up to normal operating temperature.

7   Place the air conditioning temperature selector at the coldest setting and put the blower at the highest setting.

8   After the system reaches operating temperature, feel the larger pipe exiting the evaporator at the firewall. The outlet pipe should be cold (the tubing that leads back to the compressor). If the evaporator outlet pipe is warm, the system probably needs a charge.

9   Insert a thermometer in the center air distribution duct **(see illustration)** while operating the air conditioning system at its maximum setting - the temperature of the output air should be 35 to 40 degrees F below the ambient air temperature (down to approximately 40 degrees F). If the ambient (outside) air temperature is very high, say 110 degrees F, the duct air temperature may be as high as 60 degrees F, but generally the air conditioning is 35 to 40 degrees F cooler than the ambient air.

10 Further inspection or testing of the system requires special tools and techniques and is beyond the scope of the home mechanic.

ADDING REFRIGERANT

> ❄❄ **CAUTION:**
>
> Make sure any refrigerant, refrigerant oil or replacement component you purchase is designated as compatible with R-134a systems.

✳ CAUTION:

Never add more than one can of refrigerant to the system. If more refrigerant than that is required, the system should be evacuated and leak tested.

11 Purchase an R-134a automotive charging kit at an auto parts store **(see illustration)**. A charging kit includes a can of refrigerant, a tap valve and a short section of hose that can be attached between the tap valve and the system low side service valve.

✳ WARNING:

Wear protective eye-wear when dealing with pressurized refrigerant cans.

12 Back off the valve handle on the charging kit and screw the kit onto the refrigerant can, making sure first that the O-ring or rubber seal inside the threaded portion of the kit is in place.
13 Remove the dust cap from the low-side charging port and attach the hose's quick-connect fitting to the port **(see illustrations).**

✳ WARNING:

DO NOT hook the charging kit hose to the system high side! The fittings on the charging kit are designed to fit only on the low side of the system.

14 Warm up the engine and turn On the air conditioning. Keep the charging kit hose away from the fan and other moving parts.

➡ **Note:** *The charging process requires the compressor to be running. If the clutch cycles off, you can put the air conditioning switch on High and leave the car doors open to keep the clutch on and compressor working. The compressor can be kept on during the charging by removing the connector from the pressure switch and bridging it with a paper clip or jumper wire during the procedure.*

15 Turn the valve handle on the kit until the stem pierces the can,

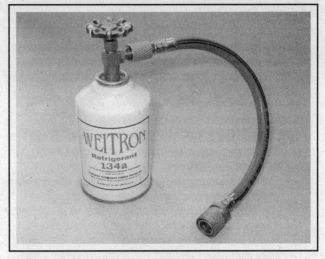

3.11 R-134a automotive air conditioning charging kit

then back the handle out to release the refrigerant. You should be able to hear the rush of gas. Keep the can upright at all times, but shake it occasionally. Allow stabilization time between each addition.

➡ **Note:** *The charging process will go faster if you wrap the can with a hot-water-soaked rag to keep the can from freezing up.*

16 If you have an accurate thermometer, you can place it in the center air conditioning duct inside the vehicle and keep track of the output air temperature. A charged system that is working properly should cool down to approximately 40 degrees F. If the ambient (outside) air temperature is very high, say 110 degrees F, the duct air temperature may be as high as 60 degrees F, but generally the air conditioning is 35 to 40 degrees F cooler than the ambient air.

17 When the can is empty, turn the valve handle to the closed position and release the connection from the low-side port. Reinstall the dust cap.

18 Remove the charging kit from the can and store the kit for future use with the piercing valve in the UP position, to prevent inadvertently piercing the can on the next use.

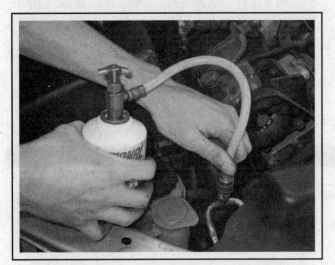

3.13a Location of the low-side charging port - 2009 and earlier models

3.13b Location of the low-side charging port - 2011 and later models

HEATING SYSTEMS

19 If the carpet under the heater core is damp, or if antifreeze vapor or steam is coming through the vents, the heater core is leaking. Remove it (see Section 12) and install a new unit (most radiator shops will not repair a leaking heater core).

20 If the air coming out of the heater vents isn't hot, the problem could stem from any of the following causes:

a) *The thermostat is stuck open, preventing the engine coolant from warming up enough to carry heat to the heater core. Replace the thermostat (see Section 4).*

b) *There is a blockage in the system, preventing the flow of coolant through the heater core. Feel both heater hoses at the firewall. They should be hot. If one of them is cold, there is an obstruction in one of the hoses or in the heater core, or the heater control valve is shut. Detach the hoses and back flush the heater core with a water hose. If the heater core is clear but circulation is impeded, remove the two hoses and flush them out with a water hose.*

c) *If flushing fails to remove the blockage from the heater core, the core must be replaced (see Section 12).*

ELIMINATING AIR CONDITIONING ODORS

21 Unpleasant odors that often develop in air conditioning systems are caused by the growth of a fungus, usually on the surface of the evaporator core. The warm, humid environment there is a perfect breeding ground for mildew to develop.

22 The evaporator core on most vehicles is difficult to access, and factory dealerships have a lengthy, expensive process for eliminating the fungus by opening up the evaporator case and using a powerful disinfectant and rinse on the core until the fungus is gone. You can service your own system at home, but it takes something much stronger than basic household germ-killers or deodorizers.

23 Aerosol disinfectants for automotive air conditioning systems are available in most auto parts stores, but remember when shopping for them that the most effective treatments are also the most expensive. The basic procedure for using these sprays is to start by running the system in the RECIRC mode for ten minutes with the blower on its highest speed. Use the highest heat mode to dry out the system and keep the compressor from engaging by disconnecting the wiring connector at the compressor.

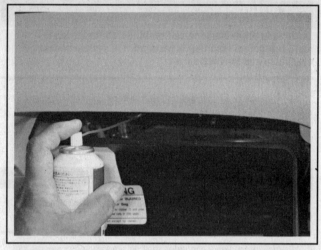

3.24 Insert the nozzle of the disinfectant can into the return-air intake behind the glove box

24 The disinfectant can usually comes with a long spray hose. Insert the nozzle into an intake port inside the cabin, and spray according to the manufacturer's recommendations **(see illustration)**. Try to cover the whole surface of the evaporator core, by aiming the spray up, down and sideways. Follow the manufacturer's recommendations for the length of spray and waiting time between applications.

25 Once the evaporator has been cleaned, the best way to prevent the mildew from coming back again is to make sure your evaporator housing drain tube is clear **(see illustration 3.1)**.

AUTOMATIC HEATING AND AIR CONDITIONING SYSTEMS

26 Some vehicles are equipped with an optional automatic climate control system. This system has its own computer that receives inputs from various sensors in the heating and air conditioning system. This computer, like the PCM, has self-diagnostic capabilities to help pinpoint problems or faults within the system. Vehicles equipped with automatic heating and air conditioning systems are very complex and considered beyond the scope of the home mechanic. Vehicles equipped with automatic heating and air conditioning systems should be taken to dealer service department or other qualified facility for repair.

4 Thermostat - replacement

❊❊ WARNING:

Do not attempt to remove the surge tank cap, coolant or thermostat until the engine has cooled completely.

REMOVAL

1 Drain the cooling system (see Chapter 1).

2 Follow the radiator hose to the thermostat housing cover and disconnect the hose **(see illustration)**.

3 Remove the thermostat housing cover mounting fasteners and remove the housing **(see illustration)**. Be prepared for some coolant to spill as the gasket seal is broken.

4 Remove the thermostat, noting the direction in which it was installed in the housing, and thoroughly clean the sealing surfaces.

5 Install a new gasket onto the thermostat. Make sure it is evenly fitted all the way around **(see illustration)**.

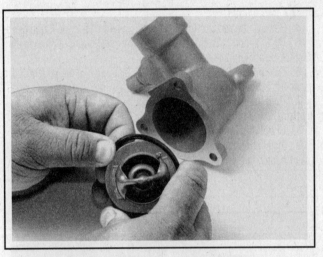

4.2 On 2011 and later 3.5L V6 models, both radiator hoses attach to the same area - the thermostat is in the housing at the end of the lower hose

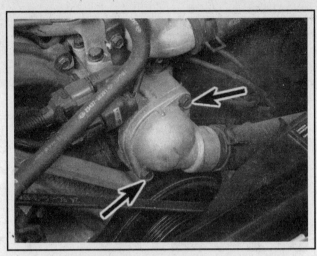

4.3 Thermostat housing bolts - 2006 and earlier V6 models (later models have three bolts)

4.5 The thermostat seal fits around the edge of the thermostat

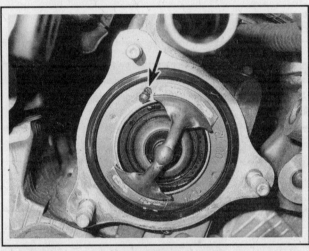

4.6 Note the position of the thermostat - the jiggle pin should be installed at the highest point

6   Install the thermostat and housing, positioning the jiggle pin at the highest point **(see illustration)**.

7   Tighten the housing cover fasteners to the torque listed in this Chapter's Specifications and reinstall the remaining components in the reverse order of removal.

8   Refill the cooling system (see Chapter 1). Run the engine and check for leaks and proper operation.

5   Engine cooling fans - check, removal and installation

CHECK

1   If the engine is overheating and the cooling fan is not coming on when the engine temperature rises to an excessive level, see Section 2. Check the fan relays in the underhood fuse/relay box (see Chapter 12).

2   If the relays are okay, check all wiring and connections to the fan motor. Refer to the wiring diagrams in Chapter 13. If no obvious problems are found, the problem could be the Engine Coolant Temperature (ECT) sensor or the Powertrain Control Module (PCM). Have the cooling fan system and circuit diagnosed by a dealer service department or a repair shop with proper diagnosic equipment.

5.6a Disconnect the wiring harnesses to the cooling fans and remove the wiring mounting bracket

5.6b Cooling fan mounting fastener locations

REMOVAL AND INSTALLATION

> ❊ **WARNING:**
>
> **Wait until the engine is completely cool before beginning this procedure.**

3   Disconnect the cable from the negative terminal of the battery (see Chapter 5). Drain the cooling system (see Chapter 1).

4   Remove the radiator upper cover fasteners and cover, if equipped.

5   On 3.3L and 3.8L V6 models, it may be necessary to remove the coolant expansion tank (see Section 6).

6   Disconnect the electrical connector, then remove the fan/shroud mounting fasteners **(see illustrations)**.

7   Hold the fan blades and remove the fan retaining nut **(see illustration)**.

8   Unbolt the fan motor from the shroud **(see illustration)**.

9   Installation is the reverse of removal. Refill the cooling system (see Chapter 1).

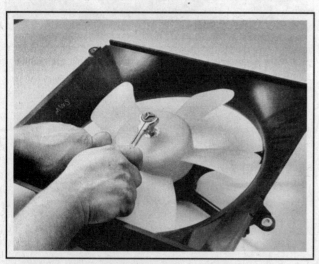

5.7 Remove the fan from the motor

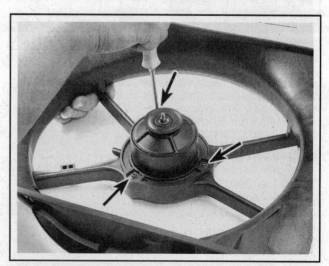

5.8 Remove the screws and separate the motor from the shroud

6 Coolant expansion tank - removal and installation

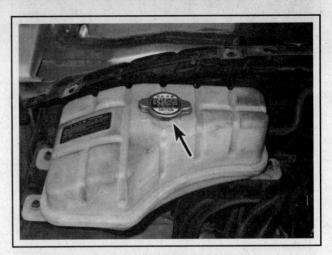

6.1 Coolant expansion tank - 2006 and earlier V6 model shown

1 On 3.3L and 3.8L V6 models, the coolant expansion tank is mounted to the cooling fan shroud; on four-cylinder and 3.5L V6 models, it's bolted to the right fenderwell **(see illustration)**.

2 Use a small clamp to pinch the hose connecting the tank to the radiator.

3 Place a drain pan under the tank and disconnect the hose.

4 Remove the mounting fasteners and lift out the tank.

5 Pour any remaining coolant into the container. Wash out and inspect the tank for cracks and chafing. Replace it if it's damaged.

6 Installation is the reverse of removal. Refill the cooling system (see Chapter 1).

7 Radiator - removal and installation

➡ **Note: Non-toxic coolant is available at local auto parts stores. Although the coolant is non-toxic when fresh, proper disposal of used coolant is still required.**

REMOVAL

1 Disconnect the cable from the negative battery terminal (see Chapter 5).

2 Remove the engine splash shield(s) from beneath the radiator and any engine covers, if equipped (see Chapter 2A or 2B).

3 On 2011 and later models, remove the air filter housing (see Chapter 4), the battery and battery tray (see Chapter 5).

4 Disconnect the wiring to both fan motor(s).

5 Drain the cooling system (see Chapter 1).

6 Detach the upper and lower radiator hoses from the radiator and the reservoir hose from the radiator filler neck. Mark the exact positions of the hoses and clamps with a dab of white paint or something similar.

7 On vehicles equipped with automatic transmission/transaxles, disconnect the transmission/transaxle oil cooler lines from the radiator. Place a drip pan to catch the fluid and cap the fittings to prevent leakage and contamination.

8 Remove the radiator upper cover fasteners and remove the cover.

9 Remove the A/C condenser mounting bolts and slightly separate

7.10a Radiator lower mounting bolt (left side) - 2009 and earlier models

7.10b Radiator upper mounting bolt (right side) - 2009 and earlier models

the condenser from the radiator.

10 Unbolt the radiator mounts and carefully remove the radiator **(see illustrations)**.

11 Remove the cooling fan shroud assembly from the radiator (see Section 5).

12 With the radiator removed, it can be inspected for leaks, damage and internal blockage. If in need of repairs, have a professional radiator shop perform the work, as special techniques are required.

13 Bugs and dirt can be cleaned from the radiator with compressed air and a soft brush. Don't bend the cooling fins as this is done.

❊❊ WARNING:

Wear eye protection.

INSTALLATION

14 Installation is the reverse of removal. Be sure the rubber mounts are correctly in place.

15 After installation, fill the cooling system with the proper mixture of antifreeze and water. Refer to Chapter 1 if necessary.

16 Start the engine and check for leaks. Allow the engine to reach normal operating temperature, indicated by the upper radiator hose becoming hot. Recheck the coolant level and add more if required.

17 Check the automatic transmission/transaxle fluid level and add fluid as needed (see Chapter 1).

8 Water pump - removal and installation

❊❊ WARNING:

Do not start this procedure until the engine is completely cool. Do not allow antifreeze to come in contact with your skin or painted surfaces of the vehicle. Rinse off spills immediately with plenty of water. Antifreeze is highly toxic if ingested. Never leave antifreeze lying around in an open container or in puddles on the floor; children and pets are attracted by its sweet smell and may drink it. Check with local authorities on disposing of used antifreeze. Many communities have collection centers, which will see that antifreeze is disposed of safely. Never dump used antifreeze on the ground or into drains.

➡ Note: Non-toxic coolant is available at local auto parts stores. Although the coolant is non-toxic when fresh, proper disposal of used coolant is still required.

1 Disconnect the cable from the negative battery terminal (see Chapter 5).

2 Remove the drivebelt (see Chapter 1) and the alternator (see Chapter 5).

3 Drain the engine coolant (see Chapter 1).

2006 AND EARLIER 3.5L V6 ENGINES

4 Remove the timing belt cover (see Chapter 2B).

5 Remove the fittings to the water pump and water outlet then remove the thermostat housing-to-engine bolts and remove the complete housing as a unit.

❊❊ CAUTION:

Every sprocket must maintain its position on the timing belt or severe engine damage can occur! If the marks are not legible later, it will be necessary to follow the timing belt installation procedure in Chapter 2B to ensure correct alignment.

➡ **Note: The belt can be secured to the pulleys with plastic zip-ties or a similar device to prevent them from coming off.**

6   Paint each sprocket with alignment marks onto the timing belt so that the belt can be installed in exactly the same position.

7   Remove the timing belt tensioner (see Chapter 2B).

❊ CAUTION:

DO NOT rotate the crankshaft with the timing belt removed!

8   Unscrew the water pump fasteners and remove the water pump. If necessary, tap the pump loose with a soft-face hammer.

9   Clean the water pump and block of any old gasket material or sealant, then clean with lacquer thinner.

10   Install a new gasket and install the water pump. Install the water pump bolts and nuts and tighten them to the torque listed in this Chapter's Specifications.

3.3L, 3.8L, AND 2011 AND LATER 3.5L V6 ENGINES

11   Remove the water pump pulley mounting bolts and remove the pulley.

12   Remove the water pump mounting bolts, then remove the pump and gaskets; it may be necessary to use a soft-face hammer to loosen the pump.

13   Install a new gasket and install the water pump. Install the water pump bolts and nuts and tighten them to the torque listed in this Chapter's Specifications.

2.4L FOUR-CYLINDER ENGINES

14   Raise the vehicle and support it securely on jackstands.

15   Remove the water pump pulley mounting bolts and remove the pulley from the pump.

16   Remove the water pump inlet tube mounting bolts.

17   Remove the water pump mounting bolts then remove the pump and inlet tube as an assembly. Once the assembly is removed, separate the inlet tube from the water pump.

18   Install new water pump gaskets to the cylinder block. If not already done, remove and discard the inlet pipe O-rings. Install new O-rings to the inlet pipe, coat the O-rings with a small amount of white grease, and insert the tube into the water pump.

19   Maneuver the pump assembly into position and insert the inlet tube into the housing at the same time the pump is placed into position. Install the bolts and tighten them to the torque listed in this Chapter's Specifications.

ALL MODELS

20   The remainder of installation is the reverse of removal.

21   On 2006 and earlier 3.5L V6 models, retract the timing belt tensioner (see Chapter 2B).

❊ CAUTION:

Verify that all sprocket marks are aligned with the marks you made on the timing belt before starting the engine!

22   Refill the cooling system (see Chapter 1), then run the engine and check for leaks and proper operation.

9   Coolant temperature indicator - check

❊ WARNING:

Wait until the engine is completely cool before beginning this procedure.

1   The coolant temperature indicator system consists of a temperature gauge on the dash and a sensor mounted on the engine. On all models, the Engine Coolant Temperature (ECT) sensor gives information to the Powertrain Control Module (PCM) that then controls the coolant temperature gauge in addition to controlling engine operation. Refer to Chapter 6 for more information on this sensor.

2   If an overheating indication has occurred, first check the coolant level in the system (see Chapter 1) and that the coolant mixture is correct (see Chapter 1). Also, refer to the *Troubleshooting* Section at the front of this manual before assuming that the temperature indicator is faulty.

3   Start the engine and warm it up for 10 minutes. If the temperature gauge has not moved from the C position, check the wiring harness connections going to the instrument cluster.

10   Blower motor - removal and installation

❊ WARNING:

The models covered by this manual are equipped with Supplemental Restraint Systems (SRS), more commonly known as airbags. Always disarm the airbag system before working in the vicinity of any airbag system component to avoid the possibility of accidental deployment of the airbag, which could cause personal injury (see Chapter 12).

1   Disconnect the cable from the negative terminal of the battery (see Chapter 5).

2   The blower unit is located under the dash and below the glove box.

3   Remove the lower trim panel fasteners and remove the panel.

4   Disconnect the electrical connector to the blower motor.

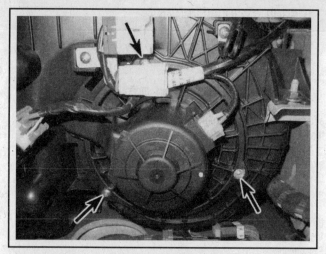

10.5 Blower motor mounting screw locations

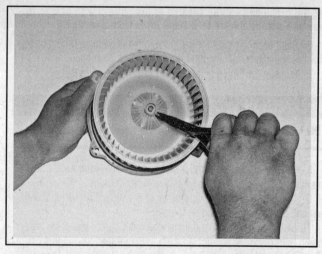

10.6 Use pliers to release and remove the clip, then lift the blower fan off the motor shaft

5   Remove the blower motor mounting screws and remove the blower motor **(see illustration)**.

6   If the motor is being replaced, transfer the fan to the new motor

prior to installation **(see illustration)**.

7   Installation is the reverse of removal. Check for proper operation.

11   Heater and air conditioning control assembly - removal and installation

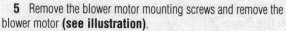

✳✳ WARNING:

The models covered by this manual are equipped with Supplemental Restraint Systems (SRS), more commonly known as airbags. Always disarm the airbag system before working in the vicinity of any airbag system component to avoid the possibility of accidental deployment of the airbag, which could cause personal injury (see Chapter 12).

1   Disconnect the cable from the negative battery terminal (see Chapter 5).

2   Remove the shift console trim panel (see Chapter 11).

3   Carefully pry out the switch panel from under the control assembly (see Chapter 12). Disconnect the electrical connectors and remove the panel.

4   On 2009 and earlier models, carefully pry the two side trim panels to disengage the clips, and remove the panel from each side of the control unit.

5   Remove the center trim panel fasteners and pry the panel away from the radio and control assembly (see Chapter 11).

6   Remove the control unit mounting screws, pull the assembly out slightly, and disconnect all electrical connectors for the control assembly **(see illustration)**.

7   Remove the screws (accessible from the rear of the panel) and remove the heater control from the panel.

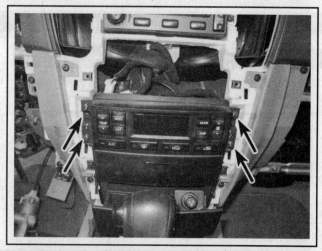

11.6 Remove the mounting screws, then disconnect the wiring harnesses from the heater controls and the lighter - there is no need to remove the knobs before prying the heater control unit out, but be careful to avoid scratching the plastic trim

8   Installation is the reverse of removal.

9   Run the engine and check for proper functioning of the heater and air conditioning.

12 Heater core - removal and installation

⁂ WARNING:

The models covered by this manual are equipped with Supplemental Restraint Systems (SRS), more commonly known as airbags. Always disarm the airbag system before working in the vicinity of any airbag system component to avoid the possibility of accidental deployment of the airbag, which could cause personal injury (see Chapter 12).

⁂ WARNING:

Do not allow antifreeze to come in contact with your skin or painted surfaces of the vehicle. Rinse off spills immediately with plenty of water. Antifreeze is highly toxic if ingested. Never leave antifreeze lying around in an open container or in puddles on the floor; children and pets are attracted by its sweet smell and may drink it. Check with local authorities on disposing of used antifreeze. Many communities have collection centers that will see that antifreeze is disposed of safely. Never dump used antifreeze on the ground or into drains.

⁂ WARNING:

Wait until the engine is completely cool before beginning this procedure.

➡ Note: Non-toxic coolant is available at local auto parts stores. Although the coolant is non-toxic when fresh, proper disposal of used coolant is still required.

➡ Note: Removal of the heater core is a difficult procedure for the home mechanic. There are numerous fasteners involved, some of which can be difficult to access. We recommend that you have considerable mechanical experience before performing a heater core replacement.

1 Take the vehicle to a dealer service department or automotive air conditioning shop, and have the air conditioning system discharged and the refrigerant recovered.
2 Disconnect the cable from the negative terminal of the battery (see Chapter 5).
3 Drain the cooling system (see Chapter 1).
4 The procedure for removal of the heater core involves removal of the heater/evaporator housing, which requires complete removal of the

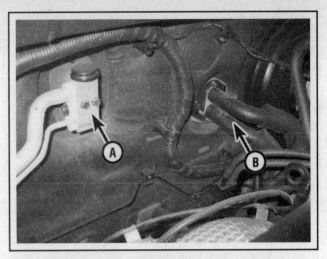

12.6 After having the air conditioning system evacuated, disconnect the refrigerant lines at the firewall (A); the heater hoses (B) must also be disconnected after draining the coolant

instrument panel and its support tube. Refer to Chapter 11 to remove the instrument panel assembly.
5 Unbolt and remove the cross-cowl support tube.
6 Disconnect both air conditioner lines at the firewall (see illustration). Seal the openings to prevent contamination.
7 Remove the instrument panel (see Chapter 11).
8 Disconnect the wiring from the blower motor.
9 Disconnect any air ducts that are attached directly to the unit.
10 Remove the mounting fasteners from the unit. Carefully pull the unit rearward until the tubes are free of the firewall openings.
11 Remove the screws and separate the halves of the heater housing, then remove the heater core from the housing.
12 Installation is the reverse of removal. Use new O-rings to seal the evaporator refrigerant connections. Make sure all of the cross-cowl support tube mounting fasteners are tightened securely before installing the instrument panel pad.
13 Refill the cooling system (see Chapter 1). Have the air conditioning system evacuated, charged and leak tested by the shop that discharged it.

13 Air conditioning receiver/drier - removal and installation

⁂ WARNING:

The air conditioning system is under high pressure. Do not loosen any hose fittings or remove any components until the system has been discharged. Air conditioning refrigerant must be properly discharged into an EPA-approved recovery/recycling unit by a dealer service department or an automotive air conditioning repair facility. Always wear eye protection when disconnecting air conditioning system fittings.

1 Have the air conditioning system discharged and the refrigerant recovered by an automotive air conditioning technician.
➡ Note: The receiver/drier is a part of the condenser and is not serviceable by itself.
2 Disconnect the cable from the negative battery terminal (see Chapter 5).
3 Remove the condenser (see Section 15).

4 Using an Allen wrench, detach the end plug **(see illustration)** and remove the desiccant from the condenser with a pair of needle-nose pliers.

5 Use new O-rings and a new bottom cap when installing the new desiccant, and tighten the end plug to the torque listed in this Chapter's Specifications. Lubricate the O-rings with R-134a compatible refrigerant oil.

6 Installation is the reverse of removal.

7 Have the system evacuated, charged and leak tested by the shop that discharged it.

13.4 After the system has been discharged, remove the Allen plug and pull the dessicant cartridge from the tube on the condenser

14 Air conditioning compressor - removal and installation

❉❉ WARNING:

The air conditioning system is under high pressure. Do not loosen any hose fittings or remove any components until the system has been discharged. Air conditioning refrigerant must be properly discharged into an EPA-approved recovery/recycling unit by a dealer service department or an automotive air conditioning repair facility. Always wear eye protection when disconnecting air conditioning system fittings.

❉❉ CAUTION:

The receiver/drier should be serviced whenever the compressor is replaced.

1 Have the air conditioning system discharged and the refrigerant recovered by an automotive air conditioning technician.

2 Disconnect the cable from the negative battery terminal (see Chapter 5).

3 Raise the vehicle and support it securely on jackstands.

4 Remove the drivebelt from the compressor (see Chapter 1).

5 Disconnect the electrical connector **(see illustration)**.

6 Disconnect the refrigerant lines at the compressor. Seal the ends to prevent contamination.

7 Unbolt the compressor and lower it from the vehicle.

8 If a new or rebuilt compressor is being installed, follow the directions,

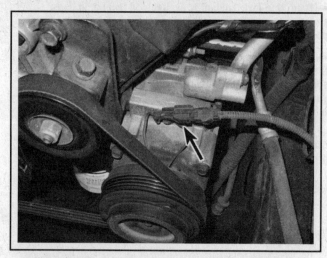

14.5 Compressor electrical connector location - 2009 and earlier models shown

which come with it regarding the proper level of oil prior to installation.

9 Installation is the reverse of removal. Replace any O-rings with new ones specifically made for the purpose and lubricate them with refrigerant oil.

10 Have the system evacuated, recharged and leak tested by the shop that discharged it.

15 Air conditioning condenser - removal and installation

REMOVAL

1   Have the air conditioning system discharged and the refrigerant recovered by an automotive air conditioning technician.

2   On 2009 and earlier models, remove the radiator and cooling fan assembly (see Section 7).

3   On 2011 and later models, remove the front bumper cover (see Chapter 11).

4   Disconnect the inlet and outlet fittings. Cap the open fittings immediately to keep moisture and dirt out of the system.

5   Remove the mounting fasteners and remove condenser from the radiator support.

INSTALLATION

6   Install the condenser, brackets and bolts, making sure the rubber cushions fit on the mounting points properly.

7   Reconnect the refrigerant lines, using new O-rings where needed.

8   The remainder of installation is the reverse of removal.

9   Have the system evacuated, charged and leak tested by the shop that discharged it.

Specifications

General

Expansion tank cap pressure rating	13 to 18 psi	93 to 122 kPa
Cooling system capacity	See Chapter 1	
Refrigerant type	R-134a	
Refrigerant capacity	Refer to HVAC specification tag	

Torque specifications	Ft-lbs (unless otherwise indicated)	Nm

➡ **Note: One foot-pound (ft-lb) of torque is equivalent to 12 inch-pounds (in-lbs) of torque. Torque values below approximately 15 foot-pounds are expressed in inch-pounds, because most foot-pound torque wrenches are not accurate at these smaller values.**

Receiver/drier plug	9 to 22 in-lbs	1 to 2.5
Thermostat housing bolts		
Four-cylinder engines	96 in-lbs	11
V6 engines	177 in-lbs	20
Water pump fasteners		
Four-cylinder engines	17	23
V6 engines		
2011 and later 3.5L		
Bolt A (G)	17	23
Bolt B (H)	96 in-lbs	11
Bolt C (I)	96 in-lbs	11
Bolt D (J)	96 in-lbs	11
Bolt E (K)	96 in-lbs	11
Bolt F (NEW bolt) (L)	19	26
All other V6 engines	16	21
Water pump pulley fasteners		
All except 2006 and earlier 3.5L V6 engines	84 in-lbs	9.5
2006 and earlier 3.5L V6 engines	Not available	

4

FUEL AND EXHAUST SYSTEMS

1 General Information

FUEL SYSTEM WARNINGS

1 *Gasoline is extremely flammable and repairing fuel system components can be dangerous. Consider your automotive repair knowledge and experience before attempting repairs which may be better suited for a professional mechanic.*

- *Don't smoke or allow open flames or bare light bulbs near the work area*
- *Don't work in a garage with a gas-type appliance (water heater, clothes dryer)*
- *Use fuel-resistant gloves. If any fuel spills on your skin, wash it off immediately with soap and water*
- *Clean up spills immediately*
- *Do not store fuel-soaked rags where they could ignite*
- *Prior to disconnecting any fuel line, you must relieve the fuel pressure (see Section 3)*
- *Wear safety glasses*
- *Have a proper fire extinguisher on hand*

FUEL SYSTEM

2 The fuel system consists of the fuel tank, electric fuel pump/fuel level sending unit (located in the fuel tank), fuel rail and fuel injectors. The fuel injection system is a multi-port system which uses timed impulses to inject the fuel directly into the intake port of each cylinder. The Powertrain Control Module (PCM) controls the injectors. The PCM monitors various engine parameters and delivers the exact amount of fuel required for efficient operation.

3 Fuel is circulated from the fuel pump to the fuel rail, through fuel lines running along the underside of the vehicle. Various sections of the fuel line are either rigid metal or nylon, or flexible fuel hose. The various sections of the fuel hose are connected either by quick-connect fittings or threaded metal fittings.

EXHAUST SYSTEM

4 The exhaust system consists of the exhaust manifold(s), catalytic converter(s), muffler(s), tailpipe and all connecting pipes, flanges and clamps. The catalytic converters are an emission control device added to the exhaust system to reduce pollutants.

2 Troubleshooting

FUEL PUMP

1 The fuel pump is located inside the fuel tank. Sit inside the vehicle with the windows closed, turn the ignition key to ON (not START) and listen for the sound of the fuel pump as it's briefly activated. You will only hear the sound for a second or two, but that sound tells you that the pump is working. Alternatively, have an assistant listen at the fuel filler cap.

2 If the pump does not come on, make sure that the inertia switch (if equipped - **see illustration)** has not opened the fuel pump circuit.

The inertia switch is a re-settable circuit breaker that automatically opens the fuel pump circuit in the event of an accident. The switch is located on the passenger's side of the engine compartment. If the inertia switch was not the problem, check the fuel pump fuse and relay **(see illustration)**. If the fuse and relay are okay, check the wiring back to the fuel pump. If the fuse, relay, wiring and inertia switch are okay, the fuel pump is probably defective. If the pump runs continuously with the ignition key in the ON position, the Powertrain Control Module (PCM) is probably defective. Have the PCM checked by a professional mechanic.

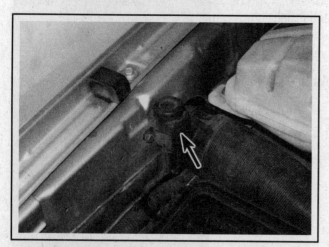

2.2a The fuel pump inertia switch is located on the passenger's side of the engine compartment. To reset it, push the button on top

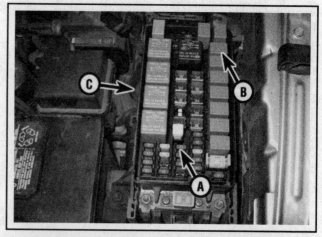

2.2b The fuel pump fuse (A) and fuel pump relay (B) are located in the engine compartment fuse box; (C) is the main relay (the locations of the fuses and relays may vary with model and year - refer to the guide on the underside of the fuse box cover and the guide in your owner's manual)

FUEL INJECTION SYSTEM

➡ **Note: The following procedure is based on the assumption that the fuel pump is working and the fuel pressure is adequate (see Section 4).**

3 Check all electrical connectors that are related to the system. Check the ground wire connections for tightness.

4 Verify that the battery is fully charged (see Chapter 1).

5 Inspect the air filter element (see Chapter 1).

6 Check all fuses related to the fuel system (see Chapter 12).

7 Check the air induction system between the throttle body and the intake manifold for air leaks. Also inspect the condition of all vacuum hoses connected to the intake manifold and to the throttle body.

8 Remove the air intake duct from the throttle body and look for dirt, carbon, varnish, or other residue in the throttle body, particularly around the throttle plate. If it's dirty, clean it with carb cleaner, a toothbrush and a clean shop towel.

9 With the engine running, place an automotive stethoscope against each injector, one at a time, and listen for a clicking sound that indicates operation **(see illustration)**.

※ **WARNING:**

Stay clear of the drivebelt and any rotating or hot components.

➡ **Note: On some models this check will not be possible, since the upper intake manifold is in the way.**

10 If you can hear the injectors operating, but the engine is misfiring, the electrical circuits are functioning correctly, but the injectors might be dirty or clogged. Try a commercial injector cleaning product

2.9 An automotive stethoscope is used to listen to the fuel injectors in operation

(available at auto parts stores). If cleaning the injectors doesn't help, replace the injectors.

11 If an injector is not operating (it makes no sound), disconnect the injector electrical connector and measure the resistance across the injector terminals with an ohmmeter. Compare this measurement to the other injectors. If the resistance of the non-operational injector is quite different from the other injectors, replace it.

12 If the injector is not operating, but the resistance reading is within the range of resistance of the other injectors, the PCM or the circuit between the PCM and the injector might be faulty.

---

3 Fuel pressure relief procedure

※ **WARNING:**

The fuel delivery system on 2012 and later 2.4L GDI models is made up of a low-pressure system and a high-pressure system. Once the pressure on the low-pressure side of the system has been relieved, wait at least two hours before loosening any fuel line fittings in the engine compartment.

2009 AND EARLIER MODELS

1 Remove the rear seat cushion (see Chapter 11).

2 Remove the fuel pump/sending unit floor service hole cover (see Section 7).

3 Disconnect the fuel pump electrical connector (see Section 7).

2011 AND LATER MODELS

4 Remove the fuel pump relay from the underhood fuse/relay box.

➡ **Note: When the fuel pump relay is removed, a trouble code will be set in the computer. Once the repairs are made, use a scan tool to erase the code.**

ALL MODELS

5 Attempt to start the engine; it should immediately stall. Crank the engine several more times to ensure the fuel system has been completely relieved. Disconnect the cable from the negative terminal of the battery before working on the fuel system.

6 It's a good idea to cover any fuel connection to be disassembled with rags to absorb the residual fuel that may leak out. Properly dispose of the rags.

4   Fuel pressure - check

➡ **Note: The following procedure assumes that the fuel pump is receiving voltage and runs.**

1   Disconnect the fuel supply line at the fuel rail, then use an adapter to connect the fuel pressure gauge between the fuel line and the fuel rail **(see illustrations)**.

➡ **Note: On 2006 and earlier 3.5L V6 models, access to the fuel line at the fuel rail is extremely difficult (it's at the back of the engine). The upper intake manifold will have to be removed to connect the fuel pressure gauge between the fuel feed line and the fuel rail (see illustration), then reinstalled to perform the pressure check. Alternatively, the pressure gauge can be installed between the fuel pump and the fuel feed line (see Section 7).**

RETURN-TYPE FUEL SYSTEMS (2006 AND EARLIER MODELS)

2   Turn off all accessories and turn the ignition switch key to ON. The fuel pump should run for about two seconds to pressurize the system. Note the reading on the gauge. After the pump stops running, the pressure should hold steady. After five minutes it should not drop below the minimum listed in this Chapter's Specifications.

3   Start the engine, allow it to warm up to its normal operating temperature, then measure the fuel pressure and compare your readings to the system pressure listed in this Chapter's Specifications.

 a) *If the pressure is high, disconnect the vacuum hose from the fuel pressure regulator and connect a vacuum gauge to the hose. Make sure there is 12 in-Hg or more vacuum present at the hose. If there isn't, check the hose for a restriction or leak.*

 b) *If there is adequate vacuum to the regulator but the pressure is high, check for a restricted fuel return hose or line. If the return hose and line are clear, replace the pressure regulator.*

 c) *If the pressure is low, pinch the fuel return hose. If the pressure goes up, replace the fuel pressure regulator. If the pressure does not increase, replace the fuel filter (see Section 8) and recheck the pressure. If it's still low, check the fuel supply hose and line for a restriction. If there is no restriction, replace the fuel pump (see Sections 7 and 8).*

 d) *Another possibility of low fuel pressure is a leaking fuel injector, but that would most likely set a trouble code and turn on the CHECK ENGINE light (because the fuel mixture would be too rich).*

4   To check the operation of the fuel pressure regulator, disconnect the vacuum hose from the regulator with the engine idling and watch the fuel pressure gauge - the fuel pressure should increase 3 to 10 psi as soon as the hose is disconnected. If it doesn't, check for vacuum at the hose. If vacuum is present, replace the fuel pressure regulator.

5   Turn the key off and observe the pressure for five minutes. If the pressure drops substantially, then there is either a leaking injector or a faulty check valve in the fuel pump.

6   Relieve the system fuel pressure (see Section 3), then disconnect the cable from the negative battery terminal (see Chapter 5). Remove the fuel pressure gauge and test hoses, then reconnect the fuel supply hose to the fuel rail. Reconnect the cable to the negative battery terminal, then start the engine and check for leaks.

RETURNLESS FUEL SYSTEMS (2007 AND LATER ENGINES)

7   Start the engine and let it warm up until it's idling at its normal operating temperature, then measure the fuel pressure and compare your reading to the fuel pressure listed in this Chapter's Specifications.

➡ **Note: At the time of writing, the fuel pressure regulator was not available separately. Check with your local auto parts store or dealer parts department to see if the pressure regulator can be purchased separately.**

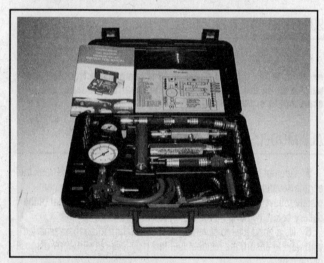

4.1a This fuel pressure testing kit contains all the necessary fittings and adapters, along with the fuel pressure gauge, to test most automotive fuel systems

4.1b Fuel line details (2006 and earlier 3.5L V6 models)

1 *Fuel feed line*	4 *Pressure regulator*
2 *Fuel return line*	*vacuum hose*
3 *Fuel pressure regulator*	

a) *If the indicated fuel pressure is low, inspect the fuel supply hose and line for an obstruction. If the hose and line are clear, replace the fuel filter, then recheck the fuel pressure. If the indicated fuel pressure is still low, replace the fuel pump/fuel pressure regulator, then recheck the fuel pressure.*

b) *If the indicated fuel pressure is high, replace the fuel pump/ fuel pressure regulator, then recheck the fuel pressure. If the fuel pressure is still high, have the fuel system diagnosed by a dealer service department or other qualified repair shop.*

8 After the test is complete, relieve the system fuel pressure (see Section 3), then disconnect the cable from the negative battery terminal (see Chapter 5).

9 Remove the fuel pressure gauge.

10 Reconnect the cable to the negative battery terminal.

11 Start the engine and check for fuel leaks.

5   Fuel lines and fittings - general information and disconnection

⚞ WARNING:

Gasoline is extremely flammable, so take extra precautions when you work on any part of the fuel system. See Fuel system warnings in Section 1.

1 Relieve the fuel pressure before servicing fuel lines or fittings (see Section 3), then disconnect the cable from the negative battery terminal (see Chapter 5) before proceeding.

2 The fuel supply line connects the fuel pump in the fuel tank to the fuel rail on the engine. The Evaporative Emission (EVAP) system lines connect the fuel tank to the EVAP canister and connect the canister to the intake manifold.

3 Whenever you're working under the vehicle, be sure to inspect all fuel and EVAP lines for leaks, kinks, dents and other damage. Always replace a damaged fuel or EVAP line immediately.

4 If you find signs of dirt in the lines during disassembly, disconnect all lines and blow them out with compressed air. Inspect the fuel strainer on the fuel pump pick-up unit for damage and deterioration.

STEEL TUBING

5 It is critical that the fuel lines be replaced with lines of equivalent type and specification.

6 Some steel fuel lines have threaded fittings. When loosening these fittings, hold the stationary fitting with a wrench while turning the tube nut.

PLASTIC TUBING

⚞ WARNING:

When removing or installing plastic fuel line tubing, be careful not to bend or twist it too much, which can damage it. Also, plastic fuel tubing is NOT heat resistant, so keep it away from excessive heat.

7 When replacing fuel system plastic tubing, use only original equipment replacement plastic tubing.

FLEXIBLE HOSES

8 When replacing fuel system flexible hoses, use only original equipment replacements.

9 Don't route fuel hoses (or metal lines) within four inches of the exhaust system or within ten inches of the catalytic converter. Make sure that no rubber hoses are installed directly against the vehicle, particularly in places where there is any vibration. If allowed to touch some vibrating part of the vehicle, a hose can easily become chafed and it might start leaking. A good rule of thumb is to maintain a minimum of 1/4-inch clearance around a hose (or metal line) to prevent contact with the vehicle underbody.

DISCONNECTING FUEL LINE FITTINGS

10 These are some of the fitting types you may encounter when working on the fuel system (**see illustrations**).

5.10a Two-tab type fitting; depress both tabs with your fingers, then pull the fuel line and the fitting apart

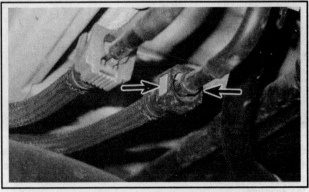

5.10b On this type of fitting, depress the two buttons on opposite sides of the fitting, then pull it off the fuel line

5.10c Threaded fuel line fitting; hold the stationary portion of the line or component (A) while loosening the tube nut (B) with a flare-nut wrench

5.10d Plastic collar-type fitting; rotate the outer part of the fitting

5.10e Metal collar quick-connect fitting; pull the end of the retainer off the fuel line and disengage the other end from the female side of the fitting...

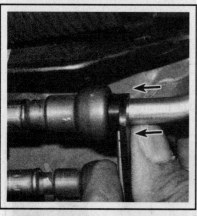

5.10f... insert a fuel line separator tool into the female side of the fitting, push it into the fitting and pull the fuel line off the pipe

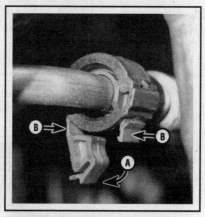

5.10g Some fittings are secured by lock tabs. Release the lock tab (A) and rotate it to the fully-opened position, squeeze the two smaller lock tabs (B)...

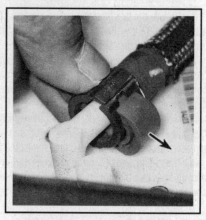

5.10h... then push the retainer out and pull the fuel line off the pipe

5.10i Spring-lock coupling; remove the safety cover, install a coupling release tool and close the tool around the coupling...

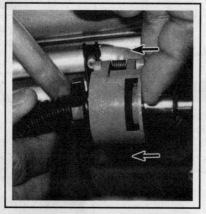

5.10j... push the tool into the fitting, then pull the two lines apart

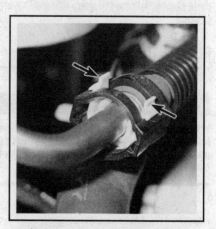

5.10k Hairpin clip type fitting: push the legs of the retainer clip together, then push the clip down all the way until it stops and pull the fuel line off the pipe

6 Exhaust system servicing - general information

1   The exhaust system consists of the exhaust manifolds, catalytic converter, muffler, tailpipe and all connecting pipes, flanges and clamps. The exhaust system is isolated from the vehicle body and from chassis components by a series of rubber hangers **(see illustration)**. Periodically inspect these hangers for cracks or other signs of deterioration, replacing them as necessary.

2   Conduct regular inspections of the exhaust system to keep it safe and quiet. Look for any damaged or bent parts, open seams, holes, loose connections, excessive corrosion or other defects which could allow exhaust fumes to enter the vehicle. Do not repair deteriorated exhaust system components; replace them with new parts.

3   If the exhaust system components are extremely corroded, or rusted together, a cutting torch is the most convenient tool for removal. Consult a properly-equipped repair shop. If a cutting torch is not available, you can use a hacksaw, or if you have compressed air, there are special pneumatic cutting chisels that can also be used. Wear safety goggles to protect your eyes from metal chips and wear work gloves to protect your hands.

4   Here are some simple guidelines to follow when repairing the exhaust system:

a) *Work from the back to the front when removing exhaust system components.*

b) *Apply penetrating oil to the exhaust system component fasteners to make them easier to remove.*

6.1 A typical exhaust system hanger. Inspect regularly and replace at the first sign of damage or deterioration

c) *Use new gaskets, hangers and clamps.*

d) *Apply anti-seize compound to the threads of all exhaust system fasteners during reassembly.*

e) *Be sure to allow sufficient clearance between newly installed parts and all points on the underbody to avoid overheating the floor pan and possibly damaging the interior carpet and insulation. Pay particularly close attention to the catalytic converter and heat shield.*

7 Fuel pump/fuel level sending unit - removal and installation

➡ **Note: On 2011 and later models, a second sub-fuel sender is used, located across from the fuel pump/fuel sending unit, and is removed and installed the same manner.**

1   Relieve the fuel system pressure (see Section 3) and remove the fuel tank cap.

2   Disconnect the cable from the negative battery terminal (see Chapter 5).

3   Remove the rear seat (see Chapter 11).

4   Pull back the carpet flap.

5   Remove the fuel pump/sending unit floor service hole cover **(see illustration)**.

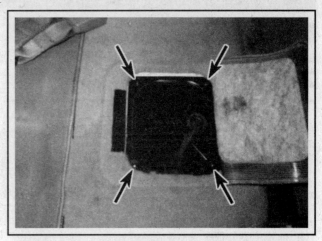

7.5 Remove the screws holding the access cover for the top of the fuel tank

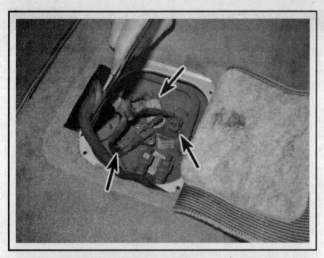

7.6 Disconnect the electrical connectors to the fuel pump module, then the fuel lines

6 Disconnect the fuel pump electrical connectors and the fuel lines from the top of the fuel pump unit **(see illustration)**.

7 On 2006 and earlier models, remove the retaining bolts from the fuel pump/fuel level sending unit mounting flange.

8 On 2007 and later models, use special service tool #09310-2B200, or use pliers engaged with the lock ring to rotate the lock ring counterclockwise and remove it.

9 Carefully lift the fuel pump/fuel level sending unit assembly from the fuel tank.

10 Inspect the fuel pump inlet strainer for contamination. If it's dirty, try cleaning the strainer with some clean solvent and an old toothbrush. If the strainer is too dirty to be cleaned while it's installed, remove it from the fuel pump/fuel level sending unit (see Section 8) and try cleaning it again. If you still can't clean it adequately, replace it.

11 Installation is the reverse of removal.

8 Fuel pump/fuel level sending unit - component replacement

1 Remove the fuel pump/fuel level sending unit assembly from the fuel tank (see Section 7).

2 Drain any residual gasoline from the fuel pump/fuel level sending unit, then place the fuel pump/fuel level sending unit on a clean workbench. Make sure that the work area is well ventilated, because there will be gasoline evaporating from the pump/sending unit for a while.

3 Check the strainer for clogging. If in doubt, replace it.

4 On 2005 and earlier models, the the fuel pump can be separated from the filter/sender assembly and replaced. On later models, the pump is not available individually.

5 Reassembly is the reverse of disassembly.

6 Install the fuel pump/fuel level sending unit in the fuel tank (see Section 7).

9 High-pressure fuel pump (2.4L GDI engines) - removal and installation

✳✳ WARNING:

Gasoline is extremely flammable, so take extra precautions when you work on any part of the fuel system. See Fuel system warnings in Section 1.

1 Relieve the fuel system pressure (see Section 3).

2 Disconnect the cable from the negative battery terminal (see Chapter 5).

3 Remove the air filter housing (see Section 11).

4 Disconnect the fuel pressure regulator valve electrical connector at the top of the valve cover.

5 Remove the ignition coil from cylinder number four (see Chapter 5).

6 Remove the canister purge control solenoid valve (see Chapter 6).

7 Disconnect the fuel supply line quick disconnect fitting.

8 Using special tool #09314-3Q100 or equivalent, remove the nut from the high pressure fuel pump and delivery pipe.

9 Remove the junction block, then remove the high pressure fuel pipe.

10 Unscrew the fuel pump mounting bolts alternately, 1/2-turn at a time, until they are removed.

✳✳ CAUTION:

If the bolts aren't removed evenly, the housing surface of the cylinder head may be broken because of the tension of the pump spring.

11 Remove the high-pressure fuel pump from the cylinder head.

12 Rotate the engine by hand until the lifter for the high pressure pump is at the lowest point.

13 Apply engine oil to the high-pressure pump O-ring and set the pump on the cylinder head.

14 Install new bolts and tighten them to the torque listed in this Chapter's Specifications.

15 The remainder of installation is the reverse of removal.

10 Fuel tank - removal and installation

※ WARNING:

Gasoline is extremely flammable, so take extra precautions when you work on any part of the fuel system. See Fuel system warnings in Section 1.

1 Relieve the fuel system pressure (see Section 3).
2 Disconnect the cable from the negative battery terminal (see Chapter 5).
3 Disconnect the hoses and electrical connectors from the fuel pump/fuel level sending unit (see Section 7). On 2011 and later models, also disconnect the wiring from the sub-fuel sending unit.
4 Remove the fuel filler hose and vent hose, and any EVAP hoses that would interfere with tank removal.

2009 AND EARLIER MODELS

5 Remove the nuts from the front of the tank and the bolts from the rear of the tank **(see illustration)** then lower the rear of the tank a few inches until the front of the tank can be lifted over the studs at the front.

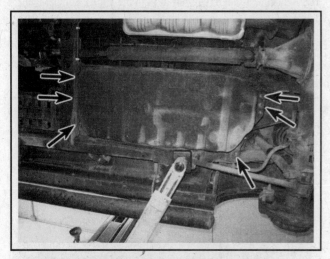

10.5 Fuel tank mounting fastener locations - 2009 and earlier models

Continue to lower the tank enough to access and disconnect any lines or electrical connectors from the top of the tank.

2011 AND LATER MODELS

6 Remove the exhaust system.
7 On 4WD models, remove the rear driveshaft (see Chapter 8).
8 Remove the nuts from the tank retaining straps **(see illustration)**.
9 Lower the tank to gain access to the top of it.
10 Disconnect any remaining hoses from the tank and EVAP canister (see Chapter 6).
11 It may be necessary to unbolt the parking brake cable brackets and move the cable out of the way.
12 Carefully lower the tank.

ALL MODELS

13 Installation is the reverse of removal. Tighten the fuel tank strap bolts securely.

10.8 Remove the nuts from the fuel tank retaining straps - 2011 and later models

11 Air filter housing - removal and installation

AIR INTAKE DUCT AND RESONATORS

1 Remove the engine cover (see Chapter 2A or 2B).
2 Disconnect the electrical connector at the sensor(s).

3 Loosen the hose clamps at both ends of the air intake duct and remove the duct.
4 Installation is the reverse of removal.

11.6 Air filter mounting nuts (2009 and earlier models)

AIR FILTER HOUSING

5 Remove the air filter housing cover and remove the filter element (see Chapter 1). On 2011 and later models, remove the air intake duct retainer and pull the duct out of the filter housing.

6 Remove the air filter housing mounting fasteners **(see illustration)**.

7 Remove the air filter housing.

8 Installation is the reverse of removal.

---

12 Accelerator cable (2006 and earlier models) - removal and installation

1 Remove the engine cover (see Chapter 2A or 2B).

2 Disengage the accelerator cable from the throttle lever **(see illustration)**.

3 Trace the accelerator cable back to the firewall, note the routing of the cable and detach any cable clips or guides.

4 Inside the vehicle, disengage the cable from the accelerator pedal **(see illustration)**.

5 Remove the bolts and detach the cable from the firewall. Pull the cable through the firewall from the engine compartment side.

6 Installation is the reverse of removal. Apply a dab of white grease to the nylon ball at the accelerator pedal end of the cable.

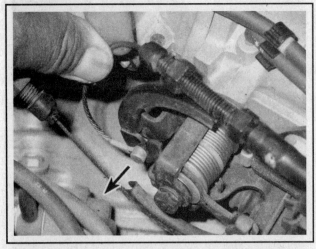

12.2 To disconnect the accelerator cable from the throttle cam, align the cable with the slot in the side of the cam, then slide the cable end plug out of the cam

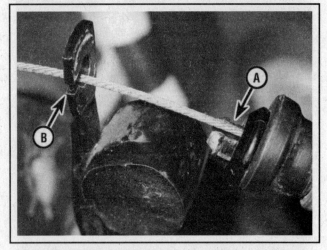

12.4 To disconnect the cable from the accelerator pedal, pull the cable end (A) out of the pedal, then guide the cable out the slot on the left (B)

---

13 Throttle body - removal and installation

❋❋ WARNING:

Wait until the engine is completely cool before beginning this procedure.

1 Disconnect the cable from the negative battery terminal (see Chapter 5).

2 Remove the air intake duct (see Section 11).

3 On 2006 and earlier models, disconnect the throttle and cruise control cables from the throttle body.

13.4 Disconnect the electrical connectors to the ISC motor (A) and TPS (B) on the throttle body

13.9 Pinch off the two coolant hoses prior to detaching them from the throttle body to avoid spillage

4 On 2006 and earlier models, disconnect the electrical connectors to the Throttle Position Sensor (TPS) and Idle Speed Control (ISC) motor **(see illustration)**.

5 On 2007 and later models, disconnect the wiring from the throttle control motor.

6 Disconnect the vacuum hoses from the throttle body.

7 Clamp off the coolant hoses to the throttle body to minimize coolant loss.

8 Remove the throttle body mounting fasteners and remove the throttle body.

9 Disconnect the coolant hoses from the throttle body **(see illustration)**.

10 Remove and discard the old throttle body gasket. Clean the gasket mating surfaces.

11 Installation is the reverse of removal. Use a new gasket and tighten the throttle body mounting nuts to the torque listed in this Chapter's Specifications. Check the coolant level, adding as necessary (see Chapter 1).

14 Fuel rail and injectors - removal and installation

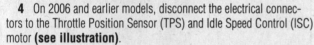

✳✳ WARNING:

Gasoline is extremely flammable, so take extra precautions when you work on any part of the fuel system. See Fuel system warnings in Section 1.

➥ Note: We recommend replacing all injector O-rings even when only one injector O-ring or seal is leaking. On most fuel rails, you have to remove the entire assembly anyway, so replace all of the O-rings/seals at one time to avoid having to remove the fuel rail later to replace another O-ring and/or seal.

1 Relieve the fuel pressure (see Section 3).

2 Disconnect the cable from the negative battery terminal (see Chapter 5). Remove the engine cover, if equipped.

3 Remove the air intake duct and air filter housing (see Section 11).

4 On V6 models, remove the upper intake manifold (see Chapter 2B).

5 On 2012 and later 2.4L four-cylinder GDI models, remove the intake manifold (see Chapter 2A).

6 On 2012 and later 2.4L four-cylinder GDI models, unscrew the tube nut and disconnect the high pressure fuel pipe from the fuel rail.

7 On V6 models, detach the fuel line from the fuel rail. On 2006 and earlier 3.5L V6 models, also detach the fuel return line from the fuel pressure regulator **(see illustration 4.1b)**.

8 Disconnect the electrical connectors from the fuel injectors **(see illustration)** and set the injector harness aside. On 2.4L GDI models, also disconnect the electrical connector from the fuel rail pressure sensor.

14.8 On 2.4L four-cylinder MPI models, disconnect the electrical connectors to the injectors (A), then disconnect the harness retainers (B) and move the harness

14.9 Fuel rail mounting bolts (2006 and earlier V6 models shown)

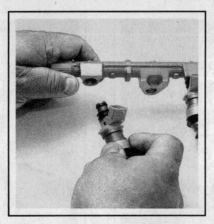

14.10 To remove each fuel injector from the fuel rail, simultaneously twist and pull it out of the fuel rail

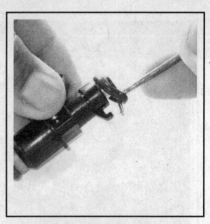

14.11 If you plan to reinstall the original injectors, remove and discard the old O-rings and grommets and replace them with new ones

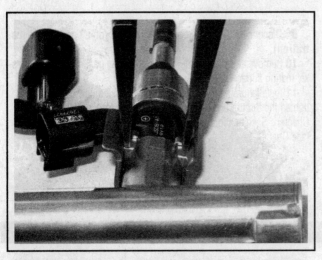

14.13 Use pliers to open up the retaining clip, then remove it

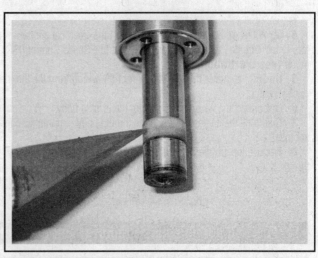

14.14 To remove the Teflon sealing ring, cut it off with a hobby knife (be careful not to scratch the injector groove)

9 Remove the fuel rail mounting bolts **(see illustration)**. On 2.4L GDI models, discard the bolts; new ones must be used on installation.

ALL EXCEPT 2.4L GDI MODELS

10 Remove the retaining clips (on models so equipped), then remove the fuel injectors from the fuel rail **(see illustration)**.

11 If you intend to re-use the same injectors, replace the washer seals (if equipped), grommets and O-rings **(see illustration)**.

12 Installation is the reverse of removal. Use new injector O-rings and tighten the fuel rail mounting bolts to the torque listed in this Chapter's Specifications.

2.4L GDI MODELS

13 Remove each fuel injector retaining clip with a pair of needle-nose pliers **(see illustration)** then remove the injector from its bore in the fuel rail. Remove and discard the upper injector O-rings. Repeat this procedure for each injector.

➡ **Note: Even if you only removed the fuel rail assembly to replace a single injector or a leaking O-ring, replace all of the fuel injector retaining clips, O-rings and Teflon sealing rings.**

14 Remove the old combustion chamber Teflon sealing ring and the upper O-ring and support ring from each injector **(see illustration)**.

✳ **CAUTION:**

Be extremely careful not to damage the groove for the seal or the rib in the floor of the groove. If you damage the groove or the rib, you must replace the injector.

15 Before installing the new Teflon seal on each injector, thoroughly clean the groove for the seal and the injector shaft. Remove all combustion residue and varnish with a clean shop rag.

Teflon seal installation using the special tools

16 The manufacturer recommends that you use the tools included in the special injector tool set described above to install the Teflon lower seals on the injectors: Install the special seal assembly cone on the

14.19 Slide the new Teflon seal onto the end of a socket that's the same diameter as the end of the fuel injector . . .

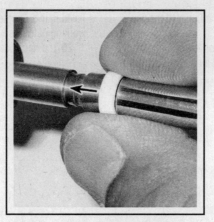

14.20 . . . align the socket with the end of the injector and slide the seal onto the injector and into its mounting groove

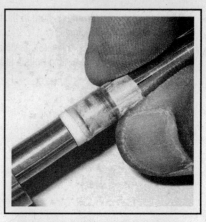

14.21a Use the socket to push a short section of plastic tubing onto the end of the injector and over the new seal . . .

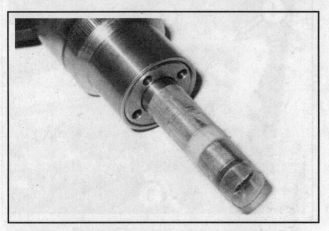

14.21b . . . then leave the plastic tubing in place for several hours to compress the new seal

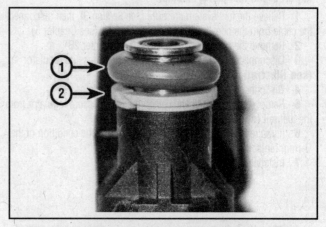

14.22 Note that the upper O-ring (1) is installed above the support ring (2)

injector, install the special sleeve on the injector and use the sleeve to push on the assembly cone, which pushes the Teflon seal into place on its groove. Do NOT use any lubricants to do so.

17 Pushing the Teflon seal into place in its groove expands it slightly. There are sizing sleeves in the special tool set with different inside diameters. Using a clockwise rotating motion of about 180 degrees, install the slightly larger sleeve onto the injector and over the Teflon seal until the sleeve hits its stop, then carefully turn the sleeve counterclockwise as you pull it off the injector. Use the slightly smaller sizing sleeve the same way, followed by the smallest sizing ring (if there are three sizing sleeves). The seal is now sized. Repeat this step for each injector.

➡ Note: Some kits only have one sizing sleeve, but with a different diameter on each end. In this case, start with the flanged-end of the tool (it is the larger diameter side), followed by the non-flanged side.

Teflon seal installation without special tools

18 If you don't have the special injector tool set, the Teflon seal can be installed using this method: First, find a socket that is equal or very close in diameter to the diameter of the end of the fuel injector.

19 Work the new Teflon seal onto the end of the socket (see illustration).

20 Place the socket against the end of the injector (see illustration) and slide the seal from the socket onto the injector. Do NOT use any lubricants to do so. Continue pushing the seal onto the injector until it seats into its mounting groove.

21 Because the inside diameter of the seal has to be stretched open to fit over the bore of the socket and the injector, its outside diameter is now slightly too large - it is no longer flush with the surface of the injector. It must be shrunk it back to its original size. To do so, push a piece of plastic tubing with an interference fit onto the end of the socket; a plastic straw that fits tightly on the injector will work. After pushing the plastic tubing onto the socket about an inch, snip off the rest of the tubing, then use the socket to push the tubing onto the end of the injector (see illustration) and slide it onto the injector until it completely covers the new seal (see illustration). Leave the tubing on for a few hours, then remove it. The seal should now be shrunk back its original outside diameter, or close to it.

Injector and fuel rail installation

22 Lubricate the new upper O-ring with clean engine oil and install it on the injector. Do NOT oil the new Teflon seal. Note that the O-ring is installed above the support ring (see illustration).

23 Thoroughly clean the injector bores with a small round nylon brush.

24 Insert each injector into its bore in the fuel rail. Install the new retaining clips on the injectors.

25 Install the injectors and fuel rail assembly on the cylinder head. Tighten the *new* fuel rail mounting bolts a little at a time, to the torque listed in this Chapter's Specifications, starting with the center bolt and working outwards.

26 The remainder of installation is the reverse of removal.

15 Fuel pressure regulator (2006 and earlier models) - replacement

➡ **Note: On 2007 and later models, the fuel pressure regulator is part of the fuel pump module.**

1 Relieve the fuel system pressure (see Section 3), then disconnect the cable from the negative terminal of the battery (see Chapter 5).

2 Remove the upper intake manifold (see Chapter 2B).

3 Disconnect the vacuum hose from the fuel pressure regulator **(see illustration)**.

4 Disconnect the fuel return line from the regulator.

5 Remove the two bolts and detach the fuel pressure regulator from the fuel rail **(see illustration 15.3)**.

6 If you're installing the same regulator, check the condition of the O-ring, replacing it if necessary.

7 Installation is the reverse of removal.

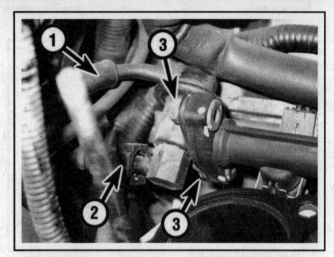

15.3 The fuel pressure regulator is located at the rear end of the left fuel rail

1 *Vacuum hose*
2 *Fuel return line*
3 *Pressure regulator mounting bolts*

Specifications

General

Fuel system pressure (at idle)		
2.4L MPI engines	46.9 to 52.6 psi	324 to 363 kPa
2.4L GDI engines		
Low pressure side	69.6 to 75.4 psi	480 to 520 kPa
High pressure side	725.2 to 1740.5 psi	5.0 to 12.0 mPa
3.5L engine		
2006 and earlier		
Vacuum hose connected to pressure regulator	38 psi	262 kPa
Vacuum hose disconnected from pressure regulator	47 psi	324 kPa
2011 and later	55 psi	379 kPa
3.3L and 3.8L engines	54.3 to 55.8 psi	375 to 385 kPa
Fuel injector resistance (approximate)	13 to 16 ohms	

Torque specifications	Ft-lbs (unless otherwise indicated)	Nm

➡ **Note: One foot-pound (ft-lb) of torque is equivalent to 12 inch-pounds (in-lbs) of torque. Torque values below approximately 15 foot-pounds are expressed in inch-pounds, because most foot-pound torque wrenches are not accurate at these smaller values.**

Fuel rail mounting bolts or nuts		
2.4L MPI four cylinder models	70 to 86 in-lbs	8 to 9.5
2.4L GDI four-cylinder models	14 to 17	19 to 23
V6 models	78 to 104 in-lbs	9 to 11.5
Throttle body mounting bolts/nuts	15 to 18	20 to 24
High pressure fuel pump bolts (2.4L GDI engines)	113 to 131 in-lbs	12.5 to 14.5
High pressure fuel pipe nut (2.4L GDI engines)	20 to 24	27 to 32
High pressure fuel pipe junction block bolt (2.4L GDI engines)	70 to 104 in-lbs	8 to 11.58

Notes

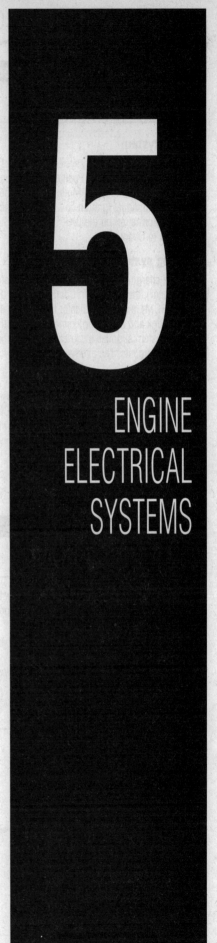

Section

5

ENGINE
ELECTRICAL
SYSTEMS

1 General information and precautions

GENERAL INFORMATION

Ignition system

1 The electronic ignition system consists of the Crankshaft Position (CKP) sensor, the Camshaft Position (CMP) sensor, the Knock Sensor (KS), the Powertrain Control Module (PCM), the ignition switch, the battery, the individual ignition coils or a coil pack, and the spark plugs. For more information on the CKP, CMP and KS sensors, as well as the PCM, refer to Chapter 6.

Charging system

2 The charging system includes the alternator (with an integral voltage regulator), the Powertrain Control Module (PCM), the Body Control Module (BCM), a charge indicator light on the dash, the battery, a fuse or fusible link and the wiring connecting all of these components. The charging system supplies electrical power for the ignition system, the lights, the radio, etc. The alternator is driven by a drivebelt.

Starting system

3 The starting system consists of the battery, the ignition switch, the starter relay, the Powertrain Control Module (PCM), the Body Control Module (BCM), the Transmission Range (TR) switch, the starter motor and solenoid assembly, and the wiring connecting all of the components.

PRECAUTIONS

4 Always observe the following precautions when working on the electrical system:

a) *Be extremely careful when servicing engine electrical components. They are easily damaged if checked, connected or handled improperly.*
b) *Never leave the ignition switched on for long periods of time when the engine is not running.*
c) *Never disconnect the battery cables while the engine is running.*
d) *Maintain correct polarity when connecting battery cables from another vehicle during jump starting - see "Booster battery (jump) starting" (at the beginning of this manual).*
e) *Always disconnect the cable from the negative battery terminal before working on the electrical system, but read the battery disconnection procedure first (see Chapter 5).*

5 It's also a good idea to review the safety-related information regarding the engine electrical systems located in "Safety first!" (at the beginning of this manual) before beginning any operation included in this Chapter.

2 Troubleshooting

IGNITION SYSTEM

1 If a malfunction occurs in the ignition system, do not immediately assume that any particular part is causing the problem. First, check the following items:

a) *Make sure that the cable clamps at the battery terminals are clean and tight.*
b) *Test the condition of the battery (see Steps 21 through 24). If it doesn't pass all the tests, replace it.*
c) *Check the ignition coil or coil pack connections.*
d) *Check any relevant fuses in the engine compartment fuse and relay box (see Chapter 12). If they're burned, determine the cause and repair the circuit.*

Check

> **⁂ WARNING:**
>
> **Because of the high voltage generated by the ignition system, use extreme care when performing a procedure involving ignition components.**

➡ **Note: The ignition system components on these vehicles are difficult to diagnose. In the event of ignition system failure that you can't diagnose, have the vehicle tested at a dealer service department or other qualified auto repair facility.**

➡ **Note: You'll need a spark tester for the following test. Spark testers are available at most auto supply stores.**

2 If the engine turns over but won't start, verify that there is sufficient ignition voltage to fire the spark plugs as follows.

3 On models with a coil-over-plug type ignition system, remove a coil and install the tester between the boot at the lower end of the coil and the spark plug **(see illustration)**. On models with spark plug wires, disconnect a spark plug wire from a spark plug and install the tester between the spark plug wire boot and the spark plug.

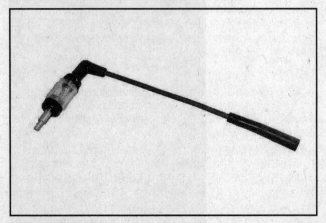

2.3 Spark tester

> ※ **CAUTION:**
>
> Do NOT crank the engine or allow it to run for more than five seconds; running the engine for more than five seconds may set a Diagnostic Trouble Code (DTC) for a cylinder misfire.

4 Crank the engine and note whether or not the tester flashes.

Models with a coil-over-plug type ignition system

5 If the tester flashes during cranking, the coil is delivering sufficient voltage to the spark plug to fire it. Repeat this test for each cylinder to verify that the other coils are OK.

6 If the tester doesn't flash, remove a coil from another cylinder and swap it for the one being tested. If the tester now flashes, you know that the original coil is bad. If the tester still doesn't flash, the PCM or wiring harness is probably defective. Have the PCM checked out by a dealer service department or other qualified repair shop (testing the PCM is beyond the scope of the do-it-yourselfer because it requires expensive special tools).

7 If the tester flashes during cranking but a misfire code (related to the cylinder being tested) has been stored, the spark plug could be fouled or defective.

Models with spark plug wires

8 If the tester flashes during cranking, sufficient voltage is reaching the spark plug to fire it.

9 Repeat this test on the remaining cylinders.

10 Proceed on this basis until you have verified that there's a good spark from each spark plug wire. If there is, then you have verified that the coils in the coil pack are functioning correctly and that the spark plug wires are OK.

11 If there is no spark from a spark plug wire, then either the coil is bad, the plug wire is bad or a connection at one end of the plug wire is loose. Assuming that you're using new plug wires or known good wires, then the coil is probably defective. Also inspect the coil pack electrical connector. Make sure that it's clean, tight and in good condition.

12 If all the coils are firing correctly, but the engine misfires, then one or more of the plugs might be fouled. Remove and check the spark plugs or install new ones (see Chapter 1).

13 No further testing of the ignition system is possible without special tools. If the problem persists, have the ignition system tested by a dealer service department or other qualified repair shop.

CHARGING SYSTEM

14 If a malfunction occurs in the charging system, do not automatically assume the alternator is causing the problem. First check the following items:

  a) *Check the drivebelt tension and condition (see Chapter 1). Replace it if it's worn or deteriorated.*
  b) *Make sure the alternator mounting bolts are tight.*
  c) *Inspect the alternator wiring harness and the connectors at the alternator and voltage regulator. They must be in good condition, tight and have no corrosion.*
  d) *Check the fusible link (if equipped) or main fuse in the underhood fuse/relay box. If it is burned, determine the cause, repair the circuit and replace the link or fuse (the vehicle will not start and/or the accessories will not work if the fusible link or main fuse is blown).*
  e) *Start the engine and check the alternator for abnormal noises (a shrieking or squealing sound indicates a bad bearing).*

2.21 To test the open circuit voltage of the battery, touch the black probe of the voltmeter to the negative terminal and the red probe to the positive terminal of the battery; a fully charged battery should be at least 12.6 volts

  f) *Check the battery. Make sure it's fully charged and in good condition (one bad cell in a battery can cause overcharging by the alternator).*
  g) *Disconnect the battery cables (negative first, then positive). Inspect the battery posts and the cable clamps for corrosion. Clean them thoroughly if necessary (see Chapter 1). Reconnect the cables (positive first, negative last).*

Alternator - check

15 Use a voltmeter to check the battery voltage with the engine off. It should be at least 12.6 volts **(see illustration 2.21)**.

16 Start the engine and check the battery voltage again. It should now be approximately 13.5 to 15 volts.

17 If the voltage reading is more or less than the specified charging voltage, the voltage regulator is probably defective, which will require replacement of the alternator (the voltage regulator is not replaceable separately). Remove the alternator and have it bench tested (most auto parts stores will do this for you).

18 The charging system (battery) light on the instrument cluster lights up when the ignition key is turned to ON, but it should go out when the engine starts.

19 If the charging system light stays on after the engine has been started, there is a problem with the charging system. Before replacing the alternator, check the battery condition, alternator belt tension and electrical cable connections.

20 If replacing the alternator doesn't restore voltage to the specified range, have the charging system tested by a dealer service department or other qualified repair shop.

Battery - check

➡ **Note: The battery's surface charge must be removed before accurate voltage measurements can be made. Turn on the high beams for ten seconds, then turn them off and let the vehicle stand for two minutes.**

21 Check the battery state of charge. Visually inspect the indicator eye on the top of the battery (if equipped with one); if the indicator eye is black in color, charge the battery (see Chapter 1). Next perform an open circuit voltage test using a digital voltmeter. With the engine and all accessories Off, touch the negative probe of the voltmeter to the negative terminal of the battery and the positive probe to the positive terminal of the battery **(see illustration)**. The battery voltage should

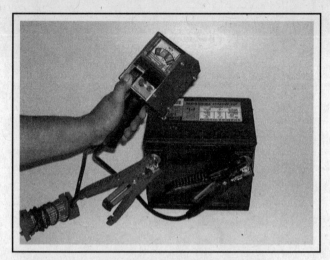

2.23 Connect a battery load tester to the battery and check the battery condition under load following the tool manufacturer's instructions

be 12.6 volts or slightly above. If the battery is less than the specified voltage, charge the battery before proceeding to the next test. Do not proceed with the battery load test unless the battery charge is correct.

22 Disconnect the negative battery cable, then the positive cable from the battery.

23 Perform a battery load test. An accurate check of the battery condition can only be performed with a load tester **(see illustration)**. This test evaluates the ability of the battery to operate the starter and other accessories during periods of high current draw. Connect the load tester to the battery terminals. Load test the battery according to the tool manufacturer's instructions. This tool increases the load demand (current draw) on the battery.

24 Maintain the load on the battery for 15 seconds and observe that the battery voltage does not drop below 9.6 volts. If the battery condition is weak or defective, the tool will indicate this condition immediately.

➡ **Note: Cold temperatures will cause the minimum voltage reading to drop slightly. Follow the chart given in the manufacturer's instructions to compensate for cold climates. Minimum load voltage for freezing temperatures (32 degrees F) should be approximately 9.1 volts.**

STARTING SYSTEM

The starter rotates, but the engine doesn't

25 Remove the starter (see Section 8). Check the overrunning clutch

and bench test the starter to make sure the drive mechanism extends fully for proper engagement with the flywheel ring gear. If it doesn't, replace the starter.

26 Check the flywheel ring gear for missing teeth and other damage. With the ignition turned off, rotate the flywheel so you can check the entire ring gear.

The starter is noisy

27 If the solenoid is making a chattering noise, first check the battery (see Steps 21 through 24). If the battery is okay, check the cables and connections.

28 If you hear a grinding, crashing metallic sound when you turn the key to Start, check for loose starter mounting bolts. If they're tight, remove the starter and inspect the teeth on the starter pinion gear and flywheel ring gear. Look for missing or damaged teeth.

29 If the starter sounds fine when you first turn the key to Start, but then stops rotating the engine and emits a zinging sound, the problem is probably a defective starter drive that's not staying engaged with the ring gear. Replace the starter.

The starter rotates slowly

30 Check the battery (see Steps 21 through 24).

31 If the battery is okay, verify all connections (at the battery, the starter solenoid and motor) are clean, corrosion-free and tight. Make sure the cables aren't frayed or damaged.

32 Check that the starter mounting bolts are tight so it grounds properly. Also check the pinion gear and flywheel ring gear for evidence of a mechanical bind (galling, deformed gear teeth or other damage).

The starter does not rotate at all

33 Check the battery (see Steps 21 through 24).

34 If the battery is okay, verify all connections (at the battery, the starter solenoid and motor) are clean, corrosion-free and tight. Make sure the cables aren't frayed or damaged.

35 Check all of the fuses in the underhood fuse/relay box.

36 Check that the starter mounting bolts are tight so it grounds properly.

37 Check for voltage at the starter solenoid "S" terminal when the ignition key is turned to the start position. If voltage is present, replace the starter/solenoid assembly. If no voltage is present, the problem could be the starter relay, the Transmission Range (TR) switch (see Chapter 7B) or clutch start switch (see Chapter 8), or with an electrical connector somewhere in the circuit (see the wiring diagrams at the end of Chapter 12). Also, on many modern vehicles, the Powertrain Control Module (PCM) and the Body Control Module (BCM) control the voltage signal to the starter solenoid; on such vehicles, a special scan tool is required for diagnosis.

3 Battery - disconnection

⁂ CAUTION:

Always disconnect the cable from the negative battery terminal FIRST and hook it up LAST or the battery may be shorted by the tool being used to loosen the cable clamps.

1 Some systems on the vehicle require battery power to be available at all times, either to maintain continuous operation (alarm system, power door locks, etc.), or to maintain control unit memory (radio station presets, Powertrain Control Module and other control units). When the battery is disconnected, the power that maintains these systems is cut. So, before you disconnect the battery, please note that on a vehicle with power door locks, it's a wise precaution to remove the key from the ignition and to keep it with you, so that it does not get locked inside if the power door locks should engage accidentally when the battery is reconnected!

⁂ WARNING:

Some memory savers deliver a considerable amount of current in order to keep vehicle systems operational after the main battery is disconnected. If you're using a memory saver, make sure that the circuit concerned is actually open before servicing it.

⁂ WARNING:

If you're going to work near any of the airbag system components, the battery MUST be disconnected and a memory saver must NOT be used. If a memory saver is used, power will be supplied to the airbag, which means that it could accidentally deploy and cause serious personal injury.

2 Devices known as memory-savers can be used to avoid some of these problems. Precise details vary according to the device used. The typical memory saver is plugged into the cigarette lighter and is connected to a spare battery. Then the vehicle battery can be disconnected from the electrical system. The memory saver will provide sufficient current to maintain audio unit security codes, PCM memory, etc. and will provide power to always hot circuits such as the clock and radio memory circuits.

3 To disconnect the battery for service procedures requiring power to be cut from the vehicle, loosen the cable end bolt and disconnect the cable from the negative battery terminal. Isolate the cable end to prevent it from coming into accidental contact with the battery terminal.

4 Battery - removal and installation

1 Disconnect the cable from the negative battery terminal first, then disconnect the cable from the positive battery terminal **(see illustration)**.

2 Remove the battery hold-down clamp.

3 Lift out the battery. Be careful - it's heavy.

➡ Note: Battery straps and handlers are available at most auto parts stores for reasonable prices. They make it easier to remove and carry the battery.

4 If you are replacing the battery, make sure you get one that's identical, with the same dimensions, amperage rating, cold cranking rating, etc. Remove the heat shield from the old battery and install it on the new battery.

5 Installation is the reverse of removal. Always connect the positive cable first and the negative cable last.

4.1 Battery details:

1 *Negative cable*
2 *Positive cable (under cover)*
3 *Hold-down bolt*

5   Battery cables - replacement

1   When removing the cables, always disconnect the cable from the negative battery terminal first and hook it up last, or you might accidentally short out the battery with the tool you're using to loosen the cable clamps. Even if you're only replacing the cable for the positive terminal, be sure to disconnect the negative cable from the battery first.

2   Disconnect the old cables from the battery, then trace each of them to their opposite ends and disconnect them. Note the routing of each cable before disconnecting it to ensure correct installation.

3   If you are replacing any of the old cables, take them with you when buying new cables. It is vitally important that you replace the cables with identical parts.

4   Clean the threads of the solenoid or ground connection with a wire brush to remove rust and corrosion. Apply a light coat of battery terminal corrosion inhibitor or petroleum jelly to the threads to prevent future corrosion.

5   Attach the cable to the solenoid or ground connection and tighten the mounting nut/bolt securely.

6   Before connecting a new cable to the battery, make sure that it reaches the battery post without having to be stretched.

7   Connect the cable to the positive battery terminal first, then connect the ground cable to the negative battery terminal.

6   Ignition coils - replacement

1   Disconnect the cable from the negative battery terminal (see Section 3).

2   Remove the engine cover (see Chapter 2A or 2B), if equipped.

3   Disconnect the electrical connector from the ignition coil, then remove the mounting fastener(s) **(see illustration)**.

➡ **Note: On 2006 and earlier 3.5L V6 engines, only three ignition coils are used; the ignition coils are mounted over cylinders 2, 4 and 6 with spark plug wires that feed to the other cylinders. The ignition coil on cylinder #2 is connected to cylinder #5, cylinder #4 is connected to cylinder #1 and cylinder #6 is connected to cylinder #3.**

4   On 2006 and earlier 3.5L V6 engines, disconnect the spark plug wire. Pull on the boot only - not on the wire.

5   On 2011 and later 3.5L V6 engines, to access the right hand or rear spark plugs, remove the upper intake manifold (see Chapter 2B).

6   Pull the coil straight up and out of the valve cover **(see illustration)**.

7   Installation is the reverse of removal.

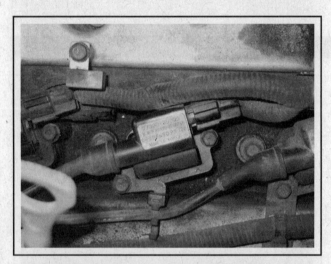

6.3 On 2006 and earlier 3.5L V6 engines, each ignition coil is secured by two bolts

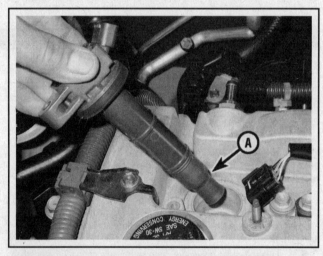

6.6 After removing the screw(s), pull the coil straight up and out. Make sure the boot (A) is in good condition

7   Alternator - removal and installation

REMOVAL

1   Disconnect the cable from the negative battery terminal (see Section 3).

2   Remove the drivebelt (see Chapter 1).

➡ **Note: Access is very limited on these models. It will be necessary to remove various components to gain access. These components vary from model to model.**

3   Disconnect the electrical connectors from the alternator **(see illustration)**.

4   Remove the mounting bolts and remove the alternator.

INSTALLATION

5 If you're replacing the alternator, take the old alternator with you when purchasing a replacement unit. Make sure that the new/rebuilt unit is identical to the old alternator. Look at the terminals - they should be the same in number, size and locations as the terminals on the old alternator. Finally, look at the identification markings - they will be stamped in the housing or printed on a tag or plaque affixed to the housing. Make sure that these numbers are the same on both alternators.

6 If the replacement alternator doesn't have a pulley installed, you might have to switch the pulley from the old unit to the replacement unit. When buying a new or rebuilt alternator, ask about the shop's policy regarding pulley swapping. Some shops will perform this service for free.

7 Installation is the reverse of removal. After the alternator is installed, check the charging voltage to verify that the alternator is operating correctly (see Section 2).

7.3 Alternator electrical connector locations - early V6 shown, other models similar

8 Starter motor - removal and installation

1 Disconnect the cable from the negative battery terminal (see Section 3).

2 Detach the electrical connectors from the starter/solenoid assembly.

3 On some V6 models it will be necessary to unbolt the front section of the exhaust system from the exhaust manifolds, disconnect the front exhaust system hanger and lower the exhaust pipes for access.

4 Remove the starter motor mounting bolts and remove the starter **(see illustration)**.

5 Installation is the reverse of removal.

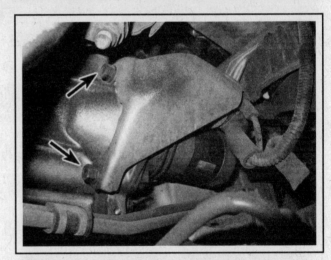

8.4 The starter is retained by two bolts - make sure the battery and the starter wiring are disconnected before removing it

Specifications

Charging system

Battery voltage	12.5 to 12.9 volts
Charging voltage	14.0 to 15.0 volts

Ignition system

Ignition coil resistance (approximate)

2.4L four-cylinder engine

Primary	0.52 to 0.72 ohms
Secondary	5.5 to 8.5 k-ohms

2006 and earlier 3.5L V6 engines

Primary	0.78 ohms
Secondary	10.4 to 15.6 k-ohms

All other V6 engines

Primary	0.52 to 0.72 ohms
Secondary	5.5 to 8.5 k-ohms

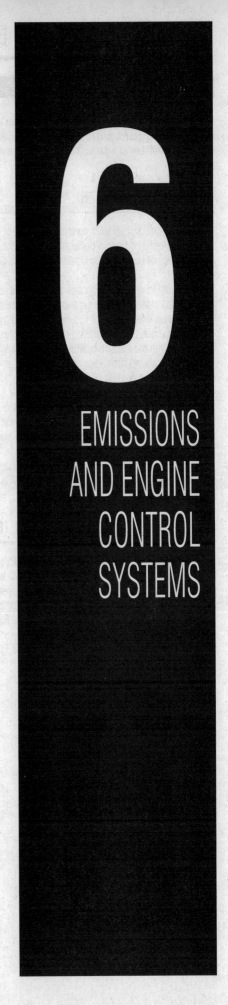

6

EMISSIONS AND ENGINE CONTROL SYSTEMS

Section

1 General Information

1 To prevent pollution of the atmosphere from incompletely burned and evaporating gases, and to maintain good driveability and fuel economy, a number of emission control systems are incorporated. They include the:

CATALYTIC CONVERTER

2 A catalytic converter is an emission control device in the exhaust system that reduces certain pollutants in the exhaust gas stream. There are two types of converters: oxidation converters and reduction converters.

3 Oxidation converters contain a monolithic substrate (a ceramic honeycomb) coated with the semi-precious metals platinum and palladium. An oxidation catalyst reduces unburned hydrocarbons (HC) and carbon monoxide (CO) by adding oxygen to the exhaust stream as it passes through the substrate, which, in the presence of high temperature and the catalyst materials, converts the HC and CO to water vapor (H_2O) and carbon dioxide (CO_2).

4 Reduction converters contain a monolithic substrate coated with platinum and rhodium. A reduction catalyst reduces oxides of nitrogen (NOx) by removing oxygen, which in the presence of high temperature and the catalyst material produces nitrogen (N) and carbon dioxide (CO_2).

5 Catalytic converters that combine both types of catalysts in one assembly are known as three-way catalysts (TWCs). A TWC can reduce all three pollutants.

EVAPORATIVE EMISSIONS CONTROL (EVAP) SYSTEM

6 The Evaporative Emissions Control (EVAP) system prevents fuel system vapors (which contain unburned hydrocarbons) from escaping into the atmosphere. On warm days, vapors trapped inside the fuel tank expand until the pressure reaches a certain threshold. Then the fuel vapors are routed from the fuel tank through the fuel vapor vent valve and the fuel vapor control valve to the EVAP canister, where they're stored temporarily until the next time the vehicle is operated. When the conditions are right (engine warmed up, vehicle up to speed, moderate or heavy load on the engine, etc.) the PCM opens the canister purge valve, which allows fuel vapors to be drawn from the canister into the intake manifold. Once in the intake manifold, the fuel vapors mix with incoming air before being drawn through the intake ports into the combustion chambers where they're burned up with the rest of the air/fuel mixture. The EVAP system is complex and virtually impossible to troubleshoot without the right tools and training.

POWERTRAIN CONTROL MODULE (PCM)

7 The Powertrain Control Module (PCM) is the brain of the engine management system. It also controls a wide variety of other vehicle systems. In order to program the new PCM, the dealer needs the vehicle as well as the new PCM. If you're planning to replace the PCM with a new one, there is no point in trying to do so at home because you won't be able to program it yourself.

POSITIVE CRANKCASE VENTILATION (PCV) SYSTEM

8 The Positive Crankcase Ventilation (PCV) system reduces hydrocarbon emissions by scavenging crankcase vapors, which are rich in unburned hydrocarbons. A PCV valve or orifice regulates the flow of gases into the intake manifold in proportion to the amount of intake vacuum available.

9 The PCV system generally consists of the fresh air inlet hose, the PCV valve or orifice and the crankcase ventilation hose (or PCV hose). The fresh air inlet hose connects the air intake duct to a pipe on the valve cover. The crankcase ventilation hose (or PCV hose) connects the PCV valve or orifice in the valve cover to the intake manifold.

INFORMATION SENSORS

10 Typical information sensors **(see illustrations)**.

1.10a Emissions and engine control system components (2.4L four-cylinder MPI engines)

1   Engine compartment fuse and relay box
2   Powertrain Control Module (PCM)
3   Multi-purpose check connector (20 pin)
4   Camshaft Position sensor (CMP) BANK 1 intake
5   Manifold Absolute Pressure sensor (MAP)/ Intake Air Temperature sensor (IAT)
6   Knock sensor (KS)

7   Variable Intake Solenoid (VIS) valve
8   Positive Crankcase Ventilation (PVC) valve
9   CVVT Oil control valve (OCV) BANK 1 intake
10 CVVT Oil control valve (OCV) BANK 1 exhaust
11 Heated Oxygen sensor (HO2S)

12 Camshaft Position sensor (CMP) BANK 1 exhaust
13 Engine Coolant Temperature (ECT) sensor
14 Crankshaft position sensor (CKP)
15 Accelerator Pedal Position sensor (APP)

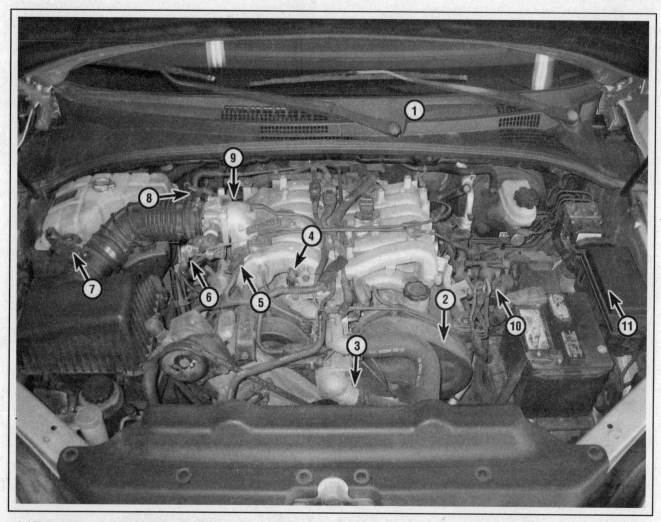

1.10b Emissions control and engine control components (2006 and earlier 3.5L engine)

1	Accelerator Pedal Position sensor (APP)	
2	Camshaft Position sensor (CMP)	
3	Crankshaft Position sensor (CKP)	
4	Engine Coolant Temperature (ECT) sensor	

5	Manifold Absolute Pressure (MAP) sensor
6	Idle Speed Control motor (ICS)
7	Air Flow sensor (AFS) & Air Temperature sensor (ATS)

8	Throttle Position sensor (TPS)
9	Positive Crankcase Ventilation valve (PCV)
10	Powertrain Control Module (PCM)
11	Engine compartment fuse and relay box

Information Sensors

Accelerator Pedal Position (APP) sensor - as you press the accelerator pedal, the APP sensor alters its voltage signal to the PCM in proportion to the angle of the pedal, and the PCM commands a motor inside the throttle body to open or close the throttle plate accordingly

Camshaft Position (CMP) sensor - produces a signal that the PCM uses to identify the number 1 cylinder and to time the firing sequence of the fuel injectors

Crankshaft Position (CKP) sensor - produces a signal that the PCM uses to calculate engine speed and crankshaft position, which enables it to synchronize ignition timing with fuel injector timing, and to detect misfires

Engine Coolant Temperature (ECT) sensor - a thermistor (temperature-sensitive variable resistor) that sends a voltage signal to the PCM, which uses this data to determine the temperature of the engine coolant

Fuel tank pressure sensor - measures the fuel tank pressure and controls fuel tank pressure by signaling the EVAP system to purge the fuel tank vapors when the pressure becomes excessive

Intake Air Temperature (IAT) sensor - monitors the temperature of the air entering the engine and sends a signal to the PCM to determine injector pulse-width (the duration of each injector's on-time) and to adjust spark timing (to prevent spark knock)

Knock sensor - a piezoelectric crystal that oscillates in proportion to engine vibration which produces a voltage output that is monitored by the PCM. This retards the ignition timing when the oscillation exceeds a certain threshold

Manifold Absolute Pressure (MAP) sensor - monitors the pressure or vacuum inside the intake manifold. The PCM uses this data to determine engine load so that it can alter the ignition advance and fuel enrichment

Mass Air Flow (MAF) sensor - measures the amount of intake air drawn into the engine. It uses a hot-wire sensing element to measure the amount of air entering the engine

Oxygen sensors - generates a small variable voltage signal in proportion to the difference between the oxygen content in the exhaust stream and the oxygen content in the ambient air. The PCM uses this information to maintain the proper air/fuel ratio. A second oxygen sensor monitors the efficiency of the catalytic converter

Throttle Position (TP) sensor - a potentiometer that generates a voltage signal that varies in relation to the opening angle of the throttle plate inside the throttle body. Works with the PCM and other sensors to calculate injector pulse width (the duration of each injector's on-time)

Photos courtesy of Wells Manufacturing, except APP and MAF sensors.

2   On Board Diagnosis (OBD) system

GENERAL DESCRIPTION

1   All models are equipped with the second generation OBD-II system. This system consists of an on-board computer known as the Powertrain Control Module (PCM), and information sensors, which monitor various functions of the engine and send data to the PCM. This system incorporates a series of diagnostic monitors that detect and identify fuel injection and emissions control system faults and store the information in the computer memory. This system also tests sensors and output actuators, diagnoses drive cycles, freezes data and clears codes.

2   The PCM is the brain of the electronically controlled fuel and emissions system. It receives data from a number of sensors and other electronic components (switches, relays, etc.). Based on the information it receives, the PCM generates output signals to control various relays, solenoids (fuel injectors) and other actuators. The PCM is specifically calibrated to optimize the emissions, fuel economy and driveability of the vehicle.

3   It isn't a good idea to attempt diagnosis or replacement of the PCM or emission control components at home while the vehicle is under warranty. Because of a federally-mandated warranty which covers the emissions system components and because any owner-induced damage to the PCM, the sensors and/or the control devices may void this warranty, take the vehicle to a dealer service department if the PCM or a system component malfunctions.

SCAN TOOL INFORMATION

4   Because extracting the Diagnostic Trouble Codes (DTCs) from an engine management system is now the first step in troubleshooting many computer-controlled systems and components, a code reader, at the very least, will be required **(see illustration)**. More powerful scan tools can also perform many of the diagnostics once associated with expensive factory scan tools **(see illustration)**. If you're planning to obtain a generic scan tool for your vehicle, make sure that it's compatible with OBD-II systems. If you don't plan to purchase a code reader or scan tool and don't have access to one, you can have the codes extracted by a dealer service department or an independent repair shop.

➡ **Note: Some auto parts stores even provide this service.**

2.4a Simple code readers are an economical way to extract trouble codes when the CHECK ENGINE light comes on

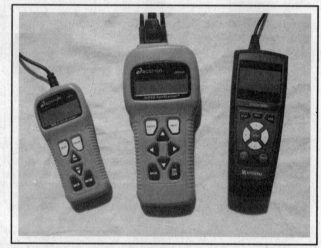

2.4b Hand-held scan tools like these can extract computer codes and also perform diagnostics

3   Obtaining and clearing Diagnostic Trouble Codes (DTCs)

1   All models covered by this manual are equipped with on-board diagnostics. When the PCM recognizes a malfunction in a monitored emission or engine control system, component or circuit, it turns on the Malfunction Indicator Light (MIL) on the dash. The PCM will continue to display the MIL until the problem is fixed and the Diagnostic Trouble Code (DTC) is cleared from the PCM's memory. You'll need a scan tool to access any DTCs stored in the PCM.

2   Before outputting any DTCs stored in the PCM, thoroughly inspect ALL electrical connectors and hoses. Make sure that all electrical connections are tight, clean and free of corrosion. And make sure that all hoses are correctly connected, fit tightly and are in good condition (no cracks or tears).

ACCESSING THE DTCS

3 The Diagnostic Trouble Codes (DTCs) can only be accessed with a code reader or scan tool. Professional scan tools are expensive, but relatively inexpensive generic code readers or scan tools **(see illustrations 2.4a and 2.4b)** are available at most auto parts stores. Simply plug the connector of the scan tool into the diagnostic connector **(see illustration)**. Then follow the instructions included with the scan tool to extract the DTCs.

4 Once you have output all of the stored DTCs, look them up on the accompanying DTC chart.

5 After troubleshooting the source of each DTC, make any necessary repairs or replace the defective component(s).

CLEARING THE DTCS

6 Clear the DTCs with the code reader or scan tool in accordance with the instructions provided by the tool's manufacturer.

DIAGNOSTIC TROUBLE CODES

7 The accompanying tables are a list of the Diagnostic Trouble Codes (DTCs) that can be accessed by a do-it-yourselfer working at home (there are many, many more DTCs available to professional mechanics with proprietary scan tools and software, but those codes

3.3 The Data Link Connector (DLC) is located at the lower edge of the dash, below the steering column

cannot be accessed by a generic scan tool). If, after you have checked and repaired the connectors, wire harness and vacuum hoses (if applicable) for an emission-related system, component or circuit, the problem persists, have the vehicle checked by a dealer service department or other qualified repair shop.

OBD-II TROUBLE CODES

➡ **Note: Not all trouble codes apply to all models.**

Code	Probable cause
P0010	Intake camshaft position actuator, open circuit (Bank 1)
P0011	Intake camshaft position timing over-advanced (Bank 1)
P0012	Intake camshaft position timing, over-retarded (Bank 1)
P0014	Camshaft "B" position sensor, over advanced
P0016	Crankshaft position-to-camshaft position correlation (Bank 1)
P0018	Crankshaft position-to-camshaft position correlation (Bank 2)
P0020	Intake camshaft position actuator, open circuit (Bank 2)
P0021	Intake camshaft position timing over-advanced (Bank 2)
P0022	Intake camshaft position timing over-retarded (Bank 2)
P0030	Oxygen sensor heater control circuit (Bank 1, Sensor 1)
P0031	Oxygen sensor heater circuit low (Bank 1, Sensor 1)
P0032	Oxygen sensor heater circuit high (Bank 1, Sensor 1)
P0036	Oxygen sensor heater control circuit (Bank 1, Sensor 2)

OBD-II TROUBLE CODES (CONTINUED)

➡ Note: Not all trouble codes apply to all models.

Code	Probable cause
P0037	Oxygen sensor heater circuit low (Bank 1, Sensor 2)
P0040	Oxygen sensor signals swapped (Bank 1, Sensor 1/Bank 2, Sensor 1)
P0041	Oxygen sensor signals swapped (Bank 1, Sensor 2/Bank 2, Sensor 2)
P0050	Oxygen sensor heater control circuit (Bank 2, Sensor 1)
P0053	Oxygen sensor heater resistance (Bank 1, Sensor 1)
P0054	Oxygen sensor heater resistance (Bank 1, Sensor 2)
P0055	Oxygen sensor heater resistance (Bank 1, Sensor 3)
P0059	Oxygen sensor heater resistance (Bank 2, Sensor 1)
P0060	Oxygen sensor heater resistance (Bank 2, Sensor 2)
P0068	Manifold Absolute Pressure (MAP) sensor/Mass Air Flow (MAF) sensor-to-throttle position correlation
P0076	Intake control solenoid valve circuit low (four-cylinder)
P0077	Intake control solenoid valve circuit high (four-cylinder)
P0079	Exhaust control solenoid valve circuit low (four-cylinder)
P0080	Exhaust control solenoid valve circuit high (four-cylinder)
P0097	Intake Air Temperature (IAT) sensor 2 circuit, low voltage
P0098	Intake Air Temperature (IAT) sensor 2 circuit, high voltage
P0102	Mass or volume air flow A circuit, low voltage
P0104	Mass Air Flow (MAF) sensor A circuit, intermittent or erratic signal
P0106	Manifold Absolute Pressure (MAP)/(BARO) Barometric Pressure sensor circuit performance problem (four-cylinder)
P0106	Manifold Absolute Pressure (MAP) sensor circuit, range or performance problem
P0107	Manifold Absolute Pressure (MAP)/(BARO) Barometric Pressure circuit low (four-cylinder)
P0107	Manifold Absolute Pressure (MAP) sensor circuit, low voltage
P0108	Manifold Absolute Pressure (MAP)/(BARO) Barometric Pressure circuit high (four-cylinder)
P0108	Manifold Absolute Pressure (MAP) sensor circuit, high voltage
P0109	Manifold Absolute Pressure (MAP) sensor circuit, intermittent signal
P0111	Intake Air Temperature (IAT) sensor circuit, range or performance problem
P0112	Intake Air Temperature (IAT) sensor circuit, low voltage
P0113	Intake Air Temperature (IAT) sensor circuit, high voltage

Code	Probable cause
P0114	Intake Air Temperature (IAT) sensor circuit, intermittent or erratic signal
P0116	Engine Coolant Temperature (ECT) sensor circuit, range or performance problem
P0117	Engine Coolant Temperature (ECT) sensor circuit, low voltage
P0118	Engine Coolant Temperature (ECT) sensor circuit, high voltage
P0119	Engine Coolant Temperature (ECT) sensor circuit, intermittent or erratic signal
P0121	Throttle Position (TP) sensor A circuit, range or performance problem
P0122	Throttle Position (TP) sensor A circuit, low voltage
P0123	Throttle Position (TP) sensor A circuit, high voltage
P0125	Insufficient coolant temperature for closed loop fuel control
P0128	Coolant temperature below coolant thermostat's regulating temperature
P0130	Oxygen sensor circuit malfunction (Bank 1, Sensor 1)
P0132	Oxygen sensor circuit, high voltage (Bank 1, Sensor 1)
P0133	Oxygen sensor circuit, slow response (Bank 1, Sensor 1)
P0134	Oxygen sensor circuit, no activity detected (Bank 1, Sensor 1)
P0135	Oxygen sensor heater circuit malfunction (Bank 1, Sensor 1)
P0138	Oxygen sensor circuit, high voltage (Bank 1, Sensor 2)
P0139	Oxygen sensor circuit, slow response (Bank 1, Sensor 2)
P013A	Oxygen sensor slow response, rich to lean (Bank 1, Sensor 2)
P013C	Oxygen sensor slow response, rich to lean (Bank 2, Sensor 2)
P013E	Oxygen sensor delayed response, rich to lean (Bank 1, Sensor 2)
P0144	Oxygen sensor circuit, high voltage (Bank 1, Sensor 3)
P0147	Oxygen sensor heater circuit malfunction (Bank 1, Sensor 3)
P0148	Fuel delivery error
P014A	Oxygen sensor delayed response, rich to lean (Bank 2, Sensor 2)
P0150	Oxygen sensor circuit malfunction (Bank 2, Sensor 1)
P0152	Oxygen sensor circuit, high voltage (Bank 2, Sensor 1)
P0153	Oxygen sensor circuit, slow response (Bank 2, Sensor 1)
P0154	Oxygen sensor circuit, no activity detected (Bank 2, Sensor 1)
P0155	Oxygen sensor heater circuit malfunction (Bank 2, Sensor 1)
P0158	Oxygen sensor circuit, high voltage (Bank 2, Sensor 2)
P0159	Oxygen sensor circuit, slow response (Bank 2, Sensor 2)

OBD-II TROUBLE CODES (CONTINUED)

➡ Note: Not all trouble codes apply to all models.

Code	Probable cause
P0161	Oxygen sensor heater circuit malfunction (Bank 2, Sensor 2)
P0171	System too lean (Bank 1)
P0172	System too rich (Bank 1)
P0174	System too lean (Bank 2)
P0175	System too rich (Bank 2)
P0180	Fuel temperature sensor circuit malfunction
P0181	Fuel temperature sensor circuit, range or performance problem
P0182	Fuel temperature sensor circuit, low voltage
P0183	Fuel temperature sensor circuit, high voltage
P0191	Fuel rail pressure sensor circuit, range or performance problem
P0192	Fuel rail pressure sensor circuit, low voltage
P0193	Fuel rail pressure sensor circuit, high voltage
P0196	Engine Oil Temperature (EOT) sensor circuit, range or performance problem
P0197	Engine Oil Temperature (EOT) sensor circuit, low voltage
P0198	Engine Oil Temperature (EOT) sensor circuit, high voltage
P0201	Injector open circuit, cylinder 1
P0202	Injector open circuit, cylinder 2
P0203	Injector open circuit, cylinder 3
P0204	Injector open circuit, cylinder 4
P0205	Injector open circuit, cylinder 5
P0206	Injector open circuit, cylinder 6
P0217	Engine coolant over-temperature condition
P0218	Transaxle fluid temperature over-temperature condition
P0219	Engine over-speed condition
P0221	Throttle Position (TP) sensor circuit, range or performance problem
P0222	Throttle Position (TP) sensor circuit, low voltage
P0223	Throttle Position (TP) sensor circuit, high voltage
P0230	Fuel pump primary circuit malfunction

Code	Probable cause
P0231	Fuel pump secondary circuit, low voltage
P0232	Fuel pump secondary circuit, high voltage
P025A	Fuel pump module control circuit open
P025B	Fuel pump module control circuit range or performance problem
P0298	Engine oil over-temperature condition
P0300	Random misfire detected
P0301	Cylinder 1 misfire
P0302	Cylinder 2 misfire
P0303	Cylinder 3 misfire
P0304	Cylinder 4 misfire
P0305	Cylinder 5 misfire
P0306	Cylinder 6 misfire
P0315	Crankshaft position system variation not learned
P0316	Misfire detected on start-up (first 1000 revolutions)
P0320	Ignition/distributor engine speed input circuit
P0325	Knock sensor 1 circuit malfunction (Bank 1)
P0326	Knock sensor 1 circuit, range or performance problem (Bank 1)
P0330	Knock sensor 2 circuit malfunction (Bank 2)
P0331	Knock sensor 2 circuit, range or performance problem (Bank 2)
P0340	Camshaft Position (CMP) sensor circuit malfunction (Bank 1 or single sensor)
P0341	Camshaft Position (CMP) sensor circuit, range or performance problem (Bank 1 or single sensor)
P0344	Camshaft Position (CMP) sensor circuit, intermittent signal (Bank 1 or single sensor)
P0345	Camshaft Position (CMP) sensor circuit malfunction (Bank 2)
P0346	Camshaft Position (CMP) sensor circuit, range or performance problem (Bank 2)
P0349	Camshaft Position (CMP) sensor circuit, intermittent signal (Bank 2)
P0350	Ignition coil primary/secondary circuit malfunction
P0351	Ignition coil A primary/secondary circuit malfunction
P0352	Ignition coil B primary/secondary circuit malfunction
P0353	Ignition coil C primary/secondary circuit malfunction
P0354	Ignition coil D primary/secondary circuit malfunction
P0355	Ignition coil E primary/secondary circuit malfunction

OBD-II TROUBLE CODES (CONTINUED)

➡ Note: Not all trouble codes apply to all models.

Code	Probable cause
P0356	Ignition coil F primary/secondary circuit malfunction
P0400	Exhaust Gas Recirculation (EGR) system flow
P0401	Exhaust Gas Recirculation (EGR) system, insufficient flow detected
P0402	Exhaust Gas Recirculation (EGR) system, excessive flow detected
P0403	Exhaust Gas Recirculation (EGR) system control circuit malfunction
P0405	Exhaust Gas Recirculation (EGR) system, differential pressure feedback sensor circuit, low voltage
P0406	Exhaust Gas Recirculation (EGR) system, differential pressure feedback sensor circuit, high voltage
P0410	Secondary Air Injection (AIR) system
P0412	Secondary Air Injection (AIR) system, switching valve circuit malfunction
P0420	Catalyst system efficiency below threshold (Bank 1)
P0430	Catalyst system efficiency below threshold (Bank 2)
P0442	Evaporative Emission (EVAP) system, small leak detected
P0443	Evaporative Emission (EVAP) system, purge control valve circuit malfunction
P0446	Evaporative Emission (EVAP) system, vent control circuit malfunction
P0451	Evaporative Emission (EVAP) system, pressure sensor range or performance problem
P0452	Evaporative Emission (EVAP) system, pressure sensor, low voltage
P0453	Evaporative Emission (EVAP) system, pressure sensor, high voltage
P0454	Evaporative Emission (EVAP) system, pressure sensor, intermittent signal
P0455	Evaporative Emission (EVAP) system, gross leak detected/no flow
P0456	Evaporative Emission (EVAP) system, very small leak detected
P0457	Evaporative Emission (EVAP) system, leak detected (fuel cap loose or off)
P0460	Fuel level sensor circuit malfunction
P0461	Fuel level sensor circuit, range or performance problem
P0462	Fuel level sensor circuit, low voltage
P0463	Fuel level sensor circuit, high voltage
P0480	Fan 1 control circuit malfunction
P0481	Fan 2 control circuit malfunction
P0483	Fan performance

Code	Probable cause
P0491	Secondary Air Injection (AIR) system, insufficient flow (Bank 1)
P0500	Vehicle Speed Sensor (VSS)
P0503	Vehicle Speed Sensor (VSS), intermittent, erratic or high signal
P0505	Idle Air Control (IAC) system
P0506	Idle Air Control (IAC) system, rpm lower than expected
P0507	Idle Air Control (IAC) system, rpm higher than expected
P050A	Cold start idle air control performance
P050B	Cold start ignition timing performance
P050E	Cold start engine exhaust temperature out of range
P0511	Idle Air Control (IAC) system circuit malfunction
P0512	Starter request circuit malfunction
P0528	Fan speed sensor circuit, no signal
P052A	Cold start camshaft position timing over-advanced (Bank 1)
P052B	Cold start camshaft position timing over-retarded (Bank 1)
P052C	Cold start camshaft position timing over-advanced (Bank 2)
P052D	Cold start camshaft position timing over-retarded (Bank 2)
P0532	Air conditioning refrigerant pressure sensor circuit, low voltage
P0533	Air conditioning refrigerant pressure sensor circuit, high voltage
P0534	Air conditioning refrigerant charge loss
P0537	Air conditioning evaporator temperature sensor circuit, low voltage
P0538	A/C evaporator temperature sensor circuit, high voltage
P053A	Positive Crankcase Ventilation (PCV) heater control circuit open
P0552	Power Steering Pressure (PSP) sensor circuit, low voltage
P0553	Power Steering Pressure (PSP) sensor circuit, high voltage
P0562	System voltage low
P0563	System voltage high
P0571	Brake switch circuit malfunction
P0572	Brake switch circuit, low voltage
P0573	Brake switch circuit, high voltage
P0579	Cruise control multifunction input circuit, ranger or performance problem
P0581	Cruise control multifunction input circuit, high voltage

OBD-II TROUBLE CODES (CONTINUED)

➡ Note: Not all trouble codes apply to all models.

Code	Probable cause
P0600	Serial communication link
P0601	Powertrain Control Module (PCM), memory checksum error
P0602	Powertrain Control Module (PCM) programming error
P0603	Powertrain Control Module (PCM), Keep Alive Memory (KAM) error
P0604	Powertrain Control Module (PCM), Random Access Memory (RAM) error
P0605	Powertrain Control Module (PCM), Read Only Memory (ROM) error
P0606	Powertrain Control Module (PCM) processor
P0607	Powertrain Control Module (PCM) performance
P060A	Internal control module monitoring processor performance
P060B	Internal control module analog/digital processing performance
P060C	Internal control module main processor performance
P060D	Internal control module accelerator pedal position performance
P0610	Powertrain Control Module (PCM) options error
P061B	Internal control module torque calculation performance
P061C	Internal control module engine rpm performance
P061D	Internal control module engine air mass performance
P061F	Internal control module throttle actuator controller performance
P0620	Alternator control circuit malfunction
P0622	Alternator field terminal, circuit malfunction
P0625	Alternator field terminal, low circuit voltage
P0626	Alternator field terminal, high circuit voltage
P0627	Fuel pump, open control circuit
P062C	Internal control module vehicle speed performance
P062F	Internal control module EEPROM error
P0642	Sensor reference voltage (VREF) circuit below VREF minimum voltage
P0643	Sensor reference voltage (VREF) circuit, high voltage
P0645	Air conditioning clutch relay control circuit malfunction
P064D	Internal control module oxygen sensor processor performance (Bank 1)

Code	Probable cause
P064E	Internal control module oxygen sensor processor performance (Bank 2)
P0657	Actuator supply voltage, open circuit
P065B	Alternator control circuit range or performance problem
P065B	Alternator control circuit range or performance problem
P0660	Intake Manifold Tuning Valve (IMTV) control circuit, open circuit (Bank 1)
P0663	Intake Manifold Tuning Valve (IMTV) control circuit, open circuit (Bank 2)
P0685	Powertrain Control Module (PCM) power relay control circuit open
P0689	Powertrain Control Module (PCM) power relay sense circuit, low voltage
P0690	Powertrain Control Module (PCM) power relay sense circuit, high voltage
P06B8	Internal control module Non-volatile random access memory (NVRAM) error
P0703	Brake switch input circuit malfunction
P0704	Clutch switch input circuit malfunction
P0705	Transmission Range (TR) sensor circuit (PRNDL) input problem
P0706	Transmission Range (TR) sensor circuit, range or performance problem
P0707	Transmission Range (TR) sensor circuit, low voltage
P0708	Transmission range sensor circuit, high voltage
P0711	Transmission fluid temperature sensor circuit, range or performance problem
P0712	Transmission fluid temperature sensor circuit, low input
P0713	Transmission fluid temperature sensor circuit, high input
P0715	Input/turbine speed sensor circuit malfunction
P0716	Input/turbine speed sensor circuit, range or performance problem
P0717	Input/turbine speed sensor circuit, no signal
P0720	Output Shaft Speed (OSS) sensor circuit malfunction
P0721	Output Shaft Speed (OSS) sensor circuit, range or performance problem
P0722	No signal from Output Shaft Speed (OSS) sensor
P0723	Output Shaft Speed (OSS) sensor circuit, intermittent signal
P0729	Gear 6 incorrect ratio
P0730	Incorrect gear ratio
P0731	Incorrect gear ratio, first gear
P0732	Incorrect gear ratio, second gear
P0733	Incorrect gear ratio, third gear

OBD-II TROUBLE CODES (CONTINUED)

➡ **Note: Not all trouble codes apply to all models.**

Code	Probable cause
P0734	Incorrect gear ratio, fourth gear
P0735	Incorrect gear ratio, fifth gear
P0736	Incorrect gear ratio, reverse gear
P0741	Torque converter clutch, circuit performance problem or stuck in Off position
P0742	Torque converter clutch circuit, stuck in On position
P0744	Torque converter clutch circuit, intermittent
P0745	Pressure control solenoid malfunction
P0751	Shift solenoid A, performance problem or stuck in Off position
P0752	Shift solenoid A, stuck in On position
P0753	Shift solenoid A, electrical problem
P0756	Shift solenoid B, performance problem or stuck in Off position
P0757	Shift solenoid B, stuck in On position
P0758	Shift solenoid B, electrical problem
P0761	Shift solenoid C, performance problem or stuck in Off position
P0762	Shift solenoid C, stuck in On position
P0763	Shift solenoid C, electrical problem
P0766	Shift solenoid D, performance problem or stuck in Off position
P0767	Shift solenoid D, stuck in On position
P0768	Shift solenoid D, electrical problem
P0771	Shift solenoid E, performance problem or stuck in Off position
P0772	Shift solenoid E, stuck in On position
P0773	Shift solenoid E, electrical problem
P0777	Pressure control solenoid "B" stuck On
P0778	Pressure control solenoid "B" electrical
P0780	Shift malfunction
P0791	Intermediate shaft speed sensor circuit malfunction
P0812	Reverse input circuit malfunction

Code	Probable cause
P0815	Upshift switch circuit malfunction
P0817	Starter disable circuit malfunction
P0830	Clutch pedal switch circuit malfunction
P0840	Transmission fluid pressure sensor circuit malfunction
P0841	Transmission fluid pressure sensor/switch "A" circuit range/performance problem
P0882	Transmission control module (TCM) power input signal low
P0894	Transmission component slipping
P0961	Pressure control (PC) solenoid A - control circuit range/performance problem
P0962	Pressure control (PC) solenoid A - control circuit low
P0963	Pressure control (PC) solenoid A - control circuit high
P0973	Shift solenoid (SS) A - control circuit low
P0974	Shift solenoid (SS) A - control circuit high
P0976	Shift solenoid (SS) B - control circuit low
P0977	Shift solenoid (SS) B - control circuit high
P0978	Shift solenoid (SS) C - control circuit range/performance problem
P0979	Shift solenoid (SS) C - control circuit low
P0980	Shift solenoid (SS) C - control circuit high
P0981	Shift solenoid (SS) D - control circuit range/performance problem
P0982	Shift solenoid (SS) D - control circuit low
P0983	Shift solenoid (SS) D - control circuit high
P0984	Shift solenoid (SS) E - control circuit range/performance problem
P0985	Shift solenoid (SS) E - control circuit low
P0986	Shift solenoid (SS) E - control circuit high
P0997	Shift solenoid (SS) F - control circuit range/performance problem
P0998	Shift solenoid (SS) F - control circuit low
P0999	Shift solenoid (SS) F - control circuit high

4 Accelerator Pedal Position (APP) sensor - replacement

➡ **Note: This procedure applies to 2007 and later models only.**

1 Disconnect the cable from the negative battery terminal (see Chapter 5).

2 Working underneath the dash, disconnect the APP sensor electrical connector at the top of the accelerator pedal.

3 Remove the sensor mounting nuts and remove the sensor.

4 Installation is the reverse of removal.

5 Camshaft Position (CMP) sensor - replacement

1 Disconnect the cable from the negative battery terminal (see Chapter 5).

2.4L FOUR-CYLINDER MODELS

➡ **Note: These models are equipped with two CMP sensors; one for the intake and one for the exhaust camshaft. The sensors are located on each end of the cylinder head.**

2 Remove the air intake duct, if necessary, to provide more room to work (see Chapter 4).

3 Disconnect the electrical connector from the CMP sensor.

4 Remove the CMP sensor mounting bolt and remove the sensor.

➡ **Note: It may be necessary to remove the engine lift bracket to access the exhaust CMP sensor.**

5 If you're going to install the same sensor, check the condition of the O-ring. Replace the O-ring if it's damaged.

6 Installation is the reverse of removal.

2006 AND EARLIER 3.5L V6 MODELS

➡ **Note: The CMP sensor is mounted under the timing belt cover, near the exhaust camshaft sprocket of the driver's side cylinder head.**

7 Remove the timing belt cover from the front cylinder head. The sensor is mounted next to the sprocket of the front exhaust camshaft.

8 Disconnect the sensor electrical connector.

9 Remove the two sensor mounting bolts and remove the sensor.

10 Installation is the reverse of removal.

ALL OTHER V6 MODELS

➡ **Note: 2007 through 2009 models use two CMP sensors, and 2011 and later models use four sensors. They are mounted on the drivebelt end of the cylinder heads.**

11 Remove the engine cover if necessary for access (see Chapter 2B).

12 Disconnect the sensor electrical connector.

13 Remove the bolt securing the sensor to the side of the cylinder head. Pull the sensor out of its socket.

14 Installation is the reverse of removal.

6 Crankshaft Position (CKP) sensor - replacement

FOUR-CYLINDER MODELS

➡ **Note: The CKP sensor is located on the back side of the engine.**

1 Raise the vehicle and support it securely on jackstands.

2 Disconnect the electrical connector from the sensor.

3 Remove the cover plate mounting nut and remove the plate.

4 Remove the CKP sensor mounting bolt and remove the CKP sensor.

5 Installation is the reverse of removal.

2006 AND EARLIER 3.5L V6 MODELS

➡ **Note: The CKP sensor is located on the front of the engine, behind the timing belt cover, next to the crankshaft sprocket.**

6 Remove the lower timing belt cover (see Chapter 2B).

7 Disconnect the sensor wiring harness.

8 Remove the two mounting bolts and lift off the sensor.

9 Installation is the reverse of removal.

ALL OTHER V6 MODELS

➡ **Note: The sensor is mounted to the rear of the engine at the top of the transmission/transaxle housing.**

10 Remove the air filter housing (see Chapter 4).

11 Disconnect the sensor wiring harness.

12 Remove the CKP sensor mounting bolt and remove the sensor.

13 Installation is the reverse of removal.

7 Engine Coolant Temperature (ECT) sensor - replacement

⁕⁕ WARNING:

Wait until the engine is completely cool before beginning this procedure.

⁕⁕ CAUTION:

Handle the ECT sensor with care. Damage to the ECT sensor will affect the operation of the entire fuel injection system.

1 Disconnect the cable from the negative battery terminal (see Chapter 5). Partially drain the cooling system (see Chapter 1).

FOUR-CYLINDER MODELS

➡ **Note: On four-cylinder models, the ECT sensor is located on the back side of the cylinder head.**

2 Remove the spring clip and pull the sensor from the coolant temperature control housing.

3 Installation is the reverse of removal. Install the spring clip once the ECT sensor is installed in the housing. Refill the cooling system (see Chapter 1).

V6 ENGINES

➡ **Note: The ECT sensor is located at the driver's end of the engine on 2006 and earlier models, and the back of the engine on 2007 and later models.**

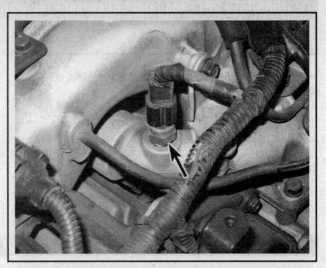

7.5 Location of the ECT sensor (2006 and earlier V6 shown)

4 On 2011 V6 models, remove the air filter housing (see Chapter 4).

5 Disconnect the electrical connector to the ECT sensor **(see illustration)**.

6 Unscrew the ECT sensor from the cylinder head.

7 Don't seal the threads of the new sensor with Teflon tape, as this will interfere with the grounding of the sensor. Apply a small amount of liquid sealer to the threads before installation.

8 Installation is the reverse of removal. Tighten the ECT sensor securely. Refill the cooling system (see Chapter 1).

8 Knock sensor - replacement

⁕⁕ WARNING:

Wait until the engine is completely cool before beginning this procedure.

FOUR-CYLINDER MODELS

➡ **Note: The knock sensor is located on the side of the engine block under the intake manifold.**

1 Disconnect the cable from the negative battery terminal (see Chapter 5).

2 Remove the intake manifold (see Chapter 2A).

3 Disconnect the knock sensor electrical connector.

4 Unscrew the knock sensor mounting bolt and remove the sensor.

5 Installation is the reverse of removal. Tighten the knock sensor

mounting bolt to the torque listed in this Chapter's Specifications.

V6 MODELS

➡ **Note: The knock sensors are located in the valley between the cylinder heads. To access them, remove the lower intake manifold.**

6 Disconnect the cable from the negative battery terminal (see Chapter 5).

7 Remove the upper and lower intake manifolds (see Chapter 2B).

8 Disconnect the electrical connectors from the knock sensors.

9 Disconnect the wiring harness retainers from the engine block.

10 Unscrew and remove the sensors.

11 Installation is the reverse of removal. Tighten the knock sensor mounting bolts to the torque listed in this Chapter's Specifications.

9 Manifold Absolute Pressure or Barometric Pressure/Intake Air Temperature (MAP/IAT - four-cylinder) (BAS/IAT - 2011 and later V6) sensor - replacement

FOUR-CYLINDER MODELS

➡ **Note: The MAP/IAT sensor is located in the intake manifold at the end of the air inlet duct.**

1 Disconnect the cable from the negative battery terminal (see Chapter 5).

2 Disconnect the electrical connector from the MAP/IAT sensor.

3 Remove the mounting bolt and remove the sensor from the intake manifold.

4 Installation is the reverse of removal.

2011 AND LATER V6 MODELS

➡ **Note: 2011 and later V6 engines use a Barometric Pressure/ Intake Air Temperature (BPS/IAT) sensor; it's located on top of the air filter housing.**

5 Disconnect the cable form the negative battery terminal (see Chapter 5).

6 Disconnect the electrical connector to the BPS/IAT sensor.

7 Remove the mounting bolts and remove the sensor from the top of the air filter housing.

8 Installation is the reverse of removal.

10 Manifold Absolute Pressure (MAP) sensor (2011 and later V6 models) - replacement

➡ **Note: The MAP sensor is located in the air inlet duct.**

1 Disconnect the cable from the negative battery terminal (see Chapter 5).

2 Disconnect the electrical connector from the sensor.

3 Remove the MAP sensor mounting bolt and remove the sensor from the air intake duct.

4 Installation is the reverse of removal.

11 Mass Air Flow/Intake Air Temperature (MAF/IAT) sensor (2007 and earlier V6 models) - replacement

➡ **Note: The MAF/IAT sensor is located in the air inlet duct.**

1 Disconnect the cable from the negative battery terminal (see Chapter 5).

2 Disconnect the electrical connector from the sensor **(see illustration)**.

3 Loosen the hose clamps and remove the sensor.

4 Installation is the reverse of removal.

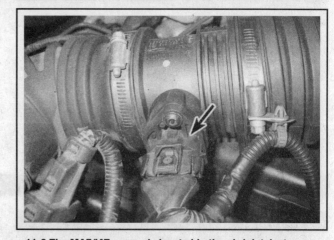

11.2 The MAF/IAT sensor is located in the air inlet duct

12 Oxygen sensors - general information and replacement

GENERAL INFORMATION

1 Use special care when servicing an oxygen sensor:

a) *Oxygen sensors have a permanently attached pigtail and electrical connector that can't be removed from the sensor. Damage to or removal of the pigtail or the electrical connector will ruin the sensor.*

b) *Keep grease, dirt and other contaminants away from the electrical connector and the oxygen sensor.*

c) *Do not use cleaning solvents of any kind on an oxygen sensor.*

d) *Do not drop or roughly handle an oxygen sensor.*

REPLACEMENT

➡ **Note: Because it is installed in the exhaust manifold/catalytic converter, both of which contract when cool, an oxygen sensor might be very difficult to loosen when the engine is cold. Rather than risk damage to the sensor, start and run the engine for a minute or two, then shut it off. Be careful not to burn yourself during the following procedure.**

2 The sensors are located at the inlet and outlet of each primary catalytic converter **(see illustration)**. These converters are bolted to the bases of the exhaust manifolds. There are two on four-cylinder mod-

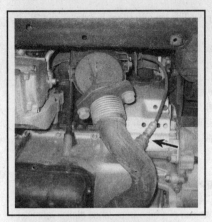

12.2 There are two heated oxygen sensors at the outlet of each exhaust manifold - before and after each catalytic converter (this is the downstream sensor for the front cylinder bank)

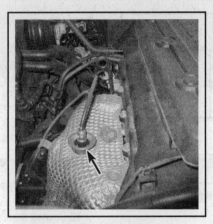

12.4a The primary (upstream) oxygen sensors on some models are accessible through holes in the heat shields - four cylinder model shown, V6 engines similar

12.4b After disconnecting the wiring, carefully unscrew the sensor with an oxygen sensor socket (shown) or with a large wrench - oxygen sensor sockets are handy where there's no room to turn a wrench

els and four on V6 models.

3   If you're working on the sensors on the rear manifold of a V6 model, raise the vehicle and support it securely on jackstands. This may ease things even if you're removing a front lower sensor.

4   Remove any interfering components to provide wrench access to the sensor. These components vary greatly depending on the year and options installed **(see illustrations)**.

5   Disconnect the sensor pigtail.

6   Unscrew the sensor.

➡ **Note: Special oxygen sensor sockets are available at most auto parts stores.**

7   Installation is the reverse of removal. Coat the threads of the oxygen sensor with anti-seize compound and tighten it to the torque listed in this Chapter's Specifications.

13   Power Steering Pressure (PSP) sensor (2009 and earlier models) - replacement

✳✳ WARNING:

Wait until the power steering fluid has cooled completely before beginning this procedure.

1   Disconnect the cable from the negative battery terminal (see Chapter 5).

2   Locate the PSP sensor on the power steering pump, then disconnect the sensor electrical connector.

3   Place a drain pain under the pump, then unscrew the PSP sensor from the pump. Be prepared for some power steering fluid to leak out.

4   Installation is the reverse of removal. Check the power steering fluid level (see Chapter 1) and add fluid as necessary.

14   Throttle Position (TP) sensor (2006 and earlier 3.5L V6 models) - replacement and adjustment

➡ **Note: The TP sensor is located on the throttle body.**

REPLACEMENT

1   Disconnect the cable from the negative battery terminal (see Chapter 5).

2   Remove the engine cover, if necessary (see Chapter 2B).

3   Disconnect the TP sensor electrical connector **(see illustration)**.

4   Mark the position of the sensor if you plan to reinstall the same one.

5   Remove the TP sensor mounting screws and remove the sensor from the throttle body.

14.3 The Throttle Position sensor has slotted mounting holes to allow for adjustment

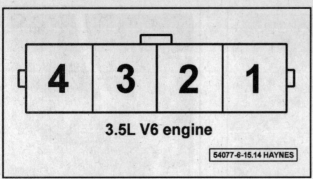

3.5L V6 engine

54077-6-15.14 HAYNES

14.12 TP sensor connector terminal designations (connector face [harness side] shown)

6 Install the sensor and rotate it until the mounting holes in the TP sensor are aligned with the mounting holes in the throttle body.

7 Installation is otherwise the reverse of removal.

ADJUSTMENT

Using a scan tool

8 Connect a scan tool to the 16-pin Data Link Connector (DLC),

then bring up the Throttle Position sensor values parameter on the screen.

9 Turn the ignition key to the On position.

10 With the throttle fully closed, note the value on the scan tool - it should be as follows:

3.5L V6 engines = 300 to 900 millivolts (mV)

11 If the sensor voltage doesn't fall within the specified range, loosen the TP sensor mounting screws and turn the sensor one way or the other until it does, then tighten the screws securely.

Using a voltmeter

➡ **Note: Use only a high-impedance digital voltmeter for this procedure.**

12 Connect the negative lead of a high-impedance digital voltmeter to a good ground and connect the positive lead to the TP sensor signal wire. It will be necessary to backprobe the sensor's connector using a straight-pin to take the voltage reading, or pierce the wire with a pin and connect the lead to it (although the latter method isn't recommended if at all possible to avoid). It may also be necessary to separate the clamshell halves of the connector to allow the connector to be backprobed. The signal wire designations are as follows **(see illustration)**:

2006 and earlier 3.5L V6 engine: Terminal 4 of the TP sensor connector (yellow wire)

13 Follow Steps 9 through 11 to check and, if necessary, adjust the TP sensor.

15 CVVT Oil Temperature Sensor (OTS) (2007 and later V6 models) - replacement

✳ **WARNING:**

Wait until the engine has cooled completely before beginning this procedure.

➡ **Note: The sensor is located on the end of the driver's side (front) cylinder head.**

1 Disconnect the cable from the negative battery terminal (see Chapter 5).

2 Remove the engine cover, if necessary (see Chapter 2B).

3 Locate the OTS sensor and disconnect the wiring harness.

4 Place rags under the sensor to minimize oil leakage.

5 Carefully clean around the sensor to avoid dropping bits of debris into the open hole.

6 Unscrew and remove the sensor.

7 Installation is the reverse of removal.

16 CVVT Oil Control Valve (OCV) - replacement

✳ **WARNING:**

Wait until the engine has cooled completely before beginning this procedure.

➡ **Note: The sensor is located on the end of the driver's side (front) cylinder head.**

1 Disconnect the cable from the negative battery terminal (see Chapter 5).

FOUR-CYLINDER ENGINES

➡ **Note: Four-cylinder models use two OCV valves; one for each camshaft.**

2 Disconnect the CVVT oil control valve electrical connector.

3 Remove the oil control valve mounting bolt.

4 Remove the oil control valve from the cylinder head.

5 Installation is the reverse of removal. Coat the O-ring with clean engine oil.

V6 ENGINES

2007 through 2009 models

6 Locate the sensor and disconnect the wiring harness.

7 Place rags under the sensor to minimize oil leakage.

8 Remove the mounting bolt and carefully clean around the sensor to avoid dropping bits of debris into the open hole.

9 Unscrew and remove the sensor.

10 Installation is the reverse of removal.

2011 and later models

Intake camshaft CVVT valves

11 Remove the lower intake manifold (see Chapter 2B).

12 Disconnect the electrical connector to the Bank 1 or Bank 2 intake CVVT valves.

13 Remove the mounting bolt(s).

14 Remove the CVVT valve(s) from the cylinder head.

15 Installation is the reverse of removal. Coat the O-ring with clean engine oil.

Exhaust camshaft CVVT valves

16 Disconnect the CVVT valve connector from the top of the valve cover.

17 Remove the valve cover (see Chapter 2B).

18 Remove the CVVT valve mounting bolts and remove the valve(s) from the front camshaft cap.

19 Installation is the reverse of removal.

17 Variable Intake Solenoid (VIS) valve - replacement

2007 THROUGH 2009 V6 ENGINES

➡ **Note: The VIS valve is mounted in the upper intake manifold.**

1 Locate and disconnect the electrical connector from the solenoid.

2 Unscrew and remove the solenoid.

3 Installation is the reverse of removal.

FOUR-CYLINDER ENGINES AND 2011 AND LATER V6 ENGINES

➡ **Note: The VIS valve is mounted to the intake manifold; V6 models use two solenoids.**

4 Disconnect the electrical connector to the solenoid.

5 Disconnect the vacuum lines to the solenoid.

6 Remove the solenoid mounting bolt and remove the solenoid.

7 Installation is the reverse of removal.

18 Transmission Range (TR) sensor - replacement

REMOVAL

➡ **Note: The TR sensor is located on the top of the transaxle, near the shift cable.**

1 Disconnect the cable from the negative battery terminal (see Chapter 5). Disconnect the fresh air intake duct from the air filter housing (see Chapter 4).

2 Remove the battery and battery tray (see Chapter 5).

3 Disconnect the electrical connector from the TR sensor **(see illustration)**.

4 Remove the nut that secures the shift control cable to the control shaft lever, and disconnect the cable from the lever.

5 Remove the nut and washer that secures the control shaft lever to the manual valve shaft and remove the control shaft lever from the manual valve shaft.

6 Remove the TR sensor mounting bolts and remove the sensor.

INSTALLATION

7 Slide the sensor onto the manual valve shaft, then loosely install the mounting bolts.

8 Install the lever on the manual valve shaft. Install the nut and tighten it securely. Turn the lever through the gears - it will click as it

18.3 Typical 2011 and later Transmission Range sensor location

changes to the next gear - until it stops at Park, then turn it two clicks. It's now in the Neutral position.

9 Connect the cable to the manual valve shaft and install the nut, but don't tighten it yet.

10 Align the holes on the manual lever and the sensor; use an appropriately sized drill bit to insert into the holes to ensure alignment, turning the sensor as necessary. When alignment is achieved, tighten the sensor mounting screws securely, being careful to avoid moving the sensor.

11 The remainder of installation is the reverse of removal.
12 Tighten the cable nut and check that the transmission and indicator operate properly. Make sure the engine only starts in Park and Neutral, and make sure the back-up lights come on when the shifter is placed in Reverse.

19 Powertrain Control Module (PCM) - replacement

✳✳ WARNING:

The models covered by this manual are equipped with Supplemental Restraint systems (SRS), more commonly known as airbags. Always disable the airbag system before working in the vicinity of any airbag system component to avoid the possibility of accidental deployment of the airbag, which could cause personal injury (see Chapter 12).

✳✳ CAUTION:

To avoid electrostatic discharge damage to the PCM, handle the PCM only by its case. Do not touch the electrical terminals during removal and installation. If available, ground yourself to the vehicle with an anti-static ground strap, available at computer supply stores, and use a special anti-static pad to store the PCM on once it is removed.

➡ Note: The PCM is located inside the engine compartment. On 2009 and earlier models, the PCM is located on the passenger's side fender; on 2011 and later models, the PCM is next to the air filter housing.

1 Disconnect the cable from the negative battery terminal (see Chapter 5).
2 Remove the air filter housing and remove the inlet pipe with the resonator (see Chapter 4).

19.3 Flip open the locking levers, then unplug the electrical connectors from the PCM - later model shown

3 Disconnect the electrical connectors from the PCM **(see illustration)**.
4 Remove the upper and lower PCM mounting bracket fasteners and carefully remove the PCM (see **Caution** above).
5 Installation is the reverse of removal.

20 Catalytic converters - replacement

✳✳ WARNING:

Do NOT service a catalytic converter until it has completely cooled down.

MANIFOLD CATALYTIC CONVERTERS

2006 and earlier 3.5L V6 models

➡ Note: On these models, the exhaust manifold catalytic converters are bolted to the undersides of the exhaust manifolds.

1 Raise the vehicle and support it securely on jackstands.

2 Unbolt the exhaust pipe from the bottom of the catalytic converter.
3 Disconnect the rubber exhaust pipe supports under the car and carefully lower the front of the pipe as much as possible for access to the catalytic converters.
4 Disconnect the oxygen sensors from the catalytic converter.
5 Unbolt the converter from the exhaust manifold and remove it from beneath the vehicle.

2007 and later models

➡ Note: On these models, the primary catalytic converters are integral parts of the exhaust manifolds.

6 Refer to Chapter 2A, Section 8 (four-cylinder engines) or Chapter 2B, Section 6 (V6 engines) for the exhaust manifold replacement procedures.

21 Evaporative emissions control (EVAP) system - component replacement

⁂ WARNING:

Gasoline and gasoline vapor is extremely flammable, so take extra precautions when you work on any part of the fuel system or EVAP system. Don't smoke or allow open flames or bare light bulbs near the work area, and don't work in a garage where a gas-type appliance (such as a water heater or a clothes dryer) is present. Since gasoline is carcinogenic, wear fuel resistant gloves when there's a possibility of being exposed to fuel, and, if you spill any fuel on your skin, rinse it off immediately with soap and water. Mop up any spills immediately and do not store fuel-soaked rags where they could ignite. When you perform any kind of work on the fuel system, wear safety glasses and have a Class B type fire extinguisher on hand.

1   Disconnect the cable from the negative terminal of the battery (see Chapter 5).

PURGE CONTROL SOLENOID VALVE

2   Remove the engine cover, if applicable (see Chapter 2A or 2B).
3   Disconnect the electrical connector from the purge valve **(see illustration)**.
4   Disconnect the vacuum hoses from the purge valve.
5   Remove the purge valve mounting fasteners and remove the purge valve.
6   Installation is the reverse of removal.

OTHER COMPONENTS (UNDER VEHICLE)

7   Raise the rear of the vehicle and support it securely on jackstands.
8   Remove the protective cover from the EVAP canister assembly, if so equipped.

Two-way valve

➡ Note: The two-way valve is located in the line between the fuel tank and the canister.

9   Disconnect the EVAP hoses from the two-way valve.
10 Installation is the reverse of removal. The valve must be installed facing the correct direction, indicated by the arrow on the valve.

EVAP canister

➡ Note: The EVAP canister is mounted to the frame rail near the fuel tank.

11 Disconnect the hoses from the canister.
12 Disconnect the wiring from the canister closed valve.
13 Remove the EVAP canister mounting bracket bolts **(see illustration)** and remove the EVAP canister and mounting bracket as a single assembly.
14 Installation is the reverse of removal.

Vapor pressure sensor

➡ Note: This sensor is mounted to the rear end of the fuel tank in the line connecting the fuel tank and the canister.

15 Disconnect the wiring harness from the sensor.
16 Disconnect the fuel hoses.
17 Remove the sensor along with its mounting bracket. The bracket can be removed from the sensor after it is out of the vehicle.
18 Installation is the reverse of removal.

Canister closed valve

➡ Note: This valve is connected to the canister.

19 Disconnect the wiring connector from the valve.
20 Remove the valve from the canister.
21 Installation is the reverse of removal.

21.3 Location of the purge control solenoid valve (3.5L V6 engine shown)

21.13 Evaporator canister mounting bolt locations - four-cylinder models

22 Positive Crankcase Ventilation (PCV) valve - replacement

1 Remove the hose clamp and disconnect the PCV hose from the valve.
2 Unscrew the PCV valve from the valve cover **(see illustrations)**.
3 Installation is the reverse of removal.

22.2a PCV location - 2006 and earlier V6

22.2b PCV location - four-cylinder models

Torque specifications	Ft-lbs (unless otherwise indicated)	Nm

→ **Note:** One foot-pound (ft-lb) of torque is equivalent to 12 inch-pounds (in-lbs) of torque. Torque values below approximately 15 foot-pounds are expressed in inch-pounds, because most foot-pound torque wrenches are not accurate at these smaller values.

	Ft-lbs (unless otherwise indicated)	Nm
Knock sensor		
V6 engines	86 to 104 in-lbs	9.5 to 11.5
Four-cylinder engine	12 to 17.5	16 to 23.5
Oxygen sensor		
Four-cylinder engines	30 to 36	40 to 49
V6 engines	26 to 33	35 to 45

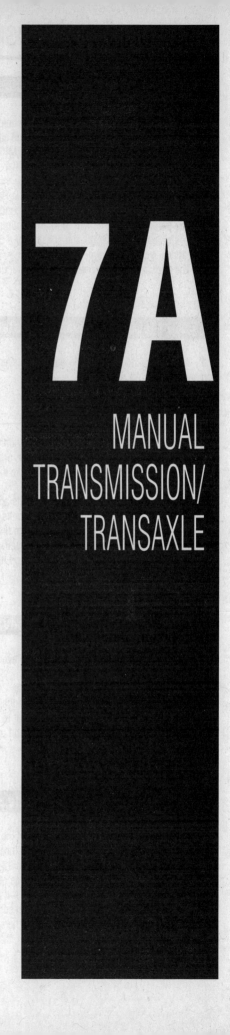

7A

MANUAL TRANSMISSION/ TRANSAXLE

1 General Information

1 The vehicles covered by this manual are equipped with either a M5UR1, 5-speed manual transmission (2006 and earlier models), a M6GF2, 6-speed transaxle (2011 and later 2.4L MPI four-cylinders) or an automatic transmission/transaxle. This Part of Chapter 7 contains information on the manual transmission/transaxle. Service procedures for the automatic transmission/transaxle are contained in Part B. Information on the transfer case used on 4WD models can be found in Part C.

2 The transmission is contained in an aluminum alloy casting bolted to the rear of the engine, and consists of a constant syncromesh type geartrain with a direct type floor shift.

3 The transaxle is contained in a cast-aluminum alloy casing bolted

to the engine's rear end, and consists of the gearbox and final drive differential. The transaxle unit type is stamped on a plate attached to the transaxle.

TRANSMISSION/TRANSAXLE OVERHAUL

4 Because of the complexity of the assembly, possible unavailability of replacement parts and special tools necessary, internal repair procedures for the transmission/transaxle are not recommended for the home mechanic. The bulk of the information in this Chapter is devoted to removal and installation procedures.

2 Shift lever - removal and installation

1 Apply the parking brake. Place the shift lever in the neutral position and unscrew the shift knob.

TRANSMISSION MODELS

2 Raise the vehicle and support it securely on jackstands.

3 Place a floor jack under the transmission or transfer case and raise the rear of the transmission enough to take the weight off of the crossmember.

4 Remove the crossmember mounting bolts and lower the rear of the transmission until the shift lever housing bolts can be accessed. Make sure nothing is being pinched against the firewall or hitting the radiator as the rear of the transmission is lowered.

5 Remove the shift lever mounting bolts and lift the lever straight

up and out.

6 Place the shift lever on to the top of the housing, making sure the end of the lever is placed in the shift rod socket, then install the bolts and tighten them securely.

7 Installation is the reverse of removal.

TRANSAXLE MODELS

8 Remove the center console assembly (see Chapter 11).

9 Use pliers to remove the shift cable pins and clips. Move the cables aside.

10 Remove the shifter assembly from the mounting bracket.

11 Remove the retainer from the shift lever.

12 Installation is the reverse of removal.

3 Transaxle shift cables - removal and installation

1 Apply the parking brake. Place the shift lever in Neutral. Unscrew and remove the shift lever knob.

2 Remove the center console assembly (see Chapter 11).

3 Use pliers to remove the pins from the ends of the shift cables.

4 Pull the cable housing retaining clips out of the shifter base.

5 Locate the shift cables at the transaxle and pull their retaining clips out.

6 Pull the pins out of the transaxle ends of the shift cables.

7 Feed the cables through the firewall grommet to remove them.

8 Check the end bushings for any signs of looseness or damage before replacing the cables.

9 Installation is the reverse of removal.

4 Driveaxle oil seals (transaxle models) - replacement

1 Oil leaks frequently occur due to wear of the driveaxle oil seals. Replacement of these seals is relatively easy, since the repair can be performed without removing the transaxle from the vehicle.

2 Driveaxle oil seals are located at the sides of the transaxle/ transfer case, where the driveaxles are attached. If leakage at the seal is suspected, raise the vehicle and support it securely on jackstands. If the seal is leaking, lubricant will be found on the sides of the transaxle below the seals.

3 Remove the driveaxles (see Chapter 8).

4 Use a screwdriver or prybar to carefully pry the oil seal out of the

transaxle bore.

5 If the oil seal cannot be removed with a screwdriver or prybar, a special oil seal removal tool (available at auto parts stores) will be required.

6 Using a large section of pipe or a large deep socket (slightly smaller than the outside diameter of the seal) as a drift, install the new oil seal. Drive it into the bore squarely and make sure it's completely seated. Coat the seal lip with transaxle lubricant.

7 Install the driveaxle(s). Be careful not to damage the lip of the new seal.

5 Manual transmission - removal and installation

REMOVAL

1 Raise the vehicle and support it securely on jackstands.
2 Disconnect the cable from the negative battery terminal (see Chapter 5).
3 Remove the shift knob and shift lever (see Section 2).
4 Remove the lower splash shield, if equipped.
5 Disconnect the hydraulic lines to the clutch release cylinder (see Chapter 8).
6 Remove the front and rear driveshafts (see Chapter 8).
7 Remove the exhaust heat shield, then remove the front section of the exhaust system.
8 Disconnect the electrical connectors to the transfer case shift motor and speed sensor.
9 Place a transmission jack that can support the transfer case and transmission assembly and slightly raise the transmission.
10 Remove the rear transmission mount-to-crossmember fasteners and the crossmember mounting bolts, and lower the crossmember from the vehicle.
11 Lower the transmission assembly slightly and remove the transmission-to-engine bolts. With the help of an assistant, pull the assembly away from the engine and slowly lower it to the ground, checking that it's not catching on other components as you do so.
12 Pull the transmission out from beneath the vehicle, remove it from the jack and set it where it can't roll over and become damaged.
13 If necessary, remove the transfer case from the transmission (see Chapter 7C).

INSTALLATION

14 If removed, install the transfer case (see Chapter 7C).
15 Lubricate the input shaft with a light coat of high-temperature grease. With the transmission secured to the jack, raise it into position behind the engine and carefully slide it forward, engaging the input shaft with the clutch. Do not use excessive force to install the transmission - if the input shaft won't slide into place, readjust the angle of the transmission or turn the input shaft so the splines engage properly with the clutch.
16 Once the transmission is flush with the engine, install the transmission-to-engine bolts. Tighten the bolts to the torque listed in this Chapter's Specifications.

✷✷ CAUTION:

Don't use the bolts to force the transmission and engine together.

17 The remainder of installation is the reverse of removal, but note the following points:
   a) Tighten the crossmember mounting bolts to the torque values listed in the Chapter 10 Specifications.
   b) Bleed the clutch hydraulic system (see Chapter 8).
   c) Fill the transmission with the correct type and amount of transaxle fluid (see Chapter 1).

6 Manual transaxle - removal and installation

➡ **Note: If you're working on a 4WD vehicle, refer to Chapter 7C for the removal procedures for the driveshaft and transfer case.**

REMOVAL

1 Loosen the front wheel lug nuts and the driveaxle/hub nuts.
2 Remove the battery and battery support tray (see Chapter 5).
3 Remove the entire air cleaner assembly along with the intake duct (see Chapter 4).
4 Disconnect the wiring from the back-up light switch. Disconnect the speedometer connection at the transaxle.
5 Disconnect the wiring from the Crankshaft Position (CKP) sensor, the oxygen sensors and the oil pressure sender. Remove their wiring harness mounting bracket.
6 Remove the concentric slave cylinder tube locking clip and separate the tube from the clutch release cylinder.
7 Disconnect both shift cables from the transaxle (see Section 3).
8 Remove the topmost transaxle mounting bolts and support bracket.
9 Remove the starter (see Chapter 5).
10 Support the engine securely from above with a fixture that mounts between the fenders. These can be rented at most rental yards if you don't own one.
11 Raise the vehicle and support it securely on jackstands. Remove both driveaxles (see Chapter 8).
12 Drain the transaxle lubricant (see Chapter 1).
13 Remove the front section of the exhaust system.
14 Make sure that the engine is solidly supported by the fixture. Remove the subframe mounting bolts and lift the subframe clear with the help of an assistant.
15 Put a transmission jack (or a floor jack with an appropriate saddle) under the transaxle. Safety chains will help steady the transaxle on the jack.
16 Remove the remaining transaxle-to-engine bolts. Check to make certain that all connections between the transaxle and the vehicle are disconnected.
17 With the help of an assistant, pull the transaxle away from the engine and slowly lower it to the ground, checking that it's not catching on other components as you do so.
18 Pull the transaxle out from beneath the vehicle, remove it from the jack and set it where it can't roll over and become damaged.

INSTALLATION

19 Lubricate the input shaft with a light coat of high-temperature grease. With the transaxle secured to the jack, raise it into position behind the engine and carefully slide it forward, engaging the input shaft with the clutch. Do not use excessive force to install the transaxle

- if the input shaft won't slide into place, readjust the angle of the transaxle or turn the input shaft so the splines engage properly with the clutch.

20 Once the transaxle is flush with the engine, install the transaxle-to-engine bolts. Tighten the bolts to the torque listed in this Chapter's Specifications.

> ❄ **CAUTION:**
>
> **Don't use the bolts to force the transaxle and engine together.**

21 The remainder of installation is the reverse of removal, but note the following points:

  a) *Tighten the suspension mounting bolts to the torque values listed in the Chapter 10 Specifications.*

  b) *Tighten the driveaxle/hub nuts to the torque value listed in the Chapter 8 Specifications.*

  c) *Tighten the starter mounting bolts to the torque value listed in the Chapter 5 Specifications.*

  d) *Tighten the wheel lug nuts to the torque listed in the Chapter 1 Specifications.*

  e) *Fill the transaxle with the correct type and amount of transaxle fluid (see Chapter 1).*

7   Manual transmission/transaxle overhaul - general information

1 Overhauling a manual transmission/transaxle is a difficult job for the do-it-yourselfer. It involves the disassembly and reassembly of many small parts. Numerous clearances must be precisely measured and, if necessary, changed with select-fit spacers and snap-rings. As a result, if transmission/transaxle problems arise, it can be removed and installed by a competent do-it-yourselfer, but overhaul should be left to a transmission repair shop. Rebuilt units may be available - check with your dealer parts department and auto parts stores. At any rate, the time and money involved in an overhaul is almost sure to exceed the cost of a rebuilt unit.

2 Nevertheless, it's not impossible for an inexperienced mechanic to rebuild a transmission/transaxle if the special tools are available and the job is done in a deliberate step-by-step manner so nothing is overlooked.

3 The tools necessary for an overhaul include: internal and external snap-ring pliers, a bearing puller, a slide hammer, a set of pin punches, a dial indicator and possibly a hydraulic press. In addition, a large, sturdy workbench and a vise or transmission/transaxle stand will be required.

4 During disassembly of the transmission/transaxle, make careful notes of how each piece comes off, where it fits in relation to other pieces and what holds it in place.

5 Before taking the unit apart for repair, it will help if you have some idea what area of the transmission/transaxle is malfunctioning. Certain problems can be closely tied to specific areas in the unit, which can make component examination and replacement easier. Refer to the *Troubleshooting* Section at the front of this manual for information regarding possible sources of trouble.

8   Transmission/transaxle mount - replacement

TRANSMISSION MOUNT

1 Raise the vehicle and support it securely on jackstands.

2 Place a floor jack at the rear of the transmission, then remove the mount-to-rear crossmember fasteners.

3 Remove the nuts and bolts and remove the mount. It may be necessary to raise the transmission slightly to provide enough clearance to remove the mount.

4 Installation is the reverse of removal.

TRANSAXLE MOUNT

5 Support the transaxle from below with a jack, remove the nuts and bolts and remove the mount. It may be necessary to raise the transaxle slightly to provide enough clearance to remove the mount.

6 Installation is the reverse of removal.

➡ **Note: Install all of the mount fasteners before tightening any of them.**

Specifications

General

Transmission/transaxle oil type	See Chapter 1
Transmission/transaxle oil capacity	See Chapter 1

Torque specifications	Ft-lbs (unless otherwise indicated)	Nm
Transmission-to-engine mounting bolts	31 to 40	42 to 55
Transaxle-to-engine mounting bolts	31 to 35.5	42 to 48

7B

AUTOMATIC
TRANSMISSION/
TRANSAXLE

1 General information

1 All information on the automatic transmission/transaxle is included in this Part of Chapter 7. Information for the manual transmission/transaxle can be found in Part A of this Chapter.

2 Because of the complexity of the automatic transmission/transaxles and the specialized equipment necessary to perform most service operations, this Chapter contains only those procedures related to general diagnosis, routine maintenance, adjustment and removal and installation.

3 If the transmission/transaxle requires major repair work, it should be left to a dealer service department or an automotive or transmission repair shop. Once properly diagnosed you can, however, remove and install the transmission/transaxle yourself and save the expense, even if the repair work is done by a transmission shop.

2 Diagnosis - general

1 Automatic transmission/transaxle malfunctions may be caused by five general conditions:

a) *Poor engine performance*
b) *Improper adjustments*
c) *Hydraulic malfunctions*
d) *Mechanical malfunctions*
e) *Malfunctions in the computer or its signal network*

2 Diagnosis of these problems should always begin with a check of the easily repaired items: fluid level and condition (see Chapter 1), shift cable adjustment and shift lever installation. Next, perform a road test to determine if the problem has been corrected or if more diagnosis is necessary. If the problem persists after the preliminary tests and corrections are completed, additional diagnosis should be performed by a dealer service department or other qualified transmission repair shop. Refer to the *Troubleshooting* Section at the front of this manual for information on symptoms of transmission/transaxle problems.

PRELIMINARY CHECKS

3 Drive the vehicle to warm the transmission/transaxle to normal operating temperature.
4 Check the fluid level (see Chapter 1):

a) *If the fluid level is unusually low, add enough fluid to bring the level within the designated area of the dipstick, then check for external leaks (see following).*
b) *If the fluid level is abnormally high, drain off the excess, then check the drained fluid for contamination by coolant. The presence of engine coolant in the automatic transmission fluid indicates that a failure has occurred in the internal radiator oil cooler walls that separate the coolant from the transmission fluid (see Chapter 3).*
c) *If the fluid is foaming, drain it and refill the transmission/transaxle, then check for coolant in the fluid, or a high fluid level.*

5 Check the engine idle speed.
➡ **Note: If the engine is malfunctioning, do not proceed with the preliminary checks until it has been repaired and runs normally.**
6 Check the shift cable.
7 If hard shifting is experienced, inspect the shift cable under the steering column and at the manual lever on the transmission/transaxle.

FLUID LEAK DIAGNOSIS

8 Most fluid leaks are easy to locate visually. Repair usually consists of replacing a seal or gasket. If a leak is difficult to find, the following procedure may help.
9 Identify the fluid. Make sure it's transmission fluid and not engine oil or brake fluid (automatic transmission fluid is a deep red color).
10 Try to pinpoint the source of the leak. Drive the vehicle several miles, then park it over a large sheet of cardboard. After a minute or two, you should be able to locate the leak by determining the source of the fluid dripping onto the cardboard.
11 Make a careful visual inspection of the suspected component and the area immediately around it. Pay particular attention to gasket mating surfaces. A mirror is often helpful for finding leaks in areas that are hard to see.
12 If the leak still cannot be found, clean the suspected area thoroughly with a degreaser or solvent, then dry it thoroughly.
13 Drive the vehicle for several miles at normal operating temperature and varying speeds. After driving the vehicle, visually inspect the suspected component again.
14 Once the leak has been located, the cause must be determined before it can be properly repaired. If a gasket is replaced but the sealing flange is bent, the new gasket will not stop the leak. The bent flange must be straightened.
15 Before attempting to repair a leak, check that the following conditions are corrected, or they may cause another leak.

➡ **Note: Some of the following conditions cannot be fixed without highly specialized tools and expertise. Such problems must be referred to a qualified transmission shop or a dealer service department.**

GASKET LEAKS

16 Check the pan periodically. Make sure the bolts are tight, no bolts are missing, the gasket is in good condition and the pan is flat (dents in the pan may indicate damage to the valve body inside).
17 If the pan gasket is leaking, the fluid level or the fluid pressure may be too high, the vent may be plugged, the pan bolts may be too tight, the pan sealing flange may be warped, the sealing surface of the transmission/transaxle housing may be damaged, the gasket may be damaged or the transmission/transaxle casting may be cracked or porous. If sealant instead of gasket material has been used to form a seal between the pan and the transmission/transaxle housing, it may be the wrong type of sealant.

SEAL LEAKS

18 If a transmission/transaxle seal is leaking, the fluid level or pressure may be too high, the vent may be plugged, the seal bore may be damaged, the seal itself may be damaged or improperly installed, the surface of the shaft protruding through the seal may be damaged or a loose bearing may be causing excessive shaft movement.

19 Make sure the dipstick tube seal is in good condition and the tube is properly seated. Periodically check the area around the sensors for leakage. If transmission fluid is evident, check the seals for damage.

CASE LEAKS

20 If the case itself appears to be leaking, the casting is porous and

will have to be repaired or replaced.

21 Make sure the oil cooler hose fittings are tight and in good condition.

FLUID COMES OUT VENT PIPE OR FILL TUBE

22 If this condition occurs, the possible causes are: the transmission/transaxle is overfilled, there is coolant in the fluid, the case is porous, the dipstick is incorrect, the vent is plugged or the drain-back holes are plugged.

3 Shift lever - replacement

TRANSMISSION MODELS

1 Remove the center console (see Chapter 11).

2 To replace the shift lever handle, loosen the two small screws on the sides of the handle, then remove it **(see illustration)**. If you remove the button and spring from the handle, be sure to note the direction the button is installed.

3 Disconnect the shift cable, the shift lock cable and the key lock cable by popping the cable ends off of the ball studs.

4 Disconnect the inhibitor switch electrical connector.

5 Remove the shift lever mounting nuts and the lever assembly.

6 Installation is the reverse of removal.

TRANSAXLE MODELS

7 Pull the shift lever knob straight up to remove it from the lever.

8 Remove the center console (see Chapter 11).

9 Disconnect the electrical connectors.

10 Disconnect the shift cable from the shift lever and bracket (see Section 4).

11 Remove the mounting bolts and shift lever assembly.

12 Installation is the reverse of removal.

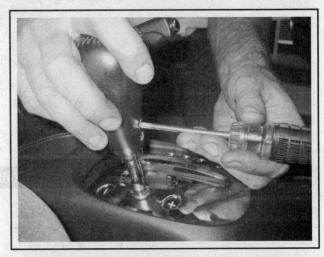

3.2 There are two small screws on the sides of the shift handle; when replacing the handle, align the push button with the plunger to allow the handle to slip into the correct position, allowing the screws to line up with their holes

4 Shift cable - replacement

1 Disconnect the cable from the negative battery terminal (see Chapter 5).

2 Remove the center console (see Chapter 11).

3 On transmission models, remove the nuts that secure the cable housing and cable to the shifter **(see illustration)**. On transaxle models remove the retaining clip and clamp that secure the cable housing to the bracket and shift lever.

4 Feed the cable through the instrument panel area and through the grommet in the firewall.

5 Disconnect the cable from retainers and interfering components.

6 On transmission models, remove the cable cover housing, remove the cable retaining pin and washer, and detach the cable.

7 On transaxle models, remove the cable bracket bolts, remove the manual lever nut, and disconnect the cable from the lever at the transaxle.

8 Remove the cable from the vehicle.

9 Installation is the reverse of removal.

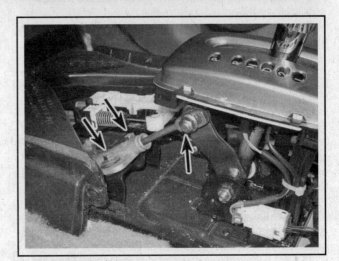

4.3 Shift cable mounting nut locations - automatic transmission model

5 Transmission cooler - replacement

1 Disconnect the cable from the negative battery terminal (see Chapter 5).

2 Remove the front bumper cover (see Chapter 11).

3 Disconnect and plug the transmission cooler lines.

4 Remove the mounting bolts **(see illustration),** and remove the cooler from the bottom of the radiator.

5 Installation is the reverse of removal.

5.4 Disconnect the cooler lines (A), then remove the transmission cooler mounting bolts (B)

6 Automatic transmission - removal and installation

REMOVAL

1 Disconnect the cable from the negative terminal of the battery (see Chapter 5).

2 Drain the fluid from the transmission (see Chapter 1).

3 Remove the entire air filter assembly, including the air duct (see Chapter 4).

4 Remove the splash shield mounting bolts and shield.

5 Disconnect the wiring harnesses from the oxygen sensors, speedometer sensor, Transmission Range sensor, solenoid connector, speed sensor, transfer case shift motor (if equipped) and the oil temperature sensor.

6 Disconnect the transmission fluid cooler hoses and seal their ends to prevent leakage and contamination.

7 Remove the front driveshaft (2009 and earlier 4WD models) (see Chapter 8).

8 Remove the rear driveshaft (see Chapter 8).

9 Disconnect the shift control cable.

10 Remove the starter (see Chapter 5).

11 Remove the upper transmission mounting bolts.

12 Remove the inspection plate, then remove the torque converter-to-driveplate fasteners. This will involve rotating the engine for access to all of the bolts. Have an assistant do this with a ratchet and socket on the end of the crankshaft. This will also hold the engine from rotating as the bolts are loosened. Mark the position of the torque converter on the driveplate with a dab of paint.

13 Remove the front section of the exhaust system.

14 Put a transmission jack (or a floor jack with an appropriate saddle) under the transmission. Safety chains will help steady the transmission and transfer case (if equipped) on the jack.

15 Remove the remaining transmission-to-engine bolts. Check that all connections between the transmission and the vehicle are disconnected.

16 Remove the crossmember bolts, then move the transmission to the rear to disengage it from the engine block dowel pins; make sure the torque converter is detached from the driveplate. Lower the transmission with the jack. Clamp a pair of locking pliers on the bellhousing case. The pliers will prevent the torque converter from falling out while you're removing the transmission.

17 Pull the transmission out from beneath the vehicle, remove it from the jack and set it where it can't roll over and become damaged.

INSTALLATION

18 Installation is the reverse of removal, but note the following points:

a) *As the torque converter is reinstalled, ensure that the drive tangs at the center of the torque converter hub engage with the recesses in the automatic transmission fluid pump inner gear. This can be confirmed by turning the torque converter while pushing it towards the transmission. If it isn't fully engaged, it will clunk into place.*

b) *When installing the transmission, make sure the matchmarks on the torque converter and driveplate line up.*

c) *Install all of the driveplate-to-torque converter nuts before tightening any of them.*

d) *Tighten the driveplate-to-torque converter fasteners to the specified torque.*

e) *Tighten the transmission mounting bolts to the specified torque.*

f) *Fill the transmission with the correct type and amount of automatic transmission fluid (see Chapter 1).*

g) *On completion, adjust the shift cable and Transmission Range sensor.*

7 Automatic transaxle - removal and installation

REMOVAL

1 Disconnect the cable from the negative terminal of the battery (see Chapter 5).

2 Remove the battery and battery tray (see Chapter 5).

3 Remove the entire air filter assembly, including the air duct (see Chapter 4).

4 Disconnect the electrical connectors from the solenoid valve and inhibitor switch.

5 On 3.5L V6 models, disconnect the electrical connector for the Crankshaft Position (CKP) sensor.

6 Disconnect the transmission fluid cooler hoses and seal their ends to prevent leakage and contamination.

7 Disconnect the shift control cable.

8 Support the engine securely from above with a fixture that mounts between the fenders. These can be rented at most rental yards if you don't own one.

9 Remove the upper transaxle mounting bolts.

10 On 2.4L four-cylinder models, remove the starter (see Chapter 5).

11 Loosen the front wheel lug nuts and the driveaxle/hub nuts. Raise the vehicle and support it securely on jackstands.

12 Remove the inspection plate, then remove the torque converter-to-driveplate fasteners. This will involve rotating the engine for access to all of the bolts. Have an assistant do this with a ratchet and socket on the end of the crankshaft. This will also hold the engine from rotating as the bolts are loosened. Mark the position of the torque converter on the driveplate with a dab of paint.

13 Make sure that the engine is solidly supported by the fixture. Remove the subframe (see Chapter 10).

14 Put a transmission jack (or a floor jack with an appropriate saddle) under the transaxle. Safety chains will help steady the transaxle on the jack.

15 Remove the remaining transaxle-to-engine bolts. Check that all connections between the transaxle and the vehicle are disconnected.

16 Move the transaxle to the rear to disengage it from the engine block dowel pins; make sure the torque converter is detached from the driveplate. Lower the transaxle with the jack. Clamp a pair of locking pliers on the bellhousing case. The pliers will prevent the torque converter from falling out while you're removing the transaxle.

17 Pull the transaxle out from beneath the vehicle, remove it from the jack and set it where it can't roll over and become damaged.

INSTALLATION

18 Installation is the reverse of removal, but note the following points:

a) As the torque converter is reinstalled, ensure that the drive tangs at the center of the torque converter hub engage with the recesses in the automatic transaxle fluid pump inner gear. This can be confirmed by turning the torque converter while pushing it towards the transaxle. If it isn't fully engaged, it will clunk into place.

b) When installing the transaxle, make sure the matchmarks on the torque converter and driveplate line up.

c) Install all of the driveplate-to-torque converter nuts before tightening any of them.

d) Tighten the driveplate-to-torque converter fasteners to the specified torque.

e) Tighten the transaxle mounting bolts to the specified torque.

f) Tighten the subframe mounting bolts to the torque listed in the Chapter 10 Specifications.

g) Tighten the driveaxle/hub nuts to the torque listed in the Chapter 8 Specifications.

h) Tighten the wheel lug nuts to the torque listed in the Chapter 1 Specifications.

8 Automatic transmission/transaxle overhaul - general information

1 In the event of a problem occurring, it will be necessary to establish whether the fault is electrical, mechanical or hydraulic in nature, before repair work can be contemplated. Diagnosis requires detailed knowledge of the transmission/transaxle's operation and construction, as well as access to specialized test equipment, and so is deemed to be beyond the scope of this manual. It is therefore essential that problems with the automatic transmission/transaxle are referred to a dealer service department or other qualified repair facility for assessment.

2 Note that a faulty transmission/transaxle should not be removed before the vehicle has been diagnosed by a knowledgeable technician equipped with the proper tools, as troubleshooting must be performed with the unit installed in the vehicle.

9 Automatic transaxle fluid level check (2011 and later models)

❈ WARNING:

This procedure is potentially dangerous and is best left to a professional shop with a safe lifting apparatus. The vehicle must be kept level while being safely raised high enough for access to the check plug on the transaxle.

➡ **Note: On 2011 and later models, checking the transaxle fluid level is not a routine maintenance item and should normally only be done if a leak is suspected.**

➡ **Note: This procedure should be performed with the vehicle at normal operating temperature. Normal operating temperature is reached after a few miles of driving.**

1 With the vehicle raised and safely supported, start the engine and allow it to idle for a minute, then move the shift lever from Park to Drive, then Park to Drive. Repeat this step one more time at idle.

➡ **Note: Incorrect fluid level readings will result if the vehicle has just been driven at high speeds for an extended period, in hot weather in city traffic, or if it has been pulling a trailer. If any of these conditions apply, wait until the fluid has cooled (about 30 minutes).**

2 With the engine running and the transaxle at normal operating temperature, locate the oil level plug. The oil level plug is located on the valve body cover on the driver's side of the transaxle.

3 Place a container under the check plug and remove it. Observe the fluid as it drips into the pan, indicating correct fluid level.

4 The fluid should flow out in a thin steady stream. If fluid pours out excessively, the transaxle may have been overfilled. Double-check to make sure the vehicle is level. If no fluid drips from the check hole, add small amounts of transaxle fluid (see Chapter 1 for the correct type) through the fill plug at the top of the transaxle, near the transmission range sensor. A long-necked funnel will be necessary to add fluid through the fill plug opening.

5 Install the check plug and tighten it securely

6 Check under the vehicle for leaks after the first few trips.

Specifications

General

Fluid type and capacity	See Chapter 1

Torque specifications	Ft-lbs	Nm
Torque converter-to-driveplate bolts		
2009 and earlier models	25 to 30	34 to 40
2011 and later models	33 to 38	45 to 52
Transmission-to-engine mounting bolts		
Upper bolts (2)	22 to 30	30 to 40
Side bolts (4) - two per side	58 to 72	79 to 98
Lower bolts (5)	25 to 30	34 to 40
Transaxle-to-engine mounting bolts		
Four-cylinder models		
Upper bolts (2)	31 to 40	42 to 54
Upper side bolts (2) - left side	36 to 47	49 to 64
Lower side middle bolts (2) - each side	58 to 72	79 to 98
2011 and later V6 models		
Upper bolts (3)	31 to 40	42 to 54
Lower front side middle		
bolts (2) - each side	36 to 47	49 to 64
Lower rear side middle bolt (1)	58 to 72	79 to 98
Lower bolts (4)	29 to 34	39 to 46

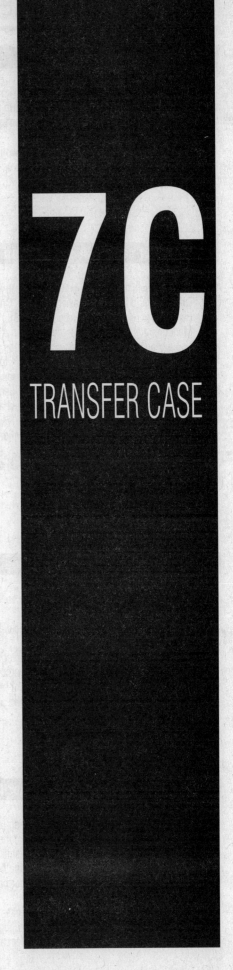

7C

TRANSFER CASE

Section

1 General information

1 Due to the complexity of the transfer case covered in this manual and the need for specialized equipment to perform most service operations, this Chapter contains only routine maintenance and removal and installation procedures.

2 If the transfer case requires major repair work, it should be taken to a dealer service department or an automotive or transmission repair shop. You can, however, remove and install the transfer case yourself and save the expense of that labor, even if the repair work is done by a transmission shop. Note that a faulty transfer case should not be removed before the vehicle has been diagnosed by a knowledgeable technician equipped with the proper tools, as troubleshooting must be performed with the transfer case installed in the vehicle.

2 Transfer case rear output shaft oil seal (2009 and earlier models) - removal and installation

1 Raise the vehicle and support it securely on jackstands.

2 Drain the fluid from the transfer case (see Chapter 1).

3 Remove the rear driveshaft (see Chapter 8).

4 Mark the relative positions of the pinion, nut and flange.

5 Use a beam- or dial-type inch-pound torque wrench to determine the torque required to rotate the pinion. Record it for use later.

6 Count the number of threads visible between the end of the nut and the end of the pinion shaft and record it for use later.

7 Remove the flange mounting nut, using a chain wrench to hold the pinion flange while loosening the locknut.

8 Remove the companion flange; a small puller may be required for removal.

9 Pry out the seal with a screwdriver or a seal removal tool. Don't damage the seal bore.

10 Lubricate the lips of the new seal with multi-purpose grease and tap it evenly into position with a seal installation tool or a large socket. Make sure it enters the housing squarely and is tapped into its full depth.

11 Align the mating marks made before disassembly and install the companion flange. If necessary, tighten the pinion nut to draw the flange into place.

12 Tighten the nut carefully until the original number of threads are exposed and the marks are aligned.

13 Measure the torque required to rotate the pinion and tighten the nut in small increments until it matches the figure recorded in Step 5.

14 Install the driveshaft, then add the specified lubricant to the transfer case (see Chapter 1).

3 Transfer case driveaxle oil seal (2011 and later models) - removal and installation

1 Break the right front hub nut loose with a socket and large breaker bar.

2 Loosen the wheel lug nuts, raise the vehicle and support it securely on jackstands. Remove the wheel.

3 Remove the driveaxle assembly (see Chapter 8).

4 Carefully pry out the oil seal with a seal removal tool or a large screwdriver; make sure you don't scratch the seal bore.

5 Using a seal installer or a large deep socket as a drift, install the new oil seal. Drive it into the bore squarely and make sure it's completely seated.

6 Lubricate the lip of the new seal with multi-purpose grease, then install a new dust shield.

7 Install the driveaxle (see Chapter 8).

8 The remainder of installation is the reverse of removal. Check the transfer case lubricant level and add some, if necessary, to bring it to the appropriate level (see Chapter 1).

4 External electronic shift motor (2009 and earlier models) - removal and installation

1 Raise the vehicle and support it securely on jackstands.

2 Remove the mounting bolt from the end of the motor, then remove the three bolts around the flange of the shift motor.

3 Remove the speed sensor bracket mounting bolt. Disconnect the electrical connector and remove the speed sensor bracket and sensor as an assembly.

4 Remove the shift motor from the transfer case.

5 Position the motor assembly so that the triangle slot in the motor will align with the shift shaft in the transfer case. Slide the motor inwards to engage the shift shaft, then rotate the motor clockwise until the motor mounting holes are aligned.

6 Install a new O-ring on to the sensor, then install the speed sensor assembly in the cover.

7 Install the speed sensor bracket over the speed sensor, then install the shift motor mounting bolts and tighten them securely.

8 The remainder of installation is the reverse of removal. Tighten the sensor bracket mounting bolts securely.

5 Transfer case - removal and installation

1 Disconnect the cable from the negative battery terminal (see Chapter 5).

2 Raise the vehicle and support it securely on jackstands.

2009 AND EARLIER MODELS

3 Disconnect the front and rear driveshaft from the transfer case (see Chapter 8). Support them temporarily with wire.

4 Disconnect the speed sensor and 4WD motor electrical connectors.

➡ **Note: On 2006 and earlier 3.5L V6 engines, it may be necessary to disconnect and remove the rear exhaust pipe.**

5 Remove the transfer case wiring harness mounting bracket fastener, and remove the bracket from the rear of the transfer case.

6 Remove the transfer case adapter mounting bolts.

7 Support the transfer case with a floor jack.

8 With the help of an assistant, use a screwdriver to pry the transfer case from the transmission and lower the transfer case from the vehicle.

2011 AND LATER MODELS

9 Remove the front exhaust pipe and muffler (see Chapter 4).

10 Remove the rear driveshaft (see Chapter 8).

11 Remove the passenger's side driveaxle (see Chapter 8).

12 Remove the transfer case right side support bracket mounting bolts, and remove the bracket.

13 Remove the transfer case-to-transaxle and transaxle-to-transfer case mounting bolts.

14 Separate the transfer case from the transaxle.

ALL MODELS

15 Installation is the reverse of removal, noting the following points:

a) *Install a new O-ring seal to the case, if necessary.*

b) *Tighten the exhaust system fasteners securely.*

c) *Tighten the driveshaft fasteners to the torque listed in the Chapter 8 Specifications.*

d) *Tighten the transfer case fasteners securely.*

e) *Refill the transfer case with the proper type and amount of fluid (see Chapter 1).*

f) *Tighten the wheel lug nuts to the torque listed in the Chapter 1 Specifications.*

6 Intelligent Torque Controlled Coupling (ITCC) (2011 and later models) - removal and installation

1 Raise the vehicle and support it securely on jackstands.

2 Remove rear driveshaft (see Chapter 8).

3 Drain the rear differential fluid (see Chapter 1).

4 Disconnect the electrical connectors to the Intelligent Torque Controlled Coupling (ITCC) magnetic clutch **(see illustration)**.

5 Remove the ITCC mounting bolts, then use a flat-blade screwdriver to separate the coupling from the differential.

6 Clean the sealing surfaces, making sure all the sealer is removed, then spray the mating surfaces with brake cleaner to remove all oil residue.

7 Apply a continues bead of sealant approximately 1/8-inch (3 mm) wide around the coupling mating surface. If the sealant is not in a continuous bead, overlap any breaks in the bead by 1/2-inch (10 mm).

8 Align the coupling with the differential, place the coupling onto the differential and install the bolts. Tighten the bolts to the torque listed in this Chapter's Specifications.

9 The remainder of installation is the reverse of removal.

6.4 Disconnect the electrical connectors to the ITCC

Specifications

Transfer case fluid type	See Chapter 1

Torque specifications	Ft-lbs	Nm
Intelligent Torque Controlled Coupling (ITCC) bolts	44 to 47	60 to 64

8

CLUTCH AND DRIVELINE

Section

1 General Information

1 The information in this Chapter deals with the components from the rear of the engine to the wheels, except for the transmission or transaxle and transfer case, which are dealt with in Chapter 7. For the purposes of this Chapter, these components are grouped into three categories - clutch, driveshaft and axles/driveaxles.

2 Since nearly all the procedures covered in this Chapter involve working under the vehicle, make sure it's securely supported on sturdy jackstands or on a hoist where the vehicle can be easily raised and lowered.

2 Clutch - description and check

1 All vehicles with a manual transmission/transaxle use a single dry plate, diaphragm spring type clutch. The clutch disc has a splined hub which allows it to slide along the splines of the transmission/transaxle input shaft. The clutch and pressure plate are held in contact by spring pressure exerted by the diaphragm in the pressure plate.

2 The clutch release system is operated by hydraulic pressure. The hydraulic release system consists of the clutch pedal, a master cylinder and fluid reservoir, the hydraulic line, a release (or slave) cylinder - which actuates the clutch release lever - and the clutch release (or throwout) bearing.

3 When pressure is applied to the clutch pedal to release the clutch, hydraulic pressure is exerted against the outer end of the clutch release lever (2004 through 2006 models) or directly to the release bearing via a concentric release cylinder (2011 and later models). The release bearing pushes against the fingers of the diaphragm spring of the pressure plate assembly, which in turn releases the clutch plate.

4 Terminology can be a problem when discussing the clutch components because common names are in some cases different from those used by the manufacturer. For example, the driven plate is also called the clutch plate or disc, the clutch release bearing is sometimes called a throwout bearing, the release cylinder is sometimes called the operating or slave cylinder.

5 Other than to replace components with obvious damage, some preliminary checks should be performed to diagnose clutch problems.

a) The first check should be of the fluid level in the clutch master cylinder. If the fluid level is excessively low, add fluid as necessary and inspect the hydraulic system for leaks (fluid level will actually rise as the clutch wears).

b) To check clutch spin down time, run the engine at normal idle speed with the shifter in Neutral (clutch pedal up - engaged). Disengage the clutch (pedal down), wait several seconds and shift into Reverse. No grinding noise should be heard. A grinding noise would most likely indicate a problem in the pressure plate or the clutch disc.

c) To check for complete clutch release, run the engine (with the parking brake applied to prevent movement) and hold the clutch pedal approximately 1/2 inch from the floor. Shift between First gear and Reverse several times. If the shift is hard or grinds, component failure is indicated. Check the release cylinder pushrod travel. With the clutch pedal depressed completely, the release cylinder pushrod should extend substantially. If it doesn't, check the fluid level in the clutch master cylinder (see Chapter 1).

d) Visually inspect the pivot bushing at the top of the clutch pedal to make sure there is no binding or excessive play.

e) Crawl under the vehicle and make sure the clutch release lever is solidly mounted on the ball stud (2004 through 2006 models only).

3 Clutch release system components - removal and installation

MASTER CYLINDER

2004 through 2006 models

1 Drain the clutch fluid through the bleeder screw. Catch the fluid in a container or with rags to prevent it from contacting painted surfaces.

2 Working under the instrument panel, disconnect the clutch pushrod from
the pedal by removing the cotter pin, washer and the clevis pin.

3 Disconnect the clutch tubing from the clutch master cylinder.

4 Remove the mounting bolts and detach the master cylinder from the firewall.

5 Installation is the reverse of removal. Bleed the system (see Section 4).

2011 and later models

6 Drain the clutch fluid through the bleeder screw at the transaxle.

7 Clamp-off the fluid feed hose coming from the brake master cylinder, then detach the hose from the master cylinder.

8 Use a flare-nut wrench to unscrew the hydraulic line fitting from the master cylinder.

9 Working underneath the instrument panel, remove the clutch pedal bracket mounting bolts and detach the bracket from the firewall.

10 Unscrew the mounting bolts and remove the master cylinder from the clutch pedal bracket.

11 Installation is the reverse of removal. Bleed the system (see Section 4).

RELEASE CYLINDER

2004 through 2006 models

12 Raise the vehicle and support it securely on jackstands.

13 Disconnect the clutch fluid hydraulic line from the release cylinder. Use a flare-nut wrench to protect the tube nut. Have rags handy, as some fluid will be lost as the line is removed. Also have a plug ready and immediately plug the line to prevent leakage.

14 Remove the two release cylinder mounting bolts.

15 Separate the release cylinder from the transmission.

16 Installation is the reverse of removal. Make sure the pushrod dust boot is in good condition and the pushrod is seated correctly in its pocket in the release lever. Tighten the release cylinder mounting bolts to the torque listed in this Chapter's Specifications.

17 Bleed the clutch hydraulic system (see Section 4).

2011 and later models

18 Remove the transaxle from the vehicle (see Chapter 7A).

19 Remove the fasteners and detach the concentric release cylinder/release bearing from the transaxle.

20 Installation is the reverse of removal.

21 Bleed the clutch hydraulic system (see Section 4).

4 Clutch hydraulic system - bleeding

1 The hydraulic system should be bled of all air whenever any part of the system has been removed, or if the fluid level has been allowed to fall so low that air has been drawn into the master cylinder. The procedure is very similar to bleeding a brake system.

2 Fill the master cylinder with new brake fluid conforming to DOT 3 specifications.

⁂ CAUTION:

Do not re-use any of the fluid coming from the system during the bleeding operation or use fluid which has been inside an open container for an extended period of time.

3 Raise the vehicle and place it securely on jackstands to gain access to the release cylinder, which is located on the left side of the clutch housing.

4 Remove the dust cap that fits over the bleeder valve and push a length of plastic hose over the valve. Place the other end of the hose into a clear container with about two inches of brake fluid in it. The hose end must be submerged in the fluid.

5 Have an assistant depress and hold the clutch pedal. Open the bleeder valve on the release cylinder, allowing fluid to flow through the hose. Close the bleeder valve when fluid stops flowing from the hose. Once closed, have your assistant release the pedal.

6 Continue this process until all air is evacuated from the system, indicated by a full, solid stream of fluid being ejected from the bleeder valve each time, and no air bubbles in the hose or container. Keep a close watch on the fluid level inside the clutch master cylinder reservoir; if the level drops too low, air will be sucked back into the system and the process will have to be started all over again.

7 Install the dust cap and lower the vehicle. Check carefully for proper operation before placing the vehicle in normal service.

5 Clutch components - removal, inspection and installation

⁂ WARNING:

Dust produced by clutch wear and deposited on clutch components is hazardous to your health. DO NOT blow it out with compressed air and DO NOT inhale it. DO NOT use gasoline or petroleum-based solvents to remove clutch dust. Brake system cleaner should be used to flush the dust into a drain pan. After the clutch components are wiped clean with a rag, dispose of the contaminated rags and cleaner in a covered, marked container.

REMOVAL

1 Access to clutch components is normally accomplished by removing the transmission/transaxle from the vehicle. If, of course, the engine is being removed for major overhaul, then check the clutch for wear and replace worn components as necessary. However, the relatively low cost of the clutch components compared to the time and trouble spent gaining access to them warrants their replacement any time the engine or transmission/transaxle is removed, unless they are nearly new. The following procedures are based on the assumption that the engine will stay in place.

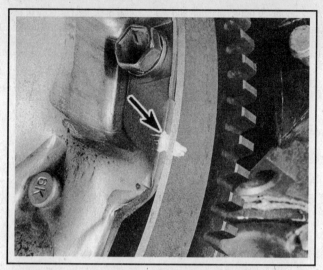

5.4 Mark the pressure plate and flywheel to ensure proper alignment during installation (this won't be necessary if a new pressure plate is to be installed)

5.8 Check the flywheel for cracks, hot spots and other obvious defects - slight imperfections can be removed by a machine shop

2   Remove the transmission/transaxle from the vehicle (see Chapter 7A). Support the engine while the transmission/transaxle is out. Preferably, an engine hoist or support fixture should be used to support it from above. However, if a jack is used under the engine, make sure a piece of wood is between the jack and the oil pan to spread the load.

✳✳ CAUTION:

The oil pump pickup is located very close to the bottom of the pan. If the pan is bent, engine oil starvation could occur.

3   The clutch fork can remain attached to the bellhousing on 2004 through 2006 models.
4   Inspect the flywheel and clutch for indexing marks **(see illustration)**. If they can't be found, scribe marks yourself so the pressure plate and flywheel will be in the same alignment during installation (if you're not replacing them).
5   Insert a clutch alignment tool through the disc and into the pilot bushing to support the disc.
6   Turn each pressure plate bolt only 1/4 turn at a time to loosen the pressure plate-to-flywheel bolts. Work in a criss-cross pattern until all spring force is relieved. Hold the pressure plate securely and completely remove the bolts, followed by the pressure plate and clutch disc.

INSPECTION

7   When a problem occurs in the clutch, it can usually be attributed to wear of the driven plate assembly (clutch disc). However, all components should be checked at this time.
8   Inspect the flywheel for cracks, heat checking, grooves and other obvious defects **(see illustration)**. If the imperfections are small, a machine shop can machine the surface flat and smooth. This is highly recommended regardless of the surface appearance. Refer to Chapter 2A for the flywheel removal and installation procedures.

9   Inspect the pilot bearing (see Section 7).
10   Inspect the lining of the clutch disc **(see illustration)**. There should be at least 1/16 inch of lining above the rivet heads. Check for loose rivets, cracks, distortion, broken springs and other obvious damage. As mentioned above, the clutch disc is routinely replaced, so if in doubt about the condition, replace it with a new one.
11   The release bearing should also be replaced along with the clutch disc (see Section 6).

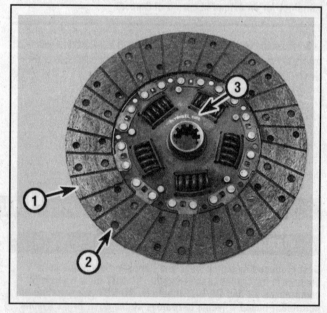

5.10 The clutch plate

1   *Lining* - this will wear down in use
2   *Rivets* - these secure the lining an will damage the flywheel or pressure plate if allowed to contact the surface
3   *Marks* - "Flywheel side" or similar

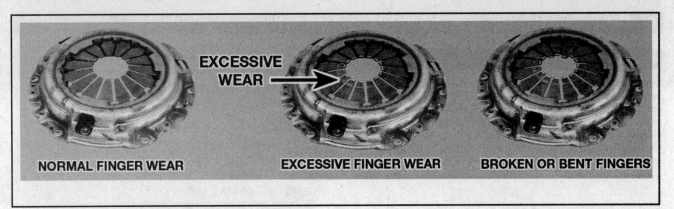

5.12a Replace the pressure plate if excessive wear is noted

5.12b Examine the pressure plate for scoring marks, cracks and evidence of overheating

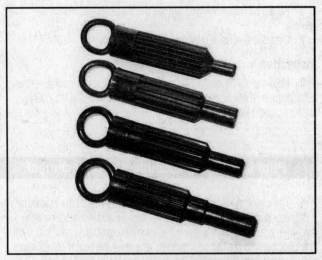

5.15 Center the clutch disc using an alignment tool

12 Check the machined surfaces and the spring fingers of the pressure plate **(see illustrations)**. If the surface is grooved or otherwise damaged, replace it. Also check for obvious damage, distortion, cracking, etc. Light glazing can be removed with sandpaper or emery cloth. If a new pressure plate is required, new and rebuilt units are available.

INSTALLATION

13 Clean the flywheel and pressure plate machined surfaces with brake system cleaner. It's important that no oil or grease is on these surfaces or the lining of the clutch disc. Handle the parts only with clean hands.

14 Position the disc onto the flywheel with the side marked "fly-wheel" against the flywheel. If there are no marks, install the clutch disc with the springs facing the transmission/transaxle.

15 Secure the disc with the alignment tool **(see illustration)**. Make sure the tool engages the pilot bearing.

16 Put the pressure plate into place, aligning the marks you previously made if you're not replacing it. Install the bolts and tighten them finger tight.

17 Tighten the bolts a little at a time, working in a criss-cross pattern to prevent distorting the cover. After all of the bolts are snug, tighten them to the torque listed in this Chapter's Specifications. Remove the alignment tool.

18 Refer to Section 6 for information on the proper installation of the release bearing.

19 The remainder of installation is the reverse of removal.

6 Clutch release bearing - removal, inspection and installation

❊❊❊ WARNING:

Dust produced by clutch wear and deposited on clutch components is hazardous to your health. DO NOT blow it out with compressed air and DO NOT inhale it. DO NOT use gasoline or petroleum-based solvents to remove clutch dust. Brake system cleaner should be used to flush the dust into a drain pan. After the clutch components are wiped clean with a rag, dispose of the contaminated rags and cleaner in a covered, marked container.

2004 THROUGH 2006 MODELS

Removal

1   Refer to Chapter 7A and remove the transmission from the vehicle.
2   Detach the release bearing from the clutch fork.

Inspection

3   Hold the center of the bearing and apply force while rotating the outer portion. If the bearing doesn't operate smoothly or if it's noisy, replace it with a new one. Wipe the bearing with a clean rag and inspect if for damage, wear and cracks. Don't immerse it in solvent - it's sealed for life and to do so would ruin it. Also check the release fork for wear on the fingertips, cracks and other damage.

Installation

4   Apply a small amount of high-temperature grease to the inside of the release bearing and to the area where the fork fingers contact it.
5   Install the bearing onto the input shaft of the transmission, engaging it with the fork fingers.
6   Install the transmission (see Chapter 7A).
7   The remainder of the installation is the reverse of removal.

2011 AND LATER MODELS

8   Refer to Chapter 7A and remove the transaxle from the vehicle.
9   Remove the fasteners and detach the release bearing/release cylinder from the transaxle.
10 Installation is the reverse of the removal procedure.
11 After installing the transaxle, bleed the clutch hydraulic system (see Section 4).

7 Pilot bearing - inspection and replacement

1   The clutch pilot bearing is pressed into the rear of the crankshaft. It is greased at the factory and does not require additional lubrication. Its primary purpose is to support the transmission/transaxle input shaft. The pilot bearing should be inspected whenever the clutch components are removed from the engine. Due to its inaccessibility, if you are in doubt as to its condition, replace it with a new one.

➡ **Note: If the engine has been removed from the vehicle, disregard the following steps which do not apply.**

2   Remove the transmission/transaxle (see Chapter 7A).
3   Remove the clutch components (see Section 5).

4   Inspect for any excessive wear, scoring, lack of grease, dryness or obvious damage. If any of these conditions are noted, the bearing should be replaced.
5   Removal can be accomplished with a slide hammer fitted with a puller attachment **(see illustration)**, which are available at most auto parts stores or equipment rental yards.
6   To install the new bearing, lightly lubricate the outside surface with multi-purpose grease, then drive it into the recess with a hammer and bearing/bushing driver. Make sure the bearing seal faces toward the transmission. If you don't have a bearing driver, carefully tap it into place with a hammer and a socket **(see illustration)**.

7.5 A small slide hammer puller is handy for removing the pilot bushing

7.6 The pilot bearing can be driven in with an appropriately sized socket

❊❊ **CAUTION:**

Be careful not to let the bearing become cocked in the bore.

7 Install the clutch components, transaxle and all other components removed previously, tightening all fasteners properly.

8   Driveshaft - removal and installation

1 Raise the vehicle and support it securely on jackstands. Place the transmission in Neutral with the parking brake off. Block the wheels to prevent the vehicle from rolling.

REAR DRIVESHAFT (ALL 2009 AND EARLIER MODELS, AND 2011 AND LATER 4WD MODELS)

Removal

2 Make matchmarks on the driveshaft and the differential flange in line with each other **(see illustration)**. This is to make sure the

driveshaft is reinstalled in the same position to preserve the balance.

3 Remove the bolts securing the flange yoke to the rear differential **(see illustration)**. Turn the driveshaft (or wheels) as necessary to bring the bolts into the most accessible position.

4 On models with a two-piece driveshaft, remove the bolts from the center support bearing **(see illustration)**.

5 Lower the rear of the driveshaft. Slide the front of the driveshaft out of the transmission on 2WD models. On 4WD models, remove the fasteners and separate the flange at the transfer case **(see illustration)**.

6 On 2WD models, wrap a plastic bag over the transmission exten-

8.2 Mark the relationship of the driveshaft flange yoke to the companion flange on the differential

8.3 Using a backup wrench to hold each bolt, break loose all four nuts securing the flange yoke to the differential

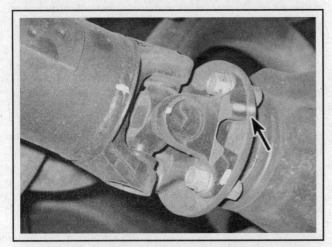

8.4 Center support bearing bolts

8.5 On 4WD models, mark the relationship of the driveshaft U-joint flange yoke to the transfer case companion flange, then remove the bolts securing the flange yoke to the transfer case

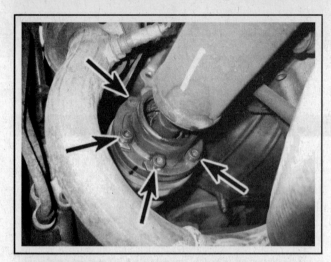

8.13 Mark the relationship of the driveshaft U-joint flange yoke to the transfer case companion flange, then remove the bolts securing the flange yoke to the transfer case

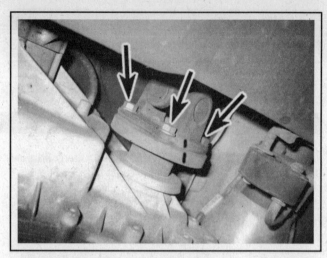

8.14 Driveshaft-to-front differential bolts

sion housing and hold it in place with a rubber band. This will prevent loss of fluid and protect against contamination while the driveshaft is out.

7 If you're replacing a U-joint, refer to Section 9. If you're replacing the center bearing on a two-piece driveshaft, see Section 10.

Installation

8 Remove the plastic bag from the transmission or transfer case and wipe the area clean. Slide the front of the driveshaft into the transmission (2WD models) or bolt the U-joint flange yoke to the companion flange, installing the fasteners finger-tight (4WD models).

9 Raise the center bearing (if equipped) into place and screw the retaining bolts in a few turns. Raise the rear of the driveshaft into position, checking to be sure the marks are in alignment. If not, turn the rear wheels to match the pinion flange and the driveshaft. Install the fasteners.

10 Tighten all fasteners to the torque listed in this Chapter's Specifications.

FRONT DRIVESHAFT (2009 AND EARLIER 4WD MODELS)

Removal

11 Support the transfer case with a floor jack and a block of wood.

12 Remove the transmission crossmember.

13 Make matchmarks on the driveshaft and the transfer case flange in line with each other **(see illustration)**. This is to make sure the driveshaft is reinstalled in the same position to preserve the balance.

14 Mark the relationship of the front CV joint to the front differential flange, then unscrew the bolts and remove the driveshaft **(see illustration)**.

Installation

15 Attach the front end of the driveshaft to the front differential companion flange and install the bolts finger-tight.

16 Extend or compress the driveshaft as necessary, attach the rear end to the transfer case flange, install the bolts and the front and rear flange bolts to the torque listed in this Chapter's Specifications.

17 Install the crossmember.

18 Remove the jackstands and lower the vehicle.

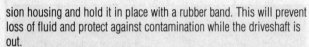

9   Universal joint - replacement

→ **Note: A large vise or a press is required for this procedure. It may be advisable to take the driveshaft to a dealer service department, service station or machine shop where the universal joints can be replaced for you.**

1 Remove the driveshaft (see Section 8).

2 Use pliers to remove the snap-rings from the spider **(see illustration)**.

3 While supporting the driveshaft, place it in position on a workbench equipped with a vise.

4 Place a piece of pipe or a large socket, with an inside diameter slightly larger than the outside diameter of the bearing caps, over one

of the bearing caps. Position a socket with an outside diameter slightly smaller than that of the opposite bearing cap over that cap, and use the vise or press to force the bearing cap out (inside the pipe or large socket). Use the vise or large pliers to work the bearing cap the rest of the way out **(see illustration)**.

5 Transfer the sockets to the opposite sides and press the other bearing cap out in the same manner.

6 Pack the new joints with grease. Usually, specific instructions will be included with the universal joint kit. Follow them carefully.

7 Position the spider into the yoke and partially install one bearing cap in the yoke.

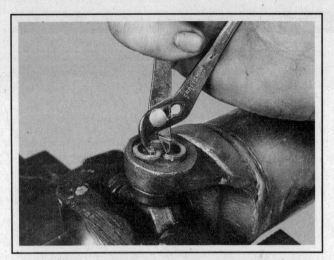

9.2 Use pliers to remove the universal joint snap-rings

9.4 To press the universal joint out of the driveshaft yoke, set it up in a vise with the small socket pushing the joint and bearing cap into the large socket

8   Start the spider into the bearing cap, then partially install the other bearing cap. Press the bearing caps into place, keeping the spider correctly centered as you do so. Be careful to avoid damaging the dust seals.

9   Use the smaller socket to press the caps fully into place. Install the snap-rings. If you have difficulty in seating them, strike the driveshaft yoke sharply with a hammer. This will spring the yoke ears slightly and allow the snap-rings to seat in their grooves **(see illustration)**.

10   If the universal joint has a grease fitting, install it now and add grease using a grease gun.

11   Install the driveshaft (see Section 8).

9.9 If the snap-ring won't seat in its groove, strike the yoke with a brass hammer - this will relieve the tension that has set up in the yoke and slightly spring the yoke ears (this should be done if the joint feels tight when assembled)

10   Center bearing - removal and installation

➡ **Note: Obtain a new yoke nut before performing this procedure.**

1   Raise the vehicle and support it securely on jackstands.

2   Remove the driveshaft (see Section 8).

3   Clamp the driveshaft securely into a bench vise lined with wood.

4   Mark the center U-joint yoke and driveshaft, then disassemble the center U-joint (see Section 9).

5   Unstake and remove the nut, then remove the yoke from the inter-mediate shaft.

6   Remove the center bearing from the rear portion of the driveshaft.

➡ **Note: A puller will usually be required to separate the center bearing from the shaft.**

7   Installation is the reverse of removal. Use a new nut and tighten it to the torque listed in this Chapter's Specifications, then stake the collar of the nut into the slot in the driveshaft.

11 Axleshaft, bearing and oil seals (rear) - removal and installation

1   Release the parking brake. Raise the rear of the vehicle, support it securely on jackstands and block the front wheels. Remove the wheels and tires.

2   Remove the brake disc (see Chapter 9).

3   Remove the ABS wheel speed sensor (see Chapter 9).

4   Disconnect the parking brake cables from the levers on the brake backing plate (see Chapter 9).

5   Remove the parking brake shoes (see Chapter 9).

6   Remove the four bearing retainer nuts (see illustration).

7   Pull the axleshaft out of the rear axle housing along with the backing plate (see illustration).

8   Remove the axleshaft inner oil seal from the axle housing with a seal removal tool or a big screwdriver (see illustration).

9   Further disassembly of the axleshaft assembly requires special tools and a hydraulic press. If the axleshaft, bearing or outer oil seal needs to be replaced, take the axleshaft assembly to an automotive machine shop.

10   Drive a new axleshaft inner seal into the end of the axle tube with a hammer and a seal installer or a big socket. Coat the lip of the seal with clean oil or multi-purpose grease.

11   Make sure the axleshaft is clean and there are no burrs or metal splinters on it. Deburr any surface irregularities so the axleshaft doesn't damage the seal during installation. Lightly coat the axleshaft with clean oil, then insert it into the axle housing. Make sure the splined inner end

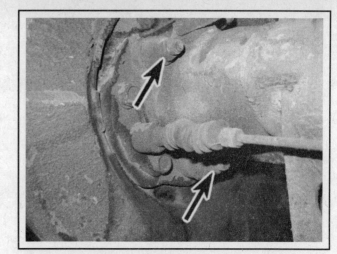

11.6 To detach the axleshaft from the rear axle housing, remove the four bearing retainer nuts

of the axleshaft doesn't damage the lip of the new axleshaft seal.

12   Installation is the reverse of removal. Tighten the four retaining nuts to the torque listed in this Chapter's Specifications.

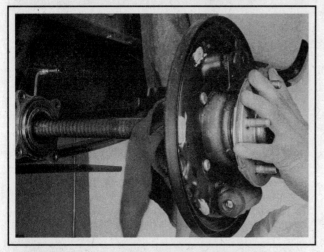

11.7 Extract the axleshaft very carefully from the axle housing, especially if you don't want to replace the axleshaft seal

11.8 Use a seal removal tool or a big screwdriver to pry out the old axleshaft seal; use a seal installer or a big socket to install the new seal

12 Axle assembly (rear, 2009 and earlier models) - removal and installation

1   Loosen the rear wheel lug nuts. Raise the rear of the vehicle and support it securely on jackstands placed under the frame (not under the axle). Block the front wheels to keep the vehicle from rolling off the stands. Remove the rear wheels.

2   Position a floor jack under the rear axle differential housing.

3   Disconnect the driveshaft from the rear axle pinion flange (see Section 8). Fasten the driveshaft out of the way with rope or wire; don't let it hang unsupported.

4   Disconnect the left and right ABS wheel speed sensors (see Chapter 9).

5 Detach the brake hose from the junction block on the axle housing, then plug the hose and lines to prevent fluid leakage.
6 Disconnect the parking brake cables from the brake assemblies (see Chapter 9).
7 Detach the vent hose from the axle housing.
8 Disconnect the shock absorbers from the axle brackets (see Chapter 10).
9 Detach the stabilizer bar links (see Chapter 10).

10 Remove the coil springs (see Chapter 10).
11 Detach the lateral control rod, upper links and trailing arm from the rear axle (see Chapter 10).
12 Installation is the reverse of removal. Tighten all suspension fasteners to the torque listed in the Chapter 10 Specifications.
13 Bleed the brakes (see Chapter 9). Check the differential lubricant level, adding as necessary (see Chapter 1).

13 Differential pinion oil seal - replacement

1 Loosen the wheel lug nuts, raise the vehicle and support it securely on jackstands. Block the front wheels and remove the rear wheels (this will allow you to obtain a more accurate pinion shaft preload reading).
2 Disconnect the driveshaft from the differential (see Section 8) and position it to the side using mechanics wire or rope.

2009 AND EARLIER MODELS

Removal

3 Using a hammer and a punch, unstake the pinion flange nut. Mark the position of the pinion nut to the flange and the flange to the pinion shaft with dabs of paint. If you have access to a beam-type inch-pound torque wrench, you can use it instead to measure the pinion bearing drag. Record your reading so the pinion nut can be tightened later to give the same amount of drag **(see illustration)**.
4 A flange holding tool will be required to keep the companion flange from moving while the self-locking pinion nut is loosened. A chain wrench will also work **(see illustration)**.
5 Remove the pinion nut.

6 Withdraw the flange. It may be necessary to use a two-jaw puller engaged behind the flange to draw it off **(see illustration)**. Do not

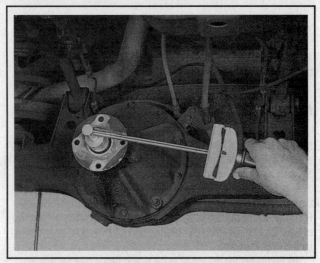

13.3 Use an inch-pound torque wrench to check the pinion bearing drag

13.4 A chain wrench can be used to hold the pinion flange while the nut is loosened

13.6 If you can't pull the pinion flange off by hand, remove it with a puller

13.7 Use a seal removal tool or a large screwdriver to remove the pinion seal (be careful not to disturb the pinion while doing this)

13.8 A large socket with a diameter the same as that of the new seal can be used to drive the pinion seal into the differential housing

attempt to pry or hammer behind the flange or hammer on the end of the pinion shaft.

7 Pry out the old seal and discard it **(see illustration)**.

Installation

8 Lubricate the lips of the new seal and fill the space between the seal lips with wheel bearing grease, then tap it evenly into position with a seal installation tool or a large socket. Make sure it enters the housing squarely and is tapped in to its full depth **(see illustration)**.

9 Install the pinion flange; if necessary, tighten the pinion nut to draw the flange into place. Do not try to hammer the flange into position. Tighten the nut until the paint marks made previously are aligned or until the original amount of bearing preload is reached as measured by the torque wrench.

10 Reconnect the driveshaft to the pinion flange (see Section 8). Check the differential lubricant level and add some, if necessary, to bring it to the appropriate level (see Chapter 1).

2011 AND LATER MODELS

Removal

11 Rotate the pinion a few times by hand. Use a beam-type or dial-type inch-pound torque wrench to check the torque required to rotate the pinion. Record it for use later.

12 Mark the relationship of the pinion flange to the shaft, then count and record the number of exposed threads on the shaft.

13 A special tool, available at most auto parts stores, can be used to keep the companion flange from moving while the self-locking pinion

nut is loosened. A chain wrench can also be used to immobilize the flange **(see illustration 13.4)**.

14 Remove the pinion nut.

15 Withdraw the flange. It may be necessary to use a two-jaw puller engaged behind the flange to draw it off **(see illustration 13.6)**. Do not attempt to pry or hammer behind the flange or hammer on the end of the pinion shaft.

16 Pry out the old seal and discard it **(see illustration 13.7)**.

Installation

17 Lubricate the lips of the new seal and fill the space between the seal lips with wheel bearing grease, then tap it evenly into position with a seal installation tool or a large socket. Make sure it enters the housing squarely and is tapped in to its full depth.

18 Install the pinion flange, lining up the marks made in Step 12. If necessary, tighten the pinion nut to draw the flange into place. Do not try to hammer the flange into position.

19 Apply a bead of RTV sealant to the ends of the splines visible in the center of the flange so oil will be sealed in.

20 Install the washer and a new pinion nut. Tighten the nut until the number of threads recorded previously are exposed.

21 Measure the torque required to rotate the pinion and tighten the nut in small increments (no more than 5 ft-lbs) until it matches the figure recorded earlier. To compensate for the drag of the new oil seal, the nut should be tightened a little more until the rotational torque of the pinion exceeds the earlier recording by 5 in-lbs.

22 Reinstall all components removed previously by reversing the removal Steps, tightening all fasteners to their specified torque values.

14 Differential (rear, 2011 and later 4WD models) - removal and installation

1 Raise the rear of the vehicle and support it securely on jackstands. Block the front wheels to prevent the vehicle from rolling. Place the transaxle in Neutral with the parking brake off. Remove the spare wheel.
2 Drain the differential lubricant (see Chapter 1).
3 Mark the relationship of the driveshaft to the pinion flange, then unbolt the driveshaft from the flange. Suspend the driveshaft with a

piece of wire (don't let it hang by the center support bearing).
4 Remove the driveaxles (see Section 16).
5 Support the differential with a floor jack. Remove the mounting fasteners **(see illustrations)**, then slowly lower the jack.
6 Installation is the reverse of removal. Tighten all fasteners to the torque values listed in this Chapter's Specifications. Fill the differential with the proper lubricant (see Chapter 1).

14.5a Differential front mounting bolts

14.5b Differential rear mounting bolts

15 Axle assembly (front, 2009 and earlier 4WD models) - removal and installation

1 Loosen the front wheel lug nuts, then raise the front of the vehicle and support it securely on jackstands. Remove the wheels.
2 Unbolt the driveshaft from the differential companion flange (see Section 8).
3 Remove the driveaxles (see Section 16).
4 Unbolt the steering gear (see Chapter 10) and position it to the

rear, supporting it with wire or rope.
5 Support the axle assembly with a floor jack.
6 Remove the fasteners from the left and right-side mounts **(see illustrations)**.
7 Pivot the axle assembly forward and lower it from the vehicle.
8 Installation is the reverse of removal.

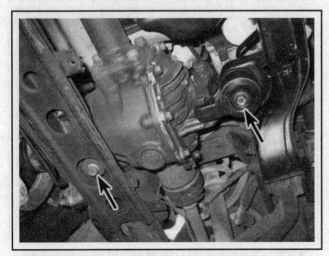
15.6a Front axle assembly left-side mounting bolts

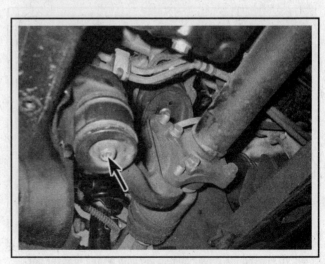
15.6b Front axle assembly right-side mounting bolt

16 Driveaxles - removal and installation

1   Loosen the wheel lug nuts, then raise the vehicle and support it securely on jackstands. Remove the wheel.

2   Unstake the driveaxle/hub nut on 2009 and earlier models **(see illustration)**; on 2011 and later models, remove the cotter pin, then unscrew the driveaxle/hub nut **(see illustration)**.

FRONT

2009 and earlier 4WD models

Removal

3   Detach the upper control arm and the tie-rod end from the steering knuckle (see Chapter 10).

4   Pry the driveaxle from the differential or axle housing **(see illustration)**.

5   Swing the steering knuckle outwards and slide the drivevaxle out

16.2a On 2009 and earlier models, use a hammer and punch to unstake the driveaxle/hub nut

16.2b Loosen the driveaxle/hub nut with a long breaker bar

of the hub. If the splines stick in the hub, push it out with a suitable puller **(see illustration)**.

Installation

6   Pry the old spring clip from the inner end of the driveaxle and install a
   new one. Lubricate the driveaxle end splines with multi-purpose grease and raise the driveaxle into position while supporting the CV joints.

7   Insert the driveaxle into the hub and install the nut finger tight.

8   Insert the splined end of the inner CV joint into the differential side gear or axle housing, making sure the spring clip locks in its groove.

➡ **Note: When installing the driveaxle, make sure the gap in the spring clip is facing down (this will allow it to compress and engage with its groove more easily).**

9   The remainder of installation is the reverse of removal. Tighten the hub nut to the torque listed in this Chapter's Specifications. Stake the collar of the nut into the groove in the driveaxle. Tighten the lug nuts to the torque listed in the Chapter 1 Specifications.

2011 and later models

Removal

10 Remove the steering knuckle (see Chapter 10).

11 Carefully pry the driveaxle from the differential.

Installation

12 Pry the old spring clip from the inner end of the driveaxle and install a new one. Lubricate the driveaxle end splines with multi-purpose grease and raise the driveaxle into position while supporting the CV joints.

13 Install the steering knuckle.

14 The remainder of installation is the reverse of removal. Tighten the hub nut to the torque listed in this Chapter's Specifications. Tighten the lug nuts to the torque listed in the Chapter 1 Specifications.

16.5 If the driveaxle sticks in the hub, it can be pushed out with a puller like this

REAR (2011 AND LATER 4WD MODELS)

Removal

15 If you haven't already done so, remove the cotter pin from the rear driveaxle/hub nut and remove the nut.

16 Remove the brake disc (see Chapter 9).

17 Detach the parking brake cable from its lever at the brake backing plate.

18 Unplug the electrical connector from the wheel speed sensor.

19 Remove the rear shock absorber (see Chapter 9).

20 Detach the trailing arm from the rear knuckle (see Chapter 10).

21 Detach the lateral control link from the rear knuckle (see Chapter 10).

22 Detach the stabilizer bar link from the rear knuckle (see Chapter 10).

23 Support the lower control arm with a floor jack, then detach the arm from the knuckle (see Chapter 10).

24 Pull out on the knuckle and tap the driveaxle out of the hub with a soft-face hammer. If the splines stick in the hub, use a puller to push it out.

25 Pry the inner end of the driveaxle out of the differential.

Installation

26 Pry the old spring clip from the inner end of the driveaxle and install a new one. Lubricate the driveaxle end splines with multi-purpose grease.

27 Insert the splined end of the inner CV joint into the differential.

➡ **Note: When installing the driveaxle, make sure the gap in the spring clip is facing down (this will allow it to compress and engage with its groove more easily).**

28 Insert the driveaxle into the hub and install the nut finger tight.

29 The remainder of installation is the reverse of removal. Tighten the lug nuts to the torque listed in the Chapter 1 Specifications. Tighten the hub nut to the torque listed in this Chapter's Specifications. Tighten the suspension fasteners to the torque listed in the Chapter 10 Specifications.

30 Check the differential lubricant level (see Chapter 1).

17 Driveaxle boot - replacement

DISASSEMBLY

➡ **Note: If the CV joint boots must be replaced, explore all options before beginning the job. Complete rebuilt driveaxles are available on an exchange basis, which eliminates much time and work. Whichever route you choose to take, check on the cost and availability of parts before disassembling the vehicle.**

➡ **Note: The procedure shown here is of a tripod-type inner joint. The basic cleaning and checking procedure is the same for all joints.**

1 Remove the driveaxle (see Section 16).

2 Mount the driveaxle in a vise with wood lined jaws (to prevent damage to the axleshaft). Check the CV joint for excessive play in the radial direction, which indicates worn parts. Check for smooth operation throughout the full range of motion for each CV joint. If a boot is torn, disassemble the joint, clean the components and inspect for damage due to loss of lubrication and possible contamination by foreign matter.

3 Using a small screwdriver, pry the retaining tabs of the clamps up to loosen them and slide them off **(see illustration).**

4 Using a screwdriver, carefully pry up on the edge of the outer boot and push it away from the CV joint. Old and worn boots can be cut off. Pull the inner CV joint boot back from the housing and slide the housing off the joint; on some joints, a wire ring retainer must be removed first **(see illustrations).**

5 Mark the tripod and axleshaft to ensure that they are reassembled properly.

17.3 Lift the tabs on the boot clamps with a small screwdriver, then open the clamps

17.4a Remove the boot from the inner CV joint and slide the joint housing from the tripod

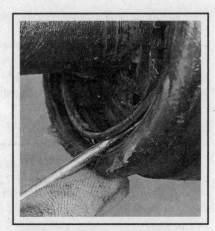

17.4b If equipped, remove the wire retainer, then pull the housing off

17.6 Remove the snap-ring with a pair of snap-ring pliers

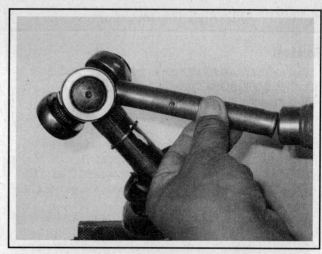

17.7 Drive the tripod joint from the driveaxle with a brass punch and hammer; be careful not to damage the bearing surfaces or the splines on the shaft

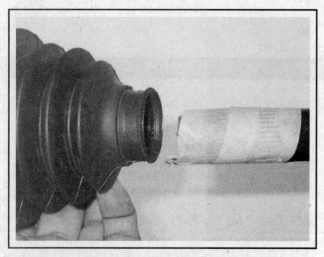

17.10a Wrap the splined area of the axleshaft with tape to prevent damage to the boots when installing them

17.10b Install the tripod with the recessed portion of the splines facing the axleshaft

6 Remove the tripod joint snap-ring with a pair of snap-ring pliers **(see illustration).**

7 Use a hammer and a brass punch to drive the tripod joint from the driveaxle **(see illustration).**

8 If you haven't already cut them off, remove both boots.

➡ **Note: Do NOT disassemble the outboard CV joint.**

CHECK

9 Thoroughly clean all components with solvent - including the outer CV joint assembly - until the old CV joint grease is completely removed. Inspect the bearing surfaces of the inner tripods and housings for cracks, pitting, scoring and other signs of wear. It's not possible to inspect the bearing surfaces of the inner and outer races of the outer CV joint, but you can at least check the surfaces of the ball bearings themselves. If they're in good shape, so are the races; if they're not, neither are the races. If the inner CV joint is worn, you can buy a new inner CV joint and install it on the old axleshaft; if the outer CV

joint is worn, you'll have to purchase a new outer CV joint and axleshaft (they're sold pre-assembled).

REASSEMBLY

10 Wrap the splines on the inner end of the axleshaft with electrical or duct tape to protect the boots from the sharp edges of the splines. Slide the clamps and boot(s) onto the axleshaft, then place the tripod on the shaft. Apply grease to the tripod assembly and inside the housing. Insert the tripod into the housing and pack the remainder of the grease around the tripod **(see illustrations).** If equipped, install the wire retainer.

11 Slide the boot into place, making sure both ends seat in their grooves. Adjust the length of the driveaxle, positioning the joint midway through its travel.

12 Equalize the pressure in the boot, then tighten and secure the boot clamps **(see illustrations).**

13 Install the driveaxle assembly (see Section 16).

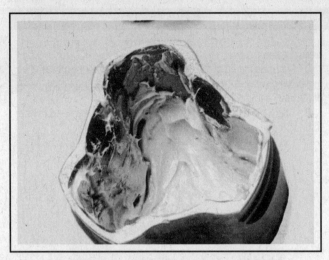

17.10c Place grease at the bottom of the CV joint housing

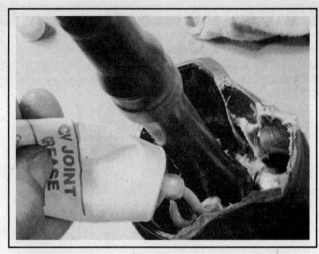

17.10d Install the boot clamps onto the axleshaft, then insert the tripod (or double-offset joint) into the housing, followed by the rest of the grease

17.12a Equalize the pressure inside the boot by inserting a small, dull screwdriver between the boot and the outer race

17.12b To install the new clamps, bend the tang down . . .

17.12c . . . then tap the tabs over to hold it in place

17.12d If your replacement boot came with crimp-type clamps, a special tool such as this one (available at most auto parts stores) will be required to tighten them properly

18 Driveaxle oil seal (rear, 2011 and later 4WD models) - replacement

1 Raise the rear of the vehicle and support it securely on jackstands. Block the front wheels to prevent the vehicle from rolling. Place the transmission in Neutral with the parking brake off.

2 Remove the driveaxles (see Section 16).

3 Carefully pry out the side gear shaft oil seal with a seal removal tool or a large screwdriver; make sure you don't scratch the seal bore.

4 Using a seal installer or a large deep socket as a drift, install the new oil seal. Drive it into the bore squarely and make sure it's completely seated.

5 Lubricate the lip of the new seal with multi-purpose grease, then install the driveaxles (see Section 16). Be careful not to damage the lip of the new seal.

6 Check the differential lubricant level and add some, if necessary, to bring it to the appropriate level (See Chapter 1).

Torque specifications	Ft-lbs (unless otherwise indicated)	Nm

→ **Note:** One foot-pound (ft-lb) of torque is equivalent to 12 inch-pounds (in-lbs) of torque. Torque values below approximately 15 foot-pounds are expressed in inch-pounds, because most foot-pound torque wrenches are not accurate at these smaller values.

Master cylinder mounting fasteners		
2006 and earlier models	15	20
2011 and later models	132 in-lbs	15
Pedal bracket fasteners (2011 and later models)	15	20
Release cylinder mounting fasteners		
2006 and earlier models	15	20
2011 and later models	144 in-lbs	16
Pressure plate-to-flywheel bolts		
2006 and earlier models	16	22
2011 and later models	25	33
Driveshaft-to-companion flange bolts/nuts		
2009 and earlier models		
To rear differential	36 to 43	50 to 60
To transfer case	36 to 43	50 to 60
To front differential		
Full-time 4WD	19 to 21	26 to 30
Part-time 4WD	36 to 43	50 to 60
2011 and later models		
To transfer case	36 to 50	50 to 68
To rear differential	36 to 50	50 to 68
Center support bearing-to-chassis bolts		
2009 and earlier models	27 to 39	37 to 54
2011 and later models	29 to 36	40 to 49
Center support bearing-to-driveshaft nut		
2009 and earlier models	115 to 130	157 to 176
2011 and later models	Not available	
Differential pinion nut		
2009 and earlier models (front and rear)	94 to 210	127 to 284
2011 and later models*	See Section 13 for procedure	
Driveaxle/hub nut		
2009 and earlier models	177 to 198	245 to 275
2011 and later models	159	215

Use a new nut

Notes

Section

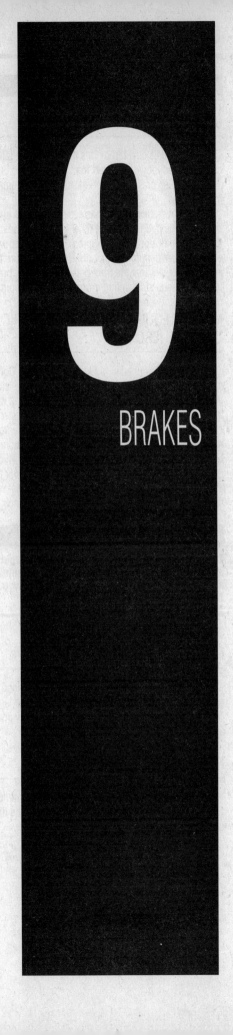

9

BRAKES

1 General Information

GENERAL

1 All models covered by this manual are equipped with hydraulically operated, power-assisted front and rear disc brakes.

2 The disc brakes are self-adjusting and automatically compensate for pad wear.

3 The hydraulic system has separate circuits for the front and rear brakes. If one circuit fails, the other circuit will remain functional and a warning indicator will light up on the dashboard when a substantial amount of brake fluid is lost, showing that a failure has occurred. However, in the event that the front brake circuit fails, braking effectiveness is greatly reduced, resulting in much longer stopping distances.

MODELS EQUIPPED WITH ELECTRONIC STABILITY CONTROL (ESC)

4 Models equipped with Electronic Stability Control (ESC) Some models may be equipped with an optional ESC (electronic stability and traction control) system. In addition to the braking control provided by the ABS (Anti-Lock Braking System), the ESC system utilizes additional electronic sensors and an advanced integrated hydraulic control system to control the engine's power output in combination with wheel specific braking control to maintain vehicle stability. The Hydraulic Electronic Control Unit (HECU) located adjacent to the master cylinder/booster assembly, receives electronic signals from the main processor and moderates the hydraulic brake line pressure to each wheel

✳✳ CAUTION:

This assembly requires special tools and expertise to diagnose and repair. Any concerns regarding this assembly should be addressed by a dealer service department or a qualified repair facility.

MASTER CYLINDER

5 The master cylinder is located under the hood, mounted to the power brake booster, and can be identified by the large fluid reservoir on top. The master cylinder has separate primary and secondary piston assemblies for the front and rear circuits.

POWER BRAKE BOOSTER

6 The power brake booster uses engine manifold vacuum to provide assistance to the brakes. It is mounted on the firewall in the engine compartment, directly behind the master cylinder.

PARKING BRAKE

7 The parking brake system works mechanically to hold the rear wheels only. The parking brake pedal or lever operates a series of cables attached to the parking brakes at each rear wheel. The cables pull on linkage that expand the parking brake shoes inside drums. The drums are integral to the rear brake discs.

SERVICE

8 After completing any procedure involving disassembly of any part of the brake system, always test drive the vehicle to check for proper braking performance before resuming normal driving. When testing the brakes, perform the tests on a clean, dry and flat surface. Conditions other than these can lead to inaccurate test results.

9 Test the brakes at various speeds with both light and heavy pedal pressure. The vehicle should stop evenly without pulling to one side or the other. Under hard braking, the ABS system may engage resulting in brake pedal pulsation. This is considered normal operation.

10 Tires, vehicle load, and wheel alignment are factors which also affect braking performance.

PRECAUTIONS

11 There are some general cautions and warnings involving the brake system on this vehicle:

a) *Use only brake fluid conforming to DOT 3 or 4 specifications.*

b) *The brake pads and linings contain fibers which are hazardous to your health if inhaled. Whenever you work on brake system components, clean all parts with brake system cleaner. Do not allow the fine dust to become airborne. Also, wear an approved filtering mask.*

c) *Safety should be paramount whenever any servicing of the brake components is performed. Do not use parts or fasteners which are not in perfect condition, and be sure that all clearances and torque specifications are adhered to. If you are at all unsure about a certain procedure, seek professional advice. Upon completion of any brake system work, test the brakes carefully in a controlled area before putting the vehicle into normal service. If a problem is suspected in the brake system, don't drive the vehicle until it's fixed.*

d) *Used brake fluid is considered a hazardous waste and it must be disposed of in accordance with federal, state and local laws.*

e) *DO NOT pour it down the sink, into septic tanks or storm drains, or on the ground.*

f) *Clean up any spilled brake fluid immediately and then wash the area with large amounts of water. This is especially true for any finished or painted surfaces.*

2 Anti-lock Brake System (ABS)/Electronic Stability Control (ESC) - general information

1 The Anti-lock Brake System (ABS) was available as optional equipment from 2003 through 2006 and became standard equipment for 2007 and later models. The Electronic Stability Control system became available as optional equipment starting in 2007. These systems are designed to help maintain vehicle steerability, directional stability and optimum deceleration under severe braking conditions on most road surfaces. The ABS system is primarily designed to prevent wheel lockup during heavy or panic braking situations. It works by monitoring the rotational speed of each wheel and controlling the brake line pressure to each wheel when engaged. Data provided by the ABS wheel speed sensors is also shared with the Electronic Stability Control (ESC) feature. This system is designed to assist in correcting over/under steering. The Traction Control System is designed to keep wheels from spinning during vehicle acceleration when road conditions are slick. Overall, these very sophisticated systems help maintain vehicle control when conditions are less than ideal.

COMPONENTS

Modulator or Hydraulic Electronic Control Unit (HECU)

2 The HECU **(see illustration)** controls hydraulic pressure to the brake calipers using two methods:

a) *An electric pump provides added hydraulic pressure to the braking system when needed.*
b) *Solenoid valves modulate brake line pressure during ABS and ESC operation.*

Wheel speed sensors

3 Generally, there is a wheel speed sensor designated for each wheel. Each sensor generates a signal in the form of a low-voltage electrical current or a frequency when the wheel is turning. A variable signal is generated as a result of a square-toothed ring (tone-ring, exciter-ring, reluctor, etc.) that rotates very close to the sensor. The signal is directly proportional to the wheel speed and is interpreted by an electronic module (computer).

4 The front sensors are mounted in the steering knuckles **(see illustrations)**. The tone-rings are integrated with the driveaxle outer Constant Velocity (CV) joints.

5 The rear sensors on 2009 and earlier models are mounted at the outer ends of the axle tubes **(see illustration)**. The sensors on 2011 and later models are mounted on the back sides of the rear knuckles.

2.2 The HECU is located at the left rear of the engine compartment, near the brake master cylinder

DIAGNOSIS AND REPAIR

6 If a dashboard warning light comes on and stays on while the vehicle is in operation, the ABS or ESC system requires attention. Although special diagnostic testing and tools are necessary to properly diagnose the system, you can perform a few preliminary checks before taking the vehicle to a dealer service department.

a) *Check the brake fluid level in the reservoir.*
b) *Verify that all electrical connectors at the master cylinder and HECU assembly are securely connected.*
c) *Check the fuses.*
d) *Follow the wiring harness to each wheel speed sensor and verify that all connections are secure and that the wiring is undamaged.*

7 If the above preliminary checks do not rectify the problem, the vehicle should be diagnosed by a dealer service department or other qualified repair shop. Due to the complexity of this system, all actual repair work must be done by a qualified automotive technician.

2.4a Front wheel speed sensor - 2009 and earlier models

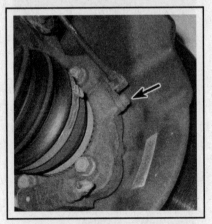

2.4b Front wheel speed sensor - 2011 and later models

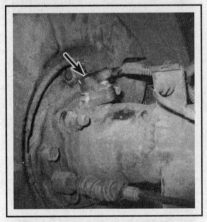

2.5 Location of the rear wheel speed sensor (2009 and earlier models)

※ WARNING:

Do NOT try to repair a wheel speed sensor wiring harness. These systems are sensitive to even the smallest changes in resistance. Repairing the harness could alter resistance values and cause the system to malfunction. If the wiring harness is damaged in any way, it must be replaced.

※ CAUTION:

Make sure the ignition is turned off before unplugging or reattaching any electrical connections.

WHEEL SPEED SENSOR - REMOVAL AND INSTALLATION

8   Loosen the wheel lug nuts, raise the vehicle and support it securely on jackstands. Remove the wheel.

9   Make sure the ignition key is turned to the Off position.

10   Follow the wiring harness from the sensor and disconnect the electrical connector **(see illustrations 2.4a, 2.4b and 2.5)**.

11   If you're replacing a rear wheel speed sensor on a 2011 or later 4WD model, remove the driveaxle (see Chapter 8).

12 All except 2011 and later rear wheel speed sensors: Remove the mounting fastener and carefully pull the sensor out from the knuckle or rear axle assembly.

13 2011 and later rear wheel speed sensors: Remove the two hub and bearing assembly mounting bolts that retain the sensor, then detach the sensor from the knuckle.

14   Installation is the reverse of removal. Tighten the mounting fastener to the torque listed in this Chapter's Specifications. On 2011 and later 4WD rear wheel speed sensors, tighten the hub and bearing assembly bolts to the torque listed in the Chapter 10 Specifications.

15   Install the wheel and lug nuts, lower the vehicle and tighten the lug nuts to the torque listed in the Chapter 1 Specifications.

3   Disc brake pads - replacement

※ WARNING:

Disc brake pads must be replaced on both front or rear wheels at the same time - never replace the pads on only one wheel. Also, the dust created by the brake system is harmful to your health. Never blow it out with compressed air and don't inhale any of it. An approved filtering mask should be worn when working on the brakes. Do not, under any circumstances, use petroleum-based solvents to clean brake parts. Use brake system cleaner only!

1   Remove the cap from the brake fluid reservoir.

2   Loosen the wheel lug nuts, raise the front or rear of the vehicle and support it securely on jackstands. Block the wheels at the opposite end.

※ WARNING:

If the vehicle is equipped with an electronically modulated air suspension, make sure that the height control switch is turned off before raising the vehicle.

3   Remove the wheels. Work on one brake assembly at a time, using the assembled brake for reference if necessary.

4   Inspect the brake disc carefully as outlined in Section 5. If machining is necessary, follow the information in that Section to remove the disc, at which time the pads can be removed as well.

5   Push the piston back into its bore to provide room for the new brake pads. A C-clamp can be used to accomplish this **(see illustration)**. As the piston is depressed to the bottom of the caliper bore, the fluid in the master cylinder will rise. Make sure that it doesn't overflow. If necessary, siphon off some of the fluid.

6   If you're replacing the front brake pads, follow the accompanying photos, beginning with **illustration 3.6a**. Be sure to stay in order and read the caption accompanying each illustration.

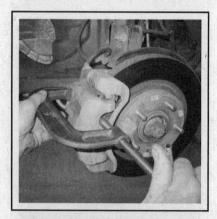

3.5 Before removing the caliper, slowly depress the piston in the caliper bore by using a large C-clamp between the outer brake pad and the back of the caliper

3.6a Always wash the brakes with brake cleaner before disassembling anything

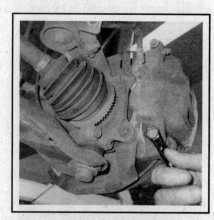

3.6b For brake pad replacement, remove the lower caliper bolt (to detach the caliper completely, remove both caliper bolts, but do not let the caliper hang by the brake hose)

3.6c Pivot the caliper up (be careful not to damage the boot for the upper slide pin)

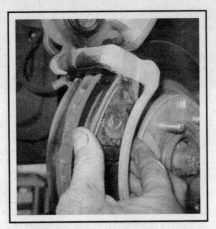

3.6d Remove the outer pad . . .

3.6e . . . and the inner pad

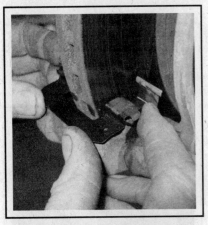

3.6f Remove the upper and lower pad support plates; make sure they are a tight fit and aren't worn. If necessary, replace them

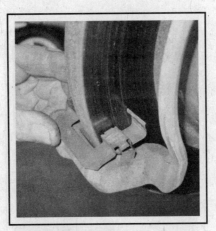

3.6g Install the upper and lower pad support plates

3.6h Pull out the upper and lower sliding pins and clean them. Apply a coat of high-temperature grease to the pins and reinstall them. Be careful not to damage the pin boots, replace any boots that are worn or damaged

3.6i Install the inner pad, making sure that the ends are seated correctly on the pad support plates

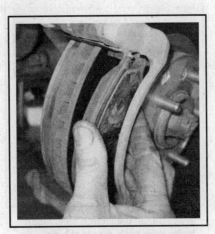

3.6j Install the outer pad, making sure that the ends are seated correctly on the pad support plates

3.6k Swing the caliper down and tighten the caliper lower mounting bolt to the torque listed in this Chapter's Specifications

3.7a Wash the brake with brake system cleaner (see illustration 3.6a), then depress the piston using a C-clamp

3.7b Remove the upper caliper mounting bolt

3.7c Pivot the caliper down for access to the brake pads

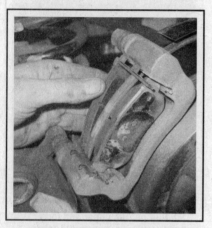

3.7d Remove the inner brake pad . . .

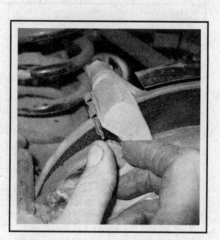

3.7e . . . and the outer brake pad

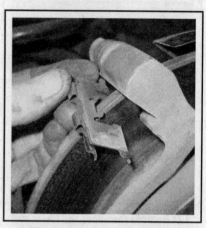

3.7f Remove the upper and lower pad support plates; make sure they are a tight fit and aren't worn. If necessary, replace them

3.7g Install the brake pads in the caliper mounting bracket

3.7h Pull out the sliding pins, clean them, then apply a coat of high-temperature grease to the pins and install them. Replace any boots that are worn or damaged

3.7i Swing the caliper back into place, install the bolt and tighten it to the torque listed in this Chapter's Specifications

7 If you're replacing the rear brake pads, wash the brake assembly **(see illustration 3.6a)**, then follow the accompanying photos, beginning with **illustration 3.7a**. Be sure to stay in order and read the caption accompanying each illustration.

8 When reinstalling the caliper, tighten the mounting bolts to the torque listed in this Chapter's Specifications. After the job has been completed, firmly depress the brake pedal a few times to bring the pads into contact with the disc. Check the level of the brake fluid, adding some if necessary. Check the operation of the brakes carefully before placing the vehicle into normal service.

4 Disc brake caliper - removal and installation

❄ WARNING:

Dust created by the brake system is harmful to your health. Never blow it out with compressed air and don't inhale any of it. An approved filtering mask should be worn when working on the brakes. Do not, under any circumstances, use petroleum-based solvents to clean brake parts. Use brake system cleaner only!

➡ **Note: Always replace the calipers in pairs - never replace just one of them.**

REMOVAL

1 Loosen the wheel lug nuts, raise the vehicle and support it securely on jackstands. Remove the wheels

2 Remove the brake hose banjo bolt and disconnect the hose from the caliper. Plug the hose to keep contaminants out of the brake system and to prevent losing any more brake fluid than is necessary **(see illustration)**.

➡ **Note: If you're just removing the caliper for access to other components, don't detach the hose, but be sure to support the caliper with a piece of wire - don't let it hang by the hose (see illustration).**

3 Remove the caliper mounting bolts **(see illustrations)**.

4 Remove the caliper. If necessary, remove the caliper bracket from the steering knuckle or rear knuckle.

INSTALLATION

5 Installation is the reverse of removal. Tighten the caliper mounting bolts (and bracket bolts, if removed) to the torque listed in this Chapter's Specifications. Install *new* sealing washers on both sides of the brake hose banjo fitting, then tighten the banjo bolt to the torque listed in this Chapter's Specifications.

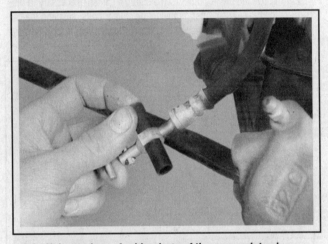

4.2a Using a piece of rubber hose of the appropriate size, plug the brake line banjo fitting to prevent brake fluid from leaking out and to prevent dirt and moisture from contaminating the fluid in the hose

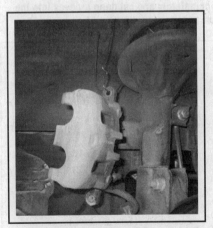

4.2b If you're just removing the caliper for access to other components, hang it from the strut bracket with a piece of wire; do not allow the caliper to hang by the flexible brake hose

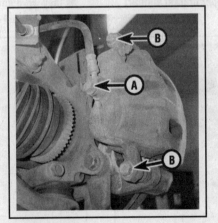

4.3a Front brake caliper mounting details

A Brake hose banjo fitting bolt
B Caliper mounting bolts

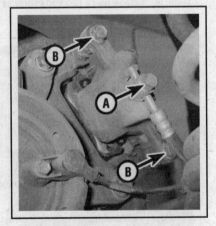

4.3b Rear brake caliper mounting details

A Brake hose banjo fitting bolt
B Caliper mounting bolts

6 Bleed the brake system (see Section 8).

7 Install the wheels and lug nuts. Lower the vehicle and tighten the lug nuts to the torque listed in the Chapter 1 Specifications.

cle to bring the brake pads into contact with the discs. Failure to do so will cause an initial loss of braking.

8 Check the operation of the brakes carefully before driving the vehicle.

5 Brake disc - inspection, removal and installation

INSPECTION

1 Loosen the wheel lug nuts, raise the vehicle and support it securely on jackstands. Remove the wheel and install the lug nuts to hold the disc in place. If the rear brake disc is being worked on, release the parking brake

2 Remove the brake caliper (see Section 4). It isn't necessary to disconnect the brake hose. After removing the caliper bolts, suspend the caliper out of the way with a piece of wire **(see illustration 4.2b)**. Remove

the caliper bracket bolts and remove the bracket **(see illustration)**.

3 Visually inspect the disc surface for score marks and other damage. Light scratches and shallow grooves are normal after use and may not always be detrimental to brake operation, but deep scoring - over 0.039-inch (1.0 mm) - requires disc removal and refinishing by an automotive machine shop. Be sure to check both sides of the disc **(see illustration)**. If pulsating has been noticed during application of the brakes, suspect disc runout.

4 To check disc runout, place a dial indicator at a point about 1/2-inch from the outer edge of the disc **(see illustration)**. Set the

5.2 To remove the front caliper bracket from the steering knuckle, remove these two bolts (rear caliper bracket similar)

5.3 The brake pads on this vehicle were obviously neglected, as they wore down completely and cut deep grooves into the disc - wear this severe means the disc must be replaced

5.4a Use a dial indicator to check disc runout; if the reading exceeds the maximum allowable runout limit, the disc will have to be machined or replaced

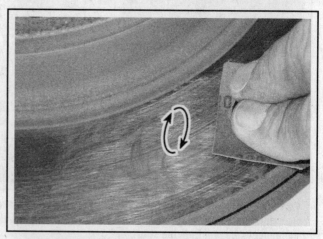

5.4b Using a swirling motion, remove the glaze from the disc surface with sandpaper or emery cloth

5.5a The minimum wear dimension is cast into the rear of the disc (typical)

5.5b Use a micrometer to measure disc thickness

indicator to zero and turn the disc. The indicator reading should not exceed the specified allowable runout limit. If it does, the disc should be refinished by an automotive machine shop.

➡ **Note: Professionals recommend resurfacing the discs whenever the pads are replaced regardless of the dial indicator reading, as this will impart a smooth finish and ensure a perfectly flat surface, eliminating any brake pedal pulsation or other undesirable symptoms. At the very least, if you elect not to have the discs resurfaced, remove the glaze from the surface with sandpaper or emery cloth using a swirling motion (see illustration).**

5   It's absolutely critical that the disc not be machined to a thickness under the specified minimum allowable refinish thickness. The minimum wear (or discard) thickness is cast into the inside of the disc **(see illustration)**. The disc thickness can be checked with a micrometer **(see illustration)**.

REMOVAL

6   Remove the lug nuts that were put on to hold the disc in place.
7   Remove the Phillips-head screws from the disc and slide the disc off the hub.

INSTALLATION

8   Place the disc in position over the threaded studs.
9   Install the caliper, tightening the bolts to the torque listed in this Chapter's Specifications. Bleeding won't be necessary unless the brake hose was disconnected from the caliper.
10   If you're installing a rear disc, check the adjustment of the parking brake (see Section 11).
11   Install the wheel and lug nuts. Lower the vehicle and tighten the lug nuts to the torque listed in the Chapter 1 Specifications.

❋❋ **WARNING:**

Depress the brake pedal several times before moving the vehicle to bring the brake pads into contact with the discs. Failure to do so will cause loss of braking at first.

12   Check the operation of the brakes carefully before driving the vehicle.

---

6   Master cylinder - removal and installation

REMOVAL

❋❋ **CAUTION:**

Brake fluid will damage paint or finished surfaces. Cover all body parts and be careful not to spill fluid during this procedure. Clean up any spilled brake fluid immediately and wash the area with large amounts of water.

1   Disconnect the cable from the negative terminal of the battery

(see Chapter 5).
2   If you're working on a 2011 or later model, remove the air filter housing and the air intake duct (see Chapter 4).
3   Remove as much fluid as possible from the reservoir with a syringe or an old turkey baster.

❋❋ **WARNING:**

If a baster is used, never again use it for the preparation of food.

6.4 Master cylinder mounting details

A   Fluid level switch electrical connector
B   Hydraulic line fittings
C   Mounting nut (one of two shown)

4 Unplug the electrical connector for the brake fluid level warning switch **(see illustration)**.

5 Place rags under the fittings and prepare caps or plastic bags to cover the ends of the lines once they're disconnected.

6 Loosen the fittings at the ends of the brake lines where they enter the master cylinder. To prevent rounding off the flats, use a flare-nut wrench, which wraps around the fitting hex.

7 Carefully move the brake lines away from the master cylinder and plug the ends to prevent contamination.

8 Remove the nuts attaching the master cylinder to the power brake booster. Pull the master cylinder off the studs to remove it. Again, be careful not to spill fluid or bend the brake lines as this is done.

➡ **Note: If necessary, remove the brake lines going to the ABS actuator from the master cylinder if they cannot be moved aside without damaging them.**

INSTALLATION

9 Bench bleed the new master cylinder before installing it. Because it will be necessary to depress the master cylinder piston and, at the same time, control flow from the brake line outlets, it is recommended that the master cylinder be mounted in a vise.

10 Attach a pair of master cylinder bleeder tubes to the outlet ports of the master cylinder **(see illustration)**.

11 Fill the reservoir with brake fluid of the recommended type (see Chapter 1).

12 Slowly push the pistons into the master cylinder (a large Phillips screwdriver can be used for this) - air will be expelled from the pressure chambers and into the reservoir. Because the tubes are submerged in fluid, air can't be drawn back into the master cylinder when you release the pistons.

13 Repeat the procedure until no more air bubbles are present.

14 Remove the bleed tubes, one at a time, and install plugs in the open ports to prevent fluid leakage and air from entering.

6.10 The best way to bleed air from the master cylinder before installing it on the vehicle is with a pair of bleeder tubes

15 Install the reservoir cover, then install the master cylinder over the studs on the power brake booster and tighten the attaching nuts only finger tight at this time.

16 Thread the brake line fittings into the master cylinder. Since the master cylinder is still a bit loose, it can be moved slightly in order for the fittings to thread in easily. Do not strip the threads as the fittings are tightened.

17 Tighten the mounting nuts to the torque listed in this Chapter's Specifications, then tighten the brake line fittings securely.

18 Fill the master cylinder reservoir with fluid, then bleed the master cylinder and the brake system (see Section 8). To bleed the cylinder on the vehicle, have an assistant pump the brake pedal several times slowly, then hold the pedal to the floor. Loosen the fitting nut to allow air and fluid to escape. Repeat this procedure on both fittings until the fluid is clear of air bubbles.

✳✳ CAUTION:

Have plenty of rags on hand to catch the fluid - brake fluid will ruin painted surfaces.

19 If it was necessary to remove the master cylinder-to-ABS actuator brake lines, also bleed the lines at the ABS control unit.

20 The remainder of installation is the reverse of removal. Test the operation of the brake system carefully before placing the vehicle into normal service.

✳✳ WARNING:

Do not operate the vehicle if you are in doubt about the effectiveness of the brake system. On models equipped with ABS, it is possible for air to become trapped in the anti-lock brake system hydraulic control unit, so, if the pedal continues to feel spongy after repeated bleedings or the BRAKE or ANTI-LOCK light stays on, have the vehicle towed to a dealer service department or other qualified shop to be bled with the aid of a scan tool.

7 Brake hoses and lines - inspection and replacement

INSPECTION

1   About every six months, with the vehicle raised and placed securely on jackstands, the flexible hoses which connect the steel brake lines with the front and rear brake assemblies should be inspected for cracks, chafing of the outer cover, leaks, blisters and other damage. These are important and vulnerable parts of the brake system and inspection should be complete. A light and mirror will be needed for a thorough check. If a hose exhibits any of the above defects, replace it with a new one.

REPLACEMENT

2   Loosen the wheel lug nuts, raise the vehicle and support it securely on jackstands. Remove the wheel.

Flexible brake hoses

➡ **Note: On 2009 and earlier models, there are two brake hoses that are routed to a bracket near the center of the axle (in addition to the caliper hoses).**

3   At the frame bracket, unscrew the brake line fitting from the hose **(see illustration)**. Use a flare-nut wrench to prevent rounding off the corners.

4   Use a pair of pliers to remove the U-clip from the female fitting at the bracket **(see illustration)**, then pass the hose through the bracket.

5   Detach any hose brackets from the coil-over shock absorber, control arm or strut, as applicable.

6   At the caliper end of the hose, remove the banjo-fitting bolt, then separate the hose from the caliper. Note that there are two copper sealing washers on each side of the fitting; they should be replaced with new ones during installation.

7   To install the hose, connect the fitting to the caliper with the banjo bolt and new sealing washers. Make sure the fitting is engaged with the casting protrusions on the caliper, then tighten the bolt to the torque listed in this Chapter's Specifications. Route the hose into the frame bracket, making sure it isn't twisted, and reconnect the hose brackets. Thread the tube nut into the fitting, then install the U-clip. Tighten the tube nut securely.

8   Bleed the caliper (see Section 8).

9   Install the wheel and lug nuts, lower the vehicle and tighten the lug nuts to the torque listed in the Chapter 1 Specifications.

Metal brake lines

10   When replacing brake lines, be sure to use the correct parts. Don't use copper tubing for any brake system components. Purchase genuine steel brake lines from a dealer or auto parts store.

11   Prefabricated brake line, with the tube ends already flared and fittings installed, is available at auto parts stores and dealer parts departments.

12   When installing the new line, make sure it's securely supported in the brackets and has plenty of clearance between moving or hot components.

13   After installation, check the master cylinder fluid level and add fluid as necessary. Bleed the brake system (see Section 8) and test the brakes carefully before driving the vehicle in traffic.

7.3 Unscrew the brake line threaded fitting with a flare-nut wrench to protect the fitting corners from being rounded off

7.4 Remove the brake hose-to-bracket U-clip with a pair of pliers

8 Brake hydraulic system - bleeding

✳ WARNING:

Wear eye protection when bleeding the brake system. If the fluid comes in contact with your eyes, immediately rinse them with water and seek medical attention.

➡ **Note: Bleeding the hydraulic system is necessary to remove any air that manages to find its way into the system when it's opened during removal and installation of a hose, line, caliper or master cylinder.**

1   You'll probably have to bleed the system at all four brakes if air

8.8 When bleeding the brakes, a hose is connected to the bleeder valve at the caliper or wheel cylinder, then submerged in brake fluid. Air will be seen as bubbles in the tube and container. All air must be expelled before moving to the next wheel

has entered it due to low fluid level, or if the brake lines have been disconnected at the master cylinder.

2 If a brake line was disconnected only at a wheel, then only that caliper must be bled.

3 If a brake line is disconnected at a fitting located between the master cylinder and any of the brakes, that part of the system served by the disconnected line must be bled.

4 Remove any residual vacuum from the brake power booster by applying the brake several times with the engine off.

5 Remove the master cylinder reservoir cover and fill the reservoir with brake fluid. Reinstall the cover.

➡ Note: Check the fluid level often during the bleeding operation and add fluid as necessary to prevent the fluid level from falling low enough to allow air bubbles into the master cylinder.

6 Have an assistant on hand, as well as a supply of new brake fluid, a clear container partially filled with clean brake fluid, a length of tubing to fit over the bleeder valve and a wrench to open and close the bleeder valve.

7 Beginning at the right rear wheel, loosen the bleeder valve slightly, then tighten it to a point where it's snug but can still be loosened quickly and easily.

8 Place one end of the tubing over the bleeder valve and submerge the other end in brake fluid in the container **(see illustration)**.

9 Have the assistant depress the brake pedal slowly, then hold the pedal down firmly.

10 While the pedal is held down, open the bleeder valve just enough to allow a flow of fluid to leave the valve. Watch for air bubbles to exit the submerged end of the tube. When the fluid flow slows after a couple of seconds, close the valve and have your assistant release the pedal.

11 Repeat Steps 9 and 10 until no more air is seen leaving the tube, then tighten the bleeder valve and perform the same procedure on the other wheels in the following order:

2003 through 2009 - *left rear wheel, right front wheel, left front wheel*
2011 and later - *left front wheel, left rear wheel, right front wheel*

➡ Note: Be sure to check the fluid in the master cylinder reservoir frequently.

12 Never use old brake fluid. It contains moisture that will deteriorate the brake system components.

13 Refill the master cylinder with fluid at the end of the operation.

14 Check the operation of the brakes. The pedal should feel solid when depressed, with no sponginess. If necessary, repeat the entire process.

✳✳ WARNING:

Do not operate the vehicle if you are in doubt about the effectiveness of the brake system. It's possible for air to become trapped in the ABS hydraulic control unit, so, if the pedal continues to feel spongy after repeated bleedings or the BRAKE or ANTI-LOCK light stays on, have the vehicle towed to a dealer service department or other qualified shop to be bled with the aid of a scan tool.

9 Power brake booster - check, removal and installation

OPERATING CHECK

1 Depress the brake pedal several times with the engine off and make sure there's no change in the pedal reserve distance.

2 Depress the pedal and start the engine. If the pedal goes down slightly, operation is normal.

AIRTIGHTNESS CHECK

3 Start the engine and turn it off after one or two minutes. Depress the brake pedal slowly several times. If the pedal depresses less each time, the booster is airtight.

4 Depress the brake pedal while the engine is running, then stop the engine with the pedal depressed. If there's no change in the pedal reserve travel after holding the pedal for 30 seconds, the booster is airtight.

REMOVAL

5 Power brake booster units shouldn't be disassembled. They require special tools not normally found in most automotive repair stations or shops. They're fairly complex and, because of their critical relationship to brake performance, should be replaced with new or rebuilt ones.

6 Remove the brake master cylinder (see Section 6). To provide room for booster removal, some models may require that the brake

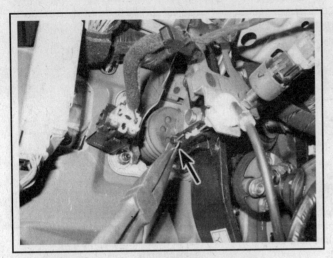

9.8 Remove the retaining clip from the clevis pin

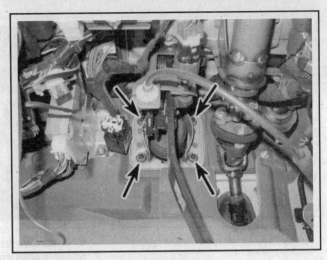

9.9 Power brake booster mounting nuts

lines that cross in front of the master cylinder be removed entirely (at both ends), and not just disconnected from the master cylinder. Other brake lines that cross in front of the brake booster can be separated from the firewall and carefully moved aside.

7 Carefully disconnect the vacuum hose from the brake booster.

8 Remove the brake pedal return spring near the top of the brake pedal. Remove the clevis pin retaining clip with pliers and pull out the pin **(see illustration)**.

9 Remove the four fasteners holding the brake booster to the firewall **(see illustration)**. Slide the booster straight out from the firewall until the studs clear the holes.

INSTALLATION

10 Installation is the reverse of removal. Tighten the booster mounting nuts to the torque listed in this Chapter's Specifications.

11 After the final installation of the master cylinder and brake hoses and lines, the brake pedal height and freeplay must be adjusted (see Section 13) and the system must be bled (see Section 8).

10 Parking brake shoes - inspection and replacement

❋❋ WARNING:

Dust created by the brake system is hazardous to your health. Never blow it out with compressed air and don't inhale any of it. An approved filtering mask should be worn when working on the brakes. Do not, under any circumstances, use petroleum-based solvents to clean brake parts. Use brake system cleaner only!

❋❋ WARNING:

Parking brake shoes must be replaced on both wheels at the same time - never replace the shoes on only one wheel.

➡ **Note: The following procedure depicts parking brake shoe replacement on a 2009 or earlier model. The replacement procedure on 2011 and later models is similar, but the components are oriented differently.**

1 Remove the rear brake discs (see Section 5). On 2011 and later models, disconnect the parking brake cable from the lever on the backing plate.

2 Inspect the thickness of the lining material on the shoes. If the lining has worn down to 1/32-inch or less, the shoes must be replaced.

3 Wash off the brake parts with brake system cleaner.

4 Follow the accompanying illustrations for the brake shoe replacement procedure **(see illustrations 10.4a through 10.4k)**. Be sure to stay in order and read the caption accompanying each illustration.

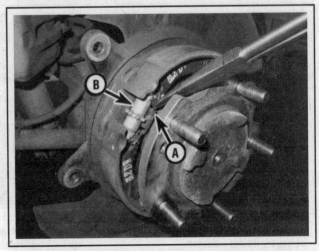

10.4a Remove the upper return spring (A), then spread the shoes and remove the adjuster (B), noting which way it is oriented

10.4b Remove the lower return spring

10.4c Remove the shoe hold-down retainers and springs

10.4d Remove the shoes from the backing plate

10.4e Clean the backing plate with brake system cleaner, the lubricate shoe contact area with a light film of high-temperature brake grease

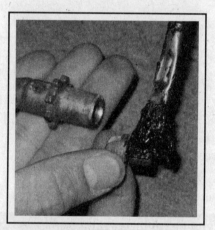

10.4f Clean the adjuster assembly and lubricate the moving components with the same grease

10.4g Place the shoes in position . . .

10.4h . . . making sure they properly engage with the actuator . . .

10.4i . . . then install the hold-down springs and retainers

10.4j Install the lower return spring

10.4k Install the adjuster, making sure it's facing the proper direction, then install the upper return spring

10.6 To adjust the parking brake shoes, remove the rubber plug, then use a screwdriver to rotate the star-wheel until the shoes lock, then back them off until the disc doesn't drag when turned

5   Install the brake disc. Temporarily thread three of the wheel lug nuts onto the studs to hold the disc in place.

6   Remove the hole plugs from the brake discs. Adjust the parking brake shoe clearance by turning the adjuster star wheel with a brake adjusting tool or screwdriver until the shoes contact the discs and the discs can't be turned **(see illustration)**. Back off the adjusters five notches, then install the hole plugs.

7   Install the brake caliper (see Section 4). Tighten the bolts to the torque listed in this Chapter's Specifications.

8   Install the wheel and tighten the lug nuts to the torque specified in Chapter 1.

9   Set the parking brake with about 45 pounds of force and count the number of clicks that it travels. It should match the number of clicks listed in the Chapter 1 Specifications - if not, adjust the parking brake (see Section 11).

11 Parking brake - adjustment

1   The parking brake is a mechanically operated system utilizing a series of cables to apply brake shoes located in the rear wheels. The parking brake system will need to be periodically adjusted to compensate for brake shoe wear. Additionally, adjustment may be needed in the event of cable stretch, which can occur as the vehicle ages.

OPERATING CHECK

2   Kia employs two different methods to apply the parking brake on the Sorento. 2009 and earlier models use a hand lever mounted in the center console. Some 2011 and later models use a foot pedal to operate the parking brake while others are equipped with the hand lever system. In either case, you will need to adjust the parking brake shoe clearance (see Section 10) prior to adjusting the hand lever or foot pedal travel.

a)   *On hand-operated systems, pull the parking brake lever using about 45 pounds of force, count the number of clicks and com-*

pare that to the specs shown for your model in the Chapter 1 Specifications. If the travel is less than that specified, there's a chance the parking brake might not be releasing completely. If it travels more than specified, the parking brake may not hold adequately on an incline, allowing the vehicle to roll.

b)   *On foot-operated systems, depress the parking brake pedal using about 45 pounds of force, observe the stroke of the parking brake pedal and compare that to the specs shown for your model in the Chapter 1 Specifications. If the travel is less than that specified, there's a chance the parking brake might not be releasing completely. If it travels more than specified, the parking brake may not hold adequately on an incline, allowing the vehicle to roll.*

3   If adjustment is needed, raise the rear of the vehicle and support it securely on jackstands. Block the front wheels, then release the parking brake.

4   Adjust the parking brake shoes (see Section 10).

HAND-OPERATED PARKING BRAKE SYSTEM

5 Remove the console cover (see Chapter 11).

  a) *On 2009 and earlier models, the parking brake adjustment nut is at the base of the handle (**see illustration**).*

  b) *On 2011 and later models, the parking brake adjustment nut is on the equalizer assembly under the console, behind the handle.*

FOOT OPERATED PARKING BRAKE SYSTEM

6 Locate the equalizer assembly under the vehicle in the area beneath the driver's seat towards the centerline of the vehicle.

ALL MODELS

7 With the parking brake released, loosen the locknut by holding the adjusting nut. Tighten or loosen the adjusting nut to achieve the proper number of clicks when the parking brake is set. Hold the flat portion of the threaded stud at the end of the cable if necessary. Tightening the nut (towards the cable) decreases the number of clicks, while the opposite is achieved by loosening the nut (turning it toward the threaded stud at the cable's end). Operate the lever or pedal several times to set the brakes between adjustments, then re-check the travel.

8 Confirm that the parking brake is fully engaged within the speci-

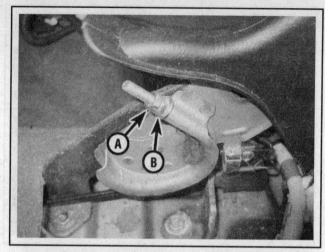

11.5 The parking brake adjustment nut is located at the base of the handle. Loosen the locknut (A) and turn the adjustment nut (B) to obtain adjustment (2009 and earlier models)

fied number of clicks, then tighten the locknut.

9 With the lever released, move the rear wheels by hand to make sure that the parking brake isn't dragging.

10 Reinstall the console cover (if removed) and lower the vehicle.

---

12 Brake light switch - removal, installation and adjustment

REMOVAL AND INSTALLATION

1 The brake light switch is located on a bracket at the top of the brake pedal (**see illustration**).

2 Disconnect the wiring harness at the brake light switch.

3 Loosen the locknut and unscrew the switch from the pedal bracket.

4 Installation is the reverse of removal.

12.1 The brake light switch is located on a bracket near the top of the brake pedal. Loosen the locknut and unscrew the switch from its bracket

ADJUSTMENT

5 Check and, if necessary, adjust brake pedal height (see Section 13).

6 Loosen the switch locknut, adjust the switch so that the plunger protrusion is as listed in this Chapter's Specifications (**see illustration**).

7 Plug the electrical connector into the switch. Make sure the brake lights come on when the brake pedal is depressed and go off when the pedal is released. If not, repeat the adjustment procedure until the brake lights function properly.

8 Check and, if necessary, adjust brake pedal freeplay (see Section 13).

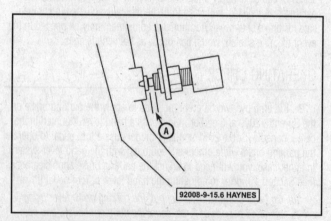

92008-9-15.6 HAYNES

12.6 To adjust the brake light switch, loosen the locknut and rotate the switch until the plunger distance (A) is within the range listed in this Chapter's Specifications, then tighten the locknut

13 Brake pedal - adjustment

BRAKE PEDAL HEIGHT

1 Disconnect the electrical connector from the brake light switch (see Section 12).

2 Loosen the locknut on the brake light switch and rotate the switch until it does not contact the brake pedal arm.

3 With the brake pedal fully released, measure the distance from the top of the pad to the floor **(see illustration)**.

4 Compare the height measurement to this Chapter's Specifications. Continue to the next Step for the pedal height adjustment.

5 Loosen the clevis locknut on the pushrod, then turn the pushrod with a pair of pliers to attain the proper pedal height.

6 With the pedal height adjusted, tighten the locknut securely.

BRAKE PEDAL FREEPLAY

7 Press the brake pedal several times with the engine OFF; this will deplete the vacuum in the brake booster.

8 Press down lightly on the brake pedal by hand and measure the distance that it moves freely before resistance is felt **(see illustration 13.3)**. The freeplay should be within the values listed in this Chapter's Specifications.

9 If there is less freeplay than specified, check to be sure the outer case of the brake light switch is not contacting the brake pedal arm.

10 If there is too much freeplay, check the clevis, clevis pin and the hole in the brake pedal arm for excessive wear and replace faulty parts as needed.

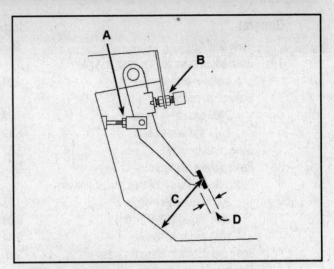

13.3 Brake pedal height and freeplay measuring and adjustment points

A   Clevis locknut
B   Brake light switch adjusting nut/locknut
C   Pedal height measurement (to steel floor)
D   Freeplay measurement point

Specifications

General	Inches	Millimeters
Brake fluid type	See Chapter 1	
Brake booster pushrod-to-master cylinder piston clearance	0.047 to 0.067 inch	1.2 to 1.7 mm
Brake pedal height		
2009 and earlier models	7.87 inches	200 mm
2011 and later models	8.19 inches	208 mm
Brake pedal freeplay	5/32 to 9/32 inch	4 to 7 mm
Parking brake adjustment	See Chapter 1	
Pedal arm-to-brake light switch outer housing		
2005 and earlier models	0.02 to 0.04 inch	0.5 to 1.0 mm
2006 through 2009 models	0.06 to 0.08 inch	1.5 to 2.0 mm
2011 and later models	0.04 to 0.08 inch	1 to 2 mm
Brake pad minimum lining thickness	See Chapter 1	
Disc lateral runout limit		
2009 and earlier models	0.0012 inch	0.03 mm
2011 and later models	0.001 inch	0.025 mm
Disc minimum (discard) thickness	Cast into disc	
Parking brake lining minimum thickness	0.06 inch	1.5 mm

Torque specifications | Ft-lbs (unless otherwise indicated)   Nm

➡ **Note:** One foot-pound (ft-lb) of torque is equivalent to 12 inch-pounds (in-lbs) of torque. Torque values below approximately 15 foot-pounds are expressed in inch-pounds, because most foot-pound torque wrenches are not accurate at these smaller values.

	Ft-lbs (unless otherwise indicated)	Nm
Brake hose-to-caliper banjo bolt		
2009 and earlier models	168 in-lbs	19
2011 and later models	20	27
Caliper mounting bolts	22	30
Front	24	32
Caliper mounting bracket bolts		
Front		
2009 and earlier models	54	73
2011 and later models	70	95
Rear		
2009 and earlier models	Not applicable	
2011 and later models	54	72
Master cylinder mounting nuts	133 in-lbs	15
Power brake booster mounting nuts	18	25
Wheel lug nuts	See Chapter 1	

➡ **Note: Replace all self-locking fasteners with new ones after removing them.**

Notes

Section

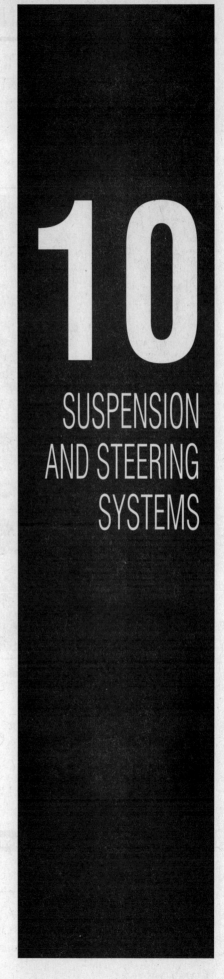

10

SUSPENSION AND STEERING SYSTEMS

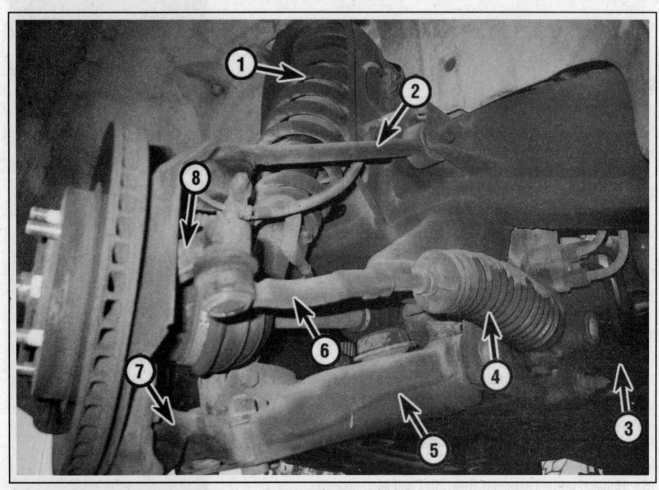

1.1 Front suspension and steering components - 2009 and earlier models

1	Shock absorber/coil spring assembly	4	Steering gear boot	7	Lower balljoint
2	Upper control arm	5	Lower control arm	8	Steering gear
3	Steering gear	6	Tie-rod end		

1 General information and precautions

FRONT SUSPENSION

2009 and earlier models

1 The front suspension on these models is fully independent. The steering knuckles are connected to upper and lower control arms by balljoints. The control arms are bolted to the frame. The shock absorbers and coil springs are integral assemblies; the upper ends are bolted to brackets on the frame and the lower ends are bolted to the lower control arms. All models use a front stabilizer bar to reduce vehicle roll during cornering **(see illustration)**.

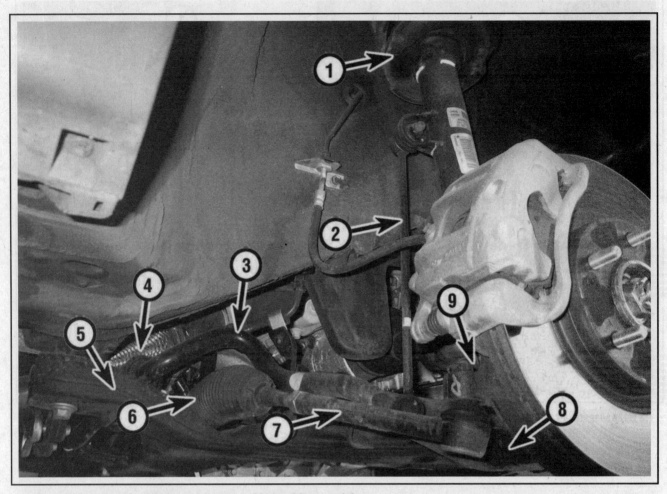

1.2 Front suspension and steering components - 2011 and later models

1	Strut/coil spring assembly	4	Stabilizer bar bushing bracket	7	Tie rod end
2	Stabilizer bar link	5	Subframe	8	Lower control arm
3	Stabilizer bar	6	Steering gear boot	9	Steering knuckle

2011 and later models

2   The front suspension on these models is a MacPherson strut design. The upper end of each strut is attached to the vehicle's body strut support. The lower end of the strut is connected to the upper end of the steering knuckle. The steering knuckle is attached to a balljoint mounted on the outer end of the suspension control arm **(see illustration)**.

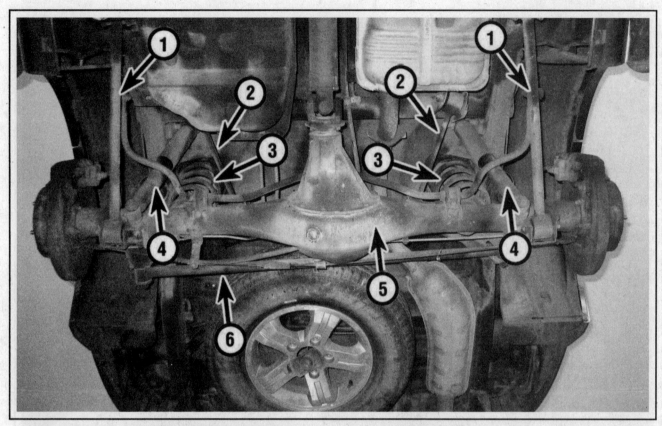

1.3 Rear suspension components - 2009 and earlier models

1	Trailing arm	3	Coil spring	5	Rear axle
2	Upper link	4	Shock absorber	6	Lateral control rod

REAR SUSPENSION

3   On 2009 and earlier models, the rear suspension on these models uses a solid rear axle, coil springs, shock absorbers, one trailing arm and upper link per side, a lateral control rod, and a stabilizer bar **(see illustration)**.

4   On 2011 and later models, the rear suspension uses a trailing arm, an upper and lower control arm, a lateral control rod, a coil spring and a shock absorber on each side. The trailing arm, control arms and lateral control rod connect to a rear knuckle and hub assembly. A stabilizer bar reduces body roll on turns **(see illustration)**.

5   The power-assisted rack-and-pinion steering gear is mounted on the frame (2009 and earlier models) or subframe (2011 and later models). The steering gear actuates the tie-rods, which are attached to the steering knuckles. The steering column is designed to collapse in the event of an accident.

PRECAUTIONS

6   Frequently, when working on the suspension or steering system components, you may come across fasteners that seem impossible to loosen. These fasteners on the underside of the vehicle are continually subjected to water, road grime, mud, etc., and can become rusted or frozen, making them extremely difficult to remove.

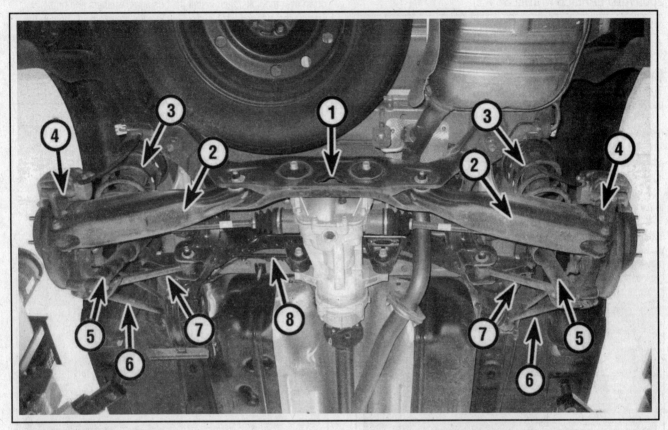

1.4 Rear suspension components

1	Subframe	4	Rear knuckle	7	Lateral control rod
2	Lower control arm	5	Shock absorber	8	Stabilizer bar
3	Coil spring	6	Trailing arm		

In order to unscrew these stubborn fasteners without damaging them (or other components), be sure to use lots of penetrating oil and allow it to soak in for a while. Using a wire brush to clean exposed threads will also ease removal of the nut or bolt and prevent damage to the threads. Sometimes a sharp blow with a hammer and punch will break the bond between nut and bolt threads, but care must be taken to prevent the punch from slipping off the fastener and ruining the threads. Heating the stuck fastener and surrounding area with a torch sometimes helps too, but isn't recommended because of the obvious dangers associated with fire. Long breaker bars and extensions, or cheater, pipes will increase leverage, but never use an extension pipe on a ratchet - the ratcheting mechanism could be damaged. Sometimes tightening the nut or bolt first will help to break it loose. Fasteners that require drastic measures to remove should always be replaced with new ones.

✷✷ WARNING:

Never, under any circumstances, rely on a jack to support the vehicle while working on it. Whenever any of the suspension or steering fasteners are loosened or removed they must be inspected and, if necessary, replaced with new ones of the same part number or of original equipment quality and design. Torque specifications must be followed for proper reassembly and component retention. Never attempt to heat or straighten any suspension or steering components. Instead, replace any bent or damaged part with a new one.

7   Since most of the procedures dealt with in this Chapter involve jacking up the vehicle and working underneath it, a good pair of jackstands will be needed. A hydraulic floor jack is the preferred type of jack to lift the vehicle, and it can also be used to support certain components during various operations.

2 Stabilizer bar bushings and links (front) - removal and installation

1 Park the vehicle with the wheels pointing straight ahead. Loosen the front wheel lug nuts, then raise the front of the vehicle and support it securely on jackstands. Remove the wheels and the under-vehicle splash shield.

2009 AND EARLIER MODELS

2 Remove the nuts and washers and bushings from the tops of the stabilizer bar links **(see illustration)**.

3 Remove the stabilizer bar bushing bracket bolts and brackets **(see illustration)**.

4 Remove the rubber bushings from the stabilizer bar, noting the position of the slit openings.

5 Inspect the rubber bushings for cracks, tears and deterioration. If they're worn or damaged, replace them.

6 Check the balljoints on the ends of each link for looseness or other signs of excessive wear. If necessary, remove the nuts from the lower ends of the links and detach them from the lower control arms.

7 Clean the bushing area of the stabilizer bar with a stiff wire brush to remove any rust or dirt.

8 Install the rubber bushings against the bushing stoppers on the stabilizer bar.

9 Position the stabilizer bar against the frame and install the bushing brackets, tightening the bolts to the torque listed in this Chapter's Specifications.

10 Install the washers and bushings onto the links, swing the bar down over the links, then install the bushings, washers and nuts. Tighten the nuts until 1/4-inch of the threads are exposed. Tighten the upper nuts against the lower nuts.

11 The remainder of installation is the reverse of removal. Tighten the lug nuts to the torque listed in the Chapter 1 Specifications.

2011 AND LATER MODELS

12 Disconnect the stabilizer bar links from the bar **(see illustration)**.

13 Lock the steering wheel in the straight-ahead position. Mark the relationship of the steering shaft to the steering gear, then remove the nut and detach the steering shaft U-joint from the steering gear input shaft (see Section 21).

14 Support the subframe with two floor jacks (one positioned on each side). Loosen the subframe mounting bolts a few turns (see Section 24), then lower the floor jacks far enough to access the stabilizer bar bracket bolts **(see illustration)**.

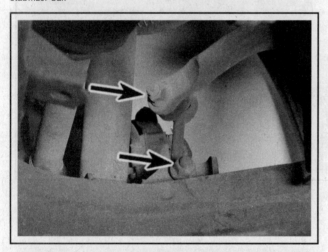

2.2 Stabilizer bar link nuts (2009 and earlier models)

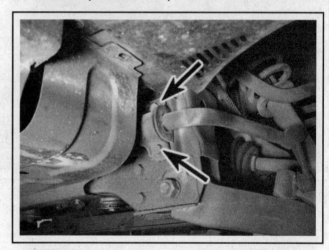

2.3 To separate the stabilizer bar from the frame, remove the bushing bracket bolts. Note the position of the bushings on the bar

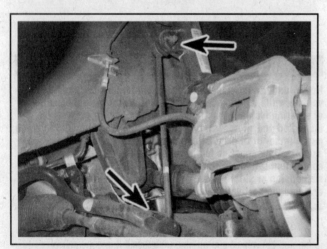

2.12 To detach the stabilizer bar link from the bar, remove the lower nut; if you're removing the strut (or replacing the link), remove the upper nut

2.14 Stabilizer bar bracket bolts (2011 and later models)

15 Maneuver the stabilizer bar out from between the subframe and the body.

16 Slide off the bushings and inspect them. If they're cracked, worn or deteriorated, replace them. Also inspect the stabilizer bar links for loose ballstuds.

17 Clean the bushing area of the stabilizer bar with a stiff wire brush to remove any rust or dirt.

18 Install the bushings onto the stabilizer bar. Guide the bar into place and install the bushing brackets, tightening the bolts to the torque listed in this Chapter's Specifications.

19 Raise the subframe against the body and tighten the bolts to the torque listed in this Chapter's Specifications.

20 Reconnect the steering shaft U-joint to the steering gear and tighten the bolt to the torque listed in this Chapter's Specifications.

21 Install the links, tightening the link nuts to the torque listed in this Chapter's Specifications .

22 The remainder of installation is the reverse of removal. Tighten the lug nuts to the torque listed in the Chapter 1 Specifications.

3   Shock absorber/coil spring assembly (front, 2009 and earlier models) - removal, component replacement and installation

✳ WARNING:

Always replace shock absorber/coil spring assemblies in pairs - never replace just one of them.

➡ Note: If the shocks or coil springs exhibit the telltale signs of wear (leaking fluid, loss of damping capability, chipped, sagging or cracked coil springs) explore all options before beginning any work. The shock absorbers or coil springs are not serviceable individually and must be replaced if a problem develops. However, complete assemblies may be available on an exchange basis, which eliminates much time and work. Whichever route you choose to take, check on the cost and availability of parts before disassembling your vehicle.

REMOVAL

1 If you're removing the left-side shock absorber, remove the battery (see Chapter 5), the junction block and, on 2006 and earlier models, the cruise control actuator.

2 Loosen the front wheel lug nuts. Raise the vehicle and support it securely on jackstands. Remove the front wheels.

3 Unbolt the brake hose bracket.

4 Remove the upper control arm (see Section 6).

5 Remove the shock absorber lower mounting bolt **(see illustration)**.

6 While supporting the shock absorber assembly, remove the upper mounting nuts **(see illustration)**.

7 Remove the shock absorber assembly.

➡ Note: It may be necessary to pry down on the lower control arm for clearance to remove the assembly.

COMPONENT REPLACEMENT

➡ Note: It is possible to replace the shocks or springs individually, but the units will have to be taken to a qualified repair shop with the proper equipment, and this will add considerable expense. You can compare the cost of replacing the complete assemblies yourself to the cost of having individual components replaced.

INSTALLATION

8 Installation is the reverse of removal. Tighten the upper and lower fasteners to the torque values listed in this Chapter's Specifications . Tighten the brake hose bracket mounting bolt securely.

➡ Note: Tighten the upper control arm pivot bolts and the shock absorber lower mounting bolt with the vehicle at normal ride height. This can be done after the vehicle has been assembled, lowered to the ground and bounced few times as if inspecting the shock absorbers. Alternatively, the normal ride height can be simulated by raising the lower control arm with a floor jack.

9 Tighten the lug nuts to the torque listed in the Chapter 1 Specifications.

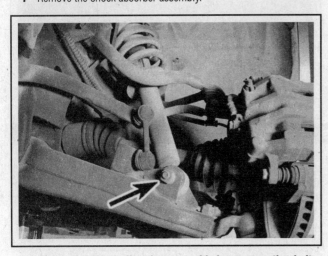

3.5 Shock absorber/coil spring assembly lower mounting bolt

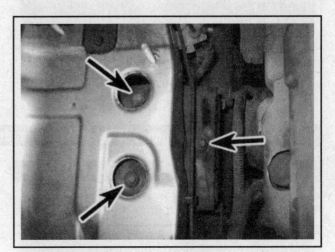

3.6 Shock absorber upper mounting nuts

4 Strut assembly (front, 2011 and later models) - removal, inspection and installation

REMOVAL

1 Loosen the wheel lug nuts, raise the vehicle and support it securely on jackstands. Remove the wheel. Support the control arm with a floor jack.

2 Disconnect the stabilizer bar link from the strut **(see illustration 2.12)**.

3 Remove the strut-to-knuckle nuts and knock the bolts out with a hammer and punch **(see illustration)**.

4 Separate the strut from the steering knuckle. Be careful not to overextend the inner CV joint. Also, don't let the steering knuckle fall outward, as the brake hose could be damaged.

5 If the strut is to be disassembled, loosen, but do not remove, the damper shaft nut (in the center of the upper mount).

6 Support the strut and spring assembly with one hand (or have an assistant hold it) and remove the three strut upper mounting nuts in the engine compartment **(see illustration)**. Remove the assembly out from the fenderwell.

❊ WARNING:

Don't remove the large nut in the center. If you are going to be disassembling the strut, you may break it loose at this time

INSPECTION

7 Check the strut body for leaking fluid, dents, cracks and other obvious damage that would warrant repair or replacement.

8 Check the coil spring for chips or cracks in the spring coating (this can cause premature spring failure due to corrosion). Inspect the spring seat for cuts, hardness and general deterioration.

9 If any undesirable conditions exist, proceed to the strut disassembly procedure (see Section 5).

INSTALLATION

10 Guide the strut assembly up into the fenderwell and insert the upper mounting studs through the holes in the shock tower. Once the studs protrude from the strut tower, install the nuts so the strut won't fall back through. This is most easily accomplished with the help of an assistant, as the strut is quite heavy and awkward.

11 Slide the steering knuckle into the strut flange and insert the two bolts. Install the nuts and tighten them to the torque listed in this Chapter's Specifications.

12 Connect the stabilizer bar link to the strut and tighten the nut to the torque listed in this Chapter's Specifications.

13 Install the wheel and lug nuts, then lower the vehicle and tighten the lug nuts to the torque listed in the Chapter 1 Specifications.

14 Tighten the three upper mounting nuts to the torque listed in this Chapter's Specifications.

4.3 Remove the nuts and drive the strut-to-knuckle bolts out with a punch

4.6 Remove the upper strut mounting nuts.

5 Strut/coil spring assembly (2011 and later models) - replacement

❊ WARNING:

Always replace strut/coil spring assemblies in pairs - never replace just one of them.

1 If the struts or coil springs exhibit the telltale signs of wear (leaking fluid, loss of damping capability, chipped, sagging or cracked coil springs), explore all options before beginning any work. The strut/shock absorber assemblies are not serviceable and must be replaced if a problem develops. However, strut assemblies complete with springs may be available on an exchange basis, which eliminates much time and work. Whichever route you choose to take, check on the cost and availability of parts before disassembling your vehicle.

5.3 Install the spring compressor in accordance with the tool manufacturer's instructions and compress the spring until all pressure is relieved from the upper spring seat

5.4 Remove the damper shaft nut

5.5 Lift the suspension support off the damper shaft

5.6 Remove the spring seat from the damper shaft

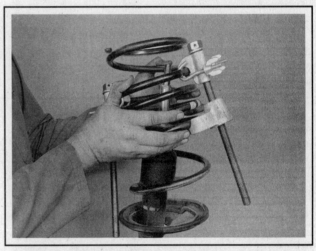

5.7 Remove the compressed spring assembly - keep the ends of the spring pointed away from your body

⁂ WARNING:

Disassembling a strut is potentially dangerous and utmost attention must be directed to the job, or serious injury may result. Use only a high-quality spring compressor and carefully follow the manufacturer's instructions furnished with the tool. After removing the coil spring from the strut assembly, set it aside in a safe, isolated area.

DISASSEMBLY

2   Remove the strut and spring assembly (see Section 4). Mount the strut assembly in a vise. Line the vise jaws with wood or rags to prevent damage to the unit and don't tighten the vise excessively.

3   Following the tool manufacturer's instructions, install the spring compressor (which can be obtained at most auto parts stores or equipment yards on a daily rental basis) on the spring and compress it sufficiently to relieve all pressure from the upper spring seat **(see illustration)**. This can be verified by wiggling the spring.

4   Unscrew the damper shaft nut **(see illustration)**.

5   Remove the nut and suspension support **(see illustration)**. Inspect the bearing in the suspension support for smooth operation. If it doesn't turn smoothly, replace the suspension support. Check the rubber portion of the suspension support for cracking and general deterioration. If there is any separation of the rubber, replace it.

6   Remove the upper spring seat from the damper shaft **(see illustration)**. Check the spring seat for cracking and hardness; replace it if necessary. Remove the upper insulator.

7   Carefully lift the compressed spring from the assembly **(see illustration)** and set it in a safe place.

⁂ WARNING:

Never place your head near the end of the spring!

5.11 When installing the spring, make sure the end fits into the recessed portion of the lower seat

5.12 The flats on the damper shaft must match up with the flats in the spring seat

8 Slide the rubber bumper off the damper shaft.

9 Check the lower insulator for wear, cracking and hardness and replace it if necessary.

REASSEMBLY

10 If the lower insulator is being replaced, set it into position with the dropped portion seated in the lowest part of the seat. Extend the damper rod to its full length and install the rubber bumper.

11 Carefully place the coil spring onto the lower insulator, with the

end of the spring resting in the lowest part of the insulator **(see illustration)**.

12 Install the upper insulator on the spring. Install the spring seat, making sure that the flats in the hole in the seat match up with the flats on the damper shaft **(see illustration)**.

13 Align the holes in the upper spring seat with those in the lower.

14 Install the damper nut and tighten it to the torque listed in this Chapter's Specifications. Don't allow the holes in the spring seats to become misaligned. Remove the spring compressor tool.

15 Install the strut/spring assembly.

6   Upper control arm (2009 and earlier models) - removal and installation

6.3 Balljoint-to-steering knuckle pinch bolt

1 Loosen the wheel lug nuts, raise the front of the vehicle and support it securely on jackstands. Apply the parking brake. Remove the wheel.

2 Support the lower control arm with a floor jack.

✳ CAUTION:

Don't allow the steering knuckle to fall outward as the brake hose may be damaged. It's a good idea to tie the steering knuckle to the coil spring so this doesn't happen.

3 Remove the upper balljoint-to-steering knuckle pinch bolt and detach the balljoint from the steering knuckle **(see illustration)**.

4 Unbolt the brake line bracket from the frame. Remove the fasteners and detach the upper control arm from the frame, then remove the arm **(see illustration)**.

5 Inspect the bushings for wear and deterioration. If they're cracked or damaged, take the arm to an automotive machine shop and have new bushings installed.

6 Installation is the reverse of removal. Tighten all suspension fasteners to the torque values listed in this Chapter's Specifications. Tighten the pivot bolt(s) with the vehicle at normal ride height. This can be done after the vehicle has been assembled, lowered to the ground and bounced few times as if inspecting the shock absorbers. Alternatively, the normal ride height can be simulated by raising the lower control arm with a floor jack.

7 Tighten the lug nuts to the torque listed in the Chapter 1 Specifications.

8 It's a good idea to have the wheel alignment checked and, if necessary, adjusted.

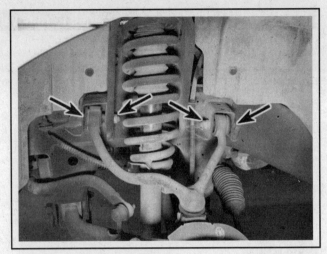

6.4 Upper control arm fasteners

7 Lower control arm (2009 and earlier models) - removal and installation

1 Loosen the wheel lug nuts, raise the front of the vehicle and support it securely on jackstands. Apply the parking brake. Remove the wheel.

2 Unbolt the shock absorber/coil spring assembly from the lower control arm (see Section 3).

3 Unbolt the balljoint from the lower control arm **(see illustration)**.

4 Unbolt the steering gear from the crossmember (see Section 21).

5 Make alignment marks to both sides of the front and rear pivot fasteners where the cam adjusters meet the frame **(see illustration)**. Remove the nuts and pivot bolts and detach the control arm from the frame.

➡ **Note: Pry the steering gear up to make clearance for pivot bolt removal.**

6 Inspect the bushings for wear and deterioration. If they're cracked or damaged, take the arm to an automotive machine shop and have new bushings installed.

7 Installation is the reverse of removal. Make sure that the alignment marks you made prior to disassembly are lined up. Tighten all suspension fasteners to the torque values listed in this Chapter's Specifications.

➡ **Note: The pivot bolt nuts should be tightened with the vehicle at normal ride height. This can be done after the vehicle has been assembled, lowered to the ground and bounced few times as if inspecting the shock absorbers. Alternatively, the normal ride height can be simulated by raising the lower control arm with a floor jack.**

8 Tighten the lug nuts to the torque listed in the Chapter 1 Specifications.

9 Have the wheel alignment checked and, if necessary, adjusted.

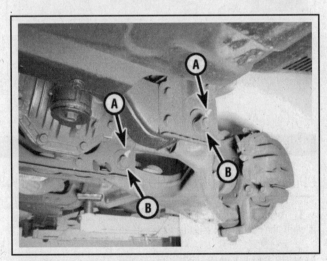

7.5 Mark the relationship of the adjusting cams to the frame - consider using different color markers or paint or label them so that they do not get mixed up. They must go back in the exact same position to maintain wheel alignment

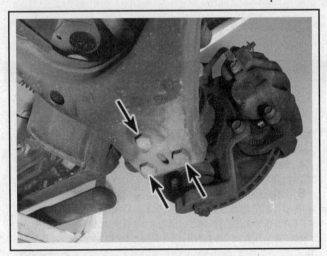

7.3 Balljoint-to-lower control arm mounting fasteners

A   *Alignment marks*   B   *Pivot bolts/nuts*

8 Control arm (2011 and later models) - removal, inspection and installation

REMOVAL

1 Loosen the wheel lug nuts on the side to be disassembled. Raise the front of the vehicle, support it securely on jackstands and remove the wheel.

2 Remove the cotter pin, nut and balljoint pinch bolt **(see illustration)**. Use a prybar to disconnect the balljoint from the control arm, being careful not to damage the balljoint boot.

3 Remove the fasteners securing the control arm to the subframe **(see illustration)**

4 Remove the front control arm-to-subframe bolts.

5 Remove the control arm.

INSPECTION

6 Make sure the control arm is straight. If it's bent, replace it. Do not attempt to straighten a bent control arm.

7 Inspect the bushings. The bushings can be removed, and the new ones installed, with a hydraulic press. If you don't have access to a press and the necessary fixtures, have the bushings replaced by an automotive machine shop.

INSTALLATION

8 Installation is the reverse of removal. Tighten all fasteners to the torque listed in this Chapter's Specifications.

➡ **Note: The pivot bolt nut should be tightened with the vehicle at normal ride height. This can be done after the vehicle has been assembled, lowered to the ground and bounced few times as if inspecting the shock absorbers. Alternatively, the normal ride height can be simulated by raising the lower control arm with a floor jack.**

9 Install the wheel and lug nuts, lower the vehicle and tighten the lug nuts to the torque listed in the Chapter 1 Specifications .

10 It's a good idea to have the front wheel alignment checked, and if necessary, adjusted after this job has been performed.

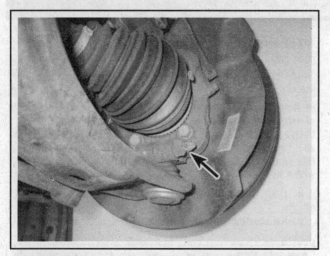

8.2 Remove the cotter pin, nut and pinch bolt that secures the balljoint and use a prybar to separate the control arm/ balljoint assembly from the knuckle

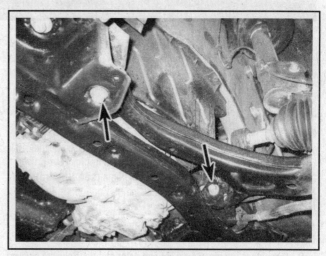

8.3 Control arm-to-subframe fasteners

9 Balljoints - replacement

UPPER BALLJOINT (2009 AND EARLIER MODELS ONLY)

1 The upper control arm balljoint is not replaceable separately; if it is worn, the control arm must be replaced.

LOWER BALLJOINT

2009 and earlier models

2 Loosen the front wheel lug nuts. Raise the front of the vehicle and support it securely on jackstands, then remove the wheel.

3 Remove the cotter pin, then unscrew the balljoint-to-steering knuckle nut a few turns. Using a balljoint separator or a puller, break the balljoint stud loose from the steering knuckle **(see illustration)**, then remove the nut and separate the balljoint from the knuckle.

4 Remove the fasteners and detach the balljoint from the lower control arm **(see illustration 7.3)**.

5 Installation is the reverse of removal. Tighten all suspension fasteners to the torque values listed in this Chapter's Specifications, and use a new cotter pin on the lower control arm balljoint castle nut. If necessary, tighten the castle nut a little more to align the hole in the ballstud with the slots in the nut - don't loosen the nut to achieve this alignment.

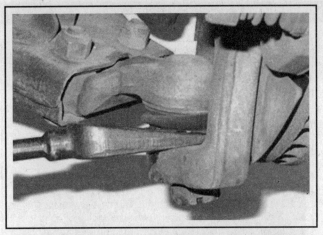

9.3 Use a puller or balljoint separator to pop the balljoint stud free of the steering knuckle. Loosening the nut a few turns (but not removing it) will prevent the components from separating violently

2011 and later models

6 The balljoints on these models are replaceable, but a balljoint press or hydraulic press and special adapters are required. If you don't have access to a press and the necessary adapters, remove the control arm and have the balljoint replaced at an automotive machine shop or other properly equipped repair facility.

10 Steering knuckle and hub - removal and installation

✳✳ WARNING:

Dust created by the brake system is harmful to your health. Never blow it out with compressed air and don't inhale any of it. Do not use petroleum-based solvents to clean brake parts. Use brake system cleaner only.

2009 AND EARLIER MODELS

Removal

1 Loosen the wheel lug nuts, raise the vehicle and support it securely on jackstands. Remove the wheel.

2 On 4WD models, remove the driveaxle/hub nut (see Chapter 8).

3 Remove the the wheel speed sensor from the steering knuckle (see Chapter 9).

4 Remove the brake caliper and brake disc. Hang the caliper with a length of wire - don't let it hang by the brake line/hose (see Chapter 9).

5 Disconnect the tie-rod end from the steering knuckle (see Section 19).

6 Disconnect the upper and lower control arms from the steering knuckle (see Sections 6 and 7), then remove the steering knuckle. On 4WD models, push the driveaxle out of the hub with a puller, being careful to not overextend the inner CV joint. Support the driveaxle with a length of wire - don't let it hang by the inner CV joint.

Installation

7 Installation is the reverse of removal. Tighten all suspension fasteners to the torque values listed in this Chapter's Specifications . Tighten the brake fasteners to the torque listed in the Chapter 9 Specifications.

8 Tighten the lug nuts to the torque listed in the Chapter 1 Specifications.

2011 AND LATER MODELS

Removal

9 Loosen the driveaxle/hub nut (see Chapter 8). Loosen the wheel lug nuts, raise the vehicle and support it securely on jackstands. Remove the wheel.

➡ Note: If your socket will not fit through the opening in the wheel, loosen the driveaxle/hub nut after the wheel is removed. To prevent the hub from turning, have an assistant apply the brake, or place a long prybar across two of the wheel studs.

10 Remove the wheel speed sensor from the knuckle and remove the brake disc from the hub (see Chapter 9).

11 Loosen, but do not remove, the strut-to-steering knuckle bolt nuts.

12 Separate the tie-rod end from the steering knuckle arm (see Section 19).

13 Separate the balljoint from the steering knuckle and pull the control arm down (see Section 8). The strut-to-knuckle bolts can now be removed.

14 Push the driveaxle from the hub (see Chapter 8). Support the end of the driveaxle with a piece of wire.

15 Separate the steering knuckle from the strut.

Installation

16 Guide the knuckle and hub assembly into position, inserting the driveaxle into the hub.

17 Push the knuckle into the strut flange and install the bolts and nuts, but don't tighten them yet.

18 Connect the balljoint to the control arm and install the pinch bolt and nut (don't tighten it yet).

19 Attach the tie-rod to the steering knuckle arm (see Section 19). Tighten the strut bolt nuts and the tie-rod nut to the torque values listed in this Chapter's Specifications. Replace all cotter pins with new ones.

20 Place the brake disc on the hub and install the caliper and wheel speed sensor (see Chapter 9).

21 Install the driveaxle/hub nut and tighten it to the torque listed in the Chapter 8 Specifications.

22 Install the wheel and lug nuts, lower the vehicle and tighten the lug nuts to the torque listed in the Chapter 1 Specifications.

11 Hub and bearing assembly (front) - removal and installation

2009 AND EARLIER MODELS

1 Due to the special tools and expertise required to press the hub and bearing from the steering knuckle, this job should be left to a professional shop. However, the steering knuckle and hub may be removed and the assembly taken to a dealer service department or other qualified repair shop. See Section 10 for the steering knuckle and hub removal procedure.

2011 AND LATER MODELS

Removal

2 Loosen the wheel lug nuts, raise the front of the vehicle and support it securely on jackstands. Remove the wheel.
3 Remove the ABS wheel speed sensor from the steering knuckle (see Chapter 9).
4 Remove the driveaxle/hub nut (see Chapter 8).
5 Remove the brake caliper, the caliper mounting bracket and the brake disc from the hub (see Chapter 9).

✳✳ CAUTION:

Suspend the caliper to the strut coil spring with a piece of wire. DO NOT let the caliper hang by the brake hose.

6 Remove the hub/bearing assembly mounting bolts from the back of the steering knuckle **(see illustration)**. Discard the mounting bolts.
7 Remove the hub/bearing assembly from the steering knuckle.
➡ **Note: If the driveaxle splines stick in the hub, push the driveaxle out of the hub with a two-jaw puller.**

INSTALLATION

8 Make sure that the mounting surface inside the steering knuckle and on the driveaxle splines is smooth and free of burrs and nicks prior to installing the hub/bearing assembly.

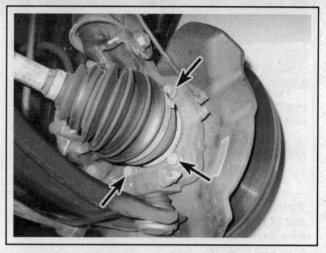

11.6 Hub and bearing assembly mounting bolts

9 Lubricate the driveaxle splines with multi-purpose grease. Install the hub/bearing assembly onto the driveaxle and into the steering knuckle until it is fully seated on the steering knuckle.
10 Install the hub/bearing assembly mounting bolts. Tighten the bolts to the torque listed in this Chapter's Specifications. Connect the wheel speed sensor harness connector and secure it to its bracket.
11 Install the brake disc, the caliper mounting bracket and the caliper; tighten the fasteners to the torque values listed in the Chapter 9 Specifications.
12 Install the driveaxle/hub nut and tighten it to the torque listed in the Chapter 8 Specifications.
➡ **Note: Have an assistant apply the brakes while tightening the driveaxle/hub nut.**
13 Install the wheel and lug nuts, remove the jackstands and lower the vehicle.
14 Tighten the lug nuts to the torque listed in the Chapter 1 Specifications.

12 Stabilizer bar and bushings (rear) - removal and installation

1 Loosen the rear wheel lug nuts. Raise the rear of the vehicle and support it securely on jackstands. Remove the wheels.

2009 AND EARLIER MODELS

2 Support the rear axle with a floor jack placed under the differential. Raise the axle slightly.
3 Disconnect the stabilizer bar links from the bar **(see illustration)**.
4 Unbolt the stabilizer bar bushing brackets **(see illustration)**.
5 The stabilizer bar can now be removed from the vehicle. Remove

the bushings from the stabilizer bar, noting their positions.
6 Check the bushings for wear, hardness, distortion, cracking and other signs of deterioration, replacing them if necessary. Check the stabilizer bar links for loose ballstuds.
7 Using a wire brush, clean the areas of the bar where the bushings ride. Lubricate the inside and outside of the new bushings with vegetable oil (used in cooking).

✳✳ CAUTION:

Don't use petroleum or mineral-based lubricants or brake fluid - they will lead to deterioration of the bushings.

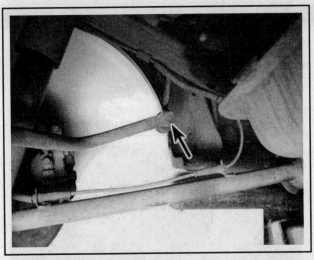

12.3 Disconnect the rear stabilizer bar links from the bar

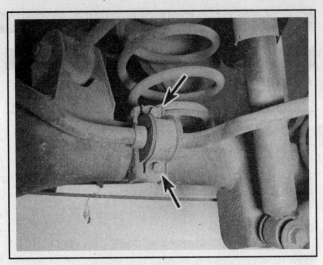

12.4 Remove the stabilizer bar bushing brackets

8 Installation is the reverse of removal. Tighten the bushing bracket bolts to the torque listed in this Chapter's Specifications. Tighten the link nuts until 5/8-inch (16 mm) of thread is exposed, then tighten the jam nuts securely.

2011 AND LATER MODELS

9 Remove the rear subframe (see Section 24).

10 Remove the nuts and detach the stabilizer bar links from the rear knuckle **(see illustration)**.

11 Remove the nuts from the stabilizer bar bushing brackets and detach the bar from the subframe **(see illustration)**.

12 Check the bushings for wear, hardness, distortion, cracking and other signs of deterioration, replacing them if necessary. Check the stabilizer bar links for loose ballstuds.

13 Using a wire brush, clean the areas of the bar where the bushings ride. Lubricate the inside and outside of the new bushings with vegetable oil (used in cooking).

> ⁂ **CAUTION:**
>
> **Don't use petroleum or mineral-based lubricants or brake fluid - they will lead to deterioration of the bushings.**

14 Installation is the reverse of removal. Tighten the bushing bracket bolts and the link nuts to the torque values listed in this Chapter's Specifications.

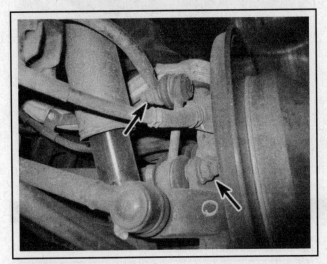

12.10 Stabilizer bar link nuts

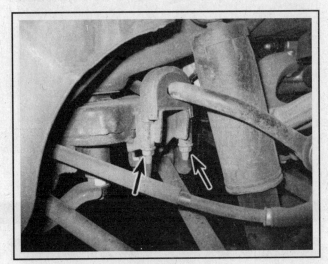

12.11 Stabilizer bar bushing bracket nuts

13 Shock absorbers (rear) - removal and installation

✳ WARNING:

Always replace shock absorbers in pairs - never replace just one of them.

1 Loosen the rear wheel lug nuts. Raise the rear of the vehicle and support it securely on jackstands. Remove the wheels.

2009 AND EARLIER MODELS

2 Support the rear axle with a floor jack nearest to the shock absorber to be removed.
3 Remove the shock absorber lower mounting bolt **(see illustration)**.
4 Remove the shock absorber upper mounting fastener and remove the shock absorber.
5 Installation is the reverse of removal. Tighten the mounting fasteners to the torque listed in this Chapter's Specifications.

2011 AND LATER MODELS

6 Support the trailing arm with a floor jack placed under the area of the coil spring.
7 Remove the bolt from the top of the shock absorber **(see illustration).**

8 Remove the bolt from the bottom of the shock absorber **(see illustration)**. Remove the shock absorber
9 Extend the new shock absorber as far as possible.
10 Installation is the reverse of removal. Tighten the fasteners to the torque values listed in this Chapter's Specifications.

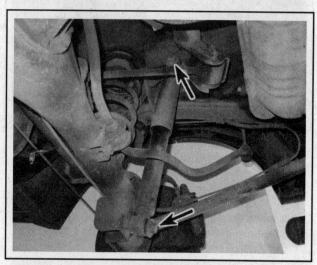

13.3 Shock absorber mounting bolts (2009 and earlier models)

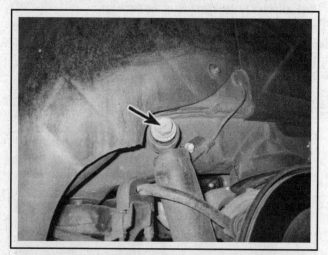

13.7 Remove the shock absorber upper mounting bolt

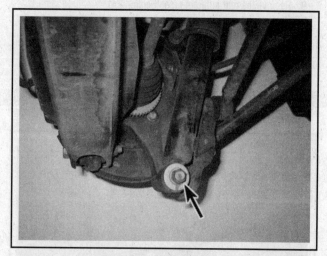

13.8 Rear shock absorber lower mounting bolt

14 Coil spring (rear) - removal and installation

✳ WARNING:

Always replace coil springs in pairs - never replace just one of them.

1 Loosen the rear wheel lug nuts. Raise the rear of the vehicle and support it securely on jackstands. Remove the wheels.

2009 AND EARLIER MODELS

2 Disconnect the stabilizer bar links from the bar (see Section 12).
3 Support the rear axle with a floor jack placed underneath the differential.
4 Remove the shock absorber lower mounting bolts.
5 Slowly lower the floor jack until the coil springs are fully

extended, then remove the coil springs and insulators.

   6 Inspect the coil spring for chips and distortion. Check the insulators for deterioration. Replace parts as necessary.

   7 Install the insulator to the top of the spring, aligning the end of the spring with the step on the insulator. Tape the insulator to the spring.

   8 Installation is the reverse of the removal procedure. Tighten the shock absorber mounting bolts to the torque listed in this Chapter's Specifications. Tighten the lug nuts to the torque listed in the Chapter 1 Specifications.

2011 AND LATER MODELS

   9 Support the lower control arm with a floor jack placed under the area of the coil spring.

   10 Unbolt and disconnect the lower control arm from the rear knuckle **(see illustration)**.

   11 Use the floor jack to slowly and carefully lower the trailing arm until the spring can be removed.

   12 Inspect the coil spring for chips and distortion. Check the insulators for deterioration. Replace parts as necessary.

   13 Installation is the reverse of removal. Tighten the lower control arm bolt/nut to the torque listed in this Chapter's Specifications. Tighten the lug nuts to the torque listed in
the Chapter 1 Specifications.

➡ **Note: The control arm bolt/nut should be tightened with the**

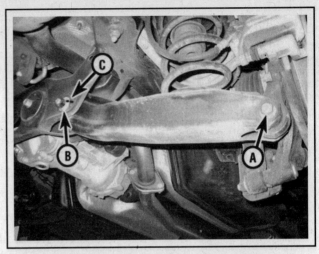

14.10 Lower control arm-to-rear knuckle nut bolt (A) and arm-to-subframe bolt/nut/adjuster cam (B). Whenever separating the lower arm from the subframe, make an alignment mark from the adjuster cam to the subframe (C)

vehicle at normal ride height. This can be done after the vehicle has been assembled, lowered to the ground and bounced few times as if inspecting the shock absorbers. Alternatively, the normal ride height can be simulated by raising the lower control arm with a floor jack.

15 Suspension arms (rear) - removal and installation

2009 AND EARLIER MODELS

   1 Loosen the rear wheel lug nuts, raise the rear of the vehicle and support it securely on jackstands placed under the frame rails. Remove the rear wheel.

Trailing arm

   2 Support the rear axle with a floor jack nearest the arm to be removed.

   3 Remove the nuts and pivot bolts from each end of the arm, then remove the arm **(see illustration)**.

   4 Check the bushings for wear and deterioration. If necessary, take the arm to an automotive machine shop or other repair facility to have the old bushings pressed out and new ones pressed in.

   5 Installation is the reverse of removal. Tighten the fasteners to the torque listed in this Chapter's Specifications. Tighten the lug nuts to the torque listed in the Chapter 1 Specifications.

➡ **Note: When installing any rear suspension arm, loosely tighten all the bolts, move the suspension to its normal ride-height angle and position (a floor jack can be used to do this), then fully tighten the bolts.**

Upper links/lateral control rod

   6 Support the rear axle with a floor jack placed under the differential.

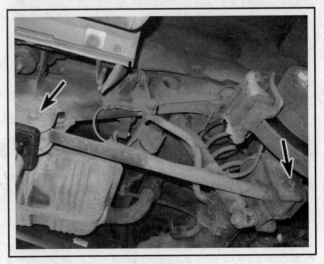

15.3 Trailing arm pivot bolts/nuts

15.7a Upper link pivot fasteners

15.7b Lateral control rod bolts

7 Remove the nuts and pivot bolts from each end of the link or rod, then remove the link or rod **(see illustrations)**.

8 Check the bushings for wear and deterioration. If necessary, take the link to an automotive machine shop or other repair facility to have the old bushings pressed out and new ones pressed in.

9 Installation is the reverse of removal. Tighten the fasteners to the torque listed in this Chapter's Specifications . Tighten the lug nuts to the torque listed in the Chapter 1 Specifications.

➡ **Note: When installing any rear suspension arm, loosely tighten all the bolts, move the suspension to its normal ride-height angle and position (a floor jack can be used to do this), then fully tighten the bolts.**

2011 AND LATER MODELS

10 Loosen the rear wheel lug nuts, raise the rear of the vehicle and support it securely on jackstands. Remove the rear wheel.

Upper control arm

11 Unbolt and lower the rear subframe (see Section 24).
12 Remove the cotter pin and unscrew the castle nut a few turns,

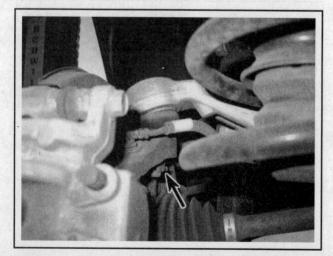

15.12 Upper control arm balljoint-to-rear knuckle nut

then break loose the balljoint stud with a balljoint separator or a suitable puller **(see illustration)**.

13 Remove the inner pivot nuts/bolts.

14 Detach the upper control arm from the subframe. Check the bushings for wear and deterioration. If necessary, take the arm to an automotive machine shop or other repair facility to have the old bushings pressed out and new ones pressed in.

15 Installation is the reverse of removal. Tighten all suspension fasteners to the torque listed in this Chapter's Specifications and use a new cotter pin on the balljoint castle nut. If necessary, tighten the castle nut a little more to align the hole in the ballstud with the slots in the nut - don't loosen the nut to achieve this alignment. Tighten the lug nuts to the torque listed in the Chapter 1 Specifications.

➡ **Note: When installing any rear suspension arm, loosely tighten all the bolts, move the suspension to its normal ride-height angle and position (a floor jack can be used to do this), then fully tighten the bolts.**

Lower control arm

16 Remove the coil spring (see Section 14).
17 Make an alignment mark on the adjuster cam to the subframe. Remove the nut and inner pivot bolt, then detach the arm from the subframe **(see illustration 14.10)**.
18 Check the bushing for wear and deterioration. If necessary, take the arm to an automotive machine shop or other repair facility to have the old bushing pressed out and a new one pressed in.
19 Installation is the reverse of removal. Tighten allsuspension fasteners to the torque values listed in this Chapter's Specifications. Tighten the lug nuts to the torque listed in the Chapter 1 Specifications.

➡ **Note: When installing any rear suspension arm, loosely tighten all the bolts, move the suspension to its normal ride-height angle and position (a floor jack can be used to do this), then fully tighten the bolts.**

Lateral control rod

20 Support the lower control arm with a floor jack. Remove the cotter pin and loosen the castle nut on the outer end of the rod several turns, then break loose the balljoint stud with a balljoint separator or a suitable puller.

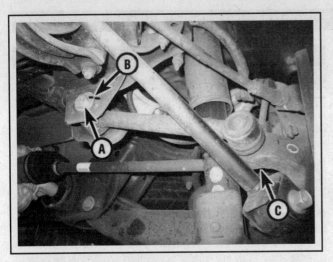

15.22 Lateral control rod details

A   Inner pivot bolt
B   Alignment marks
C   Lateral control rod-to-knuckle nut (not visible)

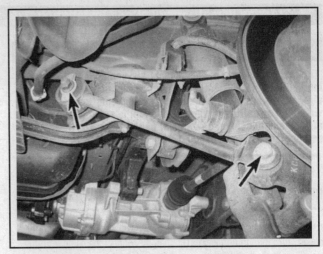

15.26 Trailing arm fasteners

21 Remove the nut and detach the rod from the knuckle.

22 Make an alignment mark on the adjuster cam to the subframe. Remove the nut and inner pivot bolt from the rod and detach the rod from the subframe **(see illustration)**.

23 Check the bushing for wear and deterioration. If necessary, take the arm to an automotive machine shop or other repair facility to have the old bushing pressed out and a new one pressed in.

24 Installation is the reverse of removal. Tighten allsuspension fasteners to the torque values listed in this Chapter's Specifications, and use a new cotter pin on on theballjoint castle nut. If necessary, tighten the castle nut a little more to align the hole in the ballstud with the slots in the nut - don't loosen the nut to achieve this alignment. Tighten the lug nuts to the torque listed in the Chapter 1 Specifications.

➡ **Note: When installing any rear suspension arm, loosely tighten all the bolts, move the suspension to its normal ride-height angle and position (a floor jack can be used to do this), then fully tighten the bolts.**

Trailing arm

25 Support the rear suspension with a floor jack placed under the *outer* end of the lower control arm.

26 Remove the fasteners securing the trailing arm to the rear knuckle and to the subframe **(see illustration)**.

27 Check the bushing for wear and deterioration. If necessary, take the arm to an automotive machine shop or other repair facility to have the old bushing pressed out and a new one pressed in.

28 Installation is the reverse of removal. Tighten all suspension fasteners to the torque values listed in this Chapter's Specifications. Tighten the lug nuts to the torque listed in the Chapter 1 Specifications.

➡ **Note: When installing any rear suspension arm, loosely tighten all the bolts, move the suspension to its normal ride-height angle and position (a floor jack can be used to do this), then fully tighten the bolts.**

16 Hub and bearing assembly (rear, 2011 and later models) - removal and installation

➡ **Note: For rear axle bearing replacement on 2009 and earlier models, see Chapter 8.**

1   Loosen the rear wheel lug nuts. If you're working on a 4WD model, loosen the driveaxle/hub nut. Raise the vehicle and support it securely on jackstands.

2   Remove the brake disc and the parking brake assembly (see Chapter 9).

3   Disconnect the rear wheel speed sensor wiring harness.

4   Remove the rear driveaxle (see Chapter 8).

5   Remove the four nuts securing the bearing assembly to the rear knuckle.

6   Detach the bearing assembly from the knuckle. On 4WD models, if the driveaxle sticks in the hub, use a two-jaw puller to push it out as the hub and bearing assembly is removed.

7   Installation is the reverse of removal. Tighten the fasteners to the torque values listed in this Chapter's Specifications.

17 Steering wheel - removal and installation

✳ WARNING:

The models covered by this manual are equipped with Supplemental Restraint Systems (SRS), more commonly known as airbags. Always disable the airbag system before working in the vicinity of any airbag system component to avoid the possibility of accidental deployment of the airbag(s), which could cause personal injury (see Chapter 12).

REMOVAL

1   Turn the steering wheel so that the wheels are pointing straight ahead. Turn the ignition key to Off, then disconnect the cable from the negative terminal of the battery (see Chapter 5).

2   Remove the airbag bolts on each side of the steering wheel **(see illustration)**.

3   Carefully pull off the airbag module.

4   Disconnect the wiring **(see illustration)** and place the airbag in a safe location with the pad facing up.

5   Make match marks on the steering shaft and the hub so the steering wheel can be replaced in exactly the same position **(see illustration)**. Remove the nut.

6   Try to remove the steering wheel by shaking the rim back and forth manually. If this fails, use a steering wheel puller.

✳ CAUTION:

Don't use a hammer in any way on the steering wheel or column.

7   Lift the wheel from the column while carefully threading the wires through it.

INSTALLATION

8   Make sure that the front wheels are facing straight ahead. If the clockspring has turned and is not centered, turn the hub in either direction until it stops (don't apply too much force). Now, rotate the hub in the other direction, counting the number of turns it takes to reach the opposite stop. Divide that number by two, then turn the hub back that many turns, approximately, until the neutral position indicator is aligned with its corresponding mark.

9   To install the wheel, align the mark on the steering wheel hub with the mark on the shaft and slip the wheel onto the shaft. Install the nut and tighten it to the torque listed in this Chapter's Specifications.

10 Plug in the electrical connectors for the airbag module and any other connectors. Make sure the module connector locks are pushed back into position.

11 Install the airbag module and tighten the bolts to the torque listed in this Chapter's Specifications.

12 Connect the negative battery cable (see Chapter 5).

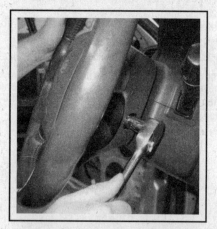

17.2 Remove the airbag module bolts

17.4 The airbag wiring has a safety latch that must be released prior to disconnecting

17.5 The steering shaft and the steering wheel must have matchmarks made so they can be assembled in the same orientation

18 Steering column - removal and installation

REMOVAL

1   Park the vehicle with the wheels pointing straight ahead. Disconnect the cable from the negative terminal of the battery (see Chapter 5).

2   Remove the steering wheel (see Section 17), then turn the ignition key to the LOCK position to prevent the steering shaft from turning.

✳ CAUTION:

If this is not done, the airbag clockspring could be damaged.

3   Remove the steering column upper and lower covers (see Chapter 11).

18.7 Make alignment marks for the orientation of the steering shaft before disassembling it

18.8 Steering column mounting fasteners

4 Disconnect the wiring and remove the multi-function switch.

5 Remove the knee bolster (see Chapter 11).

6 Mark the position of the universal joint at the steering gear pinion shaft.

7 Unscrew the steering shaft-to-universal joint pinch bolt **(see illustration)**.

8 Unscrew the mounting fasteners, then remove the steering column and shaft.

INSTALLATION

9 Guide the steering column into position, connect the intermediate shaft, then install the connecting fasteners, but don't tighten them yet.

10 Tighten the column mounting fasteners to the torque listed in this Chapter's Specifications.

11 Install the pinch bolt, tightening it to the torque listed in this Chapter's Specifications.

12 The remainder of installation is the reverse of removal.

19 Tie-rod ends - removal and installation

REMOVAL

1 Loosen the wheel lug nuts. Raise the front of the vehicle, support it securely on jackstands, block the rear wheels and set the parking brake. Remove the front wheel.

2 Hold the tie-rod with a pair of locking pliers or wrench and loosen the jam nut enough to mark the position of the tie-rod end in relation to the threads **(see illustrations)**.

3 Remove the cotter pin and loosen the nut on the tie-rod end stud.

19.2a Hold the tie-rod end with a wrench and break the jam nut loose with another wrench

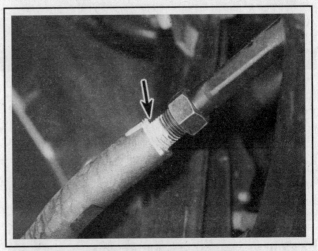

19.2b Back off the jam nut and mark the exposed threads to ensure that the new tie-rod end is threaded on the same number of turns

4 Disconnect the tie-rod from the steering knuckle arm with a puller **(see illustration)**. Remove the nut and separate the tie-rod.

5 Unscrew the tie-rod end from the tie-rod.

INSTALLATION

6 Thread the tie-rod end on to the marked position and insert the tie-rod stud into the steering knuckle arm. Tighten the jam nut securely.

7 Install the castle nut on the stud and tighten it to the torque listed in this Chapter's Specifications. Install a new cotter pin.

8 Install the wheel and lug nuts. Lower the vehicle and tighten the lug nuts to the torque listed in the Chapter 1 Specifications.

9 Have the alignment checked by a dealer service department or an alignment shop.

19.4 Use a small puller to separate the tie-rod end from the steering knuckle

20 Steering gear boots - replacement

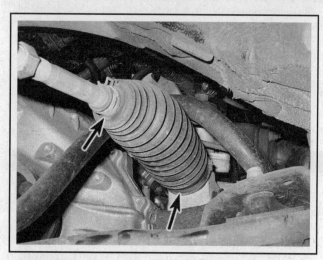

20.3 Remove the outer clamp from the steering gear boot with a pair of pliers; the inner clamp must be cut or pried off

1 Loosen the lug nuts, raise the vehicle and support it securely on jackstands. Remove the wheel.

2 Remove the tie-rod end and jam nut (see Section 19).

3 Remove the steering gear boot clamps and slide off the boot **(see illustration)**.

4 Before installing the new boot, wrap the threads and serrations on the end of the steering rod with a layer of tape so the small end of the new boot isn't damaged.

5 Slide the new boot into position on the steering gear until it seats in the groove in the steering rod, and install new clamps.

6 Remove the tape and install the tie-rod end (see Section 19).

7 Install the wheel and lug nuts. Lower the vehicle and tighten the lug nuts to the torque listed in the Chapter 1 Specifications.

8 Have the alignment checked by a dealer service department or an alignment shop.

21 Steering gear - removal and installation

REMOVAL

1 Park the vehicle with the front wheels pointing straight ahead. Loosen the front wheel lug nuts, raise the front of the vehicle and support it securely on jackstands. Apply the parking brake and remove the wheels. Remove the engine under-cover.

2 Place a drain pan under the steering gear. Detach the power steering pressure and return lines and cap the ends to prevent excessive fluid loss and contamination.

✳✳ CAUTION:

Use a flare-nut wrench for detaching the lines from the steering gear or the fittings could be damaged.

3 Mark the relationship of the intermediate shaft to the steering shaft U-joint and remove the pinch bolt.

4 Separate the tie-rod ends from the steering knuckle arms (see Section 19).

2009 and earlier models

5 Remove the steering gear mounting fasteners **(see illustrations)**.

6 Separate the intermediate shaft U-joint from the steering gear input shaft, then maneuver the steering gear down and out.

7 Check the steering gear bushings for excessive wear or deterioration, replacing them if necessary.

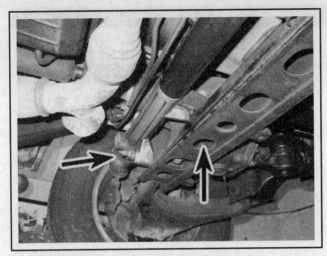

21.5a Steering gear left side mounting fasteners

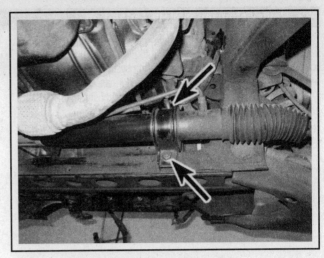

21.5b Steering gear right-side bracket bolts

2011 and later models

8 Remove the subframe (see Section 24).

9 Remove the bolts and detach the steering gear from the subframe.

INSTALLATION

10 Installation is the reverse of removal, noting the following points:

a) Align the marks on the intermediate shaft U-joint and the steering gear input shaft. If you're installing a new steering gear, center the pinion in the center of its travel by counting the number of turns lock to lock and setting the pinion midway.

b) Tighten all fasteners to the torque listed in this Chapter's Specifications.

c) Connect the power steering pressure and return hoses to the steering gear and fill the power steering pump reservoir with the recommended fluid (see Chapter 1).

d) Lower the vehicle and bleed the steering system (see Section 23).

e) Have the alignment checked by a dealer service department or an alignment shop.

22 Power steering pump - removal and installation

→ **Note: Access to the steering pump is extremely tight on most models. Remove or disconnect the components that interfere on your particular model.**

REMOVAL

1 Disconnect the cable from the negative battery terminal (see Chapter 5).

2 Using a large syringe or suction gun, suck as much fluid out of the power steering fluid reservoir as possible. Place a drain pan under the vehicle to catch any fluid that spills out when the hoses are disconnected.

3 Remove the drivebelt (see Chapter 1).

4 Detach the fluid feed hose from the pump **(see illustration)**. Disconnect the electrical connector from the power steering pressure switch.

5 Remove the banjo bolt and disconnect the pressure line from the pump.

6 Remove the mounting bolts and remove the pump.

INSTALLATION

7 When connecting the pressure line to the pump, use new sealing washers. Tighten the banjo bolt to the torque listed in this Chapter's Specifications.

8 Tighten the mounting fasteners securely.

9 Top up the fluid level in the reservoir (see Chapter 1) and bleed the system (see Section 23).

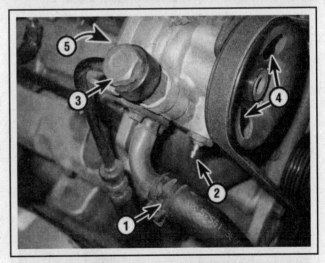

22.4 Power steering pump mounting details (2006 and earlier V6 engine, other models similar)

1 Fluid feed hose

2 Power steering pressure switch

3 Pressure line banjo fitting

4 Front mounting bolts (access through pulley holes)

5 Rear mounting bolt (not visible here)

23 Power steering system - bleeding

1 Following any operation in which the power steering fluid lines have been disconnected, the power steering system must be bled to remove all air and obtain proper steering performance.

2 With the front wheels in the straight-ahead position, check the power steering fluid level (see Chapter 1) - if low, add fluid.

3 Start the engine and allow it to idle. Recheck the fluid level and add more if necessary.

4 Bleed the system by turning the wheels fully from side to side, without hitting the stops. It may take several dozen turns to bleed the system. This will work the air out of the system. Keep the reservoir full of fluid as this is done.

➡ **Note: This procedure can be performed with the front of the vehicle raised with a jack and supported on jackstands. This makes it easier to turn the wheels back and forth during the bleeding process.**

5 When the air is worked out of the system, return the wheels to the straight-ahead position and leave the vehicle running for several more minutes before shutting it off.

6 Road test the vehicle to be sure the steering system is functioning normally and noise free.

7 Recheck the fluid level to be sure it is up to the Hot mark on the dipstick while the engine is at normal operating temperature. Add fluid if necessary (see Chapter 1).

24 Subframe (2011 and later models) - removal and installation

FRONT

Removal

1 Disconnect the cable from the negative battery terminal (see Chapter 5).

2 Loosen the front wheel lug nuts, raise the front of the vehicle and support it securely on jackstands. Remove both front wheels.

➡ **Note: The jackstands must be behind the front suspension subframe, not supporting the vehicle by the subframe.**

3 Remove any interfering front bumper trim components.

4 Disconnect the stabilizer bar links from the bar.

5 Disconnect the control arms from the steering knuckles (see Section 8).

6 Mark the relationship of the intermediate shaft to the steering shaft U-joint and remove the pinch bolt.

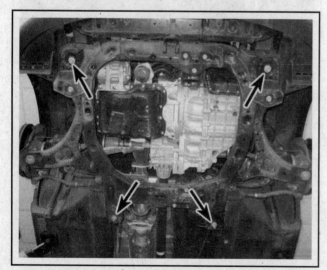

24.11 Subframe mounting fasteners

7 Inspect the subframe for any hose, line or harness brackets that may be attached, and detach them. Plug all disconnected hoses and lines.

❊❊ WARNING:

Do not disconnect any refrigerant line fittings.

8 Support the engine from above using an engine hoist or support fixture (see Chapter 2C).

❊❊ WARNING:

DO NOT place any part of your body under the engine when it's supported only by a hoist or other lifting device.

9 Detach the roll stopper (rear engine mount) from the subframe.

10 Using two floor jacks, support the subframe. Position one jack on each side of the subframe, midway between the front and rear mounting points.

11 With the jacks sufficiently supporting the subframe, remove the subframe mounting fasteners **(see illustration)**.

12 With the use of an assistant to steady the subframe, carefully lower the jacks until the subframe is sufficiently resting on the ground.

Installation

13 Installation is the reverse of removal. Tighten all suspension and subframe fasteners to the torque listed in this Chapter's Specifications. Tighten the engine mount fasteners to the torque listed in the appropriate Chapter 2 Specifications.

REAR

14 Loosen the rear wheel lug nuts, raise the rear of the vehicle and support it securely on jackstands. Remove the wheels.

15 If you're working on a 4WD model, detach the driveshaft from the rear differential.

16 Remove the rear portion of the exhaust system.

17 Remove the brake calipers (see Chapter 9). Hang the calipers with lengths of wire or rope; don't disconnect the hoses.

18 Unbolt the lower ends of the shock absorbers (see Section 13).

19 Support the crossmember with a floor jack (or a pair of floor jacks). A jack with a transmission adapter works well.

20 Remove the crossmember mounting fasteners and lower it to the floor **(see illustration)**.

21 Installation is the reverse of removal. Tighten all fasteners to the proper torque Specifications.

24.20 Crossmember mounting fasteners

25 Wheels and tires - general information

1 All vehicles covered by this manual are equipped with metric-sized fiberglass or steel belted radial tires **(see illustration)**. Use of other size or type of tires may affect the ride and handling of the vehicle. Don't mix different types of tires, such as radials and bias belted, on the same vehicle as handling may be seriously affected. It's recommended that tires be replaced in pairs on the same axle, but if only one tire is being replaced, be sure it's the same size, structure and tread design as the other.

2 Because tire pressure has a substantial effect on handling and wear, the pressure on all tires should be checked at least once a month or before any extended trips (see Chapter 1).

3 Wheels must be replaced if they are bent, dented, leak air, have elongated bolt holes, are heavily rusted, out of vertical symmetry or if the lug nuts won't stay tight. Wheel repairs that use welding or peening are not recommended.

4 Tire and wheel balance is important in the overall handling, braking and performance of the vehicle. Unbalanced wheels can adversely affect handling and ride characteristics as well as tire life. Whenever a tire is installed on a wheel, the tire and wheel should be balanced by a shop with the proper equipment.

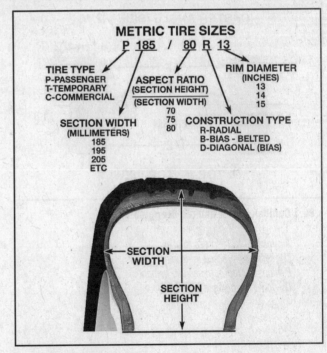

25.1 Metric tire size code

26 Wheel alignment - general information

1 A wheel alignment refers to the adjustments made to the wheels so they are in proper angular relationship to the suspension and the ground. Wheels that are out of proper alignment not only affect vehicle control, but also increase tire wear. The alignment angles normally mea-

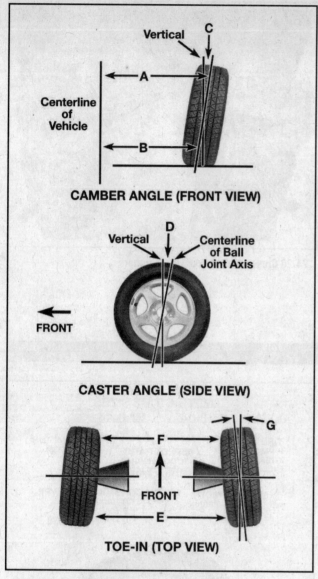

CAMBER ANGLE (FRONT VIEW)

CASTER ANGLE (SIDE VIEW)

TOE-IN (TOP VIEW)

26.1 Camber, caster and toe-in angles

A minus B = C (degrees camber)
D = caster (expressed in degrees)
E minus F = toe-in (measured in inches)
G = toe-in (expressed in degrees)

sured are camber, caster and toe-in **(see illustration)**.

2 Getting the proper wheel alignment is a very exacting process, one in which complicated and expensive machines are necessary to perform the job properly. Because of this, you should have a technician with the proper equipment perform these tasks. We will, however, use this space to give you a basic idea of what is involved with a wheel alignment so you can better understand the process and deal intelligently with the shop that does the work.

3 Toe-in is the turning in of the wheels. The purpose of a toe specification is to ensure parallel rolling of the wheels. In a vehicle with zero toe-in, the distance between the front edges of the wheels will be the same as the distance between the rear edges of the wheels. The actual amount of toe-in is normally only a fraction of an inch. On the front end, toe-in is controlled by the tie-rod end position on the tie-rod. On the rear end, it's controlled by cam bolts at the inner ends of the lateral control rod. Incorrect toe-in will cause the tires to wear improperly by making them scrub against the road surface.

4 Camber is the tilting of the wheels from vertical when viewed from one end of the vehicle. When the wheels tilt out at the top, the camber is said to be positive (+). When the wheels tilt in at the top the camber is negative (-). The amount of tilt is measured in degrees from vertical and this measurement is called the camber angle. This angle affects the amount of tire tread, which contacts the road and compensates for changes in the suspension geometry when the vehicle is cornering or traveling over an undulating surface.

5 Caster is the tilting of the front steering axis from the vertical. A tilt toward the rear is positive caster and a tilt toward the front is negative caster. Too little caster will make the front end wander, while too much caster can make the steering effort higher.

Torque specifications	Ft-lbs (unless otherwise indicated)	Nm

➡ **Note: One foot-pound (ft-lb) of torque is equivalent to 12 inch-pounds (in-lbs) of torque. Torque values below approximately 15 foot-pounds are expressed in inch-pounds, because most foot-pound torque wrenches are not accurate at these smaller values.**

Front suspension

	Ft-lbs	Nm
Stabilizer bar		
Bracket bolts	39	52
Link nuts		
2009 and earlier models		
To control arm	68	92
Upper nuts	Measure exposed thread (see Section 2)	
2011 and later models	75	104
Shock absorber/coil spring assembly (2009 and earlier models)		
Damper shaft nut	55	75
Upper mounting nuts	31	42
Lower mounting bolt/nut	90	122
Strut (2011 and later models)		
Upper mounting nuts	35	47
Lower mounting bolt/nuts	120	162
Upper control arm (2009 and earlier models)		
Pivot bolt nuts	60	81
Balljoint pinch bolt	35	47
Lower control arm		
2009 and earlier models		
Pivot bolt nuts	160	216
Balljoint-to-control arm bolt/nuts	Not available	
Balljoint-to-steering knuckle nut	120	162
2011 and later models		
Control arm-to-subframe bolt/nut	110	150
Balljoint-to-steering knuckle pinch bolt/nut	80	108
Hub and bearing assembly-to-steering knuckle bolts (2011 and later models)	80	108
Subframe mounting fasteners (2011 and later models)	115	155

Rear suspension

	Ft-lbs	Nm
Stabilizer bar		
Bracket bolts		
2009 and earlier models	16	21
2011 and later models	30	40
Link nuts		
2009 and earlier models	Measure exposed thread (see Section 12)	
2011 and later models	45	61
Shock absorber mounting bolts		
2009 and earlier models	100	135
2011 and later models		
Upper bolt	110	150
Lower bolt	80	108

Torque specifications	Ft-lbs (unless otherwise indicated)	Nm

➡ **Note: One foot-pound (ft-lb) of torque is equivalent to 12 inch-pounds (in-lbs) of torque. Torque values below approximately 15 foot-pounds are expressed in inch-pounds, because most foot-pound torque wrenches are not accurate at these smaller values.**

Rear suspension arms		
2009 and earlier models		
Trailing arm	110	150
Upper link	100	135
Lateral control rod	100	135
2011 and later models		
Upper control arm		
Pivot bolts	110	150
Balljoint-to-rear knuckle nut	60	81
Lower control arm bolts/nuts	110	150
Lateral control rod		
Pivot bolt/nut	110	150
Balljoint nut	80	108
Trailing arm bolts/nuts	110	150
Subframe mounting fasteners		
(2011 and later models)	115	155

Steering system

Airbag module bolts	88 in-lbs	10
Steering wheel nut	36	48
Steering column mounting bolts		
2009 and earlier models	15	20
2011 and later models	168 in-lbs	18
Intermediate shaft pinch bolt		
2009 and earlier models	15	20
2011 and later models	21	28
Steering gear		
2009 and earlier models		
Lower left nut and center nut	100	150
Bracket bolts	65	88
2011 and later models	70	95
Tie-rod end-to-steering knuckle nut		
2009 and earlier models	55	75
2011 and later models	30	40
Power steering pump bolts		
2009 and earlier models	16	21
2011 and later models	Not available	

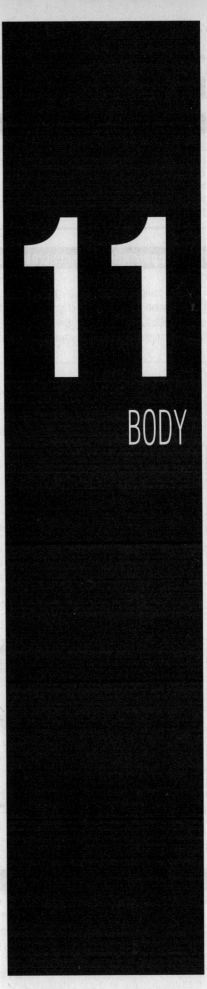

11

BODY

Section

1   General information

> ✳✳ **WARNING:**
>
> **The models covered by this manual are equipped with Supplemental Restraint Systems (SRS), more commonly known as airbags. Always disable the airbag system before working in the vicinity of any airbag system components to avoid the possibility of accidental deployment of the airbags, which could cause personal injury (see Chapter 12).**

Certain body components are particularly vulnerable to accident damage and can be unbolted and repaired or replaced. Among these parts are the hood, doors, tailgate, liftgate, bumpers and front fenders.

Only general body maintenance practices and body panel repair procedures within the scope of the do-it-yourselfer are included in this Chapter.

2   Repair minor paint scratches

No matter how hard you try to keep your vehicle looking like new, it will inevitably be scratched, chipped or dented at some point. If the metal is actually dented, seek the advice of a professional. But you can fix minor scratches and chips yourself. Buy a touch-up paint kit from a

dealer service department or an auto parts store. To ensure that you get the right color, you'll need to have the specific make, model and year of your vehicle and, ideally, the paint code, which is located on a special metal plate under the hood or in the door jamb.

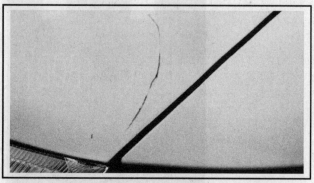

Make sure the damaged area is perfectly clean and rust free. If the touch-up kit has a wire brush, use it to clean the scratch or chip. Or use fine steel wool wrapped around the end of a pencil. Clean the scratched or chipped surface only, not the good paint surrounding it. Rinse the area with water and allow it to dry thoroughly

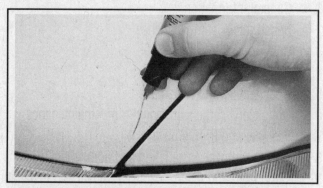

Thoroughly mix the paint, then apply a small amount with the touch-up kit brush or a very fine artist's brush. Brush in one direction as you fill the scratch area. Do not build up the paint higher than the surrounding paint

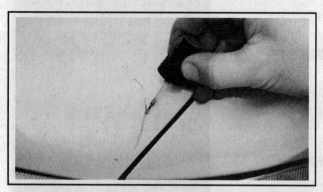

If the vehicle has a two-coat finish, apply the clear coat after the color coat has dried

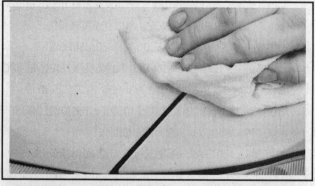

Wait a few days for the paint to dry thoroughly, then rub out the repainted area with a polishing compound to blend the new paint with the surrounding area. When you're happy with your work, wash and polish the area

3   Body - maintenance

1   The condition of your vehicle's body is very important, because the resale value depends a great deal on it. It's much more difficult to repair a neglected or damaged body than it is to repair mechanical components. The hidden areas of the body, such as the wheel wells, the frame and the engine compartment, are equally important, although they

don't require as frequent attention as the rest of the body.

2   Once a year, or every 12,000 miles, it's a good idea to have the underside of the body steam-cleaned. All traces of dirt and oil will be removed and the area can then be inspected carefully for rust, damaged brake lines, frayed electrical wires, damaged cables and other problems.

3 At the same time, clean the engine and the engine compartment with a steam cleaner or water-soluble degreaser.

4 The wheel wells should be given close attention, since undercoating can peel away and stones and dirt thrown up by the tires can cause the paint to chip and flake, allowing rust to set in. If rust is found, clean down to the bare metal and apply an anti-rust paint.

5 The body should be washed about once a week. Wet the vehicle thoroughly to soften the dirt, then wash it down with a soft sponge and plenty of clean soapy water. If the surplus dirt is not washed off very carefully, it can wear down the paint.

6 Spots of tar or asphalt thrown up from the road should be removed with a cloth soaked in kerosene. Scented lamp oil is available in most hardware stores and the smell is easier to work with than straight kerosene.

7 Once every six months, wax the body and chrome trim. If chrome cleaner is used to remove rust from any of the vehicle's plated parts, remember that the cleaner also removes part of the chrome, so use it sparingly. On any plated parts where chrome cleaner is used, use a good paste wax over the plating for extra protection.

4   Body repair - minor damage

PLASTIC BODY PANELS

The following repair procedures are for minor scratches and gouges. Repair of more serious damage should be left to a dealer service department or qualified auto body shop. Below is a list of the equipment and materials necessary to perform the following repair procedures on plastic body panels.

Wax, grease and silicone removing solvent
Cloth-backed body tape
Sanding discs
Drill motor with three-inch disc holder
Hand sanding block
Rubber squeegees
Sandpaper
Non-porous mixing palette
Wood paddle or putty knife
Curved-tooth body file
Flexible parts repair material

Flexible panels (bumper trim)

1   Remove the damaged panel, if necessary or desirable. In most cases, repairs can be carried out with the panel installed.

2   Clean the area(s) to be repaired with a wax, grease and silicone removing solvent applied with a water-dampened cloth.

3   If the damage is structural, that is, if it extends through the panel, clean the backside of the panel area to be repaired as well. Wipe dry.

4   Sand the rear surface about 1-1/2 inches beyond the break.

5   Cut two pieces of fiberglass cloth large enough to overlap the break by about 1-1/2 inches. Cut only to the required length.

6   Mix the adhesive from the repair kit according to the instructions included with the kit, and apply a layer of the mixture approximately 1/8-inch thick on the backside of the panel. Overlap the break by at least 1-1/2 inches.

7   Apply one piece of fiberglass cloth to the adhesive and cover the cloth with additional adhesive. Apply a second piece of fiberglass cloth to the adhesive and immediately cover the cloth with additional adhesive in sufficient quantity to fill the weave.

8   Allow the repair to cure for 20 to 30 minutes at 60-degrees to 80-degrees F.

9   If necessary, trim the excess repair material at the edge.

10 Remove all of the paint film over and around the area(s) to be repaired. The repair material should not overlap the painted surface.

11 With a drill motor and a sanding disc (or a rotary file), cut a "V" along the break line approximately 1/2-inch wide. Remove all dust and loose particles from the repair area.

12 Mix and apply the repair material. Apply a light coat first over the damaged area; then continue applying material until it reaches a level slightly higher than the surrounding finish.

13 Cure the mixture for 20 to 30 minutes at 60-degrees to 80-degrees F.

14 Roughly establish the contour of the area being repaired with a body file. If low areas or pits remain, mix and apply additional adhesive.

15 Block sand the damaged area with sandpaper to establish the actual contour of the surrounding surface.

16 If desired, the repaired area can be temporarily protected with several light coats of primer. Because of the special paints and techniques required for flexible body panels, it is recommended that the vehicle be taken to a paint shop for completion of the body repair.

STEEL BODY PANELS

◆ **See photo sequence**

Repair of dents

17 When repairing dents, the first job is to pull the dent out until the affected area is as close as possible to its original shape. There is no point in trying to restore the original shape completely as the metal in the damaged area will have stretched on impact and cannot be restored to its original contours. It is better to bring the level of the dent up to a point that is about 1/8-inch below the level of the surrounding metal. In cases where the dent is very shallow, it is not worth trying to pull it out at all.

18 If the backside of the dent is accessible, it can be hammered out gently from behind using a soft-face hammer. While doing this, hold a block of wood firmly against the opposite side of the metal to absorb the hammer blows and prevent the metal from being stretched.

19 If the dent is in a section of the body which has double layers, or some other factor makes it inaccessible from behind, a different technique is required. Drill several small holes through the metal inside the damaged area, particularly in the deeper sections. Screw long, self-tapping screws into the holes just enough for them to get a good grip in the metal. Now pulling on the protruding heads of the screws with locking pliers can pull out the dent.

20 The next stage of repair is the removal of paint from the damaged area and from an inch or so of the surrounding metal. This is easily done with a wire brush or sanding disk in a drill motor, although it can be done just as effectively by hand with sandpaper. To complete the preparation for filling, score the surface of the bare metal with a screwdriver or the tang of a file or drill small holes in the affected area. This will provide a good grip for the filler material. To complete the repair, see the Section on filling and painting.

Repair of rust holes or gashes

21 Remove all paint from the affected area and from an inch or so of the surrounding metal using a sanding disk or wire brush mounted in a

These photos illustrate a method of repairing simple dents. They are intended to supplement Body repair - minor damage in this Chapter and should not be used as the sole instructions for body repair on these vehicles.

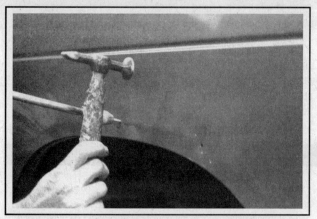

1 If you can't access the backside of the body panel to hammer out the dent, pull it out with a slide-hammer-type dent puller. Tap with a hammer near the edge of the dent to help 'pop' the metal back to its original shape, about 1/8-inch below the surface of the surrounding metal

2 Using coarse-grit sandpaper, remove the paint down to the bare metal. Clean the repair area with wax/silicone remover.

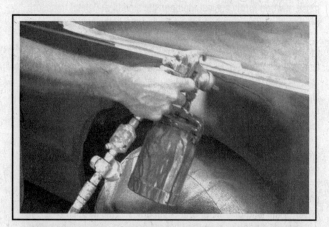

3 Following label instructions, mix up a batch of plastic filler and hardener, then quickly press it into the metal with a plastic applicator. Work the filler until it matches the original contour and is slightly above the surrounding metal

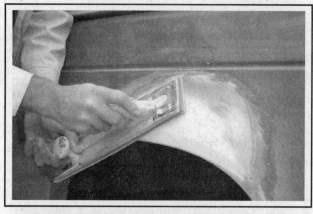

4 Let the filler harden until you can just dent it with your fingernail. File, then sand the filler down until it's smooth and even. Work down to finer grits of sandpaper - always using a board or block - ending up with 360 or 400 grit

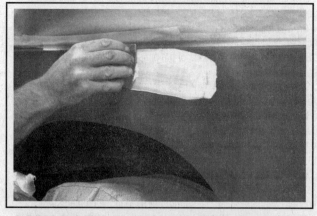

5 When the area is smooth to the touch, clean the area and mask around it. Apply several layers of primer to the area. A professional-type spray gun is being used here, but aerosol spray primer works fine

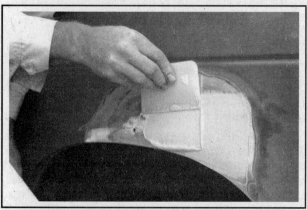

6 Fill imperfections or scratches with glazing compound. Sand with 360 or 400-grit and re-spray. Finish sand the primer with 600 grit, clean thoroughly, then apply the finish coat. Don't attempt to rub out or wax the repair area until the paint has dried completely (at least two weeks)

drill motor. If these are not available, a few sheets of sandpaper will do the job just as effectively.

22 With the paint removed, you will be able to determine the severity of the corrosion and decide whether to replace the whole panel, if possible, or repair the affected area. New body panels are not as expensive as most people think and it is often quicker to install a new panel than to repair large areas of rust.

23 Remove all trim pieces from the affected area except those which will act as a guide to the original shape of the damaged body, such as headlight shells, etc. Using metal snips or a hacksaw blade, remove all loose metal and any other metal that is badly affected by rust. Hammer the edges of the hole in to create a slight depression for the filler material.

24 Wire-brush the affected area to remove the powdery rust from the surface of the metal. If the back of the rusted area is accessible, treat it with rust inhibiting paint.

25 Before filling is done, block the hole in some way. This can be done with sheet metal riveted or screwed into place, or by stuffing the hole with wire mesh.

26 Once the hole is blocked off, the affected area can be filled and painted. See the following subsection on filling and painting.

Filling and painting

27 Many types of body fillers are available, but generally speaking, body repair kits which contain filler paste and a tube of resin hardener are best for this type of repair work. A wide, flexible plastic or nylon applicator will be necessary for imparting a smooth and contoured finish to the surface of the filler material. Mix up a small amount of filler on a clean piece of wood or cardboard (use the hardener sparingly). Follow the manufacturer's instructions on the package, otherwise the filler will set incorrectly.

28 Using the applicator, apply the filler paste to the prepared area. Draw the applicator across the surface of the filler to achieve the desired contour and to level the filler surface. As soon as a contour that approximates the original one is achieved, stop working the paste. If you continue, the paste will begin to stick to the applicator. Continue to add thin layers of paste at 20-minute intervals until the level of the filler is just above the surrounding metal.

29 Once the filler has hardened, the excess can be removed with a body file. From then on, progressively finer grades of sandpaper should be used, starting with a 180-grit paper and finishing with 600-grit wet-or-dry paper. Always wrap the sandpaper around a flat rubber or wooden block, otherwise the surface of the filler will not be completely flat. During the sanding of the filler surface, the wet-or-dry paper should be periodically rinsed in water. This will ensure that a very smooth finish is produced in the final stage.

30 At this point, the repair area should be surrounded by a ring of bare metal, which in turn should be encircled by the finely feathered edge of good paint. Rinse the repair area with clean water until all of the dust produced by the sanding operation is gone.

31 Spray the entire area with a light coat of primer. This will reveal any imperfections in the surface of the filler. Repair the imperfections with fresh filler paste or glaze filler and once more smooth the surface with sandpaper. Repeat this spray-and-repair procedure until you are satisfied that the surface of the filler and the feathered edge of the paint are perfect. Rinse the area with clean water and allow it to dry completely.

32 The repair area is now ready for painting. Spray painting must be carried out in a warm, dry, windless and dust free atmosphere. These conditions can be created if you have access to a large indoor work area, but if you are forced to work in the open, you will have to pick the day very carefully. If you are working indoors, dousing the floor in the work area with water will help settle the dust that would otherwise be in the air. If the repair area is confined to one body panel, mask off the surrounding panels. This will help minimize the effects of a slight mismatch in paint color. Trim pieces such as chrome strips, door handles, etc., will also need to be masked off or removed. Use masking tape and several thickness of newspaper for the masking operations.

33 Before spraying, shake the paint can thoroughly, then spray a test area until the spray painting technique is mastered. Cover the repair area with a thick coat of primer. The thickness should be built up using several thin layers of primer rather than one thick one. Using 600-grit wet-or-dry sandpaper, rub down the surface of the primer until it is very smooth. While doing this, the work area should be thoroughly rinsed with water and the wet-or-dry sandpaper periodically rinsed as well. Allow the primer to dry before spraying additional coats.

34 Spray on the top coat, again building up the thickness by using several thin layers of paint. Begin spraying in the center of the repair area and then, using a circular motion, work out until the whole repair area and about two inches of the surrounding original paint is covered. Remove all masking material 10 to 15 minutes after spraying on the final coat of paint. Allow the new paint at least two weeks to harden, then use a very fine rubbing compound to blend the edges of the new paint into the existing paint. Finally, apply a coat of wax

5 Body repair - major damage

1 Major damage must be repaired by an auto body shop specifically equipped to perform body and frame repairs. These shops have the specialized equipment required to do the job properly.

2 If the damage is extensive, the frame must be checked for proper alignment or the vehicle's handling characteristics may be adversely affected and other components may wear at an accelerated rate.

3 Due to the fact that all of the major body components (hood, fenders, etc.) are separate and replaceable units, any seriously damaged components should be replaced rather than repaired. Sometimes the components can be found in a wrecking yard that specializes in used vehicle components, often at considerable savings over the cost of new parts.

6 Upholstery, carpets and vinyl trim - maintenance

UPHOLSTERY AND CARPETS

1 Every three months remove the floormats and clean the interior of the vehicle (more frequently if necessary). Use a stiff whiskbroom to brush the carpeting and loosen dirt and dust, then vacuum the upholstery and carpets thoroughly, especially along seams and crevices.

2 Dirt and stains can be removed from carpeting with basic household or automotive carpet shampoos available in spray cans. Follow the directions and vacuum again, then use a stiff brush to bring back the "nap" of the carpet.

3 Most interiors have cloth or vinyl upholstery, either of which can be cleaned and maintained with a number of material-specific cleaners or shampoos available in auto supply stores. Follow the directions on the product for usage, and always spot-test any upholstery cleaner on an inconspicuous area (bottom edge of a backseat cushion) to ensure that it doesn't cause a color shift in the material.

4 After cleaning, vinyl upholstery should be treated with a protectant.

➡ **Note: Make sure the protectant container indicates the product can be used on seats - some products may make a seat too slippery.**

✳ CAUTION:

Do not use protectant on vinyl-covered steering wheels.

5 Leather upholstery requires special care. It should be cleaned regularly with saddlesoap or leather cleaner. Never use alcohol, gasoline, nail polish remover or thinner to clean leather upholstery.

6 After cleaning, regularly treat leather upholstery with a leather conditioner, rubbed in with a soft cotton cloth. Never use car wax on leather upholstery.

7 In areas where the interior of the vehicle is subject to bright sunlight, cover leather seating areas of the seats with a sheet if the vehicle is to be left out for any length of time.

VINYL TRIM

8 Don't clean vinyl trim with detergents, caustic soap or petroleum-based cleaners. Plain soap and water works just fine, with a soft brush to clean dirt that may be ingrained. Wash the vinyl as frequently as the rest of the vehicle.

9 After cleaning, application of a high-quality rubber and vinyl protectant will help prevent oxidation and cracks. The protectant can also be applied to weather-stripping, vacuum lines and rubber hoses, which often fail as a result of chemical degradation, and to the tires.

7 Fastener and trim removal

1 There is a variety of plastic fasteners used to hold trim panels, splash shields and other parts in place in addition to typical screws, nuts and bolts. Once you are familiar with them, they can usually be removed without too much difficulty.

2 The proper tools and approach can prevent added time and expense to a project by minimizing the number of broken fasteners and/or parts.

3 The following illustration shows various types of fasteners that are typically used on most vehicles and how to remove and install them **(see illustration)**. Replacement fasteners are commonly found at most auto parts stores, if necessary.

Fasteners

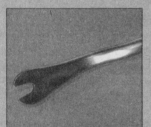
This tool is designed to remove special fasteners. A small pry tool used for removing nails will also work well in place of this tool

A Phillips head screwdriver can be used to release the center portion, but light pressure must be used because the plastic is easily damaged. Once the center is up, the fastener can easily be pried from its hole

Here is a view with the center portion fully released. Install the fastener as shown, then press the center in to set it

This fastener is used for exterior panels and shields. The center portion must be pried up to release the fastener. Install the fastener with the center up, then press the center in to set it

This type of fastener is used commonly for interior panels. Use a small blunt tool to press the small pin at the center in to release it . . .

. . . the pin will stay with the fastener in the released position

Reset the fastener for installation by moving the pin out. Install the fastener, then press the pin flush with the fastener to set it

This fastener is used for exterior and interior panels. It has no moving parts. Simply pry the fastener from its hole like the claw of a hammer removes a nail. Without a tool that can get under the top of the fastener, it can be very difficult to remove

4 Trim panels are typically made of plastic and their flexibility can help during removal. The key to their removal is to use a tool to pry the panel near its retainers to release it without damaging surrounding areas or breaking-off any retainers. The retainers will usually snap out of their designated slot or hole after force is applied to them. Stiff plastic tools designed for prying on trim panels are available at most auto parts stores **(see illustration)**. Tools that are tapered and wrapped in protective tape, such as a screwdriver or small pry tool, are also very effective when used with care.

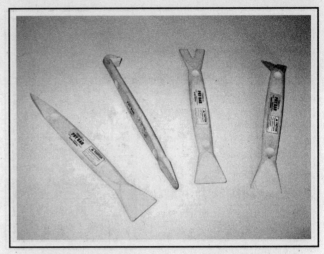

7.4 These small plastic pry tools are ideal for prying off trim panels

8 Hood - removal, installation and adjustment

➡ **Note: The hood is awkward to remove and install; at least two people should perform this procedure.**

REMOVAL AND INSTALLATION

1 Open the hood, then place blankets or pads over the fenders and cowl area of the body. This will protect the body and paint as the hood is lifted off.

2 Disconnect any cables or wires that will interfere with removal. Disconnect the windshield washer tubing.

3 Make marks around the hood hinges to ensure proper alignment during installation **(see illustration)**.

4 Have an assistant support one side of the hood then disconnect the support struts from the ball studs and lay the support down. Take turns removing the hinge-to-hood bolts and lift off the hood **(see illustration)**.

5 Installation is the reverse of removal. Align the hinge bolts with the marks made in Step 3.

ADJUSTMENT

6 Fore-and-aft and side-to-side adjustment of the hood is done by moving the hood in the hinge plate slots after loosening the bolts.

7 If you haven't done so already, mark around the entire hinge plate so you can determine the amount of movement.

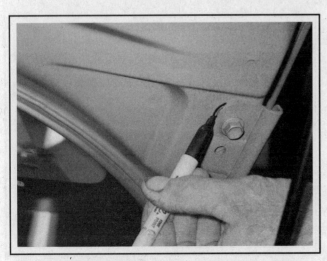

8.3 Draw alignment marks around the hood hinges to ensure proper alignment of the hood when it's reinstalled

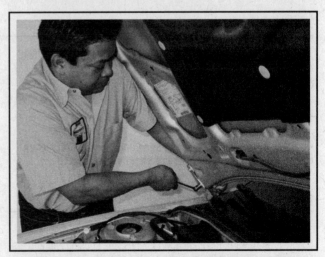

8.4 Support the hood with your shoulder while removing the hood bolts

8.9 To adjust the hood latch horizontally or vertically, loosen the mounting bolts and reposition it

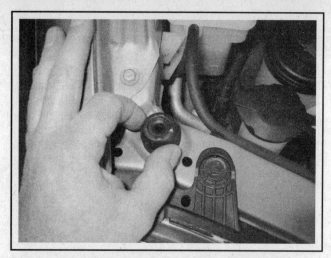

8.10 To adjust the vertical height of the leading edge of the hood so that it's flush with the fenders, rotate each edge cushion

8   Loosen the bolts and move the hood into correct alignment. Move it only a little at a time. Tighten the hinge bolts and carefully lower the hood to check the position.

9   If necessary after installation, the entire hood latch assembly can be adjusted up-and-down as well as from side-to-side on the radiator support, so the hood closes securely and flush with the fenders. Scribe a line or mark around the hood latch mounting bolts to provide a reference point, then loosen them and reposition the latch assembly, as necessary **(see illustration)**. Following adjustment, retighten the mounting bolts.

10   Finally, adjust the hood bumpers on the radiator support so the hood, when closed, is flush with the fenders **(see illustration)**.

11   The hood latch assembly, as well as the hinges, should be periodically lubricated with white lithium-base grease to prevent binding and wear.

9   Hood latch and release cable - removal and installation

LATCH

1   Scribe a line around the latch to aid alignment when installing, then remove the retaining bolts securing the hood latch to the radiator support **(see illustration 9.8)**. Remove the latch.

2   Disconnect the hood release cable by disengaging the cable from the latch **(see illustration)**.

3   Installation is the reverse of removal.

➡ **Note: Adjust the latch so the hood engages securely when closed and the hood bumpers are slightly compressed.**

CABLE

4   Working in the passenger compartment, lift the hood release handle lever upward, then pull down on the cable housing end and disengage the cable from the hood release lever handle.

5   Attach a piece of thin wire or string to the end of the cable.

6   Disconnect the hood release cable from the latch as described in Steps 1 and 2.

9.2 Pry the cable retainer from the latch and disengage the cable end

7 Remove the left inner plastic fender well.

8 Unclip all the cable retaining clips on the radiator support and the outer fenderwell **(see illustration)**.

9 Pull the cable forward into the wheel well until you can see the wire or string, then remove the wire or string from the old cable and fasten it to the new cable.

10 With the new cable attached to the wire or string, pull the wire or string back through the body until the new cable reaches the inside handle.

11 Working in the passenger compartment, install the new cable into the hood release lever, making sure the cable housing fits snugly into the notch in the handle bracket.

12 The remainder of the installation is the reverse of removal.

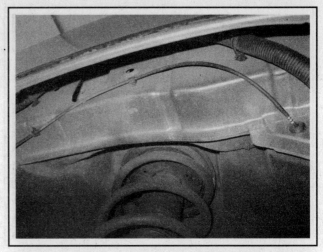

9.8 Remove the left plastic inner fender liner to get access to the hood release cable

10 Bumpers - removal and installation

FRONT BUMPER

2009 and earlier models

1 Disconnect the cable from the negative battery terminal (see Chapter 5).

2 Apply the parking brake, raise the vehicle and support it securely on jackstands.

3 Disconnect the wiring from the fog lights by reaching behind the bumper, if equipped.

4 Remove the headlight housing from each side (see Chapter 12).

5 After the headlight housing is removed, locate the bumper cover fasteners previously hidden **(see illustration)**.

6 If equipped, remove the bumper guard lower fasteners, then remove the two access hole covers and the nuts behind them. Remove the bumper guard from the bumper.

7 Remove the bumper seal board plastic type push pins and the seal board.

8 Remove the bumper cover trim upper fasteners **(see illustration)**.

10.5 Remove the corner retaining nut and fastener from each side

10.8 Upper cover trim fastener locations

10.9 Location of the bumper cover top fasteners

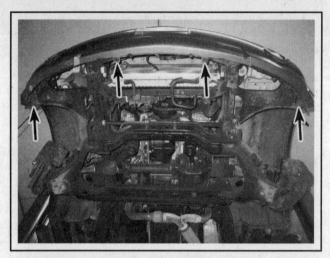

10.10 Lower front bumper cover retainer locations

10.11 Remove the fasteners from the center of the cover

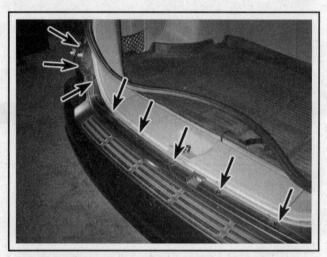

10.19 The upper bumper cover screws (8 of 11 shown) are under the weatherstrip - 2009 and earlier models shown, later models similar

9 Remove the plastic screws securing the top of the bumper cover **(see illustration)**.

10 Remove the screws securing the lower edge of the bumper cover **(see illustration)**.

11 Remove the screws from the center of the bumper cover **(see illustration)**.

2011 and later models

12 Remove the fasteners from the bottom of the bumper cover.

13 Remove the fasteners from the top of the radiator grille.

14 Remove the fastener that secures the upper rear edges of the bumper cover to the fender.

15 Disengage the clips that secure the upper rear edges of the bumper cover to the fender.

16 Using a flashlight, do a final inspection and verify that the bumper cover is completely disconnected.

17 With the assistant's help, remove the front bumper cover.

REAR BUMPER

18 Remove the rear taillight housing (see Chapter 12).

19 Open the liftgate, lift up the weatherstrip and remove the fasteners at the top of the bumper cover **(see illustration)**.

20 Raise the vehicle and support it securely on jackstands. Remove the lower screws attaching the bumper cover to the frame and the wheel well liners **(see illustration)**.

21 Remove the screws on each side attaching the bumper cover to the wheel wells **(see illustration)**.

22 Using a flashlight, make a final inspection and verify that the bumper cover is completely disconnected. Lift off the bumper cover.

23 Installation is the reverse of removal.

10.20 Lower bumper cover screw locations - left side shown on 2009 and earlier models, later models similar

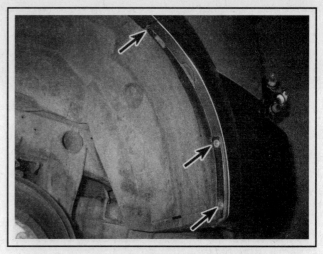

10.21 The screws for the bumper ends are in the wheel wells - 2009 and earlier models shown, later models similar

11 Front fender - removal and installation

1   Loosen the front wheel lug nuts. Raise the vehicle, support it securely on jackstands and remove the front wheel.

2   Open the hood. Remove the upper edge fender bolts **(see illustration)**.

3   Detach the inner fenderwell fasteners **(see illustration)**, then remove the inner fender splash shield. Detach the front bumper cover from the fender to be removed (see Section 10).

4   Remove the fender-to-body bolts around the edges of the fender **(see illustration)** and the nut that is recessed behind the fender.

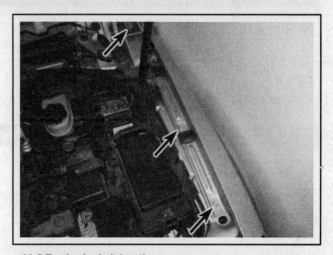

11.2 Top fender bolt locations

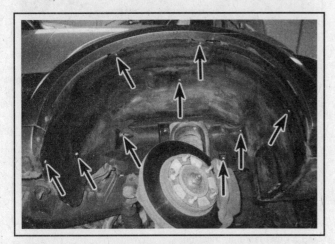

11.3 Inner fenderwell fastener locations

11.4 Inner fender nut (A) and fender lower bolt locations - the upper rear bolt is accessible after opening the door

11.5 Upper rear fender bolt

5 Open the door and remove the upper rear fender bolt **(see illustration)**.

6 Lift off the fender. It's a good idea to have an assistant support the fender while it's being moved away from the vehicle to prevent damage to the surrounding body panels.

7 Installation is the reverse of removal. Check the alignment of the fender to the hood and front edge of the door before final tightening of the fender fasteners.

12 Radiator grille (2009 and earlier models only) - removal and installation

1 Open the hood. Remove the fasteners along the top and sides of the grille.

2 Disengage the retaining clips and detach the grille from the hood.

3 Installation is the reverse of removal.

13 Cowl cover and vent tray - removal and installation

1 Remove the wiper arms (see Chapter 12). They are retained by nuts.

2 Remove the cowl weatherstrip, being careful to avoid losing the plastic retainers **(see illustration).**

3 Remove the pushpin fasteners securing the cowl cover **(see**

illustration). Use a small screwdriver to unscrew the center button up on the plastic fasteners, then pry the fasteners out (do not try to remove the center buttons; they stay in the fastener). Disengage the remaining clips and remove the cowl covers.

4 Installation is the reverse of removal.

13.2 Lift off the cowl weatherstrip - it's held in place by plastic pins

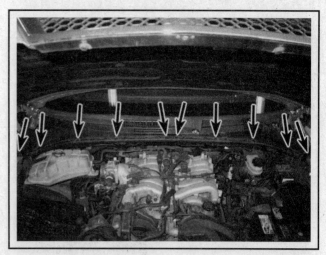

13.3 Cowl fastener locations

14 Door trim panels - removal and installation

❈ WARNING:

The models covered by this manual are equipped with Supplemental Restraint systems (SRS), more commonly known as airbags. Always disarm the airbag system before working in the vicinity of any airbag system component to avoid the possibility of accidental deployment of the airbag, which could cause personal injury (see Chapter 12).

❈ CAUTION:

Wear gloves when working inside the door openings to protect against cuts from sharp metal edges.

DOORS

1   Disconnect the cable from the negative battery terminal (see Chapter 5).

2   Remove the screw at the door latch handle, under the plastic cover **(see illustration)**.

3   Remove the screw in the front door pull handle/armrest **(see illustration)**.

4   Remove the screws at the front and rear of the panel **(see illustration)**.

5   Pry the cover from the outside mirror and speaker enclosure **(see illustration)**.

14.2 The screw for the door handle is under the plastic cover

14.3 There is a screw at the bottom of the pull handle

14.4 Door panel outer edge fastener locations

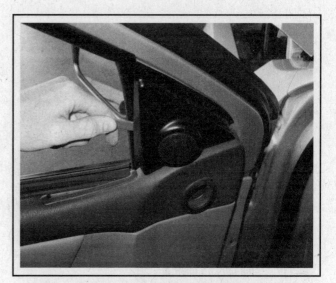

14.5 The outside mirror cover can be pried off using a trim tool or a screwdriver wrapped with electrical tape

14.6 Use a trim tool to pry the switch panel out of the door panel

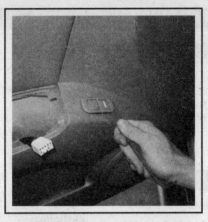

14.7 Pry the liftgate opening switch out of the panel

14.8 Use a trim tool to release the door panel - start at a corner and work slowly around the door panel

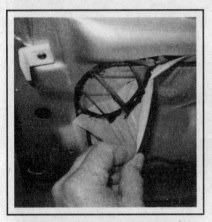

14.10 The watershield is sealed with butyl - keep it flat as you gently pull it free

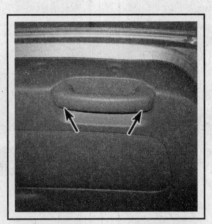

14.12 The screws for the pull handle are located under the plastic covers

14.13a Remove the trim panel fasteners (one of several shown) . . .

14.13b . . . then pry off the trim

6   Carefully pry out the window switch panel **(see illustration)** and disconnect the electrical connectors from the back side of the switch.

7   Pry the liftgate opening switch out of the door panel **(see illustration)** and disconnect the electrical connector.

8   Carefully pry the panel out until the clips disengage **(see illustration)**. Work slowly and carefully around the outer edge of the trim panel until it's free. Unplug any wiring harness connectors and remove the panel.

9   Disconnect the light at the lower rear edge as you're removing the panel.

10   For access to the door outside handle or the door window regulator inside the door, raise the window fully, then carefully peel back the plastic watershield **(see illustration)**.

11   Installation is the reverse of removal.

LIFTGATE

12   Remove the plastic covers and the two fasteners, then remove the pull handle **(see illustration)**.

13   Remove the fasteners from the liftgate window trim panel and pry the panel off **(see illustrations)**.

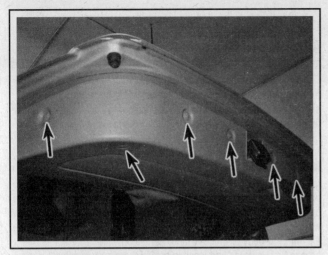

14.14 Remove the fasteners from the liftgate trim panel (left side view shown)

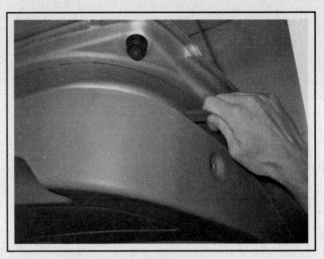

14.15 Use a trim tool to pry off the panel

14 Remove the fasteners from the trim panel **(see illustration)**.

15 Using a screwdriver or trim removal tool, pry out the clips and remove the trim panel from the liftgate **(see illustration)**. Work slowly and carefully around the outer edge of the trim panel until it's free. Unplug any wiring harness connectors and remove the panel.

16 For access to other components inside the liftgate, carefully peel back the plastic watershield **(see illustration)**.

17 Installation is the reverse of removal.

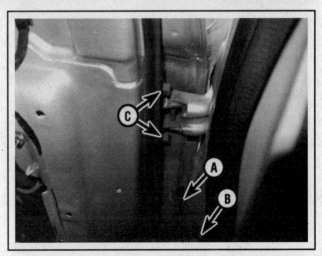

14.16 Carefully peel back the watershield from the liftgate

15 Door - removal, installation and adjustment

➡ **Note: The door is heavy and somewhat awkward to remove and install - at least two people should perform this procedure.**

REMOVAL AND INSTALLATION

1 Raise the window completely in the door and disconnect the cable from the negative battery terminal (see Chapter 5).

2 Open the door all the way and support it from the ground on jacks or blocks covered with rags to prevent damaging the paint.

3 Remove the door trim panel and watershield (see Section 14).

4 Disconnect all electrical connections, ground wires and harness retaining clips from the door.

➡ **Note: It is a good idea to label all connections to aid the reassembly process.**

5 From the door side, detach the rubber conduit between the body and the door **(see illustration)**. Pull the wiring harness through the conduit hole and remove it from the door.

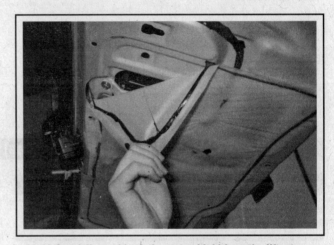

15.5 Door conduit (A), door stop strut (B) and the upper door hinge bolts (C)

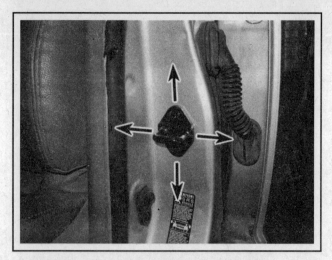

15.13 Adjust the door lock striker by loosening the mounting fasteners and gently tapping the striker in the desired direction

6 Remove the door stop strut bolt.

7 Mark around the door hinges with a pen or a scribe to facilitate realignment during reassembly.

8 With an assistant holding the door, remove the hinge-to-door bolts and lift off the door.

9 Installation is the reverse of removal.

ADJUSTMENT

10 Having proper door-to-body alignment is a critical part of a well-functioning door assembly. First check the door hinge pins for excessive play. Fully open the door and lift up and down on the door without lifting the body. If a door has 1/16-inch or more excessive play, the hinges should be replaced.

11 Door-to-body alignment adjustments are made by loosening the hinge-to-body bolts or hinge-to-door bolts and moving the door. Proper body alignment is achieved when the top of the doors are parallel with the roof section, the front door is flush with the fender, the rear door is flush with the rear quarter panel and the bottom of the doors are aligned with the lower rocker panel. If these goals can't be reached by adjusting the hinge-to-body or hinge-to-door bolts, body alignment shims may have to be purchased and inserted behind the hinges to achieve correct alignment.

12 To adjust the door-closed position, scribe a line or mark around the striker plate to provide a reference point, then check that the door latch is contacting the center of the latch striker. If not, adjust the up and down position first.

13 Finally adjust the latch striker sideways position, so that the door panel is flush with the center pillar or rear quarter panel and provides positive engagement with the latch mechanism **(see illustration).**

16 Door latch, lock cylinder and handles - removal and installation

✱✱ CAUTION:

Wear gloves when working inside the door openings to protect against cuts from sharp metal edges.

DOOR LATCH

1 Raise the window, then remove the door trim panel and watershield (see Section 14).

2 Working through the large access hole, disengage the rods from the handle and lock cylinder **(see illustration).** All door lock rods are attached by plastic clips. The plastic clips can be removed by unsnapping the portion engaging the connecting rod, then pulling the rod out of its locating hole.

3 Disconnect the electrical connectors at the latch. Disengage the handle-to-latch cable.

4 Remove the screws securing the latch to the door **(see illustration)**. Remove the latch assembly through the door opening.

5 Installation is the reverse of removal.

16.2 The control rods are attached with plastic clips

16.4 Door latch mounting screws

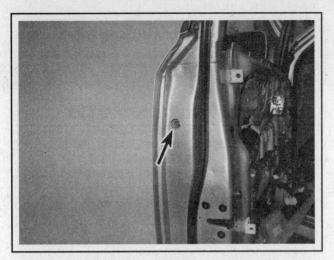

16.7 Remove the trim cap and handle retaining screw

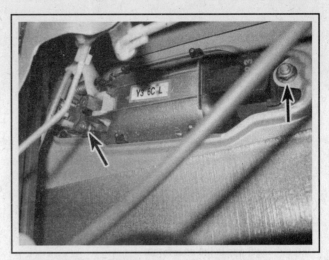

16.9 Outer door handle screw locations - 2009 and earlier models

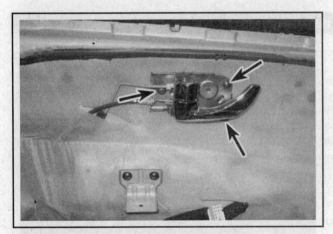

16.13 Inner door handle mounting fasteners

OUTSIDE HANDLE AND DOOR LOCK CYLINDER

6   To remove the outside handle and lock cylinder assembly, raise the window and remove the door trim panel and watershield (see Section 14).

✳ CAUTION:

Take care not to scratch the paint on the outside of the door. Wide masking tape applied around the handle opening before beginning the procedure can help avoid scratches.

17   Door window glass - removal and installation

✳ CAUTION:

Wear gloves when working inside the door openings to protect against cuts from sharp metal edges.

7   Remove the trim cap for the outside handle retaining screw and remove the screw **(see illustration)**.

8   Working through the access hole, disengage the plastic clips that secure the outside door lock-to-latch rod and the outside door handle-to-latch rod **(see illustration 16.2)**.

9   On 2009 and earlier models, remove the handle and lock cylinder retaining screws from the inside of the door, and remove the handle and lock cylinder **(see illustration)**. On 2011 and later models, remove the retaining screws from the inside of the door.

10   On 2011 and later models, working from the outside of the door, remove the cover from the outside front of the handle. Pull the handle outwards and towards the rear to disengage it from the handle reinforcement inside the door. Remove the exterior handle mounting screw and remove the handle and lock assembly from inside the door.

11   Installation is the reverse of removal.

INSIDE DOOR HANDLE

12   Remove the door trim panel (see Section 14).

13   Remove the handle retaining screws and nut, and disengage the handle from the door **(see illustration)**.

14   Disengage the handle-to-latch cable and remove the handle from the door.

15   On 2011 and later models, the inside door handle is attached to the door panel. Depress the locking hook from the rear of the handle and unclip the cable handle cage from the inside handle and disconnect the cables. Remove the inside door handle fasteners and handle from the door panel.

16   Installation is the reverse of removal.

DOOR GLASS

1   Remove the door trim panel and the plastic watershield (see Section 14).

2   Lower the window glass all the way down into the door.

3   Remove the door speaker (see Chapter 12).

17.4 Raise the window to access the glass retaining bolts through the holes in the door frame

4 Raise the window just enough to access the window retaining bolts through the holes in the door frame **(see illustration)**. Remove the two glass mounting bolts.

5 Remove the glass by pulling it up and out.

6 Installation is the reverse of removal.

LIFTGATE GLASS (WITH OPENING GLASS ONLY)

7 Remove the liftgate trim panel (see Section 14) and disconnect the rear window defroster electrical connector.

8 Release the window latch and remove the window mounting nuts.

9 Remove the window from the liftgate.

10 Installation is the reverse of removal.

18 Door window regulator and motor - removal and installation

2009 AND EARLIER MODELS

1 Remove the door trim panel and the plastic watershield (see Section 14).

2 Remove the window glass (see Section 17).

3 Disconnect the electrical connector from the window regulator motor. Detach the cables from the inside handle.

4 Remove the window glass guide bolts and the regulator/motor module mounting bolts **(see illustration).**

5 Remove the regulator/motor module assembly and unbolt the motor from the regulator.

6 Installation is the reverse of removal. Lubricate the rollers and wear points on the regulator with white grease before installation.

2011 AND LATER MODELS

7 Remove the door trim panel and the plastic watershield (see Section 14).

8 Disconnect the power window motor from the door module, then remove the mounting bolts and motor from the door module.

9 Remove the door module bolts and remove the module from the door. Unbolt the regulator from the door module.

10 Installation is the reverse of removal.

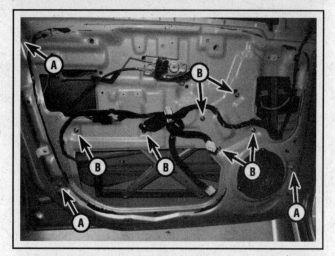

18.4 Remove the window guide bolts (A), then remove the window regulator/motor module bolts (B)

19 Mirrors - removal and installation

OUTSIDE MIRRORS

1 Remove the mirror trim panel using a panel removing tool or a screwdriver wrapped with tape **(see illustration)**.

2 Disconnect the electrical connector from the mirror, remove the three mirror retaining bolts and detach the mirror from the vehicle **(see illustration)**.

3 Installation is the reverse of removal.

INSIDE MIRROR

4 Disconnect the electrical connector from the mirror, if equipped.

5 On some models, the mirror can be removed by carefully prying between the mirror mount and the notch in the base of the mirror stalk using a screwdriver wrapped with tape. There is a hairpin-type spring holding the mirror stalk in the base. Push the screwdriver in about 3/4-inch to release the spring. On some other models, the mirror can

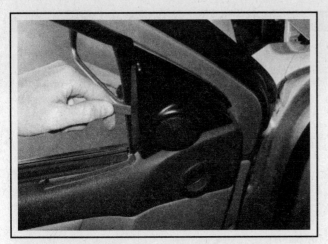

19.1 The outside mirror trim panel is simply pried off

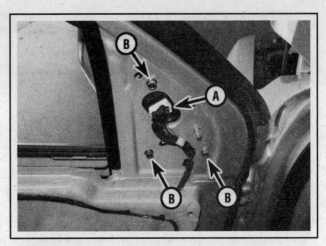

19.2 Disconnect the wiring (A) and remove the three fasteners (B) while supporting the mirror through the open window

be removed by removing the set screw located at the base of the mirror stalk.

6 On models without a set screw, to install the mirror, reinsert the spring if it was removed earlier. Insert the mirror stalk's lug into the mount, pushing downward until the mirror is secured.

7 If the mount plate itself has come off the windshield, adhesive kits are available at auto parts stores to resecure it. Follow the instructions included with the kit.

20 Liftgate - removal, installation and adjustment

➡ **Note: The liftgate is heavy and somewhat awkward to remove and install - at least two people should perform this procedure.**

REMOVAL AND INSTALLATION

1 Disconnect the cable from the negative battery terminal (see Chapter 5).

2 Open the liftgate all the way.

3 Remove the liftgate trim panel (see Section 14).

4 Disconnect all electrical connections, ground wires and harness retaining clips from the liftgate.

➡ **Note: It is a good idea to label all connections to aid the reassembly process.**

5 From the liftgate side, detach the rubber conduit between the body and the liftgate. Pull the wiring harness through the conduit hole and remove it from the liftgate.

6 Detach the liftgate support struts by either unbolting them at the top or using a small screwdriver to separate the ball socket connection. Have an assistant hold the weight of the liftgate.

7 Mark around the liftgate hinges with a pen or a scribe to facilitate realignment during reassembly **(see illustration)**.

8 With the assistant still holding the liftgate, remove the hinge-to-liftgate bolts and lift off the liftgate.

9 Installation is the reverse of removal.

ADJUSTMENT

10 Having proper liftgate-to-body alignment is a critical part of a well-functioning liftgate assembly. First check the liftgate hinge pins for excessive play. Fully open the liftgate and lift up and down on the liftgate without lifting the body. If a liftgate has 1/16-inch or more

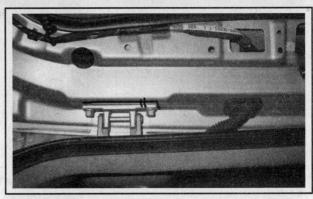

20.7 Mark around the liftgate hinges so it can be installed in the same position

excessive play, the hinges should be replaced.

11 Liftgate-to-body alignment adjustments are made by loosening the hinge-to-body bolts or hinge-to-liftgate bolts and moving the liftgate. Proper body alignment is achieved when the top of the liftgate is parallel with the roof section, the sides of the liftgate are flush with the rear quarter panels, and the bottom of the liftgate is aligned with the lower liftgate sill. If these goals can't be reached by adjusting the hinge-to-body or hinge-to-liftgate bolts, body alignment shims may have to be purchased and inserted behind the hinges to achieve correct alignment.

12 To adjust the liftgate-closed position, scribe a line or mark around the striker plate to provide a reference point, then check that the liftgate latch is contacting the center of the latch striker. If not, adjust the up and down position first.

13 Finally adjust the latch striker fore-and-aft position, so that the liftgate panel is flush with the rear quarter panel and provides positive engagement with the latch mechanism.

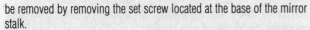

21 Liftgate latch, lock cylinder and handle - removal and installation

LIFTGATE LATCH

1 Disconnect the cable from the negative battery terminal (see Chapter 5).

2 Open the liftgate and remove the trim panel and watershield (see Section 14).

3 Working through the large access hole, disengage the outside liftgate handle-to-latch cable and the outside liftgate lock-to-latch rod. Disconnect the electrical connector for the power lock.

4 All liftgate lock rods are attached by plastic clips. The plastic clips can be removed by unsnapping the portion engaging the connecting rod, then pulling the rod out of its locating hole.

5 Remove the fasteners securing the latch to the liftgate **(see illustration)**. Remove the latch assembly.

6 Installation is the reverse of removal.

LIFTGATE LOCK CYLINDER - 2009 AND EARLIER MODELS ONLY

7 Open the liftgate and remove the trim panel (see Section 14).

8 Working through the large access hole, disengage the outside liftgate lock-to-latch rod **(see illustration)**.

9 All liftgate lock rods are attached by plastic clips. The plastic clips can be removed by unsnapping the portion engaging the connecting rod, then pulling the rod out of its locating hole.

10 Remove the lock cylinder retaining fasteners **(see illusration 21.8)**. Remove the lock cylinder.

11 Installation is the reverse of removal.

LIFTGATE OUTSIDE HANDLE

12 Open the liftgate and remove the trim panel and watershield (see Section 14).

13 Working through the large access hole, disengage the outside liftgate handle-to-latch controller rod **(see illustration),** then remove the controller mounting bolts.

14 Remove the latch controller bolts **(see illustration 21.13).** Remove the handle retaining fasteners through the holes in the frame and detach the handle from the liftgate.

15 Installation is the reverse of removal.

21.5 Liftgate latch assembly

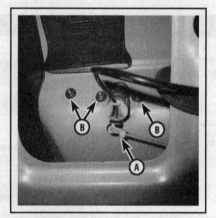

21.8 Disengage the liftgate-to-lock rod clip (A) then remove the lock fasteners (B)

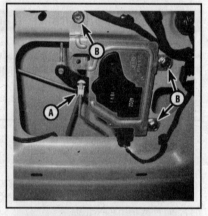

21.13 Disconnect the outside handle rod (A) the remove the latch controller fasteners (B) to access the outside handle

22 Center console - removal and installation

✳✳ WARNING:

The models covered by this manual are equipped with Supplemental Restraint systems (SRS), more commonly known as airbags. Always disable the airbag system before working in the vicinity of any airbag system component to avoid the possibility of accidental deployment of the airbag, which could cause personal injury (see Chapter 12).

1 Disconnect the cable from the negative battery terminal (see Chapter 5).

2 Using a plastic trim tool, carefully pry up the console trim panel along the outer edges of the panel **(see illustration)**.

3 Pry the storage compartment out of the console **(see illustration)**.

4 Remove the ash tray from the rear of the console, then remove the upper rear mounting screw **(see illustration)**.

22.2 Use a trim tool to pry up the outer edges of the trim panel

22.3 Remove the storage compartment from the console

22.4 Remove the console rear panel fastener and pry the panel out.

22.5 Console rear fastener locations

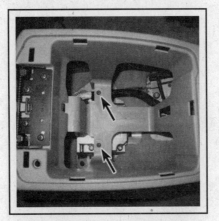

22.6 Remove the console fasteners from inside the storage compartment

22.7 Console top and side fastener locations

5 Remove the console rear mounting screws **(see illustration)**.

6 Remove any fasteners inside the console that were hidden by the storage compartment **(see illustration)**.

7 Remove the console mounting screws from the sides and top of the console **(see illustration)**.

8 Lift off the top trim panel and disconnect the power outlet electrical connector.

9 Lift off the console.

10 Installation is the reverse of removal.

23 Dashboard trim panels - removal and installation

✹✹ WARNING:

Models covered by this manual are equipped with a Supplemental Restraint System (SRS), more commonly known as airbags. Always disable the airbag system before working in the vicinity of any airbag system component to avoid the possibility of accidental deployment of the airbag, which could cause personal injury(see Chapter 12).

1 These panels provide access to various instrument panel mounting screws. Some of the covers use fasteners, and others are easily pried off with a screwdriver or trim stick. If you're going to remove the instrument panel, remove all of the covers.

2 Disconnect the cable from the negative terminal of the battery (see Chapter 5).

23.4 Instrument cluster bezel screws - 2009 and earlier models shown

23.7 Pry off the end trim panel

23.10 Hood latch mounting screws

23.11 The knee bolster is retained by screws and several concealed clips

23.13 Knee bolster reinforcement panel fastener locations

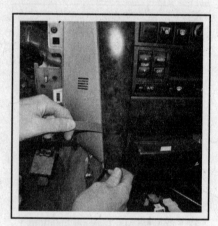

23.16 Pry out both center trim side panels

INSTRUMENT CLUSTER BEZEL

3 Remove the steering column covers (see Section 24).
4 Remove the bezel retaining screws **(see illustration)**.
5 Remove the bezel by pulling it rearward.
6 Installation is the reverse of removal.

LEFT OR RIGHT DASHBOARD END TRIM PANELS

7 Carefully pry off the end trim panel **(see illustration)**.
8 Installation is the reverse of removal.

DRIVER'S KNEE BOLSTER

9 Pry the driver's side end cap from the dashboard.
10 Remove the hood latch mounting screws **(see illustration)**.
11 Remove the retaining screws for the trim panel **(see illustration)**.
12 On 2009 and earlier models, the switch assembly can be pried

out with a trim stick or left attached to the panel and disconnect the wiring once its remove. On 2011 and later models, the switch panel can only be removed once the knee bolster panel has been removed.
13 Pull the panel rearward to disengage it from its clips. To service the instrument panel or components located under the steering column, remove the knee bolster reinforcement panel fasteners and panel **(see illustration)**.
14 On 2011 and later models, remove the switch panel fasteners and pull the switch panel forward to disconnect the electrical connectors.
15 Installation is the reverse of removal.

CENTER TRIM PANEL

16 Pry out the two center trim side panels **(see illustration)**.
17 On early models, remove the center trim panel fasteners **(see illustration)**.
18 Use a trim stick or a screwdriver with the tip wrapped with electrical tape to pry off the panel.
19 Disconnect the electrical connectors **(see illustration)**.

23.17 Remove the center trim panel fasteners - right half shown

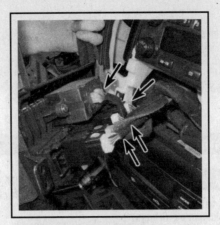

23.19 Pull the center trim panel back and disconnect the electrical connectors

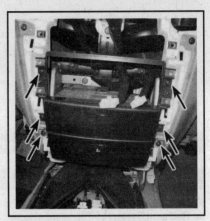

23.20 Remove the mounting screws and pull the units from the dashboard

23.21 Center lower trim panel fasteners - left side shown, right side opposite

23.23 Press the corners in to allow the glove box to be removed

23.26a Glove box trim panel front . . .

CENTER STORAGE AND ASHTRAY

20 Remove the center storage compartment and ashtray fasteners then pull them out of the dashboard **(see illustration)**. Disconnect the electrical connector to the lighter.

21 Remove the center lower trim panels from each side **(see illustration)**. On some models, it may be necessary to remove the radio (see Chapter 12) and the air conditioning/heater controller (see Chapter 3).

➡ **Note: Some models may be equipped with an audio mic attached to the rear of the center lower trim panel. Disconnect the electrical connector, but leave the mic attached to the panel.**

22 Installation is the reverse of removal.

GLOVE BOX DOOR

23 Open the glove box door and push firmly inward on both sides of the glove box to release it **(see illustration)**.

➡ **Note: On 2011 and later models, the glove box guides must be unhooked from each side of the glove box.**

24 Installation is the reverse of removal.

23.26b . . . and side mounting screw locations

GLOVE BOX SIDE TRIM PANEL

25 Remove the glove box door as previously described. Remove the right dashboard end panel (see earlier in this Section).

26 Remove the plastic screw covers at the top edge of the panel, then remove the mounting screws **(see illustrations)**.

27 On 2011 and later models, remove the right side upper trim panel fasteners and trim to access all of the glove box trim screw locations.

28 Use a trim stick or a screwdriver with the tip wrapped with electri-cal tape to pry off the panel.

29 Installation is the reverse of removal.

24 Steering column covers - removal and installation

✳✳ WARNING:

Models covered by this manual are equipped with a Supplemental Restraint System (SRS), more commonly known as airbags. Always disable the airbag system before working in the vicinity of any airbag system component to avoid the possibility of accidental deployment of the airbag, which could cause personal injury (see Chapter 12).

1 Disconnect the cable from the negative terminal of the battery (see Chapter 5). Move the column to the lowest position

2 Remove the lower screws, then separate the halves and remove the upper and lower steering column covers **(see illustrations)**.

3 Installation is the reverse of removal.

24.2a Remove the screws from the lower half . . .

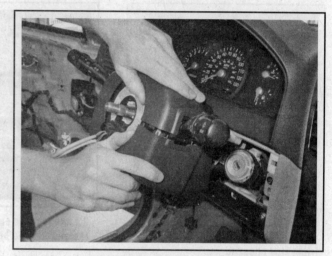

24.2b . . . then unsnap the upper and lower covers

25 Instrument panel - removal and installation

✳✳ WARNING:

Models covered by this manual are equipped with a Supplemental Restraint System (SRS), more commonly known as airbags. Always disable the airbag system before working in the vicinity of any airbag system component to avoid the possibility of accidental deployment of the airbag, which could cause personal injury (see Chapter 12).

➡ **Note:** This is a difficult procedure for the home mechanic. There are many hidden fasteners, difficult angles to work in and many electrical connectors to tag and disconnect/connect. We recommend that this procedure be done only by an experienced do-it-yourselfer.

➡ **Note:** During removal of the instrument panel, make careful notes of how each piece comes off, where it fits in relation to

other pieces and what holds it in place. If you note how each part is installed before removing it, getting the instrument panel back together again will be much easier.

➡ **Note:** It is not necessary, but it is suggested to remove both front seats to allow additional working space and lessen the chance of damage to the seats during this procedure.

1 Disconnect the cable from the negative battery terminal (see Chapter 5).

2 Remove the front seats for easier access (see Section 26).

3 Remove the multi-function switch (see Chapter 12).

4 Remove the dashboard trim panels (see Section 23) and the center floor console (see Section 22).

5 Remove the glove box (see Section 23).

6 Remove the instrument cluster (see Chapter 12).

7 Disconnect the electrical connector from the passenger's side airbag **(see illustration)**. Remove the airbag fasteners and remove the

25.7 Location of the passenger's side airbag electrical connector

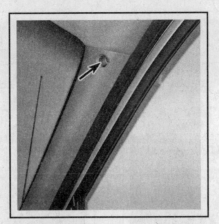

25.11 Remove the retaining screw cover, remove the retaining screw, and pry off the covers from the A pillars using a trim stick or a screwdriver wrapped with electrical tape

25.12 Pry off the scuff plates

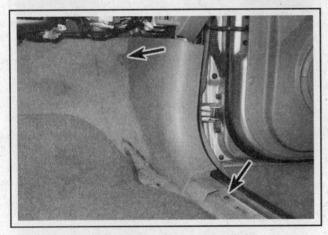

25.13 Pry off the kick panels after removing their retaining screws

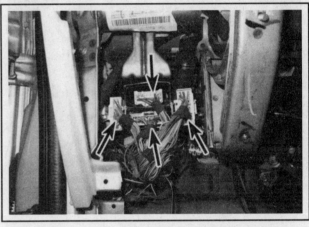

25.14a Disconnect the electrical connectors from the left . . .

airbag (see Chapter 12).

8 Remove the audio unit (see Chapter 12) and air conditioning control panel (see Chapter 3) from the center of the dashboard.

9 Remove the driver's knee bolster and reinforcement panel (see Section 23).

10 Unscrew the bolts securing the steering column to the instrument panel and lower the column (see Chapter 10).

11 Remove the front pillar trim **(see illustration)**.

12 Pry up the scuff plates from each door opening **(see illustration)**.

13 Remove the kick panels **(see illustration)**.

14 A number of electrical connectors must be disconnected in order to remove the instrument panel **(see illustrations)**. Most are designed so that they will only fit on the matching connector (male or female), but if there is any doubt, mark the connectors with masking tape and a marking pen before disconnecting them.

➡ **Note: These are just a few of the electrical connectors that need to be disconnected; take detailed notes or photos to make sure all are disconnected before removing the instrument panel**

25.14b . . . and the right of the instrument panel

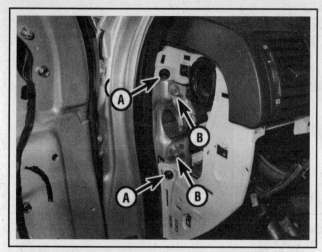

25.15a The instrument panel is secured with bolts (A) and reinforcement bolts (B) at the left end . . .

25.15b . . . the right end . . .

25.15c . . . the upper center . . .

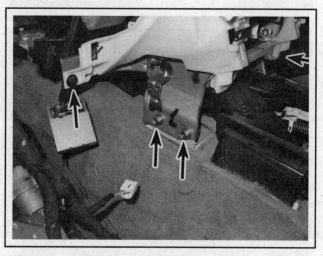

25.15d . . . and the lower center

15 Remove all of the fasteners holding the instrument panel and reinforcement to the body **(see illustrations)**. Once all are removed, lift the panel, pull it away from the windshield, and remove it through the door opening.

➡ **Note: This is a two-person job.**

16 Installation is the reverse of removal.

26 Seats - removal and installation

FRONT SEAT

⁂ **WARNING:**

The front seat belts on some models are equipped with pre-tensioners, which are pyrotechnic (explosive) devices designed to retract the seat belts in the event of a collision. On models equipped with pre-tensioners, do not remove the front seat belt retractor assemblies, and do not disconnect the electrical connectors leading to the assemblies. Problems with the pre-ten-sioners will turn on the SRS (airbag) warning light on the dash. If any pre-tensioner problems are suspected, take the vehicle to a dealer service department. Also on these models, be sure to disable the airbag system (see Chapter 12).

⁂ **WARNING:**

On models with side-impact airbags and/or seat belt pre-tensioners, disarm the airbag system before beginning this procedure (see Chapter 12).

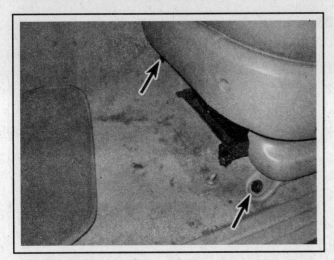

26.2a Remove the front . . .

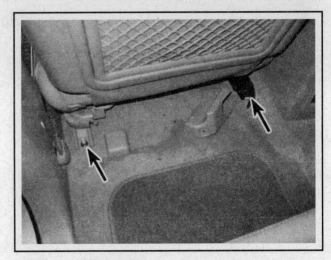

26.2b . . . and rear bolts

1 Pry off any plastic covers to access the seat tracks and their mounting bolts. Keep them in order, as they are not identical.
2 Remove the retaining bolts **(see illustrations).**
3 Tilt the seat upward to access the underside, disconnect any electrical connectors, and lift the seat from the vehicle.
4 Installation is the reverse of removal.

REAR SEAT

5 Flip the seat cushion up and forward, remove the mounting nuts, and lift out the seat cushions.
6 Remove the bolts from the bottom of the seat back.
7 Lower the seat back down. Remove the mounting bolts from the rear of the seat back and lift the cushions out.
8 Installation is the reverse of removal.

Notes

12

CHASSIS ELECTRICAL SYSTEM

1 General Information

1 The electrical system is a 12-volt, negative ground type. Power for the lights and all electrical accessories is supplied by a lead/acid-type battery, which is charged by the alternator.

2 This Chapter covers repair and service procedures for the various electrical components not associated with the engine. Information on the battery, alternator and starter motor can be found in Chapter 5.

3 It should be noted that when portions of the electrical system are serviced, the cable should be disconnected from the negative battery terminal to prevent electrical shorts and/or fires.

2 Electrical troubleshooting - general information

1 A typical electrical circuit consists of an electrical component, any switches, relays, motors, fuses, fusible links or circuit breakers related to that component and the wiring and connectors that link the component to both the battery and the chassis. To help you pinpoint an electrical circuit problem, wiring diagrams are included at the end of this Chapter.

2 Before tackling any troublesome electrical circuit, first study the appropriate wiring diagrams to get a complete understanding of what makes up that individual circuit. For instance, noting whether other components related to the circuit are operating correctly can often narrow down potential causes of trouble. If several components or circuits fail at one time, chances are the problem is in a fuse or ground connection, because several circuits are often routed through the same fuse and ground connections.

3 Electrical problems usually stem from simple causes, such as loose or corroded connections, a blown fuse, a melted fusible link or a failed relay. Visually inspect the condition of all fuses, wires and connections in a problem circuit before troubleshooting the circuit.

4 If test equipment and instruments are going to be utilized, use the diagrams to plan ahead of time where you will make the necessary connections in order to accurately pinpoint the trouble spot.

5 The basic tools needed for electrical troubleshooting include a circuit tester or voltmeter (a 12-volt bulb with a set of test leads can also be used), a continuity tester, which includes a bulb, battery and set of test leads, and a jumper wire, preferably with a circuit breaker incorporated, which can be used to bypass electrical components **(see illustrations)**. Before attempting to locate a problem with test instruments, use the wiring diagram(s) to decide where to make the connections.

VOLTAGE CHECKS

6 Voltage checks should be performed if a circuit is not functioning properly. Connect one lead of a circuit tester to either the negative battery terminal or a known good ground. Connect the other lead to a connector in the circuit being tested, preferably nearest to the battery or fuse **(see illustration)**. If the bulb of the tester lights, voltage is present, which means that the part of the circuit between the connector and the battery is problem free. Continue checking the rest of the circuit in the same fashion. When you reach a point at which no voltage is present, the problem lies between that point and the last test point with voltage. Most of the time the problem can be traced to a loose connection.

➡ **Note: Keep in mind that some circuits receive voltage only when the ignition key is in the Accessory or Run position.**

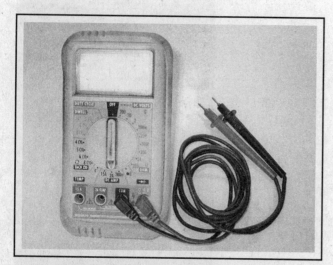

2.5a The most useful tool for electrical troubleshooting is a digital multimeter that can check volts, amps, and test continuity

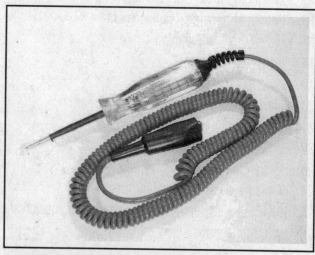

2.5b A simple test light is a very handy tool for testing voltage

2.6 In use, a basic test light's lead is clipped to a known good ground, then the pointed probe can test connectors, wires or electrical sockets - if the bulb lights, the circuit being tested has battery voltage

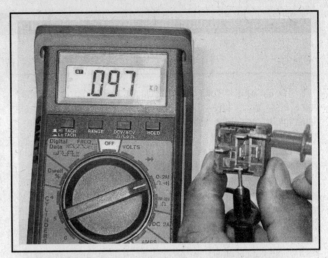

2.9 With a multimeter set to the ohm scale, resistance can be checked across two terminals - when checking for continuity, a low reading indicates continuity, a high reading or infinity indicates lack of continuity

FINDING A SHORT

7 One method of finding shorts in a live circuit is to remove the fuse and connect a test light in place of the fuse terminals (fabricate two jumper wires with small spade terminals, plug the jumper wires into the fuse box and connect the test light). There should be voltage present in the circuit. Move the suspected wiring harness from side-to-side while watching the test light. If the bulb goes off, there is a short to ground somewhere in that area, probably where the insulation has rubbed through.

GROUND CHECK

8 Perform a ground test to check whether a component is properly grounded. Disconnect the battery and connect one lead of a continuity tester or multimeter (set to the ohm scale), to a known good ground. Connect the other lead to the wire or ground connection being tested. If the resistance is low (less than 5 ohms), the ground is good. If the bulb on a self-powered test light does not go on, the ground is not good.

CONTINUITY CHECK

9 A continuity check is done to determine if there are any breaks in a circuit - if it is passing electricity properly. With the circuit off (no power in the circuit), a self-powered continuity tester or multimeter can be used to check the circuit. Connect the test leads to both ends of the circuit (or to the power end and a good ground), and if the test light comes on the circuit is passing current properly **(see illustration)**. If the resistance is low (less than 5 ohms), there is continuity; if the reading is 10,000 ohms or higher, there is a break somewhere in the circuit. The same procedure can be used to test a switch, by connecting the continuity tester to the switch terminals. With the switch turned On, the test light should come on (or low resistance should be indicated on a meter).

FINDING AN OPEN CIRCUIT

10 When diagnosing for possible open circuits, it is often difficult to locate them by sight because the connectors hide oxidation or terminal misalignment. Merely wiggling a connector on a sensor or in the wiring harness may correct the open circuit condition. Remember this when an open circuit is indicated when troubleshooting a circuit. Intermittent problems may also be caused by oxidized or loose connections.

11 Electrical troubleshooting is simple if you keep in mind that all electrical circuits are basically electricity running from the battery, through the wires, switches, relays, fuses and fusible links to each electrical component (light bulb, motor, etc.) and to ground, from which it is passed back to the battery. Any electrical problem is an interruption in the flow of electricity to and from the battery.

CONNECTORS

12 Most electrical connections on these vehicles are made with multi-wire plastic connectors. The mating halves of many connectors are secured with locking clips molded into the plastic connector shells. The mating halves of large connectors, such as some of those under the instrument panel, are held together by a bolt through the center of the connector.

13 To separate a connector with locking clips, use a small screwdriver to pry the clips apart carefully, then separate the connector halves. Pull only on the shell, never pull on the wiring harness as you may damage the individual wires and terminals inside the connectors. Look at the connector closely before trying to separate the halves. Often the locking clips are engaged in a way that is not immediately clear. Additionally, many connectors have more than one set of clips.

14 Each pair of connector terminals has a male half and a female half. When you look at the end view of a connector in a diagram, be sure to understand whether the view shows the harness side or the component side of the connector. Connector halves are mirror images of each other, and a terminal shown on the right side end-view of one half will be on the left side end view of the other half.

3 Fuses and fusible links - general information

FUSES

1 The electrical circuits of the vehicle are protected by a combination of fuses, circuit breakers and fusible links. Fuse blocks are located under the left side of the instrument panel and in the engine compartment **(see illustrations)**.

2 Each of the fuses is designed to protect a specific circuit, and the various circuits are identified on the fuse panel cover.

3 Miniaturized fuses are employed in the fuse blocks. These compact fuses, with blade terminal design, allow fingertip removal and replacement. If an electrical component fails, always check the fuse first. The best way to check a fuse is with a test light. Check for power at the exposed terminal tips of each fuse. If power is present on one side of the fuse but not the other, the fuse is blown. A blown fuse can also be confirmed by visually inspecting it **(see illustration)**.

4 Be sure to replace blown fuses with the correct type. Fuses of different ratings are physically interchangeable, but only fuses of the proper rating should be used. Replacing a fuse with one of a higher or lower value than specified is not recommended. Each electrical circuit

needs a specific amount of protection. The amperage value of each fuse is molded into the fuse body.

5 If the replacement fuse immediately fails, don't replace it again until the cause of the problem is isolated and corrected. In most cases, this will be a short circuit in the wiring caused by a broken or deteriorated wire.

FUSIBLE LINKS

6 Some circuits are protected by fusible links. The links are used in circuits that are not ordinarily fused, such as the high-current side of the charging or starting circuits. Conventional inline fusible links, such as those used in the starter cable, are characterized by a bulge in the cable. Newer cartridge-type fusible links, which are similar in appearance to a large cartridge-type fuse, are located in the engine compartment fuse and relay box **(see illustration 3.1a)**. After disconnecting the cable from the negative battery terminal, simply remove the fusible link and replace it with a unit of the same amperage.

3.1a The engine compartment fuse and relay box is located at the left side of the engine compartment. There's a guide on the cover

3.1b There's also a fuse box inside the vehicle, at the left kick panel, behind a small access door (not shown)

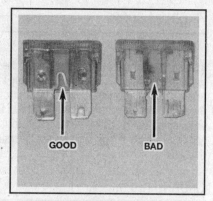

3.3 When a fuse blows, the element between the terminals melts

4 Circuit breakers - general information

1 Circuit breakers protect certain circuits, such as the power windows or heated seats. Depending on the vehicle's accessories, there might be circuit breakers in or near either of the fuse and relay boxes.

2 Because the circuit breakers reset automatically, an electrical overload in a circuit-breaker-protected system will cause the circuit to fail momentarily, then come back on. If the circuit does not come back on, check it immediately.

3 For a basic check, pull the circuit breaker up out of its socket

on the fuse panel, but just far enough to probe with a voltmeter. The breaker should still contact the sockets.

4 With the voltmeter negative lead on a good chassis ground, touch each end prong of the circuit breaker with the positive meter probe. There should be battery voltage at each end. If there is battery voltage only at one end, the circuit breaker must be replaced.

5 Some circuit breakers must be reset manually.

5 Relays - general information

1 Several electrical accessories in the vehicle, such as the fuel injection system, horns, starter, and fog lamps use relays to transmit the electrical signal to the component. Relays use a low-current circuit (the control circuit) to open and close a high-current circuit (the power cir-

cuit). If the relay is defective, that component will not operate properly. Most relays are mounted in the engine compartment and interior fuse/relay boxes **(see illustrations 3.1a and 3.1b)**.

6 Electrical connectors - general information

1 Most electrical connections on these vehicles are made with multiwire plastic connectors. The mating halves of many connectors are secured with locking clips molded into the plastic connector shells. The mating halves of some large connectors, such as some of those under the instrument panel, are held together by a bolt through the center of the connector.

2 Each pair of connector terminals has a male half and a female half. When you look at the end view of a connector in a diagram, be sure to understand whether the view shows the harness side or the component side of the connector. Connector halves are mirror images of each other, and a terminal shown on the right side end-view of one half will be on the left side end-view of the other half.

3 It is often necessary to take circuit voltage measurements with a connector connected. Whenever possible, carefully insert a small straight pin (not your meter probe) into the rear of the connector shell to contact the terminal inside, then clip your meter lead to the pin. This kind of connection is called "backprobing." When inserting a test probe into a terminal, be careful not to distort the terminal opening. Doing so can lead to a poor connection and corrosion at that terminal later. Using the small straight pin instead of a meter probe results in less chance of deforming the terminal connector.

ELECTRICAL CONNECTORS

4 To separate a connector with locking clips or tabs, use a small screwdriver to pry the clips apart carefully, then separate the connector halves. Pull only on the shell, never pull on the wiring harness, as you may damage the individual wires and terminals inside the connectors. Look at the connector closely before trying to separate the halves. Often the locking clips are engaged in a way that is not immediately clear. Additionally, many connectors have more than one set of clips.

Electrical connectors

Most electrical connectors have a single release tab that you depress to release the connector

Some electrical connectors have a retaining tab which must be pried up to free the connector

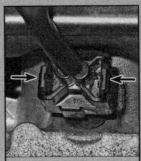

Some connectors have two release tabs that you must squeeze to release the connector

Some connectors use wire retainers that you squeeze to release the connector

Critical connectors often employ a sliding lock (1) that you must pull out before you can depress the release tab (2)

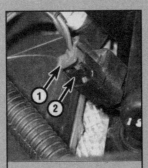

Here's another sliding-lock style connector, with the lock (1) and the release tab (2) on the side of the connector

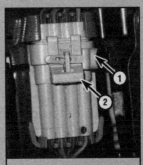

On some connectors the lock (1) must be pulled out to the side and removed before you can lift the release tab (2)

Some critical connectors, like the multi-pin connectors at the Powertrain Control Module employ pivoting locks that must be flipped open

7   Ignition switch and key lock cylinder - replacement

➡ **Note:** The ignition switch can't be replaced separately from the ignition key lock housing.

1   Disconnect the cable from the negative terminal of the battery (see Chapter 5).

2   Remove the upper and lower steering column covers (see Chapter 11).

3   Remove the driver's knee bolster trim panel (see Chapter 11).

4   Disconnect the electrical connectors from the ignition switch **(see illustration)** and detach the illumination bulb cover from the end of the key lock cylinder.

5   On 2009 and earlier models, disconnect the shift interlock cable from the bottom of the ignition lock assembly **(see illustration)**.

6   The ignition key assembly is mounted to the steering column using a pinch-bolt with a break-off head **(see illustration)**. Attach locking pliers to clamp the bolt head so the nut on the rear can be removed **(see illustration)**.

7   Pull the switch out and remove it from the key lock cylinder housing.

8   Installation is the reverse of removal.

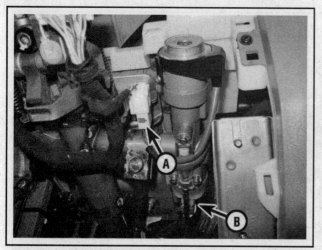

7.4 Disconnect the key warning immobilizer connector (A) and electrical wiring harnesses (B) from the switch unit

7.5 Remove the screws and detach the shift interlock cable

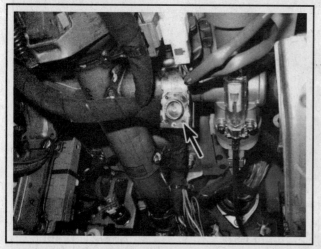

7.6a The pinch-bolt that the factory uses to clamp the ignition switch has a head that is broken off during assembly - the smooth head must be held from turning while the nut is removed

7.6b Locking pliers will secure the shear-head bolt in order for the nut on the other side of the clamp to be removed

SMART KEY MODELS

9 Disconnect the cable from the negative battery terminal (see Chapter 5).

10 Remove the center trim panels (see Chapter 11).

11 Remove the radio assembly (see Section 11).

12 Disconnect the electrical harness connector to the smart key unit.

13 Remove the smart key unit mounting fasteners, then pull the unit out of the instrument panel through the opening in the panel.

14 Installation is the reverse of removal.

8   Multi-function switches - replacement

☀ WARNING:

The models covered by this manual are equipped with Supplemental Restraint Systems (SRS), more commonly known as airbags. Always disable the airbag system before working in the vicinity of any airbag system components to avoid the possibility of accidental deployment of the airbag(s), which could cause personal injury (see Section 24).

➡ **Note: The multi-function switches (also referred to as combination switches or steering column switches) are two separate switch units connected to a central plastic housing known as the switch body, which encircles the steering column. The left multi-function switch controls the headlights and the turn signals; the right switch controls the windshield washer/wiper system. Either switch can be replaced separately.**

1 Disconnect the cable from the negative terminal of the battery (see Chapter 5).

2 Remove the steering wheel and the upper and lower steering column covers (see Chapters 10 and 11).

3 Disconnect the electrical connectors from the switch **(see illustration)**. Push the lock pin to release the headlight and turn signal switch and the other lock pin to release the windshield wiper switch from the steering column.

4 Remove the switch **(see illustration).**

5 Installation is the reverse of removal. If the clockspring has turned and is not centered, turn the hub in either direction until it stops (don't apply too much force). Now, rotate the hub in the other direction, counting the number of turns it takes to reach the opposite stop. Divide that number by two, then turn the hub back that many turns, approximately, until the neutral position indicator is aligned with its corresponding mark.

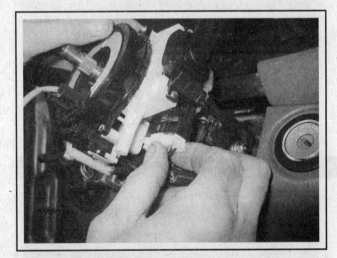

8.3 Unplug the wiring from the multi-function switch

8.4 Multi-function switch screw locations

9   Instrument panel switches - replacement

☀ WARNING:

The models covered by this manual are equipped with Supplemental Restraint Systems (SRS), more commonly known as airbags. Always disable the airbag system before working in the vicinity of any airbag system component to avoid the possibility of accidental deployment of the airbag(s), which could cause personal injury (see Section 24).

1 Disconnect the cable from the negative battery terminal (see Chapter 5).

INSTRUMENT BRIGHTNESS CONTROL AND TRACTION CONTROL SWITCH

2 Carefully pry the switch panel out of the instrument panel with a

9.2 The instrument dimmer control, TCS switch and 4WD are in a panel that can be pried out of the driver's knee bolster with a trim tool or a screwdriver wrapped with electrical tape

9.6 When the panel is loose, you will be able to disconnect the wiring and replace each switch individually

suitable trim panel tool **(see illustration).**

3 To replace the switches, disconnect the electrical connector and remove the switch from the switch panel.

4 Installation is the reverse of removal.

HAZARD WARNING LIGHT, FOG LIGHT AND REAR WINDOW DEFOGGER SWITCHES

5 Remove the center trim panel (see Chapter 11).

6 Disconnect the wiring from the switches and remove the assembly **(see illustration).**

➡ **Note: The fog light and defogger switches have identical electrical connectors. Make clear marks on them to avoid mixing them up later.**

7 Remove the individual switches as necessary.

➡ **Note: The hazard switch is held in place by screws; all other switches can be popped out from the backside of the panel.**

8 Installation is the reverse of removal.

10 Instrument cluster - removal and installation

✳ WARNING:

The models covered by this manual are equipped with Supplemental Restraint Systems (SRS), more commonly known as airbags. Always disable the airbag system before working in the vicinity of any airbag system component to avoid the possibility of accidental deployment of the airbag(s), which could cause personal injury (see Section 24).

1 Disconnect the cable from the negative battery terminal (see Chapter 5).

2 Remove the instrument cluster bezel (see Chapter 11).

3 Remove the cluster mounting screws **(see illustration)** and pull the instrument cluster towards the steering wheel.

4 Disconnect the electrical connectors from the rear of the cluster. Remove the instrument cluster.

5 Installation is the reverse of removal.

10.3 To detach the instrument cluster, remove these mounting screws - 2009 and earlier model shown, later models similar

11 Radio and speakers - removal and installation

❋ WARNING:

The models covered by this manual are equipped with Supplemental Restraint Systems (SRS), more commonly known as airbags. Always disable the airbag system before working in the vicinity of any airbag system component to avoid the possibility of accidental deployment of the airbag(s), which could cause personal injury (see Section 24).

RADIO

1 Disconnect the cable from the negative battery terminal (see Chapter 5).

2 Remove the center trim panel (see Chapter 11). Remove the audio unit mounting screws **(see illustration)**.

3 Pull out the radio and disconnect the electrical connectors from the radio assembly **(see illustration)**.

4 Installation is the reverse of removal.

SPEAKERS

5 To access the upper speakers, pry off the speaker panel from the inside of the mirror.

6 Disconnect the wiring and remove the speaker from the panel.

7 To access the main door speaker, remove the door trim panel (see Chapter 11).

8 Disconnect the electrical connector from the speaker, remove the speaker mounting screws **(see illustration)** and remove the speaker.

9 Installation is the reverse of removal.

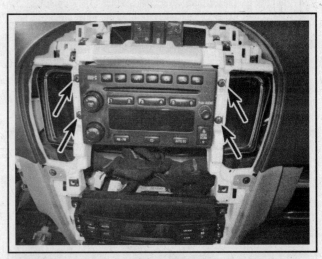

11.2 Remove the center trim panel to access the audio unit mounting screws

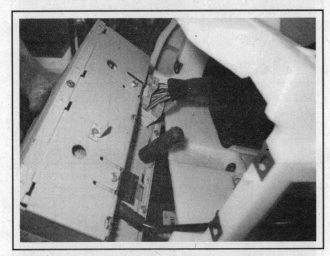

11.3 Pull out the antenna lead and disconnect the wiring harnesses

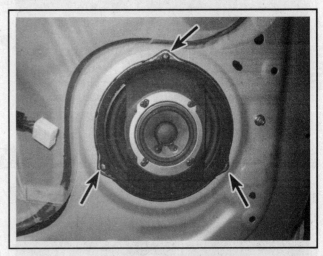

11.8 Main door speaker mounting screws

12 Antenna - replacement

1 The vehicles covered by this manual are equipped with a wire grid-type antenna attached to the rear window glass. If there's a problem with it, you can repair the antenna grid the same way that you'd repair the rear window defogger grid (see Section 14).

13 Wiper motor - replacement

WINDSHIELD WIPER MOTOR

1 Remove the wiper arm mounting nuts **(see illustration)**.

2 Mark the position of each wiper arm to its shaft, then remove the arms **(see illustration)**.

3 Remove the plastic cowl cover (see Chapter 11).

4 Disconnect the electrical connector from the wiper motor.

5 Remove the wiper motor and link assembly mounting bolts **(see illustration)**, then remove the wiper motor and link assembly from the cowl area.

6 Use a screwdriver to pry the linkage rod from the crank arm pivot of the wiper motor **(see illustration)**.

7 Remove the crank arm nut, mark the relationship of the crank arm to the motor shaft and remove the crank arm from the shaft.

8 Remove the wiper motor mounting bolts and separate the motor from the link rod assembly.

9 Installation is the reverse of removal.

REAR WIPER MOTOR

10 Remove the rear wiper arm retaining nut (see Step 1).

11 Mark the relationship of the rear wiper arm to the motor shaft, then remove the arm (see Step 2).

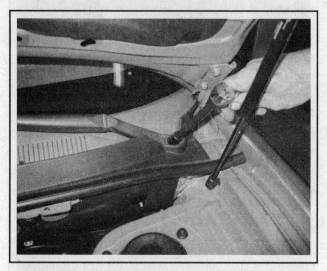

13.1 The wiper arms are secured to their shafts by nuts

13.2 Mark the positions of the arms so they can be correctly installed

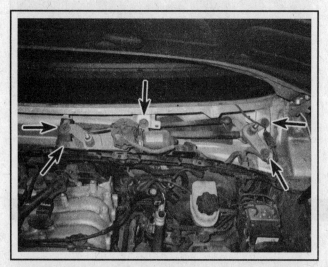

13.5 The wiper assembly is retained by three bolts - remove them after disconnecting the wiring, then lift the entire unit out of the cowl

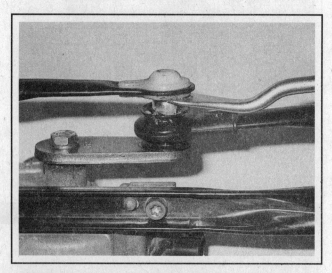

13.6 Pry the link from the crank arm; the crank arm can then be removed from the motor shaft if required

12 Remove the trim panel from the liftgate (see Chapter 11).

13 Disconnect the electrical connectors from the rear wiper motor control unit.

14 Remove the rear wiper motor control unit and motor mounting bolts **(see illustration)** and remove the motor.

15 Installation is the reverse of removal.

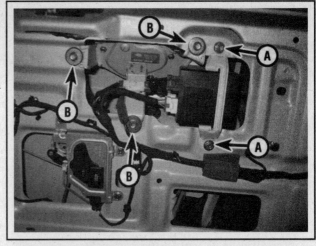

13.14 Remove the liftgate wiper motor control unit bolts (A), then the motor mounting bolts (B)

14 Rear window defogger - check and repair

1 The rear window defogger consists of a number of horizontal elements baked onto the glass surface.

2 Small breaks in the element can be repaired without removing the rear window.

CHECK

3 Turn the ignition switch and defogger system switches to the ON position. Using a voltmeter, place the positive probe against the defogger grid positive terminal and the negative probe against the ground terminal. If battery voltage is not indicated, check the fuse, defogger switch and related wiring. If voltage is indicated, but all or part of the defogger

doesn't heat, proceed with the following tests.

4 When measuring voltage during the next two tests, wrap a piece of aluminum foil around the tip of the voltmeter positive probe and press the foil against the heating element with your finger **(see illustration)**. Place the negative probe on the defogger grid ground terminal.

5 Check the voltage at the center of each heating element **(see illustration)**. If the voltage is 5 or 6-volts, the element is okay (there is no break). If the voltage is zero, the element is broken between the center of the element and the positive end. If the voltage is 10 to 12-volts, the element is broken between the center of the element and ground. Check each heating element.

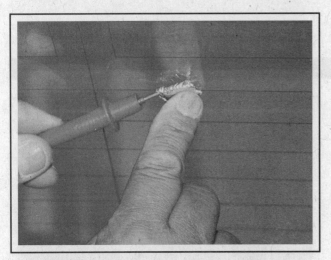

14.4 When measuring the voltage at the rear window defogger grid, wrap a piece of aluminum foil around the positive probe of the voltmeter and press the foil against the wire with your finger

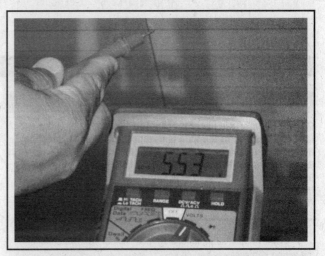

14.5 To determine if a heating element has broken, check the voltage at the center of each element - if the voltage is 5 or 6-volts, the element is unbroken; if the voltage is 10 or 12-volts, the element is broken between the center and the ground side; if there is no voltage, the element is broken between the center and the positive side

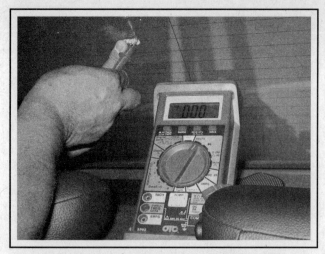

14.7 To find the break, place the voltmeter negative lead against the defogger ground terminal, place the voltmeter positive lead with the foil strip against the heating element at the positive terminal end and slide it toward the negative terminal end - the point at which the voltmeter reading changes abruptly is the point at which the element is broken

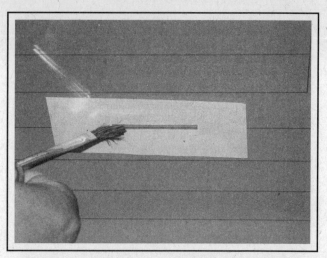

14.13 To use a defogger repair kit, apply masking tape to the inside of the window at the damaged area, then brush on the special conductive coating

6 Connect the negative lead to a good body ground. The reading should stay the same. If it doesn't, the ground connection is bad.

7 To find the break, place the voltmeter negative probe against the defogger ground terminal. Place the voltmeter positive probe with the foil strip against the heating element at the positive terminal end and slide it toward the negative terminal end. The point at which the voltmeter deflects from several volts to zero is the point at which the heating element is broken **(see illustration)**.

REPAIR

8 Repair the break in the element using a repair kit specifically recommended for this purpose, available at most auto parts stores.

Included in this kit is plastic conductive epoxy.

9 Prior to repairing a break, turn off the system and allow it to cool off for a few minutes.

10 Lightly buff the element area with fine steel wool, then clean it thoroughly with rubbing alcohol.

11 Use masking tape to mask off the area being repaired.

12 Thoroughly mix the epoxy, following the instructions provided with the repair kit.

13 Apply the epoxy material to the slit in the masking tape, overlapping the undamaged area about 3/4-inch on either end **(see illustration)**.

14 Allow the repair to cure for 24 hours before removing the tape and using the system.

15 Headlight bulbs - replacement

✳✳ WARNING:

Gas-filled bulbs are under pressure and may shatter if the surface is scratched or the bulb is dropped. Wear eye protection and handle the bulbs carefully, grasping only the base whenever possible. Do not touch the surface of the bulb with your fingers because the oil from your skin could cause it to overheat and fail prematurely. If you do touch the bulb surface, clean it with rubbing alcohol.

1 Remove the headlight housing (see Section 16), disconnecting the wiring harnesses as you do so.

➡ **Note: The bulbs are accessible without removing the entire assembly, but it's easier with the assembly on a workbench.**

2 Remove the cover from the rear of the housing **(see illustration)**.

15.2 Unscrew the cover from the rear of the headlight housing

3 Disconnect the wiring.
4 Release the retaining spring and pull out the old bulb **(see illustration)**.
5 Without touching the bulb glass with your bare fingers, insert the new bulb assembly into the headlight housing.
6 Attach the bulb retaining spring and connect the wiring.
7 Install the cover, connect the wiring harness and replace the headlight assembly.

15.4 The spring-loaded wire retains the bulb

16 Headlight housing - replacement

✳ WARNING:

These vehicles are equipped with gas-filled headlight bulbs that are under pressure and may shatter if the surface is damaged or the bulb is dropped. Wear eye protection and handle the bulbs carefully, grasping only the base whenever possible. Do not touch the surface of the bulb with your fingers because the oil from your skin could cause it to overheat and fail prematurely. If you do touch the bulb surface, clean it with rubbing alcohol.

1 Open the hood for access to the mounting bolts.
2 Remove the headlight mounting bolts and remove the headlight assembly from the bumper cover **(see illustrations)**.
3 Disconnect the wiring from the headlight assembly.
4 Installation is the reverse of removal.
5 Check headlight adjustment (see Section 17).

16.2a Remove these three bolts . . .

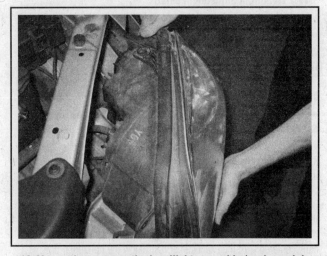

16.2b . . . then remove the headlight assembly (early model shown, later models similar)

17 Headlights - adjustment

➡ **Note:** The headlights must be aimed correctly. If adjusted incorrectly they could blind the driver of an oncoming vehicle and cause a serious accident or seriously reduce your ability to see the road. The headlights should be checked for proper aim every 12 months and any time a new headlight is installed or front-end bodywork is performed. It should be emphasized that the following procedure is only an interim step, which will provide temporary adjustment until a properly equipped shop can adjust the headlights.

1 There are several methods of adjusting the headlights. The simplest method requires masking tape, a blank wall and a level floor.

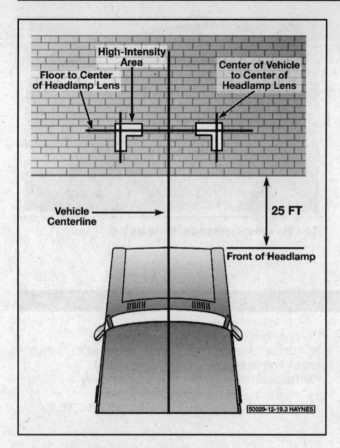

17.2 Headlight adjustment details

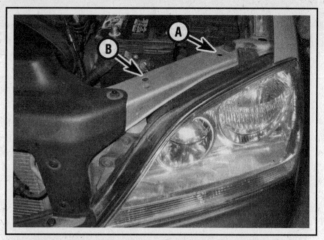

17.5a Insert a long Phillips screwdriver through the holes in the radiator support to adjust the low beam (A) and the high beam (B)

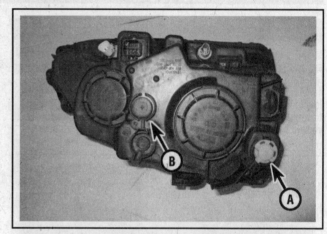

17.5b To turn the adjuster wheels for the low beam (A) and high beam (B), engage the head of the screwdriver with the teeth on the adjuster wheel and turn the wheel (housing removed for clarity)

2 Position masking tape vertically on the wall in reference to the vehicle centerline and the centerlines of both headlights **(see illustration)**.

3 Position a horizontal tape line in reference to the centerline of all the headlights.

➡ **Note: It may be easier to position the tape on the wall with the vehicle parked only a few inches away.**

4 Adjustment should be made with the vehicle parked 25 feet from the wall, sitting level, the gas tank half-full and no unusually heavy load in the vehicle.

5 With the low beams on, position the high intensity zone so it is two inches below the horizontal line. Make the adjustment by turning the adjusting screw to raise or lower the beam **(see illustrations)**.

6 With the high beams on, the high intensity zone should be vertically centered with the exact center just below the horizontal line.

➡ **Note: It may not be possible to position the headlight aim exactly for both high and low beams. If a compromise must be made, keep in mind that the low beams are the most used and have the greatest effect on driver safety.**

7 Have the headlights adjusted by a dealer service department or service station at the earliest opportunity.

18 Horn - replacement

✻ **WARNING:**

The models covered by this manual are equipped with Supplemental Restraint Systems (SRS), more commonly known as airbags. Always disable the airbag system before working in the vicinity of any airbag system components to avoid the possibility of accidental deployment of the airbag(s), which could cause personal injury (see Section 24).

1 Remove the plastic type fasteners from the radiator support trim, then remove the cover.

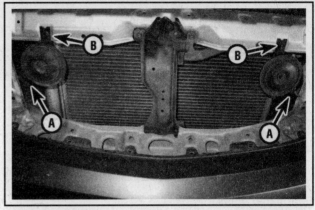

2 Disconnect the electrical connector **(see illustration)**.
3 Remove the bracket bolt and detach the horn from the radiator support.
4 Installation is the reverse of removal.

18.2 Disconnect the electrical connector to the horn (A) then remove the mounting bolt (B)

19 Bulb replacement

Bulb removal

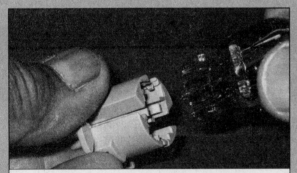

To remove many modern exterior bulbs from their holders, simply pull them out

On bulbs with a cylindrical base ("bayonet" bulbs), the socket is spring-loaded; a pair of small posts on the side of the base hold the bulb in place against spring pressure. To remove this type of bulb, push it into the holder, rotate it 1/4-turn counterclockwise, then pull it out

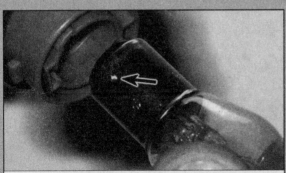

If a bayonet bulb has dual filaments, the posts are staggered, so the bulb can only be installed one way

To remove most overhead interior light bulbs, simply unclip them

EXTERIOR LIGHT BULBS

Front turn signal bulbs

➡ **Note: The front turn signal/parking and sidemarker light bulbs are located in the headlight housing.**

1 Reach behind the headlight housing. The bulbs are all accessible without removing the headlight assembly.
2 Remove the bulb holder from the headlight housing **(see illustration)**.
3 Remove the bulb from the holder.
4 Installation is the reverse of removal.

Door panel lights

5 Pry the lamp assembly from the door panel **(see illustration)**.
6 Disconnect the wiring harness from the bulb holder.
7 Turn the bulb holder counterclockwise to remove it.
8 Pull the bulb from its socket.
9 Installation is the reverse of removal.

Fog light bulbs

10 Remove the front bumper cover (see Chapter 11). Alternatively, you can remove the plastic inner fender liners - but reaching through the opening is more difficult.
11 Disconnect the electrical connector from the fog light bulb holder **(see illustration)**.
12 Turn the fog light bulb holder counterclockwise and pull it out of the fog light housing.
13 Installation is the reverse of removal.

Center high-mounted brake light

➡ **Note: The center high-mounted brake light bulb is located in the upper edge of the liftgate.**

14 Open the liftgate and remove the window trim (see Chapter 11 Section 14). Remove the screw covers **(see illustration)**, then remove the mounting screws.
15 Disconnect the electrical connector from the center high-mounted brake light bulb holder **(see illustration)**.
16 Remove the center high-mounted brake light bulb holder from the housing.

19.2 To remove the bulb holder for the front turn signal/parking light bulb, rotate it counterclockwise and pull it out of the headlight housing

19.5 Remove the lamp assembly from the door panel and disconnect the harness

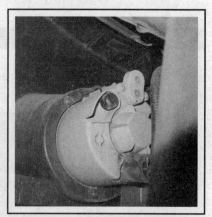

19.11 The fog lights are mounted in the front bumper cover - either remove the bumper cover or the inner fender liner for access

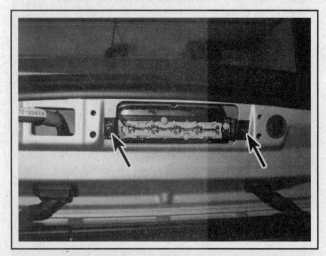

19.14 The center high-mounted brake light screws have covers that can be removed with a screwdriver

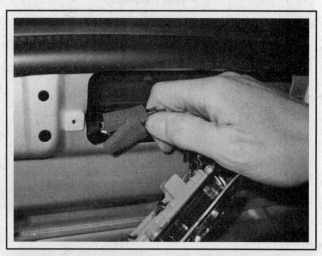

19.15 Disconnect the wiring harness and disassemble the housing to access the bulbs

17 Remove the center high-mounted brake light bulb from the holder.

18 Installation is the reverse of removal.

Rear brake/tail, turn signal, brake and back-up light bulbs

19 Open the liftgate. Use a Phillips screwdriver to remove the two mounting screws **(see illustration)**.

20 Pull the forward section of the light assembly straight out from the side of the vehicle to release the front pin **(see illustration)**.

21 Remove the bulb holder from the taillight housing by turning it counterclockwise **(see illustration)**.

22 Remove the bulb from its holder **(see illustration)**.

23 Installation is the reverse of removal.

License plate light bulbs

24 Remove the two screws securing the license plate light housing(s) and pull the housing from the liftgate. Detach the bulb holder from the housing. Pull the bulb straight out of the holder to replace it.

INTERIOR LIGHT BULBS

Luggage compartment light and dome light bulbs

25 Remove the lens from the map/reading light, dome light and cargo light housing by prying it off with a screwdriver inserted into the small slot **(see illustrations)**.

19.19 The taillight housing is retained by two screws at the rear . . .

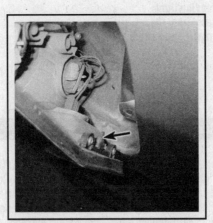

19.20 . . . and a stud at the front; pull it out to the side of the vehicle - not towards the rear

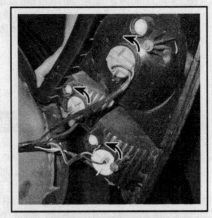

19.21 Rotate the taillight bulb holders to pull them out . . .

19.22 . . . then remove the bulbs

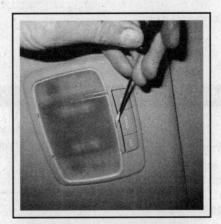

19.25a Pry down in this area of the dome light lens to avoid breaking the tabs

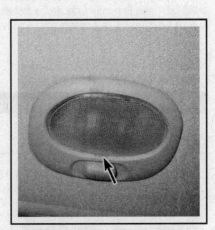

19.25b The cargo area light also has a specific area to insert a screwdriver to avoid breakage

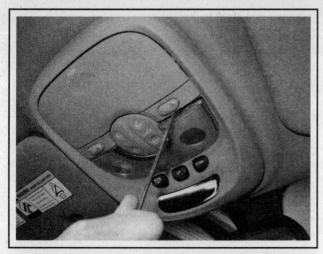

19.26 To remove a light bulb from the map/reading light housing, grasp it firmly and pull it straight down from the terminal clips. If necessary, pry only on the metal ends of the bulb, not the glass

26 Lift the lens off and remove the bulb from the terminals **(see illustration)**.
27 Installation is the reverse of removal.

Glove box light

➡ **Note: Some models have glove box light bulbs that are replaceable by prying the lens down from inside the glove compartment.**

28 Lower the glove box door fully and remove the inner glove box shell (see Chapter 11).
29 Disconnect the wiring from the light.
30 Remove the bulb holder and remove the bulb.
31 Installation is the reverse of removal.

20 Electric side view mirrors - description

1 Most electric side view mirrors use two motors to move the glass; one for up and down adjustments and one for left-right adjustments.
2 The control switch has a selector portion that sends voltage to the left or right side mirror. With the ignition ON but the engine OFF, roll down the windows and operate the mirror control switch through all functions (left-right and up-down) for both the left and right side mirrors.
3 Listen carefully for the sound of the electric motors running in the mirrors.
4 If the motors can be heard but the mirror glass doesn't move, there's a problem with the drive mechanism inside the mirror. Remove and disassemble the mirror to locate the problem.
5 If the mirrors do not operate and no sound comes from the mirrors, check the fuse (see Section 3).
6 If the fuse is OK, remove the mirror control switch from the dashboard. Have the switch continuity checked by a dealership service department or other qualified automobile repair facility.
7 Test the ground connections. Refer to the wiring diagrams at the end of this Chapter.
8 If the mirror still doesn't work, remove the mirror (see Chapter 11) and check the wires at the mirror for voltage.
9 If there's not voltage in each switch position, check the circuit between the mirror and control switch for opens and shorts.
10 If there's voltage, remove the mirror and test it off the vehicle with jumper wires. Replace the mirror if it fails this test.

21 Cruise control system - description

2006 AND EARLIER MODELS

1 The cruise control system maintains vehicle speed with a Cruise Control Module (CCM), which is connected by cable from the accelerator pedal to the CCM and a second cable from the CCM to the throttle body. The system consists of the cruise control module, brake switch, control switches, cable and Vehicle Speed Sensor (VSS). Some features of the system require special testers and diagnostic procedures that are beyond the scope of this manual. Listed below are some general procedures that may be used to locate common problems.
2 Locate and check the fuse (see Section 3).
3 Check the brake light switch (see Chapter 9).
4 Visually inspect the control cable between the cruise control module and the throttle body for free movement, replace if necessary.

5 Test drive the vehicle to determine if the cruise control is now working. If it isn't, take it to a dealer for further diagnosis.

2007 AND LATER MODELS

6 The cruise control system maintains vehicle speed with the Powertrain Control Module (PCM), throttle actuator control motor, brake switch, control switches and associated wiring. There is no mechanical connection, such as a vacuum servo or cable. Some features of the system require special testers and diagnostic procedures that are beyond the scope of the home mechanic. Listed below are some general procedures that may be used to locate common problems.
7 Check the fuses (see Section 3).

8 The Brake Pedal Position (BPP) switch (or brake light switch) deactivates the cruise control system. Have an assistant press the brake pedal while you check the brake light operation. If the brake lights do not operate properly, correct the problem and retest the cruise control.

9 Check the wiring between the PCM and throttle actuator motor for opens or shorts and repair as necessary.

10 The cruise control system uses information from the PCM, including the Vehicle Speed Sensor (VSS), which is located in the transmission or transfer case.

11 Test drive the vehicle to determine if the cruise control is now working. If it isn't, take it to a dealer service department or other qualified repair shop for further diagnosis.

22 Power window system - description

➡ **Note: 2007 and later models are equipped with a Body Control Module (BCM) that functions as a controller for many different systems. The BCM controls windshield wiper and washer signals, fog lights, tail lights, the auto-light system, the Daytime Running Lights (DRL), the interior warning systems (seat belt, parking brake, etc.), the power window delay time, power door locks, security systems and A/C heating controls. In the event of a problem with one of these systems, where no obvious problems can be found through conventional methods, have the BCM diagnosed by a dealer service department or other qualified auto repair facility.**

1 The power window system operates electric motors, mounted in the doors, which lower and raise the windows. The system consists of the control switches, relays, the motors, regulators, glass mechanisms and associated wiring.

2 The power windows can be lowered and raised from the master control switch by the driver or by remote switches located at the individual windows. Each window has a separate motor that is reversible. The position of the control switch determines the polarity and therefore the direction of operation.

3 The circuit is protected by a fuse and a circuit breaker. Each motor is also equipped with an internal circuit breaker; this prevents one stuck window from disabling the whole system.

4 The power window system will only operate when the ignition switch is ON. In addition, many models have a window lockout switch at the master control switch that, when activated, disables the switches at the rear windows and, sometimes, the switch at the passenger's window also. Always check these items before troubleshooting a window problem.

5 These procedures are general in nature, so if you can't find the problem using them, take the vehicle to a dealer service department or other properly equipped repair facility.

6 If the power windows won't operate, always check the fuse and circuit breaker first.

7 If only the rear windows are inoperative, or if the windows only operate from the master control switch, check the rear window lockout switch for continuity in the unlocked position. Replace it if it doesn't have continuity.

8 Check the wiring between the switches and fuse panel for continuity. Repair the wiring, if necessary.

9 If only one window is inoperative from the master control switch, try the other control switch at the window.

➡ **Note: This doesn't apply to the driver's door window.**

10 If the same window works from one switch, but not the other, check the switch for continuity. Have the switch checked at a dealer service department or other qualified automobile repair facility.

11 If the switch tests OK, check for a short or open in the circuit between the affected switch and the window motor.

12 If one window is inoperative from both switches, remove the trim panel from the affected door and check for voltage at the switch and at the motor while the switch is operated.

13 If voltage is reaching the motor, disconnect the glass from the regulator (see Chapter 11). Move the window up and down by hand while checking for binding and damage. Also check for binding and damage to the regulator. If the regulator is not damaged and the window moves up and down smoothly, replace the motor. If there's binding or damage, lubricate, repair or replace parts, as necessary.

14 If voltage isn't reaching the motor, check the wiring in the circuit for continuity between the switches and motors. You'll need to consult the wiring diagram for the vehicle. If the circuit is equipped with a relay, check that the relay is grounded properly and receiving voltage.

15 Test the windows to confirm proper repairs.

23 Power door lock system - description

➡ **Note: 2007 and later models are equipped with a Body Control Module (BCM) that functions as a controller for many different systems. The BCM controls windshield wiper and washer signals, fog lights, tail lights, the auto-light system, the Daytime Running Lights (DRL), the interior warning systems (seat belt, parking brake, etc.), the power window delay time, power door locks, security systems and A/C heating controls. In the event of a problem with one of these systems, where no obvious problems can be found through conventional methods, have the BCM diagnosed by a dealer service department or other qualified auto repair facility.**

1 A power door lock system operates the door lock actuators mounted in each door. The system consists of the switches, actuators, a control unit and associated wiring. Diagnosis can usually be limited to simple checks of the wiring connections and actuators for minor faults that can be easily repaired.

2 Power door lock systems are operated by bi-directional solenoids located in the doors. The lock switches have two operating positions: Lock and Unlock. When activated, the switch sends a ground signal to the door lock control unit to lock or unlock the doors. Depending on which way the switch is activated, the control unit reverses polarity to the solenoids, allowing the two sides of the circuit to be used alternately as the feed (positive) and ground side.

3 Some vehicles may have an anti-theft system incorporated into the power locks. If you are unable to locate the trouble using the following general Steps, consult a dealer service department or other qualified repair shop.

4 Always check the circuit protection first. Some vehicles use a combination of circuit breakers and fuses.

5 Operate the door lock switches in both directions (Lock and Unlock) with the engine off. Listen for the click of the solenoids operating.

6 Test the switches for continuity. Remove the switches and have them checked by a dealer service department or other qualified automobile repair facility.

7 Check the wiring between the switches, control unit and sole-

noids for continuity. Repair the wiring if there's no continuity.

8 Check for a bad ground at the switches or the control unit.

9 If all but one lock solenoid operate, remove the trim panel from the affected door (see Chapter 11) and check for voltage at the solenoid while the lock switch is operated. One of the wires should have voltage in the Lock position; the other should have voltage in the Unlock position.

10 If the inoperative solenoid is receiving voltage, replace the solenoid.

11 If the inoperative solenoid isn't receiving voltage, check the relay for an open or short in the wire between the lock solenoid and the control unit.

➡ **Note: It's common for wires to break in the section of harness that goes between the body and door because opening and closing the door fatigues and eventually breaks the wires.**

24 Airbag system - general information

1 All models are equipped with a Supplemental Restraint System (SRS), more commonly known as the airbag system. The airbag system is designed to protect the driver and the front seat passenger from serious injury in the event of a head-on or frontal collision. It consists of the impact sensors, a driver's airbag module in the center of the steering wheel, a passenger's airbag module in the glove box area of the instrument panel and a sensing/diagnostic module mounted in the center of the floorpan, in the center console. Some models are also equipped with side-impact airbags.

AIRBAG MODULES

Driver's airbag

2 The airbag inflator module contains a housing incorporating the cushion (airbag) and inflator unit, mounted in the center of the steering wheel. The inflator assembly is mounted on the back of the housing over a hole through which gas is expelled, inflating the bag almost instantaneously when an electrical signal is sent from the system. A clockspring assembly on the steering column under the steering wheel carries this signal to the module. This clockspring assembly can transmit an electrical signal regardless of steering wheel position. The igniter in the airbag converts the electrical signal to heat and ignites the powder, which inflates the bag.

Passenger's airbag

3 The airbag is mounted inside the right end of the instrument panel, in the vicinity of the glove box compartment. It's similar in design to the driver's airbag, except that it's larger than the steering wheel unit. The passenger airbag is mounted between the instrument panel reinforcement bar and the underside of the instrument panel. The trim cover (on the side of the instrument panel that faces toward the passenger) is textured and colored to match the instrument panel and has a molded seam that splits open when the bag inflates.

Side impact airbags

4 Extra protection is provided by side-impact airbags on some models. These are smaller devices, which are located on the outer sides of the seat backs, and deploy in the event of a severe side-impact collision.

SENSING AND DIAGNOSTIC MODULE

5 The sensing and diagnostic module supplies the current to the airbag system in the event of the collision, even if battery power is cut off. It checks this system every time the vehicle is started, causing the "AIR BAG" light to go on then off, if the system is operating properly. If there is a fault in the system, the light will go on and stay on, flash, or the dash will make a beeping sound. If this happens, the vehicle should be taken to your dealer immediately for service.

DISARMING THE SYSTEM AND OTHER PRECAUTIONS

✷✷✷ WARNING:

Failure to follow these precautions could result in accidental deployment of the airbag and personal injury.

6 Whenever working in the vicinity of the steering wheel, steering column or any of the other SRS system components, the system must be disarmed.

To disarm the airbag system:

a) *Point the wheels straight ahead and turn the key to the Lock position.*

b) *Disconnect the cable from the negative battery terminal.*

c) *Wait at least two minutes for the back-up power supply to be depleted.*

Whenever handling an airbag module:

7 Always keep the airbag opening (the trim side) pointed away from your body. Never place the airbag module on a bench or other surface with the airbag opening facing the surface. Always place the airbag module in a safe location with the airbag opening facing up.

8 Never measure the resistance of any SRS component. An ohmmeter has a built-in battery supply that could accidentally deploy the airbag.

9 Never use electrical welding equipment on a vehicle equipped with an airbag without first disconnecting the electrical connector for each airbag.

10 Never dispose of a live airbag module. Return it to a dealer service department or other qualified repair shop for safe deployment and disposal.

COMPONENT REMOVAL AND INSTALLATION

Driver's side airbag module and spiral cable

11 Refer to Chapter 10, *Steering wheel - removal and installation*, for the driver's side airbag module and clockspring removal and installation procedures.

Other airbag modules

12 We don't recommend removing any of the other airbag modules. These jobs are best left to a professional.

---

25 Remote keyless entry system - general information and battery replacement

1 Here's how the transmitter inside the remote keyless entry fob should work:

2 When you press the UNLOCK button, the driver's door unlocks. If you press the UNLOCK button a second time within four seconds, all the doors unlock.

3 Pressing the lock button sets the alarm and locks all of the doors and the liftgate.

BATTERY REPLACEMENT

4 When the transmitter becomes weak, operation will become intermittent and require you to be closer to the vehicle for it to work. Eventually it won't work at all.

5 To replace the transmitter battery, carefully pry open the keyless entry fob by inserting a small screwdriver into the slot in the body of the transmitter and separate the halves of the fob.

6 Using a small screwdriver, carefully pry out the old battery with the positive (+) side of the battery facing up.

7 Installation is the reverse of removal. Make sure the two halves of the cover snap together tightly to keep out dirt, dust, humidity and rain.

26 Wiring diagrams - general information

1 Since it isn't possible to include all wiring diagrams for every year covered by this manual, the following diagrams are those that are typical and most commonly needed.

2 Prior to troubleshooting any circuits, check the fuse and circuit breakers (if equipped) to make sure they're in good condition. Make sure the battery is properly charged and check the cable connections (see Chapter 1).

3 When checking a circuit, make sure that all connectors are clean, with no broken or loose terminals. When unplugging a connector, do not pull on the wires - pull only on the connector housings.

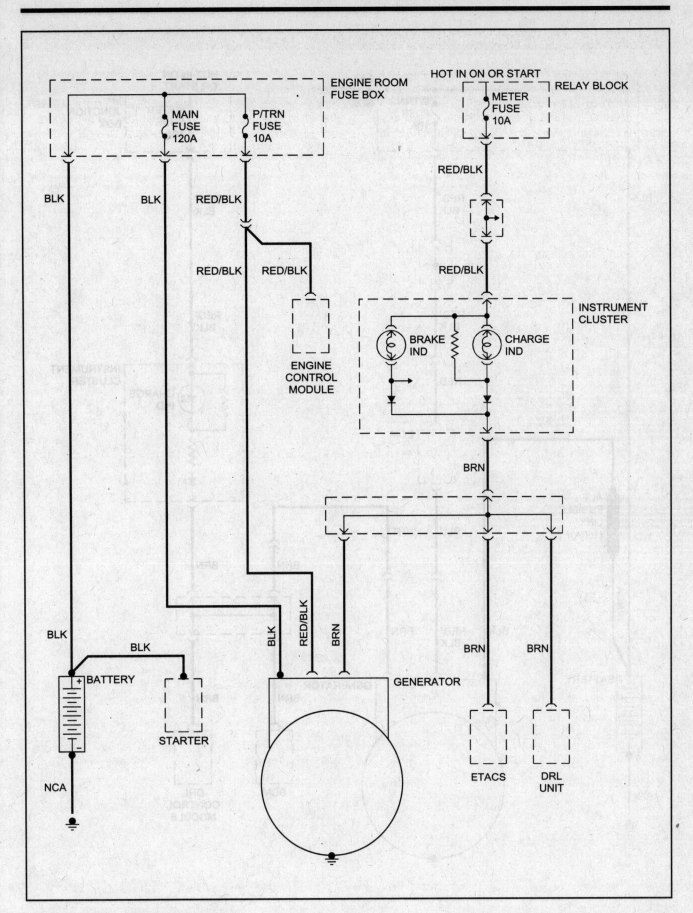

Charging system - 2006 and earlier models

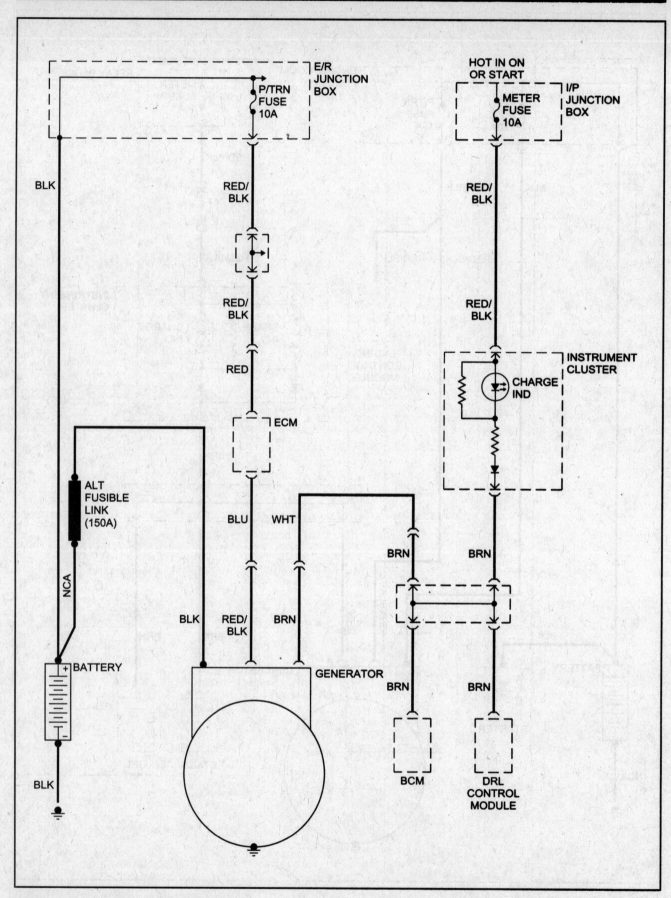

Charging system - 2007 through 2009 models

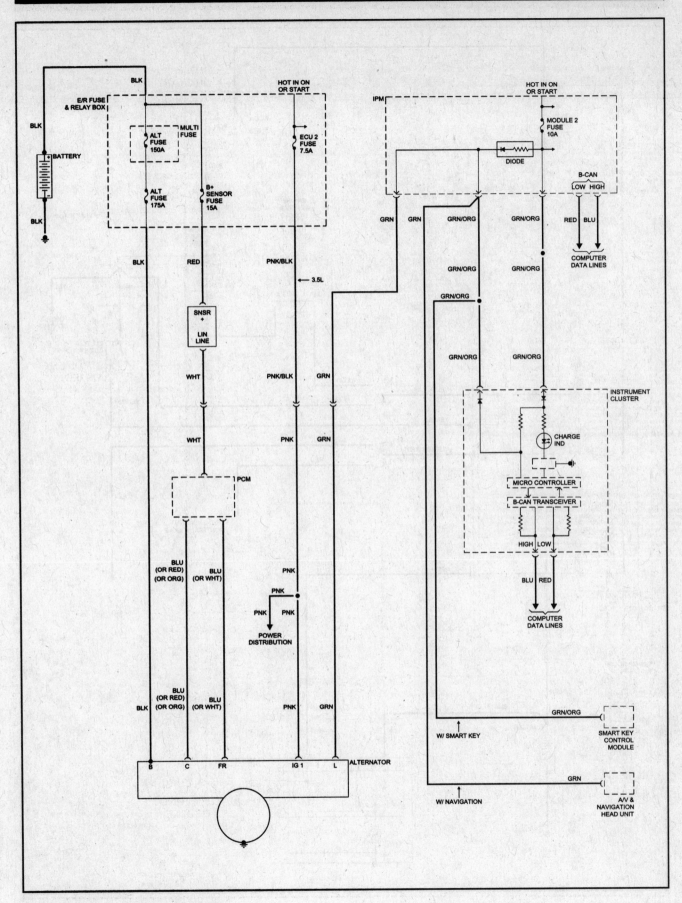

Charging system - 2011 and later models

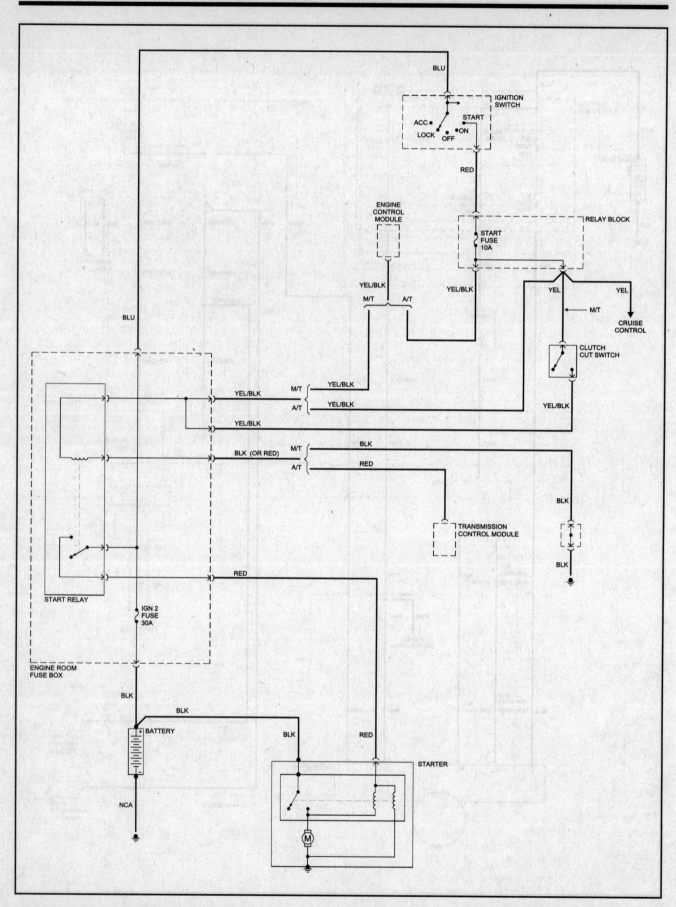

Starting system - 2006 and earlier models

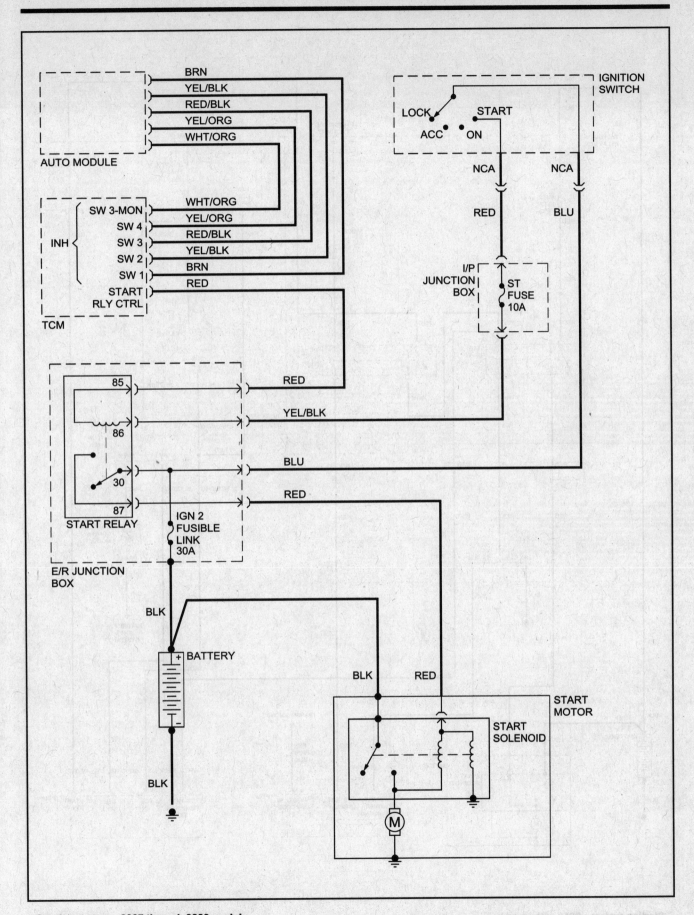

Starting system - 2007 through 2009 models

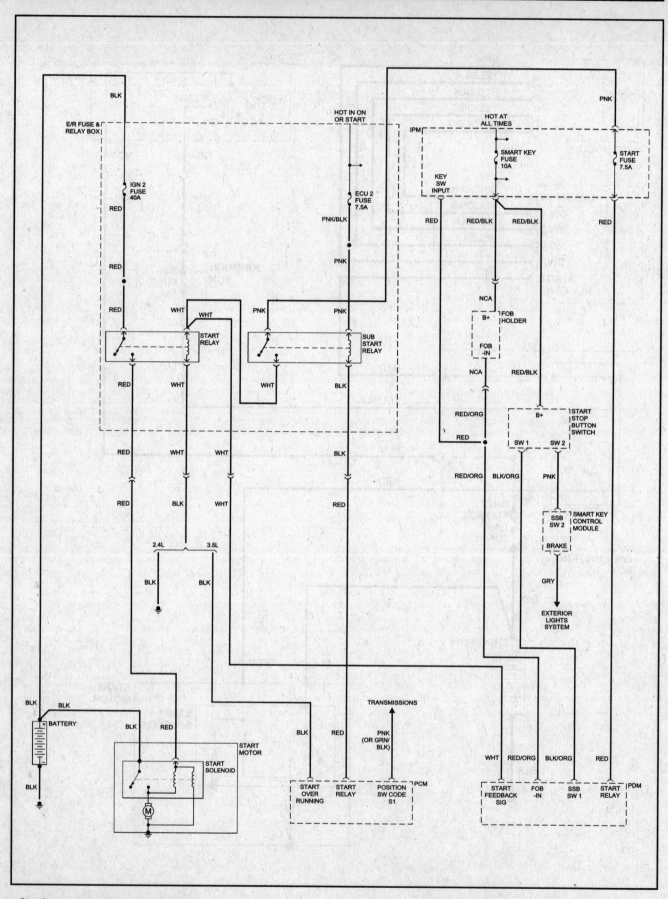

Starting system - 2011 with smart key

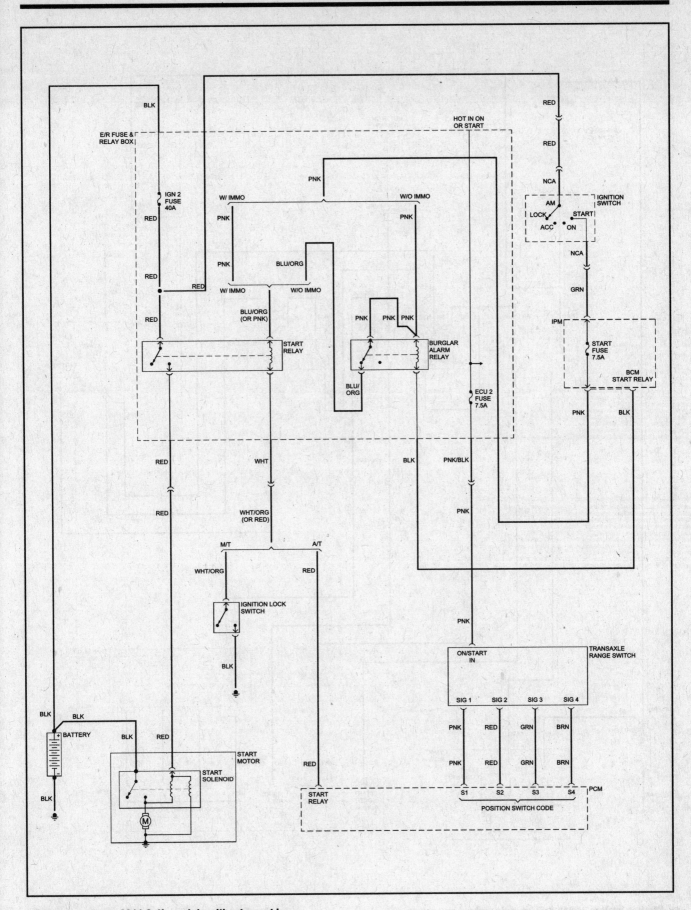

Starting system - 2011 2.4L models without smart key

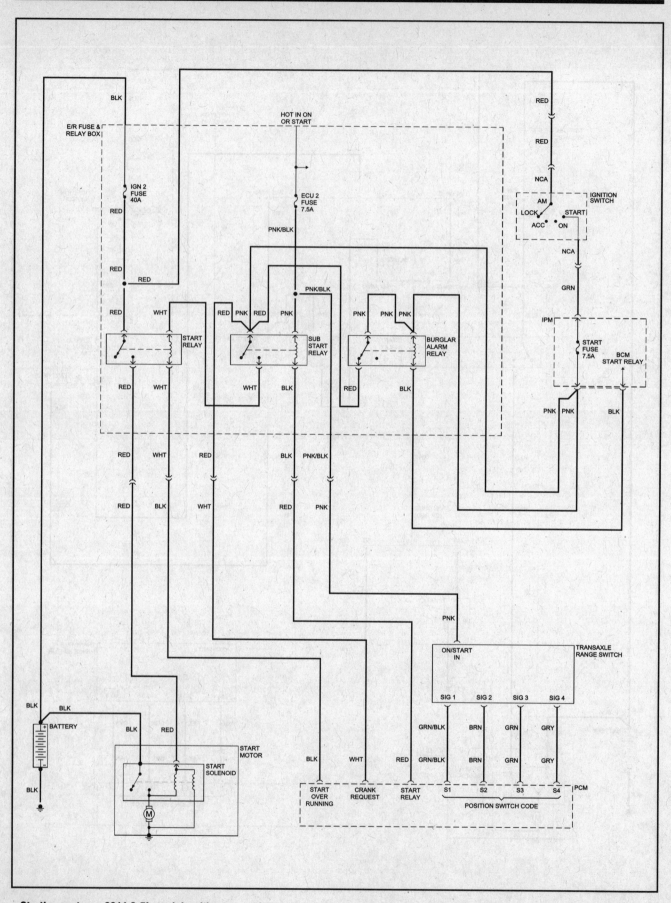

Starting system - 2011 3.5L models without smart key

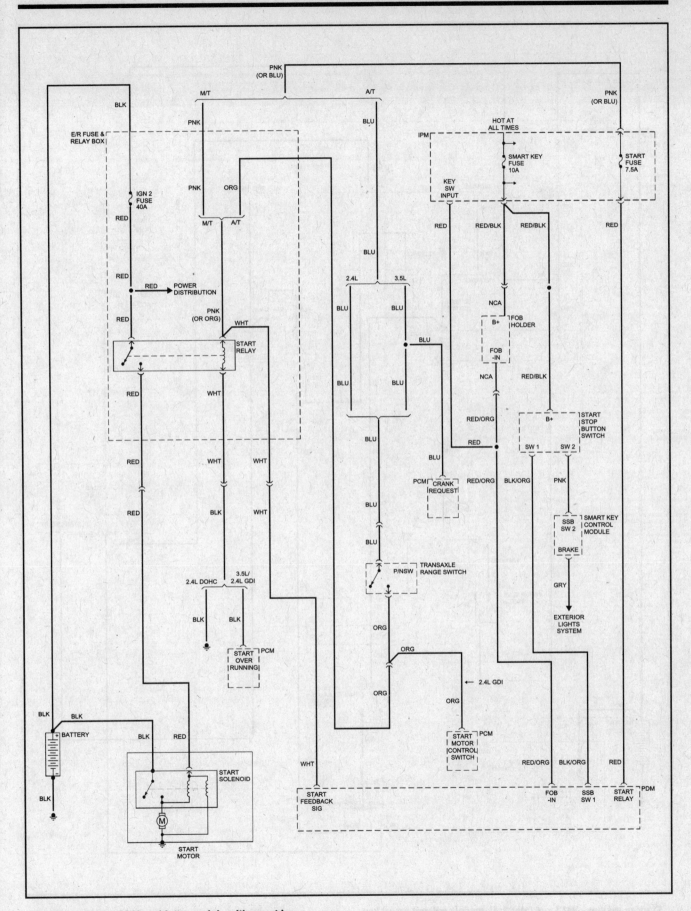

Starting system - 2012 and later models with smart key

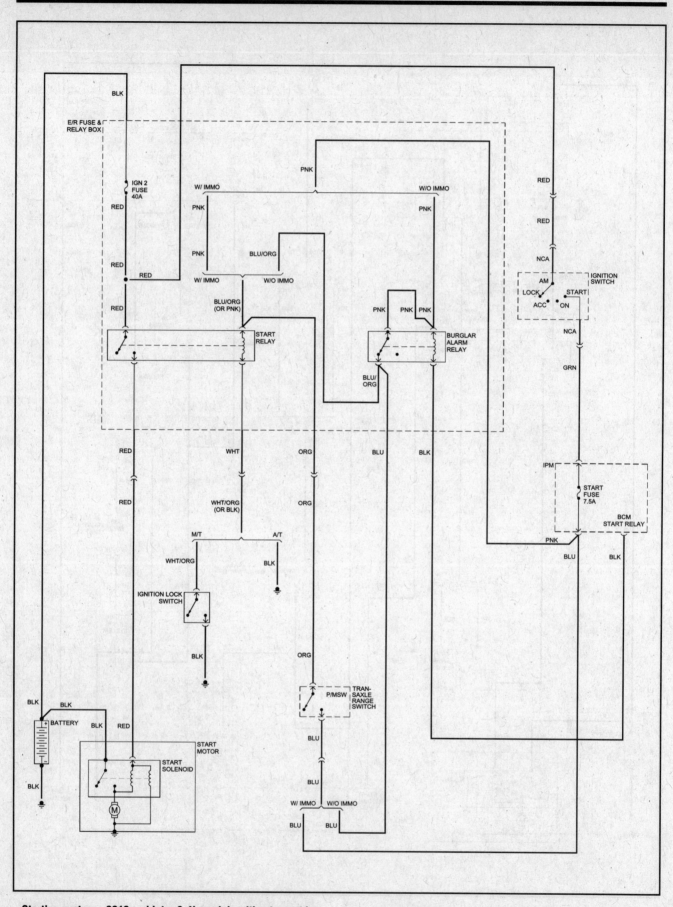

Starting system - 2012 and later 2.4L models without smart key

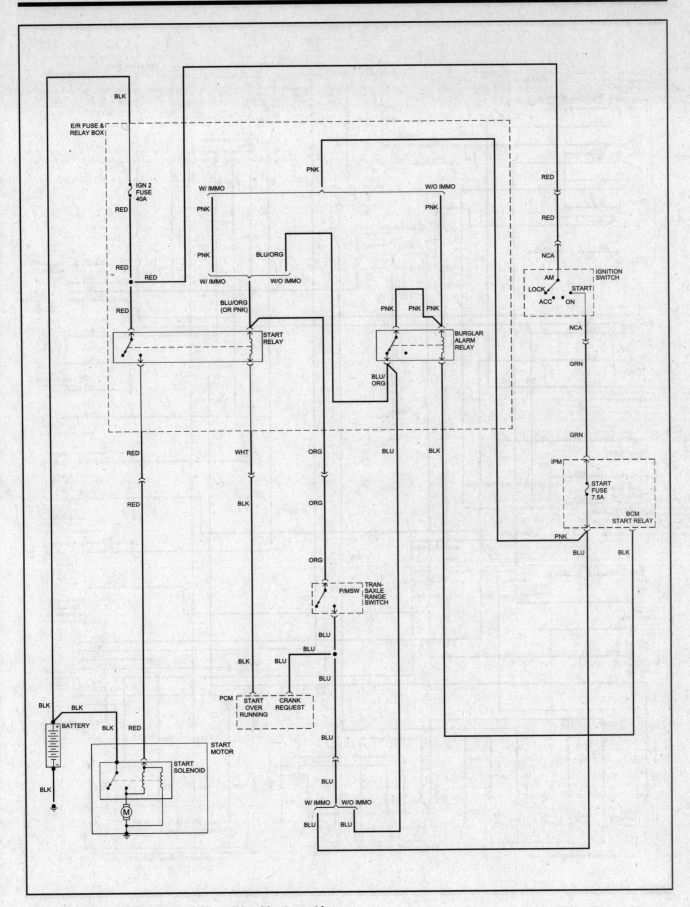

Starting system - 2012 and later 3.5L models without smart key

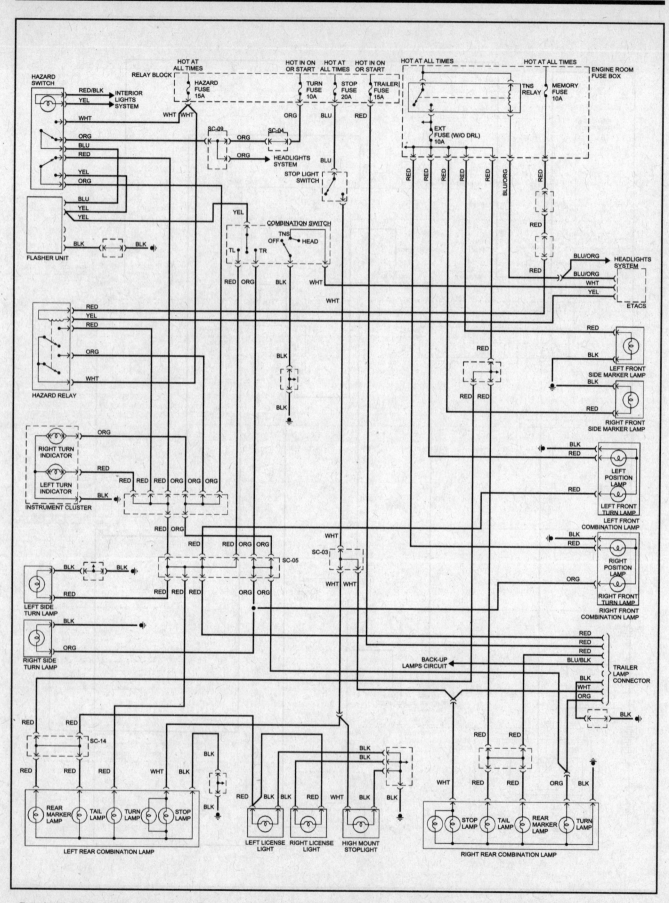

Exterior lighting system (except backup lights) - 2006 and earlier models

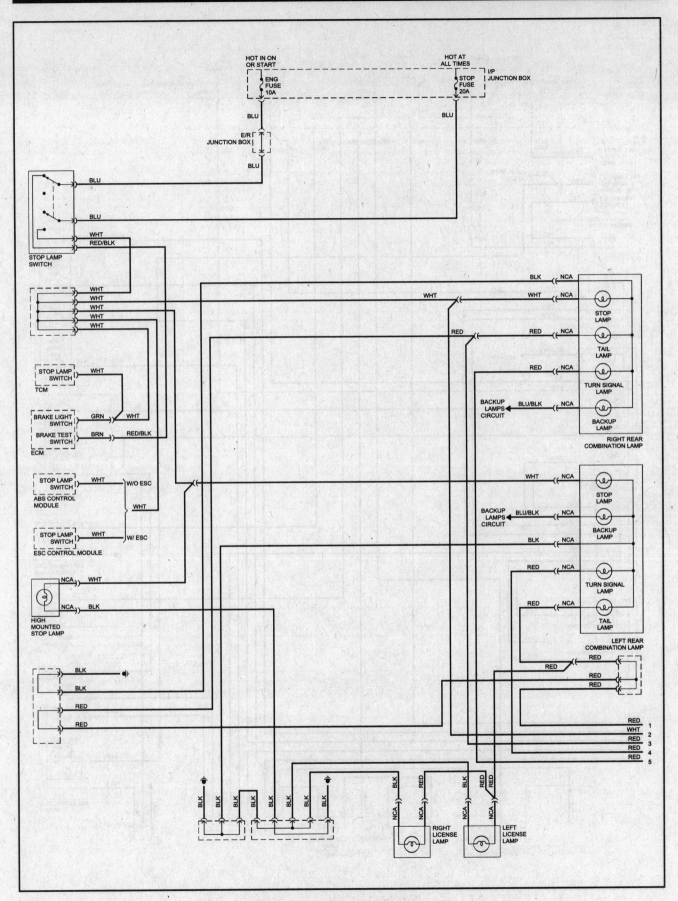

Exterior lighting system (except backup lights) - 2007 through 2009 models (1 of 2)

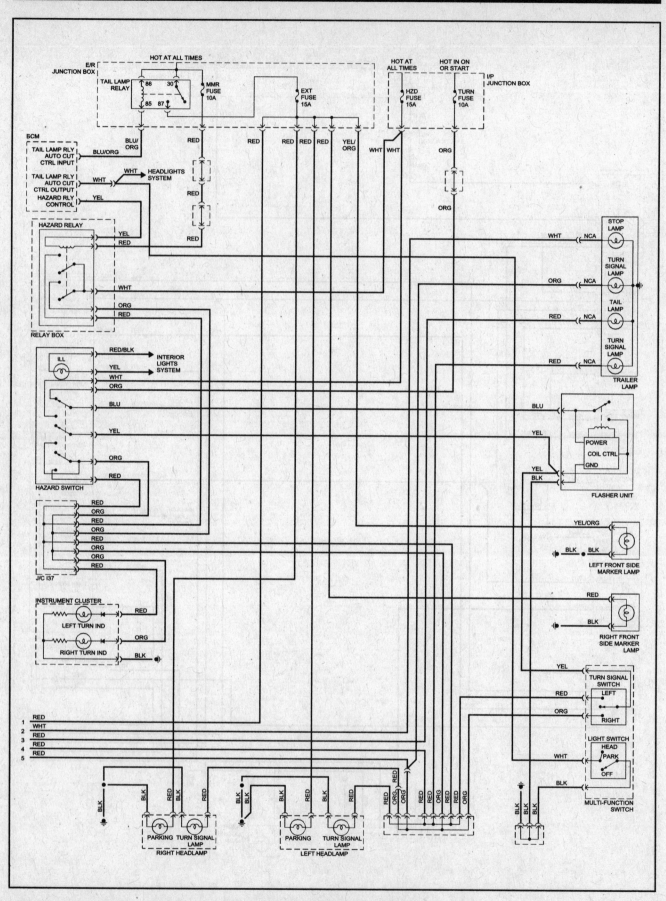

Exterior lighting system (except backup lights) - 2007 through 2009 models (2 of 2)

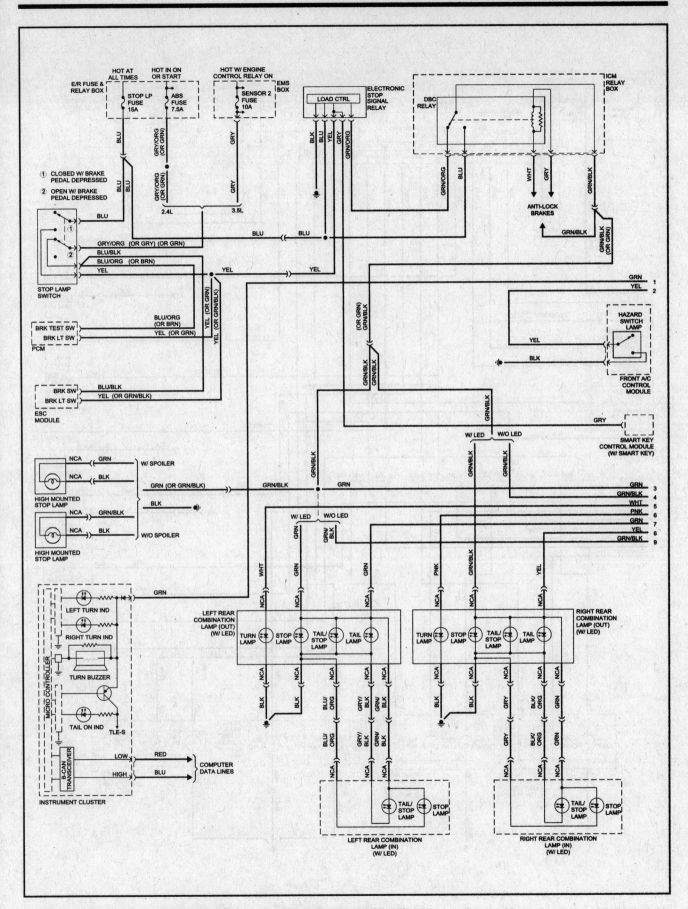

Exterior lighting system (except backup lights) - 2011 and later models (1 of 2)

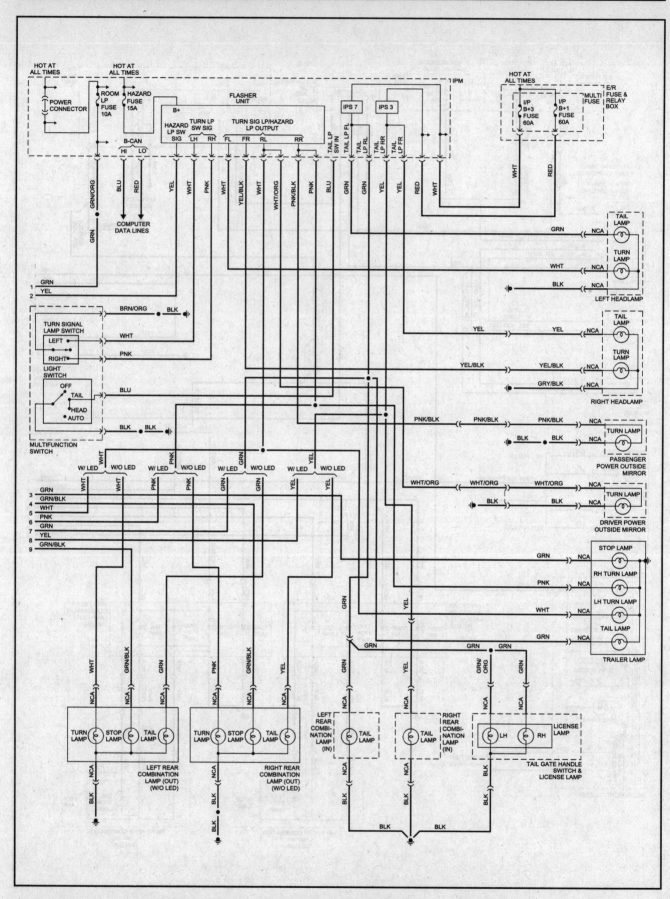

Exterior lighting system (except backup lights) - 2011 and later models (2 of 2)

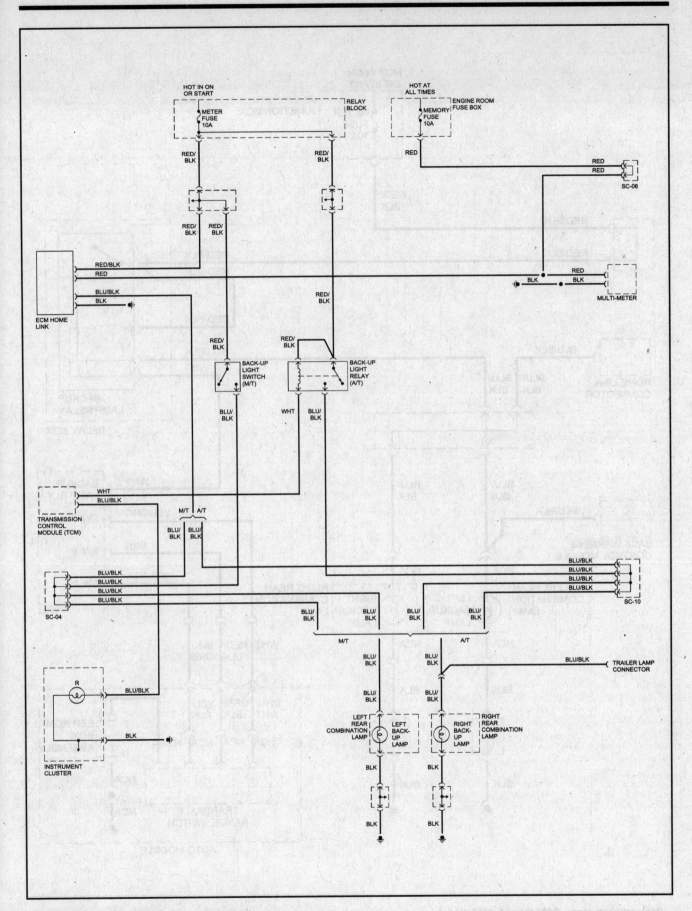

Backup light system – 2006 and earlier models

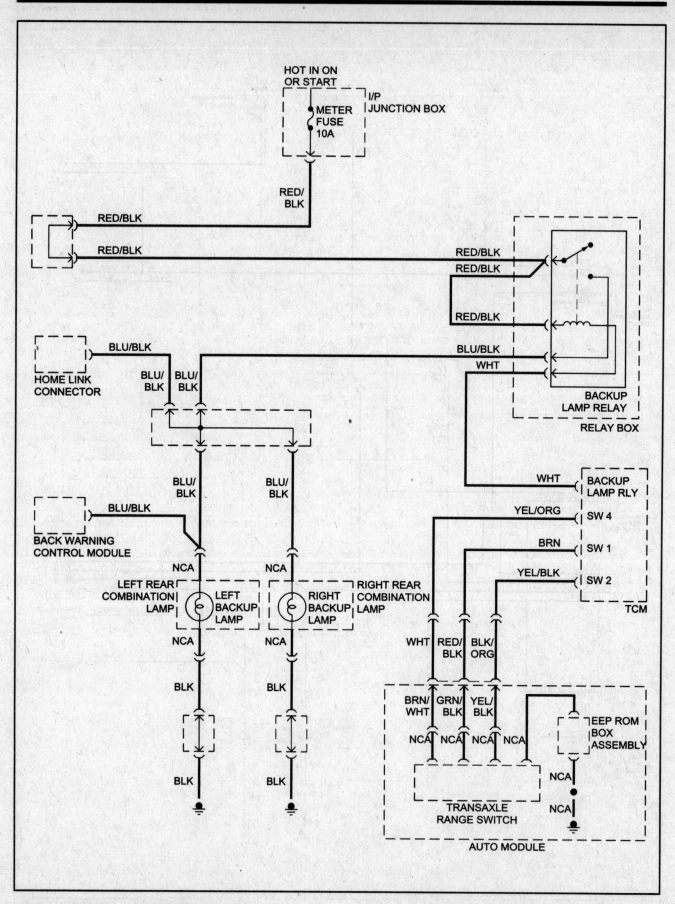

Backup light system - 2007 through 2009 models

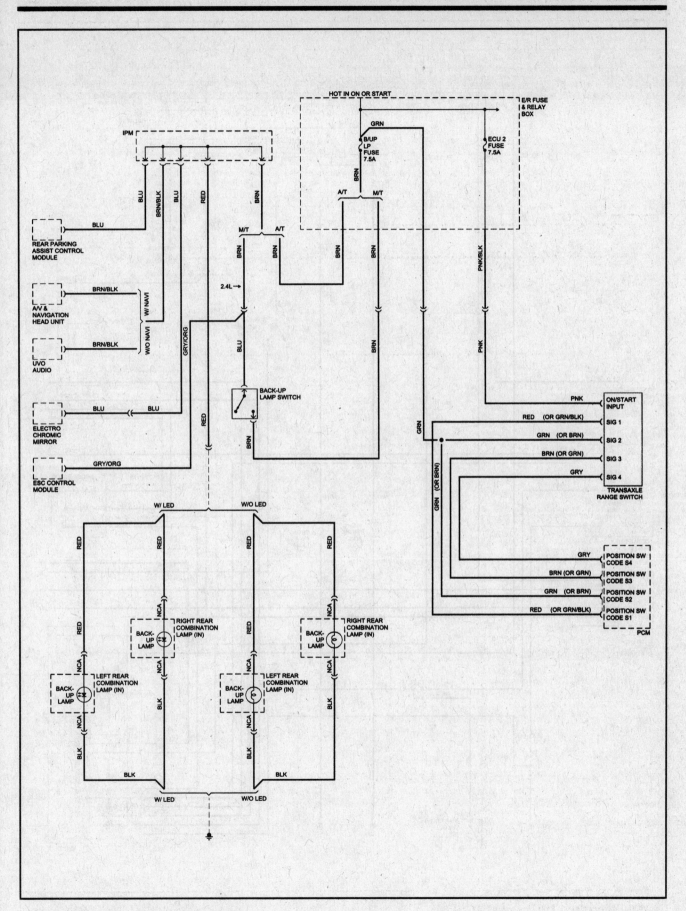

Backup light system - 2011 and later models

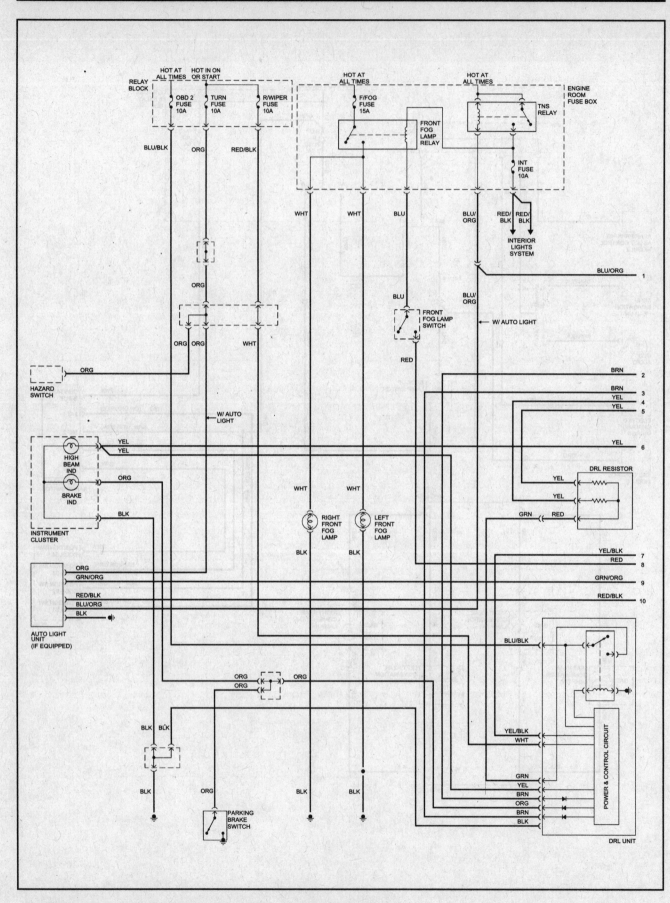

Headlight system with daytime running lights - 2006 and earlier models (1 of 2)

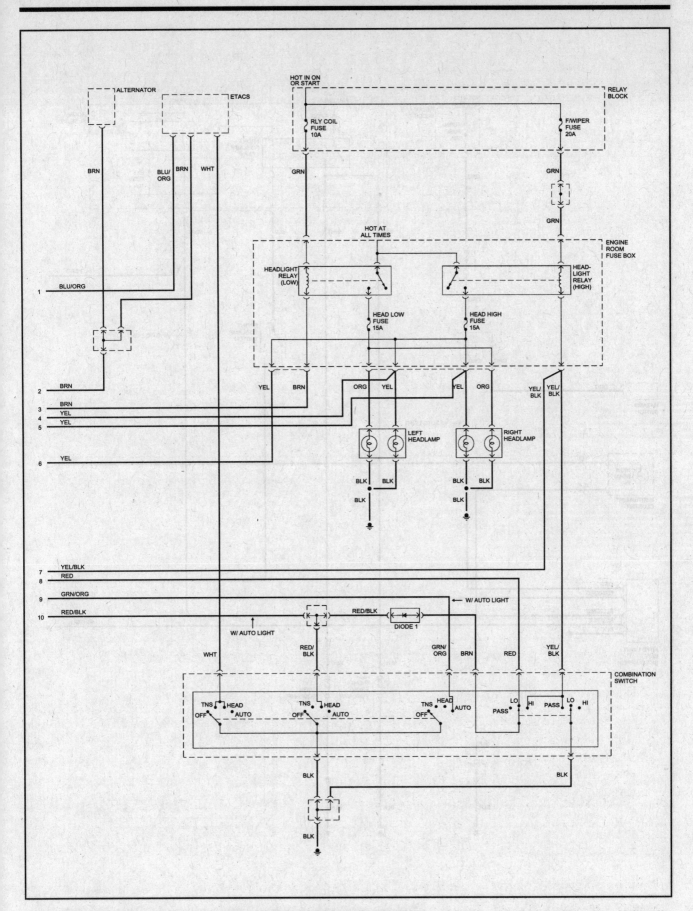

Headlight system with daytime running lights - 2006 and earlier models (2 of 2)

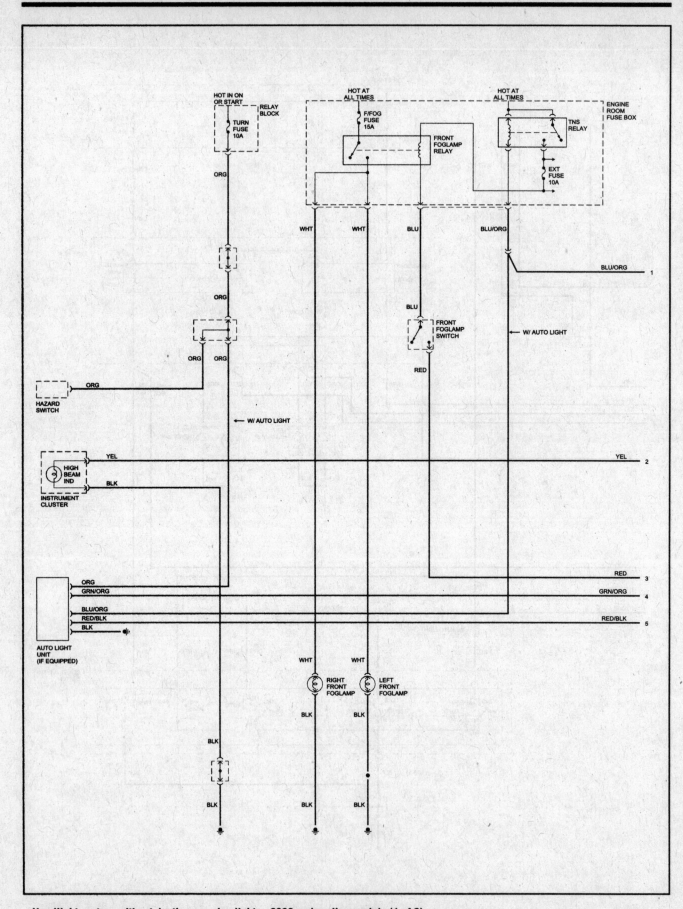

Headlight system without daytime running lights - 2006 and earlier models (1 of 2)

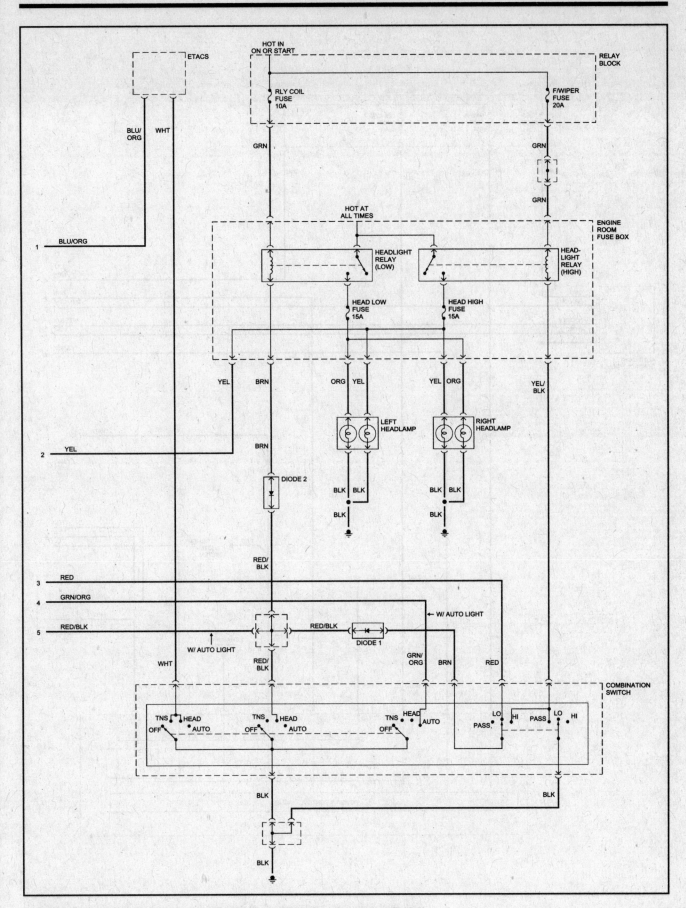

Headlight system without daytime running lights - 2006 and earlier models (2 of 2)

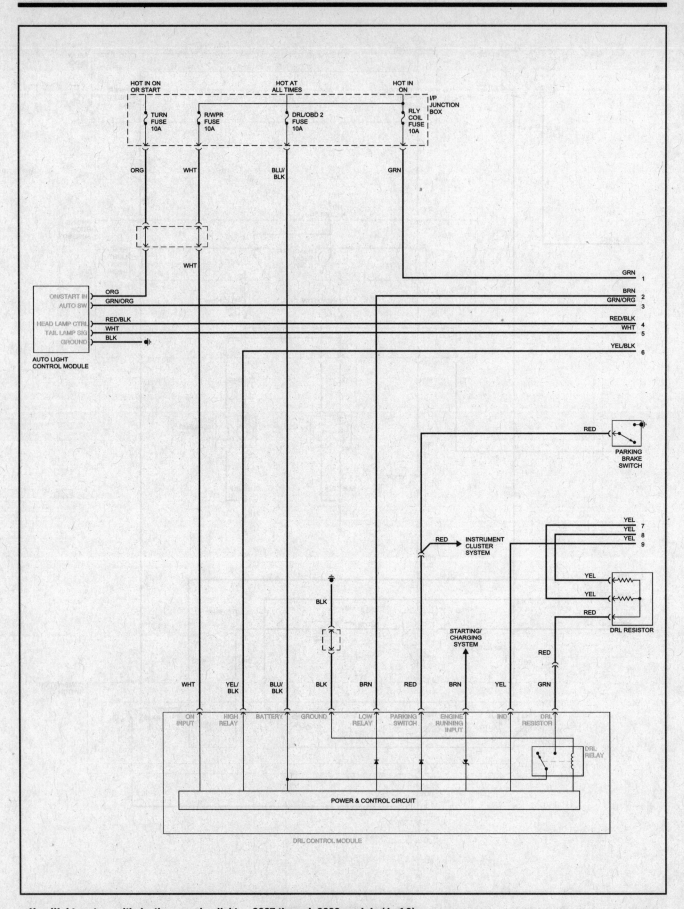

Headlight system with daytime running lights - 2007 through 2009 models (1 of 2)

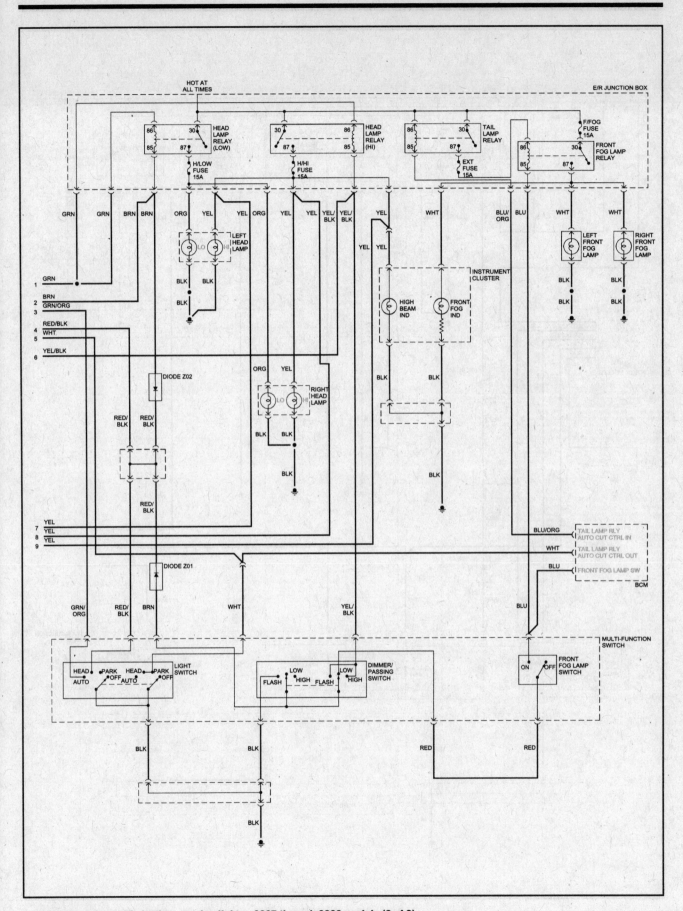

Headlight system with daytime running lights - 2007 through 2009 models (2 of 2)

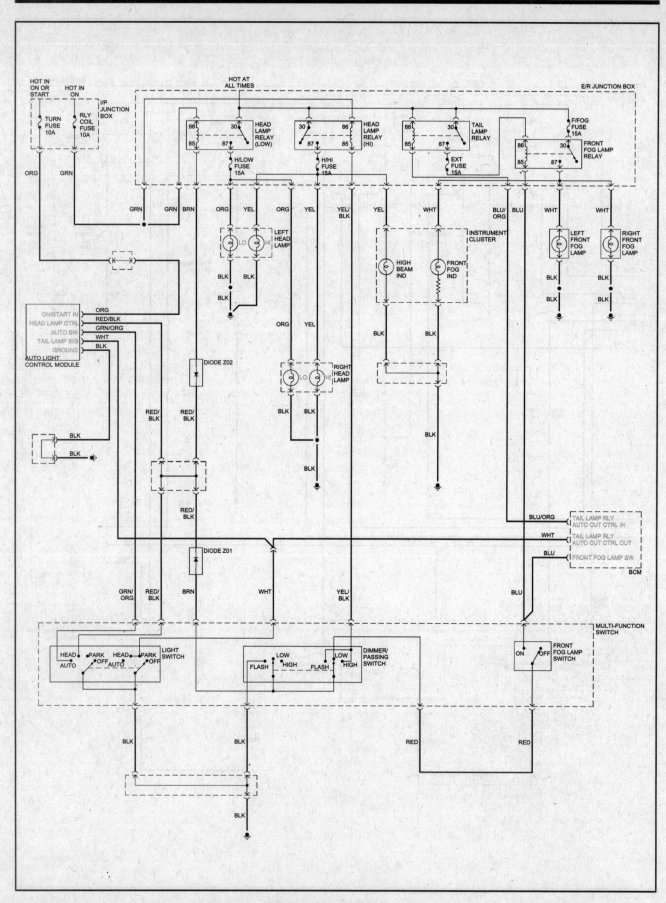

Headlight system without daytime running lights - 2007 through 2009 models

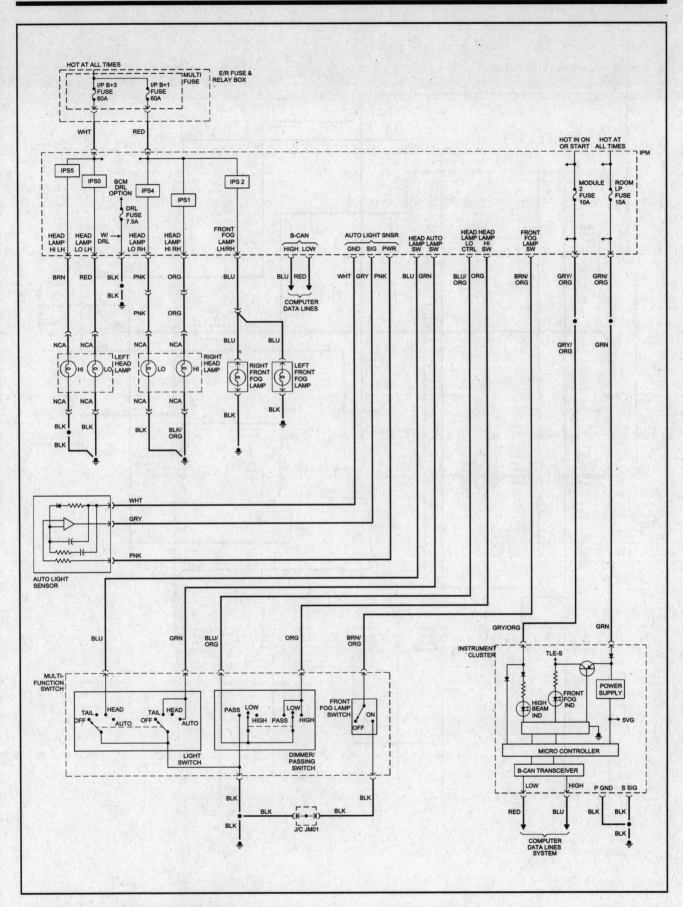

Headlight system - 2011 and later models

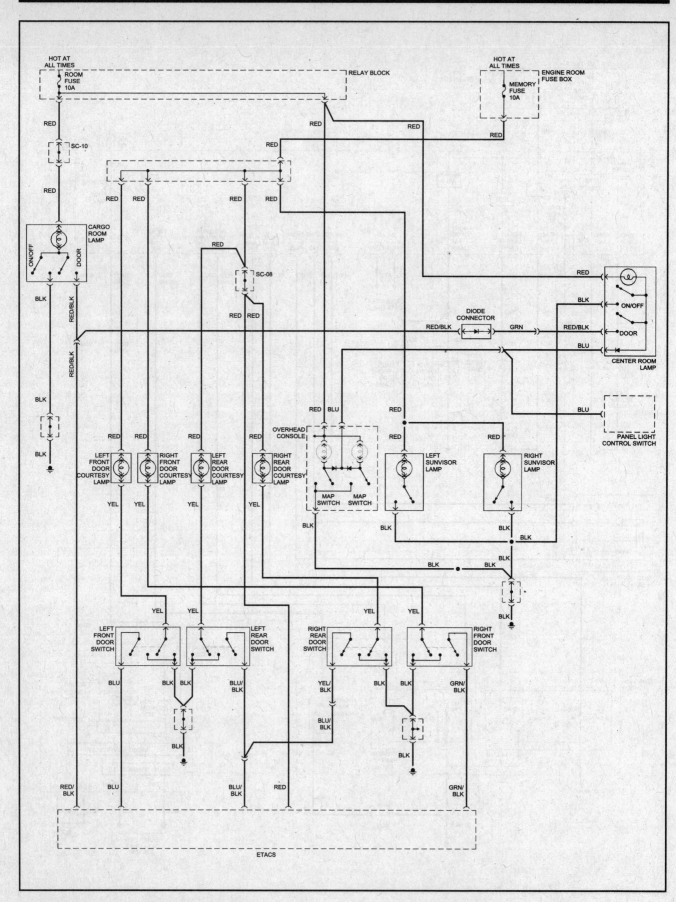

Courtesy lights system - 2006 and earlier models

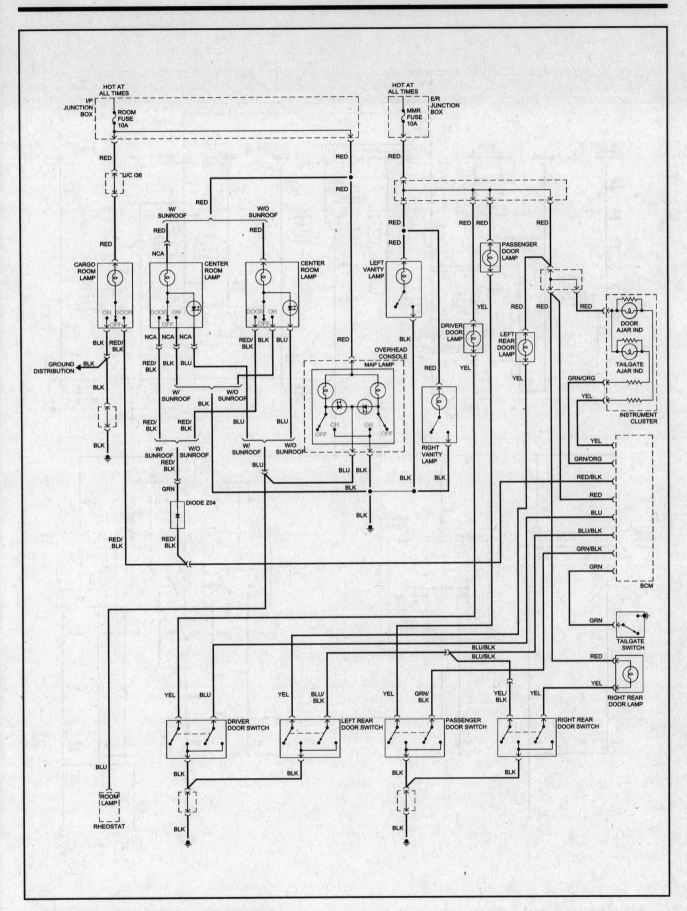

Courtesy lights system - 2007 through 2009 models

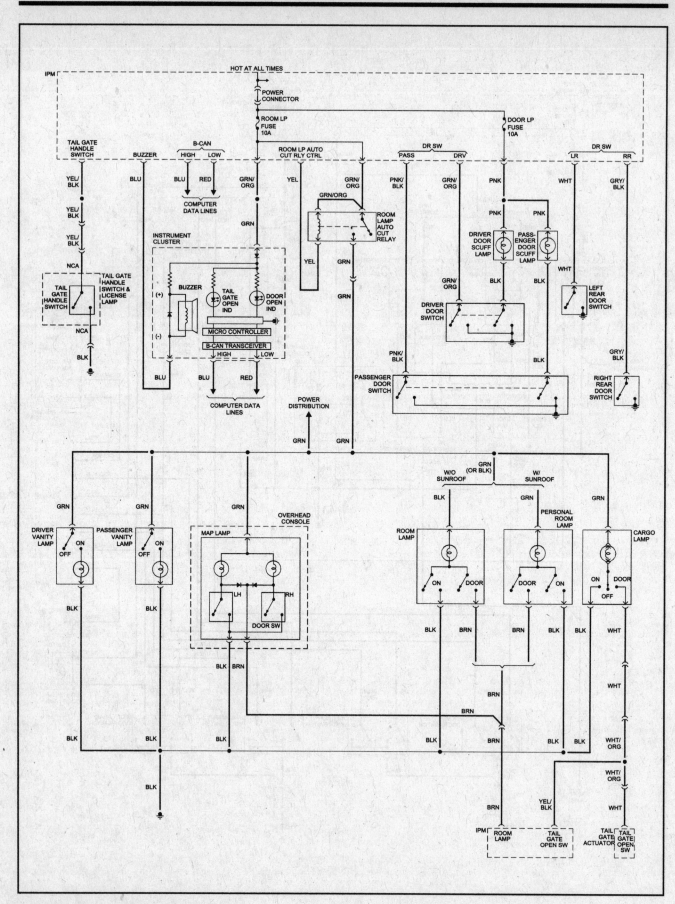

Courtesy lights system - 2011 and later models

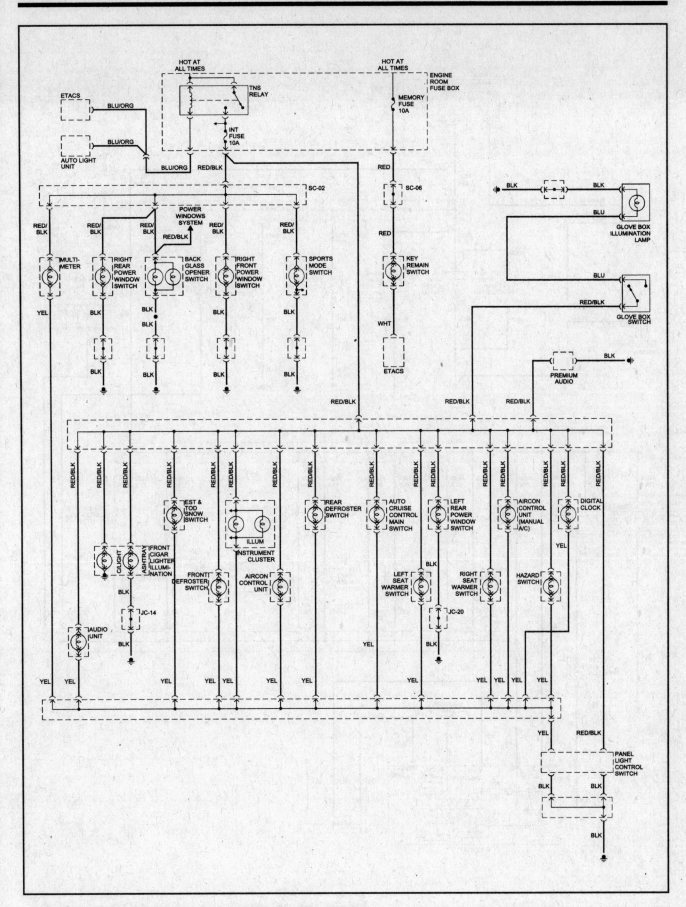

Instrument and switch illumination system - 2006 and earlier models

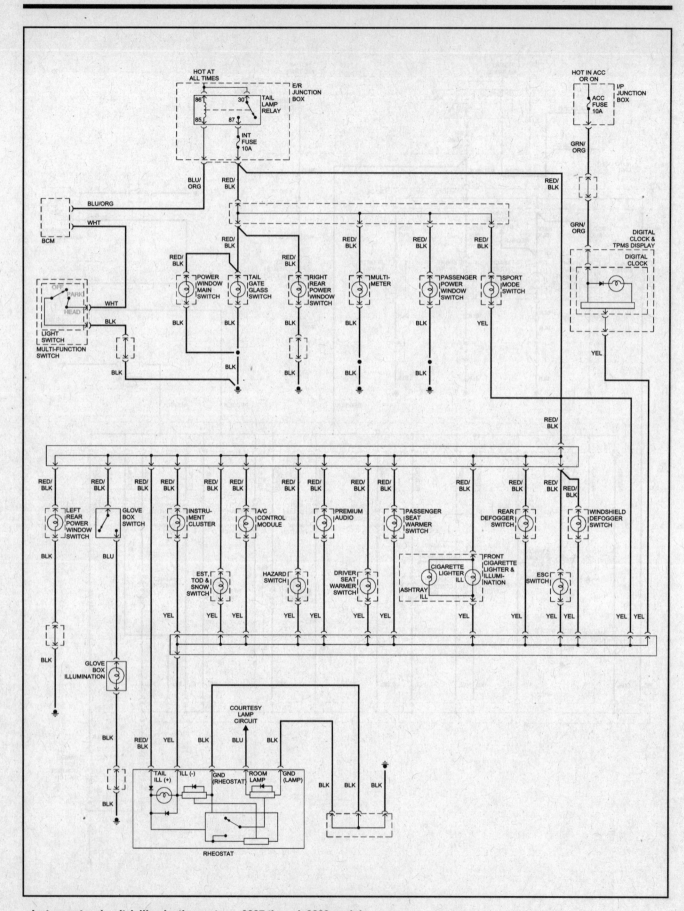

Instrument and switch illumination system - 2007 through 2009 models

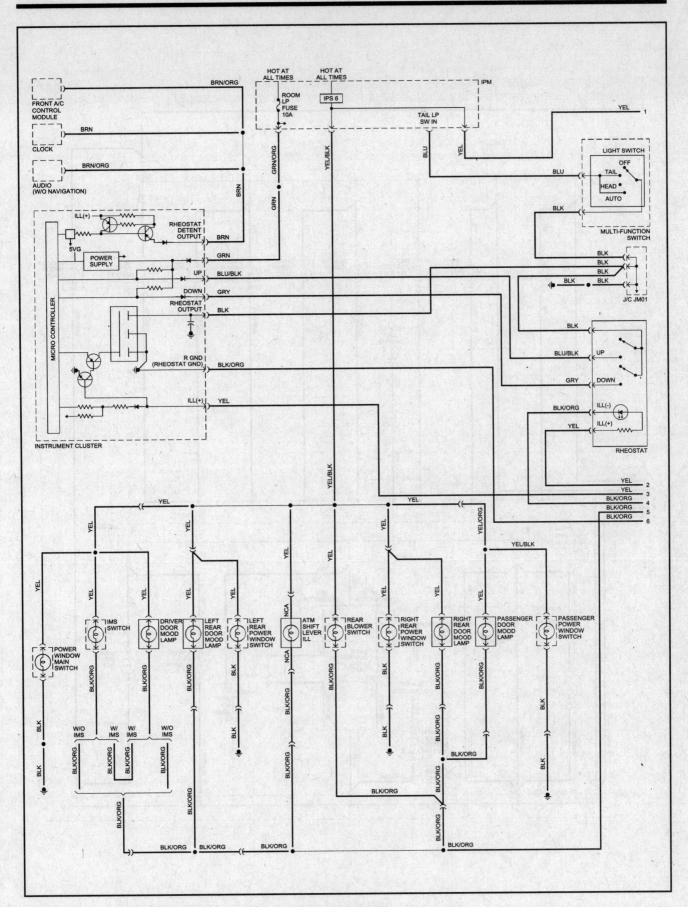

Instrument and switch illumination system - 2011 and later models (1 of 2)

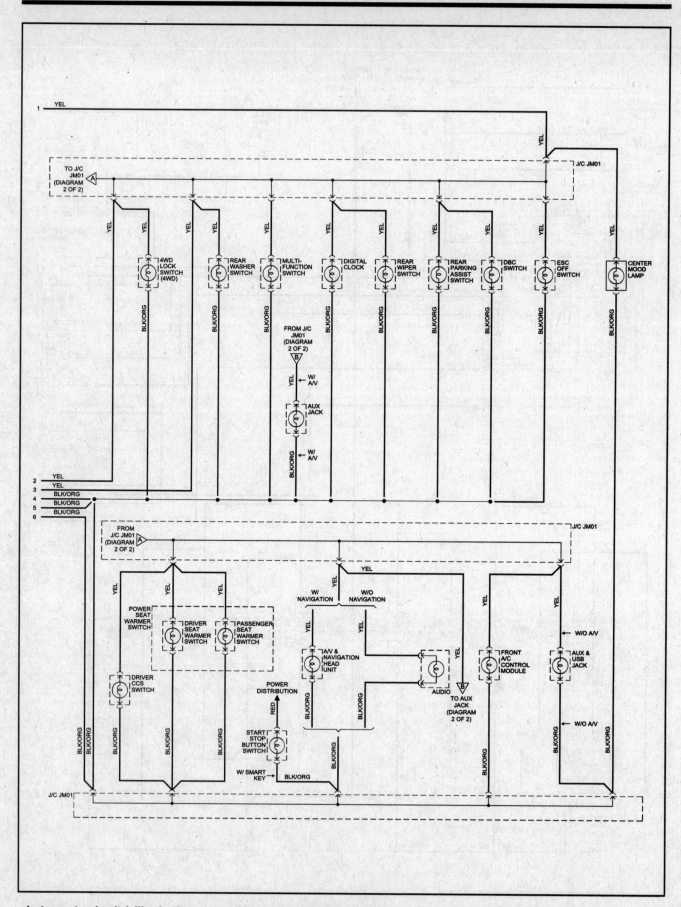

Instrument and switch illumination system - 2011 and later models (2 of 2)

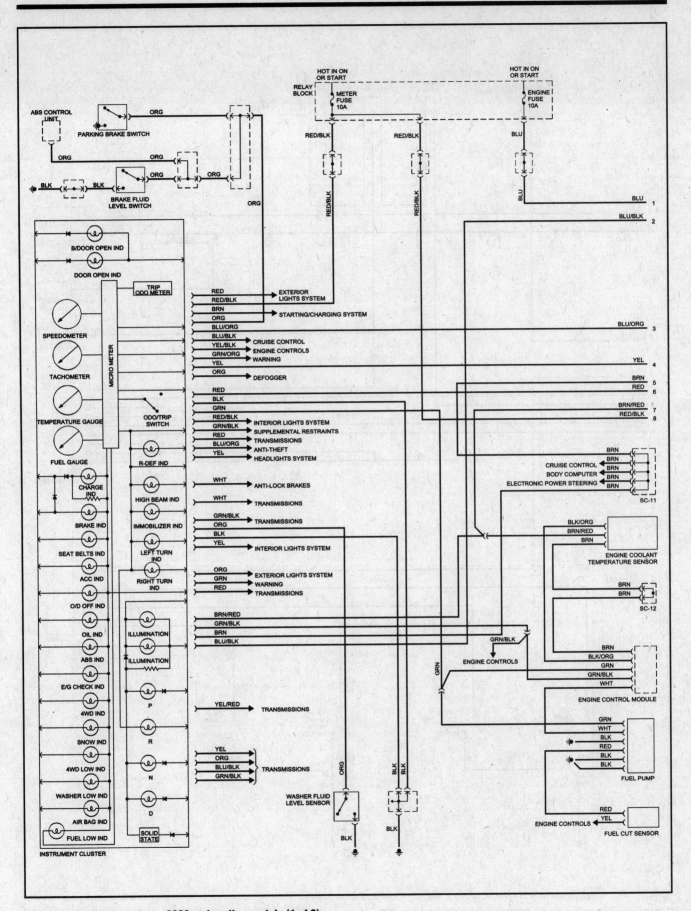

Instrument cluster system - 2006 and earlier models (1 of 2)

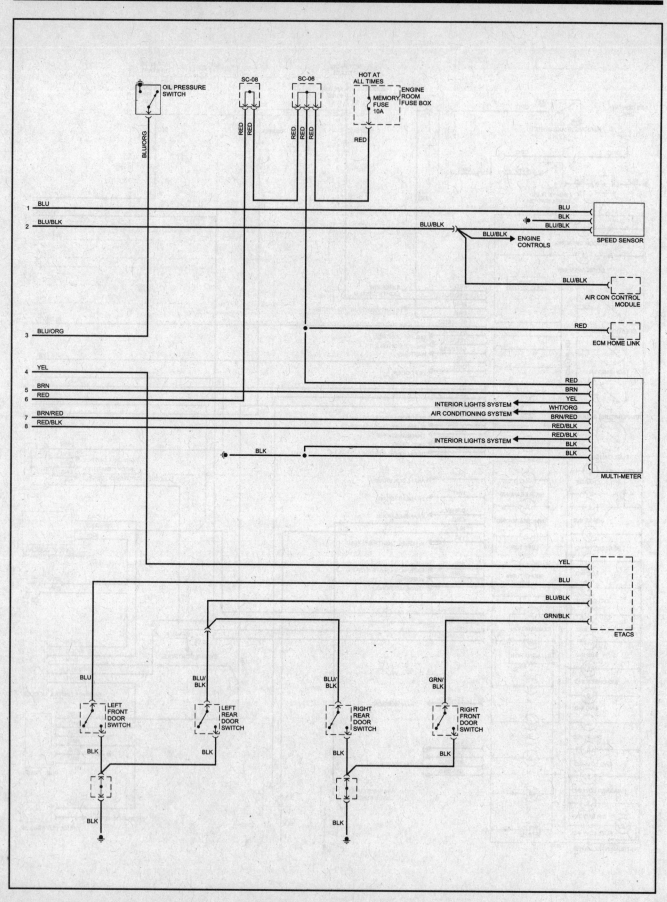

Instrument cluster system - 2006 and earlier models (2 of 2)

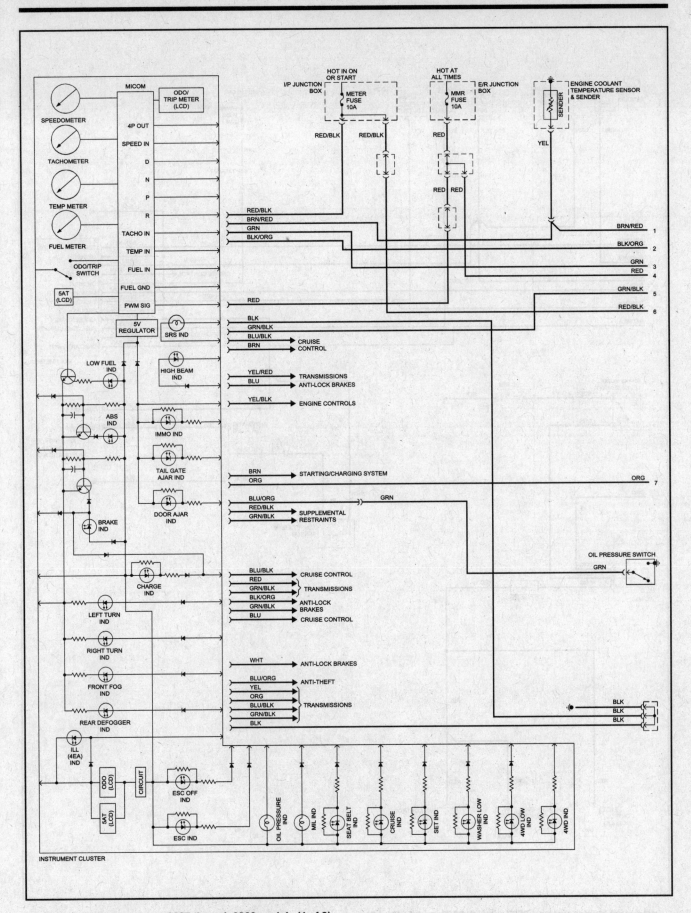

Instrument cluster system - 2007 through 2009 models (1 of 2)

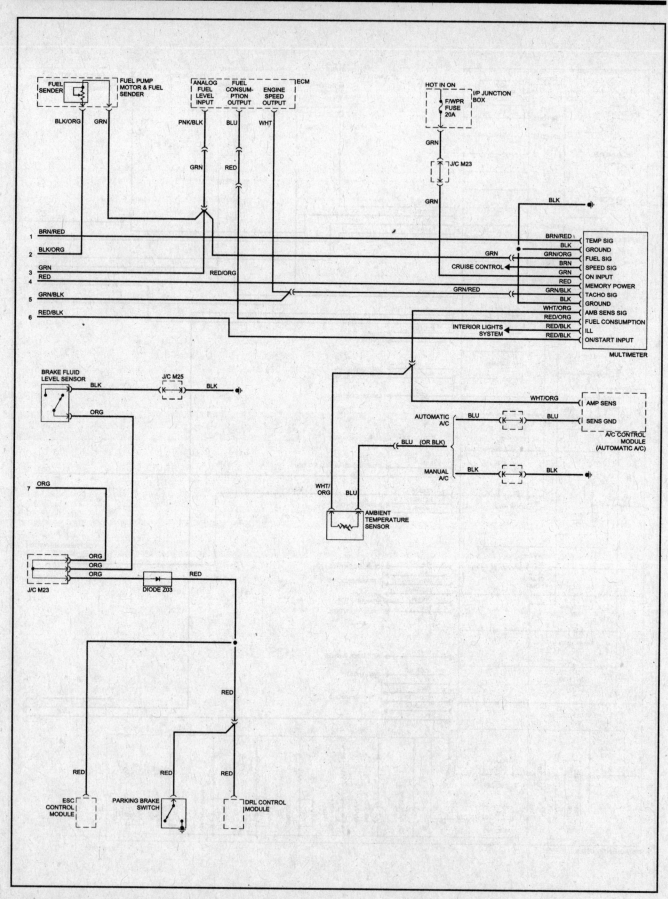

Instrument cluster system - 2007 through 2009 models (2 of 2)

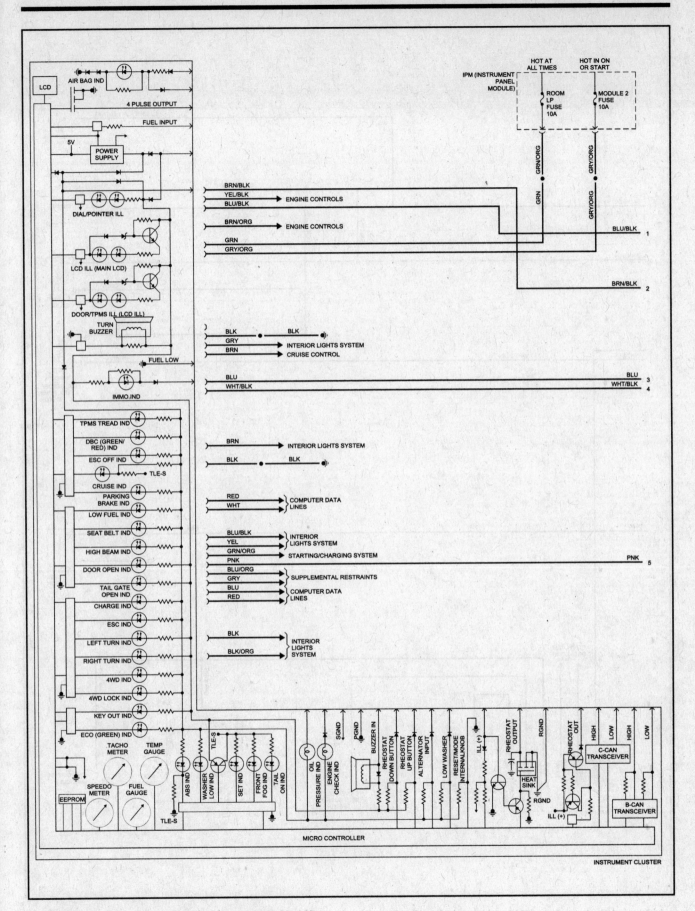

Instrument cluster system - 2011 and later models (1 of 2)

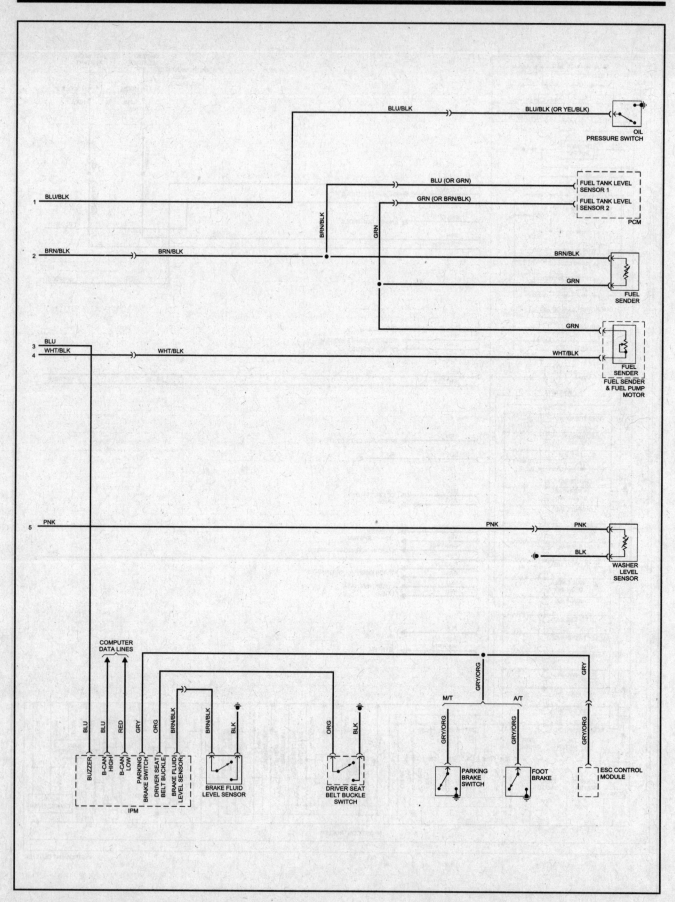

Instrument cluster system - 2011 and later models (2 of 2)

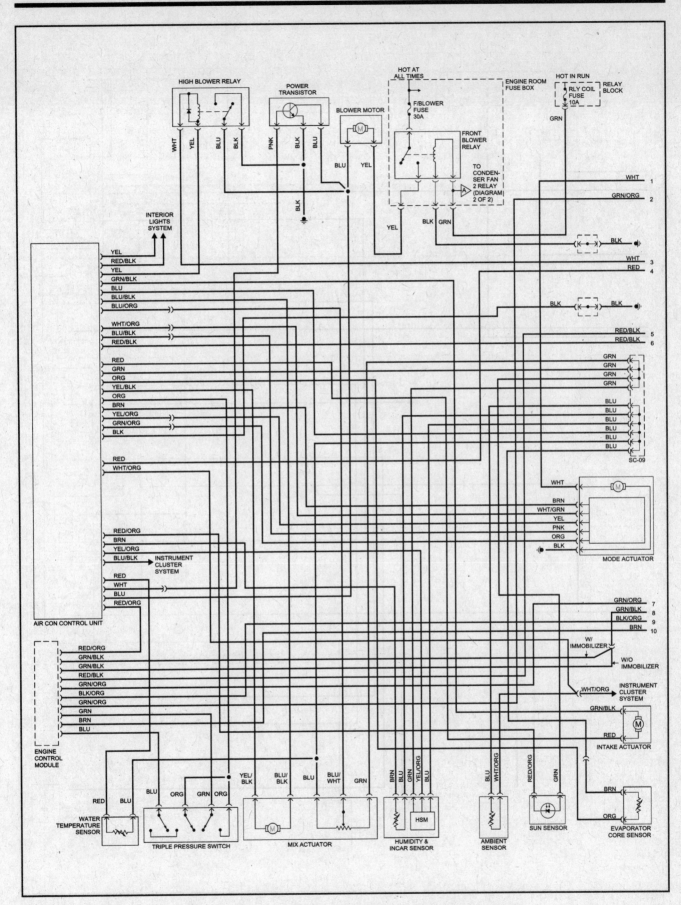

Heating, air conditioning (automatic) and engine cooling fan systems - 2006 and earlier models (1 of 2)

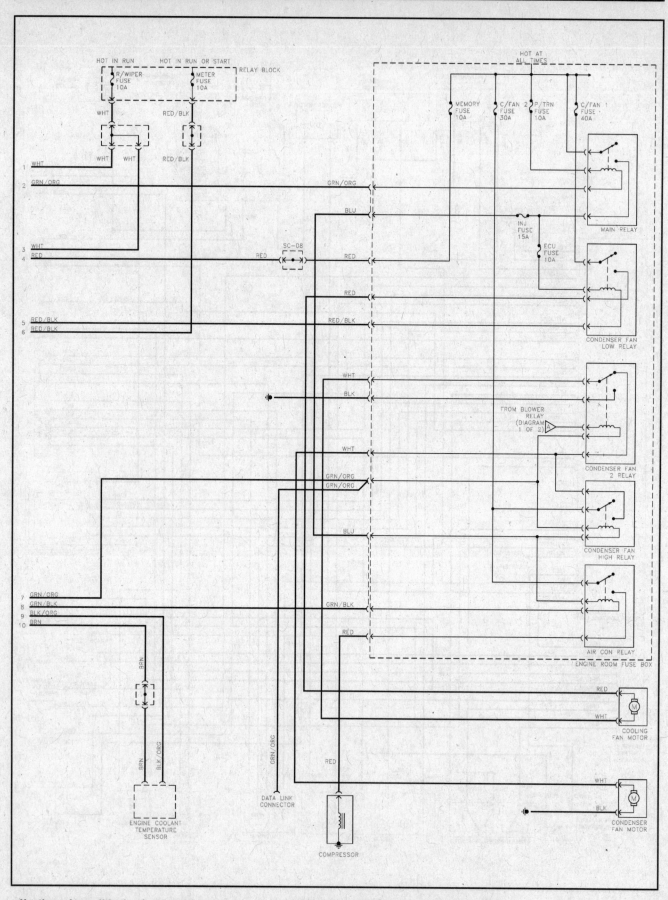

Heating, air conditioning (automatic) and engine cooling fan systems - 2006 and earlier models (2 of 2)

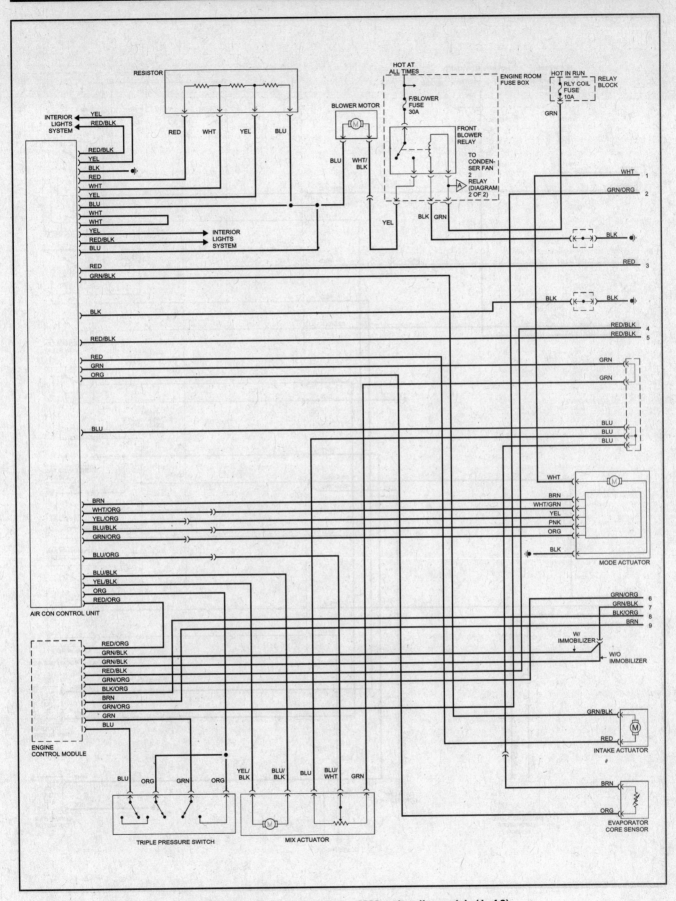

Heating, air conditioning (manual) and engine cooling fan systems - 2006 and earlier models (1 of 2)

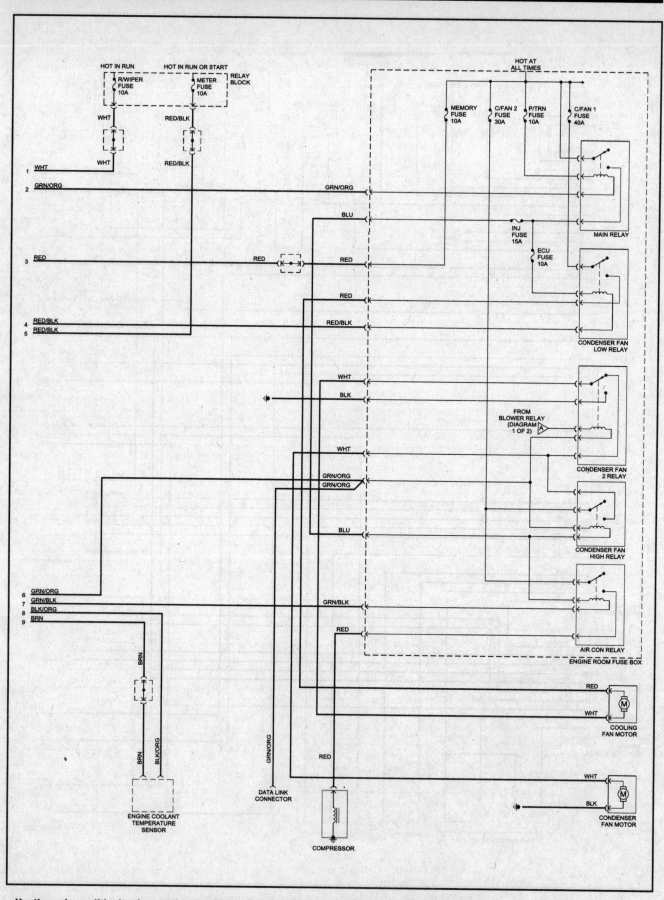

Heating, air conditioning (manual) and engine cooling fan systems - 2006 and earlier models (2 of 2)

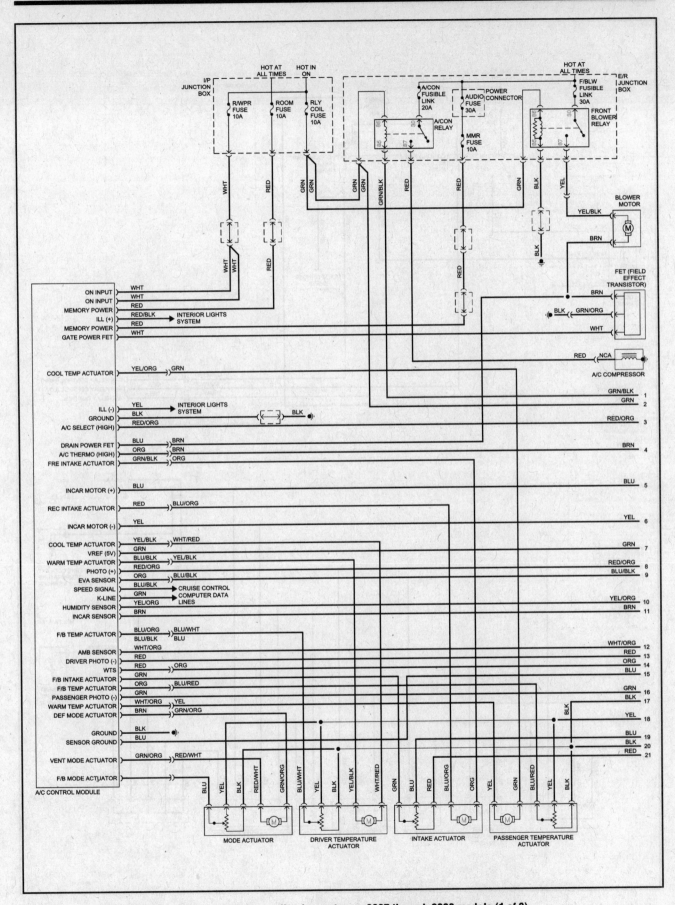

Heating, air conditioning (automatic) and engine cooling fan systems - 2007 through 2009 models (1 of 2)

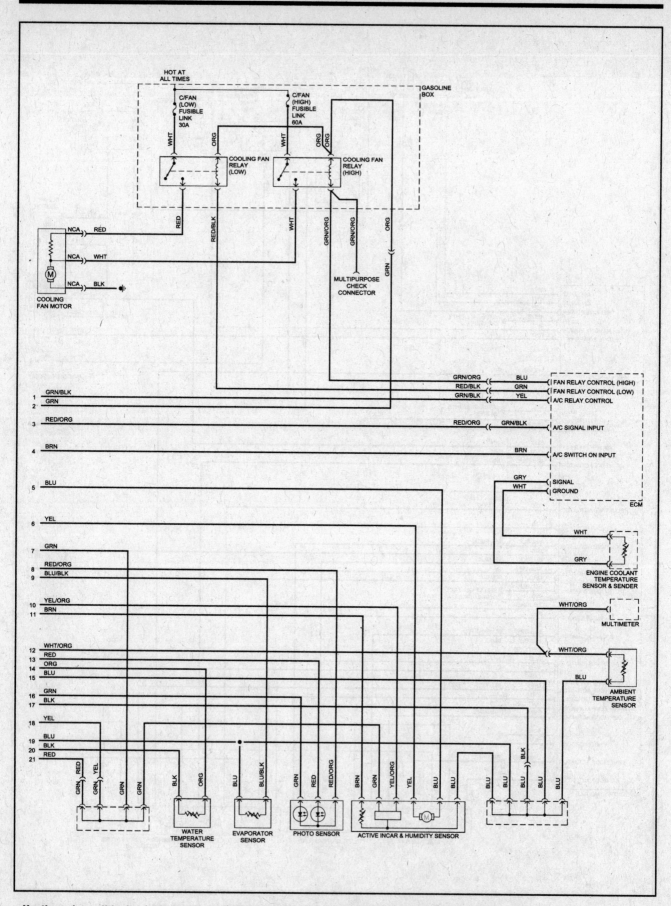

Heating, air conditioning (automatic) and engine cooling fan systems - 2007 through 2009 models (2 of 2)

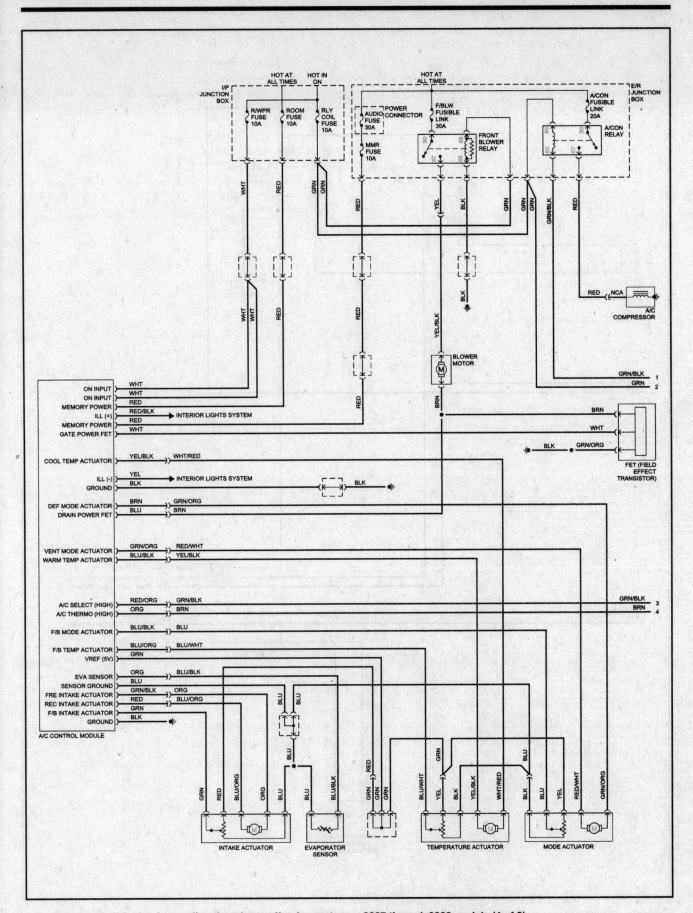

Heating, air conditioning (manual) and engine cooling fan systems - 2007 through 2009 models (1 of 2)

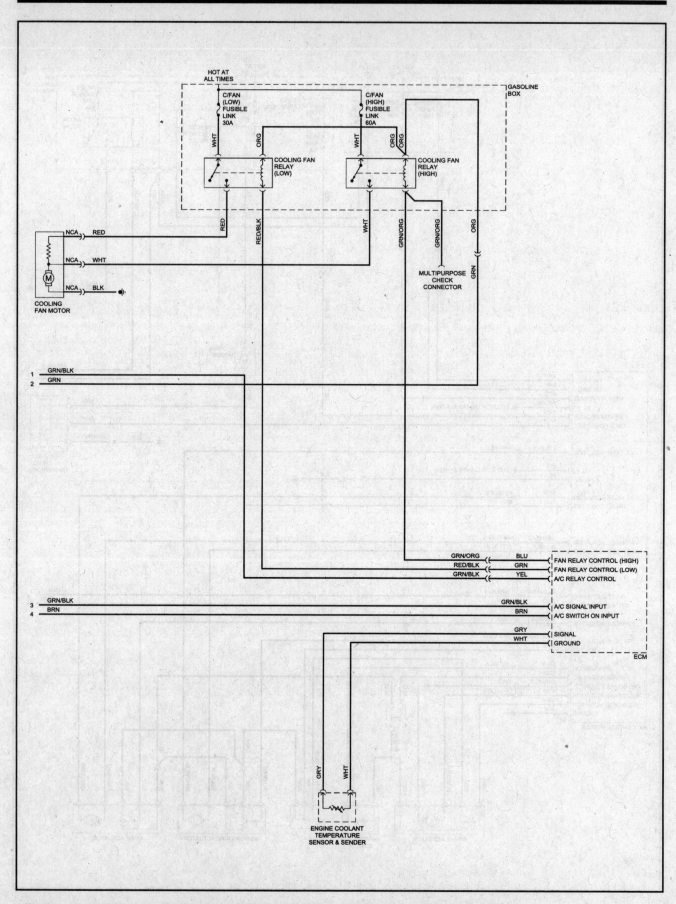

Heating, air conditioning (manual) and engine cooling fan systems - 2007 through 2009 models (2 of 2)

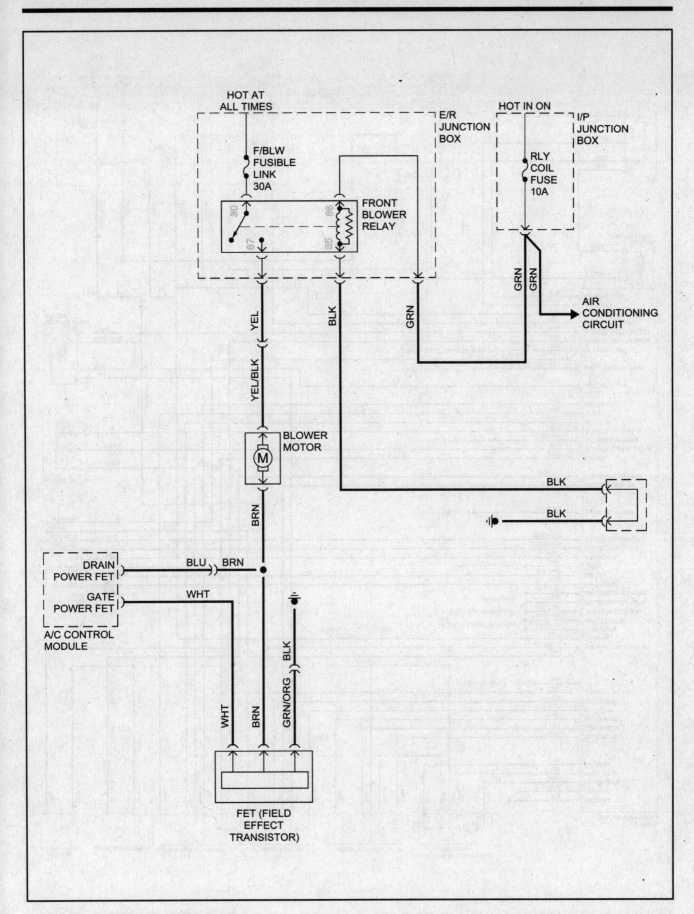

Heater circuit - 2007 through 2009 models

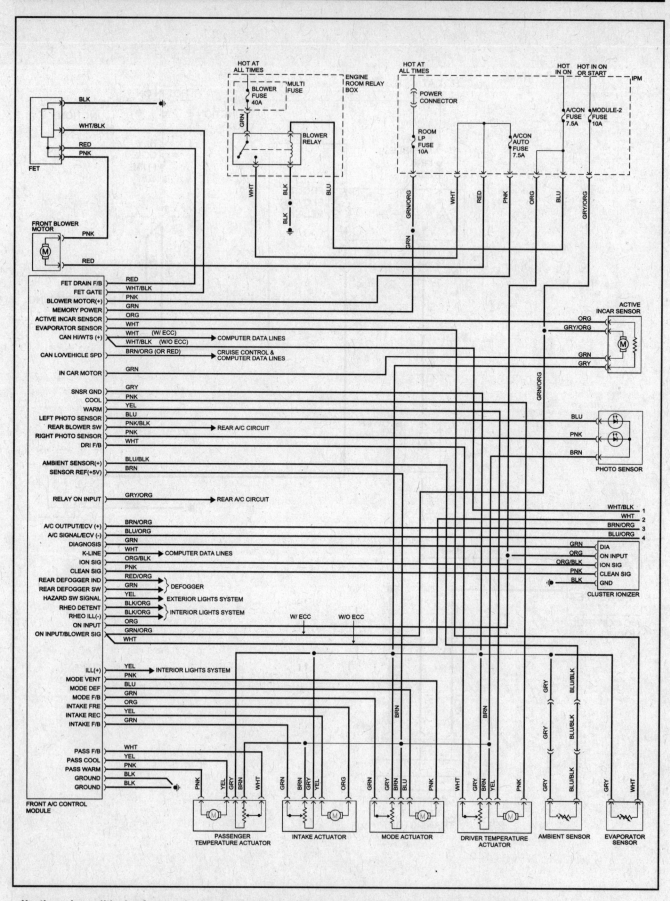

Heating, air conditioning (automatic, front) and engine cooling fan systems - 2012 and later models (1 of 2)

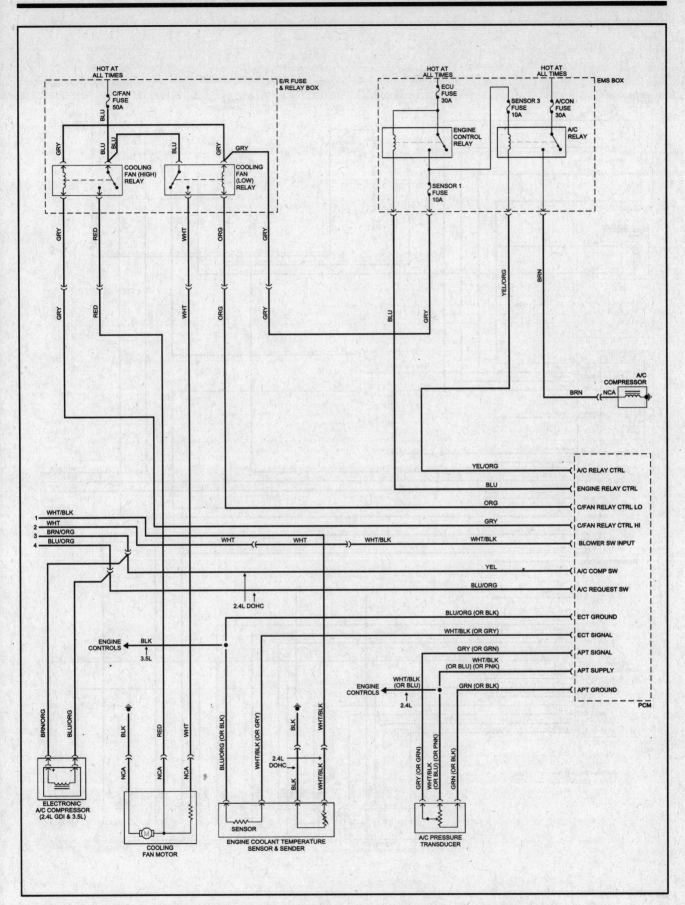

Heating, air conditioning (automatic AC, front) and engine cooling fan systems - 2012 and later models (2 of 2)

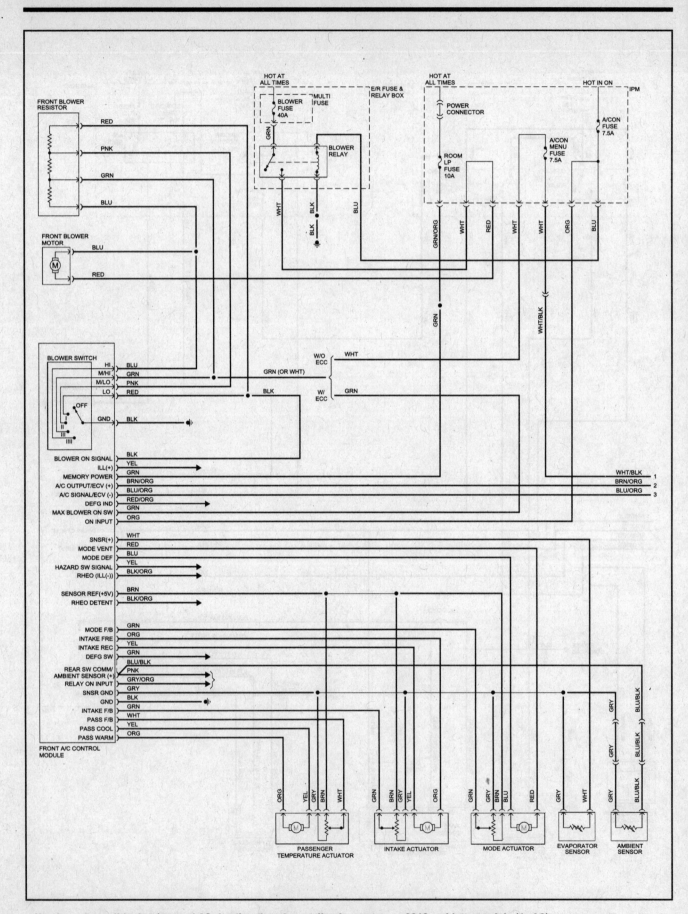

Heating, air conditioning (manual AC, front) and engine cooling fan systems - 2012 and later models (1 of 2)

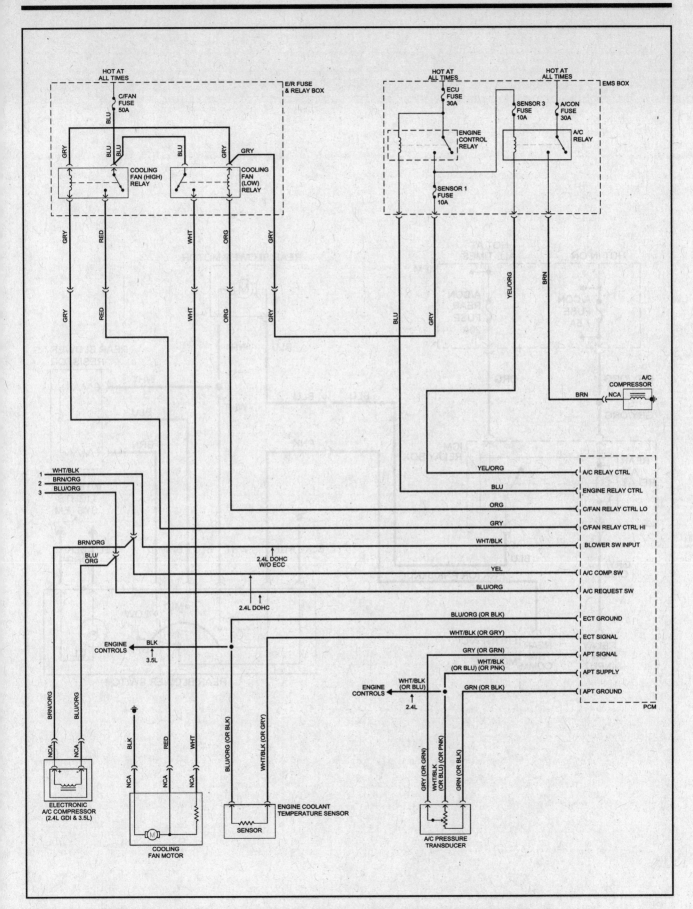

Heating, air conditioning (manual AC, front) and engine cooling fan systems - 2012 and later models (2 of 2)

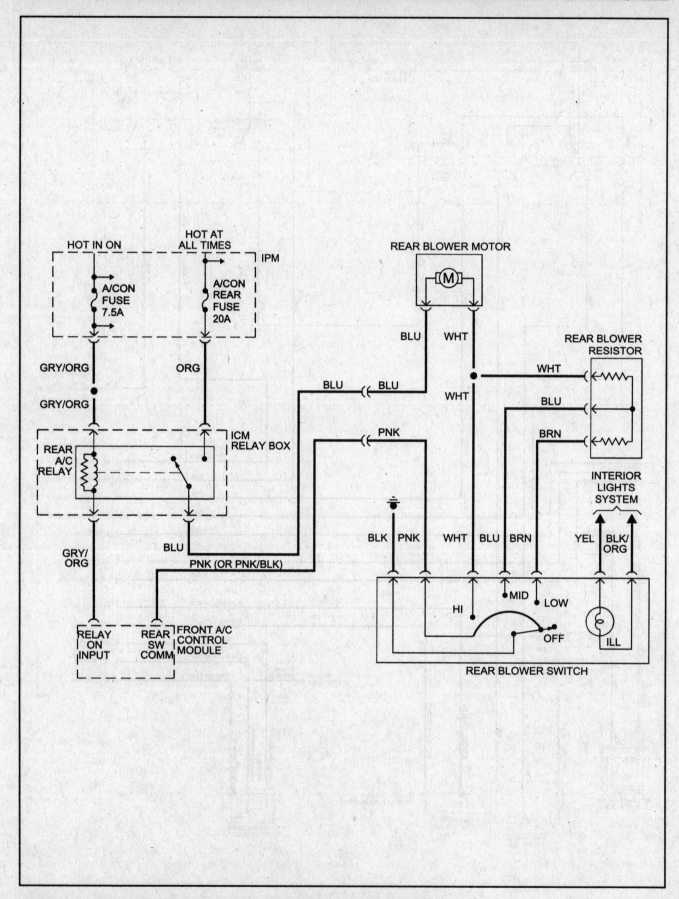

Heating, air conditioning (rear) and engine cooling fan systems - 2012 and later models

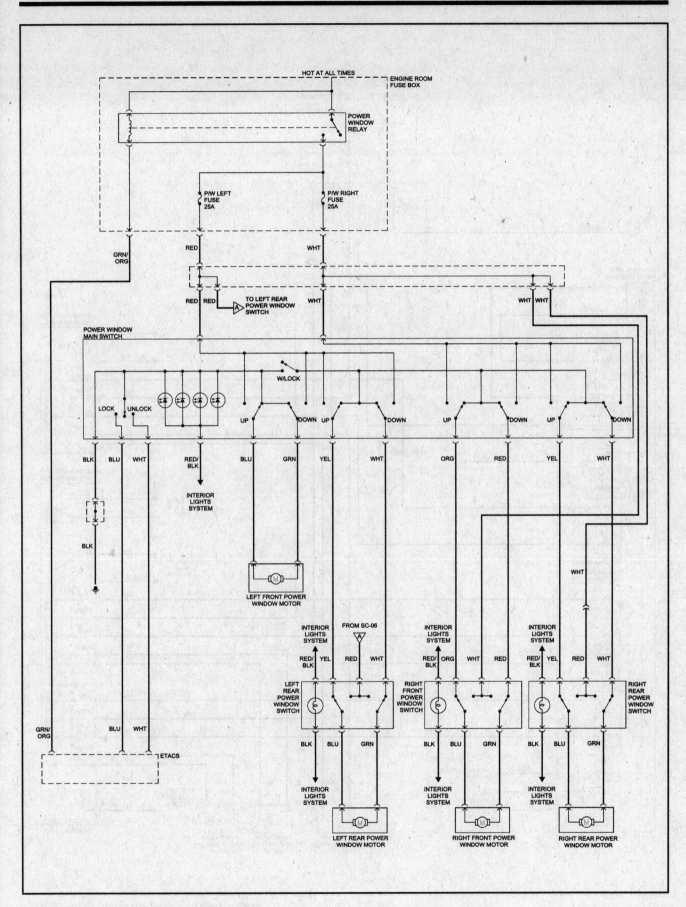

Power window system - 2006 and earlier models

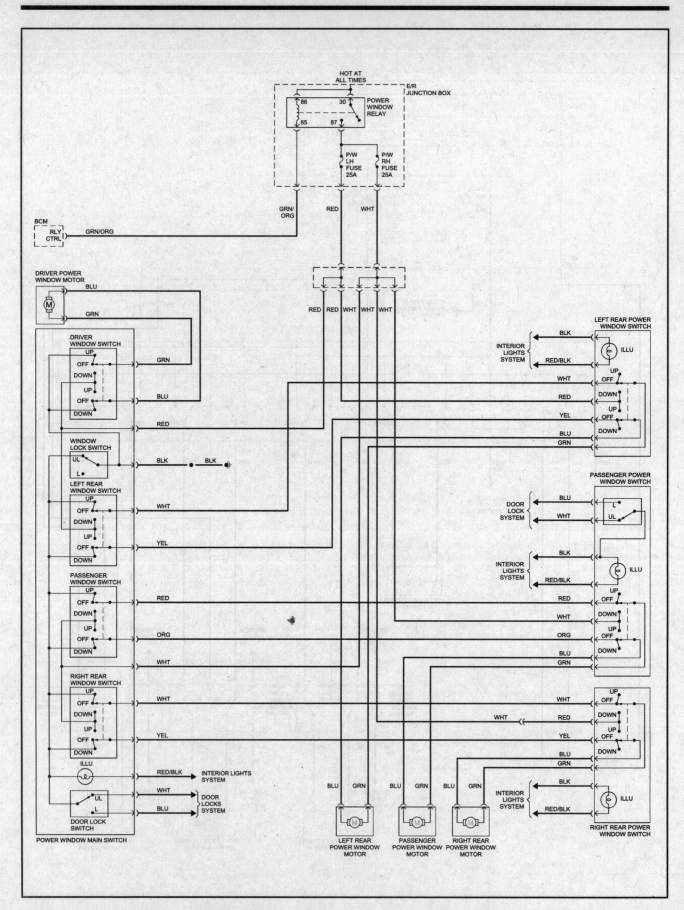

Power window system - 2007 through 2009 models

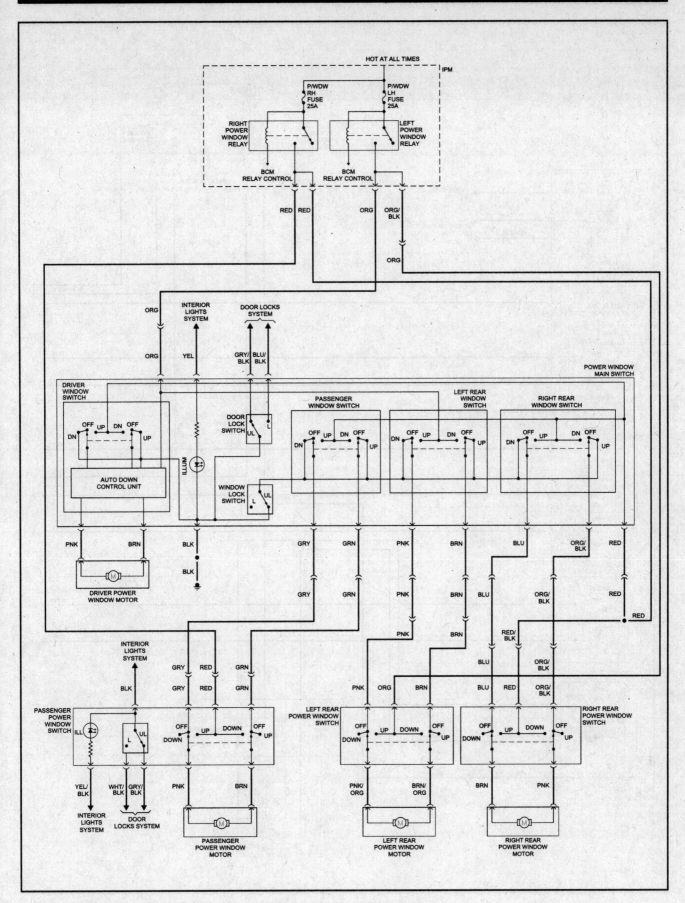

Power window system (without driver safety power windows) - 2011 and later models

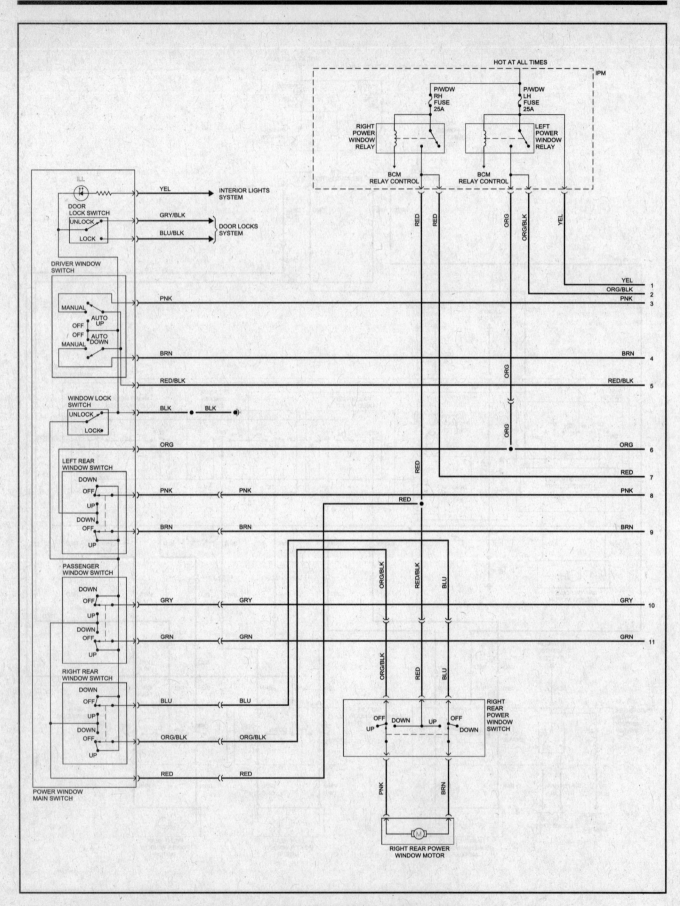

Power window system (with driver safety power windows) - 2011 and later models (1 of 2)

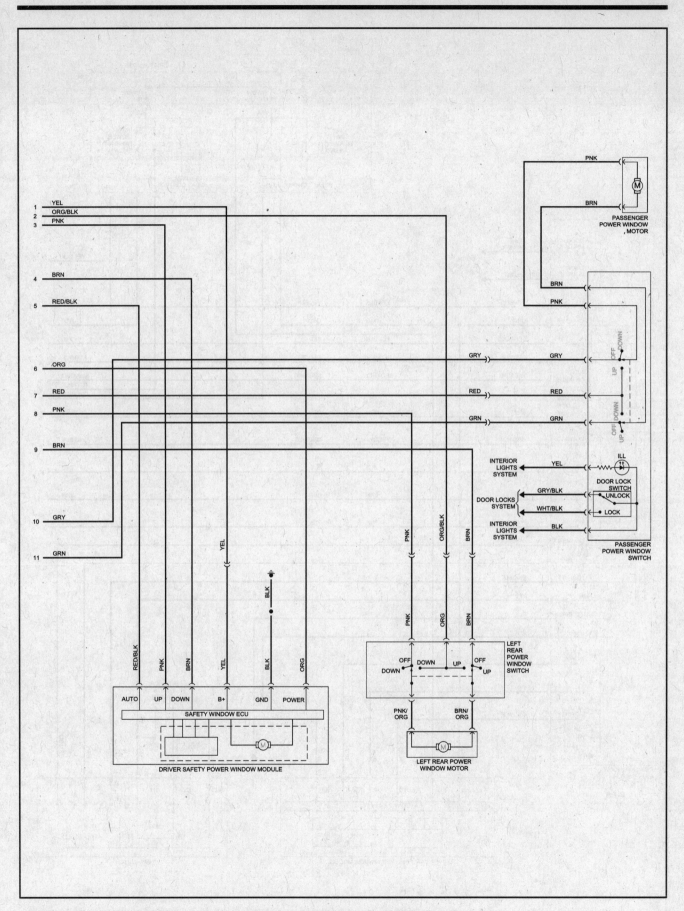

Power window system (with driver safety power windows) - 2011 and later models (2 of 2)

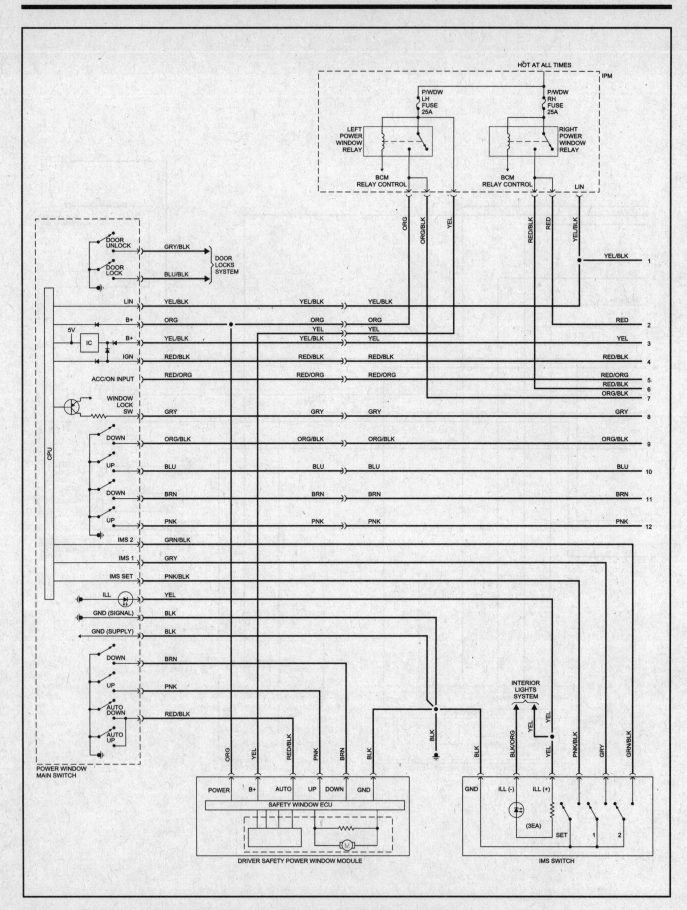

Power window system (with Integrated Memory System) - 2011 and later models (1 of 2)

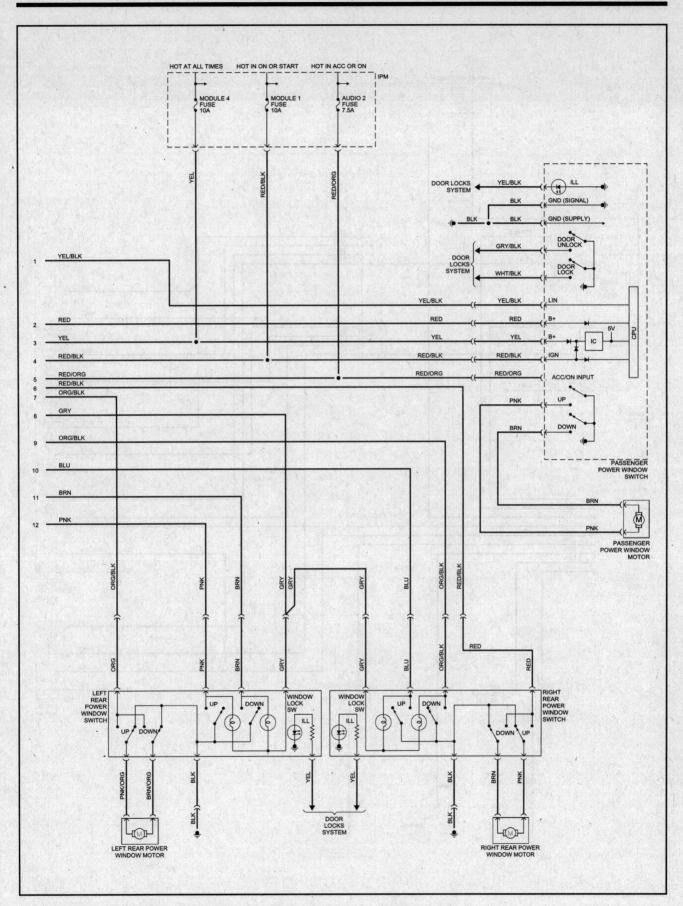

Power window system (with Integrated Memory System) - 2011 and later models (2 of 2)

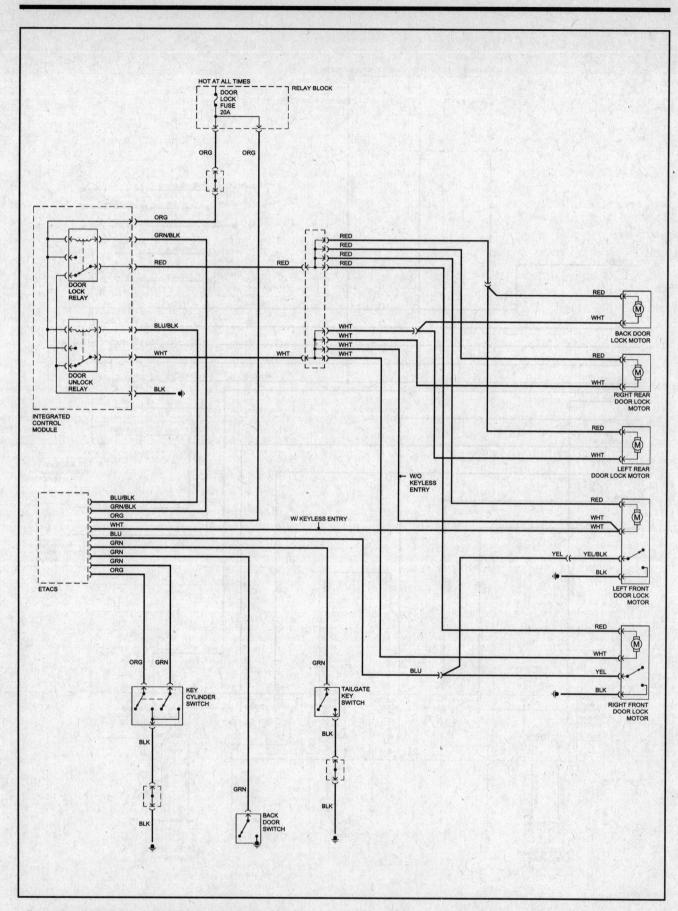

Power door lock system - 2006 and earlier models

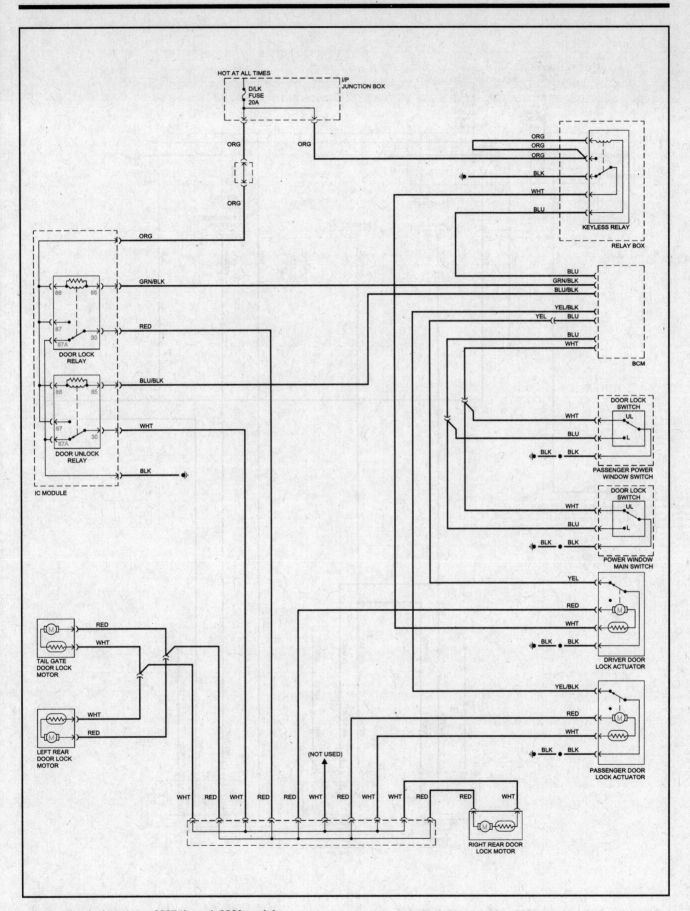

Power door lock system - 2007 through 2009 models

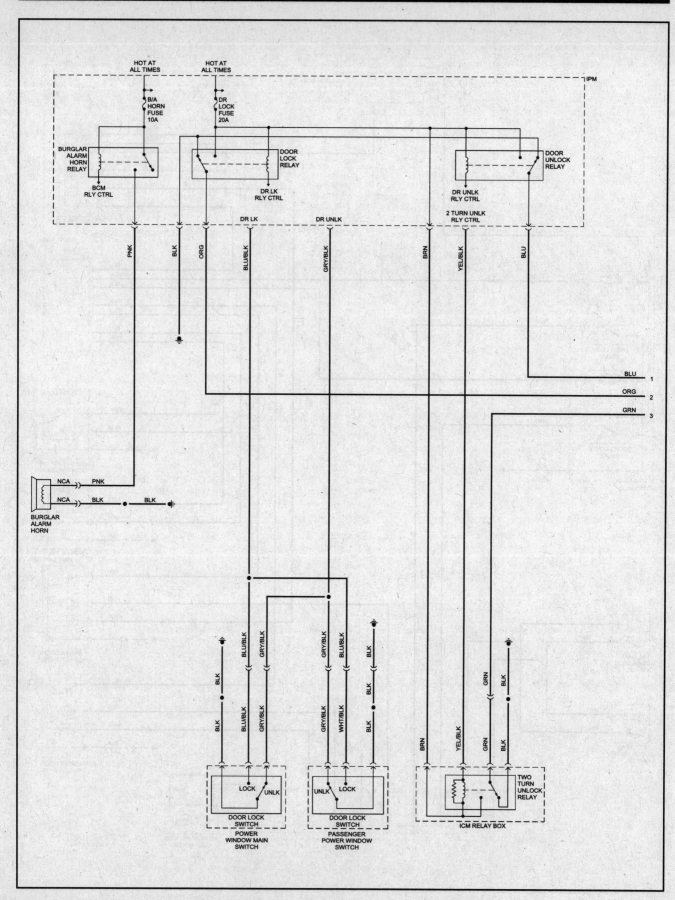

Power door lock system - 2011 and later models (1 of 2)

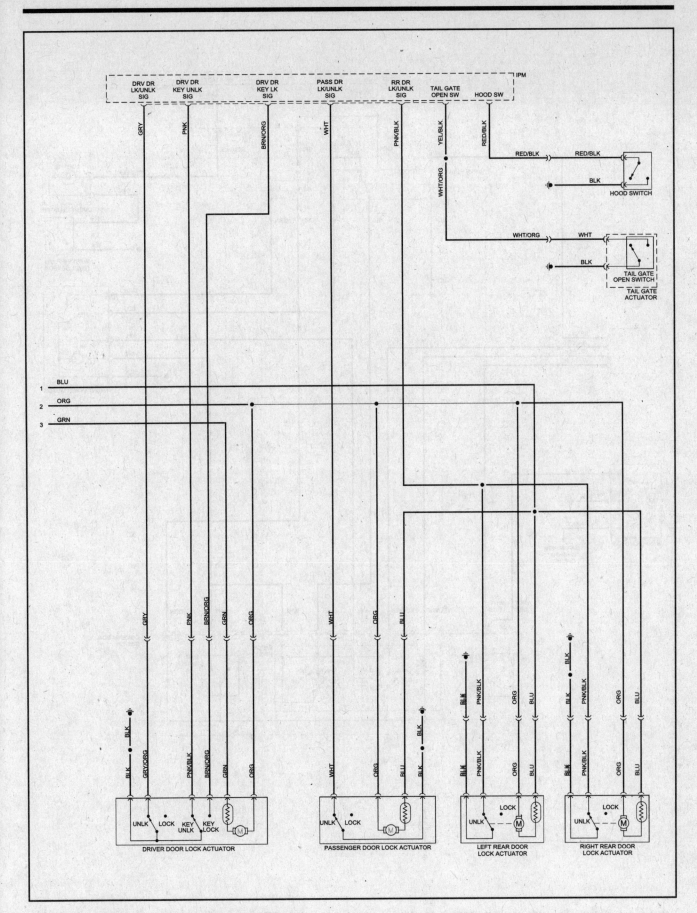

Power door lock system - 2011 and later models (2 of 2)

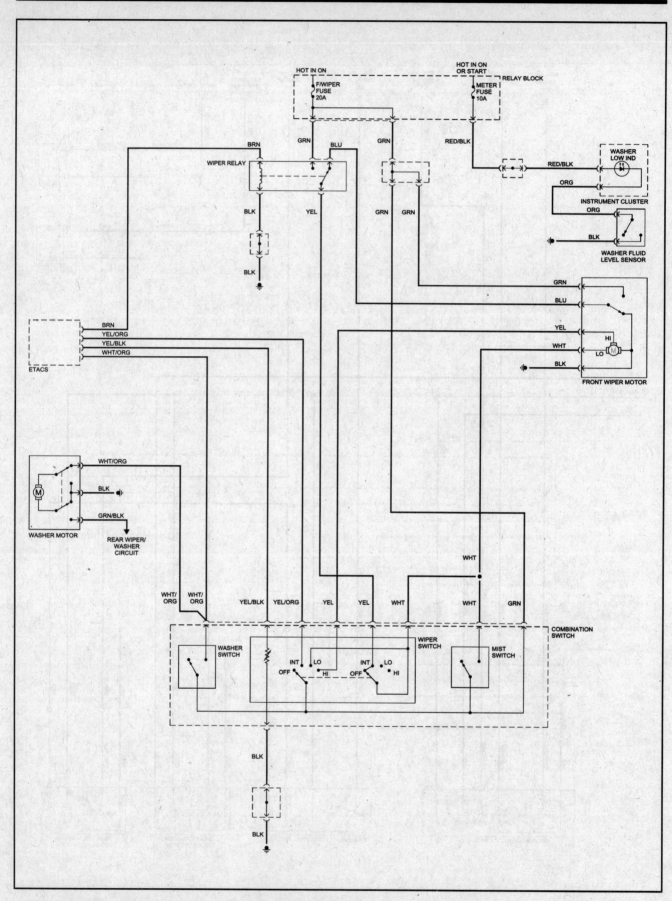

Wiper and washer system (front wiper) - 2006 and earlier models (1 of 2)

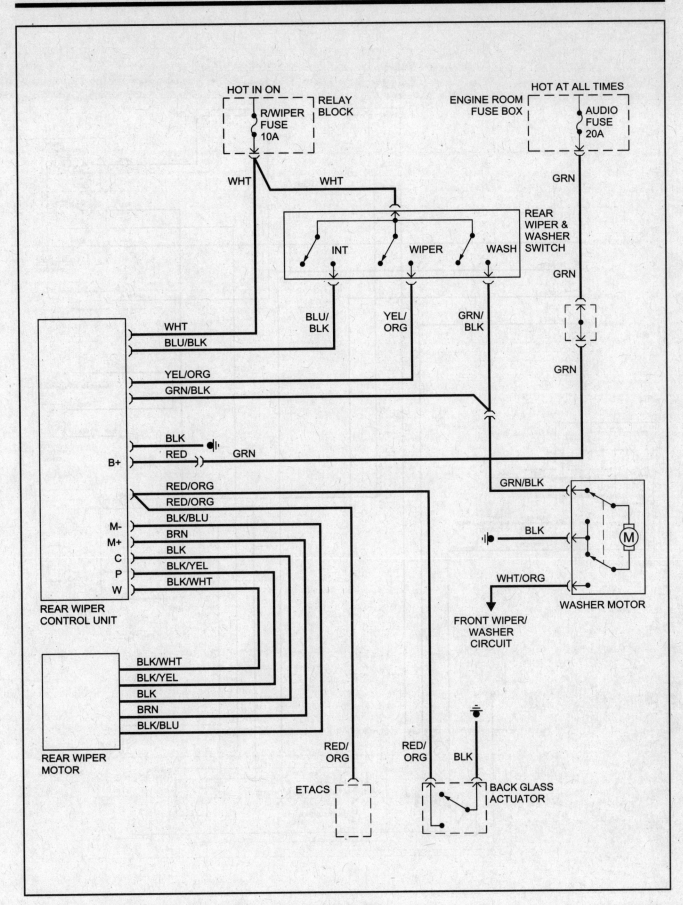

Wiper and washer system (rear wiper) - 2006 and earlier models (2 of 2)

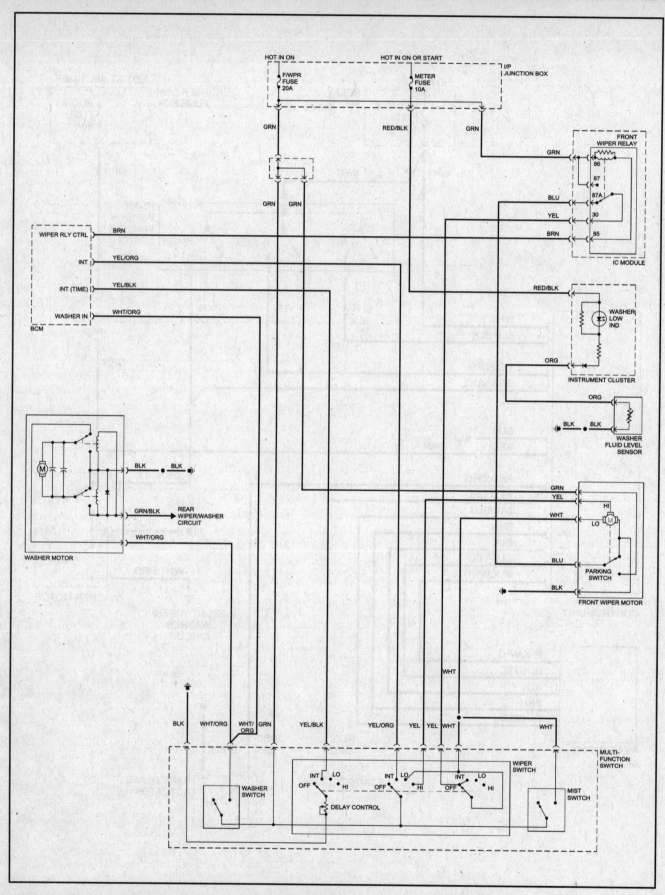

Wiper and washer system (front wiper) - 2007 through 2009 (1 of 2)

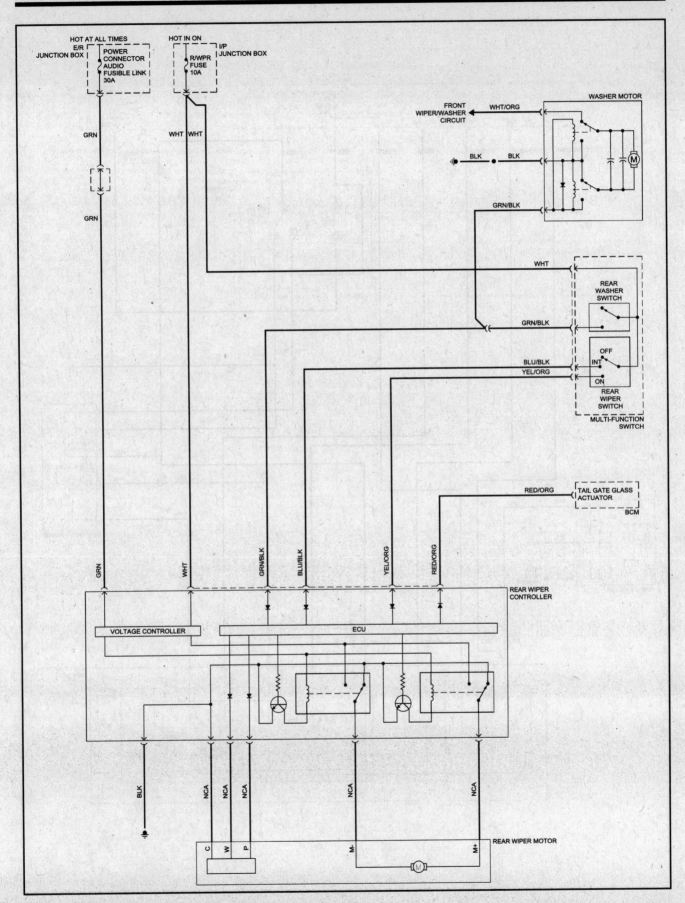

Wiper and washer system (rear wiper) - 2007 through 2009 (2 of 2)

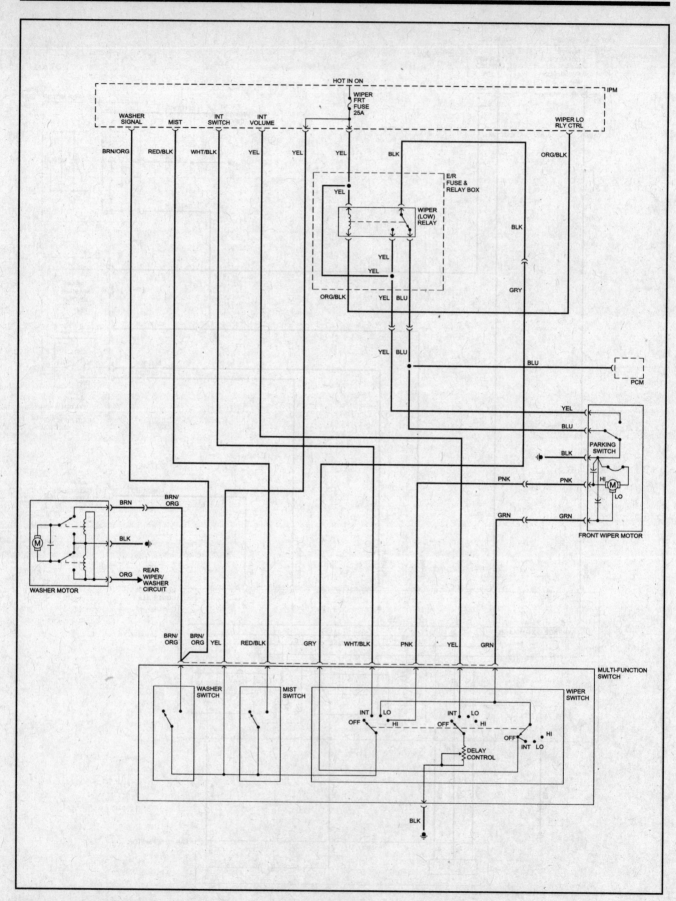

Wiper and washer system (front wiper) - 2011 and later models (1 of 2)

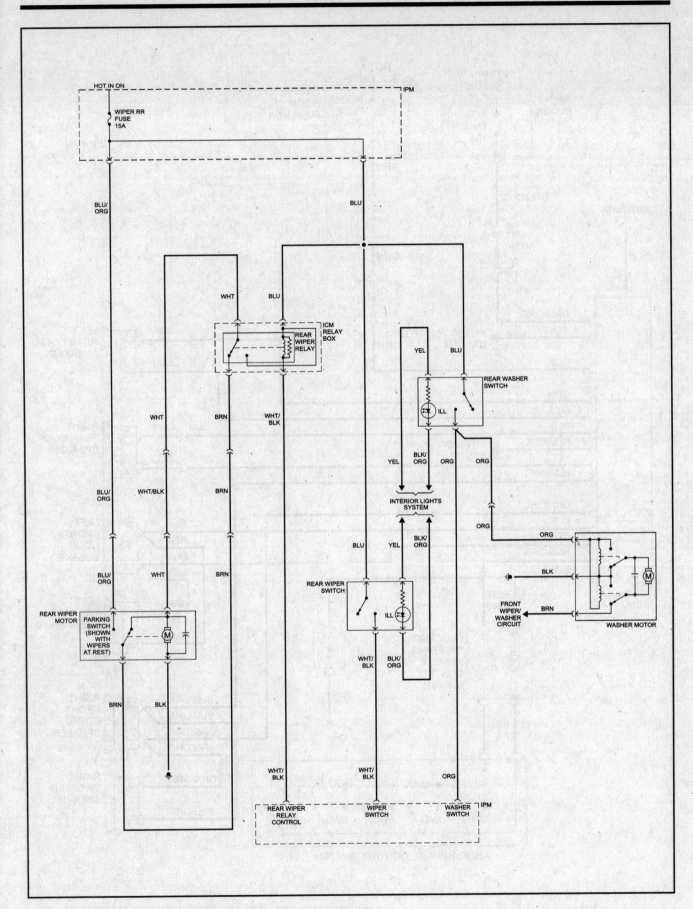

Wiper and washer system (rear wiper) - 2011 and later models (2 of 2)

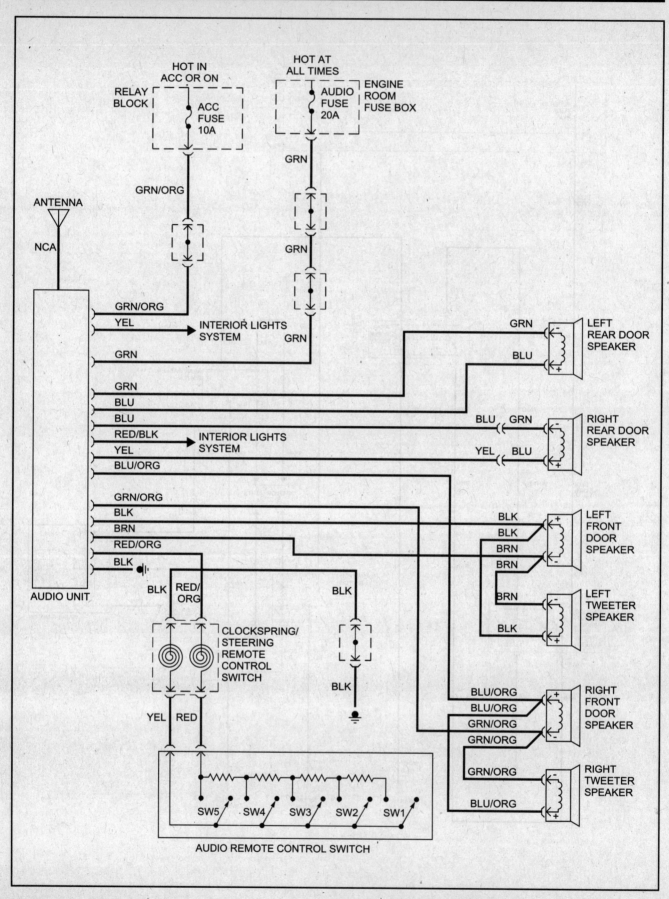

Audio system - 2006 and earlier models

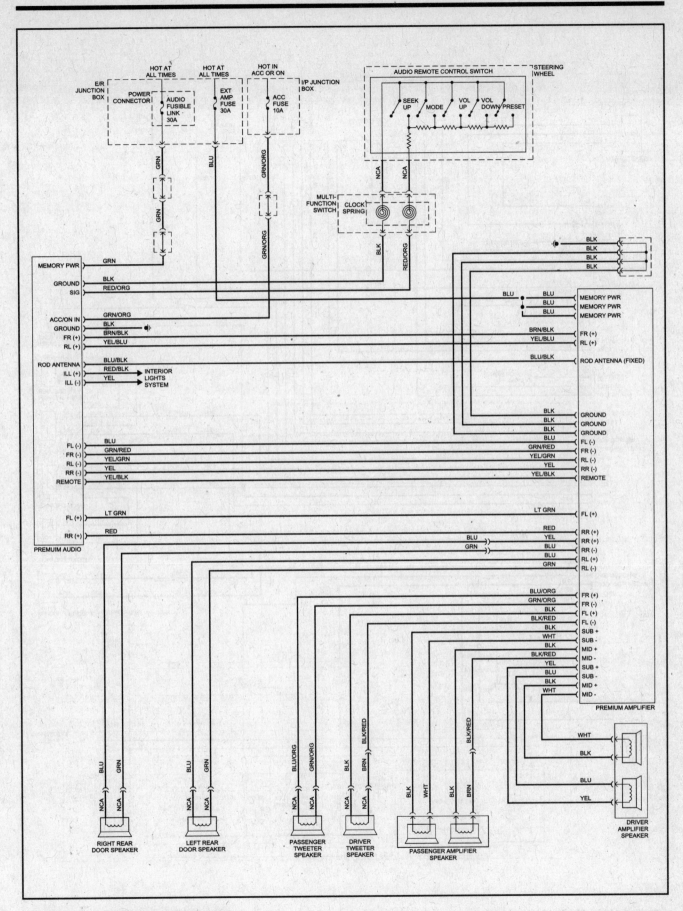

Audio system - 2007 through 2009 models

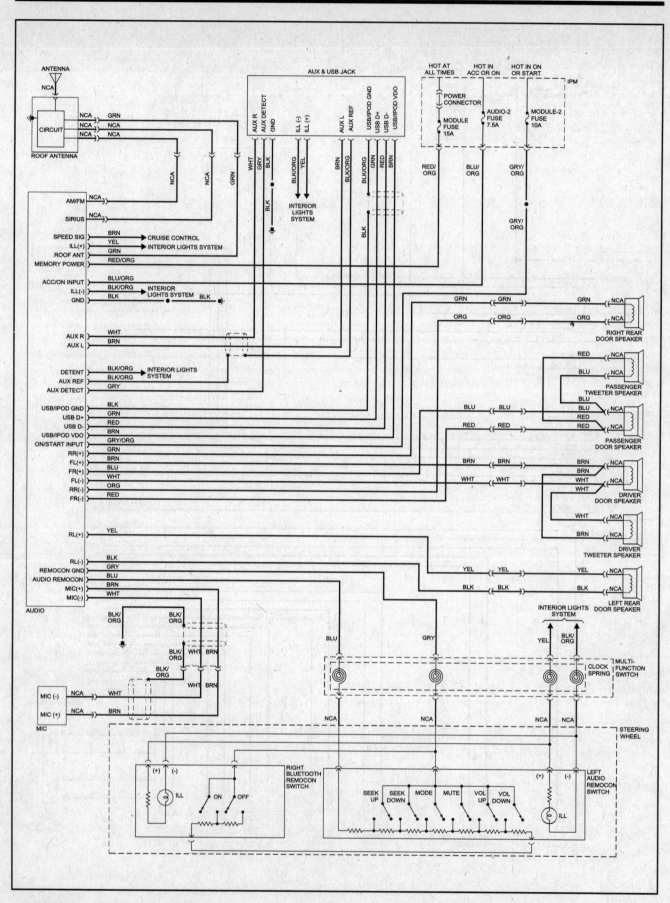

Audio system - 2011 and later models

GLOSSARY

AIR/FUEL RATIO: The ratio of air-to-gasoline by weight in the fuel mixture drawn into the engine.

AIR INJECTION: One method of reducing harmful exhaust emissions by injecting air into each of the exhaust ports of an engine. The fresh air entering the hot exhaust manifold causes any remaining fuel to be burned before it can exit the tailpipe.

ALTERNATOR: A device used for converting mechanical energy into electrical energy.

AMMETER: An instrument, calibrated in amperes, used to measure the flow of an electrical current in a circuit. Ammeters are always connected in series with the circuit being tested.

AMPERE: The rate of flow of electrical current present when one volt of electrical pressure is applied against one ohm of electrical resistance.

ANALOG COMPUTER: Any microprocessor that uses similar (analogous) electrical signals to make its calculations.

ARMATURE: A laminated, soft iron core wrapped by a wire that converts electrical energy to mechanical energy as in a motor or relay. When rotated in a magnetic field, it changes mechanical energy into electrical energy as in a generator.

ATMOSPHERIC PRESSURE: The pressure on the Earth's surface caused by the weight of the air in the atmosphere. At sea level, this pressure is 14.7 psi at 32°F (101 kPa at 0°C).

ATOMIZATION: The breaking down of a liquid into a fine mist that can be suspended in air.

AXIAL PLAY: Movement parallel to a shaft or bearing bore.

BACKFIRE: The sudden combustion of gases in the intake or exhaust system that results in a loud explosion.

BACKLASH: The clearance or play between two parts, such as meshed gears.

BACKPRESSURE: Restrictions in the exhaust system that slow the exit of exhaust gases from the combustion chamber.

BAKELITE: A heat resistant, plastic insulator material commonly used in printed circuit boards and transistorized components.

BALL BEARING: A bearing made up of hardened inner and outer races between which hardened steel balls roll.

BALLAST RESISTOR: A resistor in the primary ignition circuit that lowers voltage after the engine is started to reduce wear on ignition components.

BEARING: A friction reducing, supportive device usually located between a stationary part and a moving part.

BIMETAL TEMPERATURE SENSOR: Any sensor or switch made of two dissimilar types of metal that bend when heated or cooled due to the different expansion rates of the alloys. These types of sensors usually function as an on/off switch.

BLOWBY: Combustion gases, composed of water vapor and unburned fuel, that leak past the piston rings into the crankcase during normal engine operation. These gases are removed by the PCV system to prevent the buildup of harmful acids in the crankcase.

BRAKE PAD: A brake shoe and lining assembly used with disc brakes.

BRAKE SHOE: The backing for the brake lining. The term is, however, usually applied to the assembly of the brake backing and lining.

BUSHING: A liner, usually removable, for a bearing; an anti-friction liner used in place of a bearing.

CALIPER: A hydraulically activated device in a disc brake system, which is mounted straddling the brake rotor (disc). The caliper contains at least one piston and two brake pads. Hydraulic pressure on the piston(s) forces the pads against the rotor.

CAMSHAFT: A shaft in the engine on which are the lobes (cams) which operate the valves. The camshaft is driven by the crankshaft, via a belt, chain or gears, at one half the crankshaft speed.

CAPACITOR: A device which stores an electrical charge.

CARBON MONOXIDE (CO): A colorless, odorless gas given off as a normal byproduct of combustion. It is poisonous and extremely dangerous in confined areas, building up slowly to toxic levels without warning if adequate ventilation is not available.

CARBURETOR: A device, usually mounted on the intake manifold of an engine, which mixes the air and fuel in the proper proportion to allow even combustion.

CATALYTIC CONVERTER: A device installed in the exhaust system, like a muffler, that converts harmful byproducts of combustion into carbon dioxide and water vapor by means of a heat-producing chemical reaction.

CENTRIFUGAL ADVANCE: A mechanical method of advancing the spark timing by using flyweights in the distributor that react to centrifugal force generated by the distributor shaft rotation.

CHECK VALVE: Any one-way valve installed to permit the flow of air, fuel or vacuum in one direction only.

CHOKE: A device, usually a moveable valve, placed in the intake path of a carburetor to restrict the flow of air.

CIRCUIT: Any unbroken path through which an electrical current can flow. Also used to describe fuel flow in some instances.

CIRCUIT BREAKER: A switch which protects an electrical circuit from overload by opening the circuit when the current flow exceeds a predetermined level. Some circuit breakers must be reset manually, while most reset automatically.

COIL (IGNITION): A transformer in the ignition circuit which steps up the voltage provided to the spark plugs.

COMBINATION MANIFOLD: An assembly which includes both the intake and exhaust manifolds in one casting.

COMBINATION VALVE: A device used in some fuel systems that routes fuel vapors to a charcoal storage canister instead of venting them into the atmosphere. The valve relieves fuel tank pressure and allows fresh air into the tank as the fuel level drops to prevent a vapor lock situation.

COMPRESSION RATIO: The comparison of the total volume of the cylinder and combustion chamber with the piston at BDC and the piston at TDC.

CONDENSER: 1. An electrical device which acts to store an electrical charge, preventing voltage surges. 2. A radiator-like device in the air conditioning system in which refrigerant gas condenses into a liquid, giving off heat.

CONDUCTOR: Any material through which an electrical current can be transmitted easily.

CONTINUITY: Continuous or complete circuit. Can be checked with an ohmmeter.

COUNTERSHAFT: An intermediate shaft which is rotated by a mainshaft and transmits, in turn, that rotation to a working part.

CRANKCASE: The lower part of an engine in which the crankshaft and related parts operate.

CRANKSHAFT: The main driving shaft of an engine which receives reciprocating motion from the pistons and converts it to rotary motion.

CYLINDER: In an engine, the round hole in the engine block in which the piston(s) ride.

CYLINDER BLOCK: The main structural member of an engine in which is found the cylinders, crankshaft and other principal parts.

CYLINDER HEAD: The detachable portion of the engine, usually fastened to the top of the cylinder block and containing all or most of the combustion chambers. On overhead valve engines, it contains the valves and their operating parts. On overhead cam engines, it contains the camshaft as well.

DEAD CENTER: The extreme top or bottom of the piston stroke.

DETONATION: An unwanted explosion of the air/fuel mixture in the combustion chamber caused by excess heat and compression, advanced timing, or an overly lean mixture. Also referred to as "ping".

DIAPHRAGM: A thin, flexible wall separating two cavities, such as in a vacuum advance unit.

DIESELING: A condition in which hot spots in the combustion chamber cause the engine to run on after the key is turned off.

DIFFERENTIAL: A geared assembly which allows the transmission of motion between drive axles, giving one axle the ability to turn faster than the other.

DIODE: An electrical device that will allow current to flow in one direction only.

DISC BRAKE: A hydraulic braking assembly consisting of a brake disc, or rotor, mounted on an axle, and a caliper assembly containing, usually two brake pads which are activated by hydraulic pressure. The pads are forced against the sides of the disc, creating friction which slows the vehicle.

DISTRIBUTOR: A mechanically driven device on an engine which is responsible for electrically firing the spark plug at a predetermined point of the piston stroke.

DOWEL PIN: A pin, inserted in mating holes in two different parts allowing those parts to maintain a fixed relationship.

DRUM BRAKE: A braking system which consists of two brake shoes and one or two wheel cylinders, mounted on a fixed backing plate, and a brake drum, mounted on an axle, which revolves around the assembly.

DWELL: The rate, measured in degrees of shaft rotation, at which an electrical circuit cycles on and off.

ELECTRONIC CONTROL UNIT (ECU): Ignition module, module, amplifier or igniter. See Module for definition.

ELECTRONIC IGNITION: A system in which the timing and firing of the spark plugs is controlled by an electronic control unit, usually called a module. These systems have no points or condenser.

END-PLAY: The measured amount of axial movement in a shaft.

ENGINE: A device that converts heat into mechanical energy.

EXHAUST MANIFOLD: A set of cast passages or pipes which conduct exhaust gases from the engine.

FEELER GAUGE: A blade, usually metal, or precisely predetermined thickness, used to measure the clearance between two parts.

FIRING ORDER: The order in which combustion occurs in the cylinders of an engine. Also the order in which spark is distributed to the plugs by the distributor.

FLOODING: The presence of too much fuel in the intake manifold and combustion chamber which prevents the air/fuel mixture from firing, thereby causing a no-start situation.

FLYWHEEL: A disc shaped part bolted to the rear end of the crankshaft. Around the outer perimeter is affixed the ring gear. The starter drive engages the ring gear, turning the flywheel, which rotates the crankshaft, imparting the initial starting motion to the engine.

FOOT POUND (ft. lbs. or sometimes, ft.lb.): The amount of energy or work needed to raise an item weighing one pound, a distance of one foot.

FUSE: A protective device in a circuit which prevents circuit overload by breaking the circuit when a specific amperage is present. The device is constructed around a strip or wire of a lower amperage rating than the circuit it is designed to protect. When an amperage higher than that stamped on the fuse is present in the circuit, the strip or wire melts, opening the circuit.

GEAR RATIO: The ratio between the number of teeth on meshing gears.

GENERATOR: A device which converts mechanical energy into electrical energy.

HEAT RANGE: The measure of a spark plug's ability to dissipate heat from its firing end. The higher the heat range, the hotter the plug fires.

HUB: The center part of a wheel or gear.

HYDROCARBON (HC): Any chemical compound made up of hydrogen and carbon. A major pollutant formed by the engine as a byproduct of combustion.

HYDROMETER: An instrument used to measure the specific gravity of a solution.

INCH POUND (inch lbs.; sometimes in.lb. or in. lbs.): One twelfth of a foot pound.

INDUCTION: A means of transferring electrical energy in the form of a magnetic field. Principle used in the ignition coil to increase voltage.

INJECTOR: A device which receives metered fuel under relatively low pressure and is activated to inject the fuel into the engine under relatively high pressure at a predetermined time.

INPUT SHAFT: The shaft to which torque is applied, usually carrying the driving gear or gears.

INTAKE MANIFOLD: A casting of passages or pipes used to conduct air or a fuel/air mixture to the cylinders.

JOURNAL: The bearing surface within which a shaft operates.

KEY: A small block usually fitted in a notch between a shaft and a hub to prevent slippage of the two parts.

MANIFOLD: A casting of passages or set of pipes which connect the cylinders to an inlet or outlet source.

MANIFOLD VACUUM: Low pressure in an engine intake manifold formed just below the throttle plates. Manifold vacuum is highest at idle and drops under acceleration.

MASTER CYLINDER: The primary fluid pressurizing device in a hydraulic system. In automotive use, it is found in brake and hydraulic clutch systems and is pedal activated, either directly or, in a power brake system, through the power booster.

MODULE: Electronic control unit, amplifier or igniter of solid state or integrated design which controls the current flow in the ignition primary circuit based on input from the pick-up coil. When the module opens the primary circuit, high secondary voltage is induced in the coil.

NEEDLE BEARING: A bearing which consists of a number (usually a large number) of long, thin rollers.

OHM: (Ω) The unit used to measure the resistance of conductor-to-electrical flow. One ohm is the amount of resistance that limits current flow to one ampere in a circuit with one volt of pressure.

OHMMETER: An instrument used for measuring the resistance, in ohms, in an electrical circuit.

OUTPUT SHAFT: The shaft which transmits torque from a device, such as a transmission.

OVERDRIVE: A gear assembly which produces more shaft revolutions than that transmitted to it.

OVERHEAD CAMSHAFT (OHC): An engine configuration in which the camshaft is mounted on top of the cylinder head and operates the valve either directly or by means of rocker arms.

OVERHEAD VALVE (OHV): An engine configuration in which all of the valves are located in the cylinder head and the camshaft is located in the cylinder block. The camshaft operates the valves via lifters and pushrods.

OXIDES OF NITROGEN (NOx): Chemical compounds of nitrogen produced as a byproduct of combustion. They combine with hydrocarbons to produce smog.

OXYGEN SENSOR: Use with the feedback system to sense the presence of oxygen in the exhaust gas and signal the computer which can reference the voltage signal to an air/fuel ratio.

PINION: The smaller of two meshing gears.

PISTON RING: An open-ended ring with fits into a groove on the outer diameter of the piston. Its chief function is to form a seal between the piston and cylinder wall. Most automotive pistons have three rings: two for compression sealing; one for oil sealing.

PRELOAD: A predetermined load placed on a bearing during assembly or by adjustment.

PRIMARY CIRCUIT: the low voltage side of the ignition system which consists of the ignition switch, ballast resistor or resistance wire, bypass, coil, electronic control unit and pick-up coil as well as the connecting wires and harnesses.

PRESS FIT: The mating of two parts under pressure, due to the inner diameter of one being smaller than the outer diameter of the other, or vice versa; an interference fit.

RACE: The surface on the inner or outer ring of a bearing on which the balls, needles or rollers move.

REGULATOR: A device which maintains the amperage and/or voltage levels of a circuit at predetermined values.

RELAY: A switch which automatically opens and/or closes a circuit.

RESISTANCE: The opposition to the flow of current through a circuit or electrical device, and is measured in ohms. Resistance is equal to the voltage divided by the amperage.

RESISTOR: A device, usually made of wire, which offers a preset amount of resistance in an electrical circuit.

RING GEAR: The name given to a ring-shaped gear attached to a differential case, or affixed to a flywheel or as part of a planetary gear set.

ROLLER BEARING: A bearing made up of hardened inner and outer races between which hardened steel rollers move.

ROTOR: 1. The disc-shaped part of a disc brake assembly, upon which the brake pads bear; also called, brake disc. 2. The device mounted atop the distributor shaft, which passes current to the distributor cap tower contacts.

SECONDARY CIRCUIT: The high voltage side of the ignition system, usually above 20,000 volts. The secondary includes the ignition coil, coil wire, distributor cap and rotor, spark plug wires and spark plugs.

SENDING UNIT: A mechanical, electrical, hydraulic or electromagnetic device which transmits information to a gauge.

SENSOR: Any device designed to measure engine operating conditions or ambient pressures and temperatures. Usually electronic in nature and designed to send a voltage signal to an on-board computer, some sensors may operate as a simple on/off switch or they may provide a variable voltage signal (like a potentiometer) as conditions or measured parameters change.

SHIM: Spacers of precise, predetermined thickness used between parts to establish a proper working relationship.

SLAVE CYLINDER: In automotive use, a device in the hydraulic clutch system which is activated by hydraulic force, disengaging the clutch.

SOLENOID: A coil used to produce a magnetic field, the effect of which is to produce work.

SPARK PLUG: A device screwed into the combustion chamber of a spark ignition engine. The basic construction is a conductive core inside of a ceramic insulator, mounted in an outer conductive base. An electrical charge from the spark plug wire travels along the conductive core and jumps a preset air gap to a grounding point or points at the end of the conductive base. The resultant spark ignites the fuel/air mixture in the combustion chamber.

SPLINES: Ridges machined or cast onto the outer diameter of a shaft or inner diameter of a bore to enable parts to mate without rotation.

TACHOMETER: A device used to measure the rotary speed of an engine, shaft, gear, etc., usually in rotations per minute.

THERMOSTAT: A valve, located in the cooling system of an engine, which is closed when cold and opens gradually in response to engine heating, controlling the temperature of the coolant and rate of coolant flow.

TOP DEAD CENTER (TDC): The point at which the piston reaches the top of its travel on the compression stroke.

TORQUE: The twisting force applied to an object.

TORQUE CONVERTER: A turbine used to transmit power from a driving member to a driven member via hydraulic action, providing changes in drive ratio and torque. In automotive use, it links the driveplate at the rear of the engine to the automatic transmission.

TRANSDUCER: A device used to change a force into an electrical signal.

TRANSISTOR: A semi-conductor component which can be actuated by a small voltage to perform an electrical switching function.

TUNE-UP: A regular maintenance function, usually associated with the replacement and adjustment of parts and components in the electrical and fuel systems of a vehicle for the purpose of attaining optimum performance.

TURBOCHARGER: An exhaust driven pump which compresses intake air and forces it into the combustion chambers at higher than atmospheric pressures. The increased air pressure allows more fuel to be burned and results in increased horsepower being produced.

VACUUM ADVANCE: A device which advances the ignition timing in response to increased engine vacuum.

VACUUM GAUGE: An instrument used to measure the presence of vacuum in a chamber.

VALVE: A device which control the pressure, direction of flow or rate of flow of a liquid or gas.

VALVE CLEARANCE: The measured gap between the end of the valve stem and the rocker arm, cam lobe or follower that activates the valve.

VISCOSITY: The rating of a liquid's internal resistance to flow.

VOLTMETER: An instrument used for measuring electrical force in units called volts. Voltmeters are always connected parallel with the circuit being tested.

WHEEL CYLINDER: Found in the automotive drum brake assembly, it is a device, actuated by hydraulic pressure, which, through internal pistons, pushes the brake shoes outward against the drums.

Notes

MASTER INDEX

A

Notes